POLICING, POPULAR CULTURE AND POLITICAL ECONOMY

PIONEERS IN CONTEMPORARY CRIMINOLOGY

Series Editor: David Nelken

The titles in this series bring together the best published and unpublished work by the leading authorities in contemporary criminological theory. By drawing together articles from a wide range of journals, conference proceedings and books, each title makes readily available the authors' most important writings on specific themes. Each volume in this series includes a lengthy introduction, written by the editor and a significant piece of scholarship in its own right, which outlines the context of the work and comments on its significance and potential. The collected essays complement each other to give a retrospective view of the authors' achievements and a picture of the development of criminology as a whole.

Policing, Popular Culture and Political Economy

Towards a Social Democratic Criminology

ROBERT REINER
London School of Economics, UK

PIONEERS IN CONTEMPORARY CRIMINOLOGY SERIES

ASHGATE

Published by
Ashgate Publishing Limited
Wey Court East
Union Road
Farnham
Surrey GU9 7PT
England

Ashgate Publishing Company
Suite 420
101 Cherry Street
Burlington, VT 05401-4405
USA

Ashgate website: http://www.ashgate.com

ISBN 978 1 4094 2636 3

British Library Cataloguing in Publication Data
Reiner, Robert, 1946-
   Policing, popular culture and political economy : towards a
   social democratic criminology. – (Pioneers in contemporary
   criminology)
   1. Police. 2. Law enforcement. 3. Crime–Government
   policy. 4. Police in popular culture. 5. Criminal law.
   I. Title II. Series
   363.2-dc22

Library of Congress Control Number: 2011921395

MIX
Paper from
responsible sources
FSC® C013056
www.fsc.org

Printed and bound in Great Britain by
TJ International Ltd, Padstow, Cornwall.

Contents

Part III Political Economy of Crime and Control

Acknowledgements

The chapters in this volume are taken from the sources listed below. The editor and publishers wish to thank the authors, original publishers or other copyright holders for permission to use their material as follows:

Chapter 1: 'The Police, Class and Politics', *Marxism Today*, 1978, pp. 69–80.

Chapter 2: 'The Police in the Class Structure', *British Journal of Law and Society*, **5**, 1978, pp. 166–84.

Chapter 3: 'Fuzzy Thoughts: The Police and Law-and-Order Politics', *Sociological Review*, **28**, 1980, pp. 377–413. Copyright © 1980 Robert Reiner.

Chapter 4: 'In the Office of Chief Constable', *Current Legal Problems*, **41**, 1988, pp. 135–68.

Chapter 5: 'Policing a Postmodern Society', *Modern Law Review*, **55**, 1992, pp. 761–81.

Chapter 6: 'From PC Dixon to Dixon PLC: Policing and Police Powers since 1954', with T. Newburn, *Criminal Law Review*, 2004, pp. 601–18 [129–46]. Copyright © 2004 Taylor and Francis.

Chapter 7: 'Neophilia or Back to Basics? Policing Research and the Seductions of Crime Control', *Policing and Society*, **17**, 2007, pp. 89–101. Copyright © 2007 Taylor and Francis.

Chapter 8: 'New Theories of Policing: A Social Democratic Critique', in T. Newburn, D. Downes and D. Hobbs (eds), *The Eternal Recurrence of Crime and Control: Essays for Paul Rock*, Oxford: Oxford University Press, 2010, pp. 141–82.

Chapter 9: 'The New Blue Films', *New Society*, **43**, 1978, pp. 706–708 [204–208].

Chapter 10: 'True Lies: Changing Images of Crime in British Postwar Cinema', with Jessica Allen and Sonia Livingstone, *European Journal of Communication*, **13**, 1998, pp. 53–75. Copyright © 1998 Sage Publications.

Chapter 11: 'Media, Crime, Law and Order', *Scottish Journal of Criminal Justice Studies*, **12**, 2006, pp. 5–21.

Chapter 12: 'The State and British Criminology', *British Journal of Criminology*, **28**, 1988, pp. 138–58.

Chapter 13: 'Crime and Control in Britain', *Sociology*, **34**, 2000, pp. 71–94. Copyright © 2006 BSA Publications Limited.

Chapter 14: 'Beyond Risk: A Lament for Social Democratic Criminology', in T. Newburn and P. Rock (eds), *The Politics of Crime Control: Essays in Honour of David Downes*, Oxford: Oxford University Press, 2006, pp. 7–49.

Chapter 15: 'Law and Order—A 20:20 Vision', *Current Legal Problems*, **59**, 2006, pp. 129–60.

Chapter 16: 'Neo-liberalism, Crime and Criminal Justice', *Renewal*, **14**, 2006, pp. 10–22.

Chapter 17: 'The Law and Order Trap', *Soundings: A Journal of Politics and Culture*, **40**, 2008, pp. 123–34.

Chapter 18: 'Citizenship, Crime, Criminalization: Marshalling a Social Democratic Perspective', *New Criminal Law Review*, **13**, 2010, pp. 241–61. Copyright © 2010 by the Regents of the University of California.

Every effort has been made to trace all the copyright holders, but if any have been inadvertently overlooked the publishers will be pleased to make the necessary arrangement at the first opportunity.

Introduction

Some 30 years ago I heard an inspiring paper by our series editor, David Nelken, at a conference on Critical Legal Studies. He remarked that all scholars sought to reach two goals: to be true *and* to be good. In the contemporary culture of post- or late (perhaps post-post or late-late?) modernity either aspiration sounds anachronistic if not sclerotic. And combining the two is, of course, a perennial problem of the philosophy of science.

I believe that Max Weber's tackling of these issues remains the most credible and stimulating – shot through, as it is, with unresolved, and probably unresolvable, tensions. Weber maintains that scientists, including social scientists, have a responsibility (itself, of course, a moral judgement) to seek objectivity and value-freedom in their research, although this is never fully attainable – the influence of values seeps through or bursts out inevitably, and objectivity is an ideal that can be approached asymptotically at best. More obviously, the choice about what to study is necessarily a value judgement about what is important and interesting. And at the other end of the spectrum, people of action, only concerned with the achievement of practical objectives, need information about the likely consequences of what they plan that is based on an impartial assessment and not one that is tailored to what they want to hear. If the Light Brigade is to charge into a valley, it is better for its commanders to be correctly informed that they will face cannons than to be comfortingly told that the valley is clear. So both politics and science (including criminology) are vocations that must appease the tensely competing, voracious gods of passion *and* professionalism: 'ought' *and* 'is'.

The practical implication of this is that the researcher's values should be openly and clearly declared, so that their influence can be taken into account. But the perennial vice of social scientists is to hide behind a stance of sticking stubbornly to the facts. This is most obvious with the positivistic, largely quantitative, research that dominates criminology (at least numerically), especially in the USA, but it also characterizes what presents itself as the opposite pole – appreciative studies of deviance. Despite Becker's seminal call, more than 40 years ago, for sociologists of deviance to declare whose side they were on (Becker, 1967), much labelling theory (and its current rebirth as cultural criminology) purports to offer a tell-it-like-it-is interpretation of deviant life-worlds, coolly suspending any moral judgement.

I believe that a failure to come to terms with the moral issues that inevitably underpin its work is a major Achilles heel of criminology and indeed social science more broadly. It is also a serious lacuna for the political left, with which I (but not all and perhaps not even most criminologists) broadly identify. But, as Weber (and Freud) anticipated, the repressed returns inescapably, often in uncontrollably malignant ways. Values can only be tackled in the open.

This Introduction aims to lay out the development of my criminological career, and place in context the essays which this volume brings together. Following the injunctions above, I will begin with a brief statement of what I now see as the purposes and predicaments that have generated my work. The Owl of Minerva flies at dusk: I cannot claim that this understanding was conscious in the past, or that my work followed a consistent line. Rather my reconstruction is heavily informed by where I am now. But I don't feel it is too much of a retrospective invention to claim that the writing presented in the volume is informed by two interdependent threads: a particular moral/political position that has remained fairly consistent and a biographical experience that is dialectically intertwined with it.

When I attempted a similar biographical account some 15 years ago (Reiner, 1998) my conclusion likened these guiding threads to 'Rosebud', the sledge which is revealed in the final frames of the classic film *Citizen Kane* as the condensed symbol of childhood events, animating the eponymous protagonist's life. I was referring then to the biographical antecedents of my academic work, and I will summarize that later. But I would now add what is implicit in the sub-title of this volume. One thread, derived from biographical experiences no doubt, is a commitment to social democratic values. These two elements, biography and ethical commitments, are the underlying themes of my intellectual career and the essays collected here. So I must begin with an explicit statement of the moral/political values that have inspired my work.

Social Democracy

In my essay 'Beyond Risk: A Lament for Social Democratic Criminology' (Chapter 14) I attempt a brief characterization of social democracy. As I noted, the label has been used by a wide variety of political movements and thinkers, from Marxists such as Trotsky to the explicitly non- or anti-socialist Social Democratic Party formed in 1981 in Britain as a breakaway from the Labour Party which it criticized as unacceptably militant. Since the First World War and the October 1917 Bolshevik Revolution in Russia, the term 'social democracy' has generally been contrasted with communism. Social democracy signified at least an acceptance of democratic means to achieve socialism – a non-revolutionary, parliamentary road – and, for many, a change of ends, too: the reform of capitalism rather than its destruction.

The social democracy that I have been inspired by has its intellectual centre of gravity in the English tradition of ethical socialism (Dennis and Halsey, 1988), the quintessential exemplar of which was R.H. Tawney. This 'social democracy' was avowedly a species of socialism, although it can be said to offer a 'third way' between communism and liberalism.[1] I suggest that this social democracy was not just a middle-of-the-road compromise, 'a presentational splitting of the difference, but an anguished and internally contested terrain, an intellectual and moral Buridan's ass, torn between the powerful pulls of justice and liberty' (p. 302). In terms of a systematic attempt to ground this in philosophical first principles, the most fully developed example is John Rawls' magisterial *Theory of Justice* (1971). Rawls is normally labelled as a liberal theorist, but his powerful arguments for 'justice as fairness', based on principles that balance liberty and equality, offer the quintessential case for the values underpinning social democracy as I espouse it.

---

1   This distinguishes it from the 1990s 'third way' of the two Tonys – Blair and Giddens – which was an attempt to triangulate 'social democracy' and neo-liberalism, repudiating any identification as socialist.

The essence of this moral/political position is encapsulated in Rawls' two rules of justice: everyone should enjoy the maximum possible liberty subject only to preserving the same for others; and material welfare should be distributed equally, with inequality justified only if it benefits the least well-off.[2] Rawls' book meticulously and rigorously derives these principles from a hypothetical 'original position' in which alternatives can be assessed 'fairly' – that is, without the biasing effects of vested interests. It is so striking because at first reading (or so it appeared to me in 1971) it seems to offer an Archimedean position providing an objective grounding of these values. This is not how Rawls regarded them, nor (on reflection) is it a defensible position. The notion of 'fairness' as the absence of vested interests has been criticized cogently and most prolifically, on methodological and substantive grounds, by neo-liberals and communitarians. The neo-liberal critique, keenly promoted by Nozick (1974), questions the justice of taking property away from people who have acquired it by legitimate methods, in order to attain an idealized pattern of justice based on an *a priori* thought-experiment. A variety of philosophers loosely (and contentiously) dubbed as 'communitarian'[3] point out that people cannot be conceived of as pure decision-making entities, the 'unencumbered selves' attributed to Rawls' original position. They are always born into, and formed by, existing cultures endowing them *ab initio* with distinctive perspectives, values and tastes. So Rawls does not provide indubitable proof of an egalitarian position on liberty and welfare, although his work is the most rigorous account of such a position.

My own view is that value commitments are ultimately existential choices that can be argued for more or less convincingly but not finally established in knock-down ways, capable of converting even all well-intentioned people. But the kind of fundamental egalitarianism encapsulated in Rawls' principles has deep and ancient roots and recurs in most influential conceptions of justice in moral philosophy and theology. It is the conception that I have dubbed 'reciprocal individualism' in my book on *Law and Order* (Reiner, 2007a, pp. 18–20). I contrasted this with the 'egoistic individualism' that was encapsulated in Margaret Thatcher's notorious assertion that '[T]here is no such thing as society … and people must look to themselves first. It's our duty to look after ourselves and then, also to look after our neighbour' (interview, *Woman's Own*, 31 October 1987).

Thatcher explicitly inverts the biblical Golden Rule, 'Love your neighbour as yourself' (Leviticus 19: 18), which I take to be the moral foundation of social democracy and ethical socialism. In her version, neighbours have to wait in line while we look after ourselves first. But it should be stressed that the Golden Rule is *not* a collectivist ethos. Its bedrock value is the welfare of individuals, whose interests have to be balanced on the basis of fundamentally equal concern, including oneself ('as yourself'). Indeed, the Talmudic sage Ben Azzai specifically relates the Golden Rule in Leviticus to the earlier statement in Genesis I: 27, that all people were created in the image of God – that is, that individuals share in a common basis for equal concern and respect.[4] This derivation not only makes it clear that the Golden Rule is universal, applying to all people and not just literal 'neighbours', but also

---

2   This is, of course, a highly condensed version. I have given my own take on the vast Rawls literature in my essay on 'Justice' (Reiner, 2002).

3   The leading examples are MacIntyre (1981), Sandel (1982) and Walzer (1983).

4   The best-known Israeli human rights group derives its name from the Hebrew for 'in the image', *B'tselem*.

introduces an element of objectivity into the concrete obligations of care that flow from the injunction to 'love'. They should be based on a notion of the common 'image' of humanity, not my subjective preferences. If I am a masochist, I don't fulfil the injunction by flogging my neighbour.

Pace Mrs Thatcher, there is no simple contrast between individualism and other ethics. There are important differences between distinct forms of individualism:

> Specifically, the *egoistic individualism* that she and other neoliberals champion must be contrasted with the *reciprocal individualism* that underpins social democracy. Egoistic individualism regards individuals as responsible primarily for themselves – neighbours hold back! Reciprocal individualism sees all individuals as mutually responsible: neighbours are to be treated *as* oneself, requiring equal concern and respect. These two versions of the ethics of individualism suggest radically different notions of social policy, crime, and criminal justice. (Reiner, 2007a, p. 18)

Reciprocal individualism is the ethical basis of most – arguably all – forms of social democracy and of Rawlsian liberalism. Collectivities such as the state, trade unions and social classes may be valued as instruments for achieving justice, but they are not venerated in themselves.

My Entry into Criminology

I stumbled into criminology through what I have described elsewhere as 'a mixture of cowardice, compulsion and convenience' (Reiner, 1998, p. 75). My first degree was in economics, which I graduated in at Cambridge in 1967. Economics then was very different from what it is now. Nowadays students take it up mainly in the hope that it will prove a fast track to a well-heeled future of megabucks in the City, whereas my more innocent generation hoped to heal society. I had originally studied economics at 'A' Level and found it fascinating as my first exposure to social science. As an adolescent who voraciously read Freud in a vain effort to analyse my own inner turmoil, the idea that you could actually study human behaviour (even in the relatively limited aspects in the economics syllabus) was a revelation.

I started in economics with a genuine passion to understand the sources of poverty and inequality, and set the world to rights. In this I was far from alone. At my entrance interview I was asked what I wanted to do with my economics degree, 'and don't say you want to run off to the United Nations to solve world poverty like all the others' – pre-empting precisely that answer and leaving me speechless. Originally, my hope was to be a mathematical economist, finding rational and neat solutions to the problems of the universe. My economics tutor in the second year was the distinguished mathematical economist Frank Hahn, a privilege arranged by his wife Dorothy who was director of studies in the subject at my college. He was inspiring but daunting, with an amazingly rapid mind; he was constantly scribbling equations on scraps of paper – solutions that he had just thought of to hitherto impenetrable problems. He was somewhat isolated as a neo-classical economist in Cambridge which was then dominated by Keynesians and Marxists (and remains so more than most other economics faculties).

My ambitions as a would-be mathematical economist were soon dashed. Although I had coped well enough with maths at school up to 'A' level, I was completely thrown by the maths course I followed in the second year at Cambridge. By the Easter vacation I realized that I was completely out of my depth and heading for disaster at the end-of-year maths exam. Many of my friends were enthralled by the sociology course then taught primarily by David Lockwood and John Goldthorpe. So, as an insurance policy, I decided to enter for the sociology option as well. My college arranged a crash course of tutorials with Lee Davidoff, David Lockwood's wife. I remember doing my first essay on Merton's theory of anomie and being completely captivated by the study of deviance (a revelation given the repressive orthodoxy of my background). My conversion was confirmed by the exam results. After a year of maths I only managed to get a third, but my few weeks of enthusiastic reading of a handful of sociology texts netted me a 2.1.

During my third year I concentrated on sociology and politics options, one of which was taught by Ralph Miliband, on loan from the LSE, and father of the two front-runners in the race for the Labour Party leadership following the 2010 general election defeat. The third-year compulsory economics course, which was then called something like 'Economic and Social Relations', confirmed me in deep scepticism about what has become the mainstream in the subject. It was largely a rebuttal of the neo-classical model and, in particular, its Milton Friedmanite, Chicago School variant, which has, of course, swept the world in subsequent decades, at least until the 2007 credit crunch. The course's critique was largely directed at the neo-classical economists' 'physics envy', which drove them to increasingly elaborate mathematical model-building, based on highly simplistic and artificial assumptions about human motivation, cognition and social organization. Their perfunctorily acknowledged premises (perfect rationality, perfect competition, one-dimensional maximization of economic returns as the sole human goal and so on) blithely bracketed out any empirical research on these phenomena. The course argued for the integration of sociological research on these issues into the building of economic models, encouraging me further down the road I was already set on taking.

Following graduation, I went on to do an MSc in sociology at the LSE in 1968. By this time my central substantive interest in sociology (apart from theory, my and probably every student's first love) was criminology. This was heightened by the excellent option on deviance, inspiringly taught by Terence Morris. In 1969 I was offered a lectureship at the Sociology Department at Bristol which had recently been formed by Professor Michael Banton. It was understood that I would specialize in teaching deviance, and embark on a PhD on something in that broad area under Michael Banton's supervision. I had the summer vacation to find the precise topic.

Policing

PhD

Most of my research and publishing – at any rate until the last decade – has been on the police. They were the focus of my PhD on police unionism (Reiner, 1978/2010), my text on the politics of the police which is now in its fourth edition (Reiner, 1985, 2010), my joint research with Rod Morgan and Ian McKenzie on custody officers (McKenzie, Morgan and Reiner, 1990), my book on chief constables (Reiner, 1991), my inaugural lecture on policing a postmodern society (Chapter 5 in this volume), my joint volume with Sarah Spencer on police accountability (Reiner and Spencer, 1993), two edited volumes in the Dartmouth International Library of Criminology, Criminal Justice and Penology, and dozens of journal and newspaper articles and book chapters on a variety of aspects of policing (seven of which appear in Part I of this book).

I am pleased when police officers I meet assume that my reason for specializing in the police is because I have some sort of personal or family connection with them, as this implies to me that my accounts of police work and culture have some sense of authenticity. The truth is, however, that I do not have even the most remote personal background or involvement in policing. As far as I can remember, the first time I met or spoke to a police officer was when I was interviewing one for my PhD. Before that I had never had the occasion even to ask a policeman the time!

It was a sign of both my profound ignorance of the police, and of the neglect of policing within criminology at that time, that I did not know that Michael Banton, my PhD supervisor, was the pioneer of research on the police in the UK and the US. He had published the first sociological study of policing, *The Policeman in the Community* (1964).

During the summer vacation in 1969 I agonized over a subject for my PhD. In truth, the problem was that, as a stereotypically repressed grammar schoolboy with an orthodox Jewish upbringing, I had been fascinated to read the appreciative, tell-it-like-it-is studies of 'nuts, sluts and perverts' within the then burgeoning labelling and naturalistic approaches to deviance. But voyeuristic thrills experienced in learning about other people's forays into bohemian underworlds while cocooned in the sheltered environs of the university library, were one thing; observational field research was quite another. I realized, with increasing trepidation, that immersing myself in the front-line reality of deviant subcultures could be a more fraught and hazardous enterprise than I had bargained for.

A chance encounter in the library with Jerome Skolnick's riveting and seminal study of policing in California *Justice Without Trial* (Skolnick, 1966) seemed to offer an inspired way out. Why not study what I still, perhaps naively, thought of as the right side of the law? So when I met Michael Banton for my first supervision in the autumn of 1969 I tentatively suggested to him that I would like to do research on the police. His eyes lit up, as he pulled from his drawer a long list of possible PhD projects which he had put aside for just such an occasion. 'How about doing a study of the Police Federation?' he suggested. I did not dare confess that I had never heard of the Police Federation, which had not yet become the high-profile pressure group it now is. 'Sounds interesting,' I mumbled. 'I'll think about it.'

A couple of days later, some assiduous research had resulted in my discovery that the Police Federation was what some of its own members described as a copper's trade union with a vasectomy: it had all the equipment apart from the power to strike. I was far from certain that I wanted to spend three or more years studying it. However, the die had been cast. The next time I saw Professor Banton he asked, 'How's your thesis on the Police Federation coming along?' So there it was.

But what angle was I to take on the Police Federation? I quickly concluded that the straightforward approach, a historical account of its structure and functioning, had already been accomplished more or less definitively by Tony Judge, the editor of *Police* (the Federation's monthly magazine), in a couple of his books (Reynolds and Judge, 1968; Judge, 1968). So like many PhD students, I fell back on the safety of the intellectual pastiche of established models. As I mentioned earlier, my first sociology lecturers had been David Lockwood and John Goldthorpe, and the latter had been my supervisor during my final undergraduate year. I was steeped in their classic studies of trade union and class-consciousness, Lockwood's *The Black-Coated Worker* (1958) and *The Affluent Worker* trilogy (Goldthorpe *et al.*, 1968a, 1968b, 1969). Why not try to adopt a similar approach to the career, work situation and socio-political perspective of police officers, who were workers after all, albeit of a highly distinctive kind? To my mind, the idea had several appealing aspects. I could follow the methodological models of some of the most influential empirical studies in British sociology at that time. I could also combine the two main ingredients of my formal academic education: economic sociology and the sociology of deviance. Not least, I liked the mild *chutzpah* of calling the project *The Blue-Coated Worker* in honour of these roots. And I was delighted when, many years later, the book of the thesis appeared under that title in the same series as *The Affluent Worker* studies (Reiner, 1978a, 2010).

Post-doctoral Research

My continuation in police research after completing and publishing my thesis was once again the product of outside pressures and serendipitous opportunities. By coincidence, I finished my PhD, and began publishing papers and a book based on it, just as the Police Federation stopped being as obscure a topic as one could envisage and became front-page news, partly because it was engaged in a bitter and protracted pay dispute, including threats of police industrial action for the first time in 50 years, which culminated in the Edmund Davies pay review in 1978. Even more significantly, these were the years in which the Police Federation began a high-profile and controversial 'law and order' campaign, which became a coded 'vote for Margaret Thatcher' message in the run-up to the 1979 general election. The Police Federation, usually labelled the 'toothless tiger' by my PhD sample of officers, suddenly bit the Labour government where it hurt.

So I was in 'the right place at the right time' (the favourite explanation of career success in the police offered by my interviewees). The advantage of doing a PhD on an obscure topic is that if it ceases to be obscure, you have a monopoly of expertise on it. On the basis of my research I was well placed to comment and publish on the newly prominent pressure group that the Police Federation had become.

During the early 1970s police research had been a small cosy club with a handful of members. Apart from work by Banton himself there was the PhD and later book by Maureen Cain (Cain, 1973), John Lambert's (1970) work on police and race relations, John Martin's and Gail Wilson's (1969) study of police manpower, and Maurice Punch's study of public demand for policing (Punch and Naylor, 1973). There was also a rapidly growing body of excellent American research, the relevance of which to Britain was much debated (the American giants of police research were producing some of their major works at this time – for example, Skolnick, 1966; Wilson, 1968; Bayley and Mendelsohn, 1968; Reiss, 1971; and Manning, 1977).

The second half of the 1970s saw policing, and law and order in general, become increasingly central to political conflict (Downes and Morgan, 2007; Reiner, 2007a). Reflecting this, the police began to be studied on a significant scale in British criminology.

Following in the wake of the early research was a growing band of PhD researchers like myself, notably Mike Chatterton and Simon Holdaway. Nonetheless, as late as 1979, the extent of police research in this country was still small enough for Simon Holdaway to edit a volume that offered a definitive sampling of the state of the field at that time but was less than 200 pages long (Holdaway, 1979). The explosion of British police research only began in the early 1980s, in the wake of the Thatcherite politicization of law and order (examined in detail in Reiner, 1989b, 1992, Reiner and Newburn, 2007a, 2007b).

My first publication after my PhD was an article summarizing it, 'Reds in Blue?' (1976), which I sent to *New Society*. This proved to be fruitful in many more ways than merely being the first notch in my curriculum vitae (apart from a paper on the sociology of country music which *The New Edinburgh Review* had published in 1973). Paul Barker, the editor of *New Society*, had a remarkable eye for spotting trends before they emerged. Once I had become known to him, he kept commissioning me to write articles on aspects of policing which were about to hit the headlines. This led me to write a series of articles on different aspects of policing just as they became controversial, and eventually meant that I had covered the whole field in embryo. These articles, in effect, became the basis for the general book on policing which I wrote in the appropriate Orwellian year, 1984, *The Politics of the Police* (1985, 2010).

Critical Criminology and Policing

The period in the late 1970s, during which I was producing these papers on different aspects of the growing political debate on policing, was one in which the intellectual centre of gravity in British sociology was Marxist. The dragon of left-wing idealism had not yet even been named, let alone slain, by Saints John and Jock and the other new left realists (Lea and Young, 1984). It permeated much of deviance theory as a taken-for-granted, scarcely articulated set of attitudes, much as its counterparts did in other areas of sociology. Just as the prospect of change in a socialist direction departed from the tent of political reality into an Arctic darkness, to be gone for a very long time, academic sociology and criminology were churning out papers and debates implying that the Marxist millennium was around the corner.

This climate was reflected in my main publications in the late 1970s (especially the 1978 essays reproduced as Chapters 1 and 2 in this volume) which were heavily influenced by Marxist perspectives. These were uncharacteristic for me, in terms of my overall life and experience. Although (because?) I came from a largely conservative family background in terms of both attitude and politics, I cannot ever remember not being somehow radical in my political beliefs and commitments. I had no enemies from the Left, and an implacable moral and intellectual hostility to the Right. But perhaps an even more firmly rooted aspect of my outlook and personality has been a deep pessimism about the prospects of anything other than piecemeal progress, and scepticism about utopian enthusiasms. For reasons of personal biography which I will sketch later, I am a dyed-in-the-wool emotional Menshevik, with a perennial soft spot for heroes destined for the dustbin of history. So I was heavily suspicious of revolutionary tactics or slogans, believing that methods for achieving socialism had to abide by ethical constraints, a 'just revolution' version of the 'just war' theory (Walzer, 1977). I agreed with Steven Lukes that the ideals to which Marxists and socialists aspire are 'unapproachable through the violation in the present and in the future of the limits that basic or human rights impose' (Lukes, 1985, p. 70). The downside is, as he gloomily added, that they 'might also be unapproachable through respecting them'.

Nonetheless, when a former University of Bristol colleague Martin Jacques, who had become editor of *Marxism Today*, commissioned me in 1977 to write an analysis of recent developments in policing for his journal, I leapt at the chance. I must confess to a frisson of childish glee at the opportunity *épater mes bourgeois parents*. More seriously, I was already somewhat vexed about the root-and-branch hostility towards the police then dominant on the Left. It gave me a chance to develop my own more ambivalent, albeit still critical, analysis of the police.

My feelings on reviewing my *Marxism Today* essay (Chapter 1) are as ambivalent and contradictory as the class location I attributed to the police. On the one hand, I remain pleased with my critique of the then dominant critical criminology cliché that crime was a phenomenon of tabloid headlines rather than of the streets, with the function of ideologically legitimating more repressive social control through the generation of moral panics. I argued instead that crime was a genuine problem, albeit one that could be the basis of disproportionate fears exploited by the Right. As volume crime blighted the lives of the poorest and most vulnerable sections of society in particular, it ought to be taken more seriously by the Left. I can still reread this anticipation of 1980s left-wing realism with some satisfaction. I also remain happy with the basically structuralist diagnosis and policy recommendations about crime which I offered: that the sources of crime are rooted in wider social arrangements – above all, in the political economy and culture – so that criminal justice, however efficiently and effectively conducted, is at most marginally important in controlling crime. This perspective remains at the heart of my analysis of policing and criminal justice (as Chapters 7, 8, and 12–18 show).

What now makes me squirm with embarrassment is the section of my *Marxism Today* essay that attracted the most favourable responses at the time. These are the pages in which I attempted to sketch out the way in which the contradictory class location of the police as simultaneously workers and state agents could be politically exploited to prise them away from Conservatism to support for revolution. And to my chagrin I pursued the ultra-utopian hare of speculating on what shape the police would take in a socialist society, no doubt before they withered away altogether. Like the last few pages of Taylor's, Walton's and Young's 1973 classic text *The New Criminology* (then a bible to me as to so many criminologists of my generation – cf. Rock, 1994), these passages now seem to me almost a caricature of what Young later labelled 'left idealism' (Lea and Young, 1984).

Sociology to Law

I felt uncomfortable with the rather vulgar Marxist straitjacket that constrained the papers I wrote in the late 1970s, even at the time. But I was emotionally carried along by the wishful thinking which then dominated so much British sociology and the Left generally.

What broke this intellectual log-jam for me was an experience which I initially found traumatic and vainly resisted. As a consequence of the 1981 cuts in university finance, the University of Bristol developed a plan which included shrinking the Sociology Department, by redeployment rather than redundancy. The little local difficulty for me in their grand design was the Godfather-style 'offer' made to me that I might 'like' to be redeployed to the Law Department.

My perception of law at that time was that it was a matter only of learning rules, black-letter in the extreme. I thought of it as vocational rather than intellectual, and a bastion of authoritarianism. Nonetheless, after some futile struggle, I bowed to the pressures of the university plan and transferred to the citadel of rational legal authority in the mock-Gothic spire of the Wills Memorial Building.

I have now worked in three Law Departments as a criminologist (Brunel and the LSE after Bristol) and found the intellectual and political climate of all of them at least as liberal and theoretical as academic sociology. There is a very clear sociological basis for this. Nearly all academic lawyers have far more lucrative career opportunities open to them in legal practice than in the groves of academe. Those who choose the academic route are therefore a self-selected group of people who have made a deliberate choice to forego instrumental rewards for intellectual and political values.

I personally found the transfer intellectually liberating. I was left to my own devices academically so long as I fulfilled the basic remit of continuing to publish. My presence as a token sociologist demonstrated the department's concern to move away from its traditional black-letter approach towards a more socio-legal, contextual one. This was made clear to me at the farewell party held when I was leaving for Brunel. David Feldman (now Professor of English Law at Cambridge) gave a valedictory speech. They had wanted me, he said, to import a touch of the modern social world into the fusty corridors dominated by the Law Reports, and I had succeeded amply, bringing them slap-bang up-to-date with the culture of the 1950s (still my favourite period of pop music).

The Politics of the Police

From the late 1970s onwards, while still in the Sociology Department at Bristol, I had been planning to write a general book on the politics of the police. The title was inspired by John Griffith's *The Politics of the Judiciary* (1977), which I greatly admired. At the back of my mind was the dream of achieving a similar exposé of another arm of the state's repressive apparatus.

By the mid-1980s there was a burgeoning scholarly library on the police, but it comprised either empirical monographs or interventions on specific policy issues. The debates on policing were highly polarized, both politically and analytically. The police were either paragons or pigs – defenders of civilization as we know and love it, or the jack-booted repressive arm of the state.

For theoretical and moral/political reasons (growing out of my personal background as I will show later) I was drawn to try to bridge this increasingly gaping chasm. In general political terms I was firmly on the Left, and concurred with the criticisms of many police activities. But I felt that these were partly vitiated by an implied utopian standpoint about what was possible.

To me, the police were fated to be 'dirty workers' – to use Everett Hughes' (1962) phrase – doing the tragically inescapable job of managing, often coercively, the symptoms of deeper social conflicts and malaise. They were a necessary evil in any complex society, even if this was sometimes overdetermined by a surplus degree of malpractice or repressiveness due to the especially unjust or contradictory character of social structure and culture in particular periods. This sense of the police function as being Janus-faced was pithily captured in the title of a paper by Otwin Marenin: the police dealt with both 'Parking Tickets and Class Repression' (Marenin, 1983). Although this was a heretical view on the Left in the late 1970s, I was encouraged by E.P. Thompson's passionate and wittily eloquent espousal of it in his *Writing by Candlelight* (980).

This basically tragic perspective on the police role was the leitmotif of two theoretical analyses of policing which had an increasing influence on me. The image of the good police officer as a tragic hero was elaborated at length in a sensitively observed, Weberian analysis of the police by Ker Muir Jr entitled *The Police: Streetcorner Politicians* (1977). The inevitably thankless and ultimately Sisyphean character of police work was also implied in Bittner's celebrated theorization of the police as the wielders of the state's monopoly of legitimate force, called upon to intervene in any emergency conflict situation (Bittner, 1974). Both accounts were anticipated in a passage from Weber, which appears as an epigraph in *The Politics of the Police*:

> He who lets himself in for politics, that is, for power and force as means, contracts with diabolical powers and for his action it is *not* true that good can follow only from good and evil from evil, but that often the opposite is true. Anyone who fails to see this is, indeed, a political infant. (Weber, 1918/2004, p. 86).

The Politics of the Police was intended to do two things. My primary purpose was to contribute to the enormously impassioned political debates then raging around the police. The book was written during the miners' strike, when the political controversies about policing, which had been building up throughout the late 1970s and early 1980s, were at their height. The Thatcher government had built the police up as the battering-ram of the strong state which was the paradoxical precondition of the free economy at which it aimed (Gamble, 1994). To the Conservatives at that time the police were a beloved pet, the pampered special-case exception to their aversion to all things public.

Against this, a left-wing consensus of hostility to the police had developed. On this view the police were over-mighty oppressors who had grown far too big for their jackboots. Their powers, resources and status all needed cutting down by a 'democratization' of the police. The minimum demand was for complete subjection of policing to control by democratically elected local police authorities.

My practical purpose in writing *The Politics of the Police* was to intervene in this polarized argument in support of a middle way (not dreaming that such a 'third way' would become a cloak for abandoning socialism altogether). As I indicated above, a complex society inevitably required a body capable of regulating emergency conflicts by the use of legitimate force. The most that could be achieved was not the elimination of this necessary evil, but its subjection to values decided upon by the democratic process. In the actual context of the mid-1980s the police *were* being used to maintain and increase social injustice on behalf of an increasingly privileged minority. But what was needed was to democratize policing, not to alienate the police by viewing them as intrinsic enemies. Whilst, formally, my polemic was aimed equally at the Left and the government, the greater passion was expended against the former, with whom I identified, than the latter, whom I regarded as irredeemably morally misguided.

In order to advance my political argument, I reviewed as comprehensively as my knowledge allowed the historical and sociological literature on the police. Thus the book served an alternative function as a textbook on policing, the first to be published in this country. The polemical side of the book was quickly overtaken by political developments. Once the Conservatives had accomplished the virtual destruction of organized labour, courtesy of the rough policing directed at the miners and print workers, the police were no longer vital tools of their project. The police rapidly became as redundant as most other traditional workers, at least in the pampered style supported by the Conservatives in the mid-1980s. Already by 1988 the government was indicating in unequivocal terms that severe police expenditure cutbacks were imminent.

At the same time, the Labour Party began to woo the police with increasing ardour, eager to shed its electorally damaging image as anti-police. Neil Kinnock set the tone in 1986 with an interview in *Police Review*, in which he confessed that, as a boy, he had always wanted to be a police officer, but for some inexplicable reason had ended up as Labour leader instead. Subsequently Tony Blair's New Labour lost no opportunity to court the cops and establish their credentials as tough champions of law and order (see Chapter 5).

Life at the Top

The Politics of the Police proved popular with police officers and provided the opportunity to conduct a study of senior police, breaking the previous pattern of research which had concentrated only on the lower-ranking 'servants of power'. The ensuing 1991 book, *Chief Constables*, attracted a fair amount of attention at the time of its publication, largely because it provided some new empirical material on issues of current controversy. However, its relevance is now largely historical. I studied chief constables at a crucial point of change, when the old post-war styles (which I dubbed Bobbies, Barons and Bosses) were being replaced almost wholesale by a new breed which was being cultivated by the Home Office in the Scarman mould, whom I called Bureaucrats. These were highly educated, politically adroit, human relations sensitized managers, oriented to the cultivation of consensus, inside and outside their forces. They stood in sharp contrast to both varieties of the old school: the autocratic disciplinarians and the everyday bobbies promoted to top cop. Sadly, the post-Sheehy and Police and Magistrates' Court Act 'reforms' threatened the 'Scarmanesque' diplomatic type of chief constable with displacement by a new type, the 'Businessman' – yuppies who know the performance measures for everything and the meaning of nothing.

To me, the most interesting finding of my study was the extent of behind-the-scenes Home Office influence on chief constables. Some of the revelations made to me in interviews so contradicted official denials of this that I was tempted at times to blow the whistle. One particular afternoon in the spring of 1987, a few days before the general election, I remember standing on a station platform on my way home after an interview, wrestling with the decision whether to break all my pledges of confidentiality and phone the *Guardian*. I had just been told of direct instructions from Mrs Thatcher during the miners' strike to establish an intelligence unit to cover trade unionists who she was convinced were under Russian influence (Reiner,

1991, p. 191). In the end, fear (for myself and my informant), rather than professional ethics, persuaded me that no-one would pay any attention anyway, so I took the train and not the risk.

The finding of Home Office domination of key policing decisions was novel at the time, but has since become quite explicit in the managerialist transformation of the police, initially under the Conservatives, but accelerating under New Labour. Although my research on chief constables was fascinating to carry out and contributed some interesting empirical results, it was not informed by any new theoretical concerns, so I will not dwell on it any further here. Since the mid-1990s I have not conducted any further empirical research on policing. I have continued to publish overviews and theoretical analyses (for example, in most editions of *The Oxford Handbook of Criminology*, which I began editing in 2004 with Mike Maguire and Rod Morgan), but these are largely subsumed in broader concerns with popular culture and political economy, which I shall discuss next.

Popular Culture

I have been a film buff since at least the age of five, my main passion then being Westerns (to which I remain devoted). An uncle of mine had a huge collection of detective stories and pulp magazines like *Black Mask*. As a small boy I would gaze at these with fascination, at once terrified by the menacing murderers on the covers and mesmerized by the prospect of thrilling mysteries. Eventually, when I was about ten, I braved myself to read one, which I remember was Carter Dickson's *A Graveyard to Let* – a suitably chilling title. As a result, I became hooked into a lifelong addiction to detective stories, especially the classic sleuth mysteries that are known by fans as 'the cosies'. These two passions remained hidden hobbies until late in my undergraduate career when I encountered some sociological discussions of the mass media. I toyed with the idea of a PhD looking at the political impact of changing fashions in pop music (Bob Dylan, the Beatles, the Stones *et al.*), but eventually, as narrated above, settled on deviance as my subject.

In the mid-1970s I met Chris Frayling, subsequently rector of the Royal College of Art, but then a historian at Bath University. Together, we taught a series of evening classes for the Bristol Extra Mural department, on Westerns and detective films. I also began writing on the film and television representation of policing (see Chapter 9; Reiner, 1981 and several other short pieces in *New Society* and other magazines). This enthusiasm for combining my hobby and my day job was aborted when I moved to the Law Department and was told firmly that media writing was to be done only in my 'gardening time'. Nonetheless I did smuggle a chapter on police and the media into *The Politics of the Police*.

All this changed in 1994 when I was awarded a substantial four-year Economic and Social Research Council (ESRC) grant for a study called 'Discipline or Desubordination? Changing Media Representations of Crime since the Second World War', together with Sonia Livingstone of the LSE Media and Communications Department and a leading expert on the impact of mass media, with Dr Jessica Allen as our research associate. Our work involved a qualitative content analysis of a large sample of crime films and TV series since the Second World War and of crime news stories in *The Times* and the *Daily Mirror*. We also conducted a range of focus groups to examine how audiences perceived the changing depictions of crime.

For most of the 1990s and early 2000s my main publications were on media representations of crime and policing. Apart from the papers directly reporting our research cited below, my main writings on the media have been a chapter in most editions of *The Oxford Handbook of Criminology* (most recently Reiner, 2007b), and various chapters on representations of policing (including Reiner, 1994, 2008).

I learned much from this study. The one negative lesson was the truth of Defoe's dictum that making your hobby your work means you lose a hobby. My enthusiasm for crime movies (temporarily) abated while having to watch them with the equivalent of a clipboard and stopwatch. But what I found gripping was the systematic reading of our sample of news stories. My eyes wandered irresistibly from the crime stories to the whole of the pages in which they were embedded, and it was a wonderful chronological immersion into the history of the decades since the Second World War – and also immensely nostalgic, as the period coincided with my life thus far. The experience has informed all my subsequent work, especially on the history of crime and criminal justice policy in these decades (Reiner, 2007a, especially chs 4 and 5).

Regrettably, I have never managed to write the monograph at which we were aiming, but our results are reported in a number of essays (see Chapters 10 and 11, this volume; Allen, Livingstone and Reiner, 1997; Livingstone, Allen and Reiner, 2000a, 2000b, 2001; Reiner, 1996; Reiner, Livingstone and Allen, 2003). The study remains unique as a long-term history of media representations of crime and criminal justice across a range of media. It documents the growth in media representations of crime in both fiction and news stories and the increasingly frequent and graphic depiction of violence. It also shows that – whilst remaining mainly positive – media representations of policing and criminal justice have become ever more critical. A crucial change is the increasing focus on victims, making them the emotional pivot of narratives. This reflects a change from a taken-for-granted legalistic conception of crime, to a more individualistic one, in which the basis for opposing it is contingent on the degree of harm inflicted on sympathetic victims. Most fundamentally, there is a narrative shift from the inclusive and consensual discourse about crime, offenders, victims and state during the social-democratic era of the 1940s and 1950s to much more contingent, conflicted, zero-sum stories in more recent neo-liberal times. These increasingly portray a Nietzschean 'beyond good and evil' universe of bestial perpetrators violating sympathetic victims, in which the forces of law and order are themselves often at least as evil as the nominal criminals (Reiner, 2007a, pp. 141–51). Together with a growing sense of how to understand the basic dynamics of change in policing, the media research fed into my most recent work on political economy, which has been my main focus in the 2000s.

Political Economy

I indicated above that my Cambridge degree course in economics inoculated me against the neo-classical approach that has now become mainstream. 'Economics' today refers to a supposedly apolitical, value-free, 'scientific' enterprise, using primarily mathematical models based on highly abstract and simplified axioms about human motivation, decision-making processes and forms of social organization. It has caustically been dubbed 'autistic' economics by a growing movement of economists seeking a return to what they call 'real-world' economics, along the lines of the political economy out of which economics originally grew (Fullbrook, 2007; PAE Movement, n.d.).

What is now taught as mainstream 'economics' is very different from the 'political economy' that was its origin. The most famous work of eighteenth-century political economy, Adam Smith's *The Wealth of Nations*, was part of a much wider exploration of social structure and relations, inextricably bound up with moral philosophy. Marx saw himself as heir to this tradition, synthesizing it with Hegel's dialectical philosophy and French St Simonian socialism. Indeed, 'political economy' is sometimes used as virtually a synonym for Marxism. Political economy recognizes the *embeddedness* of the 'economic' in wider networks of political, social and cultural processes, and its ethical sources and implications.

Political economy has been an important influence in modern attempts to understand crime and its control (Reiner, 2007c, pp. 345–55), although its impact has been eclipsed at times – particularly during the last three decades of neo-liberal hegemony and also in the late nineteenth century when the term 'criminology' was first coined to refer to the emerging 'science of the criminal' pioneered by Cesare Lombroso and his associates. Thus the term 'criminology' came into being in association with the Lombrosian version of the quest for theoretical understanding of the etiology of crime, but the project of developing such an analysis using the intellectual tools of social science, partly to further policy ends of achieving order and justice, pre-dated the label. The eighteenth-century criminologies *avant la lettre*, the 'classical' school of criminal law and the 'science of police', were closely linked to political economy. They were sidelined in the later nineteenth century by the rise of the positivist 'science of the criminal', with its aura of scientific rigour, objectivity and dispassionate expertise. The late twentieth-century downplaying of political economy in criminology was the result of the opposite one-sided accentuation: an attempt to marginalize theoretical questions for the sake of 'realism' – a pragmatic pursuit of policies that 'worked', denying the value of any consideration of deeper causes.

I have argued in several recent essays that the eclectic, broad-ranging account of crime, criminals and control offered by political economy is necessary both for understanding and for effective policy (see Chapters 7, 8, 12, 13, 14, 15, 17 and 18; and Reiner, 1989a, 1993, 1999, 2007a, 2007c, 2007d, 2007f, 2010). But I feel that, like Mr Jourdain's prose, I have been speaking political economy throughout my academic career, and it has implicitly informed all my writing.

The criminological perspective most explicitly rooted in political economy was the 'fully social theory of deviance' sketched in *The New Criminology* (Taylor, Walton and Young, 1973, pp. 268–80), stressing the interdependence of macro-, meso- and micro-processes. This was explicitly intended as 'a political economy of criminal action, and of the reaction it excites', together with 'a politically informed social psychology of these ongoing social dynamics' (ibid., p. 279). It was an attempt 'to move criminology out of its imprisonment in artificially segregated specifics ... to bring the parts together again in order to form the whole' (ibid.). Most research studies inevitably focus on a narrower range of phenomena, but the checklist of elements for a 'fully social theory' is a reminder of the wider contexts in which deviance and control are embedded. This was illustrated by *Policing the Crisis*, the closest attempt to incorporate all these elements into the study of one specific phenomenon (Hall *et al.*, 1978). Hall *et al.* moved out from an account of a particular robbery in Birmingham to a wide-ranging analysis of British economic, political, social and cultural history since the Second World War, charting the deeper concerns that 'mugging' condensed, and the impact of transformations in the political economy on black young men in particular.

My book, *The Politics of the Police*, implicitly adopted this multi-layered political economy model. It moved from a historical analysis of the roots of modern policing to look at the wider structural and cultural pressures shaping it, as well as the actions of Robert Peel and the pioneer founders of the police. My account of the legitimation – and subsequent delegitimation – of the police also combined analysis of policing policy and practice with the wider political, economic, social and cultural transformations of British society. The discussions of police culture, of sociological research on what constitutes the police role, and of how effectively and fairly they perform it, emphasized the significance of contingent individual interpretations of meaning, the small-scale interactions generating specific actions, as well as the wider structural forces that bear down on police and their publics. This analytic approach, rooted in political economy, is most explicit in the third and fourth editions. These argue that the fundamental precondition of what is celebrated, by Conservatives above all, as the British style of policing by consent, is the social-democratic consensus that even the Tories accepted (however grudgingly) in the middle decades of the twentieth century, but which they have been relentlessly unravelling since 1979, aided and abetted after the mid-1990s by New Labour. This analysis is at the core of Chapters 7 and 12–17 in this volume and is most fully set out in my book on *Law and Order* (Reiner, 2007a).

Life and Times

My account of how I came to undertake the various projects on policing that have occupied most of my career emphasizes the superficial elements of chance. For many years I had no answer to my parents' frequently voiced question of how on earth I had ended up doing so much work on the police. It just seemed like one random opportunity after another. However, I eventually came to realize that, as in the Marxist cliché, it was no accident.

In this section I will try to make explicit the underlying intellectual and moral concerns which allowed the police to become my anthropological tribe – a forum for exploring a host of theoretical, moral and political issues. The police were especially suitable for this because, as I put it in my inaugural lecture at the LSE (see Chapter 5), the police are a kind of social litmus paper. They register all major changes in the broader social structure and culture because they are the specialist regulators of social conflict, both at an everyday micro level and at a macro political level. Thus the police face problems that continuously evolve as sensitive reflections of general social developments.

The police, and more broadly crime and deviance, have been congenial subjects for me because, even though they are concretely far removed from my own direct life experience, they have served as coded vehicles of other, more personal concerns. I have come to understand that my interest in policing, crime and deviance ultimately draws on deeper roots in my personal biography.

I was born in Hungary in January 1946, shortly after the Second World War, and was brought to England as a refugee in 1948. Many years ago, a senior Police Federation official thought he saw in this the source of what he perceived as my radicalism on policing. At a police conference (where he had been sampling rather too much of the Bull's Blood on offer) he warned some chief constables not to talk to me, as he had discovered that I had been born in Hungary and was therefore a 'dangerous Red'. I asked how he knew this, and he replied that he had seen my Special Branch file. If I am honoured by having such a file, it presumably does record the fact that I was born in Miscolc, Hungary. However, the Federation official's deduction from this was precisely the opposite of the truth.

My parents were both Jewish holocaust survivors, most of whose families had perished at the hands of the Nazis. They left Hungary as refugees shortly after I was born. This was just before the Soviets (who represented to them the threat of another totalitarian regime, albeit without the same genocidal intent) cemented their grip. To my parents, England, Churchill and all symbols of the British way of life – from roast beef to bobbies – represented salvation.

Perry Anderson in 'Components of the National Culture' (1968) attributes the stubbornly empiricist flavour of British social theory to the enthusiasm for pragmatism and other supposedly British values, of the generation of 'white émigrés who fled totalitarianism in the 1930s and 1940s. Many such refugees – for example, Popper and Hayek – became intellectually dominant in British social thought in the 1950s. With the enthusiasm of converts, they hallowed not just empiricism, but also all aspects of British culture and liberal-democratic political institutions.

When I read the Anderson paper I recognized this pattern in myself, although unlike the older generation of 'white émigrés', the experience did not incline me to conservatism. It did, however, inoculate me against the wilder extremes of police-bashing common on the Left from the 1960s to the 1980s. In particular, it made me contemptuous of the student radicals' trivialization in calling the British police fascists or SS. I was acutely aware of the potential for abuse which is inextricable from the police's role as the repository of the state's monopoly of legitimate force. But I was also imbued with a deep sense that the British police tradition (and others derived from it) had at least largely succeeded in minimizing the ultimately inescapable dangers. This feeling was common to those with my experience. The title of a book collecting reminiscences of child refugees from Hitler captures the point. It quotes the poignant words of one little girl on seeing a British bobby after years of the SS: *And the Policeman Smiled* (Turner, 1990).

I believe that this 'white émigré' psychology underpinned my interest in analysing the sources of the British police 'advantage'. My experience as a child refugee and a member of the 'second generation' (a child of Holocaust survivors) also underlay my affinity for the tragic, Weberian perspective on policing exemplified in the work of Bittner (also a Holocaust refugee) and Ker Muir, discussed earlier. It makes me sceptical of utopianism, and 'good enough' concepts like harm reduction and damage limitation are more congenial to me than the ambition of perfection. The negative, Rabbinic version of the Golden Rule formulated by Hillel ('do not do to others what you do not want done to yourself') offers a more realizable guide to ethical behaviour than the positive version found in Leviticus 19:18: 'love your neighbour as yourself'. This is despite the inspiration offered by the latter, and the harm wreaked by those who deny it, like Margaret Thatcher (Reiner, 2007a, p. 18).

These considerations underlie my position that, in policing, the unfortunate necessity of using evil means – violence – to attain good or at least minimize harm is ultimately inescapable in some situations – a predicament well characterized by Klockars (1980) as

'The Dirty Harry Problem'. From this perspective, the only viable political and analytic project is to minimize those situations where violence becomes tragically necessary, and to imbue the dispensers of legitimate violence with the means and culture to achieve minimal-force interventions. To me, understanding the structural and cultural conditions of good or bad policing in this sense remains a worthwhile and compelling theoretical issue.

My more general interest in understanding trends and patterns in crime, deviance and social control (including criminal justice and policing) derives partly from the same roots of my refugee and survivor experience. But it is more directly a product of my religious education and upbringing. I come from an Orthodox Jewish family, went to a strictly Orthodox primary and grammar school,[5] and then for six months (during what is now called my 'gap' year) to a Talmudical college in Gateshead. I grew up in Golders Green in what has subsequently become a self-imposed ghetto of the ultra-Orthodox. Until I went to Cambridge at the age of 18, my only contact with non-Jewish (or even Jewish secular) culture was vicariously through books and the mass media. My only contact with non-Jewish people was fleeting and impersonal – in shops or on public transport.

Despite this, I began to question my faith during my 'A'-level studies. This was especially prompted by learning about the Reformation for 'A'-level history. I identified the Jewish world I had grown up in with medieval Catholicism, and saw all the questions of the Protestant reformers as ones applicable to the Judaism I had been taught and previously absorbed without question. This led to a project that I only abandoned after some years, when it became clear that it was an unattainable chimera: trying to read all the classic works of Western, particularly modern, philosophy. I also read my way voraciously through Freud in a quixotic effort at self-analysis.

All this made me a fanatical, militant atheist and rationalist for many years. My heroes were Freud, Bertrand Russell, John Stuart Mill, Popper and the like. I enjoyed nothing better than going to my religious lessons and using their arguments in fierce contests with my teachers and more devout fellow pupils. However, during my anti-religious teen and early adult years I never lost the personal ethical code I had derived from my upbringing (encapsulated in the Golden Rule).

This underlay my early attraction to socialism, and I have never been able to understand how most religious people who claim to espouse that ethic are conservative. My major problem with the faith of my childhood was (and remains) the 'problem of evil'. How can religious individuals (not just Jewish ones, of course) hold and enforce values (for example on homosexuality, the place of women, ethnic differences, and social and economic policy) which to me seem flagrantly at odds with the Golden Rule which they claim is paramount? To me, commitment to a socialist and liberal position is an inescapable logical outgrowth of religious ethics, a position I found eloquently expressed in Isaac Deutscher's essay 'The Non-Jewish Jew' (Deutscher, 1968).

---

5   This was also the *alma mater* of several other academics who work in the criminology/criminal justice field including our series editor Professor David Nelken, the late Professor Gerald Cromer of Bar Ilan University, Professor Leslie Sebba of the Hebrew University and Professor Michael Freeman of University College, London. For an interesting discussion of the elective affinity between criminology and Jewish academics see Berkowitz (2007, pp. 7–8 and p. 237 fn. 28).

My attraction to sociology – in particular, to the sociology of crime and deviance – stemmed from all these considerations. When I first encountered the discipline in the mid- to late 1960s it was dominated by the arguments about labelling theory and its appreciative studies of deviance (now echoed in cultural criminology). These seemed to speak directly to my predicament as a young man trying (with little success) to liberate myself from guilt about deviating from the practices and beliefs with which I had been brought up. More than abstract moral philosophy, the debates about what should be criminalized and how different social groups defined and applied deviant labels in varying ways captured dilemmas with which I was struggling personally. At the time I embraced the then fashionably dominant libertarian position on matters I regarded as ones of purely private morality (sexuality, censorship, drugs and the like) while maintaining an absolutist radical stance on questions concerning how people should treat each other and how societies should be organized.

However, I found that as I left the confines of the ghetto and actually entered the world of secular academe (which I had read about in awe for so many years), I began to experience some disillusion with the latter and an increasing interest and sympathy for my roots. On the one hand, I discovered to my disappointment that progressive secular intellectuals in the flesh were far from the selflessly rational, humane and ethical beings conveyed by their books. I had always been mystified by the contrast between the theoretical Golden Rule ethic of Orthodox Judaism and the actual intolerance and lack of humane concern for others which is embodied in its moral and political conservatism. However, on the other hand, I have never been able to come to terms with the contrast between the egoism and inconsiderate treatment of people in personal relationships, which is often accepted behaviour by those who nominally espouse values of radical concern for social justice. On a small scale, this disillusion set in at my very first staff meeting. Thirsting for some debate about intellectual or political matters, I was shocked to find the agenda dominated by heated discussions about car-parking spaces and the allocation of a 'merit' increment.

At the same time, once I was living away from the Jewish world from which I had yearned to liberate myself in my teenage years, I began to pine for at least some of its aspects. In particular, I began to read assiduously on contemporary Jewish culture, which my religious education (steeped in the study of ancient texts) had neglected. I eagerly read studies of the Holocaust – the details of which my parents had tried to protect me from. I also read voraciously about the consequent establishment of the state of Israel and the history of Zionism – aspects of contemporary Jewish life which my ultra-Orthodox school had played down because of ambivalence about the secular character of most of the Zionist movement.[6]

For some years I maintained a secular Jewish identity, but gradually experienced some *rapprochement* with my childhood faith, too. This went hand-in-hand with loss of belief in the inevitability, or even likelihood, of salvation through the various rationalistic beliefs I had in turn espoused: Marxism, psychoanalysis and the like. However, just as I maintained the Golden Rule ethic of my religious upbringing during the period when I was a firm believer in atheism, my moral and emotional commitment to the values of social justice, as embodied in both the prophetic and the socialist traditions, did not waver in the face of my loss of faith

---

6   More recently, growing awareness of Israel's treatment of Palestinians has raised another set of dilemmas and contradictions between its espoused liberal-democratic ethics and its practices.

in the prospects of humanistic progress. In essence, I would now regard myself as a Jewish version of a Christian Socialist.[7]

The concerns derived from my personal background and experiences now clearly inform my work on the police (see Chapters 7 and 8; also Reiner, 2010), media and crime, and the political economy of crime and criminal justice (Reiner, 2007a, 2007c, 2007d and Part III of this volume), in a way that was only latent in my earlier years in criminology (see Reiner, 1984, 1989a, 1993). Many critics of the perspective which informs *The Politics of the Police* have pointed out that it reflects a 'golden ageism' of the kind Geoff Pearson (1983) so elegantly demolished. The book *is* structured around an account of what I call the rise and fall of police legitimacy, with the high point being the 1950s. As these were my childhood and early teenage years, characterizing this as Paradise Lost fits uncomfortably with Geoff Pearson's demonstration that middle-aged, middle-class, middle-everything men like me have always characterized the years of their youth as a lost golden age.

For many years I was touchy about this criticism, generally wriggling out of it by claiming that I was taking the 1950s to be a high point in public perceptions of the police (as represented by survey and other evidence), *not* a golden age in terms of police practice. However, since the initial publication of *The Politics of the Police* in 1985, I have been influenced by several key books (for example, Hobsbawm, 1994; Judt, 2010) which have persuaded me to come out and argue that the 1950s and 60s were a sort of golden age in objective terms, and that in the early 1970s something happened to set in train a general – though not unambiguous – decline in the quality of life.

This triggered an interest in the burgeoning literature about postmodernity which is reflected in much of my more recent writing on the police, notably my inaugural lecture (Chapter 5). Subsequently, I have come to think more in terms of neo-liberalism as the defining way of regarding the post-1970s changes.[8]

Between them, these books by Hobsbawm and Judt give me confidence in the perspective that underlies my recent work on trends in crime (summed up in Reiner, 2007a and Part III of this volume). For all the caveats about statistics and moral panics, crime *has* risen since the 1950s, and in particular it has exploded since the late 1970s. It is a major issue in its own right, but also the most visible symbol of a deeper economic, social and cultural malaise. This is reflected in the mass media representation of crime and violence and is possibly aggravated by it in turn (cf. Chapters 9 and 10). But if criminologists 'have only interpreted the world; the point is to change it' (conflating Marx's and Lenin's aphorisms), what is to be done?

Future Agendas

I have never had trouble with Gramsci's recommendation of pessimism of the intellect, but I have chronic problems with his encouragement of optimism of the will. To many, it appears that civilization is currently fighting a losing battle with barbarism. But the same could have

---

7 In the mid-1990s I dubbed myself a 'bagel-eating Blairite' as a synonym for Jewish socialist (Reiner, 1998, p. 96). I still like bagels, though on doctor's orders seldom eat any. But I shudder at the naive optimism that identified Blair as any kind of socialist!

8 Harvey (2005) succinctly sums up this perspective.

been said at almost any time in the century since the lights went out over Europe in 1914 (apart, perhaps, from the post-war decades of social-democratic consensus – and even then the shadow of nuclear Cold War was a serious threat). I remain unquenchably optimistic about the capacity of reason, research and scholarship to illuminate the sources of malaise and point to ways forward. Criminology *can* interpret the world. And if Blatcherite neo-liberalism changed it for the worse, it is possible for others to change it for the better.

There has been something of a *trahison de criminologists* (to paraphrase Benda). This is found in the relative absence of critical attention given to wider social and political–economic sources of contemporary crime and criminal justice changes, at any rate until very recently. In the early stages of neo-liberalism's rise, during the later 1970s and 1980s, conservative criminologists cheered the neo-liberal turn heralded by James Q. Wilson in his book, *Thinking about Crime* (1975). But, *soi-disant*, radical criminology also attenuated its critique of criminal justice in a variety of ways. For all their virtues, the various strands of the realist turn after the 1970s did imply a change in the subject, diverting attention from the large-scale social and cultural forces that were restructuring crime and criminal justice. Changes in funding and career opportunities for academic criminologists encouraged this (Hillyard *et al.*, 2004), but perhaps a deeper factor was an excessive intellectual modesty in the wake of the political defeats of Soviet communism and Western social democracy.

Nearly a quarter of a century ago, Zygmunt Bauman suggested that the role of intellectuals shifted from 'legislators' to 'interpreters' as modernity segued into postmodernity (Bauman, 1989). They no longer enjoyed the respect or self-confidence to lay down laws from on high, mandating new values and directions, but could at best only explain existing perspectives. In criminology, as in other disciplines, a horror of judgementalism served to eviscerate critique. Criminologists became either policy wonks or interpreters of the florid cultures of deviance. But I would argue that there is an excluded middle in this dichotomy, namely the intellectual (or criminologist) as prophet – in the meaning that prophecy has in the Old Testament, not in its contemporary usage of Mystic Megs who purport to foresee the future. As Michael Walzer puts it,[9] the Old Testament prophets' message 'is not something radically new; the prophet is not the first to find, nor does he make, the morality he expounds ... The prophet need only show the people their own hearts' (Walzer, 1993, pp. 71–74). The prophet pointed out the way for people to realize values they already shared and accepted, but which their current practices frustrated. This was always a controversial intervention – as Max Weber suggested, the prophets were pioneering political pamphleteers (Weber, 1952, p. 267) – but their admonishments were compatible with Weber's strictures about value neutrality in the scientific, as distinct from political, vocation. The prophets based their critique of people's practices by invoking, and not challenging, existing communal values. In this sense, prophecy is a paradoxical form of value-free preaching.

Many criminologists (like other social scientists) used to talk in this manner, generally presuming that a major source of crime and disorder was social injustice. For much of the twentieth century a social-democratic perspective at least implicitly informed most

---

9   I am in debt to my son Toby's thesis on the political thought of Michael Walzer for alerting to me to this aspect of Walzer's arguments for preserving a social-democratic voice in the face of the neo-liberal tsunami of recent decades (T. Reiner, 2011).

sociological criminology. This implied limited potential for criminal justice to control crime levels. Although intelligent policing and penal policy could more effectively relieve the symptoms of criminogenic political economic structures and cultures, this was what Paul Rogers has dubbed 'liddism' in the context of the 'war on terror': an ultimately futile struggle to hold the lid down on the smouldering sources of crime. Social peace required getting tough on these causes. I have tried in my essay 'Beyond Risk' (Chapter 14) to probe (and lament) the decline of this perspective, but I believe that although it has lost the political battle for the time being, it has not (as is often said) lost the argument.

My future writing plans involve taking further the analysis that I have begun in the essays included in Part III of this volume. My first intention is to write a short book on the concept of crime, which has largely been unexamined in the recent years of pragmatic 'realism' (with a few exceptions, such as David Nelken's 2007 exploration of the ambiguities of white-collar crime and Hillyard, Sim *et al*.'s 2004 'zemiological' deconstruction of criminology, with which I am largely in sympathy). This would expand on my chapter in *Law and Order*, 'An Inspector Calls: Putting Crime in its Place' (Reiner, 2007a, ch. 2).

My longer-term ambition is to attempt a thorough excavation of the sources of the eclipse of social-democratic criminology since the 1970s, taking further what I began In 'Beyond Risk' (Chapter 14). There are still mysteries surrounding the sudden rise to dominance of neo-liberalism in the 1970s, sweeping away so rapidly the post-Second World War social-democratic consensus that had delivered so much in terms of widely shared growth in material prosperity and security, as well as relatively low crime and benign control strategies by historical standards.

Even more important, and at least as mysterious: where are we going now? It is remarkable that so soon after the economic and financial crunch in late 2007 apparently discredited the neo-liberal model, its savagely deflationary prescriptions for dealing with the sovereign debt crisis (resulting from governmental support for banking) are the new orthodoxy in the UK. How can this zombie neo-liberalism be explained? And what will it mean for criminal justice in Britain, in the hands of the new Conservative–Liberal Democrat coalition?

Many liberals have been impressed and surprised by early signs of the coalition government's willingness to reverse some of the trends towards harsher punitiveness and the erosion of civil liberties under New Labour (and, of course, the Michael Howard regime at the Home Office before that). For example, a landmark speech by Justice Secretary Kenneth Clarke on 30 June 2010 at the Centre for Crime and Justice Studies harked back to the philosophy articulated by the White Paper preceding the 1991 Criminal Justice Act – that prison was an expensive way of making bad people worse. For the first time in nearly20 years a government was questioning Howard's mantra that 'prison works'. This apparent conversion is very welcome, even if it is largely prompted by economic considerations. But it is sadly predictable that these liberal ambitions will be frustrated in practice by increasing crime and disorder flowing from the financial cuts and downturn. As before, the 'freeing' of the economy will engender a strong state penal and policing response to the social dislocation it produces. Neo-liberalism entails social injustice and thus undermines liberal approaches to criminal justice, as I have tried to show in these essays and my book on law and order (Reiner, 2007a). An alternative narrative to neo-liberal instrumentalism and egoistic aspiration is needed, evoking the mutualism of Buber's ideal of 'I-thou', as argued by Benjamin (2010) in relation to financial markets. This echoes the ethics of the Golden Rule that underpins social democracy, as suggested earlier. A core criminological responsibility, I believe, is to chart a way forward to reviving the conditions for social security and peace, which social democracy gradually began to deliver and most people desire.

References

Allen, J., Livingstone, S. and Reiner, R. (1997), 'The Changing Generic Location of Crime in Film', *Journal of Communication*, **47**(4), pp. 89–101.

Anderson, P. (1968), 'Components of the National Culture', *New Left Review*, **50**, July–August, pp. 3–58.

Banton, M. (1964), *The Policeman in the Community*, London: Tavistock.

Bauman, Z. (1989), *Legislators and Interpreters*, Cambridge: Polity.

Bayley, D. and Mendelsohn, H. (1968), *Minorities and the Police*, New York: Free Press.

Becker, H. (1967), 'Whose Side Are We On?', *Social Problems*, **14**(3), pp. 239–47.

Benjamin, J. (2010), 'The Narratives of Financial Law', *Oxford Journal of Legal Studies*, **30**(4), pp. 787–814.

Berkowitz, M. (2007), *The Crime of My Very Existence: Nazism and the Myth of Jewish Criminality*, Berkeley, CA: University of California Press.

Bittner, E. (1974), 'Florence Nightingale in Pursuit of Willie Sutton: A Theory of the Police', in H. Jacob (ed.), *The Potential for Reform of Criminal Justice*, Beverly Hills, CA: Sage.

Cain, M. (1973), *Society and the Policeman's Role*, London: Routledge and Kegan Paul.

Dennis, N. and Halsey, A.H. (1988), *English Ethical Socialism*, Oxford: Oxford University Press.

Deutscher, I. (1968), *The Non-Jewish Jew and Other Essays*, Oxford: Oxford University Press.

Downes, D. and Morgan, R. (2007), 'No Turning Back: The Politics of Law and Order into the Millennium', in M. Maguire, R. Morgan and R. Reiner (eds), *The Oxford Handbook of Criminology* (4th edn), Oxford: Oxford University Press.

Fullbrook, E. (ed.) (2007), *Real World Economics: A Post-Autistic Economics Reader*, London: Anthem Press.

Gamble, A. (1994), *The Free Economy and the Strong State: Politics of Thatcherism*, London: Palgrave Macmillan.

Goldthorpe, J., Lockwood, D., Bechhofer, F. and Platt, J. (1968a), *The Affluent Worker: Industrial Attitudes and Behaviour*, Cambridge: Cambridge University Press.

Goldthorpe, J., Lockwood, D., Bechhofer, F. and Platt, J. (1968b), *The Affluent Worker: Political Attitudes and Behaviour*, Cambridge: Cambridge University Press.

Goldthorpe, J., Lockwood, D., Bechhofer, F. and Platt, J. (1969), *The Affluent Worker in the Class Structure*, Cambridge: Cambridge University Press.

Griffith, J.A.G. (1977), *The Politics of the Judiciary*, London: Fontana.

Hall, S., Critcher, C., Jefferson, T., Clarke, J., Roberts, B. (1978), *Policing the Crisis: Mugging, the State and Law and Order*, London: Palgrave Macmillan.

Harvey, D. (2005), *A Brief History of Neoliberalism*, Oxford: Oxford University Press.

Hillyard, P., Pantazis, C., Tombs, S. and Gordon, D. (eds) (2004), *Beyond Criminology*, London: Pluto.

Hillyard, P., Sim, J., Tombs, S. and Whyte, D. (2004), 'Leaving a "Stain upon the Silence"', *British Journal of Criminology*, **44**(3), pp. 369–90.

Hobsbawm, E. (1994), *Age of Extremes: The Short Twentieth Century 1914–1991*, London: Michael Joseph.

Holdaway, S. (ed.) (1979), *The British Police*, London: Edward Arnold.

Hughes, E.C. (1962), 'Good People and Dirty Work', *Social Problems*, **10**(1), pp. 3–11.

Judge, T. (1968), *The First Fifty Years*, London: The Police Federation.

Judt, T. (2010), *Ill Fares the Land: A Treatise on our Present Discontents*, London: Allen Lane.

Klockars, C. (1980), 'The Dirty Harry Problem', *The Annals*, **452**, November, pp. 33–47.

Lambert, J. (1970), *Crime, Police and Race Relations*, Oxford: Oxford University Press.

Lea, J. and Young, J. (1984), *What is to be Done about Law and Order?*, Harmondsworth: Penguin.

Livingstone, S., Allen, J. and Reiner, R. (2000a), 'Casino Culture: Media and Crime in a Winner-Loser Society', in K. Stenson and R. Sullivan (eds), *Crime, Risk and Justice: The Politics of Crime Control in Liberal Democracies*, Cullompton: Willan Publishing, pp. 175–93.

Livingstone, S., Allen, J. and Reiner, R. (2000b), 'No More Happy Endings? The Media and Popular Concern about Crime since the Second World War', in T. Hope and R. Sparks (eds), *Crime, Risk and Insecurity: Law and Order in Everyday Life and Political Discourse*, London: Routledge, pp. 107–25.

Livingstone, S., Allen, J. and Reiner, R. (2001), 'Audiences for Crime Media 1946–91: A Historical Approach to Reception Studies', *Communication Review*, **4**(2), pp. 165–92.

Lockwood, D. (1958), *The Black-Coated Worker*, London: Allen and Unwin.

MacIntyre, A. (1981), *After Virtue*, London: Duckworth.

McKenzie, I., Morgan, R. and Reiner, R. (1990), 'Helping the Police with their Enquiries: The Necessity Principle and Voluntary Attendance at the Police Station', *Criminal Law Review*, January, pp. 22–33.

Manning, P. (1977), *Police Work*, Cambridge, MA: MIT Press.

Marenin, O. (1983), 'Parking Tickets and Class Repression: The Concept of Policing in Critical Theories of Criminal Justice', *Contemporary Crisis*, **6**(2), pp. 244–66.

Martin, J.P. and Wilson, G. (1969), *The Police: A Study in Manpower*, London: Heinemann.

Muir, Jr, K.W. (1977), *The Police: Streetcorner Politicians*, Chicago, IL: Chicago University Press.

Nelken, D. (2007), 'White-collar and Corporate Crime', in M. Maguire, R. Morgan and R. Reiner (eds), *The Oxford Handbook of Criminology* (4th edn), Oxford: Oxford University Press, pp. 733–70.

Nozick, R. (1974), *Anarchy, State and Utopia*, New York: Basic Books.

PAE Movement, 'Real-World Economics Review: Real-World Economics Review Blog', at: http://www.paecon.net/.

Pearson, G. (1983), *Hooligan*, London: Macmillan.

Punch, M. and Naylor, T. (1973), 'The Police – A Social Service', *New Society*, 17 May, pp. 358–61.

Rawls, J. (1971), *A Theory of Justice*, Cambridge, MA: Harvard University Press.

Reiner, R. (1976), 'Reds in Blue?', *New Society*, 7 October, pp. 14–16.

Reiner, R. (1978/2010), *The Blue-Coated Worker*, Cambridge: Cambridge University Press.

Reiner, R. (1981), 'Keystone to Kojak: The Hollywood Cop', in P. Davies and B. Neve (eds), *Politics, Society and Cinema in America*, Manchester: Manchester University Press.

Reiner, R. (1984), 'Crime, Law and Deviance: The Durkheim Legacy', in S. Fenton with R. Reiner and I. Hamnett (eds), *Durkheim and Modern Sociology*, Cambridge: Cambridge University Press.

Reiner, R. (1985), *The Politics of the Police* (1st edn), Brighton: Wheatsheaf.

Reiner, R. (1989a), 'Race and Criminal Justice', *New Community*, **16**(1), pp. 5–21.

Reiner, R. (1989b), 'The Politics of Police Research', in M. Weatheritt (ed.), *Police Research: Some Future Prospects'*, Aldershot: Gower.

Reiner, R. (1991), *Chief Constables: Bobbies, Bosses or Bureaucrats?*, Oxford: Oxford University Press.

Reiner, R. (1992), 'Police Research in the United Kingdom: A Critical Review', in N. Morris and M. Tonry (eds), *Modern Policing: A 'Crime and Justice' Thematic Volume*, Chicago, IL: Chicago University Press, pp. 435–58.

Reiner, R. (1993), 'Race, Crime and Justice: Models of Interpretation', in L. Gelsthorpe and B. McWilliam (eds), *Minority Ethnic Groups and the Criminal Justice System*, Cropwood Papers No. 21, Cambridge: Cambridge University Institute of Criminology, pp. 1–25.

Reiner, R. (1994), 'The Dialectics of Dixon: Changing Television Images of the Police', in M. Stephens and S. Becker (eds), *Police Force, Police Service: Care and Control*, London: Macmillan.

Reiner, R. (1996), 'Crime and the Media', in H. Sasson and D. Diamond (eds), *LSE on Social Science: A Centenary Anthology*, London: LSE Publishing, pp. 135–55.

Reiner, R. (1998), 'Copping a Plea', in P. Rock and S. Holdaway (eds), *The Social Theory of Modern Criminology*, London: UCL Press, pp. 73–98.

Reiner, R. (1999), 'Order and Discipline', in I. Holliday, A. Gamble and G. Parry (eds), *Fundamentals in British Politics*, London: Palgrave Macmillan.

Reiner, R. (2002), 'Justice', in J. Penner, D. Schiff and R. Nobles, (eds), *Jurisprudence and Legal Theory*, London: Butterworths, pp. 719–78.

Reiner, R. (2007a), *Law and Order: An Honest Citizen's Guide to Crime and Control*, Cambridge: Polity Press.

Reiner, R. (2007b), 'Media Made Criminality', in M. Maguire, R. Morgan and R. Reiner (eds), *The Oxford Handbook of Criminology* (4th edn), Oxford: Oxford University Press, pp. 302–37.

Reiner, R. (2007c), 'Political Economy, Crime and Criminal Justice', in M. Maguire, R. Morgan and R. Reiner (eds), *The Oxford Handbook of Criminology* (4th edn), Oxford: Oxford University Press, pp. 341–80.

Reiner, R. (2007d), 'Criminology as a Vocation', in D. Downes, P. Rock, C. Chinkin and C. Gearty (eds), *Crime, Social Control and Human Rights*, Cullompton: Willan Publishing, pp. 395–409.

Reiner, R. (2008), 'Policing and the Media', in T. Newburn (ed.), *Handbook of Policing*, Cullompton: Willan Publishing, pp. 313–35.

Reiner, R. (2010), *The Politics of the Police* (4th edn), Oxford: Oxford University Press.

Reiner, R. and Newburn, T. (2007a), 'Police Research', in R. King and E. Wincup (eds), *Doing Criminological Research* (2nd edn), Oxford: Oxford University Press, pp. 343–74.

Reiner, R. and Newburn, T. (2007b), 'Policing and the Police', in M. Maguire, R. Morgan and R. Reiner (eds), *The Oxford Handbook of Criminology* (4th edn), Oxford: Oxford University Press, pp. 910–52.

Reiner, R. and Newburn, T. (2007c), 'Crime and Penal Policy', in A. Seldon (ed.), *Blair's Britain, 1997–2007*, Cambridge: Cambridge University Press, pp. 318–40.

Reiner, R. and Spencer, S. (eds) (1993), *Accountable Policing: Effectiveness, Empowerment and Equity*, London: Institute for Public Policy Research.

Reiner, R., Livingstone, S. and Allen, J. (2003), 'From Law and Order to Lynch Mobs: Crime News Since the Second World War', in P. Mason (ed.), *Criminal Visions: Media Representations of Crime and Justice*, Cullompton: Willan Publishing, pp. 13–32.

Reiner, T. (2011), 'Democracy, Community, Citizenship: The Political Thought of Michael Walzer', PhD thesis, University of California, Berkeley.

Reiss Jr, A.J. (1971), *The Police and the Public*, New Haven, CT: Yale University Press.

Reynolds, G.W. and Judge, A. (1968), *The Night the Police Went on Strike*, London: Weidenfeld and Nicholson.

Sandel, M. (1982), *Liberalism and the Limits of Justice*, Cambridge: Cambridge University Press.

Skolnick, J. (1966), *Justice Without Trial*, New York: Wiley.

Taylor, I., Walton, P. and Young, J. (1973), *The New Criminology*, London: Routledge.

Thompson, E.P. (1980), *Writing by Candlelight*, London: Merlin.

Turner, B. (1990), *And the Policeman Smiled: 10,000 Children Escape from Nazi Europe*, London: Bloomsbury.

Walzer, M. (1977), *Just and Unjust Wars*, New York: Basic Books.

Walzer, M. (1983), *Spheres of Justice*, New York: Basic Books.

Walzer, M. (1993), *Interpretation and Social Criticism*, Cambridge, MA: Harvard University Press.

Weber, M. (1918/2004), *The Vocation Lectures*, Indianapolis: Hackett Publishing.

Weber, M. (1952), *Ancient Judaism*, Glencoe: Free Press.

Wilson, J.Q. (1968), *Varieties of Police Behaviour*, Cambridge, MA: Harvard University Press.

Wilson, J.Q. (1975), *Thinking about Crime*, New York: Vintage.

Part I
Policing

[1]
The Police, Class and Politics

(I) INTRODUCTION: THE NEED FOR A
SOCIALIST ANALYSIS OF THE POLICE

At last year's Tory party conference, Mr. William
Whitelaw claimed that it was "part of left-wing
mythology" that "there was something despicable,
almost immoral, in discussing the prevention of
crime at all".[1] "Our Socialist rulers", he said,
"never even discussed the whole problem of crime
at their conference". He criticised their allegedly
"haphazard and fickle" attitude to "freedom under
the law".[2]

Public Concern about Crime

We may be excused for failing to notice that the
solid figures of James Callaghan and his Cabinet
constitute "our Socialist rulers". It would be less
excusable to assume that socialists have nothing to
learn from Mr. Whitelaw's words, for, as he rightly
said, ordinary people *are* concerned about questions
of crime, and look to governments to ensure their
protection.[3] If socialists are seen as either indifferent
or hostile to these concerns this is undoubtedly a
serious political liability, and deservedly so, for it is
unforgivably elitist to minimise such acutely felt
anxieties experienced by people. This is not to say,
however, that fears about the maintenance of "law
and order" must be accepted at face value. Popular
definitions and analyses of the "crime problem"
may be misguided in many ways, and socialists can
have an educative role to play. But they must not
fail to be sensitive to people's own priorities, or allow
so important an issue to be seen as a Tory one.

The Requirements of a Socialist Analysis

What is required is an analysis of the police which
recognises the need which will be faced by people in
any society short of a communist millenium for
protection of person, personal property and the
conditions of a secure, ordered and productive

existence. This does not mean that the criminal justice
system of a socialist society would simply mirror the
existing one. But it does mean that thought must be
given to the structures that should be developed.
More specifically, it is vital that the personnel of the
criminal justice system are brought into alliance
with other progressive forces. Effective reform of the
police and other criminal justice institutions cannot
be envisaged without wider changes in society which
alter the conditions generating crime, but at the
same time consideration must be given to the
structures needed in a socialist society and the ways
of moving towards these. To date there has been
little serious discussion of the police from a socialist
perspective, but they must be seen as central to
political strategy.

The Centrality of the Police to Political Strategy

The police are crucial to the prospects for socialism
in Britain and other developed capitalist countries.
This is despite the common realisation amongst
communists that an insurrectionary strategy is not
likely to succeed given the balance of social forces
and the means of coercion available, in such
societies. The police are important in three ways.
First, the danger would confront any socialist
government, even if it had majority support, that the
police and army might be used in a counter-
revolutionary coup. As Carrillo puts it, largely
drawing on the experience of the Chilean tragedy:

> "without the transformation of the State apparatus,
> every socialist transformation is precarious and
> reversible, not by an electoral result which it would be
> logical and natural to accept, but by an armed coup
> carried out by the very people theoretically respon-
> sible for defending legality".[4]

Winning the support of at least the rank-and-file of
the repressive state apparatuses is necessary to
forestall this.

Second, the police play a part in preventing the
building of majority support for socialism. As
documented in Tony Bunyan's recent book *The
Political Police in Britain*, sections of the police,
together with the army and intelligence services, are
continuously engaged in surveillance and harassment
of political activists and trade-unionists. In recent

[1] The *Guardian*, October 14th, 1977, p. 6.

2 The *Daily Telegraph*, October 14th, 1977, p. 14.

[3] This is indicated by many surveys of "public
opinion". An example is reported in Mark Abrams,
"Changing Values", *Encounter* October, 1974, p. 29-38.
He found that "the maintenance of law and order" was
ranked very high as a social value by respondents, only a
couple of percentage points behind "higher living
standards".

[4] S. Carrillo, *"Eurocommunism" and the State*, p. 13.

70

MARXISM TODAY, MARCH, 1978

years these institutions have become increasingly involved in active preparation against the possibility of insurrection, and there has been a significant development of police-military co-operation in exercises and planning, justified by the growth of **IRA** and other terrorist activity.[5] Under the guise of impartial law-enforcement and order-maintenance the police also prevent specific struggles from succeeding. Recently, for example, they have been deployed against the Grunwick pickets, and on October 9th, 1977, 6,000 police officers were fielded in a massive operation costing £0.25m. to protect the "democratic right" of National Front organiser Martin Webster to march in Hyde, Manchester.

Third, the police are the enforcement arm of the legal system which legitimises capitalist social relations. They contribute to the acceptance of a rhetoric of "law and order" as the cement of civilised existence, which abstracts from the class character of the content and application of legal rules in a capitalist society.[6]

Democratisation of the Police

A vital element of socialist strategy and the building of a socialist society is the *democratisation* of the police force, to work towards making the rhetoric of law as representing the communal interest the reality which it cannot be in a class society. This democratisation has two formal aspects: changing the internal relations in the police so as to allow police officers the same democratic rights as other workers; and bringing the police force firmly under the control of popular democratic institutions. However, neither aspect is only a question of formal institutional change in the machinery of policing. Without wider changes towards equalisation of economic and political power any reforms within the police apparatus will remain merely formal, or even prove counter-productive. Furthermore, institutional changes must be linked to debate involving both the police and public about the police role in a democratic society, a consideration of the social implications of policing activities and the meaning of "law and order". Such debates have begun among the French police as the influence of socialist ideas has spread with the growing political success of the Left.[7]

---

[5] Bunyan, *The Political Police in Britain.* The recent firemen's strike afforded another opportunity for police-military co-operation in which there was the chance to learn about co-ordination of their activities.

[6] A. Hunt, "Law, State and Class Struggle", *Marxism Today,* June, 1976, is a useful analysis of the role of law in maintaining capitalist social relations.

[7] See *Marxism Today,* July 1977, p. 193.

Police Forces Not Monolithic

The basis of such developments is the fact that police forces are not the monolithic, mechanical entities suggested by such terms as "state machine" or "apparatus". Police officers are employees who share some common interests with other workers, as shown by the development of police unions in all democratic societies. In recent years these organisations have become increasingly important politically in Britain, the US and Europe. The implications of this will be considered in the next section of this article, and the prospects for proper unionisation of the British police assessed. The third section of the article will broaden the discussion to consider the police role in society. The place of the police in class relations will be analysed to try and specify the possibilities and limits of alliance between the police and labour movement. Finally, the police conception of their role as law-enforcement agents will be considered, and the contradictions within it discussed. This will lead to suggestions about the role of the police in a society undergoing democratic transition to socialism.

(II) POLICE UNIONISATION: PROBLEMS AND PROSPECTS

Police Unions: Reactionary or Progressive?

A necessary first step towards democratisation of the police force would be the winning of the same rights of trade union representation for the rank-and-file as exist for all other occupations apart from the army. However, trade unionism is, of course, not necessarily associated with progressive or socialist ideas and practices, and this is especially so in the case of police unions.

Reactionary Political Interventions by the Police

American police associations have in the last decade and a half become increasingly militant in terms of industrial action but when their targets have gone beyond a bread-and-butter kind they have exerted their political muscle for reactionary ends.[8] In several cities police unions, for example, have been successful in defeating civilian review boards, the most famous instance being the New York Patrolmen's Benevolent Association's victory in a 1966 referendum, when it mounted a highly effective campaign combining appeals to white racism and fear of crime.

In Britain, the Police Federation in 1975 launched a "law and order" campaign which sought to influence political and public opinion to reverse what they perceived as a liberalising trend in criminal

---

[8] For a more detailed account of American police unionism see *The Iron Fist and the Velvet Glove,* Centre for Research on Criminal Justice (2nd edition) 1977, Chapter 6.

MARXISM TODAY, MARCH, 1 9 7 8   71

justice policy. Apart from this campaign, the Federation has emerged as a vocal and effective pressure-group putting forward the rank-and-file view on policies which are felt to impinge on their interests, for example abolition of capital punishment.

Progressive Police Organisations

But while police representative organisations in Britain and America have tended to put forward right-wing demands when their concerns have transcended economism, European police unions have often supported liberal policies and tried to resist being used by the state to repress dissent and the workers' movement. For example, the secretary of the main French police union dissociated it from the violence against students in May 1968 and blamed the government. He declared that the police ought never be used against a justifiable demonstration."

In Britain, too, during the only period in which there existed independent police unionism, 1913-19, the illegal Police and Prison Officers' Union gradually forged links with the labour movement, and its leaders called for the democratisation of the force. Although most rank-and-file support for the Union and the 1918-19 strikes was instrumentally motivated, the association with organised labour underlay the government and conservative press's apocalyptic analysis of the situation, and its determination to smash the Union. The Union was defeated by the granting of a substantial pay rise combined with the establishment of the Police Federation as a tame substitute.

The Need for Police Unionisation

The political character of police unionism is clearly historically variable. Although in the recent past British and American police associations have acted as right-wing pressure-groups, in the period after the First World War they showed tendencies of radicalisation in line with the general direction of the labour movements in all capitalist societies at that time. Similarly, in recent years police unions in several Continental countries, notably France, have begun to align themselves with the Left as it has grown in strength. The political character of police unionism must be seen as a reflection of the general balance of class and political forces in society, and is not necessarily a monolithic conservatism. While the immediate consequence of greater rank-and-file power today in Britain or America might be support for reactionary policies, in the longer term the police would be able to associate more freely with the labour movement, and might even seek affiliation.

9 G. Monate, *La Police, Pour Qui? Avec Qui?* EP1, Paris, 1972.

The result of such association could be a reduction in the present virulently anti-union views of many police officers, and a lessening of their enthusiasm for controlling pickets.[10]

While the achievement of trade union rights by the police is only a part of the aim of democratisation of the force and could initially take a right-wing character, it would nonetheless be a step forward. The reliability of the force as an automatic instrument of government would be reduced, it would be exposed to different views and possibly attract types of recruits presently inhibited from joining, and signify a change in the anti-union sentiments of the police.

The Prospects of Police Unionisation

Since 1976 there has been a much publicised growth of militancy in the British police arising mainly out of grievances over pay. It is expressed in demands for the right to strike and rejection of existing negotiating machinery. This contrasts sharply with previous acquiescence in the restricted legal position of police representation. However, towards the end of 1977 the steam appears to have gone out of police militancy, pending the results of an enquiry into pay and representative machinery.

To identify the prospects for police unionism it is necessary to chart the changing attitudes of the police expressed in recent years.

The Police Federation before 1960

From its inception in 1919 there has always been an undercurrent of dissatisfaction with the Police Federation, but until 1976 it was effective as a safety-valve for discontent. Before the end of the Second World War the Federation was even more shackled than now, lacking any independence or proper negotiating machinery. But the militants had been purged after the 1919 strike, and the inter-war years were a "Golden Age" for police pay and conditions. Though pay was cut together with other public sector wages it fell less than industrial earnings and prices, and security of employment and the pension made the police a highly sought-after job.

Postwar inflation eroded the attractiveness of the police occupation and heralded the problems in recruiting up to official establishment figures which police forces have experienced ever since. This was the opening for the Federation to gain a measure of independence from the early 1950s onwards, and for the establishment of negotiating machinery, the Police Council, along the lines of the Whitley Councils. It was not successful in achieving the

10 The anti-union ideology of policemen, and their resentment at some senior officers' attempts to restrain their conduct at pickets, are documented in my article "Police and Picketing", *New Society*, July 7th, 1977.

72   MARXISM TODAY, MARCH, 1978

status of a free association, however, and remained subject to tight legislative controls on its activities, forbidden to take industrial action, affiliate (and until recently even associate) with outside bodies, involve itself officially in individual discipline cases, or use its funds as it wished.

The Federation in the 1960s

Nonetheless, it was able to use the leverage provided by continuing manpower problems to gain successes in some pay and other negotiations. Outstanding among these was its persuasion of the 1960 Royal Commission on the Police, which was set up after a number of *causes celebres* raised anxiety about the constitutional position of the police, to consider pay first as an urgent priority. Its Interim Report not only recommended a level of pay almost completely conceding the Federation's case, but based this on a formula, the Willink scale, which established police pay at a relative level which has been the target of all subsequent negotiations.

Since the mid-1960s the Federation has become increasingly active and influential as a negotiating body and pressure-group. It has become involved in the process of legislation by giving evidence to Royal Commissions or committees on aspects of criminal justice and lobbying for its views.

The Federation has also become more outspoken in pursuit of pay demands. In 1966 they combined with the official side of the Police Council to protest when the July pay freeze was introduced shortly before their pay review. Their pressure was so effective that, not for the last time in years to come, the police were made a special case.

In 1970 a prolonged pay dispute produced unprecedentedly vigorous Federation tactics, with talk of industrial action at its Annual Conference.

This build-up of militant sentiment, however, was dispelled when the new Conservative government awarded the police a significant rise in February **1971**.

Police Quiescence during the Heath Government

This heralded a period of nearly four years during which the police were treated relatively favourably, in the context of the Heath government's struggle with the trade union movement. As one local Federation secretary commented to me in 1973:

> "Most policemen tend to be Conservative, at the present time especially. For one very good reason—the Tories have been more favourable to the police with pay and conditions. That's what the average policeman tends to care about, 'what's in it for me?' And you don't have to look far to see why the Tories have been so keen to make sure of a happy, contented police force. They're anticipating trouble because of strikes in the next few months".[11]

Structured Variations within the Police Force

The police force is not a monolithic body, however, and there were structured conflicts in it, as well as contradictions and tensions within individuals, which indicated a potential for change under different circumstances. Uniformed constables were more inclined to want union powers than supervisors or specialists, the CID being especially opposed (and also relatively alienated from the Federation). The Federation is constructed so as to give each rank (it includes all ranks up to chief inspector) and special division an *equal* vote on all joint bodies, despite the overwhelming numerical preponderance of the more militant constables.

Generational differences are also important. Those who had joined during or shortly after the war had often been older as recruits, with experience of outside trades and sympathies for unionism, attracted to the police by its instrumental advantages in terms of security. In particular there was a number of older uniformed constables and sergeants with experience of active trade unionism who formed the core of Federation activists at local level and campaigned unsuccessfully at several conferences for trade-union rights. During the 1950s and 1960s there was a trend for recruits to be younger with no previous work experience. They were attracted more by an intrinsic liking for policing than instrumental considerations. They were much less sympathetic to the Federation and averse to its unionisation. It is possible that the return of high unemployment has attracted more instrumentally motivated recruits in recent years, and that these are more recalcitrant to the restraints on their negotiating powers.

The Explosion of Militancy

Since 1975 there has been a dramatic upsurge of militancy among the police. The basis of this was a deterioration of police bargaining power. The "demand" for police was reduced by the decline in industrial conflict following the "social contract". The "supply" of police improved considerably between 1974-6 as rising unemployment made it a more attractive job.

At the May 1975 Annual Conference delegates and observers heckled Home Secretary Roy Jenkins to an extent that made him declare "you must not make me think I'm dealing with the International Marxists". But calls for the right to strike were once more rejected. The 4th June award fell far short of police hopes, but the leadership convinced members it was as much as could be hoped for given pay policy.

[11] Use of the masculine should not be taken as a sign of sexism. Police-women were especially reluctant to be interviewed, and of a sample of 168 only five were female.

MARXISM TODAY, MARCH, 1978

During negotiations for the 1976 pay review, the Staff Side maintained that the 1975 increase had only represented a previously recommended restructuring, with allowance for inflation since 1974. They claimed they had not yet received a Phase One award, but the official side contended that the 1976 review had to be subject to the tighter Phase Two limit. Unable to convince the Official Side, the Federation withdrew from the Police Council in July 1976, declaring they had lost faith in it and demanding direct negotiations with the Home Secretary.

In 1977 militancy developed rapidly, and the future of negotiating machinery remains an open question. The Federation lobbied Parliament, policemen's wives demonstrated with slogans like "lobby for my bobby". There were angry Open Meetings. Several motions on industrial action and trade-union status were laid down for the May Conference. By May, 31 out of the 43 forces in England and Wales had held referenda on the right to strike, supporting it with majorities ranging from 60-80 per cent. In two polls the question of TUC affiliation had also been raised, but rejected by 2:1.

At Conference feelings ran high. Anger had been aggravated rather than reduced by a Phase Two settlement imposed by the Home Secretary a few days earlier. In an intensely emotional atmosphere, large majorities voted for the right to strike and independent status. However, a motion seeking TUC affiliation was lost. About two-thirds of the delegates voted against it, despite the Central Committee's endorsement. The Home Secretary's speech was met by a wall of silence, while outside the Conference he was mobbed by plain-clothed police, one sporting a tee-shirt saying "Stuff Merlyn Rees".[12]

These events clearly open up the issue of police unionism as a live political prospect for the first time since 1919. The militant mood and support for the right to strike are an explosive shift from the past forelock-touching approach and acquiescence in statutory restrictions. But whether police industrial action or unionisation are likely immediate prospects must remain doubtful.[13]

The Ebb of Militancy

Despite the unity shown at Conference, it remains apparent that the ranks differ. Inspectors are much less keen on the right to strike, and more inclined to press for the other goal which the Federation has espoused, an independent police pay review body.

[12] For a more detailed analysis of this Conference, see my article "Scarborough Conference 1977", *Police Journal,* January 1978.

[13] This is despite reports of overtime bans by policemen in at least three forces since the summer.

An inspectors' split from the Federation should an actual strike be imminent can be anticipated. While wildcat, small-scale outbreaks are possible, a united front for industrial action still seems remote.

Unionism remains unpopular, as the votes on TUC affiliation indicated. Although the national leadership supported it, most delegates responded to the red-baiting of the speakers against affiliation, and rejected it. Anti-union sentiment is likely to have increased since May, with the wide publicity given to police injuries at Grunwick.

The possibility of a police strike continued to be threatened by the Federation, despite the setting up in July of a Committee of Inquiry under Lord Edmund Davies. But on October 31st, the Federation accepted a 10 per cent rise which was well below the 60-100 per cent they had been claiming, together with assurances that the government would accept the findings of the Inquiry. The sudden climb-down was much criticised by the rank-and-file. But despite doubts, the membership seem to have been persuaded to wait for the verdict of Edmund Davies.

Why the leadership accepted the offer in view of the strength of rank-and-file feeling, and enthusiastic support for their "special case" from the Tories, remains unclear. The prospect of actively organising militancy may have proved ultimately too frightening, especially in view of Chairman Jim Jardine's revelation on October 8th that he had been threatened with prosecution under Section 53 of the 1964 Police Act prohibiting "causing disaffection". This may have combined with a change in the police bargaining situation to make the prospects of a satisfactory rise without further militancy more promising. For during 1977 the manpower situation worsened, with increasing numbers leaving the force. The reasons for this exodus at a time of high unemployment are obscure. The Federation attributes it mainly to the relative deterioration of pay, while some Chief Constables have also blamed the violence of clashes at Lewisham, Manchester and Grunwick. The combination of police pay problems with increasing industrial and political conflict is a potent negotiating lever, as the £12,000 advertising campaign mounted by the Federation in the press on October 17th illustrated, with its juxtaposition of a photo of an injured policeman outside Grunwick and the slogan "One way to earn £40 a week".

Another development that may strengthen the police hand without unionisation is the proposal currently being touted by some politicians and the press to separate out a few occupations from ordinary collective bargaining procedures by defining them as "emergency" services. This is clearly a response to the firemen's strike, and unrest in the army as well as the police. Such groups would receive "special case" treatment by the formation of an "independent" body to review their pay and

74   MARXISM TODAY, MARCH, 1978

conditions, in return for which they would eschew industrial action. This might allow the government off the hook, when groups perceived as vital to "law and order" or public safety threaten a pay policy depending on consent, and might be especially attractive to a Tory administration if it wins the next election. There are indications from public opinion polls that it might be widely favoured.[14]

The idea of a "special case" pay review body to deal with "emergency" services has not attracted the Federation's support,[15] although it remains a distinct possibility that the idea of regular "independent" review will end up as a substitute for unionisation.

Analysis of the prospects for police unionisation cannot rest only on describing the present conjuncture, but must consider the class location of the police. Before doing this, however, I shall look at the question of democratisation of police decision-making.

Police Decision-Making and Political Accountability

At present the process of police decision-making is largely concentrated in the hands of chief constables. The precise relationship, constitutionally and in practice, between the chief constable of a police force, its police authority, and the Home Office is a complex and much debated matter. The 1964 Police Act intended to clarify and rationalise the situation, but in many ways failed to do so. The relevant sections are often self-contradictory or vague at crucial points. The police authority are explicitly empowered to appoint the chief constable, to secure his retirement (subject to the Home Secretary's agreement) "in the interests of efficiency", and to receive an Annual Report from the Chief Constable.[16] The Chief Constable may also be asked to submit further reports on "matters connected with the policing of the area" (Section 12.2). However, this is contradicted by the immediately following para-

graph, which declares that the chief constable may refuse to issue such a report if he deems it inappropriate, and refer the matter to the Home Secretary. Nor is the Act clearer about the possibility of the police authority being able to instruct the chief constable on general policy concerning law-enforcement in the area. Again, it would be up to the Home Secretary to decide in cases of conflict between the police authority and chief constable of an area.

The degree of local accountability of police forces has been further restricted by the growing size of police areas due to amalgamations in the last two decades. Although Home Office power has increased with greater dependence on central finance, provision of national support services and more regional co-ordination, successive Home Secretaries have consistently claimed that they are not responsible for specific actions of local forces, as opposed to the Metropolitan Police, for which they are the police authority. Although little is known of the relationship between the Home Secretary and Chief Constables, it is reasonable to conclude that the main beneficiaries of recent changes have been Chief Constables who have gained in autonomy.

Little is known about the process of decision-making in practice, and the real as opposed to constitutional relations between chief constables, police authorities and the Home Secretary, a sharp contrast with the relative plethora of information about lower-level police work. But a valuable recent study by Mike Brogden of the relationship between chief constable and police authority in one provincial city supports the conclusions that can be drawn from an examination of constitutional and organisational changes.[17] He documents the tenuous nature of the authority's activities as a form of lay control. Members of the authority consistently deferred to the "professional" expertise of the chief constable. Operational control seems firmly in the hands of the chief constable.

Despite this, policemen of all ranks chafe at the extent to which they feel that the police authorities, perceived as laymen ignorant of law enforcement affairs (one constable described them as a "group of plumbers and butchers"), restrict the "professional" autonomy of the chief constable. Lessening the involvement of local authorities, who are seen as introducing an unwelcome element of "political" considerations into police matters, has become a central aim of the Federation in its pursuit of a reformed machinery of negotiation and control for the police.

---

[14] The *Sun,* October 26th, 1977; *The Times,* November 2nd, 1977.

[15] *Police,* December 1977, p. 5. There is, however, some evidence of rank-and-file solidarity between police and firemen. In the recent strike, policemen contributed generously to collections for the firemen at meetings.

[16] That the wheels of justice grind exceedingly slow for chief constables is illustrated by the case of Stanley Parr, ex-chief constable of Lancashire, recently dismissed following a disciplinary tribunal. Commenting on the dilatoriness of the police authority in investigating or acting on complaints against him, *Police* comments: "their record of action or inaction is hardly an example of dynamic democratic control". (January 1978, p. 8.) The moral drawn by *Police* is, however, that the case illustrates the need for greater central control relative to local police authorities, a conclusion I would question.

[17] M. Brogden, "A Police Authority: The Denial of Conflict", *Sociological Review,* 1977, Vol. 25, No. 2, pps. 325-49.

Industrial Democracy in the Police

While they resent the perceived power of local authorities, most rank-and-file policemen would like to see themselves have a greater say in decision-making. The Federation does not enjoy a mandatory right to be consulted by either chief constables or police authorities. In practice most chief constables do afford facilities for regular consultation and access, but this is subject to their whim, and the Federation often only learns of decisions after the event. While relations with chief constables vary considerably, Federation relations with police authorities are generally tenuous. Regular consultation between the Federation and police authorities still only occurs in 23 out of the 53 forces.[18]

There is a demand for more institutionalised consultation of the rank-and-file. In my study, 52 per cent of constables felt the Federation should have more say in decision-making, and 80 per cent felt it should have some say.

Democratic Police Authorities

Allowing more scope for internal discussions of decision-making would be a step towards democratisation of the force. The immediate consequence of this would undoubtedly be that the rank-and-file would press demands or opinions of a rather reactionary kind.[19] But the dialectical result of opening up the decision-making process could be the modification of police views as they come into contact with a wider range of considerations than are experienced in the immediate work situation, with its pressures deriving from a given and already defined task. Police officers might come to see that the solution for their problems does not necessitate harsher "law and order" measures, but a rethinking of their purposes and supporting reform of the conditions which generate their difficulties. Whether this happens depends partly on social developments outside the police, but more specifically on increasing civilian involvement in police decisions. This goes against police views, but democratisation of police forces requires the involvement of a wider range of interests than at present. The full range of interests in localities must be involved in police authorities, and their control widened and made more effective.

These proposals may appear to echo the abortive bid for "community control" of the police which was an outgrowth of the American black and student movements of the 1960s. The weakness of these attempts lay primarily in a romantic conception of the homogeneity of local "communities" in a class society, and neglected the extent to which they are dominated by wider structures of power. Effective changes at local level can only take place in conjunction with wider developments, or old fallacies will be repeated in a chimerical pursuit of "socialism in one community". But such changes in local police control are an important part of any movement towards socialism.

Independent Review of Complaints against the Police

A related issue of external control is the vexed issue of ensuring an independent element in the handling of complaints against the police. Despite much criticism in the past of the lack of an independent element in judging complaints, and evidence of class and other forms of discrimination in the outcome of investigations, policemen felt that the system already gave too much scope to trivial or malicious allegations. There was consequently much opposition to the 1976 Police Act's extension of non-police control through the establishment of an "independent" Complaints Board. The introduction of a "non-police" element in the complaints procedure must be distinguished from "independence" in any meaningful sense. The new system seems in effect to give the government greater powers over the police, and despite the rhetoric of "popular" control, chief constables remain significant. The Prime Minister selects all the Board's members, and the Home Secretary has a considerable role in formulating its procedures. Disciplinary tribunals will be chaired by the chief constable and have two lay members. While guilt is found by a majority decision, the chief constable alone, after consultation, decides punishment. However, although the reform seems to fall short of what was claimed by its proponents, it does open up possibilities for greater civilian control depending on the extent of usage of the machinery and the monitoring of results. Initial indications are far from encouraging, however. The character of the Board's members is decidedly respectable and establishment, the chairman being the ubiquitous Lord Plowden, also recently appointed to the enquiry on police pay and representative machinery.[20] Contrary to expectations, the Board does not seem to have produced a rise in the number of complaints, probably because people are deterred by the threat of legal action against them for libellous complaints.[21] Under Police Federation pressure a clause was included in the Act entitling policemen complained against to see the letter of complaint. If it is libellous or

---

[18] *Police Review,* April 8th, 1977, p. 443.

[19] Some Federation officials have argued to me that continued restrictions on police political activity are needed because of growing sympathy among police officers for the National Front and other right-wing movements.

[20] D. Humphry, "Fuzzy Board", *New Statesman,* January 28th 1977.

[21] D. Humphry, "Police Complaints Face Libel Snag", *Sunday Times,* July 24th, 1977, p. 4.

76

MARXISM TODAY, MARCH, 1978

defamatory in their view, they can use Federation funds for a court action. On the other hand, the Federation has advised members not to co-operate with the new procedure because the Act failed to *compel* chief constables to show policemen letters of complaint, if he deems this "contrary to public interest". Despite these inauspicious beginnings, the new procedure must be used as a basis for extending civilian accountability of the police.

(III) THE POLICE IN SOCIETY
(a) The Place of the Police in Class Relations
The potentialities and political implications of police unionisation depend on how one analyses the place of the police in class relations, that is their location in the social division of labour as a whole. This does not explain or predict the position they take up in terms of political and ideological practice in specific conjunctures—the political cannot be simply "read off" from the economic. But it suggests the extent to which there is any basic identity of interest between the police and working-class, or whether any possible common action would be only a fragile alliance, won or, perhaps more easily, lost only by political manoeuvring. The question of identifying the class location of the police is not intended as a pigeon-holing exercise, but an exploration of political possibilities.

Broad or Narrow Working Class?
Alan Hunt has recently suggested a distinction between "broad" and "narrow" definitions of the boundaries of the working class.[22] **"The** 'broad' definition defines the working-class as all those who sell their labour-power (in return for wages and salaries) and are not owners (or controllers) of the means of production." The "narrow" definition restricts the working class to those that produce surplus-value or to manual industrial workers. Poulantzas' definition incorporates both restrictions in confining the working class to productive workers making material commodities.[23] A third possible approach which proposes that there can be *contradictory* class locations, is rejected almost out of hand by Hunt, but is the most helpful for understanding the police.[24]

The political implications of these disputes are fairly obvious. If the working class is identified with

[22] A. Hunt, "Class Structure and Political Strategy", *Marxism Today*, July 1977.

[23] N. Poulantzas, *Classes in Contemporary Capitalism*, New Left Books, 1975.

[24] This approach is associated with G. Carchedi, "On the Economic Identification of the New Middle Class", *Economy and Society*, 1975; and E. O. Wright, "Class Boundaries in Advanced Capitalist Societies", *New Left Review* 98, 1976.

the broad definition then the police would be part of it. The realisation of the unity of the working class remains a political problem, but no more so for the police than other workers who are also divided by the pursuit of sectional interests and the hegemony of ruling class ideas.

On the other hand, if the working class is defined restrictively then it is only a small minority, although it may succeed in forming more or less fragile alliances with fractions of other classes that become polarised towards it. As Hunt argues, "such a position leads inexorably towards the adoption of an insurrectionary strategy". But given the armouries at the disposal of the state if the agents of its repressive apparatuses remain loyal to it, or at best are only loosely allied to the working class, such a strategy is more likely to end in what the *Communist Manifesto* called "the common ruin of the contending classes" than "a revolutionary re-constitution of society at large".

But if the police are essentially part of the working class it becomes hard to explain why they have been so much more consistently hostile to realising this unity with it than almost any other section. This is especially so in view of the predominantly working-class *origins* of the police in all places and periods, (largely a result of deliberate strategy to make them appear representative of those they control). If, on the other hand, there are *objective* bases of division between the police and the working class, then the record of police politics becomes clearer. However, the political and ideological practice of the police has not been consistently reactionary, as we have already seen.

Contradictory Class Location of the Police
The answer to the problem of explaining the contradictory positions taken up by the police lies, I suggest, in their *contradictory* class location. Is this position untenable, as argued by Hunt and Poulantzas?[25] They claim that the idea of contradictory class location implies that some groups can be "suspended or floating between classes or have one foot in the working class and the other in the capitalist class". I would suggest that this apparent absurdity is avoided if we adopt Poulantzas' own distinction between *place* in the class structure and *positions* taken up in specific conjunctures of class struggle. The position a group takes up in a concrete conjuncture must always be on one side or the other (schizophrenia aside), or at any rate it must be divided into segments taking one or other side. But this does not apply to their place in the structure of class relations, which has different elements that

[25] N. Poulantzas, "The New Petty Bourgeoisie" in A. Hunt (ed.), *Class and Class Structure*, Lawrence and Wishart, 1977, pp. 118-9.

MARXISM TODAY, MARCH, 1978   77

may be contradictory. The place of a group in the class structure depends on economic, political and ideological elements, and these can involve contradictory pressures of an objective kind, which are manifested in their concrete conditions.

The police exemplify this. Their place in political and ideological relations is to maintain the domination of the capitalist class. They help preserve the relatively stable conditions of social life necessary for *any* form of production to take place, but at the same time they protect a system of property relations in which surplus value is realised and appropriated to one class. In some situations they defend a particular rate of exploitation by helping to break strikes or make picketing ineffective. They also control political dissent. As part of a system of law and criminal justice based on principles of formal equality within a society of substantive inequality they perpetuate an ideology of legality and fairness which veils class rule.

But they do not share to any great extent in the return on the capital they protect. They are politically dominated within a rigidly hierarchical work organisation, have accepted an ideology which denies them a significant voice in the decisions affecting their working lives, and are largely excluded from an understanding of the forces underlying their problems. In short, they are economically, politically and ideologically oppressed.

They are not, however, economically *exploited*. This would be implied by the "wide" definition of the working-class as all wage-labour. But as Eisler and Seifert point out in a critique of Hunt, workers like the police, who do not directly produce surplus value and are paid out of revenue, cannot be described as *exploited*, no matter how poor their pay.[26] Although they may indirectly contribute to the reproduction and realisation of capital, indeed in the case of the police be essential to it, they are not employed bycapital in the expectation of making aprofit.

This is important for understanding the possibilities and limitations of such groups as the police being bought off by the State to control their potential dissent. Since they are paid out of revenue their wages can be adjusted to the level required to ensure their contribution to the continued production and realisation of surplus value. The limits to this are not, in the first place, economic.

The limits to police income depend on political and ideological factors. One is the organisation and consciousness of the police themselves. Another is the organisation and consciousness of the working-class in relation to government strategy. If there is voluntary acquiescence of the labour movement with government policy, as under the "social

contract", the limits of police bargaining power will be tighter. Concessions to the police would undermine government strategy, while the police are less vital because workers are essentially policing themselves. If government policy involves the forced imposition of pay restraint, as under Heath, concessions to the police do not undermine any consensus and are necessary to ensure that the police play the vital role accorded to them of controlling militancy.

However, the police compete for a share of revenue with other unproductive workers, as well as the capitalist class. They will thus be economically oppressed to the extent possible given their own degree of organisation and militancy in relation to the political and ideological resources available to these other groups.

Thus the condition of the police is economically, politically and ideologically oppressed in ways analogous to the working class. This explains their resort to similar tactics of union action, and in some conjuctures, affiliation with the labour movement. **But** these pressures are contradicted by others deriving from their role in maintaining the domination of capital over labour. This tends to cut them off from other workers, and makes them particularly exposed to reactionary ideology and politics. It places them in situations where their immediate enemies are other oppressed groups, who they come to blame for the problems of their job. This is bolstered by the possibility that they may be bought off out of revenue, and their *immediate* economic interest become opposed to other workers.

Nonetheless, their own oppressed economic, political and ideological condition offers the possibility of their defensive strategies becoming linked with the labour movement. The main barrier to this is the way their work experiences generate a diagnosis which defines other workers as the source of their problems, and leads them to espouse reactionary solutions of repression. Pay apart, their main problems are subjectively defined in terms of "law and order", the containment of crime and dissent. I will next consider the way the police define their role in society.

(b) The Role of the Police: Repressive Apparatus or Social Service?

The Contrast between the Police Conception of their Role and the Reality

Empirical studies of police work have repeatedly shown that the vast bulk of police activity relates not to law-enforcement but the provision of a varied range of services to people in need.[27] But studies

---

[26] E. Eisler and M. Seifert, "Definitions of the Working Class", *Marxism Today*, November 1977.

[27] See, for example, M. Punch and T. Naylor, *op. cit.;* E. Cumming *et. al.,* "Policeman As Philosophers, Guide and Friend", *Social Problems,* 1965, Vol. 12, No. 3.

78   MARXISM TODAY, MARCH, 1978

have also demonstrated that in the conception of most policemen such social service aspects of their work have little importance. They see themselves as primarily concerned with preventing or detecting crime, and in more speculative moments, as "the thin blue line" separating chaos from civilisation. Increasing crime rates are usually taken as an indication of the need for more police resources, and are often used to support pay claims. However, there is little reason to suppose that this strategy of combatting crime by greater police power can succeed. The sources of crime lie deep in the social structure, beyond police control, and, as long as this remains so, increasing police resources is a Canute-like attempt to push back the debris of society.

In recent years there have been some indications in more liberal police circles that this is coming to be appreciated by them. For example, the Boston Police Commissioner, Robert J. Di Grazia has said:

> "There is relatively little the police can do about crime. We are not letting the public in on our era's dirty little secret; that those who commit the crime which worries citizens most—violent street crime—are, for the most part, the products of poverty, unemployment, broken homes, rotten education, drug addiction and alcoholism, and other social and economic ills about which the police can do little, if anything. Rather than speaking up, most of us stand silent and let politicians get away with law and order rhetoric that reinforces the mistaken notion that the police—in ever greater numbers and with ever more gadgetry—can alone control crime."[28]

Even our own Home Office has come to question the idea that increasing police activity and numbers necessarily succeed in controlling crime.[29]

The Crime Problem in Proportion
People have a quite understandable fear of crime and need to be protected. In view of the poverty of the traditional solutions, what is to be done? The first task is to get the problem into proportion. Despite the much publicised statistics showing rapidly rising crime rates, it remains the case that most officially recorded crime is not of the kind that really strikes terror into people's hearts. Of the 2,135·7 thousand indictable offences recorded as known to the police in 1976, 95 per cent were offences against property. Violence against the person accounted for 3.6 per cent of indictable offences, and another 1 per cent of the total were sexual offences. So the overwhelming majority of indictable offences are against *property* rather than the person. Against this it must be said that offences of violence against

[28] R. J. Di Grazia, "What's Wrong with America's Police Leadership", *Police,* May 1976, p. 24.

[29] *A Review of Criminal Justice Policy* 1976, Annex C.

the person have been rising rapidly in the last few years, exhibiting a rate of increase exceeded only by criminal damage. Furthermore, some property offences such as burglary and robbery may involve a degree of personal fright in the victim but without any actual violence, so that the loss cannot be calculated only in material terms. It is important to note the relatively petty amounts involved in most robberies, burglaries and thefts (the largest categories of property offence). 32 per cent involved losses under £5, and 85 per cent were of amounts under £100. This hardly indicates a prevalence of big-time crime.

While the rise in violent crime is obviously disturbing, it must be pointed out that relatively little of it fits the stereotypical fear of crime in the streets or unprovoked assault by a stranger. Of homicides, in 1976, for example, 73 percent involved suspects who were acquainted with the victim, and in 51 per cent of cases the victim was a member of the family, cohabitant or lover of the suspect. More disturbing is the fact that homicide by a stranger, although still only 18 per cent of the total in 1976, has risen over the last decade (although fluctuating from year to year).

What the above figures indicate is the connection between most crimes and the nature of social relations in our society. The vast bulk of indictable crime consists of relatively minor offences. Is it implausible to suggest that in a more egalitarian and less competitive society, which guaranteed decent minimum standards of life and the opportunity for good education and productive work to all, the number of such offences would be *drastically* reduced?

Most violent crimes also are the product of the quality of intimate interpersonal relations in our society. They are particularly insensitive to law enforcement efforts. Hopefully, a less competitive society might see a reduction in their extent. In so far as they remained a problem, might it not be that crimes in the family are more appropriately dealt with by what Griffiths has called the "family model" of criminal process, rather than the "crime control model"?

The same applies to many of the non-indictable offences processed by the police, which though more numerous are generally considered relatively minor. These can essentially be divided into six categories: traffic offences, offences by companies, vice offences like drugs or prostitution, minor assaults, public order offences like drunkeness or vagrancy, and tax offences. There is a good case for removing the category of vice offences from the statute book altogether. This is not only because there are ethical arguments against using the weight of the law to punish people for behaviour to which all directly involved parties consent, but because such offences

MARXISM TODAY, MARCH, 1978   79

have traditionally been the prime breeding ground for police corruption. While public nuisances like drunkeness or vagrancy require some form of control, the "family" model of providing effective social service help for those with personal problems is more desirable than treating weak or pathetic people as offenders.

The Police Task in a Socialist Society

I would argue that in a socialist society, which involved changes in the distribution of resources and a less competitive tone in social relations, including sexual ones, the police task would no longer be the apparently impossible endeavour of controlling a mass of human misery, degradation and brutality that it now is. Much property crime of relatively minor kinds would disappear, other offences would be decriminalised, and those which are clearly related to personal problems would be handled according to a "family" rather than "crime control" model. This would not, however, leave the police with nothing to do. On the contrary, they would be in a position to take seriously important and challenging tasks that are now relatively neglected, and attain the status of skilled "professionals" which, despite much propaganda, has eluded them in the past.

Preventive Patrol and Civilian Involvement

First, the freeing of resources as the pressure of petty crime diminished would allow concentration on the most alarming offence in terms of public fear, violent street crime. As the preventive patrol studies implied, this is the one kind of offence which might be sensitive to visible patrolling, though the level of policing required would be financially prohibitive at present. This would no longer be the case if resources could be freed from other duties. Thus one function which would remain would be the continuous patrol, on foot or in vehicles, of public places. This is essential not only for crime prevention purposes but also because it allows the police to provide the many services to people in need of varying kinds of support which studies show is the main source of calls on police time.

What must be questioned, however, is whether this kind of work requires only specialised professional police officers. Until the beginning of the last century, policing was essentially seen as a communal duty which in principle everyone had a responsibility to participate in. This principle has been honoured more in lip-service than practice. But it would seem to me desirable for several reasons that they be made a reality. On the one hand, citizens should not let the "dirty work" of society become the burden of a restricted few. They must know about, and contribute to the solution of, the extreme problems thrown up by the pressures of

living which confront the police. On the other hand, the role of society's "dirty workers" that the police now perform produces the sense of cynicism and bitterness, amounting at worst to a paranoid garrison mentality, which sociological studies have depicted as the typical police outlook, and which is portrayed at its most extreme in the novels of ex-Los Angeles policeman Joseph Wambaugh. An element of citizen participation in law enforcement is also a means of democratic control, if it is on a universal basis rather than the present self-selected Special Constabulary. This is vital if there is to be a more pervasive patrol presence.

While citizen involvement in routine patrol is desirable, it does not obviate the need for trained, experienced, professional officers. They are necessary to guide the citizens, and to cope with the more difficult and demanding jobs requiring special knowledge and experience. The ideal would be routine patrol by a combined body of citizens on a rotating basis working in conjunction with professional officers. The latter would then play an important educative and supervisory role, as well as their patrol function. The rewards for the police would be an elevated status and a removal of citizen antagonism.

Detective Work and Crime in the Suites

In addition to patrol, there would be a body of highly skilled and trained officers to handle detective work in relation to serious crimes committed in private. In a socialist society, and a transitional one, detectives would have much more demanding tasks, requiring more esoteric skills than at present. This is because priorities of enforcement would alter. Instead of dealing primarily with minor property and vice offences, much more attention would be directed to large-scale property offences of the "white collar" type, such as embezzlement. At present relatively few resources are directed to these because of the great amount of time and effort required to uncover and prove a fraud case. But the quantity of money involved in such cases typically far exceeds the property crimes of the poor. The present concentration of police resources on the crimes of the poor rather than the rich, which was recognised by a recent Police Federation Chairman, must be reversed.[30] A war against crime in the suites rather than crime in the streets requires more highly trained and skilled police officers and would give them a higher status and social importance.

Political Police

The role of the specifically political police would have to change in appropriate ways. Rather than

---

[30] "A Fair Cop—But Is It Always So?", *Daily Express*, July 20th, 1971, p. 8.

80   MARXISM TODAY, MARCH, 1978

concentrating on trade-union and left-wing activists, it would be concerned with forestalling counter-revolutionary activity and foreign subversion. But it is vital that political policing be brought firmly under the control of the elected legislature, as opposed to the present situation where it is almost entirely free from public scrutiny and account-ability.[31]

(IV) CONCLUSION

1 have argued in this article that it is dangerous for the Left to ignore the important and justified public concern about crime and the police. I have tried to show that the facts of life in this area are not necessarily Tory. The traditional "law and order"

[31] T. Bunyan, *op. cit.,* p. 131-3, p. 192, p. 291-6.

strategies for crime control cannot succeed, but in a more egalitarian and less competitive society the crime problem would have a different character. Within such a society the police function and status would be more important than at present, and they would have a more rewarding role.

Certain recent developments, notably public discussion of civilian review and accountability, and police unionisation, offer the opportunity for a widening of debate about the police role, and the pressing of the points I have argued above. However, it must continuously be remembered that no changes in police organisation are likely to prove of much value in the absence of wider social reforms. They can only be pressed in conjunction with the building of a wider democratic movement towards socialism.

[2]
The Police in the Class Structure

"Police vote for the right to strike" declared *The Times'* headline on 25 May 1977. The next morning there was a picture of a less than ecstatically happy Merlyn Rees (Home Secretary) surrounded by fist-shaking, banner-waving, plain-clothed policemen. The media gave extensive coverage that week to the militancy demonstrated at the Police Federation Annual Conference, the culmination of months of unrest. Just three weeks later the police relationship with trade unionism again hit the front pages but from a diametrically opposed angle. Readers of *The Times* on 14 June saw a photograph of three excited policemen dragging away a picket member outside the Grunwick factory gates, watched by an angry crowd held back by a line of constables.

These closely juxtaposed events illustrate this article's central contention, that the police occupy a contradictory place in the class structure. This, linked by its effects on their work and life conditions, must be taken into account in analysing the position they take up in specific political and social conjunctures. In short, while the ideological and political practice of the police is normally "conservative" (maintaining the existing social order), there are countervailing pressures which may be significant in particular historical circumstances. Police support for the *status quo*, while usually reliable, is problematic. It has to be won by the ruling class and it can be lost.

The specific focus of this article is on the class position of the police as reflected in its relationship to trade unionism. Trade union organisation is not directly connected to class position or consciousness.[1] But most sociologists would accept Lockwood's description of the trade union movement as "the main vehicle of working class consciousness".[2] While trade union organisation is neither a sufficient condition of class consciousness, nor an unequivocal index of place in the class structure, it is usually a response to at least some facets of the condition of being working class.

This article is divided into four sections. The first relates the police to some recent discussions of class. The second examines the specific conditions of police work. In the third part the consequences of the police place in the class structure will be traced in an historical account of British police unionism. Finally, the subjective reflection of this in the consciousness of policemen will be examined by looking at a study of police attitudes to unionism, which I conducted in 1973. This must be firmly located in the specific historical context in which it was carried out, rather than treated as tapping some constant or universal set of attitudes.

[1] Some would deny any such relationship e.g. G.S. Bain, D. Coates and V. Ellis, *Social Stratification and Trade Unionism* (1973). For a critique of this industrial relations approach see Crompton, "Approaches to the Study of White-Collar Unionism" (1976) 10:3 *Sociology* 407-26. Marxists would emphasise Lenin's distinction between "trade-union" and "class" consciousness. See R. Hyman, *Marxism and the Sociology of Trade Unionism* (1971).

[2] D. Lockwood, *The Black-coated Worker* (1958) 13.

My perspective, of the policeman as a worker, differs from previous sociological research, which has concentrated on the output of policing, how the police process deviance and maintain order. But before the policeman can be a labeller, peace-keeper, philosopher, guide and friend, he has first to turn up for work. As recent American experience testifies, the policeman, like other employees, may withdraw his labour.[3] Even more important is the possibility that in some situations countervailing pressures and loyalties may make the policeman a less than reliable agent of government in controlling crowds, demonstrations or pickets.[4]

The place of the police in the class structure

It is not possible to consider comprehensively the myriad ways in which class, perhaps the British sociologist's pet word, has been used. But certain distinctions must be made. First, in many treatments, the concern is not class as a structured set of social relations, but rather the background and mobility of individual agents. Second, many usages confuse class with status, in the sense of "style of life".[5]

The Weberian tradition, perhaps the most influential in academic sociological treatment of stratification, avoids that confusion.[6] But it reduces class to one dimension of stratification amongst others, effectively coequal with status. Class situation is used as a factor in explaining behaviour, but itself remains unexplained. Class is seen as a phenomenon of the market, and the underlying capitalist process of production is not explored.[7]

Class has also been the focus of much recent debate amongst Marxists. Theoretically a major issue has been to cut the Gordian knot of treating the economic as determinant in the last instance of the structure of social relations, while eschewing economism, the simplistic reduction of political and ideological structures to the economic. This is a focal concern of Poulantzas' seminal attempt to ground class economically in the process of production of surplus value, while also including political and ideological

[3] M. Levi, *Bureaucratic Insurgency* (1977); S. Bernstein *et.al. The Iron Fist and the Velvet Glove* (2nd ed., 1977) chap. 6.

[4] A valuable historical paper demonstrates how, in 19th century America, the sympathy of local police forces for strikers from their communities had to be systematically broken down by a strategy of "professionalisation". Robinson, "The Deradicalisation of the Policeman" (1978) April *Crime and Delinquency*.

[5] W.A.T. Nichols, "Social Class: Official, Sociological and Marxist" in *Demystifying Social Statistics* (ed. J. Evans, J. Irvine and I. Miles, 1978) gives a lucid account of these distinctions.

[6] H.H. Gerth and C.W. Mills (eds.), *From Max Weber: Essays in Sociology* (1948) chap. VII; D. Lockwood *op.cit.*; Goldthorpe and Lockwood, "Affluence and the British Class Structure" (1963) 11:2 *Sociol. Rev.* 133-63; J. Goldthorpe *et.al., The Affluent Worker in the Class Structure* (1969).

[7] Crompton, *op.cit.*, 409.

relations as elements in class determination.[8] This has been criticised both for treating politics and ideology as coequal with economics, and for reducing political strategy in effect to economic class interest.[9]

The practical stimulus to this debate has been the problem of locating the proliferating middle strata of 20th century capitalism, neither clearly proletarian nor bourgeois. Essentially there are two contrasting approaches. The first confines the category of worker to the unequivocal proletariat, manual producers of surplus value with no control or supervisory functions (in Poulantzas' even narrower definition only those making material commodities). Other groups of wage-labour are excluded because of economic criteria (e.g. non-productive work or function in the social division of labour), and/or their place in political and ideological relations. They constitute a new middle class or petty bourgeoisie, albeit with fractions which may have a proletarian or bourgeois polarisation. The alternative approach stresses the common condition of lack of property and lack of control to locate such middle groups in the working class, even though the contradictory pull of political and ideological factors may make their actual position in specific conjunctures a conservative one. Since the narrow view involves the concept of polarisations which may deviate from class place, and the broad view recognises contradictory locations with the same effect both concede that "position in the conjuncture" (Poulantzas' term), i.e. action in specific historical circumstances in neo-Weberian language, may not correspond to place in the social division of labour. The two viewpoints really reflect contrasting conceptions of the ultimate interests of the middle groups and working class, rather than analyses of immediate variations in behaviour.

What these discussions lack is adequate connection of place in the class structure with concrete analysis of specific conjunctures. The recent Marxist accounts have not moved back from the discussion of class place, and its consequences for the condition of different groups, to consciousness, action or organisation.

In trying to develop an account of the police in the class structure, three levels of analysis will be considered: (a) Place in the class structure i.e. the location of the police in relations of production and the social division of labour; (b) Class condition, that is, the actual correlates of their place in concretely perceptible economic, political and ideological terms; (c) Class

[8] Poulantzas, "On Social Classes" (1973) 78 *New Left Review* 27-55; *Political Power and Social Class* (1973); *Classes in Contemporary Capitalism* (1975).

[9] Wright, "Class Boundaries in Advanced Capitalist Societies" (1976) 98 *New Left Review* 18; B. Hindess, "The Concept of Class in Marxist Theory and Marxist Politics" in *Class, Hegemony and Party* (ed. J. Bloomfield, 1977) 103.

position, that is, the consequences of place, as mediated by condition, for consciousness, action and organisation.[10]

The police occupy a contradictory place in the class structure.[11] Economically, the police (at any rate all but the most senior officers) are working class. They are dispossessed i.e. wage labourers, with no control over the labour power of others, and relatively little over their own (although this varies both over time and between different specialisations). Their role is indirectly productive in that it maintains the stable social environment necessary for any production to take place. Furthermore, they facilitate the realisation of surplus value by protecting property relations. They also play an important part in affecting the rate of exploitation, when they intervene in labour disputes in such a way as to weaken union action. Even if they act impartially, they are protecting the right of capital to maintain its rate of return. While thus playing a vital part in the process of reproduction of capital, the police are not productive in the sense of directly creating value.[12] To Poulantzas and others, this would mean they must be classed as petty-bourgeois, rather than workers, despite the fact that they are wage labourers, and may indeed themselves be exploited, in the sense that they provide surplus labour power such that their wages are less than the increase in value realised by employers due to their efforts. At most, in this view, their condition of being wage labourers, subject to control of their work, and possibly exploited, may under some circumstances lead to a proletarian polarisation, expressed, for example, in industrial action, without their being working class. However, the relevance of the productive/unproductive labour distinction, so crucial to Poulantzas, is of questionable use in explaining class condition and position as opposed to theories of crisis.[13]

I would thus argue that the police can be seen as working class in economic terms, although their role in political and ideological relations, their location in the social division of labour, makes their overall class place a contradictory one. Although economically working class they contribute to the political and ideological domination of capital over labour. (This is quite independent of any specific partiality shown by policemen, and does

[10] The relationship between position and place is problematic if one foregoes economism, the view that there is a necessary and straightforward reflection. I would suggest that while relations of production have determinate ideological and political preconditions, and hence limit the possible range of variation of action, within these parameters political, legal, ideological and cultural forces operate in an irreducible way. To the extent that there are contradictory pressures operating for some groups (like the police) at the level of place, these limits, and hence the relative autonomy of action, will be wider.

[11] This is also argued by Wright, *op.cit.*, 40-1.

[12] This does not mean that they are not socially useful. The concept of productive labour is independent of any notion of utility. See Gough, ''Marx's Theory of Productive and Unproductive Labour'' (1972) 76 *New Left Review* 47-72.

[13] Wright, *op.cit.*, 16-18.

not impugn their formal and often factual neutrality — or even sympathy for labour.)

What are the consequences of this contradictory place for condition and position? The next section examines the effects of class place on police conditions.

The class condition of policemen

This will be considered in terms of market, work and status situation. Market situation refers to "economic position narrowly conceived, consisting of source and size of income, degree of job-security and opportunity for upward occupational mobility".[14] The market situation of policemen is comparable in form to other salaried employees, but their relative financial standing fluctuates.[15] Until 1919 police pay was on a par with agricultural and unskilled labour. This reflected the 19th century "deliberate policy to recruit men 'who had not the rank, habits or station of gentlemen' ".[16] It was intended to give the appearance of a separation of "constitutional authority from . . . social and economic dominance", and hence facilitate working class acceptance of the police as a force representing the communal interest embodied in the rule of law.[17] After the 1918-19 police strikes, the police gained a substantial pay advantage over most other workers, which continued through the inter-war years. After the Second World War the police fell considerably behind their "Golden Age" of the 1930's. The Royal Commission of 1960 recommended substantial rises, but during the 1960's this level was not maintained. By 1974 the constable's pay had fallen behind and there was much official anxiety about the manpower shortage. Following the 1975 Police Council Working Party the Federated ranks received an average increase of 28%, but the 1976 pay negotiations were bedevilled by conflict. The official and staff sides disagreed about what the level of pay was in 1976-7. The dispute partly concerned the value of the rent and other allowances, which form an important part of the policeman's market situation. (According to a Police Council survey in May 1974, basic pay was only 76% of average earnings of uniformed constables in England and Wales).

While the relative financial status of the policeman varies, he is economically working class inasmuch as he is dependent on the sale of his labour power. However, due to the police function in relations of production, they will under some circumstances have economic interests in opposition to other workers. Increasing state intervention in the economy with the

---

[14] Lockwood, *op.cit.*, 15.

[15] It is traced in detail in J.P. Martin and G. Wilson, *The Police: A Study in Manpower* (1969), and the 1975 *Report of the Police Council Working Party on Pay*.

[16] T.A. Critchley, *A History of Police in England and Wales* (1967) 52.

[17] A. Silver, "The Demand for Order in Civil Society" in *The Police: Six Sociological Essays* (ed. D. Bordua, 1967); W.R. Miller, *Cops and Bobbies: Police Authority in New York and London* (1977).

development of monopoly capitalism makes wage bargaining more explicitly politicised. Two strategies of wage control to protect profitability can be distinguished: the conflictual and the consensual. The consensual has been the mode typically adopted by Labour governments, with their understanding with trade unions allowing "voluntary" incomes policies. The conflictual has been the mode adopted by Conservative governments. The particular mode in operation is important to the police. A conflictual mode increases the need for police morale and loyalty making them a special case. This is recognised by policemen. As one Federation branch secretary told me in 1973: "You don't have to look far to see why the Tories have been so keen to make sure of a happy, contented police force. They're anticipating trouble because of strikes in the next few months, and they want to keep us happy". During Labour's "voluntary" policy after 1974, by contrast, it became imperative to the government that the police were *not* a "special case", which would have weakened TUC assent. Furthermore, recession in industry make the police force, with its comparative security, especially attractive, and buoyant recruitment weakens police bargaining power. These circumstances underlay the police pay dispute and militancy of 1976-7.

In terms of the other constituents of market situation, security and mobility prospects, the police fare well relative to most workers. After the first two probationary years, a constable can only be dismissed for a serious disciplinary offence or criminal conviction. Several studies have seen security as one of the major reasons motivating recruitment, but mine did not replicate this.[18] In my sample, 49% mentioned solely non-instrumental reasons for joining, 19% mentioned purely instrumental factors, and 33% both. This suggests a markedly non-instrumental initial orientation to work. However, this varies historically according to labour ·market conditions, which accounts for the contradiction with previous research. Of men who had joined before 1949, 43% gave only instrumental reasons, (mainly security), compared with 23% joining in the 1950's, and 11% of those who entered after 1960. It seems that recruits in a full employment period more often have an intrinsic attraction to policing, while in a recession the instrumental advantage of security becomes more compelling.

The mobility prospects of policemen appear good, though only a few can reach high rank. The police force is unique in that the élite is generated internally, compared to other organisations which have qualification barriers at various levels. All policemen begin with the same formal chances of promotion. In practice, people with some characteristics are more likely to succeed than others. Those with police backgrounds, better educational qualifications, cadet entry, or previous non-manual jobs, are more likely to become specialists and/or supervisors. Subjective perceptions of the

[18] My study is reported fully in R. Reiner, *The Blue-Coated Worker: A Sociological Study of Police Unionism* (1978). It was based on lengthy interviews with a representative sample of the Federated ranks of a city force in 1973-4.

promotion system reflect this. Only 25% of constables in my sample, but 52% and 57% of sergeants and inspectors respectively, saw promotion as fair. Nonetheless, all have the formal possibility of a better chance of reaching high occupational status than in other jobs drawing from the same socio-economic strata. The market situation of policemen is thus similar to working class occupations in form of income, although the relative pay level varies. It compares favourably in security and mobility prospects.

The work situation is "the set of social relationships in which the individual is involved at work by virtue of his position in the division of labour".[19] A peculiar feature of police work is the paradoxical combination of strict internal discipline of a formal kind, with considerable autonomy in the actual work situation out on the streets. The force as a whole is also largely independent of government involvement and civilian review. All these elements are historically variable, and differ within any force according to role in the internal division of labour.

In Britain, internal supervisory relationships were radically altered during the 1960's. Specialisation and the use of technology increased. Manpower deployment was restructured by the Unit Beat system of policing, and accompanied by improvements in training, especially of senior officers through the Police College. Holdaway has argued that the Unit Beat system was intended as an agent of "professionalisation".[20] However, a major motive was more economic use of manpower.[21] The change was essentially a productivity bargain which in effect intensified the rate of exploitation of police labour, increasing the work-load more than proportionately to any pay rises. The Federation encouraged and approved the changes.[22] Job interest was heightened, and the men could feel their work was more worthwhile. But recently in the general disgruntlement over pay awareness of the exploitative aspects of the change has surfaced.[23]

While there has been a relaxation of internal discipline in terms of parades, standards of physical appearance etc., the Unit Beat system was intended to tighten control over the actual labour process. Under the previous Fixed Point system, bureaucratic regulation by pre-arranged appointments with sergeants and narrowly defined beats, was superimposed upon virtually complete absence of control in between. This allowed great scope for easing behaviour, illicit devices for making the job more pleasant in the long intervals between bursts of real police activity.[24]

[19] Lockwood, loc.cit.

[20] Holdaway, "Changes in Urban Policing" (1977) 28:2 British J. of Sociol. 119-37.

[21] Home Office Reports on Police Manpower, Equipment and Efficiency, 1967.

[22] Federation Newsletter, January 1967, 3.

[23] Police September 1977, 7-9.

[24] M. Cain, Society and the Policeman's Role (1973) 46-75.

On the face of it, the Unit Beat system increased supervisory control. Instead of spasmodic meetings with sergeants, constables in Panda cars were now in continuous radio contact with the station, dispatching them to calls when needed. (Area constables or Home Beat officers, the other main component of the Unit Beat system, were explicitly granted autonomy in terms of when and how to work, but they are a minority compared to Panda drivers). Moreover, radio contact increased the likelihood that a supervisor might also attend an incident, thus allowing more control of the constable's on-the-spot discretion.

Despite this, the subjective perception of most policemen (88%) is that the net effect of the last decade's changes has been relaxation of supervision. Partly this was due to a man-management style of supervision reducing unnecessary regimentation. But it was also felt that Unit Beat policing did not effectively increase supervisory control, and certainly not in an irksome way. Continuous radio contact could be circumvented by various avoidance devices. The workload was increased, but largely in terms of real police work satisfying the men's "action orientation". Many perceived the relationship between constables, sergeants and inspectors as moving from control to teamwork. The following is a typical view from an uniformed constable:

> When I joined we were treated almost like idiots . . . but now we're treated more like men . . . I have a section sergeant, he exists, he's there, but I've been left to get on with it as an individual doing the panda driver's job . . . The supervisor's always available, if necessary, and for the most part they attend emergency calls. With the exception of one sergeant who doesn't usually bother! But the sergeant knows if he exercises too much control, he visits his men too often, they begin to think: "Doesn't he trust me? Doesn't he think I can do the job? Does he think he needs to hold my hand? . . . But he's not really in a position to exercise any control over the P.C. when he's sent out on patrol. No-one is these days. This personal radio system is a lovely advantage. If we want help we can get it immediately. And the public benefits because they have a response to their 999 calls within 2 or 3 minutes, subject to work load. But it's not perfect by any stretch of the imagination. There are vast numbers of black spots where you can't get a message in or out. If you have a piece of apparatus that's not 100% effective, there's always the man who'll take advantage, fail to receive a message — in other words, he ignores it. Because he knows nobody can prove he got the message, unless there's somebody stood on his shoulder . . . Most of the time we play fair, we answer. Not for any high-minded reasons, but we just do. But obviously there are blokes who don't come to work to do any, but just for the ride. This applies in any industry. Some of them shove off a bit quick without a radio, because there's not enough to go round. I'm not saying they're committing crime or going into people's houses, shagging the missus, or any of this nonsense. Just they may be disinterested or lazy, can't be bothered. If a nasty job comes up, a sudden death, and it's a bit pooey, he says "Oh, I don't fancy that, I shan't hear it." He points his car in the appropriate direction, and goes deaf! If the sergeant happens to see him 3 minutes later, he can pull the batteries out of the bloomin' thing and say he was just checking it. I know it's done, and to this extent supervision's impossible.

In terms of immediate supervision, then, the work group of uniformed constables has shown considerable resilience in maintaining autonomy despite attempts to tighten control. This is conducive to policemen developing a consensual image of the nature of the force as a social organisation.

Autonomy varies not only over time but also between ranks and special-isation. The CID, for example, have always enjoyed a greater degree of on-the-job autonomy than patrolling constables.

With regard to control of the force as a whole, the traditional view is that the most important facet and virtue of British police arrangements is the subtle balance of operational autonomy and ultimate account-ability.[25] The respective legal powers of chief constables, central government and local police authorities are ambiguous.[26] The net effect of recent changes has probably been to shift power away from local authorities in favour of the Home Secretary and chief constables.[27] The real, as opposed to formal, relationships are more opaque, for as with other organisations, research on lower-level personnel is more common than on the élite. Policemen advocate "professional" autonomy and resent the influence of local police authorities.[28] Operational control is firmly in the hands of chief constables. No policemen questioned the fundamental acceptability of this, though a majority of constables in my sample wanted a greater say in policy-making.

The aspect of outside control most resented by policemen is the gradual extension of facilities for civilian complaints, starting with the Police Act 1964. Despite much criticism of the lack of an independent element in judging complaints, and evidence of class and other forms of discrimination in their outcome, policemen felt that the system already gave too much scope to trivial or malicious allegations.[29] There was consequently much opposition to the 1976 Police Act's extension of control through the establishment of an independent Complaints Board. The results of the new system have yet to be seen, but the introduction of a non-police element in the complaints procedure must be distinguished from "independence" in any meaningful sense. The new system seems in effect to give the Home Secretary greater powers over the police, despite the rhetoric of community control — an inevitable outcome in view of the vacuousness of any notion of community in the context of a highly stratified society.[30] Thus the police retain a considerable autonomy at all levels, despite attempts to increase accountability. However, the ultimate outcome of recent develop-ments is still uncertain, and subject to political struggle.

[25] R. Mark, *Policing a Perplexed Society* (1977).

[26] G. Marshall, *Police and Government* (1965).

[27] G. Marshall, "The Government of the Police Since 1963" in *The Police We Deserve* (eds. J.C. Alderson and P.J. Stead, 1973) 55-67.

[28] Brogden, "A Police Authority — The Denial of Conflict" (1977) 25:2 *Sociol. Rev.* 325-49, documents the tenuous character of one Watch Committee as a form of lay control.

[29] Box and Russell, "The Politics of Discreditability" (1975) 23:2 *Sociol. Rev.* 315-46.

[30] M. Cain, "An Ironical Departure: The Dilemma of Contemporary Policing" in *A Yearbook of Social Policy 1976* (ed. K. Jones, 1977).

The status situation refers to "the position of the individual in the hierarchy of prestige in the society at large."[31] There is evidence that the police enjoy considerable esteem, though the extent accorded by different groups varies, and most policemen have experienced upward social mobility through joining the force. This is not reflected, however, in policemen's own estimation of how they are regarded.

The Registrar-General's classification of occupational groups purports to be a system of classes, but in the categories of this paper, it is a set of divisions by status.[32] Most policemen are placed in class III (Skilled Occupations), Non-manual (senior officers are in higher categories). In the 1971 Census, nearly two-thirds of the population were in lower classes. Most policemen started their lives in a lower status group, usually skilled manual. The social origins of my sample are shown below:

Registrar-General's Social Class

I	II	III (non-manual)	III (manual)	IV	V	Military/ agriculture	Total
%	%	%	%	%	%	%	%
2.4	14.9	16.7	36.9	19.1	3.6	6.5	100

The Registrar-General's scale is essentially based on status in the sense of culture or style of life.[33] The police come out at least as high on scales based on explicit rankings by population samples, such as the Hall-Jones index.[34] This graded police above skilled manual workers, at the same level as routine clerks, but below most non-manual and professional occupations. The Young and Willmott study of grading by manual workers placed the police even higher, above routine non-manual occupations, though still below professionals.[35]

Numerous polls show that the police occupy a high place in public estimation.[36] However, surveys indicate that the police themselves perceive public opinion as hostile.[37] This discrepancy may be the result of

[31] Lockwood, *loc.cit.*

[32] Nichols, *op.cit.*

[33] *Ibid.*

[34] Hall and Caradog-Jones, "Social Grading of Occupations" (1950) 1:2 *British J. of Sociol.* 31-55.

[35] Young and Willmott, "Social Grading by Manual Workers" (1956) 7:4 *British J. of Sociol.* 337-45.

[36] Appendix IV to the *Minutes of Evidence, Royal Commission on the Police* (1962; Cmnd. 1728, H.M.S.O. London); Abrams, "Changing Values" (1974) 253 *Encounter* 29-38; W. Belson, *The Public and the Police* (1965); *Daily Express* 18 May 1972, 4; *The Times* 1 February 1977; *The Sun* 2 February 1977, 9.

[37] e.g. Belson, *op.cit.*, 7.

a difference between people's responses to a survey, and when actually being processed by a police officer, and to the fact that the police come into contact disproportionately with hostile groups.[38]

Appreciation of the police varies between different groups. Several surveys find young people to be more suspicious of the police. Another study found that attitudes to the police varied by class, with those in the higher Registrar-General's categories being more sympathetic.[39] However, it should be stressed that these are variations around a favourable estimation of the police by all classes. Altogether, such findings indicate that the police have a high status consistently over a period of time.

Class: place and condition

Although the condition of being a policeman is the subject of struggle, and varies over time, it can only do so within limits set by the place the police occupy in the class structure. In economic terms they are similar to other workers with only their labour power to sell. The price of this will largely be determined by factors beyond their control, though trade union organisation may influence it. An example of the effects of their place in the class structure on their market situation is the relationship of police bargaining power to their role in different modes of restricting the share of wages through incomes policies.

Their part in maintaining the hegemony of the ideology of the impartial rule of law was also seen to contribute to another facet of their market situation — the unique extent of mobility prospects for all recruits to reach élite levels, a reflection of the need to maintain the appearance of a police force representative of society as a whole. (Vigorous Federation opposition to plans for direct entry to higher rank plays a part, but many other trade unions have not been able to resist lateral entry). Their high status reflects their centrality, in practice and symbolically, to the maintainance of the economic, political and ideological structure. The contrast between police status in opinion polls and officers' own perception suggests a contradiction between their image as agents of the community, presented by the ruling ideology, and the conflictual character of their actual work. This is reflected in class variation in opinion, though the hegemony of the dominant ideology is manifested in the high esteem given the police by all classes in interviews.

Class place, as linked by its effects on observable condition, influences class position i.e. consciousness, behaviour and organisation in particular historical conjunctures. Place does not, however, determine position. The character of political and ideological forces is not ensured by their place in class relations. The next two sections will consider the position the police have taken in response to their condition, by examining the historical

[38] M. Banton, *The Policeman in the Community* (1964) 9.

[39] Shaw and Williamson, "Public Attitudes to the Police" (1972) 7:26 *The Criminologist* 18-33.

development of their union organisation in Britain, and the subjective consciousness of a group of policemen.

The historical development of police unionism in Britain

The history of police unionism reflects the contradictory place of the police in the class structure. On the one hand, their economic situation as wage-labour without property has often resulted in grievances, stimulating union organisation as a collective defence. On the other hand, their function in political and ideological domination has meant that their unionisation has been officially opposed to a greater extent than for other workers, and also facilitated an ideology among policemen which accepts that their special role demands special restraints on collective action.

The development of the Police Federation, the present negotiating body, has been narrated in several works.[40] During the First World War inflation eroded the real value of police pay and drove sufficient numbers into the illegal "National Union of Police and Prison Officers" to make it a serious movement, despite official harassment. Money was not the only problem. Conditions were poor and deteriorated with wartime efforts to intensify the use of available manpower. Discipline was arbitrary and dictatorial, and there were no channels for the expression of grievances. In the later war years the "demonstration effect" of unprecedented labour and political militancy fuelled the Police Union's membership.

The government was especially alarmed by the development of links between the Police Union and the labour movement. The Union was affiliated to the Labour Party, TUC and many local trade councils. Against the background of the 1917 Russian Revolution, and political turmoil throughout Europe, the government viewed the unionisation of the police, and the Metropolitan police strike of 1918, in apocalyptic terms.

In accordance with its view that the police ought to be organised on militaristic lines, with a strict and unquestioned hierarchy of authority, the government set out to smash the Union. It succeeded by combining a generous pay rise, the establishment of a tame, official representative body (the Federation), and the victimisation of militants. The labour movement condemned the destruction of an independent union, but to no avail. The Union was outlawed, and the 1919 strike it called to save itself was unsuccessful. The few strikers were dismissed.

The Federation was weak between the wars not only through legal emasculation but also because the police force was a highly sought after occupation in the Depression. After the Second World War policing became less attractive an occupation, and manpower shortages relative to official

---

[40] Allen, "The National Union of Police and Prison Officers" (1958) 11:1 *Economic History Review* 133-43; A. Judge, *The First Fifty Years* (1968); G.W. Reynolds and A. Judge, *The Night The Police Went On Strike* (1968); G. Picton-Davies, *The Police Service of England and Wales Between 1918 and 1964* (1973 Unpublished Ph.D. dissertation, London School of Economics); Reiner, *op.cit.*, chap. 2.

establishments became a perennial problem. This facilitated the emergence of the Federation as a fully fledged negotiating body, and the institution of machinery for collective bargaining, the Police Council. The Federation still remained restricted compared to trade unions. Industrial action was forbidden, affiliation (and until 1972 association) with outside unions was illegal, and its constitution was shackled in many ways.

During the 1970's two important developments have occurred, illustrating the contradictory class place of the police. Inflation has continuously eroded the real value of pay, even after generous awards. The 1970 pay negotiations were accompanied by considerable bitterness, and talk of industrial action. This was taken up in an increasingly serious way in the 1975 and much publicised 1976-7 negotiations. The crucial difference from previous pay disputes (e.g. 1960) was the combination of inflation and unemployment. In earlier years dissatisfied policemen would have quit the force, thus putting pressure on the government to increase pay, but now police officers were compelled to stay despite their grievances. Militancy seemed the only option. (Announcements in mid-1977 that wastage was again becoming a serious problem suggested that the fall in real value of pay was beginning to overcome the effect of unemployment as a deterrent to resignations.) The 1976-7 pay dispute stimulated unprecedented police militance, manifested in stormy Open Meetings, lobbying of Parliament by policemen and their wives, referenda in local police forces showing overwhelming support for the right to strike, and finally the 1977 Conference vote supporting this. In July 1977 the government implemented its commitment to set up a body to review police negotiating machinery, under Lord Edmund-Davies. The outcome was not known at the time of writing, but is not likely to be trade union status for the police representative body.

The growth of militancy manifested in the 1977 votes for the right to strike is momentous, but it does not constitute the emergence of a fully fledged trade union consciousness. In those referenda which included the question of TUC affiliation, it was opposed by majorities of two-thirds. A Conference motion on affiliation was defeated by "red-baiting" rhetoric.[41]

Anti-union sentiment among policemen has increased since then, especially after the wide publicity given to police injuries at Grunwick. Although the possibility of a police strike continued to be threatened in the autumn of 1977, the Federation accepted a 10% rise on October 31st, together with government promises to implement Edmund-Davies' recommendations.

The climb-down by the Federation was abrupt, but encouraged by several factors. Chairman Jim Jardine was threatened with prosecution, under S.53 of the Police Act prohibiting "causing disaffection".[42] The

[41] Reiner, "Scarborough Conference 1977" (1978) 1 *The Police Journal* 18-23.

[42] *Sunday Telegraph* 9 October 1977.

1977 deterioration in manpower strengthened the Federation's bargaining hand, as has increasing industrial unrest, and growing Tory emphasis on "law and order" as an election issue. The defeat of the firemen's strike indicated that police industrial action might prove futile, while there was political and press support for giving to the emergency services "special case" treatment. These factors seem to have persuaded the Federation against unionisation. If the Tories win the next election, the strategy of presenting a responsible image in return for "special case" treatment appears more enticing to policemen, as well as more resonant with their social philosophy. Nonetheless, the 1977 militancy has placed police unionism on the political agenda, and provided a rhetoric which can be drawn upon in future conflicts.

While their economic situation may press the police towards unionisation, their political and ideological function exerts a contrary pressure. This is manifested in the Federation's emergence into the political arena as rank-and-file spokesman on questions of social and penal policy.

In 1975, the Federation launched an unprecedented "law and order" campaign "to harness the public's growing concern about the state of crime and public order in Britain into a programme for positive action".[43] The Chairman declared the aim of reversing "the drift into a lawless society. . . . We have gone too far with the liberal, lenient approach". The campaign was conducted in a highly organised way, informed by systematic research into public opinion to determine the most effective strategy. It was immediately criticised by several Labour M.P.s, magistrates, the British Association of Social Workers, and a few police officers, who opposed both the campaign's reactionary implications for penal policy and the incipient political activism of the police which it signalled. However, it met a long-felt need among most policemen, who have an almost universally pessimistic assessment of social trends. The following quote typifies the police perspective:

> The permissiveness of society has gone so far now that as time goes on the police job won't be workable. People want the police force purely for their own ends, not because it's representative of law and order for society. They look on it as an unnecessary evil . . We're the whipping boys of society. We can do no right . . . The public neither wants nor deserves a police force, in my opinion.[44]

The "law and order" campaign was temporarily shelved because of the pressure of the 1977 dispute on Federation resources. It was launched again in February 1978 with the aim of making it an election issue.[45]

This assertion of a police voice in policy making should not be interpreted as a straightforward transmission of right wing philosophy into action. It reflects an attempt to maintain autonomy on the job, and is in this

[43] *Police* November 1975, 13-14.

[44] Reiner, *The Blue-Coated Worker op.cit.*, chap. 11.

[45] *State Research Bulletin* 5 April/May 1978, 81-2.

sense analogous to other workers' struggles on the "frontier of control".[46] The paradox is that because of their contradictory class location, the police demand for "workers' control" asks that they be unrestrained in control of other workers.[47] Police Federation history shows that while the economic place of the police drives them to adopt trade unionism, and at times even an incipient working class consciousness, their involvement in the maintenance of political and ideological domination exerts contradictory pressures towards alignment with conservative, or even reactionary, political forces. These contradictory pressures, deriving from their place in the class structure, are manifested not only in the historical record, but also the consciousness of policemen in specific conjunctures. This will be illustrated in the final section.

The trade union consciousness of policemen
The general picture that emerged from my 1973-4 study was of a force that was content on the whole both with the job and the system of representation. But analysis of the reasons for this shows contradictory facets of satisfaction and tension, balanced out in that particular historical conjuncture to yield an overall quiescence. The changing economic condition of the police in the political circumstances which developed after 1974 made the elements of conflict more salient in the consciousness of many policemen who previously had accepted their lot. This added weight within the force to the views of those men, a minority in 1973, who had a fully developed trade union consciousness. The police force must not be seen as monolithic. While at any time a certain orientation may appear dominant, variations in outlook exist both in a structured way between different roles in the police division of labour and in terms of individual idiosyncrasy.

In 1973-4 the majority (52%) accepted the Federation as an adequate representative body for policemen. The principle of unionism for the police was rejected by 57% and only 14% supported the right to strike.

What were the sources of this acquiescence in the status quo? It must first be stressed that the above figures are for all Federated ranks, and inspectors were far more satisfied with the existing system and hostile to unionism than constables, with sergeants in between (reflecting inspectors' and sergeants' role as middle-managers and supervisors). But even among constables, 46% felt the Federation was adequate, and only 44% supported the principle of a police union.

The source of rejection of unionism was a blend of the ideas that it was morally illegitimate, inefficacious or even counter-productive, and unnecessary. The special illegitimacy of police unionism was related to a hostile image of general trade unionism. Unions were seen as too powerful

[46] C.L. Goodrich, *The Frontier of Control* (1920) Pluto Press edition (1975).

[47] Reiner, "Police and Picketing" (1977) 770 *New Society* 14-15, documents the common rank-and-file view that senior officers restrain proper law-enforcement at pickets.

in the double sense that they could inflict great harm on the public by irresponsible industrial action, and that they usurped authority at both work-place and government levels by trying to dictate policy. Furthermore, they were dominated by unwholesome political elements, responsive, as an inspector intimated darkly, "to people across the sea". Police unionism was even more objectionable because of their special role in society. The industrial action a police union could organise would "leave the country open to anarchy". It would also expose the force to undesirable political influences in the trade unions and threaten its impartiality, especially in industrial disputes. "You can't have brothers throwing brothers about", as one constable said.

Underlying the moral rejection of unionism was the view that it was unnecessary and/or inefficacious in the police case. Whereas the principled arguments against police unionism reflect a common ideology within the force, the extent of perceived necessity for union representation varied systematically according to rank, specialism and orientation to work. Most policemen had been attracted by intrinsic aspects of the job rather than instrumental advantages. They had an image of police work as interesting, varied, exciting, a man's job. For some of the older generation with experience in the armed forces, the attractions of a disciplined service had been paramount, although among the older men a higher proportion had been drawn by the instrumental advantage of security. Few had been recruited with a motivation to maximise financial rewards.

In different ways these initial orientations encouraged policemen to feel unionism was unnecessary for them. Among the younger men, with their primarily action orientation, grievances about pay and conditions were not very salient. They were relatively satisfied and involved with police work. Among the CID particularly, the Federation and its concerns were looked down on patronisingly as petty and irrelevant. As one detective inspector put it "they're banner wavers trying to stir up trivialities. I haven't got time, I'm too busy doing my job". The relatively low salience of instrumental concerns to these men made them unconcerned about the Federation's lack of power. They were anxious about the position of policemen, especially the "active" ones like themselves. But their worries were about the extent to which they were defended against public complaint and could control the job. Neither concern made them want a more union-like representative body. The main sense in which these men wanted a stronger representative body was to act as a political pressure group for their ideas on penal policy, a sentiment activated in the "Law and order" campaign. As the American example has shown, such issues can lead to industrial action, and a mild form has occurred here with the Federation policy of non-cooperation with the implementation of the new complaints procedure. But it is not a type of grievance that leads in the direction of unionisation. Despite the non-instrumental orientation to work of the generation of policemen recruited in the 1950's and 60's, they could become sufficiently dissatisfied with pay to alter their views, as happened to some extent in 1977. But in 1973 their experience of "special case" treatment made them feel typically that "the government realise we're the prime law and order force in the country. As it's been shown in the past, they seem to give you pay rises every now and then which weren't as hard going with us as others". So unionisation was simply unnecessary.

The older generation did contain a higher proportion who had been recruited because of the instrumental advantages of a secure occupation like the police after the war, when memories of mass unemployment lingered. However, theirs was not a maximising orientation. Furthermore, ideas of loyalty to the oath taken on joining were more common than in the younger generation. While there were more men in the older generation who accepted authority without question, there were also more who had worked outside before becoming policemen. Among these, some had been ardent trade unionists and maintained their commitment to the union tradition. They formed the hard-core of Federation activists, and were prominent in the minority who supported the idea of a police union.

Another group of older constables were the "uniform-carriers", who had become disillusioned and cynical about all aspects of the job, and were tied to it solely by the cash nexus. While they were bitter about their condition this did not lead to support for union activism. They regarded Federationists as pursuing a "gimmick" for their own ends. Although many detectives and action-seekers also derided representatives as shirkers or clock-watchers, the Federationist's concern for the rights of policemen has to be distinguished from malingering. Union activism demands a commitment to the importance, at least potentially, of the work being done and faith in the possibility of change, which the total cynicism of the "uniform carriers" precluded.

While most policemen in 1973-4 felt unionism was unnecessary, they also believed it would not be effective. The importance of the police to government and society was thought to give them adequate bargaining power. But essential to this was the respect and confidence placed in the force by politicians and public. This would be undermined by police militancy, which could thus be counter-productive. As one sergeant put it "the police have got to be seen as being above this sort of thing in order to retain any respect. Militancy brings us into great disrepute. I live in a kind of Fairyland, where I'd like to see the government say to the police: 'we want to keep you happy . . . so we'll look after you quietly and you'll get your pay award.' " This almost touching faith in the cash-value of public respect and government appreciation has taken a few knocks lately. But despite the 1977 votes for the right to strike, it remains the ideal for many policemen.

Unionism was also opposed because the instrumental concern of most younger policemen was status mobility, rather than immediate financial return. A desire for collective status mobility is shown by the view, held by 74%, that the police should be seen as a profession. The achievement of this was thought to be hindered by unionisation. As one constable said "it adds

182

a bit of status to the force, the fact that we can't strike''. The majority also had individual aspirations for promotion. While most felt that being a Federation representative did not hold back a person's career chances nowadays, this was only if he was responsible and eschewed militancy. Thus the concentration of ambition on individual and collective status mobility inhibited unionism, which was irrelevant or even inimical to these goals. However, those who felt they had missed out in the promotion stakes usually came to view the system as unjust and to support unionism.

The 1973-4 acceptance of the system of representation and opposition to unionism was rooted largely in the conditions of the time. The principled rejection of police unionism as illegitimate was inextricably mingled with the belief that it was unnecessary and/or counter-productive. These arguments were undermined by economic and political developments in 1976-7 which weakened police bargaining-power, and made policemen increasingly receptive to the unionism which a handful of Federation activists had long been advocating. (The recent years of unemployment may also have drawn in instrumentally oriented recruits less conducive to police socialisation). But the change that the 1977 militancy signified is not towards full trade union, let alone class, consciousness. While espousing the right to strike, the majority rejected TUC affiliation, signifying that they did not see themselves as aligned with other working class forces, even though they had come to recognise that they are subject to similar economic pressures and need similar weapons to defend the price of their labour power. This recognition itself was fragile, as the rapid decline of militancy after the autumn of 1977 indicated.

Conclusion

It has been argued that the position taken up by the police in particular historical conjunctures, specifically their consciousness and practices in relation to trade unionism and other forces of class struggle, must be understood in terms of the contradictory place which the police occupy in the class structure, as linked by its consequences for their condition. Their contradictory place in class relations i.e. the social division of labour as a whole, structures the elements of condition — market, work and status situation — which are the immediate bases of their experience. On the one hand, their economic location as property-less wage earners exposes them to exploitation analogous to other workers, and they are subject to managerial control. On the other hand, their function in maintaining political and ideological domination pushes them away from unionism. It means that under some circumstances the determination of the price of their labour is inversely related to that of other workers. It also gives them advantages in terms of the security and mobility aspects of market situation. Their work situation is affected by government attempts to increase the rate of exploitation of their labour power, and to ensure they work effectively as agents of the state. Their status is influenced both by the image of their role as "communal defenders" presented in the hegemonic ideology and by the conflictual character of their contacts with working class and racial minority groups. While these elements are structured by the class place of the police, the situation is, within limits, open to struggle, and affected by the organisation of the police themselves and other groups. Their contradictory location in class relations is shown in the history of police unionism. In certain conjunctures the proletarian aspects of their place as property-less workers is dominant and support for union organisation develops, though normally their political and ideological role ensures their quiescence. The contradictions are also manifest in the subjective consciousness of policemen. Neither the consciousness of individuals nor the composition of the force are monolithic. While traditionally the police have acted and thought in a conservative way, circumstances and struggle can bring to dominance the facets and tendencies reflecting the proletarian aspects of their place. The radicalisation of the police remains a possibility.

R. REINER*

*Department of Sociology, University of Bristol.

[3]
Fuzzy Thoughts: The Police and Law-and-Order Politics

1 Introduction: the Politicization of The Police

The purpose of this paper is to discuss an important development in British and American police forces in recent years—their emergence as *overtly* political. The politicization of the American police since the mid-1960s has received a fair amount of attention.[1] But the development of pressure-group activity by the British police has not been subject to any sustained analysis.[2]

What must be seen as new is *overt* political activity by police officers. This is not to suggest that policing could ever be non-political. It is, of course, a revered article of faith of British police tradition that they are and should be separate from politics. Robert Mark, for example, claims for the British police a

> long tradition of constitutional freedom from political interference in our operational role. Notwithstanding the heavy responsibilities for the policing of England and Wales given to the Home Secretary by the 1964 Police Act, it is important for you to understand that the police are not servants of government at any level. We do not act at the behest of a minister or any political party, not even the party in government. We act on behalf of the people as a whole and the powers we exercise cannot be restricted or widened by anyone save Parliament alone.[3]

In this traditional view the role of the police is solely to enforce the laws which are determined by Parliament. There is a strict separation between the functions of law-*making*, law-*enforcement*, adjudication and dealing with convicted offenders. To quote Mark again, the criminal justice system has

> four successive stages. First comes the enactment by Parliament of the criminal laws, secondly the task of the police to enforce them. The third stage is the criminal trial, where the question of guilt is decided. Finally, there is the problem of what to do with the guilty. Each of these four stages has usually been considered in isolation. Each tends to be the province of a different group of people. Politicians make the laws, police enforce them, lawyers run the trials, and the prison or probation services deal with convicted offenders.[4]

Fuzzy Thoughts: *The Police and Law-and-Order Politics*

This conventional assertion that the police are non-political rests, of course, on a very narrow conception of the 'political'—what Worsley has called 'Politics II', which 'restricts the term to the specialized machinery of government, together with the administrative apparatus of state and party organization'.[5] As Worsley says, this 'vulgar' usage of the term politics is 'a dying conceptual apparatus, the prerogative predominantly of a few formal constitutional theorists and legal theorists', and has been eclipsed by 'what we may call Politics I. By this definition, the exercise of constraint in any relationship is political'.[6]

In the wider sense police work is inherently and inescapably political. The enforcement of laws, themselves the products of 'Politics II', involves the exercise of constraint and is thus a part of 'Politics I'. Moreover, the police, through the exercise of their discretion (both in terms of explicit policy decisions at various levels of the hierarchy of command and because of the inevitably open-ended texture of general rules in their application to concrete situations), are a major force determining the content of 'law in action' as opposed to 'law in the books'.[7] Valuable as it has been, however, the tradition of research on the police which focuses on the issue of discretion— the problematic of the gap between 'law in the books' and 'law in action'—has crucial limitations, which McBarnet has shown recently.[8] It restricts analysis of the source of police action to the level of police occupational culture and attitudes, and the organizational pressures of the police bureaucracy. But the 'Law in the books'—as McBarnet puts it, 'the powers, duties and sanctions of the formal legal system itself'[9]—fundamentally structures the pattern of police behaviour. This points analysis beyond concentration on the immediate situational determinants of police action to the level of the State as the source of substantive and procedural law.

One problem in talking of the 'politicization' of the police is to separate out lobbying and other activities which are intended to benefit the bread-and-butter interests of policemen from the pursuit of 'political' ends. As I have argued elsewhere, a sharp dividing line between instrumental concern about job conditions and ideological issues cannot be drawn.[10] Demands for, say, tougher police weaponry involve both an 'instrumental' anxiety about personal safety, an aspect of work conditions, and an 'ideological' belief in harsher repression of dissidents or criminals. But in recent years it seems

Robert Reiner

that the manifestly ideological or political content of police activity has increased. I would define the object of my analysis, the 'politicization' of the police, as their *overt* intervention into the *public* political arena in order to change the *content* of rules both within the police organization and at the societal level.

The concern of this paper is with the emergence of the police as parts of the law-making process itself, as part of 'Politics II', a development which represents a significant departure from tradition —the politicization of the police in the most explicit sense. While clearly police officers have always had political views, the fiction of neutrality has been maintained by denying them any means of overt expression, though their political ideology must have influenced the exercise of discretion. In Britain policemen were not even enfranchised until 1887, and are still forbidden to belong to any political party, or affiliate to the T.U.C., on the grounds that this would threaten impartiality.[11] Even exploring the political views of policemen has been prohibited by the Home Office.[12] In fact, of course, policemen's sympathies are pretty apparently right of centre.[13] The recent overt politicization of the police has involved a translation of their values into political action.

The rest of this paper will be divided into two parts. In the next section some aspects of recent police politicization in Britain and the U.S. will be described, concentrating on rank-and-file activism. The final section will consider possible explanations of this development, and its significance.

II *The Politicization of the Police*

(a) *The 'Police Rebellion' in the United States*

The police and urban political machines

In one sense the American police have always been closely involved in politics. As Miller's comparative history of the establishment of the New York and London police forces demonstrates, the democratic and anti-professional ideology which America inherited from the Jacksonian era was translated into a partisan control structure, sharply contrasting with the contemporaneous British model of impersonal police authority.[14]

> Although not themselves elected, policemen were originally appointed by the aldermen of the wards in which they were to serve and had a fixed term of office. Reformers, mainly commercial and professional men con-

Fuzzy Thoughts: The Police and Law-and-Order Politics

cerned with improving the efficiency of municipal services, sought to move the force closer to London's non-partisanship. Reorganization of the police in 1853 secured good-behaviour tenure for the men and gave control of the force to the mayor and two elected judical officials. This change simply centralized partisan domination of the police. Mayor Ferdnando Wood, elected as a reformer in 1854, soon became one of America's first urban bosses, controlling the force for his own ends through his power of appointment, promotion, and assignment of the men. Unable to escape politics, the police became a political issue.[15]

By the end of the 19th century, control of the city police forces by the political machine was a deeply ingrained pattern. The boss of the machine controlled hiring and firing and deployment of manpower. The election of a new political slate was often followed by wholesale sackings. Surmounting minimum entrance requirements was no problem for those who had given their services to the victorious party, for the medical and other examiners were themselves political appointees.

'Hence some recruits were overweight, undersize, and overage; others were illiterate, alcoholic, and syphilitic; still others had outstanding debts and criminal records; and one Kansas City policeman had a wooden leg.'[16]

The Police Reform Movement

Control of the police by political machines not only affected the calibre of personnel but produced the systematic corruption of the law-enforcement and electoral processes which was revealed by the Lexow Committee (1894-5) in New York and similar enquiries in other cities.[17] These committees heralded a movement for police reform which over the next two generations transformed the rhetoric and, to a lesser extent, the reality of policing.[18] Fogelson has distinguished two phases of this campaign. The first, from about 1890 to 1930, was led by commercial, civic and religious groups, and emphasised a *military* model of policing. It reflected the wider stuggle for control of cities between political machines and Progressive élites. The second wave was characterized by the leadership of prominent members of the law-enforcement community itself, and centred around a conception of the police force as a *professional* body. Whereas the first phase was motivated primarily by concern about the effectiveness of law enforcement as defined by the Progressive élites, the second was mainly anxious to raise police status. The second wave was initiated by prominent reforming police chiefs like August Vollmer of Berkeley,[19] and their 'pro-

Robert Reiner

fessional association', the International Association of Chiefs of Police.[20]

Both phases of the reform movement shared certain assumptions rejecting the 19th-century legacy of policing. The police and other public agencies should provide the best possible service at least possible cost, rather than constituting a channel of mobility for immigrants loyal to the party machine. Varying ethnic life-styles could not be permitted, and the criminal law should be used to impose a uniform WASP morality. Above all, policing must be insulated from 'politics' and given a large measure of professional autonomy. Consequently, police departments have been centralized and bureaucratized, and standards of personnel upgraded. Although chiefs of police continue to be appointed by mayors or other politicians, the reformers succeeded in achieving 'good-behaviour' security of tenure in many cities, and the dismissal of a chief on partisan grounds has become a comparative rarity, as has political control of day-to-day policing.[21]

While the Progressive era reformers saw themselves as championing a value-neutral conception of technical efficiency against partisanship, their struggle with the urban machines reflected the political interests of conflicting class and ethnic groups. As the social historian Samuel P. Hays puts it:

> 'The movement for reform in municipal government, therefore, constituted an attempt by upper-class, advanced professional, and large business groups to take formal political power from the previously dominant lower- and middle-class elements so that they might advance their own conceptions of desirable public policy.'[22]

In essence the police reform movement constituted a bid for political power by the class and ethnic élite, not a purging of politics from police forces.

However, the reform movement was ultimately a failure in achieving its stated ends. The most obvious indicator of this failure is the similarity between the revelations by the 1973 Knapp Commission on corruption in the New York City Police and those in the 1895 Lexow Committee Report.[23]

The major beneficiaries of Progressive era reforms were the police themselves, not the upper-class élites which launched the movement's first phase. Police forces gained autonomy, and some of the material and status perquisites of 'professionalism'. The reforming police chiefs were not the sole beneficiaries. The unintended con-

Fuzzy Thoughts: The Police and Law-and-Order Politics

sequence of the professionalizing movement has been the growth of the lower-rank organization. Like a Frankenstein's monster, rank-and-file power has developed into an independent force challenging the newly-won autonomy of the police chiefs. While the involvement of American police in politics prior to the Reform movement meant the responsiveness of police to politicians, the police have now emerged as a political force in their own right.[24]

The development of rank-and-file organization

Until the 1960s, rank-and-file police organization in the U.S. was aimed primarily at securing material advantages and establishing collective bargaining rights. To achieve these ends, police associations did engage in lobbying, but they kept a low profile. Rank-and-file police organization was concentrated in three growth periods.[25] In the latter years of the 19th century city police forces began to form fraternal and benevolent societies (for example, the New York Patrolmen's Benevolent Association (P.B.A.) in 1894). In 1897 the American Federation of Labour refused an application for a union charter from a police group on the grounds that police were 'not within the province of the trade union movement' as they were 'too often controlled by forces inimical to the labour movement'. But the economic and social pressures of the First World War provided a stimulus to police unionization.

> 'Hurt by the severe inflation which accompanied World War I and spurred by the renewed militancy of the working class, local police organizations turned to the A.F.L. for charters in the fall and winter of 1917.'[26]

This incipient police union movement was destroyed by the image of 'anarchy' associated with the Boston police strike in September 1919.[27] Although the violence and disorder that ensued in Boston was blamed on the union (Woodrow Wilson called it 'a crime against civilization'), it is probable that the Police Commissioner, and in particular Governor Calvin Coolidge, deliberately allowed the situation to get out of hand and delayed mobilizing available alternative forces in order to discredit police unionism.[28] Coolidge was the strike's only beneficiary—he rode to the White House on the strength of his image as the man who beat Boston's cops, and his much quoted statement 'There is no right to strike against the public safety by anybody, anywhere, at any time'.

Robert Reiner

After the Boston débâcle police unionism remained in the doldrums for twenty years. But the renewed working-class militancy of the Depression years and the general growth of the trade union movement were reflected in the police force. In 1937 the American Federation of State, County and Municipal Employees began a police organizing drive. This achieved some success, but police chiefs frowned on unionization of their forces and most of them managed to direct their men into autonomous associations.

During the 1950s many of these consolidated their positions as effective bargaining units. For example, the New York P.B.A. succeeded in transforming itself from a pressure-group into a *de facto* union.[29]

The rise of 'blue power'

It was these associations which during the latter half of the 1960s formed the organizational springboards for the politicization of the police. Their intervention into the political arena was largely a reaction to the liberalizing changes in social and penal policy of the 1960s, and most specifically, the attempt in many cities to establish civilian review of the police, a major demand of civil rights groups. As the National Commission on the Causes and Prevention of Violence declared: 'The major impetus to police politicization . . . was without doubt the attempt to impose a civilian review apparatus to adjudicate complaints against police officers by aggrieved citizens and attempts of citizen groups to restrict police use of firearms'.[30]

In Bopp's analysis the 'police rebellion' had four triggers: the 1964 Berkeley Free Speech movement; the 1965 New York Civilian Review board controversy; the violence at the 1968 Democratic Convention in Chicago; and the July 1968 'shoot-out' in Cleveland. 'Berkeley crystallized police opinion; New York showed them they had political muscle; Chicago drove them together; and Cleveland created the new militancy'.[31]

The New York Civilian Review Board controversy

The New York P.B.A.'s destruction of the Civilian Review Board was perhaps the main single stimulus to police political intervention.[32] In 1964 a bill was sponsored to add one or two civilians to the New York Police Department Board for reviewing citizen complaints. Pressure by civil rights groups for civilian involvement in reviewing complaints against the police had been mounting for

Fuzzy Thoughts: The Police and Law-and-Order Politics

some time, and was spurred by the 1963 killing of two Puerto Ricans in police custody and the 1964 Harlem riots. The plan was opposed by Commissioner Murphy and the P.B.A. On 29th June, 1965 the police were given the chance to present their case at the Council hearings in City Hall. An amazing spectacle ensued:

> The scene at City Hall that day was one that few New Yorkers who saw it will soon forget. Thousands of off duty policemen in uniform, with service revolvers strapped on and wearing P.B.A. buttons (the buttons were later removed at the request of the police commissioner), tightly ringed City Hall and packed its corridors. Many carried signs with such slogans as 'WHAT ABOUT CIVIL RIGHTS FOR COPS', 'DON'T TIE OUR HANDS', 'SUPPORT THE POLICE DEPT.', and 'DON'T LET THE REDS FRAME THE POLICE'. Adding to the spectacle were dozens of American Nazis and John Birch Society members toting American flags and shouting encouragement to the police. Some of the police pickets yelled at a quiet group of C.O.R.E. counter-pickets, 'Go home, finks', 'Send em to Vietnam where they belong', 'Wave a bar of soap at them and they'll all run', and other epithets and obscenities. Over the police radio crackled unauthorized messages urging as many police as possible to join the demonstration; one anonymous voice sang off-key the civil rights song 'We Shall Overcome', at the conclusion of which another remarked sourly, 'They already have'.[33]

Shortly after his victory in the 1965 mayoral election, John Lindsay appointed a new Police Commissioner, Howard Leary, who had a record of support for civilian review.[34] Lindsay established a review board on 7th July, 1966, with civilian domination.

The P.B.A. won a court ruling that the Civilian Review Board be made a referendum issue. It organized its campaign to win public support around the paradoxical slogan 'Keep Politics Out of Police Work'. The New York Conservative Party (which had promoted its 1965 mayoral candidate William Buckley on the platform 'Support Your Local Police')[35] backed the P.B.A. Wealthy ultra-conservatives poured money into P.B.A. coffers—one Texas oil millionaire contributed $10,000. A Madison Avenue public relations firm was hired to prepare a $1½ million campaign.[36]

Support for the Board was organised by F.A.I.R. (Federated Associations for Impartial Review). Among the groups backing it were the Anti-Defamation League of Bnai B'rith, the New York Civil Liberties Union, the State Trial Lawyers Association, the N.A.A.C.P. and the C.R.E. Despite lustrous liberal political support from Mayor Lindsay, Senators Javits and Robert Kennedy, as well as Commissioner Leary, the pro-Board forces lacked equivalent resources to the P.B.A.

Robert Reiner

The P.B.A. campaign basically exploited the public's fear of crime, and played on racism and the claim that F.A.I.R. was communist-dominated.

> One poster depicted damaged stores and a rubble-strewn street and read: 'This is the aftermath of a riot in a city that *had* a civilian review board'. Included in the text was a statement by J. Edgar Hoover that civilian review boards 'virtually paralysed' the police. Another poster showed a young girl fearfully leaving a subway exit onto a dark street: 'The Civilian Review Board must be stopped! . . . Her life . . your life . . . may depend on it'.[37]

Police spokesmen made speeches like this:

> No matter what names are used by the sponsors of the so-called 'Police Review Boards' they exude the obnoxious odour of communism. This scheme is a page right out of the communist handbook which says in part, '. . . police are the enemies of communism, if we are to succeed we must do anything to weaken their work, to incapacitate them or make them a subject of ridicule.[38]

P.B.A. President John Cassesse illustrated the campaign's racism when he declared:

> Racial minorities would not be satisfied until you get all Negroes and Puerto Ricans on the board and every policeman who goes in front of it is found guilty . . . I am sick and tired of giving in to minority groups.[39]

The operational policemen themselves pressed home the cause at every opportunity.

> Bluecoats buttonholed pedestrians on Manhattan sidewalks, giving them the anti-review-board message and handing out literature. Patrol cars were converted into rolling billboards decrying civilian review. Police used their citation powers discriminately: automobiles bearing pro-review-board signs were ticketed at the slightest real or imagined infraction, while those with anti-review-board signs were indulged to the point of absurdity. It became an 'in' game to fasten an 'anti' sticker to one's bumper and park all day in a meter zone.[40]

The Campaign was successful in winning the referendum by a majority of 63% voting against the board. The board was defeated in every borough except Manhattan (which has the largest black concentration).

The social characteristics of the vote have been analysed by Rogowsky *et al.*[41] Catholics overwhelmingly opposed the Board (over 70 per cent of the New York police are Catholic). Despite the prominence of Jewish groups in F.A.I.R. Jewish voters came out against the Board, heralding the demise of their traditional liberalism on civil rights questions. Class was an important factor, with the mid-

Fuzzy Thoughts: The Police and Law-and-Order Politics

dle class being more supportive of the Board than working-class voters. There was no difference between Democrats and Republicans on this issue, but 80 per cent of Liberal Party supporters voted for the Board, while no Conservative Party supporters did. The success of the P.B.A. campaign was reflected in the fact that 48 per cent of those who were favourable to the civil rights movement voted for the Board, compared to only 23 per cent of those who were not favourable to the civil rights movement. Race was a more salient issue than fear of crime, which hardly affected the vote. 78 per cent of those who felt 'very unsafe' in the city opposed the Board, but so did 69 per cent of those who felt 'very safe'. As Rogowsky *et al.* conclude, 'Race was the most significant factor in the C.R.B. contest'.[42]

Police power and political authority

This controversy marked the most overt political intervention of American police rank-and-file organizations until that time.[43] It was, however, only the precursor of many similar struggles. The P.B.A. won a significant victory, which encouraged further actions to control the political process.[44] Partly under pressure from a newly formed ultra-rightist faction (the Law Enforcement Group, L.E.G.), the P.B.A. upped the level of its criticism of Lindsay and Leary's 'mollycoddling' of criminals and demonstrators. In 1968 Lindsay attempted to prevent black protests in Harlem escalating into full-scale rioting by ordering a low police profile. Cassesse threatened he would issue his own 'get tough' guidelines for '100% law enforcement . . . regardless of what orders we may get from a superior officer'. However, when Commissioner Leary warned of disciplinary action against this flagrant incitement to disobey orders, Cassesse backed down by issuing as his 'guidelines' excerpts from the Police Department's official rules.[45] L.E.G. initiated a policy of court-watching and demanded the removal of a judge who had supposedly permitted disorderly conduct during the trial of two Black Panthers. Later in 1968 Cassesse managed to curb the growing power of L.E.G. after some of its members beat up Black Panther supporters inside the Brooklyn Criminal Court Building. But L.E.G. had succeeded in pushing the P.B.A. into a more aggressively militant stance.[46] In 1969, Lindsay and Leary proposed a bill which would abolish a 1911 law prohibiting the Police Commissioner organizing his men

Robert Reiner

into more than three shifts. They aimed to establish a fourth platoon to provide extra manpower at peak-crime periods. The P.B.A. vigourously opposed this initiative. This time the Mayor and the Commissioner could pose as officials concerned to fight crime but impeded by the sectional interest of the rank-and-file, a stance which won them victory against the P.B.A.[47]

The New York struggle for control of policy and legislation was paralleled in many other cities. In Philadelphia, for example, the Police Advisory Board was vigorously opposed by the local lodge of the Fraternal Order of Police (F.O.P.).[48] At first Mayor Tate supported his Commissioner Howard Leary (of later New York fame) in retaining the Board. But facing an uphill struggle for re-election in 1967, Tate adopted a new 'get tough' policy on racial unrest. He appointed Frank Rizzo, a 'no-nonsense' cop, as Commissioner, and with Rizzo's support won an unexpected, narrow victory. As Rizzo said, 'Tate won by only 12,000 votes and we think it's because we went out on a limb. Police and firemen, wives and families— that's 50,000 votes'. Henceforth, Tate was the 'cop's mayor', governing only with Rizzo's support. The extent of police power in Philadelphia is demonstrated by the fact that when Tate's second term as Mayor ended in 1971, Rizzo himself won the Democratic nomination and won a crushing victory on a 'law and order' platform. Mayor Rizzo has used the police force for overtly political ends such as arresting without charges anti-Nixon demonstrators, and 'court-watching' to pin-point 'liberal' judges in order to use such information against them when they stand for re-election.[49]

Similar cases of police revolt against political authority occurred in many other cities. For example, in Cleveland during the ghetto riots of summer 1968, when Mayor Stokes withdrew the police to allow black leaders to quell the rioting with less bloodshed, the police refused to answer other calls and abused the Mayor on their radios.

> This came in response to a report of a heart-attack case within the cordoned area: 'White or nigger? Send the Mayor's Committee'. When a report was broadcast that a child had fallen off a second-floor porch, the return call came: 'Tell the Mayor's Committee to handle it'. When the police dispatcher requested cars to respond to a fire call, an anonymous voice suggested that Mayor Stokes 'go piss on it'. Responses to other calls included 'Fuck that nigger Mayor'.[50]

In Atlanta, Georgia, the late 1960s saw the emergence of deep conflict between liberal police chief Herbert Jenkins and his sub-

Fuzzy Thoughts: The Police and Law-and-Order Politics

ordinates organized in a lodge of the F.O.P.[51] Part of the struggle concerned material demands and Jenkins' refusal to recognise the F.O.P. for collective bargaining. But a major source of conflict was the rank-and-file's criticism of Jenkins' liberal and pro-civil rights stance. Jenkins, by contrast, felt that the police union 'was not a union at all but in fact a thinly-veiled cover for (Ku Klux) Klan membership'.[52] On at least two occasions they initiated job actions in protest against Jenkin's liberal policies. In October 1969 the F.O.P. started 'Operation No Case'—a traffic ticket slowdown and refusal to arrest for minor violations—in protest against the city's 'go easy' policy on hippy law-breakers. In 1970 there was a similar wildcat action, largely against Jenkins' objecting to F.O.P. demands for increased weaponry including mace, black-jacks and shot-guns.

> In protest, one police officer reported to duty wearing only the equipment officially listed by Jenkins—he appeared without his shoes, socks, underwear or holster! One F.O.P. leader described what so upset the force: 'Preferential arrests. So-called immunities of certain groups during the major conflicts that occurred on the street. One-man cars vs. two-man cars. Numerous officers injured during that period of time. Equipment problems . . . A man's guilty until proven innocent. Pay cut off before you have a chance to even explain yourself. You have to make statements and swear and take a lie-detector test, yet the accuser doesn't. The belief that a man wearing wing-tips and carrying a .357 magnum who's your superior officer tells you, who are wearing a pair of plain-toed boots and a snubnose, that you're out of uniform. No qualifications. No examinations. Political promotions. These are the things that cause a strike.[53]

This list of grievances encapsulates the issues over which police associations throughout the country were engaging in militant action. Boston Mayor Kevin White summed up the situation: 'Are the police governable? Yes. Do I control the police, right now? No.'[54] By contrast with the experience of these liberal mayors, however, Chicago's police during the incumbency of Mayor Daley were the 'mayor's cops'.[55] The reason is not hard to find. As shown by Ruchelman's comparative analysis of Chicago, New York and Philadelphia,[56] even the P.B.A. would have found it difficult to act tougher than Daley—the Mayor who issued 'shoot to kill' orders in 1968, and was thus largely responsible for the 'police riot' later that year at the Democratic Convention.[57]

Black versus blue in the station-house

Police politics are not monolithic. One consequence of the rightward political mobilization of the main police organizations in the

Robert Reiner

late 60s was the emergence of counter-organizations of Black police officers, who have opposed the double-racism of police departments —discrimination in employment and promotion opportunities, and in law enforcement operations.[58]

> For example, in 1969 the Connecticut Guardians (a black police association) called a mass sick call to end departmental discrimination. The next year, the Guardians defended a Black police officer charged with assaulting a white policeman who abused a Puerto Rican girl, and they warned that Black police would physically restrain white officers exercising brutality towards citizens.[59]

The New York Guardians opposed the P.B.A. in the civilian review board fight. In Atlanta, the Afro-American Patrolman's League denounced the F.O.P. job action in 1970.[60] In 1972 a number of black police associations founded the National Black Police Association to counter the 'law and order' campaigns of their white confrères, opposing indiscriminate stop-and-frisk policies and preventive detention, and supporting civilian review. Senior Black police officers founded the National Organization of Black Law Enforcement Executives in 1976 to press for such liberal goals as increased minority recruitment and civilian complaint procedures.[61]

Police power institutionalized

In the 1970s overtly militant action in support of political demands has declined. Undoubtedly part of the explanation is 'the institutionalization of class conflict'. Halpern, on the basis of a comparative study of the relationship between police association and department leaders in Baltimore, Buffalo and Philadelphia, argues that 'militant tactics stem from organizational weakness'.[62] The struggles of the 1960s gave police associations greater recognition and collective bargaining rights, and this has removed the need for militancy. This decline in militancy is manifested both over political and bread-and-butter issues.[63] However, the continued readiness of the American police to engage in job actions is illustrated by stoppages in several cities in recent years. Nor has pressure-group activity by police relented—court-watching, partisan campaigning in elections, and lobbying on specific 'law and order' issues like the successful 1972 initiative in California for restoration of the death penalty or against the Berkeley community-control plan continues.[64] I would argue that the decline in overt political campaigns cannot be explained by an ahistorical general relationship between institutionali-

Fuzzy Thoughts: The Police and Law-and-Order Politics

zation and the absence of militancy.[65] The relative lack of militancy over political issues in recent years reflects rather the rightward shift in the political complexion of city governments in the 1970s and hence the absence of non-economic issues stimulating conflict with the police.[66] The decline in police militancy in Philadelphia after Rizzo became the dominant political influence in the city illustrates this. Police vigilantism is less apparent because the whole society has become pervaded by the vigilante spirit.[67]

(b) *The Politicization of the Police in Britain*

During the 1970s the British police have also emerged as an overtly political force. The crucial turning points here were Robert Mark's much-publicized Dimbleby lecture on B.B.C. T.V. in November 1973, and the Police Federation's 'law and order' campaign launched in November 1975.[68]

Top of the Cops: The politics of chief constables

Chief constables have traditionally had an important voice in policy-making at national level, as well as control of operational policing in their areas—an autonomy increased by the vagueness of the 1964 Police Act's definition of their role, and the growth in size of police forces brought about by amalgamations.[69] Chief constables' autonomy has increased not only relative to local police authorities, but also *vis-à-vis* the Home Office.[70] The discretion of chief constables to implement varying priorities in detection and prosecution policy is considerable. The recent crackdown on pornography and gay clubs in Manchester by Anderton is only one obvious example. (See his 5th December, 1977 letter to *The Times*).

In addition to their local power, chief constables have influence over the Home Office both individually and through the Association of Chief Police Officers.[71] A.C.P.O. influences government through the medium of the Central Conference of Chief Constables (established by the Home Office in 1918). This now concentrates,

> 'as an entirely professional body, on operational matters. It meets two or three times a year, and provides a permanent link between the Home Office and police forces, and also a means of bringing other Government departments into touch with the police.'[72]

Since 1918 there have also been district conferences of chief constables, which are attended by Home Office officials. These now

Robert Reiner

meet at least quarterly 'to discuss common problems and to promote common action'.[73] They have also generated a number of specialist subcommittees on such matters as detection, traffic, regional crime squads etc.

Examples of the role of chief constables in influencing law and penal policy are the 1966 introduction of legislation requiring pre-trial disclosure of defence alibis and permitting the finding of guilt in jury trials by majority (as opposed to unanimous) verdicts. Both were measures which Robert Mark, then Chief Constable of Leicester had urged.[74] Mark's inclusion the same year on the Standing Advisory Council on the penal system, and the Mountbatten enquiry into prison security, furnish other examples.[75]

Mark's Capital

Mark's Dimbleby Lecture, however, constituted an important departure from tradition in heralding public intervention into legal and policy debates by a chief officer, as opposed to the making of private representations. As Mark himself states: 'The Dimbleby Lecture was the first occasion on which a senior policeman had publicly voiced at length comment about the reality of criminal justice'.[76] Mark's example has since been followed by other chief constables (notably his successor, David McNee, and James Anderton) who now seem ready to preach at the drop of a helmet about the evils of the 'permissive' society and the moral state of the nation.[77]

Mark would represent his stance as 'non-political'. In the Dimbleby Lecture itself he justified it by the personal stake of the police in the laws they enforce because of the difficulty and danger of the job, and their expertise in criminal matters.[78] However, the meaning of Mark's concept of political neutrality is made clear in his recent autobiography.[79]

Throughout the book there are numerous examples of Mark's contempt for most institutions in society other than the police (or rather, chief officers—the Federation is often included in his scorn).[80] His notion of police 'professionalism' is compatible with a disturbing contempt for the law. Criticism of corrupt lawyers is only a part of Mark's general view that the police are unduly hampered in dealing with criminals by the due process of law. He claims that since 1967 'virtually every change in laws relating to criminal

Fuzzy Thoughts: The Police and Law-and-Order Politics

procedure and policy has been favourable to the wrong-doer'. This conveniently overlooks two major changes which in another mood Mark would see as cornerstones of his own achievement, majority verdicts and pre-trial disclosure of alibi defences. But these victories have merely served to encourage his attack on democratic rights like the right to silence and jury trial.

Mark explicitly regards the law as an unwelcome hindrance to the zealous policeman. As he puts it:

> 'I am one of those who believe that if the criminal law and the procedures relating to it were applied strictly according to the book, as a means of protecting society it would collapse in a few days.' (p. 57).

Mark is not hesitant to quote examples of his own bending of the rules. He would excuse as youthful indiscretions such incidents as breaking a navvy's leg with an illicit truncheon during his days as a Manchester constable. But as Commissioner of the Yard Mark still believed that the end justified the means, for example when he held suspected I.R.A. bombers incommunicado for four days, and when he contemplated spiriting away the body of an I.R.A. member en route to burial.

Perhaps the most disturbing aspect of Mark's book is the partisanship it displays. In the press view the internal conflict at the Yard preceeding Mark's appointment as Commissioner was a fight between 'liberals' and 'hardliners'. But Mark's reputation as a liberal rested entirely on a contrast with the stone-age views of the hang-'em-and-flog-'em-brigade opposing him, epitomised by the notorious 1971 *Times* interview with two reactionary senior yard officers.[81]

It must be emphasized that Mark's position is clearly conservative, in both the general and party senses of the word (even though he claims never to have voted in a postwar election!). It is especially insidious because his is the kind of social philosophy that identifies conservatism with non-partisanship. Only socialists are 'political'! His politics emerge clearly from his railing against a variety of left targets. 'Socialist philosophy' is condemned for advocating the reduction of all to 'the lowest common denominator'. This champion of individual liberty, however, dismisses the National Council for Civil Liberties as 'a small, self-appointed political pressure group'. His heroes are men like 'National Association for Freedom' founder Ross McWhirter, dubbed as 'a notable upholder of freedom for the individual', and George Ward, 'an Anglo-Indian running a small

Robert Reiner

business' who 'courageously and successfully stood firm against politically motivated violence'. Mark's rejection of adequate independent complaints machinery protects from investigation the kind of police violence shown in the Newsreel Collective's film about Grunwick. Peregrine Worsthorne had a point when he asked in the *Sunday Telegraph* (22 October) whether Mark 'intends to become a future Tory politician—changing one blue uniform for another'.

Mark's whole career must be seen as an attempt to increase the political autonomy of police chiefs under the guise of 'professionalism'. It is true that, as Mark frequently reminds us, his achievements in dealing with corruption at Scotland Yard are impressive. He ended the organizational autonomy of the C.I.D., and established a specialist internal investigations unit A 10, thus suppressing the blatant corruption which had been exposed by a series of scandals in the early 1970s. But rooting out 'the firm within a firm' was the price of business as usual for the firm itself. The essence of Mark's contribution was to protect the legitimacy, and hence autonomy, of the police force in the face of crisis. His reforms were part of a package deal in which the reward for sacrificing unprecedented numbers of bent policemen was to be the continued independence of police chiefs.

This is demonstrated by Mark's opposition to any effective system of independent review of complaints against the police. Mark himself would deny this. He points to his repeated recognition of the need for an independent element in the complaints process. But this is contradicted by his objections to many schemes, including the one embodied in the 1976 Police Act which prompted his resignation, on the ground that they undermine the disciplinary responsibility of chief officers. To have an effective independent review which does not weaken chief constables' sole disciplinary power is as impossible as squaring the circle, even for Robert Mark.

Mark's panacea is police 'professionalization'. The police will keep their own house in order, avoiding the scandals of the past, but in return the public must rely on the professional integrity of such principled men as himself, and not demand any concrete institutions of control that dilute the authority of the 'professional' commanders.

Thus under Mark's leadership chief constables have emerged as important public political figures, seeking changes in law and social policy and enhanced autonomy in their own organizational domain. An important example of how this can prevent a democratically

393

Fuzzy Thoughts: The Police and Law-and-Order Politics

elected government implementing the policies it wants to is given by Mark's successful effort to prevent the 1975 Employment Protection Act including a right for pickets to stop vehicle drivers in order to make a reality of the right of 'peaceful persuasion'. Mark informed the Home Office,

> in no uncertain terms that if there was any danger of this proposal reaching the statute book I would declare in *The Times* that this was an unjustifiable infringement of individual liberty and an inexcusable requirement for the police to abandon the impartiality in industrial disputes to which they have always been dedicated.[82] We were fortunate indeed in our Home Secretary Roy Jenkins. He clearly must have shared our feelings to some extent because the Home Office arranged a meeting between representatives of all chief officers and Michael Foot's senior civil servants at which we left them in no doubt that the proposals would be publicly opposed by every chief officer. Happily they were abandoned and no harm was done. But the prospect caused every senior policeman to reflect on the differing interpretation of freedom. To some of us, the Shrewsbury pickets had committed the worst of all crimes, worse even than murder, the attempt to achieve an industrial or political objective by criminal violence, the very conduct, in fact, which helped to bring the National Socialist German Workers Party to power in 1933.[83]

The police revolution: rank-and-file involvement in policy-making

It was not only police *chiefs* who became politicized in the 70s. The rank and file, as organized in the Police Federation, also made a bid for influence in the political arena.[84] Until the 1950s the Federation played little part in trying to influence internal police policy, let alone more general social questions.[85] In 1955 their increasing independence (the legacy of the 1949 Oaksey Report) was used to employ a parliamentary Consultant. (James Callaghan was the first to hold this post—the Consultant is always an Opposition M.P.). But the main use of the Consultant at this time was to present the police case for better pay and conditions.[86]

However, during the 1960s and 70s the Federation has begun to pay increasing attention to more fundamental matters of police policy, as well as general problems of society. During the first fifty years of its existence the Federation's terms of reference, 'all matters affecting welfare and efficiency' (laid down in the 1919 and 1964 Police acts) had been interpreted mainly as implying that, in pressing its claim for 'welfare', the Federation ought also to have regard to the requirements of 'efficiency', i.e. it was to act 'responsibly', and only make 'reasonable' claims. But a widening of its interest was presaged in 1965 when the Federation document 'The Problem' was launched at a press conference. This was intended

Robert Reiner

to show that 'owing to manpower difficulties, the police forces of Great Britain are in grave danger of losing the fight against crime'. The manifesto argued not only for pay rises to cope with this, but also better equipment and new approaches in management, of a less dictatorial kind. The authorities were furious at this Federation initiative, which they saw as 'unprecedented' and a 'breach of faith'.[87] One member of the Official Side of the Police Council declared 'I never thought I would see the day when the representatives of law and order would be advocating anarchy'.[88]

In 1966, however, the new Home Secretary, Roy Jenkins, demonstrated that he accepted their claim to greater involvement in force policy by establishing three working parties on 'Manpower, Equipment and Efficiency' which included Federation representatives.

Their Report was acclaimed by the *Federation Newsletter* as 'the chance of a lifetime'. It was 'mainly a product of the initiative taken by the Federation in 1965'. The proposals included a new system of policing, the Unit Beat, involving the introduction of modern equipment, notably personal radios and panda cars.

> Those who are talking about a 'revolution' in the police are quite right. In their proposals on management and especially in their call for the replacement of the almost universal system of beat patrol with more flexible and imaginative policing methods, the working parties have pointed the way to modernization and to a status for the constable never achieved in the past.[89]

1966 did not only mark the first significant involvement of the Federation in policy-making, but was also a harbinger of its later entry into 'law-and-order' politics. It joined in the spirited public debate on capital punishment which followed the murder of three policemen in August. Not for the last time it warned that without the death penalty the police would lose the 'War against Crime'.[90]

The late 1960s and the 1970s show mounting police concern about what was perceived as a trend to lawlessness, disorder and increasing violence, manifest not only in rising rates of crime but also growing problems of crowd control arising out of political demonstrations, industrial militancy, and the spread of terrorist tactics internationally and in Britain. The concern with these social issues pervades Federation meetings, documents and actions in the 1970s. Pay demands come to be seen as morally justified by the danger and difficulty, as well as crucial social importance of the police.

Fuzzy Thoughts: The Police and Law-and-Order Politics

During the early 70s the police were relatively favourably treated in pay negotiations. The reason was the wish to preserve police manpower and morale in the context of the Health government's struggle with the trade union movement.[91] One prominent Joint Central Committee official even intimated to me that the Federation had reached an understanding with the Conservative leaders before the 1970 election. In return for giving James Callaghan a rough ride in his appearance as Home Secretary at the Annual Conference (which was believed to be damaging to Labour's prospects), the police would receive sympathetic attention in pay negotiations. Whatever the truth of this conspiracy theory, the police certainly did enjoy a series of awards which 'pleasantly surprised' both Federation negotiators and members.

In the first half of the 1970s the police were in a strong bargaining position because of the 'demand' for their services in the face of concern about crime and disorder, while the 'supply' of policemen was unfavourable. Anxiety about police manpower and morale were the 'weapons' used by the Federation in gaining generally satisfactory pay rises. Between 1974 and 1977, however, the rapid increase in unemployment altered the situation considerably. The buoyant manpower situation, despite the relative deterioration of pay and conditions, undercut the traditional Federation argument for better pay to cope with shortages. The result was the militancy of the 1975 and even more dramatically the 1976-7 pay negotiations.[92]

The 'law and order' campaign

The 1970s have also been notable for the emergence of the Federation as spokesman for the rank-and-file policeman on matters of penal and social policy. The Federation has been increasingly consulted at national level on legislation and proposed changes in penal and force policy. (It remains far less institutionalized in this respect at local level.)[93] In 1970, the Chairman began his speech to Conference with the statement 'we have been eyeball to eyeball with the fanatics, the lunatics and the hooligans'.[94] In September 1970, *Police* drew attention to the institution of a 'Pig of the Month' contest in an 'underground' newspaper.

> 'Should we be upset? Not at all. The pig has made a notable contribution to our national well-being over the centuries. As such, it has a great

396

Robert Reiner

advantage over hippy squatters . . . whose concepts of sanitation are often far more primitive than its own . . . In America, they say P-I-G stands for Pride, Integrity and Guts.'[95]

During the 1970s policemen grew increasingly frustrated by what they saw as too great an influence of anti-police elements on society, reflected in what were seen as lenient penal and sentencing policies, and the demand for independent review of complaints against the police.[96]

At the end of November 1975, in response to this feeling, the Federation launched an unprecedented campaign for 'law and order'. The general aim, as outlined to members in *Police*, was 'to harness the public's growing concern about the state of crime and public order in Britain into a programme for positive action'.[97] The more detailed list of specific objectives was to publicize:

> (1) Concern about the growing *volume* of crime and the burdens thus thrown upon the police service. (2) Anxiety about *violence*, particularly the large number of assaults on police officers, 'mugging' of innocent members of the public, hooliganism and vandalism. (3) Concern about the effectiveness of existing criminal legislation . . . (4) the attitude of the courts at all levels towards the punishment of offenders . . . (5) The need for changes in criminal justice administration procedures . . . (6) The attitude of some people and some bodies in public life towards the rule of law, instancing the sympathy shown to law breakers whose crimes have allegedly 'political' overtones. The need for the 'silent majority' to assert itself in order that politicians and judges fully understand the true feelings of the public. (7) The need for public support for the police to be more positive.

The campaign was inspired by the example of the activities and success of pressure groups supporting liberalizing reforms of the law. 'The pattern of recent years has seen the dominant influence of pressure groups, often representing a minority view, able to secure major changes in the law.' Examples were given: the abolition of capital punishment, homosexual law reform, changes in the law affecting children and young persons, abortion law reform, legislation for sexual equality, race relations, independent examination of complaints against the police, etc. The police were to learn from these bodies, and seek to influence 'opinion-makers' in support of the 'rule of law'. The national campaign was to be backed up by local activity by branch boards. Suggested organizations to contact were: ratepayers' and residents' associations, chambers of trade and commerce, employers' organizations and trade unions, branches of political parties, magistrates' associations, councils of social service and community relations, Rotary clubs, women's institutes, churches,

Fuzzy Thoughts: *The Police and Law-and-Order Politics*

youth organizations, parent-teacher associations, MPs, and local newspapers.

In response to this suggestion, local branches urged the public to write to MPs and councillors supporting a reversal of 'soft' penal policies. Letters were sent to branches of trade unions, the C.B.I., and political parties around the country, seeking talks to discuss the problems of crime. The campaign was supported by various bodies, including the Superintendents' Association and various chief constables.

The campaign was condemned by many other sections of opinion. This was not only on the grounds of substance, but even more because of the departure from the established policy of non-involvement in politics that it seemed to signal. A group of 25 Labour MPs laid down a motion regretting the campaign and the incipient political activity of the police.[98] Magistrates and social workers defended themselves against allegations that they were over-indulgent to criminals.[99] Some policemen dissociated themselves from the political implications of the campaign and felt it might be counter-productive.[100] However, the campaign seems to meet a long-felt need among rank-and-file policemen.[101]

The Federation defended itself against these accusations, by arguing:

> 'What is "political" about crime? So far as we know, all responsible political parties are committed to the rule of laws enacted by elected Parliaments. [The Federation had a right to comment on legislation and on crime, which] 'affected the working lives of police officers who might have strong views on it.'[102]

The Federation also gave much publicity to a public opinion survey it had commissioned, which it claimed 'reveals strong support for the Police Federation's views'.[103] In fact, the questions tended to be worded with such ambiguity as to defy meaningful interpretation. For example, '82 per cent of the sample either agreed or strongly agreed with the statement "too much is done for criminals and not enough for their victims" '. It is by no means clear that 'doing something' for 'criminals' precludes effective concern for the 'victim'. By the same token, the 82 per cent may be concerned that more be done for 'victims', without wanting less to be done for 'criminals'. Many of the other questions similarly lumped together various issues, so that it is not clear to which one respondents are replying. None the less, the Federation's conclusion was that 'support for action does

398

Robert Reiner

indeed come from a moderate, and perhaps silent, majority'. The survey did seem to locate resistance to the campaign amongst 'younger people, those in the upper socio-economic groups and those with the highest level of educational attainment'. It therefore recommended that a special effort be made 'to address those *least* likely to provide support', e.g. University societies, '*as well* as those groups who might be more immediately in sympathy' (e.g. 'Rotary clubs, Townswomen's Guilds'). It was also found that there was widespread support for 'more liberal sexual attitudes'. Members were therefore urged to dissociate the campaign from any taint of a more general attempt to impose moral standards.

> Be careful not to confuse acceptance of violence with 'declining standards of morality', particularly sexual morality . . . The Federation would be in danger of alienating support . . . if it tried to equate support for public order with an overly conventional view of sexual or other personal morality. It would be right to stress the value of the family and family togetherness and a respect for conventional discipline as a support for combating crime but, for younger people, this does not entail what they might conceive of as a repressive attitude to freedom in personal behaviour.

In April 1976, the Federation held a seminar on 'The Challenge of Crime' at Cambridge, attended by 'politicians, church leaders, magistrates and trade unionists, leaders of voluntary bodies and members of the police service'. Among the main speakers were Enoch Powell and Mr. Justice Melford Stevenson. The decision to invite Powell was attacked by representatives of black people's organizations.[104] This criticism is understandable in view of Powell's previous image with regard to race relations. This cannot have been improved by his speech itself, with its references to 'the introduction of these alien wedges into the population of our cities' as a major source of the increase of violence represented by 'mugging'.[105] The criticism of the Federation's invitation to Powell was attacked by the Chairman as 'ill-conceived and totally misdirected . . . In a free society an organization must be free to hold what meetings it wishes and invite which speakers it wants, without having to submit them to the Community Relations Commission for prior approval'.[106]

This campaign marks a significant departure for the Federation. Whatever its success, it is clearly the result of a careful consideration of pressure-group tactics, and a judicious appraisal of strategy, informed by 'scientific' study of public opinion. It is the climax of

Fuzzy Thoughts: The Police and Law-and-Order Politics

ten years of change in which the Federation has sought to broaden its scope beyond the confines of a narrow, collective bargaining body, and a very tame one at that.

The 'law and order' campaign was temporarily shelved at the end of 1976, owing to the pressures of the acrimonious 1976-7 pay dispute, during which police unionization became a serious issue for the first time in over fifty years.[107] However, with the cooling-off of militancy over pay after the government's acceptance of the Edmund Davies Committee recommendations, the 'law and order' campaign has been revived. The political implications of this during a pre-election year in which the Conservatives are seeking to make 'law and order' a central issue scarcely need underlining, despite Federation disclaimers.[108] Labour ministers condemned the Tories for exploiting public fear of crime in blatant electioneering.[109] The similarity of the rhetoric used by Tory politicians and Federation spokesman makes the Federation's claims of non-partisanship somewhat disingenuous.[110] It is certainly a rank-and-file belief that the police are better served by Tory than Labour governments.[111]

III *Conclusion: an analysis of police politicization*

At the level of ideological content the 'law and order' political interventions by both American and British police were clearly reactions to the liberalizing changes in penal and social policy and the moral climate of the 1960s. In fact, of course, this liberal moment lasted for a briefer time, and achieved less solid or sweeping reform, than the police, with their constant railing against the 'permissive society', would recognize. The backlash set in early. 1968, the *annus mirabilis* of student protest, was also the year of Nixon's election as president after a campaign built largely on the 'law and order' issue.[112] Hall *et al.*, in their analysis of the drift towards authoritarianism as a response to deepening social and economic crisis, trace the origins of backlash in Britain to 1966 (and Wilson's 'red-scare' about the seamen's strike).[113] 1970, the year in which Heath became Prime Minister after his 'Selsdon Man' campaign, can be seen in retrospect as marking the 'birth of the "law and order" society'.[114]

Law-and-order politics: three perspectives

Why did the police become an independent political force in this period? Previous analyses of political interventions by the police have

Robert Reiner

mainly looked at limited campaigns by specific specialist organizations, perhaps the best known being the Federal Narcotics Bureau's 1937 crusade for legislation controlling marijuana. Becker's classic analysis of this regards the campaign as essentially an example of moral entrepreneurship, the expression of an ideology in political action.[115] Dickson has reinterpreted it as resulting from bureaucratic self-interest, a response to a decline in the Bureau's business owing to its success in curbing heroin traffic.[116] Bureaucratic aggrandisement by law-enforcement agencies is perhaps the prevailing explanation of their lobbying activities.[117]

Certainly the ideology of policemen and the bureaucratic interest of police agencies go some way towards explaining the sort of political interventions described earlier. But the ideological account fails to explain why policemen sometimes go *against* political or departmental authority. Similarly, the notion of bureaucratic self-interest assumes a consensus *within* the police. Neither explanation considers the relationship between the police and the social structure as a whole, save in terms of random conflict between the police and other organized or disorganized interest groups (say civil liberties organizations or drug users). In other words, they assume a pluralistic model of society in which there are no systematic or structural forces shaping the ideologies and power resources of different groups. I would argue, by contrast, for a *class* analysis which locates the police as one institution of the state system (itself not monolithic) and would permit the explanation both of internal conflicts and linkages between police and other class agents. This also allows the exploration of some differences between police action in Britain and the U.S.

Towards a class analysis of police politics

The 'police rebellion' in the U.S. during the later 1960s can be seen as a reaction to certain changes which made the rank-and-file policemen the meat in the sandwich of conflicting social forces. Juris and Feuille, for example, pinpoint as factors generating police militancy: increased public hostility, greater law-and-order demands by citizens, perceived poor pay in relation to increased difficulty of the job, poor managerial personnel practices, the demonstration effect of other groups' militancy, and the influx of younger police-

Fuzzy Thoughts: The Police and Law-and-Order Politics

men less socialized into the obedience mentality.[118] But this is merely a descriptive catalogue. Which sections of the population increased hostility to the police and made greater law and order demands? Why was there an erosion of commitment to institutionalized procedures by other groups? These questions require an analysis of the whole social and political conjuncture in the U.S. But as a beginning it can be suggested that the influx of blacks from the South into Northern cities following rural mechanization 1940-60 made them a significant political force.[119] The threat and reality of rioting to secure basic civil rights for blacks who were excluded from the rewards of the established system was augmented by the breakdown of traditional social controls due to migration. This made political élites in some cities, e.g. New York, concede a measure of reform—such as civilian review of the police. These same changes threatened working-class whites, materially and symbolically. One expression of resentment was a demand for law and order. In many cities this led to a configuration in which the rank-and-file police and working-class whites were pitted against blacks and the WASP élite—the line-up seen in the analysis of voting on the 1965 New York civilian review board referendum.

This pattern of political forces is a recurrent one in American history, explaining the recalcitrance of the police to reform movements. As Johnson has argued, 'the whole history of local public police in America suggests that the essential constituency of today's urban police is the working class'. The police subculture on which so much attention has focussed is not free-floating—it 'is largely ethnic and working-class in character'.[120] The roots of this situation lie in the early 19th-century origins of the police. The enfranchisment of the working-class in America and the absence of serious political crises allowed the police to be trusted with a personal authority without the framework of controls from above which were imposed in London.[121]

In England, by contrast, the police have traditionally been subjected to a tight regime of discipline within the organization, in order to present an image of impersonal authority as the agents of the law, not government. This was a necessity as the modern police force was established in a context of intense class conflict and political crisis, epitomised by Chartism and the struggle for the franchise. Acceptability of the police required their presentation

Robert Reiner

as embodiments of the law, an impersonal body of rules supposedly independent of politics.[122]

The continuation of this tradition is reflected in the fact that the contemporary English police's 'law and order' campaign was not directed *against* the police hierarchy. Rather it followed in the wake of similar initiatives by police chiefs. It also came after government policy had already moved towards greater repression to cope with the social consequences of economic crisis. In this context the Federation campaign functions as a legitimation for changes that might otherwise be more readily seen as political. It lends the 'common-sense' authority of the bobby on the beat, the 'practical' man doing his job, to attacks on traditional civil liberties which were the fruits of past popular struggles. A particularly important stimulus to British police reaction was working-class militancy against the Industrial Relations Act and the Heath government. English police ideology reflects the peculiar concerns of the petty bourgeoisie, rather than as in the U.S. the working class. It is perhaps no coincidence that the Federation 'law and order' campaign originated at the same moment as a number of schemes to establish vigilante private armies to cope with a possible breakdown resulting from industrial conflict.[123] The Federation itself condemned these plans (partly on obvious trade-union grounds), but its 'law and order' campaigning reflects the same concern that the new Labour government of 1974 might not be sufficiently tough on dissident elements.

Whatever their ideology, however, the police are neither petty-bourgeois nor working-class. As I have argued elsewhere, they occupy a contradictory place in the class structure.[124] While their social and political role underlines the political ideology and initiatives described above, at the same time their conditions as wage-earners subject to managerial control exerts contradictory pressures towards unionism and in some conjunctures identification with the labour movement.

The implications of their political activity are themselves ambiguous. While the content of their present demands clearly carries dangerous connotations of threat to democracy and a 'police state', it does not therefore follow that they must restrict themselves to their traditional stance of non-involvement in policy.[125] Indeed, the ideal of political neutrality of the police is the argument always

Fuzzy Thoughts: *The Police and Law-and-Order Politics*

raised by conservatives against police unionization. As has been shown above, the police are not politically neutral, and it is hard to see how they could be. However, if the police are given the same rights as other workers should be for participation in the formulation of policy which affects their working lives, their power makes is especially important that this is balanced by democratic external control.[126] This implies not only a vigorous utilization of existing machinery, like police authorities and the complaints board set up by the 1976 Police Act, but also further reforms such as greater openness about structure and procedures. What is insidious is the bid for unilateral power represented by the police initiatives I have discussed, and the notion that policies which have profound political implications should be determined by a supposedly neutral and technical 'professional' expertise.

University of Bristol.   *First received 19th June 1979*
                                   Finally accepted 12th September, 1979

[1] For example, in J. Skolnick: *The Politics of Protest*, Ballantine, New York, 1969, Chap. VII; W. J. Bopp: *The Police Rebellion*, C. C. Thomas, Springfield, 1971; H. A. Juris and P. Feuille: *Police Unionism*, D. C. Heath, Lexington, 1973; L. Ruchelman: *Who Rules the Police?*, New York University Press, New York, 1973; L. Ruchelman: *Police Politics: A Comparative Study*, Ballinger, Cambridge, 1974; S. Halpern: *Police Association and Department Leaders*, D. C. Heath, Lexington, 1974; A. E. Bent: *The Politics of Law Enforcement*, D. C. Heath, Lexington, 1974; M. Levi: *Bureaucratic Insurgency: The Case of Police Unions*, D. C. Heath, Lexington, 1977; S. Bernstein *et al.*: *The Iron Fist and the Velvet Glove* (2nd ed.), Centre for Research On Criminal Justice, Oakland, 1977, Chap. 6; C. D. Robinson: 'The Deradicalization of the Policeman', *Crime and Delinquency*, Vol. 24, No. 2, 1978, pp. 129-151.

[2] The phenomenon is described briefly, however, in T. Bunyan: *The Political Police in Britain* (2nd. ed.), Quartet, London, 1977; R. Reiner: *The Blue-Coated Worker: A Sociological Study of Police Unionism*, Cambridge University Press, Cambridge, 1978; and *State Research*, April-May, 1978, pp. 81-82.

[3] R. Mark: *Policing A Perplexed Society*, Allen and Unwin, London, 1977, p. 24.

[4] ibid. It should be noted that this quote is taken from Mark's notorious (or celebrated) Dimbleby Lecture on B.B.C. television in November 1973, which was itself a milestone in the politicization process I am concerned with, and in which Mark himself criticizes this traditional ideal of separation of functions.

[5] P. Worsley: 'The Distribution of Power in Industrial Society' in Sociological Review Monograph No. 8, *The Development of Industrial Societies* (ed. P. Halmos), Keele University, 1964, p. 17.

Robert Reiner

[6] ibid.

[7] For a succinct summary of studies of police discretion, and its determinants and consequences, see S. Box: *Deviance, Reality and Society,* Holt, Rinehart and Winston, New York, 1971, Chap. 6.

[8] D. J. McBarnet: 'Pre-trial Procedures and the Construction of Conviction' in Sociological Review Monograph No. 23, *The Sociology of Law* (ed. P. Carlen), Keele University, 1976, pp. 172-201; D. J. McBarnet: 'The Police and the State' in *Power and the State* (ed. G. Littlejohn *et al.*), Croom Helm, London, 1978, pp. 196-216; D. J. McBarnet: 'False Dichotomies in Criminal Justice Research' in *Criminal Justice* (eds. J. Baldwin and A. K. Bottomley), Martin Robertson, London, 1978, pp. 23-40.

[9] McBarnet 1976, op. cit., p. 177.

[10] Reiner, op. cit., pp. 68-72 and Chap. 6.

[11] Until 1972 the Police Federation was even forbidden to 'associate' with outside trade unions.

[12] Reiner, op. cit., p. 11 and p. 283.

[13] The social perspective of policemen as described in ibid., Chaps. 8 and 11 bears this out. See also R. Reiner: 'How Deeply Are the Police Getting Into Politics?', *Tribune*, Vol. 42, No. 38, 1978, p. 20. I have recently seen an unpublished dissertation by a police officer who interviewed a sample of colleagues using the questions I was prohibited from asking. He found that 80 per cent described themselves as Conservative—18 per cent to the right of the party. The remainder were evenly divided between Labour, Liberal and Don't know. 80 per cent of his sample had voted in all recent elections. A slight rightward shift in recent years is indicated by the fact that 9 per cent had moved from Labour or Liberal to Conservative between 1974-77, with no movement in the opposite direction. Despite this (or perhaps because of it!) 64 per cent affirmed that the police should remain politically neutral at all times (the identification of neutrality or non-politicality with Conservatism is a familiar phenomenon), 21 per cent wished the right to join a political party without taking an active role, while 12 per cent wished to to be able to take an active part in politics. Interestingly, I have recently been told by a number of Police Federation activists who had previously resented the restraints on their political activism that they now welcomed these because of a growth in support for the National Front which they perceived among other policemen. For data on right-wing political attitudes of police in other countries see, for example, D. H. Bayley and H. A. Mendelsohn: *Minorities and the Police*, Free Press, New York, 1968, pp. 14-30; S. M. Lipset: 'Why Cops Hate Liberals—and Vice Versa', *Atlantic Monthly*, 1969 (reprinted in Bopp, op. cit., pp. 23-39); Bent, op. cit., esp. Chap. 5; T. Bowden: *Beyond the Limits of the Law*, Penguin, London, 1978, pp. 31-34.

[14] W. R. Miller: *Cops and Bobbies*, Chicago University Press, Chicago, 1977, pp. 16-24.

[15] ibid., p. 17.

[16] R. Fogelson: *Big-City Police*, Harvard University Press, Cambridge, Mass., 1977, p. 28.

[17] 'Corruption' is, of course, a highly value-laden term. In a society characterized by a plethora of varying life-styles based on different ethnic and class cultures, what the view from the WASPish apex of the pyramid saw as

Fuzzy Thoughts: The Police and Law-and-Order Politics

'corruption' was often an accomodation by the policeman on the ground to the mores of his own social group. This is most importantly the case in those numerous instances in the 19th century when local police officers sided with strikers from their communities against the interests of outside capitalists. This 'unreliability' and 'inefficiency' of local police forces from the standpoint of national capital was a major stimulus for one aspect of the 'professionaliz-ation' of the police, the establishment of State police forces. (See Robinson op. cit., pp. 135-142). Robinson also enters a caveat against taking the oft-reiterated complaints about the poor quality of policemen at face value. Citing the conventional imagery of the constable as a bumbling buffoon which was an important element in the rhetoric of the English and American early 19th-century police reformers, he argues: 'They have the scent of upper-class contempt of lower-class life and may actually hide upper-class dissatisfaction with the close association of the constable and his assigned victims.' (ibid., pp. 133-134 footnote).

[18] Fogelson, op. cit., S. Walker: *A Critical History of Police Reform*, D.C. Heath, Lexington, 1977; G. E. Carte and E. H. Carte: *Police Reform in the United States*, University of California Press, Berkeley, 1975; Bernstein *et al.*, op. cit., Chap. 3.

[19] For a study of his career and ideology see Carte and Carte, op. cit.

[20] Founded in 1893. See Walker op. cit., pp. 56-59 and Bernstein *et al.*, op. cit., p. 67. Long regarded as the spearhead of the professionalization move-ment, the I.A.C.P. is now under something of a cloud. Not only is its grant from the federal Law Enforcement Assistance Administration currently suspended pending investigation for the rather unprofessional conduct of fraud, but a split has developed within its ranks. The highly educated and professionalized chiefs of the large urban police departments have criticized the Association for being dominated by the far more numerous 'chiefs' of the more than 15,000 police agencies in the U.S. (80 per cent of which have ten or fewer personnel). In 1976, these big-city chiefs organized themselves into the Police Executive Research Forum, and criticised the I.A.C.P. for being over-responsive to the personal and political concerns of the Chiefs without Indians, rather than 'professionalization'. The P.E.R.F. has strong links with the controllers of the national police jackpot which was unearthed as a response to the 'law and order' panic after the late 1960s, notably the L.E.A.A. and the Police Foundation. See the remarks of Patrick Murphy, President of the Police Foundation (and formerly Commissioner of the New York City Police in the early 1970s) before the P.E.R.F. meeting in New York, 10th October, 1978 (Police Foundation, mimeo).

[21] Fogelson op. cit., p. 176. Partisan control was still defined as the major police problem until the 1930s. The 1931 Report of the Wickersham Commission appointed by President Hoover to study police abuses and corruption in the heyday of Prohibition gangsterism argued: 'The chief evil lies in the insecure, short term of service of the chief or executive head of the police force and in his being subject while in office to the control of politicians in the discharge of his duties'. (The National Commission on Law Observance and Enforcement, *Report on the Police*, Washington D.C., 1931, p. 1).

[22] S. P. Hays: 'The Politics of Reform in Municipal Government in the Progressive Era', *Pacific Northwest Quarterly*, October 1964, p. 162.

[23] *Report of the Commission to Investigate Allegations of Police Corruption in New York City*, Whitman Knapp, Chairman, Braziller, New York, 1973.

Robert Reiner

[24] To say that the police have become an independent political influence is not to claim that they are unrelated to other political interests or constituencies. These links will be analysed below.

[25] For fuller accounts of the development of American police associations see Bernstein *et al.* op. cit., Chap. 6; Levi op. cit.; Juris and Feuille, op. cit.; Bopp, op. cit.; J. H. Burpo: *The Police Labour Movement*, C. C. Thomas, Springfield, 1971; A. Z. Gammage and S. L. Sachs: *Police Unions*, C. C. Thomas, Springfield, 1972; R. M. Ayres and T. L. Wheeler (eds.): *Collective Bargaining in the Public Sector*, International Association of Chiefs of Police Inc., Gaithersburg, Md., 1977.

[26] Bernstein *et al.*, op. cit., p. 62.

[27] The standard account is given in F. Russell: *A City in Terror*, Viking, New York, 1975. But for a more illuminating 'revisionist' analysis see Walker, op. cit., pp. 110-120.

[28] Walker, ibid., pp. 116-8.

[29] Levi, op. cit., Chaps. 3 and 4.

[30] J. S. Campbell, J. R. Sahid, D. P. Stang: *Law and Order Reconsidered*, Praeger, New York, 1970, p. 294. A parallel example of citizen-'professional' conflict over policy-making occurred in relation to education. See M. E. David: *School-Rule in the U.S.A.*, Ballinger, Cambridge, Mass., 1975.

[31] Bopp, op. cit., p. 11. The Supreme Court rulings of the early 60s which limited police powers, such as the Mapp, Miranda and Escobedo decisions, were also important catalysts of discontent.

[32] For fuller accounts see Bopp, ibid., Chap. 16; W. Turner: *The Police Establishment*, Putnam's, New York, 1968, pp. 221-233; E. Rogowsky *et al.*; 'The Civilian Review Board Controversy' in *Race and Politics in New York* (J. Bellush and S. David eds.), Praeger, New York, 1971; Ruchelman 1973, op. cit., Part IV, Chap. 2; J. P. Viteritti: *Police, Politics and Pluralism in New York City*, Sage Professional Paper 03-004, Sage, Beverly Hills, 1973; Ruchelman 1974, op. cit., pp. 83-86.

[33] Turner, op. cit., p. 223.

[34] Leary had previously been Commissioner of the Philadelphia police and supported their Civilian Review Board. He replaced serving senior police officers with more liberal men. Thus the police élite was now pro-civilian review and sided with Lindsay.

[35] In November 1966 an editorial in *Nation* commented: 'In crude shorthand "support your local police" means "rally in support of the right wing". It is another of the numerous phrases which bemuse politics. It means backlash.' (Vol. 203, p. 468).

[36] Viteritti, op. cit., p. 25.

[37] Skolnick, op. cit., p. 280.

[38] Ibid.

[39] Viteritti, op. cit., p. 27.

[40] Turner, op. cit., p. 233.

[41] Rogowsky *et al.*, op. cit., pp. 69-91.

Fuzzy Thoughts: The Police and Law-and-Order Politics

[42] ibid., p. 91.

[43] Specialized police units had engaged in overt political campaigning before this. But these efforts were confined to a few élite units, and were organized by the formal leadership of the organization. The most obvious example is the unrelenting series of campaigns by F.B.I. director J. Edgar Hoover who was a national political figure for half a century from the early 1920s to the early 1970s His main targets were a variety of supposed subversive conspiracies—anarchists in the 20s following the 1919-20 Red Scare, communists in the 30s and 50s, Nazis for a brief period during World War II, and Black Panthers and urban terrorists in the 60s and 70s. As well as the threat to all-Americanism, Hoover utilized public anxieties about crime to boost his organization materially and build for it a reputation as the nation's main bulwark against crime which has only recently been tarnished by post-Watergate revelations. In the 30s especially, Hoover captured the public imagination by shrewd exploitation of F.B.I. successes in killing or capturing such fabled hoodlums as Dillinger, Pretty Boy Floyd, Baby Face Nelson, Ma Baker and Alvin 'Creepy' Karpis. Hollywood faithfully co-operated in elevating the 'G-Man' to folk-hero status. Hoover assiduously cultivated the notion of a crime wave—'an infamous, vicious, cancerous growth' of 'mad dogs' and 'human vultures'—to gain for the police political autonomy and lavish equipment. The sober statistics of criminologists like Sutherland who questioned the existence of a 'crime wave' stood no chance against such rousing rhetoric. (See Walker, op. cit., Chap. 6 and I. Silver: *The Crime-Control Establishment*, Prentice-Hall, New Jersey, 1974, Introduction and Chap. 1).

Another well-known example is the influence of the Federal Bureau of Narcotics in shaping drugs legislation. (See H. Becker: *Outsiders*, Free Press, New York, 1963, Chap. 7; D. T. Dickson: 'Bureaucracy and Morality: An Organizational Perspective on a Moral Crusade', *Social Problems*, Vol. 16, No. 2, pp. 143-156; Silver, op. cit., Part II.) Despite their importance, these earlier efforts to affect the political process must be distinguished from the 1960s politicization of the police. First, they are confined to highly specialized units. Second, they are interventions by police leaders, unlike the recent development of rank-and-file organization *against* political authorities and often against police chiefs themselves (as in the New York Review Board struggle).

[44] The P.B.A. victory was more symbolic than real. As Viteritti shows (op. cit., Chap. VIII) Lindsay replaced the outlawed Civilian Review Board with an internal review board to which he appointed civilian members of the Police Department staff. The investigative arm of the board remained the same. The operations of the later board seem identical with that of the discredited Civilian Review Board in its few months of active existence, in terms of volume, character and disposition of citizen complaints (ibid., p. 56).

[45] Ruchelman 1974, op. cit., pp. 42-43 and 58-59; Levi, op. cit., pp. 66-67.

[46] Ruchelman op. cit., pp. 60-61.

[47] Viteritti op. cit., Chaps. V and IX; Levi, op. cit., pp. 67-76. The P.B.A. had, however, successfully prevented such a bill even being debated on several occasions in previous years by behind-the-scenes lobbying at Albany. This provides a classic illustration of the superior potency of Bachrach and Baratz's 'second face' of power.

[48] The P.A.B. was the nation's first civilian review board, established in 1958. For an account of the controversy see Ruchelman 1974, op. cit.

[49] Ruchelman op. cit., p. 105.

Robert Reiner

[50] *Shoot Out in Cleveland.* Report to the National Commission on the Causes and Prevention of Violence, Bantam, New York, 1969, pp. 78-79.

[51] Levi, op. cit., Chap. 6.

[52] ibid., p. 133.

[53] ibid., p. 139-140.

[54] Quoted in Skolnick, 1969, p. 286.

[55] Ruchelman 1974, op. cit., p. 99.

[56] ibid.

[57] More recently, however, even Chicago policemen showed signs of growing independence. In 1972 they instituted a ticket-writing spree to support such demands as collective bargaining rights and an end to polygraph examination of police under charges. Ruchelman ibid., p. 107.

[58] N. Alex: *Black in Blue*, Appleton, Century, Crofts, New York, 1969; N. Alex: *New York Cops Talk Back*, Wiley, New York, 1976; Bernstein *et al.*, op. cit., pp. 70-72.

[59] Bernstein *et al.*, ibid., p. 70.

[60] Levi, op. cit., p. 140.

[61] Bernstein *et al.*, op .cit., p. 71.

[62] Halpern, op. cit., p. 94.

[63] Between 1966-69 there were 127 police work-stoppages, compared to only 16 in the previous seven years. There were 13 between May 1970 and January 1971. Juris and Feuille, op. cit., p. 19.

[64] Bernstein *et al.*, op. cit., p. 66. J. B. Wolf: 'Police Employee Association: Management Relationships', *Police Studies*, Vol. 1, No. 1, 1978, pp. 73-77, gives some recent examples of militancy over both economic demands and policy issues such as the wearing of police name tags.

[65] In the 1960s the New York P.B.A. was one of the most strongly organized police associations in terms of collective bargaining rights, but this did not dampen its militant reaction to Lindsay's policies. Indeed it could be argued that the strength of the organization was the basis for its political efforts.

[66] Economic demands, of course, also have political implications, as illustrated by the black Officers for Justice organization in San Francisco which condemned the 1976 police strike on the ground that the police did not deserve pay rises when some of the communities they patrolled suffered 40 per cent unemployment.

[67] See the March/April 1976 issue of *Society* on 'American Vigilantes'. One article, by K. Kotecha and J. Walker on 'Police Vigilantes' defines this as 'acts or threats by police which are intended to protect the established sociopolitical order from subversion but which violate some generally perceived norms for police behaviour' (p. 48). Police vigilantism found an interesting ideological reflexion in the glut of cop movies, novels and T.V. shows (R. Reiner: 'The New Blue Films', *New Society*, Vol. 43, No. 808, 26 March 1978, pp. 706-708).

Fuzzy Thoughts: The Police and Law-and-Order Politics

[68] Mark's lecture 'Minority Verdict' is reprinted as Chap. 5 of his 1977 book. I have described the background to the Federation campaign in Reiner, op. cit., pp. 45-49 and Chap. 11. S. Hall et al.: *Policing the Crisis*, Macmillan, London, 1978, indicates the period 1972-74 as a crucial watershed in the move towards a 'law and order' society (p. 309). As Nat Hentoff commented at the time: 'If you liked "1984", You'll Love 1973'. (*Playboy*, May 1973, quoted in Bent, op. cit., p. 73).

[69] For an account of the constitutional position of chief constables see G. Marshall: *Police and Government*, Methuen, London, 1965 and G. Marshall: 'The Government of the Police Since 1963' in *The Police We Deserve* (eds. J. C. Alderson and P. J. Stead), Wolfe, London, 1973, pp. 55-67. M. Brogden: 'A Police Authority: The Denial of Conflict', *Sociological Review*, Vol. 25, No. 2, 1977, pp. 325-349, documents how the power in practice of a chief constable exceeds the formal position due to the habitual deference of the police authority to 'professional expertise'.

[70] Brogden ibid., p. 346. Also, M. Kettle: 'Anderton's Way', *New Society*, No. 857, 8 March, 1979, pp. 550-552.

[71] A.C.P.O. was formed in 1948 by the fusion of previously separate organizations for county and borough or city chief constables. It now represents all provincial chief and assistant chief constables, the Commissioner and all ranks down to deputy commander in the Metropolitan police, and the Commissioner and Assistant Commissioner of the City of London police. (T. A. Critchley: *A History of Police in England and Wales*, Constable, London, 1967, p. 195).

[72] ibid., pp. 195-196.

[73] ibid.

[74] R. Mark: *In the Office of Constable*, Collins, London, 1978, pp. 67-70.

[75] ibid., p. 74.

[76] ibid., p. 148.

[77] Anderton has literally taken to the pulpit on occasion. ('Police chief's pulpit appeal', *The Guardian* 16th February, 1978.)

[78] Mark 1977, op. cit., p. 72.

[79] Mark 1978, op. cit., See also the reviews in *News Release*, Winter 1978, pp. 6-8; *State Research* pp. 32-34; *Sunday Times*, 15th October 1978 (by Robert Kilroy-Silk); by myself in *Police Review*, 29th September 1978, p. 1442 and *Marxism Today*, December 1978, pp. 365-366.

[80] For example, on p. 151 he claims 'much harm has been done in recent years to the police image by irresponsible and ill-informed comment by police spokesmen whose only real concern is with the negotiation of pay and conditions of service'. Professional autonomy thus means freedom from both outside and rank-and-file pressure.

[81] Quoted in P. Evans: *The Police Revolution*, Allen and Unwin, London, pp. 110-112.

[82] Reiner, op. cit., Chap. 8 illustrates the anti-union bias which in fact informs police attitudes.

[83] Mark 1978, op. cit., p. 152. Mark also demonstrates here his contemptuous attitude to the Police Federation which was mentioned in note 79

Robert Reiner

above. They had made strong representations on this issue, but their role in changing government policy is ignored.

[84] For an account of the development of the Federation see Reiner, op. cit., Chap. 2. In brief, the Federation was an official representative body established under the 1919 Police Act as part of the government's successful struggle to smash the illegal Police Union which had emerged during World War I in response to the same economic and social pressures as those which stimulated the contemporaneous unionization of the American police. To this day it remains an emasculated body without full union status or independence, though a considerable advance was made after World War II by establishment of collective bargaining machinery—again a response to similar postwar pressures as the second wave of American police unionization. The economic and social pressures of the last decade have stimulated both the politicization documented below, and renewed demands for unionism which have so far been abortive.

[85] In the 30s the Metropolitan branch had unsuccessfully tried to prevent Trenchard's schemes to introduce a separate officer corps based on alumni of his Hendon Police College, but this only brings home their degree of impotence in this period.

[86] Notably in the case for a police pay increase presented to the 1960 Royal Commission.

[87] See the 3rd February 1965 statement by the Official Side of the Police Council. (*Police Federation Newsletter*, January 1965, p. 17.)

[88] *Police Federation Newsletter*, April 1965, p. 40.

[89] *Police Federation Newsletter*, January 1967, p. 3.

[90] *Police Federation Newsletter* September 1966, pp. 215-216. Hall *et al.*, op. cit., also see this moment in 1966 as a significant point in the backlash towards a 'law and order' society, 'a sort of early turning point in the passage Gramsci describes from the "moment of consent" through to the "moment of force"'. (p. 239).

[91] Reiner op. cit., pp. 36-37, pp. 60-62.

[92] ibid., pp. 39-45 and Postcript.

[93] ibid., p. 121.

[94] Edited proceedings, p. 31.

[95] *Police*, September 1970, p. 6.

[96] Rank-and-file attitudes on these questions are documented in Reiner, op. cit., Chap. 11.

[97] *Police*, November 1975, pp. 13-14.

[98] *The Times*, 21st November 1975.

[99] *The Times*, 19th February 1976.

[100] See the letter from Inspector G. Marsden, *The Times*, 6th April 1976.

[101] Reiner, op. cit., Chap. 11.

[102] *Police*, December 1975, p. 3. In the same issue the cover carried a cartoon which attracted much Press comment. It showed a courtroom in

Fuzzy Thoughts: The Police and Law-and-Order Politics

which all the legal functionaries, the jury and the accused were depicted as grotesquely deformed, while the lone policeman in the witness-box was drawn as a clean-cut, stalwart young man. This cover marked a considerable departure for *Police*. It was the first ever to refer in any way to police involvement in law-enforcement. All the previous covers depict policemen in friendly contact with members of the public. Prominently featured are policemen with children, animals, old people, pretty girls, or sports, frequently in an idyllic rural setting.

[103] *Police*, March 1976, pp. 18-19; *The Times*, 22nd January 1976.

[104] 'Police assault bolsters claim of "racial bias"'. *The Observer*, 18th April 1976.

[105] See the transcript of his speech ' "The Thing" that swept the world', *Police*, April 1976. 'The Thing' was the spread of political protest. Lumped in with a catalogue of 'folk-devils' were 'race and immigration', obviously to Mr. Powell intrinsic elements of 'The Thing'.

[106] 'Police leader rejects criticism over Powell' *Daily Telegraph*, April 15th, 1976. However, the contrast with the members of the 'public' invited to previous Federation seminars, e.g. one at Kenilworth in 1969, which included representatives of more liberal bodies like the N.C.C.L., Race Relations Board and N.U.S., signifies the change in its approach.

[107] Reiner, op. cit., pp. 40-45; Postcript pp. 273-276.

[108] Announcing the campaign, Chairman Jim Jardine declared: 'We are anxious to make it a big election issue. We want the political parties to give serious and urgent thought to the problems of law and order and to say what they are going to do to stem the tide of lawlessness in their manifestoes. We are strictly non-political and we will not become involved in campaigning on behalf of any party'. ('Police see lawlessness as big election issue', *Daily Telegraph* 6th February 1978). See also 'Tory Law and Order Challenge', *Daily Telegraph* 23rd February 1978; 'Back the police plea by Tories, *Daily Mail* 22nd June 1978.

[109] 'Rees Crime Plea leads Cabinet counter-attack', *Guardian* 15th February 1978; 'Labour hits back at Tory campaign on crime', *Guardian*, 10th March 1978.

[110] Especially when the Federation Parliamentary Advisor, Eldon Griffiths, is one of the leading Tory law-and-order campaigners. ('Public opinion must alter to beat crime, MP says', *Daily Mail*, 7th March 1978). The contribution of the Federation towards a previous Tory 'Law and order' election campaign in 1970 should also be remembered.

[111] Reiner, op. cit., pp. 60-62. This reinforces the ideological conservatism of policemen. (See note 12 above). L. McDonald: *The Sociology of Law and Order*, Faber, London, 1976, gives a convincing refutation of the mythology that the Conservatives provide better for 'law and order' than Labour (Chap. 6, esp. p. 193-197).

[112] R. Harris: *Justice: The Crisis of Law, Order and Freedom in America*, Bodley Head, London, 1970, outlines this.

[113] Hall *et al.*, op. cit., pp. 238-239. See also S. Hall: 'The Great Moving Right Show', *Marxism Today*, Vol. 23, No. 1, 1979, pp.14-20.

[114] Hall *et al.*, op. cit., p. 273.

Robert Reiner

[115] Becker, op. cit., Chap. 7.

[116] Dickson, op. cit.

[117] For other examples see Silver, op. cit., on the F.B.I. (Part I); W. Chambliss and R. Seidman: *Law, Order and Power*, Addison-Wesley, Mass., 1971, pp. 328-330. I. Taylor, P. Walton, J. Young: *The New Criminology*, Routledge, London, 1973, Chap. 8, is a general critique of this position.

[118] Juris and Feuille, op. cit., pp. 18-24.

[119] R. Cloward and F. Piven: *The Politics of Turmoil*, Vintage, New York, 1974.

[120] B. Johnson: 'Taking Care of Labour: The Police in American Politics', *Theory and Society*, Vol. 3, No. 1, 1976, p. 103.

[121] Miller, op. cit., pp. 16-24.

[122] ibid., Chap. 1.

[123] C. Ackroyd *et al.*, *The Technology of Political Control*, Penguin, London, 1977, p. 110.

[124] R. Reiner: 'The Police in the Class Structure', *British Journal of Law and Society*, Vol. 3, No. 1, 1976, p. 103.

[125] As, for example, *State Research* argues (April-May 1978, p. 82).

[126] For an expansion of this argument see R. Reiner: 'Police, Class and Politics', *Marxism Today*, Vol. 22, No. 3, 1978, pp. 69-80, as well as M. Cain: 'An Ironical Departure: The Dilemma of Contemporary Policing', *Yearbook of Social Policy 1976*, (ed. K. Jones), Routledge, London, 1977.

[4]
In the Office of Chief Constable

Introduction

> "Policing in this country is run by an extra-constitutional
> and (in theory) informal body—the Association of Chief
> Police Officers."

This was the dramatic claim made a couple of years ago by an
editorial in the *New Statesman*, under the graffiti-inspired headline
"ACPO Rules is not OK."[1] The editorial encapsulates the most
conspiratorially inclined pole in the spectrum of concern about the
accountability and control of police forces which has developed
apace amongst civil libertarians in the last decade.[2]

As I tried to show in my 1985 book *The Politics of the Police*,
policing in Britain has become thoroughly politicised, the subject
of acute political controversy and debate. I hesitate to say a
political football, because the ball seems to be so consistently
hogged by one side.

There is nothing novel about the politicisation of policing in the
grand sweep of British history. But the recent clashes over the
police follow an era in which the police had come to be "like the
Royal Family...regarded as above politics," in the words of
Leslie Curtis the Police Federation Chairman.

Bipartisan accord over the principles of policy governing crime,
"law and order," and policing has been rudely shattered, and is
now just one more relic of the lost age of cosy consensus.[3] Many
specific issues about the police have aroused concern and
controversy: methods of dealing with public order, the use of
firearms, corruption, violations of the rules protecting suspects'
rights, rising levels of serious crime and the declining proportion of
crimes which are cleared up, the treatment of ethnic and other

minorities. These and many other questions have been pin-pointed by a series of *causes célèbres*. But underlying them all is the issue of the accountability, or more bluntly, the control of policing. It is a question of the greatest possible constitutional significance, and indeed is the litmus test of the quality of a political order—for policing, the application of the state's monopoly of legitimate force, is the sharp end, the bottom line of all governance.

The *Final Report of the Royal Commission on the Police* in 1962 summed up its view in a celebrated sentence. "The problem of controlling the police can, therefore, be restated as the problem of controlling chief constables."[4] Much of the sociological research which has been done on the processes of law-enforcement in action have called this unidirectional, top-down approach into question. It has come to be generally understood that the impact of organisational and legal rules on police practices on the ground is tenuous and problematic, mediated by a complex filter of immediate situational pressures, and by the cop culture of the canteen and the streets.[5] Nonetheless, the policies and organisational structures constructed by chief officers are a crucial, if not complete, determinant of policing practices. Chief constables have been at the nub of debate, most luridly in the conspiratorial versions of their role encapsulated in the quotes with which the article began. In the last two decades systematic research on the lower ranks of police organisations has accumulated rapidly, and remains one of the few growth centres in today's impoverished social science world. But our knowledge of the senior ranks, of the policy-making levels, remains sketchy and anecdotal, a pot-pourri of chance revelation, scandal and the much-publicised remarks of arguably unrepresentative media celebrities in the rent-a-quote business. If I may humbly follow Lord Denning's precedent and cite my own past statements as authority:

> "The character of police work at the senior levels of the organisation is the greatest gap in the growing body of knowledge which social scientists have accumulated about the police."[6]

If it is true that chief constables have become, in Duncan Campbell's words "a power in the land,"[7] then we ought at the very least to know who chief constables are, and what they think. But "while we have some knowledge of the social origins and previous careers of recruits, we do not have this information for senior officers."[8] In this paper I will present some preliminary results from an empirical study of contemporary chief constables, which I have conducted over the last year, with the aid of a grant from the Nuffield Foundation. In some respects, as will emerge, the conclusions I have come to so far, paradoxically, undercut the obvious importance of my subject of study. In a nutshell what I will argue is that debate has tended to under-emphasise the growing control of policing by central government. Critics and supporters of the status quo have underlined the autonomy of chief officers, understandably in view of some well-publicised clashes with local police authorities which have been much ventilated. But in the process the role of central government has been occluded by the emphasis on constabulary independence. Even in the conspiratorial views it is the influence of ACPO on government which is stressed, not the reverse. In the 1962 Royal Commission's Report there was a long memorandum of dissent by Professor A. L. Goodhart.[9] It argued for a national police force, regionally administered. At the time it was widely regarded (not least by the majority on the Commission) as powerfully argued, but politically unacceptable. This may well remain the verdict today. But with hindsight it seems as if the alternative to Professor Goodhart's *de iure* national force, with explicit structures of accountability, has turned out to be covert national influence, with no accountability for the *de facto* co-ordinating role of central government. I will return to these considerations at the end. But first I want to review what is known about the history and legal powers of the office of chief constable, and the preliminary results of my own recent research. I must emphasise that these results are tentative ones. I have not yet completely finished my fieldwork, and have only begun the analysis of the mass of material gathered.

(i) *The History of the Office of Chief Constable Until 1964*

The term "chief constable" was only applied uniformly to all (provincial) chief officers of police after the Police Act of 1919.[10] Prior to 1919, the term "chief constable" was only standard in referring to county forces. In borough forces the usual term was "head constable," although there was a variety of other nomenclature: "superintendent," "head officer of police," as well as "chief constable" in a growing number of boroughs.[11] The difference in title corresponded to differences both in formal legal position, and in social status and background, between county and borough chiefs. These differences remained after the assimilation of names by the 1919 Police Act, right down to the Police Act of 1964, albeit in more attenuated form after the Second World War.

The first modern police force, the Metropolitan Police, was established by the 1829 Police Act on a pattern which was not followed for provincial forces, and remains unique. Its administration was placed in the hands of two justices, (later called commissioners in 1839; since 1856 there has only been one). The police authority to whom the commissioner was (and remains) accountable is the Home Secretary. When in 1888 the London County Council was set up providing elected local government for London, it was specifically decided that the control of the police should remain with the Home Secretary, because of the unique national and "imperial" functions of the Met., a decision which was the subject of much partisan controversy at the time.[12]

When the first provincial borough forces were established, by the 1835 Municipal Corporations Act, no mention was made of chief or head constables. The new municipal corporations elected as a result of the Act were required to appoint a sufficient number of their members to constitute a watch committee (together with the mayor, appointed as a justice). The watch committee in turn was instructed to appoint a "sufficient number of fit men" to act as constables. The watch committee had the power to appoint and dismiss the constables, and to frame regulations governing them, although the common law powers of the office of constable were preserved.

There rapidly emerged a wide range of differences between the borough forces. The largest city forces—Manchester, Bristol, Birmingham and Liverpool—had chief or head constables who were figures of power and importance in their forces and in the local community. At the other extreme, in the smallest forces, most obviously those with only one or two men, the office of chief constable was indistinguishable from that of constable.

> "The 'chief constable,' in any case, held no exceptional position comparable with that of the county man: he was simply the constable who held the highest rank in the force, and his status depended on the numbers under him."[13]

The locus of control in the nineteenth century between borough chief constables and watch committees has been much debated of late. The standard view,[14] supported recently by Lustgarten, holds that in the nineteenth century "the subordination of the police to elected representatives in the boroughs was part of common understanding."[15] This view has been challenged in recent years by Brogden[16] in the specific case of the Liverpool head constable, and Jefferson and Grimshaw.[17] These authors argue that the doctrine of constabulary independence was already in being for borough chief officers, and offer a reinterpretation of some of the examples of watch committee instructions to chief officers which

In the Office of Chief Constable   139

Critchley proposed as support for the subordination view. The Jefferson and Grimshaw argument about the 1880 Birmingham case is an example of the rather forced nature of their attempted reinterpretation. Following clashes about the chief constable's policies concerning the prosecution of drunks and of "improper" music-hall performances, the Watch Committee passed a resolution that he should not take proceedings "likely to affect a number of ratepayers, or to provoke public comment" without first informing them of his intentions. The chief constable refused to comply unless instructed to by the Home Secretary and the justices. The Home Secretary would not intervene directly, but referred the chief constable to the Municipal Corporations Act which gave the Watch Committee power to make regulations "for preventing neglect or abuse, and for rendering constables efficient in the discharge of their duties," and to dismiss any constable "whom they shall think negligent in the discharge of his duty, or otherwise unfit for the same." In the end, the chief constable gave way, after the Council resolved that it was not desirable to retain a chief officer who was "not subordinate to or not in harmony with" the Watch Committee and threatened him with a requirement to resign. The plain-as-pikestaff interpretation of this is that it demonstrates that watch committees *were* seen as empowered to give chief constables lawful orders about law enforcement priorities. Jefferson and Grimshaw's contrary reading is somewhat tenuously stretched. They claim first that the chief constable's compliance with the Watch Committee's directions does not mean he accepted the *idea* that he lacked independent power to decide on law enforcement. But surely the point is that irrespective of what ideas the chief constable may or may not have entertained (and who is to know?), his ideas did not prevail. Further, they argue that all the Watch Committee claimed was the right to be *informed* of the chief's intentions, not to direct them. But they evidently wanted to be informed of his intentions in order to control them, to be able to ensure that they were "subordinate to" and "in harmony with" the Watch Committee's views (as the Council resolutions put it). I would submit that the orthodox view is correct in holding that in the nineteenth century it *was* generally accepted that watch committees *did* have the power to instruct their chief officers on law enforcement policy. The revisionist reinterpretations establish no more than the obvious limitation that watch committees could only give *lawful* orders, and that especially in the case of experienced heads of large forces (as in Liverpool) the chief constable commanded a certain respect based on professional expertise, but that this was not necessarily deferred to.

In the counties, however, the office of chief constable was not only labelled as such from the outset, but had much of the autonomy of his present-day heirs. The County Police Act of 1839 was a permissive measure, empowering, but not requiring, magistrates in quarter sessions to establish forces for counties (or parts of them). From the outset the county constabularies were under greater Home Office regulation, and also more autonomous of *all* outside influences, than borough forces. The Home Secretary maintained the right to decide whether or not a force should be established, and to approve its size, rules, rates of pay, and the appointment of the chief constable. Guidelines for the selection of chief constables for county forces were issued by the Home Secretary, Lord Normanby, under the 1839 Act, and continued to be enforced until the 1919 Desborough Committee's recommendations superseded them. But "once in post the county chief constable was an autocrat over whom the justices had no power other than the ultimate sanction of dismissal . . . Thus he fulfilled many of the duties which in the borough were assigned to the watch committee."[18] These included appointments, discipline and law enforcement policy. This remained the position without substantial alteration down to the 1964 Police Act. The 1856 County and Borough Police Act, which introduced the Home Office grant and the Inspectorate, the 1888 Local Government Act which established Standing Joint Committees consisting 50 per cent. of elected councillors and 50 per cent. of justices, and the 1919 Police Act which implemented the Desborough Committee's recommendations following the police strikes, all enhanced the role of central government in regulating common basic standards. While they reduced police autonomy *vis-à-vis* central government, they did not substantially diminish the independence of the county chief from *local* electoral control.

This difference in legal status between county and borough chiefs of police is reflected in their social calibre. The county chiefs were drawn from the same landed gentry backgrounds as the justices who appointed them (and so were the elected members who formed the Standing Joint Committees together with the Justices after 1888). It was this congruence of background and outlook with the local elite which made the autonomy of the county chief unproblematic.[19] In recent historical research on the social origins of chief constables, David Wall has noted that three-quarters of the county chiefs in office in 1905 are included in contemporary directories of elites, *e.g. Who's Who* or *Kelly's*

In the Office of Chief Constable   141

Handbook of Official and Titled Classes.[20] This was because of *who* they were rather than *what* they were (unlike the 50 per cent. of present-day chiefs who also find themselves in these exalted pages).

> "The inclusion of county chief constables in such director-ies was by virtue of their background rather than their occupation. The county chief constableship became a popular occupation for the younger sons of the landed gentry in the same way that the army and the cloth had done."[21]

This same social cachet which integrated county chiefs with the local elite, cut them off from their men. Together with their experience as army officers this enhanced their image as autocrats.

By contrast only 5 per cent. of the borough chiefs in office in 1905 feature in the elite directories, and these were usually the heads of the very large city forces, whose origins were more exalted than those of their subordinates (albeit usually they were recruited from professional rather than military careers). But the majority of borough chiefs were men who had worked their way up the police ranks, and came from the same working (or at most lower-middle) class backgrounds as their subordinates. A common pattern was for boroughs to recruit their chiefs from the middle ranks of larger forces—usually the Met.

The Desborough Committee in 1919 examined the case for a fully professional police service with internally recruited chiefs. It recommended a movement towards this:

> "No person without previous police experience should be appointed as chief constable in any force unless he possesses some exceptional qualification or experience which specially fits him for the post, or there is no other candidate from the police service who is considered sufficiently well-qualified." (para. 139).

This was embodied in Regulation 9 of the rules which the 1919 Police Act empowered the Home Secretary to make governing the pay, conditions of service and appointments of the police. But the effect of the regulation was circumvented by the county forces. They either appointed men of the traditional type with colonial police backgrounds, or ex-military men to Assistant Chief Const-able posts (not covered by Reg. 9) to give them the "police experience" required. The result was that while in 1908 it was found that only three of the 44 English county chief constables had risen through the ranks (the rest being ex-army officers or colonial policemen), by 1939 this had only increased to four of the then 42

142   *In the Office of Chief Constable*

English county chiefs.[22] By contrast, only 15 of the 123 borough
chiefs in 1908, and six of the 117 in 1939 had *not* risen through the
ranks.

During and after the Second World War, the policy of only
recruiting chief constables who *had* served as police throughout
their careers became effective (*Postwar Committee on the Reconstruction of the Police Service*). However, county forces were able
to stave off the full effects of this until the early 1970s, because of
the legacy of the short-lived Trenchard scheme in the 1930s which
provided for direct entry of (mainly middle-class) graduates to the
Hendon Police College as "officer material" with automatic
promotion to Inspector.

> "In 1965, the Commissioner, Deputy Commissioner, 4
> Assistant Commissioners in the metropolitan Police, 19
> county chief constables, 6 borough chief constables, the Chief
> Inspector of the Constabulary and three of his colleagues
> were all trained at Hendon."[23]

What is clear is that down to the 1964 Police Act there remained
a substantial divide in legal and social status between county chief
constables and their borough namesakes (with the partial exception of the largest city forces). While the latter were upwardly
mobile career police officers from humble origins, the former were
firmly parts of the county social elite. Moreover, they were
extremely well-established parts of the local elite. Usually
appointed in their 30s, it was common for them to die in office
after extremely long periods as chief constable. The Surrey
Constabulary, for example, was not unusual in having only two
chiefs during its first 80 years: its first chief constable retired in
1899 at the age of 86, after 48 years in office, followed by his
successor who retired in 1930.[24] Such longevity was matched by a
few borough forces: Chester City, for example, which had only
four chief constables in the whole 113 years of its existence (1836–
1949), or Oxford City which also had only four chief officers from
1869 (when Charles Head, a Metropolitan Inspector became its
"Superintendent") to 1968, when it was amalgamated into Thames
Valley.[25] Evidently there would be much more scope for such chief
officers to stamp a personal style of leadership upon their forces
than would be usual today, and the potential for autocratic
command is clear.

One final, most important aspect of the development of the
office of chief constable before 1964 was the evolution of effective
representative machinery. A Chief Constable's Association was
founded in 1896 for city and borough chiefs, and a County Chief

In the Office of Chief Constable　　143

Constables' Conference in 1920. The present Association of Chief Police Officers was formed in 1948 by the merger of the earlier bodies. It includes deputy and assistant chiefs, the Metropolitan ranks from Commander upwards, and the City of London Commissioner and Assistant Commissioner. The vehicle for these bodies to influence (and be influenced by) central government has been the Central Conference of Chief Constables, dating back to the First World War, under the chairmanship of the Home Secretary or a senior Home Office official. These meet two or three times a year. In addition there are district conferences which meet at least quarterly, also dating back to 1918. These are conduits both for the formation of a collective voice, and communication with the Home Office.

(ii) *The Office of Chief Constable Since 1964*

The statutory basis of the office of chief constable now, and of its relationship with local and central government, is the Police Act of 1964, together with the case law this has generated. The Act largely implemented the recommendations of the 1962 Report of the Royal Commission on the Police, which had been established in the wake of a series of cases raising concern about the accountability of the police generally and chief officers in particular.[26] The Royal Commission was faced by two conflicting and cogent lines of argument. The first was the view (articulated most explicitly by the Association of Municipal Corporations) that local police authorities should be (and watch committees were) able to issue instructions on policy matters in the same way as to other local officials (but not in individual cases of law enforcement). On the other hand, several representative bodies of professional legal opinion (the Law Society, the Inns of Court Conservative and Unionist Society, and Professor E. C. S. Wade who was consulted as an expert witness) all argued for a centrally controlled force, under parliamentary supervision, both on grounds of efficiency and accountability. This view was accepted in the dissenting memorandum by Professor Goodhart. Interestingly, it was also supported by the *New Statesman*, now the champion of the ACPO/police state conspiracy theory. An article by C. H. Rolph saw the report as

> "22 pages by Dr. Goodhart, with a preface seven times as long by a faintly admiring syndicate of diplomats."[27]

The majority of chief constables rejected the case for national control, but also reasserted the notion of constabulary independ-

144   *In the Office of Chief Constable*

ence from local control. A few chief constables (notably Eric St. Johnston of Lancashire), as well as the Police Federation, went along with the arguments for nationalisation, or at least regionalisation.

In the end, as C. H. Rolph's comments intimate, the Commissioner's Report, and the ensuing Act was a diplomatic compromise, the "tripartite" system of control by chief officers, Home Office and local police authorities. The latter were essentially a hybrid of the old watch and standing joint committees, consisting of two-thirds elected councillors, and one-third J.P.s. As critics remarked at the time (notably Geoffrey Marshall) the boundaries of function, responsibility and power between the points of the triangle were ill-defined and contained the seeds of future conflict once the political and social consensus about policing broke down, as it did increasingly after the late 1960s. There have been several excellent recent statements of the statutory position and case law, so this can be summarised briefly.[28]

The main duty of the police authority is to maintain "an adequate and efficient" force for its area. (s.4(1)). It is responsible for providing buildings, vehicles and other equipment, "as may be required for police purposes of the area." (ss.4(3), 4(4)). Subject to the approval of the Home Secretary, it also appoints, and "in the interests of efficiency" may dismiss, the chief constable, his deputy and assistants. (ss.4(2), 5(1), 5(4), 6(4), 6(5)). Again with the Home Secretary's approval, the police authority determines the establishment of the force. (s.4(2)). It controls force revenue and expenditure, although it can be required to pay sums necessary to give effect to regulations issued by the Home Secretary, or a court order, or to implement statutory changes. (s.8(1), s.8(4)). Central government meets 50 per cent. of policing costs directly, and also contributes to the local 50 per cent. through rate support grant. The chief constable is obliged to make an annual report to the police authority, and the authority may ask for further reports on any matter connected with the policing of the area. (s.12). But the chief constable may refuse such a report if it appears to him not to be in the public interest, or not to be "needed for the discharge of the functions of the police authority." In the event of such disagreement, the Home Secretary decides what should be done.

This apparently substantial list of functions begins to evaporate when the allocation of powers and duties to the chief constable and the Home Secretary is considered. The role of the chief constable is described almost parenthetically in the Act.

In the Office of Chief Constable   145

"The police force maintained for a police area under s.1 of this Act shall be under the direction and control of the chief constable appointed under s.4(2) of this Act." (s.5(1)).

Geoffrey Marshall argued in 1965 that this "merely describes the existing situation."[29] As seen above, this meant that chief constables, arguably, would be obliged to follow the lawful instructions of the police authority. But Lustgarten's critique of this interpretation of the Act seems more convincing. He argues, first, that when establishing other local government services (*e.g.* Education Act 1944; Social Services Act 1970) the terminology "direction and control" is not used to describe the function of the director. The other Acts establish a special local authority (*e.g.* education) or instruct the local authority to establish a special committee (*e.g.* social services), who are responsible for providing the service, to which end they are required to appoint a chief officer who is clearly subordinate to them. This argument by itself is not totally convincing. The main difference in the structure of the statutes is the terminology "direction and control," the meaning of which is precisely what is at issue.

However, Lustgarten's interpretation is further supported by a consideration of the case law. It must be stressed at once that, as is common ground between Marshall and Lustgarten, no case since the Act (and arguably none before it) *directly* has in point the issue of whether a chief constable has to follow lawful instructions from a police authority. The doctrine of constabulary independence has emerged in case law without ever being centrally at issue. *Obiter* on *obiter*. Of the pre-Act cases, the most often cited is *Fisher* v. *Oldham*.[30] As Marshall, Lustgarten and numerous other commentators have argued, this only establishes that constables and police authorities do not have a master/servant relationship for the specific question of vicarious liability in tort (on which the 1964 Act in substance reverses the effect of *Fisher* by explicitly making chief constables vicariously liable for their subordinates' torts in section 48(1) and exposing the police fund controlled by the police authority to the obligation to pay damages). This limited decision about the absence of a specific master/servant relationship in the tort sense, has come to stand as authority in later cases for the broader constitutional doctrine of constabulary independence from any instructions about law-enforcement methods and policy.

The most influential and often cited, post-1964 Act, judicial statement of the independence doctrine is that by Lord Denning in the first *ex p. Blackburn* case.[31] Mr. Blackburn was seeking an order of mandamus directing the Metropolitan Commissioner to

146   *In the Office of Chief Constable*

reverse a policy of not enforcing the law on gaming. The Court of Appeal[32] found that the police have a public duty to enforce the law, which the courts could, if necessary, compel them to perform. But within this they have a broad discretion about methods and priorities. The courts would only countermand this if it was a policy of complete non-enforcement of a law, amounting to a chief officer "failing in his duty to enforce the law," *e.g.* by a directive saying no one would be prosecuted for thefts worth less than £100.

In the course of this judgment remarks were made about the independence of chief constables.

> "No minister of the Crown can tell him that he must or must not keep observation on this place or that; or that he must or must not prosecute this man or that one, nor can any police authority tell him so . . . he is not the servant of anyone save of the law itself. The responsibility for law enforcement lies on him. He is answerable to the law and to the law alone."[33]

With respect to this particular passage, Lustgarten has remarked "seldom have so many errors of law and logic been compressed into one paragraph."[34] He counts no fewer than six separate fallacies in Lord Denning's remarks. Whether or not he is correct, however, it is clear in any event that the remarks are strictly *obiter*.[35] The relationship between a chief officer, and either a police authority or the Home Secretary was simply not at issue in this case (or any of the later *Blackburn* cases). Nonetheless, these remarks have been used as authority for later judgments in the same vein, *e.g.* by Lord Denning himself in the *C.E.G.B.* case, where he cited, his own earlier words to support the proposition that "it is of the first importance that the police should decide on their own responsibility what action should be taken in any particular situation."[36] In the *C.E.G.B.* case the Board applied for an order of mandamus, after being prevented by protestors from carrying out a survey which they were statutorily empowered to conduct. The chief constable had refused to take action to remove the protestors, claiming no breach of the peace had occurred or was threatened. The court's sympathies clearly seem to have been with the Board, rather than the chief, and they found that the conduct of the protestors in unlawfully obstructing the Board's survey was itself a breach of the peace. However, the Court of Appeal did not grant mandamus. In Lord Denning's argument, this was on the grounds of constabulary independence: "The decision of the chief constable not to intervene in this case was a police decision with which I think the courts should not

In the Office of Chief Constable   147

interfere,"[37] citing his own words in *Blackburn* as authority. However, it is not clear that this view is the basis of the judgment. Lord Lawton uses another argument, and Lord Templeman seems to concur with it. Lord Lawton argued that the application for mandamus

> "showed a misconception of the powers of chief constables. They command their forces but they cannot give an officer under command an order to do acts which can only lawfully be done if the officer himself with reasonable cause suspects that a breach of the peace has occurred or is imminently likely to occur or an arrestable offence has been committed. In July 1981 the Chief Constable of Devon and Cornwall could have, and probably did, order some of his constables to watch what was going on in the field ... but what he could not do was to give unqualified orders to his officers."[38]

In other words, no one, whether a senior officer, police authority, or court, can order a constable to exercise a power which can only be exercised lawfully if certain factual conditions precedent are satisfied, and this can only be ascertained by the constable on the spot. If this is the ground of the judgment then it too does not really establish independence of constables from being given lawful instructions by police authorities, an issue not directly in question in any event.

The same applies to the more recent case *R. v. Oxford, ex p. Levey*.[39] Mr. Levey lost substantial amounts of jewellery in a robbery by thieves who escaped when the pursuing police car was called back by the Force control room after entering Toxteth. The pursuers had informed the control room of this, in compliance with a Force Order. The order to call off the chase was given by the control room inspector after the police car "encountered a group of some 50 youths armed with bricks, iron bars and pieces of metal" and "one of these youths threw a house-brick at and hit P.C. Bark's car." Mr. Levey sought (i) a declaration that it was *ultra vires* for the chief constable to adopt a policy whereby an area was deemed to be a "no-go" area; (ii) a declaration that it was *ultra vires* for the chief constable to call off the chase when the police car entered Toxteth; (iii) an order of mandamus directing the chief constable to rescind any order or decision to treat Toxteth or any part of the city as a "no-go" area, which would be counter to his statutory and common law duties; (iv) damages for breach of statutory duty. Mr. Levey failed in his action, the decision turning on the specific facts. It was found that the order to call off the chase was motivated primarily by concern for the safety

148   *In the Office of Chief Constable*

of the pursuing officer. The obligation to inform the control room when entering Toxteth did not amount to a "no-go" policy, as remarks made by some P.C.s to Mr. Levey wrongly implied. Arguably such a policy *would* amount to the total abdication from the duty to enforce the law with which the courts have consistently said they would interfere. The policy to inform the control room was intended to ensure that any law enforcement activities in the sensitive area of Toxteth could take full account of the current situation there. This was a matter about the appropriate *methods* for enforcing the law, a choice over which "chief constables have the widest possible discretion."[40] So the judgment amounts to confirmation of the view that chief constables will not be told by the courts *how* to enforce the law, provided they do not totally abdicate from their duty to do so. Once again, however, while the constabulary independence doctrine is bolstered, the relationship specifically with police authorities was not at issue.

The recent *Northumbria* case[41] *did* concern the powers of police authorities. However, it involved all three parties to the tripartite relation, so consideration will be postponed until after looking at the Home Secretary's powers under the 1964 Act.

The cases considered so far do establish a strong judicial tradition of support for the doctrine of "constabulary independence." Arguably, as Marshall claims, the statements containing this are *obiter*, at any rate as concerns the chief constable/police authority relationship which was never directly at issue. Nonetheless, Lustgarten is surely right that however deficient its initial basis, the doctrine of constabulary independence

> "has ... embedded itself in the lore and learning of both judges and police, and it is inconceivable that, without parliamentary intervention, the courts would resile from the position they have reached."[42]

The third party to the tripartite system, the Home Secretary, has also grown in power, together with chief constables, at the expense of local police authorities, at any rate as compared with pre-1964 watch committees. The Royal Commission and the 1964 Act clearly *intended* to tilt the balance towards the centre. The history of legislation concerning police organisation and accountability reflects a perennially repeated clash of rhetorics, re-emerging in the debates around the 1829, 1835, 1839, 1856, 1888, 1919, and 1964 Acts. On the one hand, there is a clear Benthamite vision of a rationally structured, bureaucratic police organisation, controlled by, and accountable to, the centre. On the other side, there is a chorus of opposition to this, invoking fear of the trampling of

In the Office of Chief Constable   149

hallowed British liberties by a foreign-inspired Leviathan. At each turn, the Benthamites have had much of their way, as evidenced by the very fact of the passage of the legislation. But the libertarian fears result in compromises and concessions from the clear centralist form. Since 1964 the Benthamite vision has had undisputed sway in practice, while, paradoxically, explicit support for it has faded away to such a degree that Lustgarten can remark

> "The one point that commands near-universal agreement is that a national police force is undesirable."[43]

The Royal Commission Report was clearly impressed by the Goodhart centralising line. This is most evident in the way they firmly refuted the main bulwark of the localist position: the fear of a centralist and totalitarian "police state."[44] The reasons for rejecting the central control argument are much more tenuous and amount to no more than respect for tradition, and the importance of local ties and identity for policing. The latter point was in fact recognised by the advocates of nationalisation, and various attempts to preserve local links were incorporated in their schemes for change.[45] The accountability argument was stressed by the advocates of centralisation[46] rather than the localists. The description of the benefits of local police authorities by the Commission[47] sees them not so much as a means of accountability but only as consultative devices, and as administrative dogs-bodies. What the Commission seems to be saying, almost explicitly, is that the argument for central control is basically sound, but that it would be better to provide the means while maintaining a semblance of local accountability, than to come clean on the issue. With hindsight, is that too cynical an interpretation of its concluding comment on the matter, where they speak of proceeding by

> "accelerating the pace at which the police service moves towards greater unity, rather than by any abrupt and radical change which might not be readily understood."[48]

The means for beefing up central control were two-fold. First, the role of Home Secretary as arbiter in conflicts between police authorities and chief constables. More fundamentally, the Commission wanted the Home Secretary to be made statutorily responsible for the efficiency of the police.[49] This formulation was objected to by the Home Secretary during the Parliamentary debates, on the ground that it would give responsibility without power (an argument which had been anticipated in Professor Goodhart's dissenting memorandum.[50] Instead, it might be

150   *In the Office of Chief Constable*

argued, he has ended up with power without responsibility. The 1964 Act specifies the general duty of the Home Secretary as being to

> "exercise his powers...in such manner and to such extent as appears to him to be best calculated to promote the efficiency of the police." (s.28).

For this purpose he is given a variety of powers:

(i) to require a police authority to exercise their power under Part 1 of this Act to call upon the chief constable to retire in the interests of efficiency, (s.29(1));

(ii) to require a report from a chief constable on any matter connected with the policing of any area, and to receive an annual report, (s.30);

(iii) the power to make grants of expenses, (s.31), and related to this, the power to appoint the Inspectorate to monitor and advise on efficiency, (s.38);

(iv) the power to establish special inquiries into the policing of local areas, (s.32);

(v) the power to make regulations concerning all aspects of the government, administration and conditions of service of police forces, (s.33) and concerning standards of equipment, (s.36) (and of course the continuing practice of issuing circulars);

(vi) the power to provide a wide array of central services, (s.41), a power which was to prove crucial in the recent *Northumbria* case.

Outside the 16 very long sections (ss.28–43) detailing the Secretary of State's functions and powers, others crop up elsewhere in the Act. Of potentially great importance in the context of a national policing operation such as occurred during the miners' strike of 1984–1985, sections 13 and 14 on collaboration and mutual aid arrangements give the Home Secretary the clear power to direct that such agreements be made if necessary (s.13(5)), to order a force to receive or provide reinforcements (s.14(2)), and to arbitrate on inter-force disputes about the allocation of the financial burden of such co-operation (s.13(3), s.14(4)).

In the event, these powers were never used. Instead, the most extensive mutual aid operation to date, in the 1984 miners' strike, was co-ordinated by the National Reporting Centre under the control of the President of ACPO, implicitly to the satisfaction of

In the Office of Chief Constable   151

the Home Secretary or presumably he *would* have invoked his powers.[51] The accountability implications are significant. Had the operation been directed by the Home Secretary under his Police Act powers, he would have been answerable to Parliament for their exercise. As it was, no one was.

Several recent developments accentuate this centralising trend clearly evident in the 1964 legislation. The statutory requirement to establish consultative arrangements in each police area, which section 106 of the Police and Criminal Evidence Act 1984 introduces, at first sight appears an exception. But whatever the virtues of these arrangements, the form they took was uniformly shaped by Home Office Circular 54/1982.[52] Paradoxically this move to local consultation reveals the way that nominally advisory Home Office Circulars are interpreted as binding.

The Local Government Act 1985 which abolished the six Metropolitan County Councils considerably increased the statutory powers and the *de facto* influence of the Home Secretary. The rate-capping powers of central government allow it to determine the budget, and manpower levels of the Metropolitan Forces, which means the Home Secretary in effect

> "now directly controls the financial resources for nearly half of the entire police strength in England and Wales."[53]

A further consequence of the new Joint Boards which replaced the former Metropolitan police authorities is to increase the likelihood of a "hung" Board, with the magistrates thus having the last say.

> "In the Metropolitan areas the tripartite structure must be viewed as little more than a legal fiction...The 1985 Local Government Act represents the most significant and overt shift in responsibility for the police service, from local to central government, since the passage of the 1964 Police Act."[54]

The point is underlined in the highly significant recent case of *R. v. Secretary of State for the Home Department, ex p. Northumbria Police Authority*.[55] This concerned Home Office Circular 40/1986 which stated that in pursuance of the Home Secretary's 1981 announcement to make available baton rounds and CS gas to chief officers of police "for use in the last resort," it was proposed that such requirements would be met from a central store. This would extend to "cases where a chief officer has been unable to obtain his police authority's agreement to purchase," subject to endorsement by H.M. Inspectorate of Constabulary. The Divisional Court upheld the circular by accepting that the Home Secretary had the power to supply equipment without the police authority's permission under the Royal Prerogative. But it rejected the view that he was also empowered to do this under section 41 of the Police Act which permitted him to supply equipment "for promoting the efficiency of the police." To do this when the police authority objected would be incompatible with its own responsibility for efficiency under section 4(1). The Court of Appeal confirmed the Royal Prerogative argument. But it also held that the power to supply common services under section 41, and the general requirement to use his powers so as to promote the efficiency of the police—section 28—entitled him to provide such services, including riot equipment, even without the police authority's consent. What this seems to amount to is that if the local and the national view of "efficiency" conflict, the Act gives priority to the interpretation by central government. In any event, this same conclusion would be available as a result of the Royal Prerogative powers.

What seems abundantly clear is that in the law in the books as well as the law in action, if there is disagreement about policing policy between local police authorities and the chief constable or central government, the latter parts of the supposed tripartite structure regularly prevail. With regard to the police authority/chief constable relationship, this is legitimated by the doctrine of constabulary independence.

But what if chief constables and the central government disagree? What becomes of constabulary independence then? The answer is, we don't know. We don't know because, unlike the many well-publicised cases of conflict between chief constables and local authorities,[56] clashes between chief constables and central government have not surfaced. To find out why, we must consider more closely who chief constables are, a question to which my recent empirical research has been addressed.

(iii) *Who Are the Chief Constables? A Social Profile*

The position of chief constables is now quite different from either the county or borough chiefs of the past. County chiefs then had a local elite position stemming from background rather than office. They elevated the standing of the office, rather than vice versa. Borough chiefs (with the possible exception of the very largest cities) were men of humble origins who had worked their way up to gain membership in the local municipal elite.[57] They were not especially prominent locally, and certainly not actors on a national stage.

In the Office of Chief Constable   153

Today's chief constable typically comes from a relatively humble background, not very different from the men and women he commands, or the general population he is responsible for policing. But he has worked himself up into a professional elite body, which is an important if unusual and unsung part of the national power elite.

Both terms "national" and "elite" may be questioned. In the letter of introduction to chief constables which I sent out last year seeking an interview, I said I was interested in them as "an elite group with considerable power and influence." One chief I interviewed questioned my use of the word elite. He could not see this word as appropriate to describe a group of people many of whom came from ordinary working-class backgrounds. While these origins distinguish chief constables from most groups traditionally thought of as elites, I would maintain the term is appropriate.

Following Weber, most sociologists would analyse position in the social stratification hierarchy in terms of three dimensions: economic class, social status or prestige, and political power. On all three chief constables now rank high.

(a) *Economic.* They command very large resources. In 1983/1984 the net expenditure of police forces ranged from a low of £16.3m (Dyfed-Powys) to a high for the Met. of £667.1m, and in the provinces £131.5m. (G.M.P.). Chief constables also command large salaries, ranging around £40,000 p.a. (depending on the size of their forces).

(b) *Status.* Perhaps the clearest index of the rise in chief constables' social standing is their move up the New Year's Honours lists of recent years. Last year Sir Philip Knights, former chief of West Midlands, became the first chief constable to be given a peerage. This year, one chief constable and one former chief (now an H.M.I.) were knighted, and this seems to be an annual pattern.

(c) *Power.* The review of the legal position showed that chief constables are given the direction and control of their forces, and power to determine policing methods and priorities in their areas. This gives them at any rate formal power of an extensive kind. Police forces range in size from 934 (Dyfed-Powys), to the largest provincial force (G.M.P.) 6,943, and the Met. with 27,165. The populations over which they police range from 440,000 (Gwent) to

154   *In the Office of Chief Constable*

the largest provincial force population, 2,647,000 (West Midlands), and 7,202,000 for the Met.

If they are in these terms an elite group of substantial importance, are they a *national* power elite? Or just 43 separate elite individuals with the same title? In his sociological classic *The Power Elite* C. Wright Mills specifies three conditions for saying that a number of separate elites at the top of different institutions may be considered as a unitary power elite.[58]

(1) *Psychological similarity and social intermingling.*

Are they men of similar origin, education, career, style of life? Is there "considerable traffic of personnel" between the institutions? Does this lead to a convergence of outlook?

(2) *Structural blending of commanding position and common interests.*

Do the institutions and the commanding positions have similar interests, problems, structural pressures?

(3) *Unity of a more explicit co-ordination.*

Do the common outlook, background, interests sometimes coalesce into united action?

The last of these can only be considered in terms of specific historical episodes, but seems confirmed by the 1984 miners' strike, and the complex, co-ordinated policing operation conducted despite lack of central coercive power by the National Reporting Centre. The second criterion is whether common interests override the inter-force and inter-personal rivalries found in any job. Since 1964 many structural differences between forces, particularly the county/borough divide have disappeared or narrowed. The first question requires systematic social research on the demography and perspectives of a group. It is the answer to this question which I have been addressing.

The research was aimed at discovering the demographic characteristics and the policing philosophy of today's chief constables. The views and background of a few chiefs (or perhaps more accurately, one chief) receive widespread media attention and are well-known. But I wanted to determine whether there was a characteristic outlook and background, or substantial variations, and if so, how these would be characterised and explained. To this end, I set out to interview all 43 chief constables in office in England and Wales, about their careers, background and views on

In the Office of Chief Constable   155

a wide range of policing issues. I will not elaborate here on the process of gaining access and setting up these interviews. Suffice to say that I was successful in obtaining the agreement of ACPO and the Home Office to approach individual chief officers. Despite dire warnings from cognoscenti I received an overwhelmingly positive amount of co-operation, and in most cases a warm, occasionally eager, welcome.[59] Four chiefs immediately refused to be interviewed when approached. One other agreed initially, but then declined following widespread controversy about some much publicised remarks of his. To date I have completed interviews with 38 chiefs. I have two more arranged in the near future, having succeeded in negotiating co-operation from two erstwhile refusals. I therefore hope to end up with at least 40 completed interviews. The data not only constitute a representative sample but a virtual census. The interviews lasted for an average of one-and-a-half hours, none appreciably less, and some considerably more. With one exception they were taped. The result is a high pile of transcripts, which since many of the questions were open-ended, is a long and laborious process to analyse. I have fully analysed so far only the demographic parts of the interview. The opinions are still in the process of being analysed, so any conclusions I give about these are tentative and subject to revision.

The background of chief constables

Table 1 shows that the social backgrounds of chief constables are not wildly divergent from police officers in general, nor the population at large. The majority (55.3 per cent.) had fathers whose work careers were spent mainly in skilled manual jobs, with 68.4 per cent. having fathers who were in manual jobs for most of their careers. The majority of the rest (21 per cent. overall) were in routine non-manual jobs. However nearly half (45 per cent.) of their fathers experienced occupational mobility during their own careers, and by the time the chiefs were 18, only 50 per cent. remained in manual work. About a third had fathers who ended up in managerial or professional positions (31.5 per cent. and 2.5 per cent. respectively).

This experience of upward social mobility is a characteristic of the police in general.[60] But it is far more marked amongst chief officers. Not only have they themselves moved up into the Registrar General's Class II. Their initial pre-police occupations were predominantly non-manual (51 per cent. overall, with 29 per cent. having no previous job). Their own adult children exhibit even more marked mobility (allowing for the distortions of parental pride). None are in manual occupations, and over two-thirds are in professional or managerial ones.

Comparing this with the sample of the Federated ranks in an earlier study in terms of father's occupation at age 18, Table 1 shows that the chiefs differed slightly but not enormously in the direction of having higher status fathers. But the difference is not marked, and is the result of the chiefs' father's own occupational mobility.

The proportion of chief constables with police fathers (13 per cent.) is the same as in the Federated ranks (14 per cent.). But 37 per cent. mentioned some police relative as an influence on joining. Interestingly 17 per cent. of their children have followed their footsteps into the police (18 per cent. have at least one child in the police, and there are a few three-generation police families).

The conclusion is clear: the chief constables of today are drawn predominantly from skilled working-class backgrounds, and have a family tradition very much marked by upward social mobility, over three generations. Chief constables can fairly be characterised as a "working-class elite."

This is reflected in their educational experiences, shown in Table 2. The chiefs show a remarkable level of educational achievement compared to the norm for their class of origin, and to the general police level. I found in an earlier study that

> "policemen . . . have done rather better educationally than other children from manual or lower level backgrounds."

Twenty per cent. of lower grade non-manual and skilled manual children born in the late 1930s went to grammar or independent schools but half of the lower-ranked police in that study had done so. But of current chief constables, Table 2 shows 85.1 per cent. had. Moreover, my earlier study showed that while the Federated ranks had done better than normal for their class of origin in terms of type of school attended, they did not do well in terms of school-leaving qualifications. But this is not true of chief constables. Only 13 per cent. of chief constables left school with no qualifications, compared with 28.6 per cent. of the lower ranks. Most chief constables left with some "O" levels or school certificate passes.

In the 1962 Royal Commission, anxiety was expressed that there was "no recent instance of a university graduate entering the service" (para. 308). This has been partly rectified because 12 per cent. of the current intake of recruits are graduates, and 4.45 per cent. of all police are.[61] But the chief constables are from earlier generations, and none entered the police with a degree. However,

In the Office of Chief Constable   157

over a quarter acquired degrees during their service. Half of these degrees were obtained through the Bramshill Scholarship scheme, whereby the most successful students on the Special Course at Bramshill go to University on police scholarships. The majority of the other degrees were either London externals or Open University degrees, with a few gained by force secondments. In addition, to these degrees, several chief constables have university diplomas, usually in criminology or management.

All this confirms the image of chief constables derived from looking at their social origins. They are predominantly drawn from the upwardly mobile, meritocratically achieving, skilled working class.

Orientation to work

Most of the chiefs were set on a police career from a relatively young age. Although 71 per cent. had worked outside the force before joining, only five had worked for more than two years at anything else. 90 per cent. had experience of military service, but of these the overwhelming majority (85 per cent.) had only done National Service.

Career histories

84 per cent. of the chiefs had joined by the age of 22, and all before the age of 25, as Table 3 shows. However, my earlier study showed that of the same generation in the Federated ranks, over one-third joined *after* the age of 25. Most of the current chief constables (68 per cent.) joined before 1954, and only one later than 1960. Their reasons for joining are predominantly an attraction to the job itself: 54 per cent. gave purely non-instrumental reasons, 30 per cent. mixed, with only 16 per cent. instrumental. This is unusual in their generation. My earlier research found that of recruits joining before 1960, 41 per cent. gave non-instrumental, and 30 per cent. instrumental reasons. Furthermore, while the main instrumental reason mentioned by the lower ranks was security, for the chief constable it was more likely to be the attraction of a career. (Though only two thought they would end up as a chief constable).

Most of the chiefs were overwhelmingly satisfied with their careers. All said they were, and 76 per cent. said they would rejoin if starting all over again.[62]

Thus most of the chiefs had looked to policing for an intrinsically interesting career, and had found what they were looking for.

158   *In the Office of Chief Constable*

Experiences in the job

Most police officers are "locals" not "cosmopolitans" in the sociological jargon. They have spent most if not all of their lives in the force area where they work. This is decidedly not true of chief constables. Indeed this is explicit policy. Regulations prevent a person serving more than two of the three ACPO ranks in the same force.

Consequently all chiefs will have served in at least one other force during their careers. In fact only four have served in only one other force, *i.e.* the minimal movement necessary. As Table 4 shows 50 per cent. have served in two others, and 40 per cent. in three or more others. Most will have experience of a mixture of city and county forces. Nine have only worked in city forces, but only three have only county experience although most forces are county ones. Interestingly, as many as 40 per cent. have served in the Met. (usually as the Force they initially joined and worked most of their careers in). It still seems to be the pattern, as in the early history of provincial city policy, that the Met. provides their senior officers!

Almost all will have had experience of at least one of the command courses at the Police Staff College, Bramshill. Only two of the present chiefs have not been on the Senior Command Course. 16 per cent. have been on the Special Course for potential high-flyers amongst constables, which since it only started in 1962, is a high proportion of those chiefs young enough to be eligible for it. In addition to these national elite training courses several (16 per cent.) have been on the Royal College of Defence Studies Course, an invitations-only one-year course primarily for senior military officers, diplomats and civil servants.

In terms of careers and training, chief constables, unlike their subordinates, are decidedly (and by design) "cosmopolitans" not "locals." By the time they reach ACPO rank they will have developed a network of national contacts and experiences.

Most will have had a variety of work experience within their forces. It is a commonly held myth that specialist detectives are unlikely to reach the top. In fact, 34 per cent. of my sample have been detectives for more than half of their careers. But the majority had a mixed bag of operational experience, albeit predominantly in uniform territorial patrol work.

For most, promotion was rapid, at any rate after the first hurdle of promotion to sergeant, which took seven years on average. The average time for all other promotions was two–three years. The

In the Office of Chief Constable   159

average age of appointment as chief constable was 50. The youngest appointment was 42, and the oldest 56. Only four were appointed chief constable before 45, and most were appointed in their late 40s. They had been chief constables for somewhere between a few months and 12 years, and on average had been in post for five years. The longevity in service of earlier generations has disappeared.

53 per cent. had been appointed chief constable while being deputy in another force, and 24 per cent. had been promoted from deputy in the same force. Three had been chief constables in smaller forces, three had held ACPO rank in the Met. when appointed, and two had been respectively Commandant and Deputy Commandant at Bramshill.

What conclusions can be drawn from the demographic profile of chief constables? It seems that their origins, education, occupational socialisation, and career patterns indicate that they do satisfy Mills' first criterion of a unitary elite. They overwhelmingly come from a similar background, the upwardly mobile, educationally successful, skilled working class. They had similar (though atypical) education experiences; had similar initial approaches to the police, and were singled out comparatively early on for rapid advancement. They will have got to know each other through moving between forces, and passing through the Police Staff College, and other shared training experiences. They will have been exposed to the same nationally designed curriculum for senior officers. If this is not enough, none will have been appointed chief constable unless they have first been approved by the Home Office as suitable to be on the short-list interviewed by the Police Authority, and after selection their appointment must be formally approved by the Home Secretary.[63]

Small wonder there are no publicly aired disputes between chief constables and central government. The chances of a rogue appointment being made are clearly miniscule.

In the interview material, the orientation to central rather than local government comes through fairly consistently. While most chiefs wish to cultivate good relations with their police authorities, and indeed believe they enjoy them, at best this means they will seek to persuade them to accept their views if disagreements arise, not that they will accept the authority's approach. This comes out clearly, for example, in a question I asked about the use of plastic bullets. Most chief constables would use them if necessary, even in the face of police authority opposition, although they would prefer to carry them along by persuasion. The following approach is typical:

160 *In the Office of Chief Constable*

"A lot depends on the circumstances. To start with I wouldn't be concerned about the police authority. If it came down to my professional judgment. It all depends, the scenario is not always the same . . . If you do have your elected members at the scene . . . your community relations council, there is nothing like them seeing what the situation is . . . If not, what you're going to do is make the decision, go ahead, use it, and then provide the evidence afterwards."

This indicates that while consensus is preferred, when the buck has to stop the decision is the chief constable's regardless of the police authority's views.

This is not the attitude taken towards the Home Office. While many rail at this, often bitterly, it is recognised that the Home Office issues many regulations which in effect have to be obeyed. Even its nominally advisory circulars can be ignored only at the chief constable's peril. While disagreements may be strongly argued, this time when the buck stops, it is normally the chief who backs down. Again a typical quote:

"We would all stand and fight our corner to the death if we felt that we were right and they (the Home Office) were wrong, and they were trying to manipulate us or instruct us, but on the other hand one would wish certainly to not be too far out of step with the thinking of the Home Office, who of course are influenced by the government of the day."

For all the pride that chief constables express in their independence, and all the testimony they pay to the value attached to good relations with local authorities, the overall sense I have is that their professional colleagues—and it is ACPO and the HMI that are seen as their peers—are the prime reference group. The Home Office is often resented, and its authority may not be respected. But at the end of the day it has power, as well as the legitimacy of an electoral mandate. The local authority is not seen in this light. Preferably it can be educated to understand the professional point of view. But if not it is that professional judgment which counts. To an extent this picture is overdrawn and oversimplified. There are individual variations, and some chiefs are more fiercely independent, and more locally oriented, than others. But in the main the prime reference group is the national professional one, and the Home Office is accepted as boss, however resentfully.

Conclusion

In a sense my conclusion confirms the conspiracy theory with

In the Office of Chief Constable   161

which I began. Chief constables are a national power elite of considerable significance, though I do not think ACPO itself is their unequivocally supported mouthpiece in the way the Duncan Campbell thesis implies. But I believe the influence is predominantly government over chiefs, rather than the reverse. The main two examples offered by the counter-thesis are:

(1) Robert Mark's account in his autobiography of how he and ACPO succeeded in making Michael Foot as Employment Secretary back down over a proposed change in picketing law. But the power here derived not from ACPO *per se*, but the threat to "go public" over an issue where populist sentiment would back the police, and the result would damage Labour electorally.[64]

(2) The Tactical Options Manual, developed by ACPO without parliamentary or public knowledge or discussion. But here (as with the more robust approach to public order generally) the police were responding to government anxiety about public disorder after 1972 and 1981, and often rather reluctantly.[65]

The issue is hard to resolve finally, because of the general lack of profound disagreement on crunch issues between central government (especially a Conservative one?) and chief constables. What if this did come? What if a Labour Government implemented the policy to give local authorities clear operational control of policy? Some chiefs no doubt would resign, as did Robert Mark over the 1976 Police Act establishing the Police Complaints Board. But those (the majority I suspect) who remained in post would simply have to go along with the new arrangements, however reluctantly, as they have done with such central initiatives (unwelcome in many forces) as consultative committees, lay visitors and the procedures of the Police and Criminal Evidence Act.

If my conclusions are correct, the implication is that what the Inns of Court Conservative and Unionist Society, Professor Goodhart and others forecast in 1962 has come about. Rejecting a *de iure* national police force, we have ended up with the substance of one. But without the structure of accountability for it which the explicit proposals embodied. You cannot have accountability for something that is not supposed to be there.

Arguably attempts to relocalise control are like pushing a stream uphill. The key impetus for central influence has come not so much over routine crime, law enforcement or order maintenance, though the pressures are there too in the name both of efficiency, and of fairness as uniformity. The main sources of central control have been in the course of national labour disputes and other serious public disorder. This is not only true of the last 15 years. Jane Morgan's recent study of the police and labour

162   *In the Office of Chief Constable*

disputes in 1900–1939 demonstrates the covert nationalisation of control of public order policing occurring already in the first three decades of this century.[66]

My final submission is that this trend cannot really be reversed. Only by recognising it and accepting it can some accountability over national policies be achieved. Partly this would be to Parliament. But beyond that, John Alderson's suggestion during the miners' strike should be seriously considered: "a national (emergency) police committee" comprising the Home Secretary, representatives of local police authorities, ACPO and arguably the Police Federation.[67] This should not only be an emergency committee, but be responsible for reviewing and formulating national policies and guidelines for policing. (These would also be discussed in Parliament of course, though detailed work would be done by the Committee.)

It is unlikely, however, that such a proposal would be politically feasible, any more than local control, in the present climate. Why should the Government change a position which gives it power without responsibility, a most unroyal prerogative?

In the Office of Chief Constable   163

Table 1: Social Origins and Mobility of Chief Constables

Father's Class When Son 18 (%)

I	II	IIIN	IIIM	IV	V	NA
2.6	31.5	15.7	44.7	2.6	2.6	—

N=38

Father's Class Earlier (%)

I	II	IIIN	IIIM	IV	V	NA	Police
—	5.3	21	55.3	5.3	7.8	5.3	16.9

Own Pre-Police Jobs (%)

I	II	IIIN	IIIM	IV	V	None
11	8	32	21	—	—	29

N=38

Adult Children's Jobs (%)

I	II	IIIN	IIIM	IV	V	NA	Police
16.9	52.1	12.7	—	—	—	1	16.9

N=71

Police Fathers: 13%   Police Family: 37%

Mobile Fathers: 45%

Federated Ranks (Reiner 1978)
N=168

Father's Class When 18 (%)

I	II	IIIN	IIIM	IV	V	NA	Police
2.9	14.9	16.7	36.9	19.1	3.6	6.5	14

Table 2: Education of Chiefs

School	Elementary	Secondary	Comprehensive	Technical	Grammar	Private
Chiefs N=38	7.9	5.2	—	5.2	78.9	5.2
Federated Ranks N=168	34		6.5	7.7	45.9	6

Age left School	Elementary	Secondary	Comprehensive	Technical	Grammar	
	14	15	16	17	18	
Chiefs	7.9	7.9	42.1	15.8	23.7	
Federated Ranks	19.6	14.9	45.8	11.9	7.7	

School Leaving Qualification	None	School Cert.	'O'	'A'	CSE
Chiefs	13.1	50	23.7	15.8	—
Federated Ranks	28.6	—	54.8	4.2	12.5

Degrees %	Chiefs	Deputy Chiefs	Assistant Chiefs	Current Recruits	All Police
	26	40	37	12	4.45
	N=43	N=43	N=89		

In the Office of Chief Constable   165

Table 3: Career

Date Joined

	-1949	1950-4	1955-9	1960-
% N=38	22	46	30	3

Aged Joined

	19	20	21	22	23	24	25
% N=38	5	30	30	19	8	5	3

When Serjeant

	-5 years	6/7 years	8/9 years	10+ years
%	26	29	37	8

Age When Chief

	-45	46-50	50+
	4	17	17

Present Age

	46-9	50-4	55-59	60+
	3	12	18	5

Years As Chief

	-3	4/5	6-9	10+
	12	13	7	6

166   *In the Office of Chief Constable*

Table 4: Work Experience

No. of Previous Forces	1	2	3	3	
	4	19	12	3	
Types of Forces	County only	City only	Mix	Met.	
	3	9	26	15	
Specialist or Uniform	CID	CID=Uniform	Uniform		
	13	4	21		
National Courses	Senior Command Course	Other Command Course	Special	Royal College of Defence Studies	
	36	34	6	6	
Previous Post When Appointed Chief	Deputy Chief Elsewhere	Deputy Chief Same Force	Chief in Other Force	ACPO in Met.	Other
	20	10	3	3	2

In the Office of Chief Constable   167

NOTES

[1] *New Statesman* May 23, 1986, pp. 3–4.

[2] *cf.* also Duncan Campbell's programme on ACPO in his celebrated *Secret Society* BBC2 series, and his accompanying article "Policing: A Power in the Land" *New Statesman* May 8, 1987, pp. 11–12.

[3] Freeman, M.D.A. (1984) "Law and Order in 1984" *Current Legal Problems* (1984), London: Stevens, pp. 175–231.

[4] Para. 102, p. 34.

[5] Reiner, R. *The Politics of the Police* (1985) Brighton: Wheatsheaf.

[6] Reiner, R. "Who Are The Police?" (1982), *Political Quarterly*, 53:2, April–June, pp. 165–180.

[7] *New Statesman*, May 8, 1987, p. 11.

[8] Reiner, *op. cit.*, p. 174.

[9] pp. 157–181.

[10] The Metropolitan and City of London chiefs have the title Commissioner, and hold neither the offices of "constable" nor "chief constable," as defined by the Police Act 1964. *cf.* Lustgarten, 1986, p. 34. Their everyday role is, however, substantially the same as provincial chief constables, and they belong to ACPO, despite the differences in constitutional position.

[11] *cf.* Critchley 1978, p. 125.

[12] Lustgarten, L. *The Governance of Police*, (1986) London: Sweet and Maxwell, pp. 36–37.

[13] Critchley, T.A. *A History of the Police in England and Wales*, (1978), London: Constable, p. 125.

[14] Found for example in Critchley 1978, pp. 131–133 and Marshall, 1965 pp. 28–29.

[15] Lustgarten, *op. cit.* p. 39.

[16] Brogden, M. *The Police: Autonomy and Consent*, (1982), London: Academic Press, p. 62.

[17] Jefferson, T. and Grimshaw, R. *Controlling the Constable*, London: Muller, pp. 41–44.

[18] Critchley, *op. cit.* p. 124.

[19] Steedman, C. *Policing the Victorian Community*, (1984), London: Routledge.

[20] Wall, D. "Chief Constables: A Changing Elite" in Mawby, R. (ed.) *Policing Britain*, Plymouth Polytechnic: Department of Social and Political Studies, pp. 84–100.

[21] *Ibid.* p. 87.

[22] *Ibid.* p. 93.

[23] *Ibid.* p. 95.

[24] Critchley, *op. cit.* p. 142.

[25] Ross, G. *Oxford City Police 1869–1968* (1979), Oxford: Oxford Publishing Co., pp. 35–36.

[26] Marshall, G., Critchley, *op. cit.* Chap. 9; Reiner 1985: 48–51; Oliver: "Police Accountability Revisited" in Butler, D. and Halsey, A.H. (eds.) *Policy and Politics* London: Macmillan, Chap. 2.

[27] *New Statesman*, June 8, 1962.

[28] Lustgarten: *The Governance of Police* (1986), London: Sweet and Maxwell; Lambert: *Police Powers and Accountability*, (1986), London: Croom Helm, Chap. 2; Leigh, L. *Police Powers in England and Wales* (2nd ed.) (1985), London: Butterworths, Chap. 1; Clayton, R. and Tomlinson, H. *Civil Actions Against the Police* (1987), London: Sweet and Maxwell, Chaps. 1 and 13.

168   *In the Office of Chief Constable*

[29] Marshall, G. *Police and Government*, (1965), London: Methuen, p. 98.

[30] [1930] 2 K.B. 364.

[31] [1968] 2 Q.B. 118.

[32] *Per* Lord Denning, *ibid.* at 136.

[33] [1968] 2 Q.B. 118 at 135–136.

[34] *Op. cit.* pp. 64–65.

[35] Marshall, G. "Police Accountability Revisited" in Butler, D. and Halsey, A.H. (eds.) *Policy and Politics* (1978), London: Macmillan, pp. 58, 59.

[36] *R. v. Chief Constable of the Devon and Cornwall Constabulary, ex p. C.E.G.B.* [1981] 3 All E.R. 826 at 833.

[37] *Ibid.* at p. 833.

[38] *Ibid.* at p. 835.

[39] *The Times*, November 1, 1986 and *Police* December 1986, 16–18.

[40] *Per* Sir John Donaldson M.R.

[41] See below, note 55.

[42] *Op. cit.* p. 67.

[43] *Op. cit.* p. 177. But for some recent support for centralisation *cf.* Zellick; 1986: p. 19.

[44] pp. 45–46.

[45] *e.g.* paras. 121, 122.

[46] *e.g.* the Inns of Court Conservative and Unionist Society: para. 122, p. 42.

[47] Para. 144, para. 146.

[48] Para. 150, p. 50.

[49] Para. 230, p. 72.

[50] Critchley *op. cit.* 286.

[51] Loveday, B. *The Role and Effectiveness of the Merseyside Police Committee* (1985), Merseyside County Council, pp. 131–132. "Central Co-ordination, Police Authorities and the Miners' Strike," (1986), *Political Quarterly*, 57:1, January–March, pp. 60–61.

[52] Morgan, R. "Police Consultative Groups: The Implications for the Governance of the Police (1986) *Political Quarterly* 57:1, January–March, pp. 83–87. Morgan and Maggs: *Setting the P.A.C.E. Police-Community Consultation Arrangements in England and Wales* (1985) University of Bath: Centre for the Study of Social Policy.

[53] Loveday, B. "The Joint Boards," *Policing* (1987), 3:3, Autumn, pp. 196–213.

[54] *Ibid.* pp. 211–212.

[55] *The Times* November 19, 1987, *The Independent* November 19, 1987.

[56] *e.g.* Loveday 1985. *op cit.* n. 51.

[57] Wall, *op. cit.* p. 98.

[58] Mills, C.W. *The Power Elite* (1956), New York: Oxford University Press, pp. 18–20.

[59] The details will be elaborated in a forthcoming book to be published by Oxford University Press.

[60] Reiner, R. *The Blue-Coated Worker*, (1978), Cambridge: Cambridge University Press, p. 150.

[61] H.M.I. Report 1985.

[62] This is a level that compares with professionals, and is far more than the norm for police 51 per cent.: Reiner 1978, p. 173.

[63] Police Act 1964, s.4(2).

[64] In the way that American police have acted as a powerful lobby by mobilising "law and order" sentiment. (Reiner 1980).

[65] Reiner, R. *The Politics of the Police* (1985), Brighton: Wheatsheaf, pp. 71, 72.

[66] Morgan, J. *Conflict and Order: The Police and Labour Disputes in England and Wales 1900–39* (1987), Oxford: Oxford University Press.

[67] *The Guardian* September 13, 1984, p. 16.

[5]
Policing a Postmodern Society

Introduction: Paradise Lost?

Four decades after his first appearance, PC George Dixon, eponymous hero of the long-running TV series *Dixon of Dock Green*, remains for many the embodiment of the ideal British bobby. Dixon, more than any other symbol, conjures up a cosier era when thanks to the wonders of glorious nostalgiavision, life — like TV — was better in black and white.

The Dixon character was unique as a cultural phenomenon, historically and comparatively.[1] In no other country, at no other time, has the ordinary beat-pounding patrol officer been seen as a national hero. If the police were represented as heroic figures at all, it was the glamorous crime-busting detective.[2] The enormous influence and popularity of the Dixon character speaks volumes about the peculiarity of the English veneration of their police in what is often described as the 'Golden Age' of policing.

Public attitudes towards the police in Britain have changed dramatically since the Dixon era. The erosion of the Dixon image is a long process, with roots going back to the late 1950s, the last years of the 'Golden Age' itself, but it has become increasingly precipitous in the last decade of the century. This article will describe and attempt to explain this process of demystification. It will be suggested that underlying the immediate symptoms and causes is a more fundamental transformation of social structure and culture, the advent of what is often described as a 'postmodern' society. The conclusion will assess the ways in which the police have tried to tackle this problem and their chances of success.

The question of why the image and substance of policing in Britain has changed is of fundamental importance to understanding current social change in general. The function of policing is essentially to regulate and protect the social order, using legitimate force if necessary.[3] The dominant theoretical analyses of the state, deriving from Weber, see the hallmark of the modern state as the monopolisation

---

*Professor of Criminology, London School of Economics and Political Science.
This is a revised version of an inaugural lecture given at the School on 7 May 1992.

1 For fuller discussions see Clarke, 'Holding the Blue Lamp: Television and the Police in Britain' (1983) 19 *Crime and Social Justice* 44, and Sparks, *Television and the Drama of Crime* (Milton Keynes: Open University Press, 1992) pp 25–30.
2 Reiner, *The Politics of the Police* (Hemel Hempstead: Wheatsheaf, 2nd ed, 1992) Ch 5.
3 Bittner, 'Florence Nightingale in Pursuit of Willie Sutton: A Theory of the Police' in Jacob (ed), *The Potential for Reform of Criminal Justice* (Beverly Hills: Sage, 1974).

The Modern Law Review   [Vol. 55

of legitimate force in its territory. The police are the domestic specialists in the
exercise of legitimate force. Thus policing is at the heart of the functioning of the
state, and central to an understanding of legal and political organisation. The character
and style of policing, in particular the extent to which resort has to be made to
legitimate force, will be affected by most changes in the social order. The police
are like social litmus-paper, reflecting sensitively the unfolding exigencies of a society.
Thus understanding policing requires a consideration of the broadest features of
social structure and change. Although the almost complest neglect of the police by
social science twenty years ago has now been remedied by an explosion of research
and comment, almost all of this is narrowly policy-oriented, governed by the
immediate practical concerns of the police and police authorities.[4] This is valuable
and welcome, but there is also a need for more fundamental social analysis of the
determinants, nature and consequences of policing, apart from anything else to make
sense of the disparate body of research studies.

This requires a return to the eighteenth-century notion of 'police science,' when
it was regarded by Adam Smith, Bentham, Colquhoun, and other major social and
political thinkers, as a fundamental aspect of political economy. Indeed, Adam Smith
referred to it as 'the second general division of jurisprudence . . . which properly
signified the policy of civil government.'[5] The term 'police' then had a much
broader connotation than its contemporary one of large people in blue uniforms,
but the eighteenth-century conception of police science as the art of 'governmentality'[6] sensitises us to the mutual interdependence of policing and political economy
as a whole. This is obscured by the narrow focus on specific technical aspects of
policing which all too often pervades current research and policy. An analysis of
the troubled state of policing today, and the sources of the malaise, will have to
range much further than the police themselves.

I   Singing the Blues: The Police in a Millennial Malaise

The modern British police were established in the 19th century in the face of
protracted and widespread opposition.[7] But as new police forces spread out from
the Metropolitan heartland established by Sir Robert Peel in 1829 to encompass
the whole of England and Wales by the mid-nineteenth century, gradually and
unevenly they began to cultivate increasing public consent and support. Painstakingly
the police leadership, beginning with Rowan and Mayne, the first two Commissioners
of the Metropolitan Police, strove to develop an image of the British bobby as the
impartial embodiment of the rule of law and the ethic of public service. This rapidly
became the prevailing conception of the police amongst the middle and upper classes,
who had little direct personal experience of their stalwart servants in blue. The
working class, who were far more likely to encounter what contemporaries dubbed
'the plague of the blue locusts,'[8] held more negative attitudes towards the new
regulators of their social and political activities.

---

4 Reiner, 'Police Research in the United Kingdom: A Critical Review' in Morris and Tonry (eds), *Modern
   Policing* (Chicago: Chicago University Press, 1992).
5 Smith, *Lectures on Jurisprudence* (Oxford: Oxford University Press, 1978. Originally published 1763).
6 In Foucault's terminology: cf M. Foucault, 'On Governmentality' (1979) 6 *Ideology and
   Consciousness* 5.
7 For syntheses of recent research on the origins and development of the British police see Emsley,
   The English Police (Hemel Hempstead: Wheatsheaf, 1991) and Reiner, *op cit* n 2, Chs 1 and 2.
8 Storch, 'The Plague of Blue Locusts: Police Reform and Popular Resistance in Northern England,
   1840—57' (1975) 20 *International Review of Social History* 61.

As the working class came gradually to be incorporated into the political, social and economic fabric over the next century, so acceptance of the police spread down throughout the social order. The economically and socially marginal — the 'rough' residuum of the reserve army of labour and indeed young men in general — continued to bear the brunt of the moral street-sweeping which constitutes the core of practical police-work. But the bulk of the settled and respectable working class followed in the footsteps of those higher up the social scale, and began to join in their veneration of the bobby as the very embodiment of the citizenly ideal. This support was brittle, and always fragile at times of industrial conflict. However, in the long social peace of the mid-twentieth century, symbolised successively by the Battle of Britain and the Festival of Britain, the bobbies had their finest hour in terms of popular affection.

Much contemporary evidence, apart from the Dixon myth, underlines the status as totems of national pride which the police enjoyed in the 1950s.[9] The most solid evidence is provided by the major survey conducted for the 1962 Royal Commission on the Police Report. This found 'an overwhelming vote of confidence in the police . . . No less than 83% of those interviewed professed great respect for the police.'

In the three decades since then, there has been a growing questioning of the institution, culminating in recent years in a veritable haemorrhage of public confidence. Optimists could, if pressed, still tell the story another way. The 1988 British Crime Survey (BCS) for instance found that 85 per cent of the public rated the police as very or fairly good in the job they did.[10] Most institutions (including universities and the legal profession) would be delighted with such approval ratings. But there is evidence of continuing erosion of confidence throughout the 1980s. This has now become precipitous in the wake of the great escape of miscarriage of justice skeletons from the Home Office cupboard since the 'Guildford Four' opened the door in 1989.

The regular *British Social Attitudes* surveys conducted by Jowell and his colleagues,[11] as well as the series of national *British Crime Surveys* by the Home Office,[12] show a clear decrease in the standing of the police. One-off surveys conducted since the series of miscarriage of justice scandals came to light, and during the current boom in the crime rate, suggest yet further decline. The *Operational Policing Review* conducted in 1990 for the three police staff associations found that only 18 per cent of a national sample considered that their local police did a 'very good' job.[13]

All these surveys show that opinion of the police is most negative amongst particular groups, those who are routinely at the receiving end of police powers: the young, males, the economically marginal, especially if they are also black and live in the inner-cities. Local surveys in city areas have for many years indicated that amongst these groups, who have been graphically described as 'police property,'[14] rejection

---

9 Royal Commission on the Police, *Final Report*, Cmnd 1782 (London: HMSO, 1962) pp 102–103. For other contemporary evidence of the high status of the British police in the 1950s, see Gorer, *Exploring English Character* (London: Cresset, 1955) and Almond and Verba, *The Civic Culture* (Princeton: Princeton University Press, 1963).

10 Skogan, *The Police and Public in England and Wales: A British Crime Survey Report* (London: HMSO, 1990).

11 Jowell, Witherspoon and Brook (eds), *British Social Attitudes: The 5th Report* (Aldershot: Gower, 1988) pp 117–118.

12 Skogan, *op cit* n 10, p 1.

13 Joint Consultative Committee of the Police Staff Associations, *Operational Policing Review* (Surbiton, Surrey: The Police Federation, 1990).

14 The term was coined by Cray, *The Enemy in the Streets* (New York: Anchor, 1972). It was developed analytically by Lee, 'Some Structural Aspects of Police Deviance in Relations with Minority Groups' in Shearing (ed), *Organisational Police Deviance* (Toronto: Butterworth, 1981).

The Modern Law Review [Vol. 55

of the practices of the police (though not the principles of law and order) is the norm.[15]

Most significantly of all for the police, they seem to have become increasingly estranged from the Conservative Government, whose pet public service they were not many years ago. The police fear a 'hidden agenda' in which they are to be made the scapegoats for the failure of the party of law and order to deliver on its election promises. The screws of financial and managerial accountability to the centre have been tightening remorselessly for several years and, much worse from the police point of view is fearfully anticipated.[16]

II The Deconstruction of Dixon

The declining status of the police is related to a number of changes in organisation and policy which have had the unintended effect of undermining legitimacy of the police. These will be considered, prior to analysis of the underlying causes.[17]

(i) Recruitment, Training and Discipline

The first element in the undermining of police legitimacy was the erosion of the image of an efficient, disciplined bureaucracy. Partly this was a question of standards of entry and training which had not kept pace with general educational improvements.

There have been many attempts in the last thirty years to raise police educational and training standards. Since the 1960s, various schemes have been introduced to attract graduates to the service and encourage higher education for serving police officers. However, significant results have only been achieved during the 1980s, when as a result of pay increases (and unemployment outside the service) the intake of graduates has accelerated sharply to about 12 per cent of recruits per annum. There has also been increasing interest from serving officers in specialist criminal justice degrees.[18] Significant changes have occurred in recruit training as well, largely following from the 1981 Scarman Report.[19] Despite the merit of these developments, they have not prevented an erosion of public confidence in police professional standards.

The main way that the image of the police force as a disciplined, rule-bound bureaucracy came to be dented was by the series of corruption scandals which rocked Scotland Yard in the early 1970s. Although there have been no major cases alleging

---

15 Smith, Small and Gray, *Police and People in London* (London: Policy Studies Institute, 1983); Kinsey, *The Merseyside Crime Survey* (Liverpool: Merseyside County Council, 1984); Jones, MacLean and Young, *The Islington Crime Survey* (London: Gower, 1986); Crawford, Jones, Woodhouse and Young, *The Second Islington Crime Survey* (Middlesex Polytechnic: Centre for Criminology, 1990); McConville and Shepherd, *Watching Police, Watching Communities* (London: Routledge, 1992).

16 Police concern was accentuated by the fact that the 'Inquiry into Police Responsibilities and Rewards,' recently announced by the Home Secretary Kenneth Clarke, consists almost entirely of people from industrial and commercial rather than legal backgrounds, under the chairmanship of Sir Patrick Sheehy of British and American Tobacco. ('Clarke sends for BATman,' *Police*, July 1992, pp 8–9; Loveday, 'A Murky Business,' *Police Review*, 17 July 1992, pp 1318–1319; Butler, 'Paying the Service Charge,' *Police Review*, 24 July 1992, pp 1360–1361.)

17 The organisational and policy changes are discussed in more detail in R. Reiner, *op cit* n 2, Ch 2.

18 Brogden and Graham, 'Police Education: The Hidden Curriculum' in Fieldhouse (ed), *The Political Education of Servants of the State* (Manchester: Manchester University Press, 1988); Tierney, 'Graduating in Criminal Justice' (1989) 5 *Policing* 208.

19 Scarman, *The Brixton Disorders*, Cmnd 8427 (London: HMSO, 1981); Fielding, *Joining Forces* (London: Routledge, 1988); Southgate (ed), *New Dimensions in Police Training* (London: HMSO, 1988).

personal corruption since Sir Robert Mark's clean-up of the Yard and the 'Country-man' inquiry in the 1970s, it is undoubtedly true that those scandals damaged severely the image of the police as disciplined law enforcers. While in the 1962 Royal Commission survey 46.9 per cent of the public did not believe bribe-taking occurred, by 1981 the Policy Studies Institute study of Londoners found that only 14 per cent believed that the police 'hardly ever' took bribes.[20] During the 1980s, personal corruption has become less of an issue, and attention has switched to abuses of police powers undermining the rule of law.

(ii) The Rule of Law

The issue of police violations of legal procedures in the course of dealing with offences has become acutely politicised since the 1970s. On the one hand, civil liberties groups have publicised much evidence of police malpractice, while on the other, the police have lobbied for greater powers to aid the 'war against crime.'

The Police and Criminal Evidence Act 1984 (PACE)[21] purported to provide a balanced codification of police powers and safeguards over their exercise, synthesising the concerns of the 'law and order' and the civil liberties lobbies. It is highly debatable how far it succeeds.[22] What is certain is that the issue of police abuse of powers has increased rather than abated, especially in the late 1980s and early 1990s. Between 1989 and 1991, public confidence in the police was further shaken by an unprecedented series of scandals revealing serious malpractice. The cases of the 'Guildford Four', the 'Birmingham Six' and Judith Ward are only the most prominent of a large number of miscarriage of justice scandals which have surfaced in the 1990s.

Although these cases profoundly shook public opinion, police representatives often argued that they had occurred before the recent reforms and could not happen under the procedures now in force. This argument was itself weakened by a number of *causes célèbres* which have involved more recent abuses,[23] as well as by the implications of academic research on PACE.

The anxiety produced by these revelations of abuse was enough to make the Home Secretary announce in March 1991 (after the release of the 'Birmingham Six') the establishment of a Royal Commission on Criminal Justice, chaired by Lord Runciman, the first Royal Commission in twelve years.

(iii) The Strategy of Minimal Force

The preparedness of the police to cope with public order problems began to be expanded and refined during the 1970s, as political and industrial conflict increased.

---

20 Smith *et al, op cit* n 15, p 249.
21 PACE was itself the product of a complex political balancing act, unevenly incorporating the major recommendations of the 1981 Report of the Royal Commission on Criminal Procedure. Cf Symposium on the Police and Criminal Evidence Act, *Public Law*, Autumn 1985, pp 388–454, and Leigh, 'Some Observations on the Parliamentary History of the Police and Criminal Evidence Act 1984' in Harlow (ed), *Public Law and Politics* (London: Sweet and Maxwell, 1986).
22 McConville, Sanders and Leng, *The Case for the Prosecution* (London: Routledge, 1991); Reiner, 'Codes, Courts and Constables: Police Powers Since 1984' (1992) 12 *Public Money and Management* 11; Reiner and Leigh, 'Police Power' in Chambers and McCrudden (eds), *Individual Rights in the UK since 1945* (Oxford: Oxford University Press/The Law Society, 1992).
23 Such as the series of cases involving the West Midlands Serious Crimes Squad (disbanded by the then Chief Constable Geoffrey Dear in 1989) and the Court of Appeal decision to uphold the appeals of the 'Tottenham Three,' who had been convicted of the murder of PC Keith Blakelock during the 1986 Broadwater Farm riots.

The Modern Law Review   [Vol. 55

This militarisation of policing proceeded apace in the 1980s in the wake of yet more serious disorder, beginning with the 1981 urban riots in Brixton and elsewhere.[24]

Without much public debate *de facto* 'third forces' have developed, specifically trained and readily mobilisable to cope with riots. They are coordinated in a crisis by the National Reporting Centre, established in 1972 and located at Scotland Yard. When in operation it is controlled by the current President of the Association of Chief Police Officers (ACPO). Its most controversial and prominent use was during the 1984—85 miners' strike, when a massive, centrally coordinated policy operation was directed by the Centre, amid much criticism of 'police-state' tactics.[25] During the trial of miners on riot charges, it was revealed that in the early 1980s ACPO had produced a secret document, the Tactical Options Manual,[26] setting out the blueprint for a finely graded response to public disorder.

Neither the tougher methods available since the 1981 riots, nor the wider reforms inspired by Lord Scarman's Report, were able to avert the even more serious urban riots of 1985, on the Broadwater Farm estate in Tottenham and elsewhere. Serious public disorder occurred again in an industrial context at Wapping in 1986—87, during picketing outside the News International plant. Many complaints of undue violence were made against the police and the Police Complaints Authority upheld some of these after an investigation.[27] Other controversial uses of public order tactics have occurred in the late 1980s during the policing of hippy convoys converging on Stonehenge.[28] During 1990, anti-poll demonstrations were the source of severe public order clashes, especially following a rally in Trafalgar Square on 31 March.

In recent years, however, the greatest public order concerns have not been industrial or political conflicts. A 'moral panic' has developed about disorder occurring in a variety of leisure contexts. In 1988, ACPO raised fears about growing disorder in rural areas caused by so-called 'lager louts.'[29] In 1989—90, there was great police concern about the spread of 'acid-house' parties. During the summers of 1991 and 1992, serious violence and disorder has broken out on a number of housing estates in different parts of the country, ranging from Bristol to Tyneside, after police attempts to curb 'joy-riding.'[30] The police were subject to criticism, both for under-reacting to the joy-riding and from other quarters, for harassing teenagers suspected of joy-riding. Although the police response to riots remains lower in profile than most foreign forces, there has undoubtedly been a stiffening of strategy and more resort to technology, equipment and weaponry.

Apart from the growing use of riot control hardware, there has been a rapid proliferation of use of firearms by the police. Although still unarmed (apart from the traditional truncheon) on routine patrol, the number of occasions in which firearms are issued to the police has escalated inexorably. Many forces now deploy cars

---

24 For conflicting assessments of the militarisation of public order policing, see Jefferson, *The Case Against Paramilitary Policing* (Milton Keynes: Open University Press, 1990) and Waddington, *The Strong Arm of the Law* (Oxford: Oxford University Press, 1991).

25 McCabe, Wallington, Alderson, Gostin and Mason, *The Police, Public Order and Civil Liberties* (London: Routledge, 1988).

26 Northam, *Shooting in the Dark* (London: Faber, 1988).

27 Police Complaints Authority, *Annual Report 1989* (London: HMSO, 1990).

28 Vincent-Jones, 'The Hippy Convoy and Criminal Trespass' (1986) 13 *Journal of Law and Society* 343.

29 Subsequent Home Research has challenged the police view of growing disorder in rural areas, as distinct from towns inside what are formally county force boundaries, of M. Tuck, *Drinking and Disorder: A Study of Non Metropolitan Violence*, Home Office Research and Planning Unit Study 108 (London: HMSO, 1989).

30 cf the reports in *Police Review*, 24 July 1992, pp 1356—1357, and 31 July 1992, pp 1404—1405.

carrying guns in their lockers, which can be used on orders from headquarters. The number of occasions when guns are fired by the police remains small, and the rules are tight. Nonetheless, the traditional unarmed image of the British bobby has faded.

(iv) Non-Partisanship

The spectacle of James Anderton (Manchester's former Chief Constable) or representatives of the Police Federation preaching at the drop of a helmet about the sinking state of our national moral fibre first became familiar in the 1970s. By 1980 the police, at all levels from Chief Constable down to the rank and file, almost seemed to set the terms of debate on law and order and social policy.

In 1975, the Police Federation launched an unprecedented campaign for 'law and order,' which was revived in 1978 specifically to influence the 1979 general election. This proved to be an investment which reaped handsome dividends. The new Conservative government immediately implemented in full the pay increase recommended in 1978 by the Edmund-Davies committee. There ensued a prolonged honeymoon period in which the police were the Conservatives' most favoured public service. This love affair cooled as public expenditure cuts began to bite on the police and a 'hidden agenda' of incipient privatisation, coupled with strict central financial control, began to emerge in the late 1980s.[31]

For its part, Labour has tried hard to repair bridges which had been broken in the early 1980s, following the election of radical local authorities in the metropolitan areas, who adopted policies which were often perceived as 'anti-police.' The high-point of tension between Labour and the police came during the 1984—85 miners' strike.[32]

There is now a tendency to return to cross-party consensus on law and order (accentuated in this and other areas by the replacement of Margaret Thatcher by John Major as Prime Minister in late 1990). The prototype of the outspoken Chief Constable, Sir James Anderton, retired in 1991. He had become ever more controversial in the late 1980s for his supposedly divinely inspired utterances on AIDS and other topics. By then, most other Chief Constables had come to believe overt police interventions in political and social debates were unwise.[33] Nonetheless, the years of partisanship had tarnished, possibly irretrievably, the sacred aura hitherto enjoyed by the British police of being, like the Queen, above party politics.

(v) The Service Role

The dominant current of police thinking stresses that, contrary to the popular image of the police as primarily crime-fighters, much if not most of uniformed police work (measured by time or number of incidents dealt with) consists of calls for help, in response to which the police act as a social service more than as law enforcers. The community policing philosophy, which emphasises this, has become influential amongst police chiefs in the UK, the USA and elsewhere.[34] There is evidence,

---

31 Rawlings, 'Creeping Privatisation? The Police, the Conservative Government and Policing in the Late 1980s' in Reiner and Cross (eds), *Beyond Law and Order: Criminal Justice Policy and Politics Into the 1990s* (London: Macmillan, 1991).
32 Reiner, *op cit* n 2, Preface and Ch 7.
33 Reiner, *Chief Constables* (Oxford: Oxford University Press, 1991) pp 210—219.
34 *ibid* Ch 6, and Skolnick and Bayley, *The New Blue Line* (New York: Free Press, 1986) and *Community Policing: Issues and Practices Around the World* (Washington DC: National Institute of Justice, 1988).

The Modern Law Review   [Vol. 55

however, that most rank-and-file policemen believe the service aspects of the work should have low or no priority.[35] Since the Scarman Report in 1981 endorsed a kind of community policing philosophy, this has become the orthodox analysis of the police role for all Chief Constables. The evidence of recent decline in public support has led to a redoubling of the effort to define policing in service terms, in the Plus Programme of the Metropolitan Police and the ACPO Statement of Common Purpose and Values.[36] The success of these worthy attempts at relegitimation has yet to be seen, but initial research evaluations have not been optimistic.[37]

(vi) Preventive Policing

Peel's original conception of policing emphasised preventive patrol by uniformed constables as fundamental. The notion of the bobby on the beat as the essential bedrock of the force, to which all other specialisms are ancillary, remains a philosophy to which most Chief Constables pay homage. But in practice, specialist departments have proliferated and foot patrol has been downgraded.[38]

The meaning of prevention shifted away from the scarecrow function of uniform patrol to the development of specialist crime prevention departments, whose function is to provide advice to citizens on methods of minimising the risk of victimisation and alerting them to the dangers of some kinds of offences. At first, crime prevention departments were Cinderellas of the service, low status, low budget and low key. However, as crime prevention became increasingly central to the Government's law and order policy in the 1980s, so they blossomed into belles of the ball. A proliferation of specialist and plain clothes units, reversing the original Peelite philosophy, has been one consequence of an apparent crisis of police effectiveness in controlling crime.

(vii) Police Effectiveness

Police effectiveness is a notoriously slippery concept to define or measure. But the official statistics routinely produced by police forces and published by the Home Office seem to record an inexorable rise in serious criminal offences and decline in the clear-up rate since the mid-1950s, and especially since the late 1970s. Whereas in the mid-1950s there were less than half a million indictable offences recorded as known to the police in most years, by 1977 this was over 2 million and, by 1991, over 4 million. Before the war, the percentage of crimes recorded as cleared-up was always over 50 per cent. By the late 1950s, it had dropped to about 45 per cent and it is currently around 38 per cent.[39]

The inadequacy of these figures is well known.[40] Many crimes are not reported

---

35 For a recent national survey, see the *Operational Policing Review, op cit* n 13, s 6.
36 See the statements by the HM Chief Inspector of Constabulary, Sir John Woodcock, ACPO president Brian Johnson, 1991 and Michael Hirst, Chief Constable of Leicestershire (and one of the main architects of the 'quality of service' initiative) in *Policing*, Autumn 1991.
37 McConville and Shepherd, *op cit* n 15. But for a vigorous defence see Hirst, 'We're Getting It Right,' *Police*, July 1992, pp 40–42.
38 Jones, *Organisational Aspects of Police Behaviour* (Farnborough: Gower, 1989), and McConville and Shepherd, *op cit* n 15.
39 *Report of Her Majesty's Chief Inspector of Constabulary 1991* (London: HMSO).
40 Bottomley and Pease, *Crime and Punishment: Interpreting the Data* (Milton Keynes: Open University Press, 1986).

to the police, so increases in the rate may indicate a greater propensity to report rather than suffer victimisation.[41] The clear-up rate is affected by many other determinants apart from detective effectiveness, including massaging the figures. Nonetheless, it is hard to argue that the recorded trends do not correspond to basic changes in the same direction, and they are certainly associated with a growing public fear of crime and a popular sense that police effectiveness is declining. In addition to the direct effect on public confidence of apparently declining police efficiency, concern about crime has led to the controversial new tactics and law and order campaigns which have already been discussed.

(viii) Accountability

All the above concerns have converged on the central issue of accountability: how can the police be brought to book for poor performance? This was the nub of controversy for most of the 1980s. The independence of the British police force from control by any elected governmental institutions has usually been seen as a virtue, although there has also been a long-standing radical critique arguing that it was anomalous in a democracy.[42]

As policing has become more controversial in Britain in the last two decades, so the perception of the mechanisms of accountability has changed. The old mystical substitute of police identification with the public came under strain as the police were seen increasingly as unrepresentative in terms of race, gender and culture, and alienated from the groups they typically dealt with as offenders and victims.[43]

At the bottom of every specific conflict, critics pinpointed the problem of the police being out of control by any outside bodies and hence unresponsive to the popular will. They have sought to reform the structure of police governance so as to make police policy-making fully accountable to the electoral process. Sophisticated critiques of the existing system by constitutional lawyers appeared[44] and the view that the police were not adequately accountable came to be the orthodoxy of mainstream liberal as well as radical analysis of the police. While the police themselves have strongly resisted the full radical package, they have conceded increasingly the legitimacy of some aspects of the critique, especially about the complaints system and the absence of a local police authority for London.[45] For their part, the Conservatives have wanted to maintain the constitutional *status quo*. They have, however, become increasingly concerned to render the police more accountable for their use of powers and, even more crucially, the effective use of resources.

At the same time, it is becoming increasingly evident that local accountability to police authorities has atrophied. It is being replaced by a degree of central control amounting to a *de facto* national force.[46] Thus, accountability has been transformed, rather than simply reduced. What is clear is that the perceived lack of adequate local accountability has been a major factor undermining police legitimacy in recent years.

---

41 Hough and Mayhew, *The British Crime Survey* (London: HMSO, 1983); Mayhew, Elliott and Dowds, *The 1988 British Crime Survey* (London: HMSO, 1989).

42 Jefferson and Grimshaw, *Controlling the Constable* (London: Muller, 1984); Lustgarten, *The Governance of the Police* (London: Sweet and Maxwell, 1986) are the seminal discussions.

43 Hanmer, Radford and Stanko (eds), *Women, Policing and Male Violence* (London: Routledge, 1989); Cashmore and McLaughlin (eds), *Out of Order?: Policing Black People* (London: Routledge, 1991).

44 Notably L. Lustgarten, *op cit* n 42.

45 Reiner, *Chief Constables*, *op cit* n 33, Ch 11.

46 *ibid.*

The Modern Law Review   [Vol. 55

III   The Calculus of Consent: Social Divisions and Desubordination

These eight aspects of police organisation and policy have all been specific, concrete issues of controversy and concern in recent years, symptoms of the erosion of the public standing of the police. Underlying them, however, are a combination of deeper social changes which form the social context of the declining legitimacy of the police.

Police activity has always borne most heavily on the economically marginal elements in society, the unemployed (especially if vagrant), and young men, whose lives are lived largely in the street and other public places, 'police property.'[47] Whereas the historical incorporation of the working class modified their resentment of policing, police conflict with the residuum at the base of the social hierarchy remained. Studies of policing in all industrial societies show this to be a constant. The police themselves recognise this and their argot contains a variety of derogatory epithets for their regular clientèle drawn from this stratum. In California they are 'assholes,' in Toronto 'pukes,' in London 'slag' or 'scum' and on Tyneside 'prigs.'[48] Drawn mostly from the respectable working class, the police are responsive to their moral values and adopt a disdainful scorn for those whose lifestyles deviate from or challenge them. But however conflict-ridden, relations between the police and 'slag' have not usually been politicised. Membership in the marginal strata is temporary (youths mature, the unemployed find jobs) and their internal social relations are atomised, so a sense of group identity is hard to develop.

One important factor which politicised policing in the 1960s and 1970s was the development of social groups with a clear consciousness of antagonism towards (and from) the police. This owes something to the development of more self-conscious youth cultures, the return of long-term unemployment and the increasing militancy of industrial conflict.

The most crucial change, however, has been the catastrophic deterioration of relations with the black community. There is a long history of police prejudice against blacks and complaints of racial harassment. By the mid-1970s, clear evidence had mounted of blacks (especially black youths) being disproportionately involved in arrests for certain offences, largely but not only because of police discrimination.[49] A vicious cycle of interaction developed between police stereotyping and black vulnerability to the situations that attract police attention, resulting from racial discrimination in society generally.

The burden of recent research on police-public relations suggests that while these still remain relatively harmonious with the majority of the population (including most of the working class), they are tense and conflict-ridden with the young, the unemployed, the economically marginal and blacks.[50] What has happened to politicise policing since the 1970s is a growth in the size of these vulnerable groups, primarily due to economic failure and a heightening of their self-consciousness as targets of policing.

This is due to structural changes in the political economy of Western capitalism.

---

47 E. Cray, *op cit*, J. Lee, *op cit*.
48 Skolnick, *Justice Without Trial* (New York: Wiley, 1966); Ericson, *Reproducing Order: A Study of Police Patrol Work* (Toronto: University of Toronto Press, 1982); Smith *et al*, *op cit* n 15; Young, *An Inside Job: Policing and Police Culture in Britain* (Oxford: Oxford University Press, 1990).
49 Lea and Young, *What Is To Be Done About Law and Order?* (Harmondsworth: Penguin Books, 1984) Ch 4; T. Jefferson, 'Race, Crime and Policing: Empirical, Theoretical and Methodological Issues' (1988) 16 *International Journal of the Sociology of Law* 521; Reiner, 'Race and Criminal Justice' (1989) 16 *New Community* 5.
50 Smith *et al*, *op cit* n 15; Jones *et al*, *op cit* n 15; Skogan, *op cit* n 10.

Long-term structural unemployment (increasingly never-employment) has re-emerged, leading to the *de-incorporation* of increasing sections of the young working class, especially amongst discriminated against minorities, 'who are being defined out of the edifice of citizenship.'[51] A new underclass has formed which is not simply a result of unemployment, but of its seeming structural inevitability. 'The majority class does not need the unemployed to maintain and even increase its standard of living ... The main point about this category — for lack of a better word we shall call it the "underclass" — is that its destiny is perceived as hopeless.'[52] There is much debate about the now popular concept of an underclass, and its conservative culturalist version has unacceptable connotations of 'blaming the victim.'[53] But the structurally generated formation of a completely marginalised segment of society is a major source of the huge growth recently of crime, disorder and tensions around policing.

Unemployment is certainly not linked to crime or disorder in any straightforward automatic way, as the Conservatives are ever ready to tell us. But there is now much evidence that in the present period at any rate it is a factor in the emergence of a young underclass which has the motive, the opportunity and the lack of those social controls which are brought by social integration, and thus becomes a key part of the explanation of crime and disorder.[54]

The conflicts between the socially marginal and the police are perennial, although they are now more extensive and structural than during the postwar boom. However, the key to how this is translated into political debate is a long-term cultural change in the articulate opinion-forming middle class.

The police have lost the confidence of certain small but influential sections of the 'chattering classes,' what may be described roughly as *The Guardian* or *The Independent* reading circles. This process of a developing gulf with some educated middle-class opinion has a variety of roots, stretching back to the invention of the car. But the most significant are the growth of middle-class political protest since the early 1960s (CND, the anti-Vietnam War demonstrations, the 1960s' student movement and counter-culture) and the politicisation of forms of marginal deviance which involve some middle-class people, notably drug-taking and homosexuality. This conflict with highly articulate and educated sections of the population has been of enormous significance in converting policing into an overt political issue.[55]

Underlying the change in educated middle-class opinion is a broader cultural trend: the decline of traditional patterns of deference and unquestioning acceptance of authority, a process which has been aptly termed 'desubordination.'[56] This is reflected both in the attitudes of those at the receiving end of police powers and the general public audience of policing. Arrests are much less likely to be perceived as the legendary 'fair cop,' either by arrestees or by others. The police as symbols of social authority evidently suffer from a culture of desubordination.

The sources of declining public confidence in the police thus lie deeper than any

---

51 Dahrendorf, *Law and Order* (London: Sweet and Maxwell, 1985) p 98.

52 *ibid* pp 101–107.

53 Murray, *The Emerging British Underclass* (London: Institute of Economic Affairs, 1989); Field, *Losing Out: The Emergence of Britain's Underclass* (Oxford: Blackwell, 1989).

54 Farrington, Gallagher, Morley, St Ledger and West, 'Unemployment, School-Leaving and Crime' (1986) 26 *British Journal of Criminology* 335. Box, *Recession, Crime and Punishment* (London: Macmillan, 1987); Field, *Trends in Crime and their Interpretation*, Home Office Research Study 119 (London: HMSO, 1990).

55 Waddington, 'Why the "Opinion-Makers" No Longer Support the Police,' *Police*, December 1982.

56 Miliband, 'A State of Desubordination' (1978) 29 *British Journal of Sociology* 399.

The Modern Law Review [Vol. 55

changes in police tactics or policies. We can postulate an equation predicting public consent to policing in which public acceptance is largely a function of the extent of social and cultural consensus. Increasing social divisions and declining deference equal a decline in the public standing of the police. This is because police tactics will move up the menu of coerciveness to deal with the symptoms of division and to overcome the decline of consent. At the same time, controversial tactics, as well as outright abuse, are more likely to be perceived as malpractice by recipients, opinion-formers and policy makers, as well as the general public, due to declining deference.

One possibility this raises is that the obvious response to increasing police scandals and falling public sympathy may be misguided. The conventional assumption across the political spectrum is that standards of police behaviour have declined since the 'Golden Age' of the mid-century. But is this really so?

It is inevitably difficult to assess the extent of police abuse at any particular time, let alone to measure changes over time. Police malpractice, like all deviance, is covert and subterranean. All we know is the amount which comes to light by the uncertain processes of revelation or detection. Criminologists have long stressed this issue when interpreting recorded crime trends, but they have been prepared to accept at face value the apparent increase in deviance amongst the police.

It is clear, however, that there was an enormous amount of hidden police deviance lurking behind the Dixon façade in the middle of this century. This is shown clearly by the evidence of memoirs and oral histories, both from the side of the police and the policed.[57] That most of this police deviance did not come to light was testimony to the more deferential if not authoritarian culture of the policed, as well as the legal establishment.

Whilst there was probably considerable under-reporting of police deviance in the 'good old days,' there is reason to believe that today there may actually be less gross malpractice. One reason is that there has been a set of changes which are likely to have diluted, although far from eliminated, the 'canteen cop culture' which numerous studies have pinpointed as the engine of abuse.[58] As mentioned above, the educational background and training standards of officers have been transformed out of all recognition, although much scope for improvement remains. In addition, whilst they remain grossly under-represented from an equal opportunities standpoint, the proportion of women and ethnic minority officers has risen substantially. So too have the number of part-time volunteers (the 'Specials') and civilian employees. The result is that the backstage areas of police stations now regularly contain people who are far removed from the identikit white macho working-class model of traditional police culture. In addition, a set of legal and policy reforms has tried, with partial success, to make police work more 'transparent' in order to secure more effective stewardship by courts and managers of the exercise of police powers.[59] These include the extensive recording requirements (by tape as well as paper records)

---

57 Mark, *In the Office of Constable* (London: Collins, 1978); Cohen, 'Policing the Working Class City' in Fine *et al* (eds), *Capitalism and the Rule of Law* (London: Hutchinson, 1979); White, *The Worst Street in London* (London: Routledge, 1990); Brogden, *On the Mersey Beat* (Oxford: Oxford University Press, 1991).

58 Holdaway, *Inside the British Police* (Oxford: Blackwell, 1983); Reiner, *op cit* n 2, Ch 3; Young, *op cit* n 48.

59 Morgan, 'Police Accountability: Developing the Local Infrastructure' (1987) 27 *British Journal of Criminology* 87. These measures may, however, have the ultimate function of preserving police autonomy as Morgan has also argued, cf Morgan, 'Policing by Consent: Legitimating the Doctrine' in Morgan and Smith (eds), *Coming to Terms with Policing* (London: Routledge, 1989).

of the Police and Criminal Evidence Act 1984, the introduction of lay station visiting schemes and the rise in access to legal and social work advisers facilitated by PACE. There have also been relevant advances in forensic science, such as DNA profiling and ESDA testing.

Many of the miscarriages of justice and allegations of malpractice which have been substantiated in recent years have come to light because of these changes. The role of scientific developments in clearing Stefan Kiszko, the Tottenham Three and the Irish cases is well known. The recent conviction of several Metropolitan Police Constables for a brutal assault was the product of evidence from a woman Special Constable, illustrating the importance of the dilution of cop culture.[60] The crucial change, however, is a general cultural one. There is a greater willingness on the part of those in power, in the media and the legal system, to pursue cases and seek the relevant evidence, and to believe it when it is found. The new Lord Chief Justice, Lord Taylor, revealed as much when he recently admitted that judges had been too ready to believe the police without question in the past, but should and would not be prepared to do so in the future.[61] Several reviews of the case law interpreting PACE have underlined the greater propensity of judges to apply the requirements of its Codes of Practice against the police, rather than the permissive approach which prevailed with respect to breaches of the old Judges' Rules.[62]

These changes all suggest that the apparent wave of police deviance may really be the product of a change in social reaction, not of a real increase in police wrongdoing. This chimes in with the general view of many experienced police officers who believe there is now less flagrant and regularised malpractice than in the not very distant past.[63] They feel somewhat frustrated at the paradox that public trust in them is at its lowest ebb precisely when professional standards are at an all-time high. This may or may not be a more valid view than the conventional one of a rotting of the police institutional framework. What is certain is that the relationship between the extent of police wrongdoing and the revealed amount is as problematic as that between all offending and the official crime rate. There are many mediating processes of perception, labelling, reporting and recording.

The decline in the public standing of the police is thus far from straightforward and due to complex and social changes rather than simply an increase in police malfeasance. The key roles played by increasing social divisions, and declining cultural deference, have already been emphasised. It is in theorising these processes that the concept of postmodern society is helpful.

IV Policing a Postmodern Society

In the last decade, the related clutch of terms 'postmodern,' 'postmodernism,' 'postmodernity' and 'postmodernisation' have become increasingly fashionable as labels for what is widely seen as a qualitative break in the development of contemporary society. The earliest usage of 'postmodern,' in precisely the sense in which it tends

---

60 See the report in *Police Review*, 10 April 1992, p 662.
61 *The Guardian*, 29 April 1992, p 1.
62 Feldman, 'Regulating Treatment of Suspects in Police Stations: Judicial Interpretations of Detention Provision in the Police and Criminal Evidence Act 1984,' *Criminal Law Review*, July 1990, p 452.
63 It must be emphasised that whilst gross malpractice may have declined, subtle forms no doubt remain rife, as indeed is shown by much of the research evaluating PACE: see for example M. McConville, A. Sanders and R. Leng, *op cit* n 22.

The Modern Law Review   [Vol. 55

to be used today,[64] was by the late C. Wright Mills in a public lecture delivered at the LSE in 1969.[65] Mills' uncanny prophetic ability to anticipate the shape of things to come gives him a fair claim to be regarded as the H.G. Wells or Jules Verne of social science. Mills declared 'We are at the ending of what is called The Modern Age. Just as Antiquity was followed by several centuries of Oriental ascendancy, which Westerners provincially call the Dark Ages, so now The Modern Age is being succeeded by a postmodern period.'[66]

Mills' characterisation of this 'postmodern period' captures the gist of what contemporary analysts mean by the term: 'Our basic definitions of society and of self are being overtaken by new realities.' This is not, argues Mills, merely because of the pace of change and the struggle to grasp the meaning of it. Fundamentally, Mills claims, the explanatory and ethical frameworks which we inherited from the Enlightenment and which have dominated the 'modern' age, primarily liberalism and socialism, 'have virtually collapsed as adequate explanations of the world and of ourselves.' Referring to common threads in the work of Bentham, Mill, Freud and Marx, the giant shapers of modern understanding, Mills concludes: 'the ideas of freedom and of reason have become moot . . . increased rationality may not be assumed to make for increased freedom.'[67]

The rate at which new volumes bearing the word 'postmodern' in their titles appear on library shelves is alarming, and it is impossible here to deal systematically with all the varying interpretations, diagnoses, periodisations, explanations and political reactions in the debate.[68] The basic idea is, of course, that what is now occurring is a qualitative transformation from one kind of social order to another, as Mills' prescient remarks indicate. The use of the term 'postmodern' itself implies that, while it is claimed that there is a break from the 'modern' (itself variously interpreted), the precise contours of the new social formation are hard to pinpoint other than in the negative: they are fundamentally different from the 'modern.'

The key aspect of what is different is usually said to be epitomised by a concept developed by Lyotard.[69] Whereas the hallmark of 'modern' culture was its underpinning by 'grand' or 'meta-narratives,' such overarching stories about the direction

---

64 The term 'postmodern' itself has been in use for a long time. Arnold Toynbee used it before the Second World War in his *A Study of History*, but to refer to the whole period since the eighteenth century Enlightenment and Industrial Revolutions, ie precisely the heyday of 'modernism' in most current accounts. The *reductio ad absurdum* of attempts to find antecedents for postmodernism was the claim by Kroker and Cooke that the 'postmodern scene . . . begins in the fourth century . . . everything since the Augustinian refusal has been nothing but a fantastic and grisly implosion of experience as Western culture itself runs under the signs of passive and suicidal nihilism.' (Kroker and Cooke, *The Postmodern Scene*, London: Macmillan, 1988) p 127. No doubt we shall soon be told that postmodernism began with the Big Bang itself.

65 Published as 'On Reason and Freedom' in Mills, *The Sociological Imagination* (Glencoe: Free Press, 1959) pp 165–176.

66 *ibid.*

67 *ibid.*

68 For some recent general surveys and discussion of the issue, see Bauman, *Legislators and Interpreters: Modernity, Postmodernity and Intellectuals* (Cambridge: Polity Press, 1987); Bauman, *Modernity and the Holocaust* (Cambridge: Polity Press, 1989); Bauman, *Intimations of Postmodernity* (London: Routledge, 1992); Harvey, *The Condition of Postmodernity: An Inquiry into the Origins of Cultural Change* (Oxford: Blackwell, 1989); Turner (ed), *Theories of Modernity and Postmodernity* (London: Sage, 1990); Giddens, *The Consequence of Modernity* (Cambridge: Polity Press, 1990); Rose, *The Post-Modern and the Post-Industrial* (Cambridge: Cambridge University Press, 1991); Rosenau, *Postmodernism and the Social Sciences* (New Jersey: Princeton University Press, 1992); Crook, Pakulski and Waters, *Postmodernisation: Change in Advanced Society* (London: Sage, 1992). An excellent critique is provided by Callinicos, *Against Postmodernism* (Oxford: Blackwell, 1989).

69 Lyotard, *The Postmodern Condition: A Report on Knowledge* (Manchester: Manchester University Press, 1984).

and meaning of history have lost credibility. In one sense, of course, this claim is evidently self-defeating. For the notion of a breakdown of grand narratives is itself a meta-narrative. But clearly what is meant is the exhaustion of such grand-narratives as the ideas of Progress or Enlightenment, the unfolding of Reason or Revolution, which purported to give a positive and unitary meaning to the historical process as a whole.

Claims about the development of postmodernity falls into three distinct yet related thematic clusters. The origin of the recent fashionable use of the term was primarily in aesthetics and art criticism, where commentators like Baudrillard and Lyotard discerned the emergence of a fundamentally new set of styles which they labelled 'postmodernism.'[70] Another line of thought has primarily been philosophical, suggesting an epistemological break in conceptions of knowledge and ethics. This is often referred to generally as 'post-structuralism' or 'post-objectivism.'[71] Finally, analysts from a variety of theoretical and political persuasions have argued that there has occurred a basic transformation in the political economy, culture and social order of contemporary societies. These may be labelled as theories of 'post-industrialism' or 'post-capitalism.'[72] All these theories point to profound changes in knowledge, popular culture and social order, and the relationship between these.

Knowledge

In a vivid image, Bernstein has characterised the history of modern theories of knowledge as a variety of attempts to cope with 'Cartesian anxiety.' The twin harbingers of the modern — the Renaissance and the Reformation — undermined the absolute framework of understanding provided by Catholicism in the Middle Ages.[73] Descartes provides the prototypical example of a modern philosopher seeking a rational first principle, an Archimedean leverage point for knowledge after the removal of the absolute guarantees of religious revelation. From Descartes' *cogito*[74] to the twentieth-century positivists' falsification principle and logical coherence, modern philosophy has sought some secular substitute for clerical authority. Lurking behind the pursuit of a basis for objectivism was the fear that the only alternative was relativism and cognitive chaos.

MacIntyre tells a similar story about modern moral philosophy in his influential *After Virtue*.[75] The Enlightenment shattered the common language and conceptual framework which allowed meaningful discourse about morality. Although the simulacra of moral discourse remain, words are used with no shared conception of what they refer to. The concept of virtue lacks an agreed underpinning, just as knowledge does. In the postmodern era we have become conscious of what was always implicit in the project of modernity.

To this predicament there are two main responses. It can be celebrated as liberation from authoritarian epistemological or moral shackles. All that counts is what works

---

70 *ibid*; Poster (ed), *Jean Baudrillard: Selected Writings* (Cambridge: Polity Press, 1989).

71 Bernstein, *Beyond Objectivism and Relativism* (Oxford: Blackwell, 1983).

72 Bell, *The Coming of Post-Industrial Society* (New York: Basic Books, 1973).

73 This does not mean that all people in medieval times shared a monolithic world view any more than that in modern times there was a single hegemonic dominant ideology, cf Abercrombie, Hill and Turner, *The Dominant Ideology Thesis* (London: Unwin, 1980). But the Church did provide the basic parameters within which disputes and divergences occurred.

74 Hintikka, '*Cogito, Ergo Sum*: Inference or Performance?' in Doney (ed), *Descartes: A Collection of Critical Essays* (New York: Anchor Books, 1967).

75 MacIntyre, *After Virtue: A Study in Moral Theory* (London: Duckworth, 1981).

The Modern Law Review   [Vol. 55

for particular protagonists in specific contexts, as implied by the pragmatism of philosphers like Rorty.[76] Alternatively, it is only possible to adopt a stoic stance in these new Dark Ages, as recommended by MacIntyre, and shelter in congenial small communities awaiting some new charismatic restorer of the grand tradition of the virtues.[77]

In either optimistic or pessimistic variants, postmodernity is the realisation of the relativist potential implicit in modernity from the beginning. It is the realisation that 'Cartesian anxiety' will not be dispelled by the discovery of some new Archimedean point but has to be lived with. As Bauman, one of the foremost theorists of postmodernity puts it, the role of intellectuals changes from 'legislators,' mapping a brave new world, to 'interpreters' of pluralism.[78]

These changes in intellectual culture do not just trickle down into the culture of people in general. However, the abandonment of absolutes is paralleled in popular culture. As Bauman puts it, in postmodern culture the 'pleasure principle' displaces Puritan asceticism and discipline.[79] Consumerism becomes the driving force of social action and the brittle basis of social order.

However, instead of a single dominant conception of the good life, postmodernity is characterised by cultural pluralism and ambivalence. A mosaic of different lifestyles is on offer, none able to trump the others in legitimacy. The exclusion of an underclass from participation in the opulent spectacle needs and can have no ideological justification. Religion is no longer the opium of the people, so they will have to make do with opium itself (or its cheaper substitutes).

Social Structure and Political Economy

The theorists of postmodern society depict it as following a similar path of disorganisation, structural pluralism and decentring. In Giddens' words: 'The postmodern order is split into a multitude of contexts of action and forms of authority ... The nation state declines in importance and the cohesive totality is replaced by a multiplicity of sites of social reproduction.'[80]

Many analysts have offered similar accounts of the dispersion and fragmentation of the concentrated and centralised structure of economic organisation which reached a climax in the corporatist state regulation of the post-Second World War period up to the 1970s. Western societies are now experiencing a transition from 'organised' to 'disorganised' capitalism, in the terminology of Offe.[81]

The influential analysis of 'New Times' by writers associated with *Marxism Today* echoes similar themes.[82] In their account, contemporary capitalism is witnessing the erosion of 'Fordism.' 'Post-Fordism' is consumption not production-led. It involves the disaggregation of the market into specialised sectors, with design as a major selling point, based on the connotation of varying lifestyles rather than simply use-value. This is made possible by the development of information technology to

---

76 Rorty, *Philosophy and the Mirror of Nature* (Oxford: Blackwell, 1979); *Contingency, Irony and Solidarity* (Cambridge: Cambridge University Press, 1989).
77 MacIntyre, *op cit* n 75.
78 Bauman, *op cit* n 68.
79 *ibid.*
80 Giddens, 'Uprooted Signposts at Century's End,' *The Higher*, 17 January 1992, pp 21–22.
81 Offe, *Disorganised Capitalism* (Cambridge: Polity, 1985). See also Lash and Urry, *The End of Organised Capitalism* (Cambridge: Polity, 1987).
82 Hall and Jacques (eds), *New Times: The Changing Face of Politics in the 1990s* (London: Lawrence and Wishart, 1989).

coordinate far-flung and specialist markets and labour processes.[83]

Instead of a mass labour force of mainly semi- or un-skilled workers, a smaller multi-skilled core workforce is required.[84] The peripheral workforce of unskilled workers is low-paid, temporary, often part-time, and increasingly consists of women and ethnic minorities.[85] An underclass of the permanently excluded develops while the core labour force increases its income and freedom, though not security: the so-called 'two-thirds' society.[86] Instead of the primarily bifurcated class structure of competitive or monopoly capitalism, a much more complex system of stratification with cross-cutting lines, such as gender, ethnic identity and region, develops.[87] New forms of oppositional politics emerge, but the position of Conservative parties becomes more secure as the two-thirds of beneficiaries from 'New Times' consistently outvote the one-third who are excluded.[88] The nation state becomes a less significant locus of power, usurped by a growing internationalisation of capital and division of labour on the one hand, whilst the vitality of local identities also increases as the sites of production and reproduction become more scattered and fragmented.[89]

The themes of pluralism, contingency, the undermining of absolutes, ambivalence and disintegration pervade accounts of postmodern society, culture, knowledge and morality. There is much room for argument about the interpretation and significance of all this. What, if any, is the relationship between the material, social and cultural developments? Is there really a 'break' in capitalism, or just an unfolding of its logic to a new stage, as many Marxists argue.[90] Is the project of the Enlightenment unfinished in its emancipatory potential, although threatened by current developments, as Habermas would argue?[91] Or does the present malaise just make explicit the relativist dark side of Enlightenment liberalism, as MacIntyre implies?[92]

Whatever the outcome of such debates, what is clear is that the factors which were outlined earlier as underlying the police fall from grace — deepening social divisions and a less deferential culture — are not temporary aberrations changeable by an election, an upturn in the economy, calls for a return to Victorian values or changes in Government or police policy. They are deeply rooted structural trends, not a passing *fin de siècle* malaise.

V The Prospects of Police Reform

What are the implications for the prospects of success of current police initiatives to restore their legitimacy? During the late 1970s and 1980s, as the creeping crisis

83 Murray, 'Fordism and Post-Fordism' and 'Benetton Britain' in Hall and Jacques, *op cit* n 82; Allen, 'Fordism and Modern Industry' in Allen, Braham and Lewis (eds), *Political and Economic Forms of Modernity* (Cambridge: Polity, 1992).
84 Braham, 'The Divisions of Labour and Occupational Change' in Allen, Braham and Lewis, *op cit* n 83.
85 *ibid*; McDowell, 'Social Divisions, Income Inequality and Gender Relations in the 1980s' in Cloke (ed), *Policy and Change in Thatcher's Britain* (Oxford: Perganion, 1992).
86 Dahrendorf, *op cit* n 51, p 103; Therborn, 'The Two-Thirds, One-Third Society' in Hall and Jacques, *op cit* n 82.
87 Bradley, 'Changing Social Divisions: Class, Gender and Race' in Bocock and Thompson (eds), *Social and Cultural Forms of Modernity* (Cambridge: Polity, 1992).
88 Galbraith, *The Culture of Contentment* (London: Sinclair-Stevenson, 1992).
89 Held, 'The Decline of the Nation State' in Hall and Jacques, *op cit* n 82.
90 Jameson, *Postmodernism: Or the Cultural Logic of Late Capitalism?* (London: Verso, 1992); Callinicos, *op cit* n 68.
91 Habermas, 'Modernity — An Incomplete Project?' in Foster (ed), *Postmodern Culture* (London: Pluto Press, 1985).
92 MacIntyre, *op cit* n 75.

The Modern Law Review   [Vol. 55

of confidence in the police began to unfold, there emerged a succession of competing agendas for reform. In the late 1970s and early 1980s, debate became increasingly polarised between a conservative 'law and order' approach advanced by the police themselves and the Thatcher Government, and a radical rejectionist position, the organisational heart of which was in the Left-wing Labour Metropolitan local authorities elected in 1981.[93] Whilst the Conservatives advocated greater powers for the police, Labour saw the problem as the unfettered autonomy the police enjoyed and sought to reinforce their accountability to elected local authorities. The Scarman Report in 1981 proposed a sophisticated synthesis of these two positions, but with strict law enforcement subordinate in the last analysis to the diplomatic requirements of keeping the peace. This was a policy of back to the future. The ideals of the British police tradition epitomised by Dixon remained intact in principle but had been undermined in practice. Scarman advocated a blend of community consultation and police professionalism, predicated upon an adequately maintained iron fist, to deal with disorder should the velvet glove tactics fail.[94]

Scarmanism rapidly became the orthodox wisdom of government and police policy makers, to which at least lip-service had to be paid. In the hands of such influential police leaders as Sir Kenneth Newman and Sir Peter Imbert, it gave rise to a host of interrelated reforms throughout the 1980s. These were implemented in conjunction with innovations in management style which owed much to the new emphasis on professional management techniques and especially the concern for value for money, which increasingly pervaded the whole public sector. The style of the contemporary police chief correspondingly changed from bobby to bureaucrat.[95]

Opposition to these approaches was rapidly won over, or bludgeoned over. Middle of the road opinion could not resist the *bien pensant* tones of the new philosophy of community policing. The radical end of the spectrum was subject to cruder tactics. The Local Government Act 1985 dealt with the radical critique of policing by abolishing its material base — the Metropolitan local authorities — and replacing them for police purposes with the more manipulable Joint Boards.[96]

The problem with this accumulating avalanche of reforms was that while much changed in the leadership styles and presentational front of policing, the desired end products were not achieved. As discussed above, the end of the 1980s saw all-time record crime increases, renewed public disorder, spectacular scandals involving miscarriages of justice and plummeting public confidence in the police.

The leadership of the service has responded by seeking to model the mission of policing on the service style which their own research suggests is what the majority of the public wants. As described earlier, it has also sought to introduce a variety of managerial changes to monitor and improve the quality of service delivered.[97] The key is seen as changing police culture to incorporate quality of service values. In short, the police elite has turned to the language and style of consumerism — market research, prominently displayed mission statements, codes of ethical service and the like. This chimes in with the general approach to the public sector promulgated by John Major, and is policing designed for the age of the Citizen's Charter.[98]

Like its ideological first cousin, community policing, this consumerist ethos has

93 Reiner, *op cit* n 2.
94 Scarman, *op cit*.
95 Reiner, *op cit* n 33.
96 Loveday, 'The New Police Authorities in the Metropolitan Counties' (1991) 1 *Policing and Society* 193.
97 Woodcock, *op cit* n 36; Johnson, *op cit* n 36; Hirst, *op cit* n 36.
98 Barron and Scott, 'The Citizen's Charter Programme' (1992) 55 MLR 526.

the great virtue that it is almost impossible to be against it in principle. The issue is whether it fully confronts the realities of policing in the postmodern age. In so far as an emphasis of theorists of postmodern culture is on the centrality of style, design and image rather than use-value, it is clear that the consumerist tack is itself a prime expression of postmodernism.

However, neither this nor any other conceivable strategy will restore the police to the status they enjoyed in Britain in the middle years of this century. This was based on unique social and cultural conditions which are unlikely to re-occur and have certainly never been replicated elsewhere. In all other countries, the police have wielded power rather than authority (in the traditional Weberian distinction). The power of the British police was transmuted into authority primarily because they came to stand for a (largely mythical) national culture of order, harmony and restraint. Their power was legitimated by tradition. In other countries, any legitimation the police have achieved has been rational-legal or charismatic (again using Weber's famous ideal-typical categories).[99] These are more brittle and tenuous sources of legitimacy for the police than the authority of tradition. A first condition for the police to re-attain legitimacy is for them and the public to recognise that the traditional British bobby myth is anachronistic — indeed, it never corresponded to reality.

Beyond this, however, the deeper social changes of postmodernity are transforming the role of the police institution within the whole array of policing processes. The rise of *the* police — a single professional organisation for handling the policing function of regulation and surveillance, with the state's monopoly of legitimate force as its ultimate resource — was itself a paradigm of the modern. It was predicated upon the project of organising society around a central, cohesive notion of order. In Storch's striking phrase, the police were 'domestic missionaries.'[100] The role of the police, especially in Britain, was always more important for its dramaturgical function, symbolising social order, than for any instrumental effects in successfully controlling crime.[101] The changes in social structure and culture which have been labelled postmodernisation render this conception of policing increasingly anachronistic. There can be no effective symbol of a unitary order in a pluralistic and fragmented culture.

Nor can the instrumental functions of the police be straightforward in the 'two-thirds' society. The United States, as the Los Angeles riots of 1992 dramatically showed, indicates the dark end-point of processes which can be seen in less stark form throughout the Western world. The police are confronted with a social order bifurcated between the 'dreadful enclosures' of the underclass (often constructed on racial lines) and the castles of conspicuous consumerism in which the majority live, work and play.[102] The latter are increasingly taking the form of what the Canadian criminologists Shearing and Stenning have called 'mass private pro-

---

99 For a recent general discussion of the Weberian tradition in the analysis of power and legitimacy, see Beetham, *The Legitimation of Power* (London: Macmillan, 1991).

100 Storch, 'The Policeman as Domestic Missionary' (1976) IX *Journal of Social History* 481.

101 Manning, *Police Work* (Cambridge, Mass: MIT Press, 1977) is the most cogent presentation of a dramaturgical analysis of policing.

102 As Davis put it in his account of Los Angeles as prism of the postmodern future (written before the 1992 riots), 'the historical world view and quixotic quest of the postwar LAPD' (Los Angeles Police Department) was 'good citizens, off the streets, enslaved in their high security private consumption spheres; bad citizens, on the streets (and therefore not engaged in legitimate business), caught in the terrible jehovan scrutiny of the LAPD's space programme.' Davis, *City of Quartz* (London: Vintage, 1992) p 253.

The Modern Law Review   [Vol. 55

perty,'[103] huge privately owned facilities like shopping centres, leisure parks, office
or educational campuses, large private residential estates or apartment blocks. The
role of the police in regulating the order of these areas is residual at most. A police
officer is seldom, if ever, seen in Disneyland or indeed Brent Cross (except as a
customer). Instead, control is maintained by architecture, the technology of
surveillance and informal social mechanisms, with even the specialist input of private
security personnel being vestigial, and primarily concerned with maintaining
perimeter security.[104] The role of the police is the rump one of maintaining the
order of public spaces, which increasingly are the preserve of the excluded social
residuum.[105]

In addition, there remain higher level policing functions which the state must
exercise: the control of serious professional and international crime, and the
maintenance of state security. But these are increasingly remote from the world
of the beat police.

In short, policing now reflects the processes of pluralism, disaggregation and
fragmentation which have been seen as the hallmark of the postmodern. Hitherto,
the British police have been unique in combining within a single omnibus organisation
the disparate functions of patrol, public order, serious criminal investigation, political
policing and regulating corporate crime. In most other countries, a variety of specialist
organisations cope with these separately. It would seem, indeed, that they call for
very different skills and tactics of mobilisation. It is most unlikely that the British
police will survive the pressures towards an organisational division of policing labour
in the last decade of the millennium. There will probably be a fundamental reorgani-
sation, bifurcated between a variety of high-level units for national and international
crime, public order and security functions, with local police forces on the other
hand increasingly focused on small-scale crime, order and service tasks.[106] The
latter will find it increasingly difficult to find a suitable niche in the face of competition
from private and environmental security mechanisms. The local police role will
increasingly be the Fort Apache syndrome: patrolling the borders between respectable
and rough reservations. These processes have been referred to by several commentators as the 'greying' of policing: its diffusion between a variety of institutional
processes, with the human element increasingly not clad in blue uniforms.[107]
Sadly, Dixon is dead. Unlike his first demise in *The Blue Lamp*, we shall wait in
vain for a second coming.

---

103 Shearing and Stenning, 'Private Security: Implications for Social Control' (1983) 30 *Social Problems*
     493.
104 As Davis puts it, 'In cities like Los Angeles, on the bad edge of postmodernity, one observes an
     unprecedented tendency to merge urban design, architecture and the police apparatus into a single,
     comprehensive security effort . . . Los Angeles in its usual prefigurative mode, offers an especially
     disquieting catalogue of the emergent liaisons between architecture and the American police state.'
     Davis, *op cit* n 102.
105 Important accounts of the increasing role of private security in contemporary social control are Shearing
     and Stenning (eds), *Private Policing* (Beverly Hills: Sage, 1987); South, *Policing for Profit* (London:
     Sage, 1988); Johnston, *The Rebirth of Private Policing* (London: Routledge, 1992).
106 Anderson, *Policing the World* (Oxford: Oxford University Press, 1989); Dorn, South and Murji,
     'Mirroring the Market? Police Reorganisation and Effectiveness Against Drug Trafficking' in Reiner
     and Cross, *op cit* n 31.
107 Hoogenboom, 'Grey Policing: A Theoretical Framework' (1992) 2 *Policing and Society* 17; Johnston,
     op cit n 105.

Postscript: Postmodern Policing

There are three strategies which must be adopted if the police are to achieve what legitimacy is available in the postmodern period. All are already in place as policy aspirations of the more progressive police leaders. The first is the recognition of the chimerical character of the Dixon ideal and its replacement by more pragmatic conceptions of acceptability. The police are providers of a mundane public service, not sacred totems of national pride.

Second, the personnel of the police must reflect the more diverse and plural demographics of postmodern societies. Specifically, the proportions of women and ethnic minorities must parallel at all levels in the police their numbers in the population policed.[108] Third, local policing must be adjusted to the plural priorities and cultures of a much more diverse social world. Disaggregation downwards of policy making is already the main aspect of leading reforms such as the sector policing experiments in the Metropolitan Police.[109] One vital ingredient which must be taken on board, however, is the integration of elected local authorities into the policy-setting process. For London, this means the creation of such a local authority. Opinion polls and market research techniques, on which the police increasingly rely, cannot substitute for the electoral process as a means of registering public opinion.

The above analysis contains much intellectual pessimism. Is there room for optimism of the will?[110] Postmodern culture may have eclipsed the Enlightenment's modern conceptions of social justice, as well as the more ancient prophetic religious ideas of justice which modernism had displaced earlier. But certain harsh realities will not be pushed aside. As Los Angeles, the modern world's dream factory, showed us in May 1992, the backlash of the oppressed can turn complacent reveries into nightmare. To paraphrase Rosa Luxemburg,[111] in the final analysis the only alternatives are social justice or barbarism. Unfortunately at present, the odds seem strongly to favour barbarism.

---

108 For accounts of the formidable obstacles to achieving this, see Heidensohn, *Women in Control? The Role of Women in Law Enforcement* (Oxford: Oxford University Press, 1992); Holdaway, *Recruiting a Multi-ethnic Police Force* (London: HMSO, 1991).

109 Although this may not be how it is working out in practice. Weeks, 'Sector Policing,' *Police*, July 1992, p 38.

110 In Gramsci's famous formulation, cf Anderson, *Considerations on Western Marxism* (London: New Left Books, 1976) p 89.

111 Luxemburg, *Political Writings* (New York: Monthly Review Press, 1971) p 24.

[6]
From PC Dixon to Dixon PLC: Policing and Police Powers since 1954

Subject: Police

Keywords: Accountability; Police powers and duties

Legislation: Police Act 1964
Police and Criminal Evidence Act 1984 Part IX, s.36 , s.76 , s.77 , s.78 , s.106
Criminal Law Act 1967
Emergency Powers Act 1964
Anti-terrorism, Crime and Security Act 2001
Police Reform Act 2002
Police Act 1996 s.37 , s.38
Criminal Justice Act 1991
Crime and Disorder Act 1998

Crim. L.R. 601 Introduction: A Transformation of Policing?

Many analysts have claimed in recent years that contemporary policing is entering a fundamentally new era. Perhaps the best-known version of this thesis is a celebrated article by David Bayley and Clifford Shearing, two leading policing scholars,[1] who argue that "Modern democratic countries like the United States, Britain and Canada have reached a watershed in the evolution of their systems of crime control and law enforcement. Future generations will look back on our era as a time when one system of policing ended and another took its place."[2] This is clearly one aspect of much broader debates about the nature of contemporary social and political change, and the widespread sense that a deep transformation is occurring, although there are profound disagreements about how to characterise and understand it.

In terms of policing the arguments focus on two dimensions of change: (a) the so-called pluralisation of policing, the more complex relationship between the police and other policing mechanisms; (b) shifts in the mandate and legitimacy of the police themselves. Perhaps the clearest index of these changes is the now almost universal usage of the term *policing* rather than *the police* in academic and policy discussion. This reflects the growing recognition that the police, the state financed and organised body that specialises in policing, is only one

---

[1]   D. Bayley and C. Shearing (1996) 30 *Law and Society Review* 583. For a recent critical discussion see T. Jones and T. Newburn (2002) 42 B.J.Crim. 129.
[2]   Bayley and Shearing, *op. cit.,* p. 585.

aspect – and possibly a diminishing aspect – of an ensemble of policing institutions and processes.[3] Independently of (but also related to) the pluralisation of policing, the police have also been subject to profound transformations in their mandate and legitimacy in the last half century. The police have changed in what they do and what they are expected *Crim. L.R. 602* to do, the tasks and powers they are given and how they are held to account for them, and how they are seen and see themselves.

I. The Dialectics of Policing History since 1954

During the 1950s (and up to the late 1960s) most police patrol was on foot, and officers on long, lonely night shifts would sometimes relieve their tedium and tiredness by taking a nap in a hospitable building on their beat. If an extra-lethargic Constable R. Van Winkle woke up in 2004 he would find his job bewilderingly different. At least two very deep social transformations have altered the fields of crime control and policing. In terms of the global political economy since the mid-1970s, the "first world" of advanced mixed economy capitalism, the "second world" of state socialist societies, and the "third world" of industrially non-developed countries, have merged into a single, globalised, neo-liberal economy – albeit with deep differences in levels of development. A much longer period of cultural change also came to a head in the late 1960s. During the twentieth century there has taken place a gradual diffusion through the mass culture of the Western world and beyond of the values of enlightenment liberalism such as individual autonomy, self-realisation and scepticism about claims of authority. This became increasingly apparent during the 1960s and after, generating ferocious culture wars about what has widely come to be referred to as "permissiveness".[4] However characterised, there does seem to have been a general trend towards desubordination and declining deference to traditional forms of authority.[5]

In Britain and the rest of the Western industrial world these transformations underlie three distinct periods of political and social discourse. The post-World War II mixed economy, welfare state, Keynesian consensus that predominated up to the late 1960s became increasingly challenged and by the late 1970s was displaced by conservative governments pursuing a neo-liberal economic agenda, initially against considerable domestic and international opposition. Finally, by the early 1990s neoliberalism had emerged as the clear victor in these conflicts, signalled by the collapse of the Soviet Union and in most Western countries by the election of nonconservative, often nominally social democratic, governments that clearly espoused neo-liberal economics although trying to modulate this with some continuing commitment to more inclusive social policies (often under the banner of "the third way"[6]).

These broad socio-economic developments have generated a host of specific social changes that bear upon policing and crime control in complexly interdependent ways. Throughout the last 50 years there has been a growth of prosperity and mass consumerism. A concomitant

---

[3]   R. Reiner, *The Politics of the Police* (3rd ed., Oxford University Press, Oxford, 2000), 1-7.

[4]   T. Newburn, *Permission and Regulation: Law and Morals in Post-War Britain* (1991, Routledge, London).

[5]   R. Reiner, (1992) "Policing a Postmodern Society" (1992) 55 M.L.R. 761.

[6]   T. Blair, *The Third Way: New Politics for a New Century* (Fabian Pamphlet 588, The Fabian Society, London, 1998).

of this has been the spread of the consumer durables that are the most common target of the high volume property crimes that constitute the overwhelming majority of the recorded crime rate. The major changes in family life over the same period have significant consequences for informal social control. The advent of neo-liberal economics added further criminogenic pressures in the 1970s. Long-term unemployment returned and *Crim. L.R. 603* economic inequality began to widen,[7] reversing two centuries of gradually increasing social inclusion into an ideal of common citizenship. The growing problem of social exclusion both generates increasing motivations to commit crime and erodes informal controls traditionally provided by legitimate career prospects.

These economic, social and cultural transformations have had two clear results shaping the immediate context of policing. The first is the advent of what David Garland has called "high-crime society".[8] This refers both to the apparently inexorable and huge rise of recorded crime rates from the mid-1950s onwards and to the impact of this on popular consciousness and patterns of everyday life as people try and adjust to new fears of victimisation. The second is the growing centrality of "law and order" as a political and public concern. Crime control and policing have moved from being largely seen as non-controversial albeit important policy areas to fiercely contested and pivotal issues in partisan politics.[9]

These social trends have had clear consequences for the police and policing. In 1954 the British police were at a pinnacle of popular legitimacy.[10] The BBC was planning a new television series that would resurrect a character first introduced (and murdered) in a 1949 Ealing film, *The Blue Lamp.* Launched in July 1955 *Dixon of Dock Green* ran for over 20 years and its eponymous hero became the quintessential representation of the ideal British bobby, resonating in policy discussions even 50 years later.[11] P.C. George Dixon was the fictional embodiment of the "citizen in uniform" concept that underpinned the deliberations of the Royal Commission on the Police, and many other policy debates.[12]

This pinnacle of police legitimation in popular opinion[13] was the achievement of a combination of policies initiated by Sir Robert Peel and other architects of modern British policing in the early nineteenth century in the face of widespread opposition. These included subordination to the rule of law, minimal force tactics, crime prevention through uniform patrol, separation from direct government control and partisan politics whilst seeking popular accountability in the sense of responsiveness to public opinion, and personnel policies aimed at ensuring high standards of personal discipline and integrity. The success of these strategies

---

[7]   Joseph Rowntree Foundation, *Income and Wealth: Report of the JRF Inquiry Group* (JRF, York, 1995), Summary.

[8]   D. Garland, *The Culture of Control* (Oxford University Press, Oxford, 2001).

[9]   D. Downes and R. Morgan, "The Skeletons in the Cupboard: the Politics of Law and Order at the Turn of the Millenium" in M. Maguire, R. Morgan and R. Reiner (eds), *The Oxford Handbook of Criminology* (3rd ed., Oxford University Press, Oxford, 2002).

[10]   G. Gorer, *Exploring English Character* (Cresset, London, 1955), 311.

[11]   N. Hopkins, "It's Time to Bring Back Dixon, Says Met", *Guardian,* February 28, 2003, p.15.

[12]   Royal Commission on the Police *Final Report,* Cmnd.1728 (1963) (HMSO, London), para.30.

[13]   Beneath the rosy view of the police that dominated popular perspectives of the period there was undoubtedly a more sordid reality of corruption and abuse, as documented by memoirs and oral histories; *cf.* B. Weinberger, *The Best Police in the World* (Scolar Press, London, 1995).

in winning popular consent was made possible by the wider process of gradually increasing social inclusion into common citizenship rights.[14]

Threats to this high-point of police legitimacy were already apparent during the late 1950s in the shape of a series of scandals and controversies, resulting in the establishment of the 1960 Royal Commission on the Police, with a remit of *Crim. L.R. 604* reviewing the constitutional position of the police. Despite a fair degree of contemporary criticism, the Police Act of 1964 that ensued from the Royal Commission did seem for a time to settle fundamental controversy. However, after the late 1960s the era of consensus policing seemed to unravel, with conflict centring on the issues of corruption, abuse of suspects, excessive use of force, partisanship, militaristic public order tactics, race and gender discrimination, lack of individual and organisational accountability, declining efficiency and increasing alienation from the public. Political conflict over policing became most heated in the decade after the mid-1970s. The focal points of these controversies were the militaristic police tactics adopted to deal with the urban riots and the bitter industrial struggles of the early 1980s, and the apparent growth of police powers in the Police and Criminal Evidence Act 1984 ("PACE").

Since the early 1990s, however, fundamental political conflict about policing has abated, and a new basic consensus has emerged, although paradoxically policing and crime remain central political issues. This new consensus centres on a prioritisation of crime control as the mandate of the police, with organisational reforms modelled on private business enterprise as the intended mechanism for efficient and effective delivery. The new consensus resulted from both Labour and the Conservatives abandoning key elements of their 1980s' positions, not least as signalled by then Shadow Home Secretary Tony Blair's legendary 1993 pledge to be "tough on crime, tough on the causes of crime". The crucial change on the part of the Conservatives was the increasingly tough application to the police in the late 1980s of public expenditure disciplines, prompted by worries about the apparently meagre results from the relatively generous resourcing of the police earlier in the decade.

Overall the development of policing since 1954 can be seen as a dialectic of three models. The first was a consensus policing model of the police officer as exemplary "citizen in uniform", keeping the peace primarily through activating informal self-policing processes. Although hardly realised at the time, the precondition for the apparent success of the police in crime control terms was the effectiveness of the much broader informal control processes of deference, family, stable employment, and social inclusion. As these were eroded, and crime and disorder increased, so policing became embroiled in conflict as tactics became more coercive. In the 1990s, however, a new consensus was achieved around the model of crime-oriented business like policing, not only by the police but by a growing variety of public and private bodies. Nonetheless, the police remain at any rate the symbolic embodiment of security to the public,[15] however much concern there may be about specific lapses.

---

[14]   R. Reiner, *op. cit.*, Ch.2.
[15]   I. Loader and A. Mulcahy, *Policing and the Condition of England* (Clarendon Press, Oxford, 2003).

II. Police Powers since 1954

The concept of the police officer as "citizen in uniform" was pivotal to the legitimacy of the police at its height in 1954. This involved the idea that a police officer had no special legal powers that ordinary citizens lacked. They were different only in that they were employed to do tasks that any citizen could do as a moral duty. This has never been completely accurate even in law. Soon after the establishment *Crim. L.R. 605* of the modern police, Parliament began giving constables special powers, such as in relation to stop and search (via the Metropolitan Police Act 1839) or in relation to particular offences. The courts, however, especially in the nineteenth century were anxious to ensure that police powers were not exceeded, and police chiefs generally saw this as important for public anxiety even if they chafed at specific rulings restricting their actions.[16] In practice the police were able to exercise more power than they strictly had. They used a variety of tactics to achieve compliance with their requests, relying mainly on deference to their uniform and authority, and citizens' ignorance of their rights, to carry out "voluntary" stops and searches, and interviews "assisting with inquiries".

Any truth the "citizen in uniform" ideal may have had in 1954 has been eclipsed by the steady accretion of legal powers to the police since then. The key landmark in this development is the Police and Criminal Evidence Act of 1984 which gave the police a comprehensive set of powers to investigate crime which vastly exceeds the powers of the ordinary citizen, however much they may be balanced by adequate safeguards. However, PACE had been preceded by at least two decades in which police powers had already been steadily, though somewhat unevenly, extended by statute and case law, and the two decades since have also seen a continuing increase in statutory police powers.

A crucial statutory extension was the Criminal Law Act 1967 which specified that constables could arrest on reasonable suspicion that an arrestable offence had occurred, whilst citizen powers only existed when such an offence actually had taken place. The Misuse of Drugs Act 1973 gave the police a uniform national power to stop and search on reasonable suspicion in relation to drug offences. It also foreshadowed PACE's attempt to specify what constituted "reasonable suspicion". Although some cases in the 1960s seemed to continue the courts' traditional keen watchdog role in relation to police actions seeming to exceed their powers, the general trend was to legitimise such initiatives as necessary for effective policing.

PACE undoubtedly represents a landmark in the modern development of police powers. Its origins were in the 1981 Report of the Royal Commission on Criminal Procedure ("RCCP"). The immediate trigger was the publication in 1977 of the Fisher report on the Confait case which had revealed that suspects' rights as specified by the non-statutory Judges' Rules were commonly violated.[17] But another stimulus for the establishment of the RCCP was undoubtedly the growing law and order lobby campaigning for greater police powers to fight crime. The RCCP Report was greeted with dismay by civil liberties groups as it increased the powers of the police with what appeared to them to be inadequate safeguards for suspects, even though the Report claimed to aim at "a fundamental balance" between the two. The first version of the Police and Criminal Evidence Bill launched by the Conservative Government

---

[16] J. Davis, "A Poor Man's System of Justice: the London Police Courts in the Second Half of the 19th Century" (1984) 27 *Historical Journal* 328; W. Miller, *Cops and Bobbies* (2nd ed., Ohio State University Press, Ohio, 1999), 4-12, 56-94.

[17] *Report of the Royal Commission on Criminal Procedure,* Cmnd.8092 (1981) (HMSO, London).

in 1983 strengthened these criticisms. In the face of widespread opposition, not only from civil liberties groups and the opposition parties but also lawyers' and doctors' professional bodies (and even some members of the RCCP itself), the Bill was modified as it went through Parliament. The resulting Act passed in 1984 moved back to something closer to the RCCP's notion *Crim. L.R. 606* of balance. Nonetheless, it was seen by civil libertarians as based on a "draconian" increase in police powers and a new strategy of "policing by coercion".[18]

PACE gave the police a plethora of powers that they had not possessed before, at any rate on a statutory basis. In part this extension of powers was nominal rather than real, for much was a rationalisation of hitherto haphazard statute and common law, or a legitimation of what was already police practice. On the other hand, the exercise of statutory powers was governed by safeguards set out partly in the Act itself, partly in the accompanying Codes of Practice. These Codes provided detailed procedures regulating stop and search; search and seizure; detention and questioning of suspects; identification procedures; and tape-recording of interviews – Codes that have been revised several times since.

The Act also implemented the RCCP's solution to the difficulties of reviewing police actions due to the low visibility of routine police work. This was to establish a variety of recording requirements for each exercise of a police power, giving reasons for what is done. There was also a requirement that interviews be contemporaneously recorded. The Act also included sections purporting to strengthen police accountability, by obliging police authorities to consult local communities (s.106), and establishing the Police Complaints Authority (Pt IX).

A combination of extension and rationalisation of powers with procedural safeguards resting fundamentally on reporting requirements characterises all the major provisions of PACE. The detention and questioning sections, for example, contained a particularly complex set of safeguards, resting on the custody officer ("CO"), a new police specialism with a duty to supervise the detention of suspects (s.36). The CO (normally a sergeant) has the duty of informing a new detainee of his rights (to see a solicitor, to have someone informed of his arrest, and to consult the Codes of Practice). The CO must maintain a custody record on which is entered all significant events in the period of detention. A complex timetable of reviews of the necessity of detention, and of processes that can extend it up to an absolute maximum of 96 hours in exceptional cases, was elaborated in the Act and Code C.

Perhaps the most significant general safeguard was the possible exclusion of evidence obtained in violation of PACE procedures. Confessions are admissible only if the prosecution can show they were not obtained by oppression, or by any methods rendering them unreliable (s.76). Judges are obliged to warn juries of the dangers of convicting a mentally handicapped person on the basis of a confession (s.77). Section 78 gave judges discretion to exclude evidence if it appears that "the circumstances in which the evidence was obtained" mean it would have "an adverse effect on the fairness of the proceedings" (a watered-down version of an amendment introduced by Lord Scarman). However, since PACE the judiciary in general have displayed a tougher approach to police breaches of the Codes, implying acceptance of a regulatory role in maintaining a balance between police powers and safeguards.

Empirical studies of police work prior to PACE had suggested that the powers of the police were formulated and interpreted so permissively that police practice frequently departed from the rule of law. This informed much of the opposition to PACE. Civil libertarians feared that

---

[18]   A. Sanders and R. Young, *Criminal Justice* (2nd ed., Butterworths, London, 2000).

the police would exceed their new extended powers, and the safeguards would be ineffective as they relied mainly on police *Crim. L.R. 607* internal procedures. The controversial character of the Act has generated a considerable body of empirical research evaluating its effects, as well as of subsequent changes such as the Criminal Justice and Public Order Act 1994.[19] This evidence suggests a more complex picture than implied by the polarised polemics that attended the birthpangs of PACE.

PACE certainly seems to have had a marked effect on the nature and outcomes of police handling of suspects. Routine practice has incorporated much of the rituals and procedures of the Codes of Practice, and many indices of suspects' access to rights indicate improvement. On the other hand, assimilation of the PACE rules into police culture and working practices has been uneven and incomplete. Much is ritualistic and presentational and affects little of substance in the experience of suspects. On the plus side, research evidence suggests that suspects are normally informed of their rights on reception at the police station. As a result, the proportion receiving legal advice has increased between two and four times, and is now about a third of all suspects. Forty per cent of suspects interviewed now receive legal advice. The use of dubious "tactics" to extract incriminating statements by interrogation has declined. Tape-recording of interviews has reduced arguments in court about what occurred, and is now welcomed by the police who were long opposed to it.

On the other hand, the research also suggests that detention is authorised almost automatically and invariably, and the establishment of the custody officer as an independent check on this has proved chimerical. The information to suspects about their rights is often given in a ritualistic way, with active discouragement observed in some cases. This may account for the fact that a majority of suspects still do not take them up. Relatively few offenders have ever exercised their right of silence, in part or completely, and the proportion has declined since the Criminal Justice and Public Order Act 1994 permitted adverse inferences to be drawn. Later stages in the detention process (such as reviews, or regulating access to suspects by investigating officers) are less punctiliously followed than the reception rituals. Custody officers also seem less scrupulous about monitoring pre-detention events (such as delay between arrest and arrival at police stations). PACE procedures can frequently be side-stepped by securing "voluntary" compliance by suspects with police requests. Such "consent" is especially important for the stop and search powers, where it is often circumvented. The provision of "appropriate adults" and defence solicitors to assist vulnerable suspects like the mentally disordered is inadequate. In many cases no "appropriate adult" is called or attends. The socially discriminatory pattern of use of police powers remains as marked as before. The burden of police powers still falls disproportionately on the young, economically marginal, ethnic minority males, who are the overwhelming majority of those who are arrested and detained.

The resilience of the social pattern of policing and its basic practices in the face of PACE is due to the unchanging role of the police, primarily as regulators of public space and those who live their lives there predominantly. PACE can do little to alter the impact of this on the culture and organisation of policing. Nonetheless, the Act *Crim. L.R. 608 has* impacted

---

[19] For reviews see D. Brown, *PACE Ten Years On: a Review of the Research* (Home Office Research Study, London, 1997), 155; D. Dixon, *Law in Policing* (Oxford University Press, Oxford, 1997); A. Sanders and R. Young, "Police Powers" in T. Newburn (ed.), *Handbook of Policing* (Willan Publishing, Cullompton, 2003).

on police practices, albeit unevenly and patchily. This is partly because of the symbolic consequences of giving safeguards a statutory basis, carrying more weight in police culture than the Judges' Rules did. It is also because of a variety of changes making sanctioning of breaches more likely. These include: the tougher line taken by the courts, and the deterrent value of internal disciplinary sanctions. Of particular importance has been a variety of devices which have begun to open up the "low visibility" back-stage areas of routine policing, albeit patchily and inadequately. Key examples are the recording requirements, lay station visitors, enhanced access to solicitors and "appropriate adults" in cases involving juvenile or mentally disordered suspects, and in some stations CCTV.[20] The legislation has achieved far more than its civil libertarian critics initially expected, if far less than they would wish.[21]

Deterrence, symbolism, organisational and training changes are all important in understanding how PACE has affected police culture and practice. If powers are precisely rather than permissively formulated, procedures to render visible occasions of use are constructed, and supervisors and courts determined to police the police, the law in action may become more closely aligned to the law in the books. Thus, the custody reception procedures, which are precise, relatively visible to supervisors, and clearly enjoined in training, are religiously followed. However, the danger of precisely formulated rules is also evident here. They may be satisfied by ritualistic observance with little meaning, defeating their intended objectives. Although PACE has probably made impossible some of the horrors of the past in the treatment of detained prisoners, it is doubtful that it has achieved "balance" between powers and safeguards even if it has moved further towards it. It is also likely that the crime control emphasis of the 1990s, which has resulted in a series of Acts adding further to the powers of the police and diluting the safeguards (notably the Criminal Justice and Public Order Act 1994) has tilted the "balance" back to the powers side.

In the past 20 years or so, a gradual accretion of powers has also occurred through the passage of special legislation designed, on the surface at least, to deal with the policing of terrorism. The emergency powers that were introduced in the first half of the twentieth century were largely incorporated into the Emergency Powers Act 1973.[22] Police powers have increased time and time again as new legislation has been passed, most usually in response to specific terrorist activities – initially Irish republican terrorism and, more recently, in the aftermath of the September 11, 2001 attacks on the World Trade Centre and Pentagon in the United States. Legislation has broadened the definition of "terrorism", created new acts of conspiracy, extended police powers of arrest without a warrant and, via the Anti-Terrorism, Crime and Security Act 2001, considerably increased powers of *Crim. L.R. 609* detention of immigrants suspected of terrorism.[23] Responding to terrorism, now increasingly central to

---

[20]   T. Newburn and S. Hayman, *Policing, Surveillance and Social Control* (Willan Publishing, Cullompton, 2001).

[21]   Definitive reviews can be found in L. Lustgarten, *The Governance of the Police* (Sweet and Maxwell, London, 1986); N. Walker, *Policing in a Changing Constitutional Order* (Sweet and Maxwell, London, 2000); T. Jones, "The Governance and Accountability of the Police" in T. Newburn (ed.), *Handbook of Policing, op. cit.*

[22]   C. Walker, "Briefing on the Terrorism Act 2000" (2000) 12 *Terrorism and Political Violence* 1-36

[23]   M. Matassa and T. Newburn, "Policing and Terrorism" in T. Newburn (ed.), *Handbook of Policing, op. cit.* Although specific legislation has also been introduced with the aim of regulating the

public debates and to the shape of contemporary policing, raises important questions about the extent (legally and temporally) of "special" police powers, their potential (mis)use in "normal" policing[24] and, by extension, how best the public police and other related agencies are to be held accountable.

III. Police Governance since 1954

The problem of holding the police to account, controlling the controllers, is one of the thorniest problems of achieving democratic governance. It has two interdependent levels: procedures for remedying misconduct by individual officers, and for governing the whole organisation and its policies. The principal means of holding individual officers to account are the courts and the complaints system. Police officers are rarely prosecuted for crimes arising out of wrongful performance of their duties. During the 1990s there was an increase in the number of officers convicted of criminal offences (other than traffic offences) from 35 in 1992 to 65 in 1998 (though this had dropped to 60 by 2001).[25] However, the number remains small when compared with the approximate 35,000 complaints against the police recorded per annum, or the 1,367 people awarded damages for police wrongdoing after a civil action was settled or won. The burden of proof in civil actions is the lesser standard of "balance of probabilities" but the problems of cost, time and access to lawyers mean that such actions are rarely resorted to (and rarely successful), even though they have significantly increased in recent years.[26]

The Police Act 1964 laid down the basic system for making complaints against the police. From the start it was subject to severe criticism for relying on entirely internal police investigation and adjudication of complaints. After many years of pressure to introduce an independent element into the complaints system, resisted by most police opinion, the Police Act 1976 established the Police Complaints Board. The Board could recommend that disciplinary charges be brought, but only on the basis of the report of the internal police investigation. PACE replaced the Board with the Police Complaints Authority ("PCA"), which was required to supervise the investigation of complaints alleging death or serious injury, and empowered to do so in any other case where it considered this is in the public interest. The Act also established procedures for resolving minor complaints informally. While enhancing the degree of independent scrutiny of complaints the PACE reforms fell far short of a fully independent system and both the PCA and the system as a whole lacked public confidence.[27]

Crim. L.R. 610 In late 1997 the Parliamentary Home Affairs Committee ("HAC") began an inquiry into police discipline and complaints. Its Report, *Police Disciplinary and Complaints Procedures,* was published in January 1998 and recommended radical overhaul of the system. It supported the principle of independent investigation, and also concluded that

---

use of police powers including, for example, the Regulation of Investigatory Powers Act 2000 and the Human Rights Act 1998.

[24]   C. Walker, "Terrorism and Criminal Justice: Past, Present and Future" [2004] Crim.L.R. 311.

[25]   *Police Complaints and Discipline England and Wales, 12 Months to March 2002,* Home Office Statistical Bulletin 04/03 (Home Office, London).

[26]   B. Dixon and G. Smith, "Laying Down the Law: the Police, the Courts and Legal Accountability" (1998) 26 *International Journal of the Sociology of Law* 419.

[27]   M. Maguire and C. Corbett, *A Study of the Police Complaints System* (HMSO, London, 1991).

the terms on which officers were investigated were as important as who did the investigating. Implementing this, in 1999 Police Conduct Regulations lowered the standard of proof required to substantiate a complaint to the "balance of probabilities" rather than the criminal "beyond reasonable doubt". The Police Reform Act 2002 replaced the PCA by a new Independent Police Complaints Commission with its own investigative capacity. This overhaul of the complaints system finally introduces many procedures long called for by civil libertarians. However, the results may not be as dramatic as many hope. A key factor in the low rates of substantiation of complaints against the police (currently around three per cent) is the "low visibility" of the operational situations that give rise to most complaints. Frequently they turn on conflicts of testimony between complainants and police officers, with no independent evidence. Irrespective of who does the investigating and adjudicating, many are unlikely to be sustained even on a civil balance of probabilities standard of proof, still leaving many complainants with a sense of grievance.

In the light of the poor prospects of substantiation of complaints against the police, it is hardly surprising that civil actions have become a major growth industry as an alternative means of redress. The door was opened in effect when s.48 of the Police Act 1964 made chief officers and thus police forces vicariously liable for wrongs committed by police officers, reversing the common law position established by *Fisher v Oldham Corporation* in 1930. This made it financially worthwhile to sue officers for torts they may have committed. The means for suing frequently came from legal aid. The lower burden of proof in civil actions compared to the criminal standard required for complaints also made the prospects of success much greater. In the Met in particular, settlements and damages for civil actions rose from £471,000 to 127 claimants in 1991 to £2,309,000 to 295 claimants in 1998/99. Small wonder that the Commissioner's policy appears to have changed in the mid-1990s from settling to contesting actions wherever possible.[28]

Some of the most contentious issues of police accountability arise in relation to the quasi-legislative and executive functions of determining the priorities and efficiency of force policy. The Police Act 1964 consolidated and rationalised the governance structure for provincial policing which had developed in the previous century. The two London forces (the Met and the City of London) retained their own accountability structures (in the former to the Home Secretary alone, in the latter to the Common Council of the City of London as well as the Home Secretary).[29] The 1964 Act defined the general duty of the police authority as being "to secure the maintenance of an adequate and efficient police force for the area" *Crim. L.R. 611* (s.4(1)). The precise relationship constitutionally and in practice between police authority, Chief Constable and Home Office has long been a complex and much debated matter. The terms of the 1964 Act were self-contradictory or vague at the crucial points. Crucially, the 1964 Act was unclear about the possibility of the police authority being able to instruct the Chief Constable on general policy concerning law enforcement in the area (as distinct from

---

[28]   In the 1997 Appeal Court case *Thompson and Hsu v Commissioner of Police of the Metropolis* the Met was successful in getting the court to suggest more restrictive guidelines for damages in such cases.

[29]   The Greater London Authority Act 1999 finally established the Metropolitan Police Authority along the same lines as other local police authorities. The MPA Board is made up of 23 members: 12 members from the London Assembly (including the Deputy Mayor), four magistrates and seven independents. One of the independents is a direct appointment by the Home Secretary.

the immediate, day-to-day direction and control of the force which is clearly precluded). Again, in cases of conflict it was for the Home Secretary to arbitrate, but the Act's thrust was to limit responsibility for "operational" matters to the Chief Constables.

In practice, most police authorities did not even use the limited powers envisaged by the Act, deferring normally to the Chief Constable's "professional" expertise. Where conflict arose, for example, in the much-publicised battles between their police authorities and Chief Constables during the 1984/85 miners' strike, chief constables were almost always backed by the Home Office and emerged the victors, indicating the virtual impotence of the police authorities. The Local Government Act 1985 abolished the six Metropolitan councils, replacing their police authorities by more quiescent joint boards. The Court of Appeal in 1988 rejected a judicial review brought by the Northumbria Police Authority challenging the Home Secretary's right to issue plastic bullets after the authority had refused to sanction their purchase.[30] This seemed to underline the impotence of local police authorities *vis-à-vis* the other two legs of the tripartite system of police governance, making them a fig leaf of local influence in a highly centralised, *de facto* national structure.

In the late 1980s and early 1990s a number of other developments continued this centralising trend. The cutting-edge of the thrust to greater centralisation has been the Government's tightening control of the police budget. The Audit Commission, the independent body established by the Government to monitor local authority spending, became a key player in the policing field with a series of hard-hitting reports aimed at enhancing value for money.[31] The role of HM Inspectorate of Constabulary was considerably enhanced after the mid-1980s, as the pivot of a more centralised co-ordination of standards and procedures. The Home Office has also encouraged the Association of Chief Police Officers ("ACPO") to develop a much higher profile and expand its role, as a means of enhancing the standardisation and centralisation of policing. ACPO is the linchpin of what has become a central "policing policy network".[32]

There has been a proliferation of specialist national policing units. The most significant have been the National Criminal Intelligence Service ("NCIS") and National Crime Squad ("NCS"), established by Pts I and II of the Police Act 1997. One of the key sources of the impetus towards centralised units and the tighter national control of policing generally is the belief that it was an essential requirement of European integration after 1992. More generally there has been concern about the growth of international crime – and more recently of international *Crim. L.R. 612* terrorism – leading to a perceived need for higher level national (and indeed international) police bodies to cope with it.[33] The centralising trend became more apparent still as a result of a profound restructuring of police governance in the 1990s. The Police Act 1996 consolidated the Police Act 1964, the Police and Criminal Evidence Act 1984, Pt IX, and the Police and Magistrates' Courts Act 1994 into the currently

---

[30]   *R. v Secretary of State for the Home Department Ex p. Northumbria Police Authority* [1988] 1 All E.R. 556.

[31]   For example, Audit Commission, *Pounds and Coppers: the Financing of Provincial Police Forces* (Police Paper No.10, Audit Commission, London, 1991).

[32]   S. Savage, S. Charman and S. Cope, *Policing and the Power of Persuasion: the Changing Role of ACPO* (Blackstone Press, London, 2000).

[33]   J.-P. Brodeur, "High Policing and Low Policing: Remarks about the Policing of Political Activities" (1983) 30 *Social Problems* 507.

definitive statutory statement of the structure of police governance. The most controversial changes were to the structure of police authorities. Section 4 of the 1996 Act limits the normal size of police authorities to 17 (although the Home Secretary has discretion to increase this under s.2). This uniform size, regardless of the area or population covered, itself signified a departure from the conception of police authorities as primarily *representative* local bodies. The specified functions of police authorities are subtly altered from the 1964 Act formulation, which was the "maintenance of an adequate and efficient" force to "efficient and effective" (in s.6 of the 1996 Act). The precise scope of this responsibility remains as gnomic as in the 1964 version, but the symbolism is obvious.

The prime motif of the new-fangled police authorities is that they are to be "business like" bodies–the local watchdogs of the managerialist, value-for-money, private enterprise ethos underpinning the whole reform package.[34] The new police authorities have new duties to issue an annual policing plan for their area (Police Act 1996, s.8) and local policing objectives (s.7). The Chief Constable has the same general function of "direction and control" of the force as in the 1964 Act, but this must now be exercised with regard to the local policing plan and objectives that the authority draws up in liaison with her (s.10). This is an empowerment of the police authority compared to the 1964 Act, but it has to act as a conduit for the Home Secretary's priorities primarily. The Home Secretary decides the codes of practice for police authorities (s.39), sets national objectives and performance targets which local plans must incorporate (s.37, s.38), determines the central government grant to police forces which covers most of their expenditure according to formulae which are at his discretion (s.46), and can direct police authorities about the minimum amount of their budgetary contribution (s.41) and any other matters (s.40).

The Conservative Government's aim was radically to extend central control over policing. Not only did the original Police and Magistrates' Courts Bill seek to enhance the Home Secretary's powers, the Sheehy Inquiry into Police Responsibilities and Rewards which reported in 1993 recommended that all police officers should be appointed on short-term contracts and subject to performance-related pay. Although the Act reached the statute book in considerably modified form, and many of Sheehy's recommendations were also resisted, the changes nevertheless constituted a formidably centralised system of control over policing. Without abandoning the constabulary independence doctrine in any formal way, the Home Secretary can colour the use of discretion by constables by setting and assessing the criteria for performance that determine pay and job security. The police are no longer accountable in the gentlemanly "explanatory and co-operative" style that *Crim. L.R. 613* characterised the impact of the 1964 Police Act.[35] Nor are they subject to the "subordinate and obedient" style of accountability to democratically elected local authorities demanded by the Act's radical critics. Instead they are subject to a new market-based "calculative and contractual" style of accountability.[36]

---

[34]   T. Jones and T. Newburn, *Policing After the Act* (Policy Studies Institute, London, 1996).

[35]   G. Marshall, "Police Accountability Revisited" in D. Butler and A.H. Halsey (eds), *Policy and Politics* (Macmillan, London, 1978).

[36]   R. Reiner, "Police Accountability: Principles, Patterns, Practices" in R. Reiner and S. Spencer (eds), *Accountable Policing* (IPPR, London, 1993).

In 1998 a House of Lords' decision underlined the significance of the Home Secretary's national policing plan and objectives in setting the framework for operational policing throughout the country.[37]

This upheld the legality of a Chief Constable's restriction of the level of police protection for live animal exporters against protestors. The judgment was based in part on the Chief Constable's statutory obligation to pursue the objectives set by government under ss.37 and 38 of the Police Act 1996. In the case in question these were held to over-ride both the general police duty to keep the peace (which had to be reasonably balanced against other concerns including budgetary limitations) and also EC Treaty obligations to protect the free movement of goods.

The traditional common law doctrine of constabulary independence was given lip service in the House of Lords' judgment. However, there was also recognition of the way that the Police and Magistrates' Courts Act 1994 and subsequent legislation obliged the Chief Constable to pursue objectives specified by central government. This leaves the doctrine of police operational independence an empty shell. In currently fashionable terminology, the police are free to "row" in any way they decide, so long as it is in the direction "steered" by the Home Secretary.[38]

More recent changes have largely served to reinforce this trend. The 2001 White Paper,[39] and subsequent Police Reform Act 2002, respectively flagged up and then introduced the first national Annual Policing Plan, gave the Home Office significantly increased powers (partly through the creation of the Police Standards Unit) to manage "good practice" through statutory codes of practice and regulations, as well as the means to require a police force to take remedial action where they are judged by HMIC to be inefficient or ineffective. Further centralisation–particularly through a reduction in the number of forces and possible rationalisation of small specialist forces–is also raised by the more recent Government consultation paper, *Policing: Building Safer Communities Together.*[40]

Whatever the eventual impact of the reforms in practice, there has certainly been a profound transformation in the formal organisation of police governance in the years since 1994. Almost as much criticism was levelled at the style in which these changes have been carried out as their substance. Unlike previous major changes in police accountability there has been no preceding Royal Commission or major public deliberations. The reforms emanated from internal Home Office inquiries with minimal outside consultation. There was no public debate about this narrowing of the traditional police mandate. In theory and practice this had hitherto been **Crim. L.R. 614* seen as encompassing a much broader spectrum of concerns, including crime prevention and management, order maintenance and peace-keeping, emergency and other services. The narrow emphasis on crime detection had hitherto been seen by most official enquiries (notably, the Scarman Report of 1981[41]) as a departure from the traditional Peelian peace-keeping remit of British policing.

Arguably, attempts to re-localise control now are like pushing a stream uphill. As "law and order" becomes increasingly politicised it is ever more unlikely that governments

---

37 *R. v Chief Constable of Sussex Ex p. International Trader's Ferry Ltd* [1998] 3 W.L.R. 1260.

38 D. Osborne, and T. Gaebler, *Reinventing Government* (Penguin, Harmondsworth, 1993).

39 *Policing a New Century: a Blueprint for Reform* (Home Office, London).

40 Home Office, *Policing: Building Safer Communities Together* (Home Office, London, 2003)

41 Lord Justice Scarman, *The Scarman Report* (Penguin Books, Harmondsworth, 1982).

will relinquish ultimate control over policing. On the other hand, the complexly mediated mechanisms that ensure central government dominance also shield it from responsibility for mishaps. Why should any government relinquish a position which gives it power without responsibility? The myth of a tripartite structure of governance for essentially local policing, with constabulary independence for operational decisions, is useful for legitimating a system of *de facto* national control. Nonetheless, concern to give local communities effective control over policing remains a live issue. Given the proliferation of policing agencies and processes apart from the state police, discussed in the next section, the issue has become even more complex.

IV. Privatisation and Pluralisation

Arguably, the most profound shift in the past 50 years in policing has been the ending of the idea of a police "monopoly" in policing as a broadening array of private, municipal and civilian guards, officers and wardens become ever more visible. An increasingly complex division of labour has emerged in which private security personnel far outstrip police in numerical terms in which civilian employees and auxiliaries have become an accepted part of state policing – and have access to increased powers in some cases – and in which the police and numerous other agencies – public, private and voluntary – work in "partnership".

The proliferation of private security has involved the spread of new technologies, such as closed-circuit television ("CCTV"), and the growing incursion of the private sector into forms of work, or areas of activity, more usually associated with public policing. The latter includes privatised enforcement of parking and traffic regulations, the transport and guarding of prisoners, and most importantly – certainly for the way we view policing – the patrolling of public streets. It would be a mistake in considering the past 50 years, however, to assume that it is only relatively recently that the private security sector outstripped the public. In fact, there is good evidence to suggest that by the late 1950s, early 1960s, the numbers employed in the private security industry were already in excess of the number of police officers.[42] Despite this, it is arguably only in the last two decades that the police service's dominant position in the public mind as the sole occupier of the "thin blue line" protecting the public from crime and lawlessness has come under serious challenge.

Although much discussion of private security focuses on the manned guarding sector, arguably the most significant growth area in recent times has been in the proliferation of security hardware and, in particular, the expansion of the use of *Crim. L.R. 615* CCTV. The first major city-centre CCTV systems were introduced as part of the "Safer Cities" initiative in the mid-1980s and a small number of towns went ahead with such installations at around the same time using local authority rather than central government funding. By the mid-1990s fewer than 80 towns and cities had CCTV schemes.[43]

By May 1999 there were over 530 town and city-centre CCTV systems in operation and additional government funding since then has further fuelled expansion with the latest

---

[42]   T. Jones and T. Newburn, *Private Security and Public Policing* (Clarendon Press, Oxford, 1998).

[43]   N.R. Fyfe and J. Bannister, "City Watching: Closed Circuit Television in Public Spaces" (1996) 28 *Area* 37.

estimates suggesting that there are now in excess of four million cameras in operation in Britain.[44]

Although the private security sector was a very substantial presence much earlier, it was not until the 1980s that privatisation emerged as a formal element of government policy and began to have an effect on the police. The initial battleground was police funding. From 1982-83 onwards the Government began vigorously to pursue its "Financial Management Initiative" ("FMI"), designed to encourage efficiency and cost savings by applying private sector management methods to the public sector, and imposing market disciplines on them. Although initially it looked as if the police might be safe from such scrutiny, the publication of Home Office Circular 114/1983 (and later the even tougher 106/1988), largely without consultation with police representative bodies, signalled that the financial climate had changed. Privatisation and the FMI were of course linked, for as police representatives were quick to point out, restrictions on human and financial resources increase the opportunities for competitors to provide services hitherto the preserve of the police.

The pace of change really picked up in the 1990s, beginning with the 1993 White Paper on Police Reform[45] and the Sheehy Inquiry that followed close on its heels.[46] The most explicit consideration of privatisation came with the establishment of a further inquiry in 1993 – The Core and Ancilliary Tasks Review whose terms of reference were: *To examine the services provided by the police, to make recommendations about the most cost-effective way of delivering core police services and to assess the scope for relinquishing ancillary tasks.* The starting point for the review team was the suggestion that "some of the resources needed to improve performance in core areas of work supporting key and national objectives will have to be found by releasing resources currently absorbed by peripheral non-essential tasks or by finding more cost-effective ways of delivering core tasks." Although the initial aims of the Inquiry were modified as work progressed, the underlying rationale continued to be the desire to limit public expenditure in this area. In the event, the final report of the Inquiry was a damp squib, merely recommending the contracting out of a small number of peripheral duties, such as escorting wide loads, although it did also suggest that a national crime reporting system should be established and that force crime pattern analysis should be standardised.[47]

In fact, privatisation – directly or by contracting out – has been a more minor factor in the changing face of policing in contemporary Britain than appeared likely **Crim. L.R. 616* in the early 1990s. Some functions have been transferred entirely to the private sector. The Criminal Justice Act 1991 (ss.80-86), for example, transferred responsibility for security arrangements for prisoners in transit from the police and prison service to private contractors, and also (s.76) made provision for magistrates' courts to contract-in security officers. In addition, individual forces have contracted out such activities as the construction and management of custody centres, reception duties, and post-charge administration – including the taking of fingerprints, photographs, DNA samples and PNC checks. Rather than direct privatisation, it has been growing civilianisation, the encouragement of police partnership with other providers and,

---

44   M. Frith, "Big Brother Britain" *Independent,* January 12, 2004.

45   Home Office, *White Paper on Police Reform* (Home Office, London, 1993).

46   P. Sheehy, *Report of the Inquiry into Police Responsibilities and Rewards,* Cm.2280 (1993) (HMSO, London).

47   Home Office, *Final Report of the Review of Core and Ancilliary Tasks* (HMSO, London, 1995).

most recently, the introduction of a new tier of auxiliaries that has had the greatest impact on the contemporary policing landscape.

From the 1980s onwards there were successive waves of civilianisation. Increases in police pay made police officers relatively expensive commodities and from 1983 onward the Government's FMI reversed the policy of the previous decade and sought to increase the number of civilian employees. This move was further stimulated by the Audit Commission and the last 20 years have seen considerable expansion of civilian employment in the police service, not simply in administrative support roles but, increasingly, at senior levels including senior management within forces.

A central feature of the New Labour modernisation project, and central to the delivery of its criminal justice policies, has been partnership working. In coming to power in 1997 the new administration accepted the 1991 Morgan Report's[48] recommendation that greater responsibility for local crime prevention ought to be invested in local authorities[49] – a position continually resisted by previous Conservative administrations. In due course, the Crime and Disorder Act 1998 (ss.5-6) placed a statutory duty on chief police officers and local authorities, in co-operation with police authorities, probation committees and health authorities, to formulate and implement a strategy for the reduction of crime and disorder in the area. Through the creation of multi-agency forums – known generally as Crime and Disorder Reduction Partnerships ("CDRPs"), the Act sought to stimulate considerable changes in the working practices of the main organisations responsible for crime control and the administration of crime prevention. Since the implementation of the Act, these crime and disorder (reduction) partnerships (over 370 of them), involving local police services, local authorities, probation, health, education and other bodies, have been responsible for carrying out audits of local crime and disorder issues, to consult widely with the community on the basis of these audits, publish a local crime and disorder strategy based on the audit and consultation, identify local performance targets and report annually on progress in relation to the targets. The Crime and Disorder Act 1998 will potentially have far-reaching consequences for policing.[50] At the very least, it has further reoriented the way in which police services are managed and provided.

Crim. L.R. 617 The last decade has seen the mushrooming of what has been the termed the "new public auxiliaries".[51] It was the introduction of community support officers that was the most radical of the proposals, however. Almost a decade earlier, a committee established by the Police Foundation and the Policy Studies Institute had recommended experimentation with alternative forms of police patrol,[52] only to be roundly criticised by ACPO and by New

---

[48]   Standing Conference on Crime Prevention, *Safer Communities: the Local Delivery of Crime Prevention through the Partnership Approach* (Home Office, London, 1991).

[49]   See, for example, Home Office, *Getting to Grips with Crime* (Home Office, London, 1997), pp.3-5.

[50]   T. Newburn, "Community Safety and Policing: Some Implications of the Crime and Disorder Act 1998" in G. Hughes, E. McLaughlin and J. Muncie (eds), *Crime Prevention and Community Safety: New Directions* (Sage, London, 2002).

[51]   A. Crawford and S. Lister, *The Extended Policing Family* (Joseph Rowntree Foundation, York, 2004).

[52]   Police Foundation/Policy Studies Institute, *Inquiry into the Role and Responsibilities of the Police* (PSI, London, 1994); see also, R. Morgan and T. Newburn, *The Future of Policing* (Oxford

Labour in opposition for recommending "policing on the cheap". By 2002, however, the fiscal realities were such that it was difficult for any politician to avoid the conclusion that the level of policing seemingly demanded by the public could not easily be provided from within the public purse. A form of public-private partnership was proposed – not that such language was used. Using the more mellifluous idea of "an extended police family", and underpinned by the Broken Windows philosophy,[53] the White Paper proposed, and the Police Reform Act 2002 incorporated, proposals that agents and agencies such as neighbourhood and street wardens, security guards in shopping centres, park keepers and "other authority figures"[54] could be accredited by, and work alongside, the police in a formal capacity. More controversially, the Government included a power to enable Chief Constables to appoint support staff to provide a visible presence (*i.e.* to patrol) in the community. These "(police) community support officers" are under the control of the Chief Constable and have limited powers (Pt 1(2) of Sch.4) to detain suspects, to require the name and address of persons acting in an anti-social manner, and to stop vehicles and to issue fixed-penalty notices.[55]

Directly and indirectly, through a number of its measures, New Labour has stimulated further moves in the direction of a more complex and fragmented policing division of labour. The Police Reform Act 2002, via the creation of community support officers and the accreditation of extended police family members is the most visible of these. Arguably, however, the Crime and Disorder Act, in conjunction with Best Value and the increasing emphasis placed upon consumer demand, will prove to be just as important in the process of extending and formalising the mixed economy of policing.

Conclusion: Policing Futures

Though much of the future is, of course, uncertain, one thing we may say with a reasonable degree of confidence is that the era in which the public police somehow came to symbolise nationhood has passed and will not return. The past 50 years have witnessed some very significant changes in the pattern, focus and governance of policing – just as the society being policed has itself altered culturally and politically. There are a number of areas in which – looking to the medium term – issues central to the future development of policing in the United Kingdom might be expected to be most obviously identified. We focus very briefly on three: **Crim. L.R. 618* pluralisation; centralisation and managerialism; and, diversity and accountability. We began by noting Bayley and Shearing's contention that we are in a transitionary period in which one system of policing is being replaced by another. Although it is possible to argue about both the precise nature and timing of these changes, it is undoubtedly the case that the future of policing in the United Kingdom is likely to be characterised by the increasing visibility of a broad, and possibly broadening, array of providers of policing services.

University Press, Oxford, 1997).
   [53]   J.Q. Wilson and G. Kelling, "Broken Windows: the Police and Neighbourhood Disorder" (1982) *Atlantic Monthly.*
   [54]   Home Office, *Policing a New Century: a Blueprint for Reform* (Home Office, London, 2001), para.2.31.
   [55]   L. Jason-Lloyd, *Quasi-Policing* (Cavendish Publishing, London, 2003).

Moreover, during a period in which the "war on terrorism" looks set to be an important influence on domestic security policy and politics, it is not just plural policing that is set to become more complex, but also the intertwined – and often hidden – relationships between public police bodies, private security, the security services (MI5 and MI6), GCHQ and army intelligence.

The last 50 years have seen the gradual rationalisation of the number of police forces in England and Wales, the emergence of national (and international) policing bodies, the increased co-ordinating ability of the police service itself, largely via ACPO, together with vastly expanded central government control and management of local policing. Again, it is difficult to see how this centralising and managerialising tide is to be turned back. Although there are simultaneous pressures on government to stimulate greater local responsibility (and accountability) in policing, they sit in very uneasy tension with what appears currently at least to be the overwhelming political desire to micro-manage from the centre. This tension is visible in the Government's most recent discussion paper[56] which examines a number of proposals for increasing local accountability, including floating the idea of local policing boards advanced by the Patten Commission,[57] whilst also exploring means of enhancing government scrutiny of, and oversight over, local police performance through such approaches as "earned autonomy" (greater freedom as a result of good performance[58]) and workforce modernisation.

Finally, the last 50 years have been punctuated by expressions of concerns about the policing of minority communities. Most recently, the Macpherson Inquiry,[59] established in the aftermath of the murder of Stephen Lawrence, again highlighted the gulf between the police service and some minority ethnic communities. It is not difficult to predict that attempting to improve the understanding of, and responses to, the needs of such communities will probably be both a central issue, and a significant problem, in the future. Moreover, all this will occur within the context of a policing environment that is both more diverse and seemingly more fragmented. The language of "responsiveness", of "community", of "partnership" and the seemingly almost continuous expansion of surveillance and privatised security raise functional (who does what?), normative (what do we want them to do?) and political questions (how do we resource and hold accountable these bodies?), the responses to which are fundamental to the future shape of policing in the United Kingdom.

Crim. L.R. 2004, Aug, 601-618

---

[56]   Home Office, *op. cit.* (2003).

[57]   C. Patten, *A New Beginning: Policing in Northern Ireland: a Report of the Independent Commission on the Policing of Northern Ireland* (TSO, London, 1999).

[58]   The consultation document suggests that, in practice, this might mean the possibility of certain specific ring-fenced Home Office grants might be made non-specific; and a "lighter touch" inspection regime might be introduced for high performing forces (para.7.6).

[59]   Sir W. Macpherson, *The Stephen Lawrence Inquiry: Report of an Inquiry by Sir William Macpherson of Cluny,* Cm.4262-1 (1999) (HMSO, London).

[7]
Neophilia or Back to Basics? Policing Research and the Seductions of Crime Control

Policing: Key Readings, Tim Newburn (Ed.). Cullompton: Willan, 2005, xiv+834 pp. ISBN

In a recent study of citation practices in British criminology, Paul Rock demonstrated the prevalence of what he calls "chronocentrism"—the "doctrine that what is current must somehow be superior to what went before, that ideas, scholars and scholarship inevitably become stale and discredited over time" (Rock, 2005: 474). "Criminology has proceeded in a series of fits, being marked by radical discontinuities; a recurrence of new beginnings; and a quest for the seemingly distinctive", under the spell of this chronocentric bias (Rock, 2005: 473).

Not the least of the merits of this excellent collection of readings edited by Tim Newburn is that it largely evades the chronocentric tendency. It offers a selection of 45 extracts and articles, ranging in time from Michael Banton's pioneering *The Policeman in the Community* (Banton, 1964)—the first empirical study of contemporary policing to be published in book form on either side of the Atlantic—to recent debates about current transformations in policing. It is well organized into six sections on historical emergence and development; role and function; culture; strategies; deviance, ethics and control; and the emerging pattern of policing. In his introduction, Tim Newburn acknowledges that, despite the volume's heftiness, painful choices inevitably had to be made, that readers will doubtless think of pieces they would have put in, and he invites discussion and suggestions—and I will take this up later.

Yet it must be said first that the volume offers a definitive and invaluable resource for students (and scholars) who wish to learn about the development and content of policing research. It is a fitting companion to Newburn's 2003 *Handbook of Policing*, which provided a state-of-the-art collection of contemporary papers on the main aspects of contemporary policing in the United Kingdom. Newburn's editorial introductions to each section of both volumes are exceptionally judicious and helpful, drawing out the core points of each contribution and its relationship to the others. *Policing: Key Readings* offers not only a wealth of material for students new to the

90

field, but an opportunity to assess the development and future(s) of policing research. For me, studying the papers selected from a range of nearly a half-century repeatedly gave me a frisson of shocked pleasure at rediscovering the quality of the classics of the field, which I have referred to, but not properly re-read for many years.

The First Half-Century of Policing Research: An Overview

In earlier overviews of the development of policing research I have distinguished several different phases (Reiner, 1989, 1992, 2000a), but what is most apparent, looking back over the past fifty years, is a sharp break in the problematics of policing research in the early 1990s. This reflects much broader shifts in political economy and culture that can be summed-up as "neo-liberal triumphalism" and its impact on the fields of crime, criminal justice and policing. While there are many harbingers of these developments in the 1970s and 1980s, the early 1990s mark a particular watershed in discourse and research on policing.

As Newburn's readings show, empirical research on policing emerged in the early 1960s, in both the United States and the United Kingdom. The pioneers included William Westley (who conducted his trail-blazing fieldwork in the late 1940s, reported in a couple of seminal early 1950s journal articles, but not in book form until 1970), Michael Banton, Jerome Skolnick, Egon Bittner, Herman Goldstein, James Q. Wilson, Al Reiss, Donald Black, David Bayley, Maureen Cain and others. They were followed in the 1970s by Mike Chatterton, Peter Manning, Simon Holdaway, Maurice Punch, Lawrence Sherman, Gary Marx, John Van Maanen, Richard Ericson, Clifford Shearing, Tank Waddington and many others (including myself). The work of many of these is reproduced in this volume. What is striking compared to most of the recent papers is that the research of the 1960s and 1970s is research *on* rather than *for* the police.[1] Although many researchers were interested in policy issues (above all civil libertarian concern about police violations of the rule of law), their work was primarily aimed at understanding the nature, dynamics, sources and impact of policing through "thick" ethnographic description and theoretical analysis.

The emergence of policing research itself reflected the epistemological break in criminology in the 1960s marked by the advent of the "labelling" perspective and symbolic interactionism. These rendered intellectually problematic the practices of criminal justice, and the social construction of categories of deviance and crime. Another remarkable feature of the early classic fieldwork studies is the high proportion that originated as doctorates and other "lone scholar" studies, with minimal external funding. In the 1970s, more radical frameworks supplanted the predominantly liberal political and theoretical perspectives of the 1960s' researchers. These drew on Marxism above all, reflecting the broader dominance of radical criminology in this period, with feminism and Foucault becoming more influential in the late 1970s.

Policing & Society   91

During the 1970s and early 1980s academic research on policing began to be joined increasingly by official research undertaken by police themselves, by government agencies responsible for policing, and by specialist think tanks (e.g. the American government's National Institute of Justice, the British Home Office, the RAND Corporation, the American and British Police Foundations). This was driven, but not dictated, by policy concerns. Official research could often be sharply critical of policing—noteworthy examples being the research conducted for the 1979 Royal Commission on Criminal Procedure by the Police Foundation's Barrie Irving and others (Irving & Mackenzie, 1989) and the negative assessments of the crime control effectiveness of traditional policing strategies by Ron Clarke, Mike Hough and others for the British Home Office (Clarke & Hough, 1984). Academic research was also increasingly commissioned and financed by official bodies, and becoming more policy-oriented.

A significant break in the general politics of law and order occurred in 1992–1992. Law and order first became a partisan political issue during the 1970s as the Conservatives under Margaret Thatcher used it to undermine the Labour Government. This contributed greatly to the Tories' 1979 General Election victory. In the early 1980s, political polarization over law and order and policing became even sharper, culminating in the bitter arguments over the policing of the inner city disorders and the 1984–1985 miners' strike (Reiner, 2000b: Chapter 2). There was the emergence of a new "second order" consensus on law and order in 1992–1993, in which both the Conservatives and Labour competed to be the toughest in their crime control policies (Downes & Morgan, 2002). The police mandate was specified in narrow crime control terms (most explicitly by the 1993 Police Reform White Paper), and this was to be delivered by a businesslike management regime of targets, performance measurement and financial sanctions.

The policing changes reflected the broader transformation of criminal justice politics and policy that David Garland has analyzed as the "culture of control" and the domination of public services in general by the "New Public Management" model (Garland, 2001; McLaughlin & Murji, 2001; Long, 2003). In turn, the criminal justice and policing developments are related to broader shifts in political economy and culture, above all the triumph of neo-liberalism. During the 1980s (the Reagan/ Thatcher era), neo-liberalism was dominant in the West, but nonetheless con-tinuously challenged. Its triumph was marked above all in the early 1990s when the social democratic parties of the Western world accepted the neo-liberal economic framework as both inevitable and broadly desirable in the new era of globalization, symbolized by their espousal of "third way" politics. This expelled from the political agenda any discussion of social democratic policies to tackle the "root causes" of crime. Crime had to be controlled primarily by policing and criminal justice. The police were expected to deliver what they had always symbolized but in reality had little to do with: effective protection of the public against crime. Policing research since the early 1990s has become bifurcated into two contrasting although far from

92

unrelated modes: "abstracted empiricism" and "grand theory", in C. Wright Mills's celebrated terminology (Mills, 1959). Most policing research now consists of narrowly focused evaluations of specific policy issues and initiatives. At the same time, there has been a number of ambitious attempts to theorize the new constellation of policing.

The "Classics" of Police Research: The Core Results

The classics of early research on policing in the 1960s and 1970s built up a core set of results that implicitly call into question more recent analyses. I will now review these briefly.

Police Marginal to Social Order, not Sovereign

"The police are only one among many agencies of social control" (Banton, 1964: 1). This is the first line of the first book reporting empirical research on policing. *Pace* the extensive discussions of the contemporary transformation of policing by pluralization, ending the supposed sovereign state and police monopoly of crime control, it has always been recognized by most social theorists that order is created and reproduced by a diverse array of processes to which the formal machinery of "codes, courts and constables" are marginal. This was true both before and after the emergence of modern police forces in the eighteenth and nineteenth centuries (Zedner, forthcoming).

The Police Role is not Primarily Law Enforcement or Crime Control

Empirical research on calls for police help and on how patrol officers spent their time and reacted to calls showed that most police work did not involve law enforcement or crime control. Different studies agreed on that, but expressed what the police *did* do in somewhat different (although related) terms: peace-keeping (Banton, 1964), acting as "philosopher, guide and friend" to the troubled (Cumming et al., 1965), order maintenance or reproduction (Wilson, 1968; Ericson, 1982), "secret" social service (Punch, 1979), street-corner politics (Ker Muir Jr, 1977), discretionary deployment of legitimate force to control *"something-that-ought-not-to-be-happening-and-about-which-someone-had-better-do-something-now!"* (Bittner, 1974). As research became more influenced by radical perspectives, these characterizations of the police role were challenged as obfuscatory and bland—the police were really servants of power, repressing challenges to ruling class dominance. Or in more sophisticated formula-tions they reproduced both general and specific order—"parking tickets and class repression" (Marenin, 1982). What everyone agreed upon was that policing had little to do with crime, contrary to popular and police mythology.

Policing & Society   93

The Police Exercise Considerable Discretion

A key finding of early empirical work was the extent of police discretion, the routine under-enforcement of law (Reiner, 1994: 723–731). This contradicted statutory requirements of full-enforcement in many of the United States (though not in Britain). Police discretion, whether prohibited by law or not, was not only normal practice, but inevitable, as researchers emphasized. What was especially problematic about the routine exercise of police discretion was that its pattern of operation appeared to deviate from the principles of due process of law—for example because police powers were more frequently used against the less powerful and ethnic minorities. Much empirical work and analysis was directed at this problem of the "gap" between the "law in action" and the "law in the books", the routine deviation of policing from the principles of legality (Skolnick, 1966; McBarnet, 1979).

Police Work is Shaped by Cultural/situational Factors rather than Legal Ones

Police operations had "low visibility" (Goldstein, 1960) because they were physically dispersed and their targets were weak in the politics of credibility (Box & Russell, 1975). They were thus only formally accountable to law and management. Police work was primarily influenced by police sub-culture(s) and situational factors (such as the social characteristics, location and demeanour of those encountered), not legal considerations. Legal powers were resources for police action, shaping after-the-event accounts to protect officers from sanctioning (Chatterton, 1979; Holdaway, 1979). Police organizations were peculiar in that "discretion increases as one moves down the hierarchy" (Wilson, 1968: 7). This directed attention to the culture(s) of the rank-and-file, which developed to cope with characteristic structural features of the police role and predicament such as authority, danger, pressure to produce "results" and their place in the reproduction of social power and inequality (Skolnick, 1966).

Policing Mainly Targets the Powerless

From early on, research on policing indicated that the use of police powers was directed primarily at groups who were low in the structure of power and advantage. Young, black, economically marginal men were (and remain) disproportionately subject to stop and search, arrest, detention, charge and prosecution (and, ultimately, incarceration, and in the United States, execution). There has been extensive debate about how far this is the result of police bias and discrimination as distinct from differential offending rates or other legally relevant factors—or interaction between these (Bowling & Phillips, 2002, 2003; Phillips & Bowling, 2002). Underlying differential policing and offending patterns are deeper structural processes that shape both, such as economic and educational disadvantage and discrimination (Fitzgerald, 2004). The basic institutions of privacy and property make the economically disadvantaged more vulnerable to police attention (Stinchcombe, 1963). Not only

94

are the poor and powerless more likely to be exposed to police suspicion and coercive powers, they are less likely to be able to have their version of encounters believed (Box & Russell, 1975). Altogether, groups weak in social power and credibility become "police property" (Cray, 1972; Lee, 1981). It is this rather than physical "low visibility" of encounters per se that makes street-level policing hard to govern or make accountable to law and policy.

Traditional Policing has Little Crime Control Effectiveness

During the 1970s, empirical research showed not only that crime was relatively marginal to policing, but that conversely traditional policing tactics ("preventive" uniform patrol and after-the-event investigation by detectives) had little impact on crime levels (Clarke & Hough, 1984; Reiner, 2000b: 115–124). This was not a problem of lack of policing skills or effort, but intrinsic to policing and the nature of most crimes. Preventive patrol at any feasible level of resourcing is simply too stretched in relation to the vast number of potential perpetrators and targets of crime to encounter or uncover more than a tiny proportion (Clarke & Hough, 1984; Reiner, 2000b: 115–124; Audit Commission 1996). Successful detection of offenders by investigators is heavily dependent on the quality and quantity of initial information at the scene, which is negligible for most routine crimes (Greenwood et al., 1977; Tarling & Burrows, 1985; Innes, 2003a; Maguire, 2003). This pessimistic conclusion of studies of traditional methods has prompted the development of a variety of innovative methods, predicated primarily on more meticulous analysis of risk patterns in victimization and offending, leading to smarter, "intelligence-led" prevention, investigation and "problem-solving" (Sherman, 1992; Maguire, 2000, 2003; Cope, 2003; Tilly, 2003; Part D of the work under review). Coupled with a widespread trend towards lower crime rates in many countries during the 1990s, these have stimulated a new "can-do" confidence about the potential for crime reduction by effective policing.

Policing has Symbolic rather than Instrumental Value

The implications of the early empirical research on policing were certainly debunking of much popular and police mythology. Crime, law and policing were marginal to each other. Policing involved a combination of mundane peacekeeping and the reproduction of unequal structures of power and advantage. This did not mean that the police were not of general and fundamental social value. They were of practical help to people who called the police in a variety of small-scale troubles and conflicts. More broadly, they have dramaturgical and symbolic significance. They represent the promise and possibility of security through the rule of law, however little they may actually contribute to it in practice because the fundamental sources of order or deviance lie in social, economic and cultural processes beyond the reach of policing (Manning, 1977; Loader & Mulcahy, 2003).

Policing & Society   95

Post-classical Pluralization, 1992–

As argued above, since the early 1990s there has been a major change in the politics of law and order in the United Kingdom (paralleling similar changes in the United States), reflecting the broader triumph of neo-liberalism through its incorporation by the parties of the centre left, notably New Labour. The new consensus in law and order politics is the need and the possibility of crime control through "tough" and/or "smart" criminal justice. This is related to an eclipse of faith in the existence of "root causes" of crime, or at any rate in the possibility of affecting them by rehabilitation or social reform. Concerns about discrimination, the rule of law and human rights do remain politically potent, although their salience relative to fears about security varies with what is the latest crisis. These issues now focus at least as much on inequalities in protection from criminal victimization as on the disproportionate targeting of particular groups as suspects, as the Stephen Lawrence case illustrated most clearly.

In this era, policing research has become increasingly bifurcated and pluralized. Most studies are policy oriented and managerialist, focusing on evaluations of specific initiatives, strategies and developments, or emerging special areas of interest. Many are extremely valuable, and indeed continue the critical agenda of earlier work—for example, the Home Office and Metropolitan Police studies of stop and search arising out of the Macpherson Report on the Stephen Lawrence murder (Fitzgerald, 1999; Miller et al., 2000; Quinton et al., 2000), the Met-sponsored partial replication of the seminal 1983 PSI study (Smith et al., 1983; Fitzgerald et al., 2002) and the Home-Office-sponsored evaluation of the impact of the Macpherson Report itself (Foster et al., 2005). Some are informed by theoretical work, even though they are directed at assessing very specific policy initiatives—for example, the reassurance policing studies inspired by the concept of "signal crimes" (Innes & Fielding, 2002; Innes, 2003b; Hough, 2005) and the Nuffield-Foundation-sponsored research on plural policing (Crawford et al., 2005). These are all valuable and rigorous studies of particular issues—and there are many other examples. However they are focused on limited aspects of policing: specialized units, practices or initiatives. Unlike the earlier ethnographic studies, they cannot tell us much about routine policing practice or culture(s).

Co-existing with this proliferation of specific policy-oriented studies, and indeed partly growing out of them, are a number of "grand theory" analyses of overall trends in policing. Two of the latter figure in the first half of Newburn's final section on "The Emerging Pattern of Policing" in the form of two pairs of articles in which the second is a critique of the first. The first pair is my 1992 paper "Policing a Postmodern Society", which attracted a critique by Pat O'Malley in 1997. The other is Bayley and Shearing's very influential 1996 paper "The Future of Policing", which Trevor Jones and Tim Newburn analyzed critically in a 2002 article entitled "The Transformation of Policing?" In addition to these, Richard Ericson and Kevin Haggerty's work on policing risk society is an influential theorization of current trends and is included in Section D on "Policing Strategies". I will consider these further below.

96

First I would like to point out that the concluding section of this book on "The Emerging Pattern of Policing" itself illustrates the post-1992 bifurcation of research between the specific and the grand theoretical. Apart from the four theoretical papers I mentioned above, the section consists of four papers on particular important current aspects of policing: Frances Heidensohn on women police officers, Gary Marx on police surveillance, Colonel Charles Dunlap Jr on increasing military involvement in domestic policing and Jean-Paul Brodeur on the growing links between police and the security services. The last three are linked in being aspects of "high" policing, but nonetheless these four more concrete chapters appear somewhat random a selection of current emerging patterns. All are important, but so would be work on say ethnic minority officers, transnational policing, police use of the media, policing by agencies and processes other than the public police, policing of hate crimes and racism, and many other developments. This is not intended as a criticism of Newburn's selection. On the contrary, I believe it faithfully reflects the current bifurcation between studies of specialist issues and grand theory (it should be stressed also that some current specialist areas are given extended treatment in earlier sections, such as problem-oriented, community, "zero-tolerance", information processing and risk-related policing in the "Strategies" section).

Conclusion: Chronocentric Neophilia or Back to the Future?

Current policing research exemplifies the chronocentrism that Paul Rock's paper with which I began this review found in criminology more generally. As I said at the outset, Tim Newburn's excellent collection is largely free of this. He gives considerable space to the work of the pioneering empirical work of the 1960s and 1970s, especially in the sections on police history, role and function, and culture. There is nonetheless a blind spot in his selection in my view. There is almost nothing reflecting the phase of research in which radical and Marxist analyses were prominent. This occludes a level and form of analysis that raises questions that are still pertinent, and transcend the specific politics of Marxism. This missing dimension is the overall *macro* function of the police and policing in reproducing social order, their place in fundamental structures of power and (in)justice. Although big questions about policing continue to be asked, most obviously in the grand theories I mentioned earlier, they do so from positions (neo-liberal, Foucauldian, communitarian) that deny the reality or relevance of the classical sociological perspectives (Marxism and those who debated with its ghost).

These issues are not totally absent from the articles in this volume. In particular, the first six historical chapters raise these macro questions, as do Bittner's "Florence Nightingale in Pursuit of Willie Sutton" paper (to my mind still *the* all time no. 1 classic in the field) and Banton, Manning and Ericson in the second section on role and function. However, without examples from the Marxist literature there is an implication that the issues raised are past problems that have been resolved, or peripheral and soluble by limited, specific reforms. The historical chapters necessarily

Policing & Society   97

analyze in detail the establishment, legitimation and consolidation of modern policing in the nineteenth century in the face of considerable class and political conflict, but their focus is on the *successful* establishment of policing by consent (at least outside the colonial dimension analyzed by Brogden), although the opening chapter, Allan Silver's "The Demand for Order in Civil Society" (a *tour de force* that retains enormous power some fifty years after it was written), raises issues about policing liberal democracy that remain acute today.

If I might at this point accept Newburn's invitation to suggest missing pieces, I think that just two more papers would directly provide the points that I feel are absent. One is Otwin Marenin's "Parking Tickets and Class Repression" (Marenin, 1982), which draws out the important theme that policing simultaneously reproduces order in general (the conditions of existence of social order *per se*) and "specific" order (particular structures of power, domination, advantage, inequality). This inextricably Janus-faced function of policing is what makes analysis and policy so complex and essentially contested,[2] and renders the current exclusive concerns with crime control, risk and security one-dimensional. All this is implied by the papers in the first two sections here, but Marenin makes the point sharp and explicit. The second paper I would add is Phil Cohen's "Policing the Working-class City" (Cohen, 1979). I think the thesis of this vivid history of inner-city working-class opposition to the police somewhat overdrawn in asserting a direct line of continuity from the early nineteenth century to the late twentieth, but it does sharply underline the continuing deep structural sources of conflicts that might otherwise be seen as a miscellany of particular issues, such as ethnic or generational tensions, rather than abiding exclusion and division, which may be ameliorated from time to time, but not eliminated.

While Newburn's collection successfully avoids chronocentrism, I was struck by how chronocentric the recent papers in the volume were—especially the more theoretical ones. There is a clear tendency to misrepresent or overlook the significance of the classical studies, often by the very people who produced them. To sum up the core classical findings in an even smaller nutshell than my earlier account, policing is marginal to crime and vice versa—and this is for deep structural reasons about the sources of crime and disorder, not remediable failings of particular policing strategies. Yet this is overlooked and misrepresented in most of the recent work reproduced in this volume. For example, Ericson and Haggerty claim that the "risk-communication view of policing we are advancing here obviously decenters the criminal law and criminal justice aspects of police work" (p. 553). Yet Chapter 15, extracted from Richard Ericson's 1982 book on police as reproducers of order, shows that crime was always marginal to police work, except in mythology. Similarly, in their paper on "The Future of Policing" (Chapter 40), Bayley and Shearing say: "Police are no longer the primary crime-deterrent presence in society" (p. 717). Yet David Bayley's 1994 book *Police for the Future* (extracted in Chapter 11) eloquently summarizes why they never were or could be. Janet Chan's critique of studies of police culture (Chapter 21) suggests they fail to "situate culture in the political and social context of policing" and introduces Bourdieu's concept of "field" (as distinct from "habitus") to supply this. The terminology is new in the research on police culture, but the concept is not. To go back to the tradition's origins, Skolnick's analysis of the police "working personality" (Chapter 17), police culture is clearly located in the characteristics of the police role as shaped by the structural features of law and particular social orders. While in liberal democracies these have certain fundamental features (authority, danger, pressure to produce), they vary in intensity and scope in different social structures, explaining both commonalities and variations—and the limited possibilities of reform without wider social transformation.

The fundamental source of this chronocentrism is the sense of hopelessness about fundamental social transformation since the political triumph of neo-liberalism in the early 1990s, following two decades of contest. This expelled "root cause" analyses of crime from practical politics, as conservative criminologists such as James Q. Wilson had sought to do since the 1970s. For both conservative and liberal criminologists, however, the 7th Cavalry seemed to ride to the rescue at just the right time in the form of the widespread fall in crime rates after the early 1990s. There was a widespread tendency to attribute this to criminal justice and especially policing changes. More conservative voices emphasized the "tough" dimensions of these ("zero-tolerance" policing, harsher sentencing), liberals the "smart" aspects (intelligence-led crime analysis, more effective targeting of prevention, problem-solving policing and punishment). A full selection of views is found in Part D of this collection, from the told-you-so triumphalism of Chief William Bratton's "Crime is Down in New York City: Blame the Police" (Chapter 28) to the more cautious analyses of problem-solving, community policing and COMPSTAT (Chapters 7, 23, 24, 25, 30, 31). The claims that the police caused the crime drop in New York or elsewhere are cogently demolished in David Dixon's excellent "Beyond Zero Tolerance" (Chapter 29) (see also Bowling, 1999; Karmen, 2000; Smith, 2004).

The new "can-do" optimism of the police and their cheerleaders in the 1990s is reflected in a paler form in the theoretical analyses of transformation, forgetting the lessons of the past. Bayley and Shearing, for example, explicitly argue that a combination of "the profit motive" generating more private security and "smarter enforcement tactics ... community policing with a hard edge" can make policing "more effective in truly preventing crime" (pp. 716–718). The combination of market-based reforms of private and public policing is explicitly turned to because of a perceived impossibility of wider "root cause" changes (pp. 726, 729; cf. also p. 712). The problems of equity are recognized: markets alone would generate a "Clockwork Orange world" of greater divisions between the affluent and the poor, so some sort of redistributive voucher system is needed to level up the protection of poorer communities (p. 730).

To me the prospects of market-based solutions are like the attempts of the sharks in *Finding Nemo* to become vegetarian. Markets are unrivalled means of allocating private consumer goods efficiently and of generating innovation and growth

Policing & Society   99

(Kay, 2003), but they also have fundamental pathologies that have long been identified above all, but not only, by socialists of all varieties. Most crucially for criminological purposes, unfettered markets remorselessly generate inequality and encourage egoistic and anomic cultures, feeding crime at all levels. O'Malley rightly accuses me of pessimism (p. 711), but I still concur with the bleak closing lines of my 1992 essay in this volume (Chapter 38): "To paraphrase Rosa Luxemburg, in the final analysis the only alternatives are social justice or barbarism. Unfortunately, at present, the odds seem strongly to favour barbarism" (p. 693).[3] Recent events, in New Orleans and elsewhere, only seem to underline this stark choice.

ROBERT REINER

Law Department, London School of Economics

Notes

[1]   John Lambert stressed the distinction between sociology of and for the police in his contribution to the first of three influential conferences for British and American researchers organized by Michael Banton in the early 1970s, and this issue was much discussed at all of them (Reiner, 1994: Footnote 8).

[2]   Neil Walker's recent text on police governance and accountability draws out the implications of this distinction for the "paradoxes of policing" and their regulation (Walker, 2000: 4–6).

[3]   I have elaborated on this more fully in Reiner (2000c, 2006).

References

Audit Commission (1996), *Streetwise: Effective Police Patrol*, HMSO, London.

Banton, M. (1964), *The Policeman in the Community*, Tavistock, London.

Bittner, E. (1974), "Florence Nightingale in pursuit of Willie Sutton: A theory of the police", in: Jacob, H. (ed.) *The Potential for Reform of Criminal Justice*, Sage, Beverly Hills, CA.

Bowling, B. (1999), "The rise and fall of New York murder", *British Journal of Criminology*, Vol. 39, no. 4, pp. 531–554.

Bowling, B. & Phillips, C. (2002), *Racism, Crime and Justice*, Longman, London.

Bowling, B. & Phillips, C. (2003), "Policing ethnic minority communities", in: Newburn, T. (ed.) *Handbook of Policing*, Willan, Cullompton.

Box, S. & Russell, K. (1975), "The politics of discreditability", *Sociological Review*, Vol. 23, no. 2, pp. 315–346.

Chatterton, M. (1979), "The supervision of patrol work under the fixed points system", in: Holdaway, S. (ed.) *The British Police*, Arnold, London.

Clarke, R. & Hough, M. (1984), *Crime and Police Effectiveness*, Home Office, London.

Cohen, P. (1979), "Policing the working-class city", in: Fine, B., et al. (eds) *Capitalism and the Rule of Law*, Hutchinson, London.

Cope, N. (2003), "Crime analysis: Principles and practice", in: Newburn, T. (ed.) *Handbook of Policing*, Willan, Cullompton.

Crawford, A., et al. (2005), *Plural Policing*, Policy Press, Bristol.

Cray, E. (1972), *The Enemy in the Streets*, Anchor, New York.

Cumming, E., Cumming, L. & Edell, L. (1965), "The policeman as philosopher, guide and friend", *Social Problems*, Vol. 12, no. 3, pp. 276–286.

100

Downes, D. & Morgan, R. (2002), "The skeletons in the cupboard: The politics of law and order at the turn of the Millenium", in: Maguire, M., Morgan, R. & Reiner, R. (eds) *The Oxford Handbook of Criminology*, 3rd edn, Oxford University Press, Oxford.

Ericson, R. (1982), *Reproducing order*, University of Toronto Press, Toronto.

Fitzgerald, M. (1999), *Searches in London under Section 1 of the Police and Criminal Evidence Act*, Metropolitan Police, London.

Fitzgerald, M. (2004), "Understanding ethnic differences in crime statistics", *Criminal Justice Matters*, Vol. 55, pp. 22–23.

Fitzgerald, M., et al. (2002), *Policing for London*, Willan, Cullopmton.

Foster, J., Newburn, T. & Souhami, A. (2005), *Assessing the Impact of the Stephen Lawrence Inquiry*, LSE Mannheim Centre, London.

Garland, D. (2001), *The Culture of Control*, Oxford University Press, Oxford.

Goldstein, J. (1960), "Police discretion not to invoke the criminal process: Low visibility decisions in the administration of justice", *Yale Law Journal*, Vol. 69, pp. 543–594.

Greenwood, P., Chaiken, J. & Petersilia, J. (1977), *The Criminal Investigation Process*, Heath, Lexington, KY.

Holdaway, S. (ed.) (1979), *The British Police*, Arnold, London.

Hough, M. (2005), "Policing, new public management and legitimacy in Britain", in: Fagan, J. & Tyler, T. (eds) *Legitimacy, Criminal Justice and the Law*, Russell Sage Foundation Press, New York.

Innes, M. (2003a), *Investigating Murder: Detective Work and the Police Response to Criminal Homicide*, Oxford University Press, Oxford.

Innes, M. (2003b), "'Signal crimes': Detective work, mass media and constructing collective memory", in: Mason, P. (ed.) *Criminal Visions*, Willan, Cullompton.

Innes, M. & Fielding, N. (2002), "From community to communication policing: 'Signal crimes' and the problem of public reassurance", *Sociological Research Online*, vol. 7, no. 2. Available online at: www. socresonline.org.uk.

Irving, B. & Mackenzie, I. (1989), *Police Interrogation*, Police Foundation, London.

Karmen, A. (2000), *New York Murder Mystery*, New York University Press, New York.

Kay, J. (2003), *The Truth About Markets*, Penguin, London.

Ker Muir Jr, W. (1977), *Police: Streetcorner Politicians*, University of Chicago Press, Chicago, IL.

Lee, M. (1981), "Some structural aspects of police deviance in relations with minority groups", in: Shearing, C. (ed.) *Organisational Police Deviance*, Butterworth, Toronto.

Loader, I. & Mulcahy, A. (2003), *Policing and the Condition of England*, Oxford University Press, Oxford.

Long, M. (2003), "Leadership and performance management", in: Newburn, T. (ed.) *Handbook of Policing*, Willan, Cullompton.

Maguire, M. (2000), "Policing by risks and targets: Some dimensions and implications of intelligence-led social control", *Policing & Society*, Vol. 9, no. 4, pp. 315–337.

Maguire, M. (2003), "Criminal investigation and social control", in: Newburn, T. (ed.) *Handbook of Policing*, Willan, Cullompton.

Manning, P. (1977), *Police Work*, MIT Press, Cambridge, MA.

Marenin, O. (1982), "Parking tickets and class repression", *Contemporary Crises*, Vol. 6, no. 2, pp. 241–266.

McBarnet, D. (1979), "Arrest", in: Holdaway, S. (ed.) *The British Police*, Arnold, London.

McLaughlin, E. & Murji, K. (2001), "Lost connections and new directions: Neo-liberalism, new public managerialism and the 'modernisation' of the British police", in: Stenson, K. & Sullivan, R. (eds) *Crime, Risk and Justice*, Willan, Cullompton.

Miller, J., Bland, N. & Quinton, P. (2000), *The Impact of Stops and Searches on Crime and the Community* (Police Research Paper 127), Home Office, London.

Mills, C.W. (1959), *The Sociological Imagination*, Oxford University Press, New York.

Policing & Society   101

Phillips, C. & Bowling, B. (2002), "Racism, ethnicity, crime and criminal justice", in: Maguire, M., Morgan, R. & Reiner, R. (eds) *The Oxford Handbook of Criminology*, 3rd edn, Oxford University Press, Oxford.

Punch, M. (1979), "The secret social service", in: Holdaway, S. (ed.) *The British Police*, Arnold, London.

Quinton, P., Bland, N. & Miller, J. (2000), *Police Stops, Decision-making and Practice* (Police Research Paper 130), Home Office, London.

Reiner, R. (1989), "The politics of police research", in: Weatheritt, M. (ed.) *Police Research: Some Future Prospects*, Avebury, Aldershot.

Reiner, R. (1992), "Police research in the United Kingdom", in: Morris, N. & Tonry, M. (eds) *Modern Policing*, University of Chicago Press, Chicago, IL.

Reiner, R. (1994), "Policing and the police", in: Maguire, M., Morgan, R. & Reiner, R. (eds) *The Oxford Handbook of Criminology*, Oxford University Press, Oxford.

Reiner, R. (2000a), "Police research", in: King, R. & Wincup, E. (eds) *Doing Research on Crime and Justice*, Oxford University Press, Oxford.

Reiner, R. (2000b), *The Politics of the Police*, 3rd edn, Oxford University Press, Oxford.

Reiner, R. (2000c), "Crime and control in Britain", *Sociology*, Vol. 34, no. 1, pp. 71–94.

Reiner, R. (2006), "Beyond risk: A lament for social democratic criminology", in: Newburn, T. & Rock, P. (eds) *The Politics of Crime Control*, Oxford University Press, Oxford.

Rock, P. (2005), "Chronocentrism and British criminology", *British Journal of Sociology*, Vol. 56, no. 3, pp. 473–491.

Sherman, L. (1992), "Attacking crime: Police and crime control", in: Morris, N. & Tonry, M. (eds) *Modern Policing*, University of Chicago Press, Chicago, IL.

Skolnick, J. (1966), *Justice without Trial*, Wiley, New York.

Smith, D., Small, S. & Gray, J. (1983), *Police and People in London*, PSI, London.

Smith, G. (2004), "What's law got to do with it? Some reflections on the police in light of developments in New York City", in: Burke, R.H. (ed.) *Hard Cop, Soft Cop*, Willan, Cullompton.

Stinchcombe, A. (1963), "Institutions of privacy in the determination of police administrative practice", *American Journal of Sociology*, Vol. 69, no. 2, pp. 150–160.

Tarling, R. & Burrows, J. (1985), "The work of detectives", in: Heal, K., Tarling, R. & Burrows, J. (eds) *Policing Today*, HMSO, London.

Tilly, N. (2003), "Community policing, problem-oriented policing and intelligence-led policing", in: Newburn, T. (ed.) *Handbook of Policing*, Willan, Cullompton.

Walker, N. (2000), *Policing in a Changing Constitutional Order*, Sweet & Maxwell, London.

Wilson, J.Q. (1968), *Varieties of Police Behaviour*, Harvard University Press, Cambridge, MA.

Zedner, L. (forthcoming), "Policing before and after the police" *British Journal of Criminology*.

[8]
New Theories of Policing:
A Social Democratic Critique

Introduction: The Death of Disciplines?

The academic study of policing is just about 50 years old, venerable enough to seem an ancient edifice to most of the growing numbers studying it today but still fairly young by comparison with most disciplines. Yet it has lately been threatened with fundamental paradigm change, perhaps even extinction. In a contribution to a volume of essays exploring 'Criminology and Social Theory' at the turn of the millennium, John Braithwaite explicitly characterized criminology and sociology, the disciplines most closely associated with the study of policing, as crumbling relics, smacking of Shelley's *Ozymandias*. He claimed that 'criminology . . . is destined for decline. Most contributors . . . . Come from the discipline of sociology, which is already in decline. The risk is that in 20 years our collection will be read as a dialogue between a dead and a dying discipline' (Braithwaite, 2000: 223). And we are half-way through the 20-year warning already—so are criminology and the sociology of policing dead men walking? Such terminal pronouncements about the death of particular perspectives always remind me of the well-known 1960s exchange: '"God is dead"—Nietzche: "Nietzche is Dead" —God.'[1] The stock of the neo-liberal analysis and prescriptions that informed Braithwaite's death sentence on criminology, always dubious in my view, has become very

---

[1] 'EpistemeLinks—Philosophy Resources on the Internet' offer a colourful range of mugs and T-shirts bearing this dialogue.

low indeed since credit crunched—although in light of the Rums-feldian warning that stuff happens I am wary of donning the black cap for neo-liberalism.

This paper will review and criticize the attempts in recent years to develop a fundamentally new perspective on policing. It will argue that they misrepresent older perspectives and are mistaken in their characterization of current crises. They arise in part out of a commendable thirst for can-do answers to the manifest problems of order and justice in recent times. But they involve putting faith in market solutions without recognizing their fundamental perils. A lesson of policing history, I will suggest, is that democratic polic-ing can be approximated to only in a context of social, not just liberal—and certainly not neo-liberal—democracy.

The first part of the paper offers a sketch of the new theories, with some critical comments about their formulation, largely derived from the perspectives that the new theories aim to replace. In the conclusion the case will be made for a social democratic analysis of policing.

New Policing Theories: A Critical Synthesis

The common theme of all the new perspectives is what Jones and Newburn (in a pioneering critique of this argument) called the 'transformation thesis' (Jones and Newburn, 2002): that policing has changed so fundamentally since the 1960s that it has trans-muted into a qualitatively different system. In the words of its most influential exponents:

Modern democratic countries like the United States, Britain and Canada have reached a watershed in the evolution of their systems of crime con-trol and law enforcement. Future generations will look back on our era as a time when one system of policing ended and another took its place. (Bayley and Shearing, 1996: 585).

This has further developed into the claim that a new theoretical paradigm is needed to make sense of these developments, replac-ing the concepts of police and policing altogether by a framework based on 'the governance of security' (Johnston and Shearing, 2003).[2] The main exemplar of the new theoretical perspectives on

---

[2] For example, McLaughlin's thorough review of 'the innovative scholarship that has transformed our understanding not only of the defining characteristics of contemporary policing but also its theoretical approaches and methodologies' leads him to claim there is an 'urgent need to rethink the assumptions and registers on which police scholarship have been based' (McLaughlin, 2007: 87).

policing is without doubt the celebrated work of Clifford Shearing and a number of associates, which has most explicitly and enthusiastically argued the case not only for the 'transformation thesis' but for a complete paradigm shift from policing to security governance.[3] There is also a growing body of work advocating a 'new police science', spearheaded by Markus Dubber's acclaimed historical analysis of the 'police power' (Dubber, 2005; Dubber and Valverde, 2006. For an incisive sympathetic critique see Loader and Zedner, 2007), which although it has developed without reference to Shearing *et al* has a common inspiration in Foucault's ideas about governmentality. Richard Ericson and Kevin Haggerty's highly influential account of shifts in policing in the 'risk society' is a third important strand of the new theoretical perspectives, and has been largely incorporated into the wider transformation and paradigm shift theses which are heavily informed by it (Ericson and Haggerty, 1997; Johnston, 2000). Other 'new policing' theses (McLaughlin, 2007) include a variety of discussions about the impact of post- or late-modernity on policing (Reiner, 1992; McLaughlin and Murji, 1999; De Lint, 1999), and Pat O'Malley's claim that policing is now 'post-Keynesian' (O'Malley and Palmer, 1996; O'Malley, 1997).

In Bayley and Shearing's 1996 formulation the transformation thesis rests on two elements: that 'policing is no longer monopolized by the public police, that is, the police created by government', and that 'the public police are going through . . . an identity crisis' (Bayley and Shearing, 1996: reprinted in Newburn, 2005: 714). In recognition of the empirical changes indicated by the first of these transformations, the widely discussed 'pluralization' of policing, it has become normal to refer to 'policing' rather than 'the police' in the titles of books and papers. The 'new police science' explored by Dubber and others is an exception to this terminological trend, speaking of 'police' rather than policing in an explicit harking back to the eighteenth century usage, before the advent of '*the* police' and a narrowing of the word's connotations.

Despite this terminological difference, the 'new police science' has elements in common with the security governance perspective.

---

[3] In addition to the references already given to Bayley and Shearing, 1996, Braithwaite, 2000 and Johnston and Shearing, 2003, there are many other works developing the arguments including Cooley, 2005; Wood and Dupont, 2006; and Wood and Shearing, 2007. Henry and Smith, 2007 is a valuable eclectic collection of essays exploring different interpretations of transformations in policing since the seminal PSI study of London published as Smith, 1983.

144   New Theories of Policing: A Social Democratic Critique

Above all, they share a rejection of what Johnston and Shearing call 'mainstream criminological discourse', said to be 'still preoccupied with issues relating to the administration of security and justice by states' (Johnston and Shearing, 2003: 10). Similarly the 'new police science' castigates 'the trap of twentieth century criminology, which tries to think of policing in isolation from other practices of power' (Neocleous, 2006: 19). In an otherwise sophisticated and scholarly analysis of the 'Theoretical Foundations of the "New Police Science"', Neocleous starts from a caricature of research on policing, that is echoed in much of the new theoretical literature. He speaks of:

the backwater of a very narrowly conceived 'police studies' .... Reduced to the study of crime and law enforcement ... most research on the police eschewed any attempt to make sense of the concept itself or to explore the possible diversity of police powers in terms of either their historical origins or political diversity (Neocleous, 2006: 17).

The main thrust of his essay is to relocate the idea of police within a framework of political economy and broader issues of governance, harking back to the eighteenth century 'police science' that preceded the coming of the modern police. I am entirely in sympathy with this call for a political economy of policing—but I will suggest this grows out of the mainstream of the sociology of the police,[4] *pace* Neocleous' dismissal of this as a 'backwater'. Much more turns on this than a dispute over past scholarship, however, for in their wholesale dismissal of the importance of the empirical sociological research on policing the new theories lose the baby with the backwater.

Theories of policing: the analytic dimensions

A theory of policing has to tackle a number of related questions. In characteristically crisp fashion Lenin famously reduced all political issues to 'Who? Whom?' These certainly are core questions for policing. But elaborating on this crisp couplet I would suggest that

---

[4] During the 1980s the bulk of research on the police became 'sociology *for* the police', increasingly policy-oriented and focused on the immediate concerns of government and police management (Reiner 1989, 1992; Reiner and Newburn, 2006). But much policy-oriented work was critical and has contributed to sociological understanding of policing, for example the Home Office evaluations of the Police and Criminal Evidence Act 1984 (summarized in Brown, 1997).

theorizations of policing must include analysis of the following eight dimensions at least:

1. What is policing?
2. Who is involved in policing?
3. What do they actually do?
4. What are the means and powers of policing?
5. What social functions do they achieve?
6. How does policing impact on different groups?
7. By whom are the police themselves policed, by what means and to what ends?
8. How can the developing purposes and practices of policing be understood?

The new policing theorists' answers to these questions are of course diverse, complex and evolving. Nonetheless they can be ideal—typically represented as follows.

What is policing?

As indicated earlier, the main plank of the transformation thesis is the supposed end of the state monopoly of policing ie its principal concern is *who* does policing. The seminal texts are surprisingly coy or bland about the prior theoretical issue of defining policing, although they are clear—but wrong! —about what policing *was* pre-transformation and in the reviled traditional police studies. It is common ground that policing (an activity) must be distinguished from the police (a specific type of institution[5]). As I have put it elsewhere:

'Police' refers to a particular kind of social institution, while 'policing' implies a set of processes with specific social functions. 'Police' are not found in every society, and police organizations and personnel can have a variety of shifting forms. 'Policing', however, is arguably a necessity in any social order, which may be carried out by a number of different processes and institutional arrangements. A state-organized specialist 'police' organization of the modern kind is only one example of policing. (Reiner, 2000: 1–2).

Defining the specificity of policing is more problematic. Two kinds of definition can be distinguished: functional and tactical. Most common attempts to define policing are functional—what policing

---

[5] Or in the Dubber analysis a particular type of power, contrasted with liberal legalism (Dubber, 2005).

146   New Theories of Policing: A Social Democratic Critique

achieves, or rather, is supposed to achieve. This is largely true of the new theories.

We are interested in all explicit efforts to create visible agents of crime control, whether by government or by non-governmental institutions. So we are dealing with polic*ing*, not just *police*. At the same time, we say *explicit* attempts to create policing institutions so as not to extend our discussion to all the informal agencies that societies rely on to maintain order . . . So the scope of our discussion is bigger than the breadbox of the police but smaller than the elephant of social control. Our focus is on the self-conscious processes whereby societies designate and authorize people to create public safety. (Bayley and Shearing, 1996 in Newburn, 2005: 715–6).

Thus policing is defined by a variety of intended functions: crime control, order maintenance, public safety. Somewhat surprisingly, the reconceptualization of policing as security governance does not change this much:

In this book when we talk of the governance of security we will be referring, in particular, to programmes for promoting peace in the face of threats (either realized or anticipated) that arise from collective life rather than from non-human sources. . . that have their origin in human intentions and actions (Johnston and Shearing, 2003: 9).

Such functional definitions of policing are problematic because they have little fit with what police (public or private) actually do or can do. As the new theorists (and many other researchers) have shown in their empirical work, police are called upon to deal with many tasks other than crime or disorder, and they can make little contribution to crime control or social peace—however effective they are—because the threats to these are shaped by larger political, economic, social and cultural forces beyond their reach (Shearing, 1984; Bayley, 1985: 120–7, 1994: 29–41; Johnston, 2000: ch 3; Reiner, 2000: ch 4). It is the 'elephant' of social control rather than the 'breadbox' of policing agencies which accomplishes the functions attributed to policing (in so far as they are met at all). To paraphrase Durkheim's epigram about the contract, 'not all that is policing lies in the police'. (Reiner, 2000: xi). This is because: 'The sources of order lie outside the ambit of the police, in the political economy and culture of a society. To the extent that these provide most people with meaningful and rewarding lives, conflict, crime, and disorder will be relatively infrequent. Subtle, informal social controls, and policing processes embedded in other institutions' do the heavy work of policing (*ibid*). The 'breadbox' of overt policing

New Policing Theories: A Critical Synthesis   147

agencies is important in its impact on many people's lives, but its contribution to overall social order and peace is symbolic rather than instrumental (Manning, 1977).

The functionalist definitions also bracket out a key aspect of policing—that it deals with conflict and hence has a perpetual Janus-face, helping some by controlling others. Thus one party's functional policing may be another's repression. The order that the police are charged to protect always has a double aspect. *General* order, the requirements of any coordinated and complex civilization, is conceptually distinct from but inextricably intertwined with *particular* order—specific patterns of inequality and dominance. Policing deals simultaneously with 'parking tickets and class repression' (Marenin, 1982), and it is this tension that bedevils attempts to regulate policing (Walker, 2000). This is glossed over by talking, as the above definitions do, of 'societies', as opposed to dominant social powers (democratic or otherwise), authorizing policing.

It is thus problematic to define policing mainly in terms of supposed functions. A more satisfactory alternative analysis identifies tactics or capacities rather than functions as specifying the distinctive character of policing (Klockars, 1985), as Egon Bittner argued some 40 years ago. Police are called upon routinely to perform a bewildering miscellany of tasks, from controlling traffic to controlling terrorism (Bittner, 1970, 1974). The common feature of the tasks that come to be seen as police work is not that they are aspects of a particular social function, whether depicted as crime control, social service, order maintenance, or political repression. Rather it is that they all involve 'something that ought not to be happening and about which someone had better do something now!' (Bittner, 1974: 30). In other words, most policing tasks arise in emergencies, usually with an element of at least potential social conflict.[6] The police may invoke their legal powers to handle the situation, but more commonly they resort to a variety of ways and means, primarily verbal. But underlying policing tactics for consensual peace-keeping is their bottom-line power to wield sanctions and constraints, ultimately the use of legitimate force (Jones, 2007). 'A benign bobby ... still brings to the situation a uniform, a truncheon,

---

[6] Strangely the thought-provoking recent attempt by Rikagos to develop a typology of policing based on different police labour activities, omits responding to emergencies from the account altogether, although in quantitative terms, and in Bittner's persuasive theoretical analysis, it is the heart of the matter (Rikagos, 2005).

148   New Theories of Policing: A Social Democratic Critique

and a battery of resource charges . . . which can be employed when appeasement fails and fists start flying' (Punch, 1979b: 116).

The distinctiveness of the police lies not in their performance of a specific social function but in being the specialist repositories for the state's symbolic monopolization of legitimate force in its territory. This should not be construed to imply that all policing is about the use of force. On the contrary, 'good' policing can be seen as the craft of handling trouble without resort to coercion, usually by skilful verbal tactics (Muir, 1977; Bayley and Bittner, 1984).

Nor are the police the only people who can use legitimate force. This remains the right (and in some circumstances the moral duty) of every citizen. There are many occupations in which the potential for the legitimate use of force may arise with a fair degree of frequency, most obviously in the case of private security officers, although their main legal police powers are only those of the private citizen (Button, 2007, 2008: 177–9[7]). Legitimate force may also regularly need to be wielded by people not exercising a primarily policing role, for example workers in the health or social services handling disturbed patients, or public transport staff who may have to deal with disorder. However, they are not 'equipped, entitled and required to deal with every exigency in which force may have to be used' as specialist police are (Bittner, 1974: 35). Indeed, other workers are likely to 'call the cops' at the earliest opportunity in troublesome situations, and use legitimate force themselves only as an immediate emergency measure in the interim.

What agencies and agents are involved in policing?

As the above suggests, many other agents and agencies can and do perform policing tasks. Policing may be done by professionals employed by the state in an organization with an omnibus policing mandate—the archetypal modern idea of the police—or by state agencies with primarily other purposes (like the Atomic Energy Authority Police, parks constabularies, the British Transport Police, and other 'hybrid' policing bodies; see Johnston, 1992: ch 6). Police may be professionals employed by specialist private policing firms (contract security) or security personnel hired by

---

[7] The Police Reform Act 2002 does establish Community Safety Accreditation Schemes by which private security officers could be given some policing powers (issuing fixed penalty notices for minor offences or antisocial behaviour cf Crawford and Lister, 2004; Crawford, 2006: 116–7).

an organization whose main business is something else (in-house security; see Shearing and Stenning, 1987a; South, 1988; Johnston, 1992, 2007; Jones and Newburn, 1998, 2006; Michael, 1999; Forst and Manning, 1999; Loader, 1999; Button, 2002, 2007, 2008; Wakefield, 2003; Loader and Walker, 2007; Crawford, 2008; Zedner, 2009: ch 5). Patrol may be carried out by bodies without the full status, powers, equipment or training of the core state police, such as Police Community Support Officers (Crawford *et al*, 2005; Johnston, 2008). Policing functions may also be performed by citizens in a voluntary capacity within state police organizations (like the Special Constabulary), in association with the state police (like Neighbourhood Watch schemes), or in completely independent bodies (like the Guardian Angels, and the many vigilante bodies which have flourished at many times and places). Policing functions may be carried out by state bodies with other prime functions, like the army in Northern Ireland, or by employees (state or private) as an adjunct of their main job (like concierges, bus conductors, or shop assistants, *inter alios* guarding against theft). Policing may be carried out by technology, such as CCTV cameras or listening devices (Norris and Armstrong, 1999; Sheptycki, 2000a; Goold, 2004, 2009). Policing may be designed into the architecture and furniture of streets and buildings, as epitomized by Mike Davis's celebrated example of the bum-proof bench (Davis, 1990; Jones, 2007). It is increasingly carried out by transnational agencies (Sheptycki, 2000b, 2007; Walker, 2008; Bowling, 2009).

All these policing strategies are proliferating today, even though it is only the state agency with the omnibus mandate of order maintenance that is still popularly understood by the label 'the police'. The question is whether the new theories are correct in asserting that the shift away from state policing towards private, citizen, and transnational forms amounts to a fundamental and qualitative transformation. This claim has been subject to some cogent critiques. Although the personnel employed by private security have indeed grown to be more numerous than public constabularies in many countries (Button: 5–6), they were already coming close in the supposed heyday of state policing in the post-war decades (Jones and Newburn, 2002). Moreover part of the increase in private security numbers occurred because corporations have increasingly substituted contract for in-house security thus boosting the private security employment statistics. More broadly, Jones and Newburn show that the growth of private security represents

150   New Theories of Policing: A Social Democratic Critique

an increasing formalization of social control as the number of employees with *secondary* but still substantial security functions (bus and rail conductors and inspectors, park-keepers, roundsmen, etc has declined sharply (*op cit*: Table 41.1). This directly contradicts the new theorists' claim that such secondary security functions have proliferated (Johnston and Shearing, 2003: 126). Some forms of citizen auxiliary police like the Special Constabulary have declined not increased in numbers (Jones and Newburn, 2002 in Newburn, 2005: 741–2), though the recent introduction and rapid proliferation of Police Community Support Officers indicates the diversity of the 'extended policing family'. The mushrooming of private security performing an increasing array of functions, and the internal diversification of state policing, certainly are significant developments, but what is debatable is whether they amount to a qualitatively new model of policing requiring an entirely new analytic paradigm (cf the arguments in Johnston, 2007; Shearing, 2007 versus Newburn, 2007; Jones, 2007).

The state has never had a monopoly of security arrangements (Zedner, 2006), even though in stable liberal democracies it has claimed control over *legitimate* force—but there is no evidence that this domination of *legitimacy* is under challenge. The new theorists claim that the status and image of private security has been transformed, not just their quantitative presence (Bayley and Shearing, 1996 in Newburn, 2005: 716–7). Whilst they are certainly more in demand it is far from clear that they have become viewed more positively by the mass of the public. It is noteworthy that until the Second World War in popular fiction and entertainment the public police hardly figured as heroic characters, and the protagonists of crime stories were private sleuths of various kinds (from the cerebral confreres of Sherlock Holmes and Poirot to the hard-boiled gumshoes depicted by Hammett and Chandler). Since World War II, and especially since the 1960s, when the new theorists claim the public police monopoly has come under increasing challenge, public police heroes have come to dominate popular culture (Reiner, 2008: 320, 326). Private police have become marginalized in popular culture, scarcely appearing except as residual and unheroic characters, like the brutal security guards of *Pulp Fiction* and the comic *Paul Blart Mall Cop*. Although for primarily economic reasons it has been government policy to develop civilianization and auxiliaries like the Police Community Support Officers (PCSOs), these do not threaten the hold over the mainstream 'sworn' constables in the public imagination. Indeed the popular media have regularly reviled PCSOs ('Blunkett's Bobbies') and similar initiatives. Whilst there has undoubtedly been a pluralization of policing in recent decades, in neither substance nor symbolism does it amount to qualitative transformation.

What do police actually do?

One of the earliest findings of sociological research on policing, replicated time and time again over the last 50 years, is that—contrary to popular images—most police work does not involve crime or at any rate law enforcement. Police routinely underenforce the law, using their discretion to deal with incidents in a variety of other 'peace-keeping' ways even if an offence may have been committed. Discretion may be operated in a variety of discriminatory or other controversial ways, although it may often be the consensually wise way to deal with troubles. But although the way discretion is exercised may often be problematic, it is inevitable and necessary, if only for pragmatic reasons of the limited capacity of the criminal justice system. Calls to the police for help only involve clear references to crime in a minority of cases, although the exact proportion varies between places, over time, and above all according to different definitions of the categories and research methodologies. What was once commonly referred to by researchers in the 1960s and 70s as 'service' calls, a category that includes a high proportion of 'domestic' and other disputes, have come to be redefined as largely order maintenance and potential crimes. Nonetheless, what is beyond dispute is that most policing does not involve any use of their law enforcement powers. The police may be the normal gateway to the criminal justice process but it is one they open relatively seldom.

Altogether the police are marginal to the control of crime and the maintenance of order, and always have been. Only a tiny fraction of crimes ever come to their attention or are recorded by them, and the overwhelming majority of these are not cleared up (apart from serious violent offences like homicide).[8] This does not mean

---

[8] The poor success of police in clearing up crime is adduced by Bayley and Shearing as a major failing of the old arrangements (Bayley and Shearing, 1996 in Newburn 2005: 717). They cite data showing that 'regrettably few villains are caught in relation to crimes committed' and even fewer punished. The figures cited are of recorded crimes—we simply do not know how many more crimes are actually committed (Reiner, 2007: ch 3), but this of course reinforces their conclusion that the police 'scarecrow has grown tattered'. What is debatable is whether their solutions would help matters.

152   New Theories of Policing: A Social Democratic Critique

that the police do not play a useful role in managing the crimes that they do deal with, nor that they could not boost their performance by exploring new tactics as they have done in recent years. But seeing the police as major players in crime control is an 'impossible mandate', and their primary contribution is and remains symbolic not instrumental (Manning, 1977, 2003).

The basic reason for this is the huge array of potential offences and offenders relative to any conceivable resources for policing. This is well encapsulated in two much quoted official calculations: (a) 'A patrolling policeman in London could expect to pass within 100 yards of a burglary in progress roughly once every eight years—but not necessarily to catch the burglar or even realize that the crime was taking place'. (Clarke and Hough, 1984: 7); (b) on current police strengths, a patrolling officer typically covers an area containing: 18,000 inhabitants, 7,500 houses, 23 pubs, 9 schools, 140 miles of pavement, 85 acres of parks or open space, and 77 miles of road (Audit Commission, 1996). The toughest zero-tolerance or the smartest intelligence-led approaches cannot do more than chip away at the edges of this sea of potential targets.

The marginality of crime to policing and policing to crime was a staple conclusion of the sociology of the police, and several new theorists themselves contributed seminal research studies confirming it (Ericson, 1982; Shearing, 1984; Bayley, 1985, 1994). So it is somewhat disconcerting to find statements like 'The risk-communication view of policing we are advancing here obviously decenters the criminal law and criminal justice aspects of police work' (Ericson and Haggerty, 2002 in Newburn, 2005: 553)—as if it had formerly been central. Or 'Police are no longer the primary crime-deterrent presence in society' (Bayley and Shearing, 1996 in Newburn, 2005: 717)—as if they ever had been, outside media made mythology and police hucksterism.

The transformation thesis juxtaposes contemporary policing forms with a depiction of the past not in terms of its reality but its mythical representation, which the theorists' earlier empirical work had done much to deconstruct. This is a fascinating example of what Paul Rock has called 'chronocentrism' in criminology:

[the] doctrine that what is current must somehow be superior to what went before, that ideas, scholars and scholarship inevitably become stale and discredited over time . . . [so that] criminology has proceeded in a series of fits . . . a recurrence of new beginnings; and a quest for the seemingly distinctive (Rock, 2005: 473–4).

As Freud taught long ago in *The Psychopathology of Everyday Life*, memory lapses are seldom innocent or meaningless. The misrepresentation of past policing as primarily concerned with crime fighting is linked to a particular account of the supposedly contrasting means and powers of policing before and after the postulated transformation.

What are the means and powers of policing?

A pivotal theme of the new policing theorists is that the alleged change in responsibility for crime, order, and security from the public police alone to the pluralized marketplace of contemporary policing is linked to a fundamental and welcome shift in style, programmes, and practices. 'It seems reasonable to conclude . . . that pluralising has made communities safer.' (Bayley and Shearing, 1996 in Newburn, 2005: 720).

One argument adduced for this is quantitative: pluralization has been associated not only with a huge expansion of private security personnel, public police auxiliaries and a 'responsibilized' citizenry, but a considerable (albeit proportionately slower) growth of public police officers (*ibid*; Johnston, 2007: 28–9; Newburn, 2007: 232). This is assumed to enhance public safety in itself, despite the huge volume of research questioning the impact of increasing police numbers on crime (Bayley, 1994, 1998; Reiner, 2000: 115–124). But their main line of argument concerns alleged qualitative changes in policing resulting from pluralization. This thesis rests primarily on differences in technique and style between private and public police.

The core of the new policing perspective is that pluralization represents a qualitative and desirable shift because state policing embodies a 'punishment mentality and coercive technologies', whilst corporate security rests on 'the risk paradigm' (Johnston and Shearing, 2003: chs 3, 6). They say that:

> private police emphasise the logic of security, while public police emphasise the logic of justice. The major purpose of private security is to reduce the risk of crime by taking preventive actions; the major purpose of the public police is to deter crime by catching and punishing criminals. (Bayley and Shearing, 1996 in Newburn, 2005: 721).

The supposedly more effective, efficient and benign private corporate style is also seen as a model that is positively transforming public police, both in terms of internal governance under the

154   New Theories of Policing: A Social Democratic Critique

influence of the 'New Public Management' and operating strategies through the adoption of innovative tactics such as community,
risk and problem-oriented policing (O'Malley, 1997; Johnston,
2000: chs 4, 5, 10; McLaughlin, 2007: ch 4). The paradox, they
claim, is that Anglo-American public policing was originally established after 1829 on a Peelian model with an explicit preventive,
forward-looking philosophy, but over time has degenerated into a
reactive, coercive, punitive justice mentality (Johnston and Shearing,
2003: 15). It would now benefit from further moves restoring the
private model that Peelian policing displaced.[9]

This analysis involves some mischaracterization of the techniques, programmes, and resources of both old and new policing.
As argued above, the portrayal of policing in the past as primarily
concerned with crime is questioned by a host of research evidence.
Although the defining feature of state policing is the symbolic
monopolization of legitimate force, the tendency of police was to
minimize actual use of force, for principled and pragmatic reasons,
although the *abuse* of force—particularly against those marginal
and powerless groups that have aptly been called 'police property'
(Lee, 1983)—has also been a perennial problem. Nonetheless the
predominant style of policing observed in ethnographies of policing was peace-keeping and 'secret social service' (Punch, 1979).
The prevailing analysis emphasized that the police were *not* themselves responsible for the effective containment of crime and disorder, indeed that this would be an 'impossible mandate' (Manning,
1977). Security, crime control, and order maintenance depended
on a complex network of informal social, economic, and cultural
controls of which the police were only one part, primarily important symbolically rather than instrumentally (Banton, 1964; Cain,
1973; Walker, 1996; Loader, 1997; Reiner, 2000, 2008; Loader and
Mulcahy, 2003). This is uncannily prescient of the image of 'nodal
governance' ('that governance takes place through nodes and nodal
arrangements . . . the police constitute one node amongst many
nodes engaged in governance of security' (Shearing, 2007: 252),

---

[9] The way that current transformations are in many ways a reversion to the policing landscape pre-Peel has been pointed out by several analysts, notably Zedner
(2006), who mainly regard this as problematic in terms of the public good. This was
the stance taken also by the first generation of writers on the rebirth of public policing,
including some of the new theorists themselves (Spitzer and Scull, 1977; Shearing
and Stenning, 1983; South, 1988; Rawlings, 1991; Johnston, 1991, 1992).

postulated as a rebuttal of the old idea that 'policing belongs to the police' (*ibid*). The new theorists promote this as the image of the *future* (although their notion of nodal governance is seen as a network of explicit security providers, not general processes conducive to social peace such as the maintenance of full-employment or stable families and communities with cultural capital cf Johnston, 2007: 32–3). But the idea of the police as one 'node' of security amongst many is a well trodden theme of the sociology of policing from its beginnings.

If the new theorists exaggerate the element of crime control by the public police pre-transformation, they also minimize the coercion implicit in their own accounts of the practices of private security. It is true that private police (and indeed police auxiliaries like the PCSOs) generally lack the special police powers and the arms available to public police (Stenning, 2000; Button, 2007), although this is gradually changing (Crawford, 2006: 114–7). But this does not mean that their capacity to control the areas they are responsible for is based on a superior mentality of risk analysis and intelligent problem-solving. Certainly the individual calibre of security officers in terms of selection and training is far below the public police (Michael, 2002, Button, 2007, 2008, ch 4). Against this, however, corporate security has enormous advantages stemming from the powers of private property ownership, as well as a much narrower remit. The new theorists have illuminated the recent trajectory of social control enormously by their account of the huge expansion of 'mass private property' (Shearing and Stenning, 1983, 1987b), areas which are legally private but function largely as public spaces accessible to many people, such as shopping malls, 'gated' residential estates, entertainment complexes, theme parks, industrial or commercial estates.[10] They are right to emphasize that the extent of crime and disorder in such places is generally low (although in part this may be because it is not reported to or recorded by police). But their accounts themselves indicate the extent to which such internal peace results in large measure from exclusive tactics depending ultimately on forms of coercion. The key point is that the owners of mass private property, and the security officers who are their agents, enjoy the power to exclude

---

[10] These are expanding in significance in most parts of the world although there is considerable variation in the extent to which countries even begin to approximate to the USA in this regard (Jones and Newburn, 1999).

156   New Theories of Policing: A Social Democratic Critique

without the legal hurdle of reasonable suspicion (Crawford, 2006: 124–34; Jones, 2007: 848–9). As a condition of entry they can and frequently do require searches and checks that are far more intrusive and often discriminatory than their controversial counterparts exercised by the public police on the streets, and without even the minimal degree of accountability to law that the latter are circumscribed by. Potential sources of trouble and conflict can be swept out—possibly onto the public streets (a burgle-my-neighbour tactic that means that enhanced private security may directly reduce public safety). The nodal theorists themselves speak of such areas as 'security bubbles'. But as they depend largely on the exclusivity provided by the power of property and the purse, the bubbles vary in scope and desirability. They are positional goods, stretching from champagne bubbles through beer bubbles to toxic waste bubbles.

Shearing and Stenning's fascinating and rightly celebrated analysis of Disney World as the exemplar of future security itself shows clearly the importance of exclusion in safeguarding the tranquillity of that hedonistic idyll. Exclusion derives from the cost of entry, its physical seclusion, a myriad of devices inscribed into its architecture and routines, and when these fail, the power of the guards in the Mickey Mouse costumes to expel the deviant (as in the anecdote about the threat to send away the researcher's young daughter unless she complied with the rule prohibiting going barefoot). The similar 'Club Med' example given by Johnston and Shearing (*op cit*: 9) makes explicit that the security of such enclaves is a 'club good' depending on the barring of all but a privileged few (Hope, 2000; Crawford, 2006). The familiar cliché of the iron fist in the velvet glove applies to private security at least as much as to public policing, belying the purported sharp contrast between mentalities and practices. The apparently superior success of corporate security derives from its power to coerce compliance as a condition of being in the bubble, as well as its much narrower remit: to maximize the bottom-line of profitability, not any notions of public good. The excluded are of no concern to them, unlike the way they are, at least in principle and potentially in practice, for public police.

What social functions do they achieve?

To the new theorists the bottom-line is plain: 'Both quantitatively and qualitatively, then, the pluralising of policing should increase public safety.' This claim rests on two dubious assumptions: that increasing numbers of policing agents, and their increasing deployment in forward-looking, risk-based styles, results in greater public safety. As argued earlier, increasing police numbers by itself is unlikely to have much impact on crime levels.[11]

The more plausible aspect of the case is that qualitative changes in strategy may increase public safety. The popular image of policing is what I have called 'police fetishism', that they are the vital 'functional prerequisite of social order so that without a police force chaos would ensue' (Reiner, 2000: 1). This myth has been constructed over the last two centuries by a complex of cultural processes, not least campaigning by the police themselves and the endless reproduction in the media of story-lines depicting heroic police as 'the thin blue line' battling (usually successfully) to protect or restore order and justice (McLaughlin and Murji, 1998; Reiner, 2000, 2008; Loader and Mulcahy, 2003; McLaughlin, 2007: ch 1). But for reasons already indicated earlier, the police are marginal to the control of crime and disorder. Public peace and security are primarily a function of deeper processes in political economy and culture. This does not mean, however, that strategic changes in police tactics cannot have a crime reducing effect, and there are many such claims.

Most notably, the police have, of course, popularly been credited with the huge drop in crime in New York City in the 1990s, not

---

[11] In an econometric analysis of falling crime in the USA that became famous as part of his best-selling book *Freakanomics* Steven Levitt attributed 'between one-fifth and one-tenth of the overall decline in crime' to a 14% increase in (public) police per capita in the 1990s (Levitt, 2004: 176–7). But no causal mechanisms are suggested for why this increase—in the absence of qualitative changes in tactics which Levitt explicitly dismisses—could have this result, contradicting decades of earlier findings (Reiner, 2007: 156–8). It is plausible that at the extremes—no police at all, or saturation policing such as during terror alerts—police numbers could affect crime levels. The popular gut feeling that if only there was a police officer at every doorstep crime would disappear (however undesirable and indeed impossible such omnipresent policing might be) is supported by recent econometric studies showing reductions of routine crime during saturation policing in the wake of terrorist attacks or alarms (Di Tella and Schargrodsky, 2004; Klick and Tabarrok, 2005; Draca, Machin, and Witt, 2008). Fascinating as the recent terrorism policing results are it is problematic to extrapolate from the limited very sharp visible increases in police that they analyse to the consequences of the much more modest variations in cover that are economically and politically feasible as long-run levels. The notion that there is a calculable elasticity of crime rates in relation to changes in police numbers that is constant at all levels from zero police to saturation, including the rather thin cover that is the normal experience, is dubious. It is hard to see why relatively marginal changes in numbers alone, scarcely discernible to most people, could have much effect.

158   New Theories of Policing: A Social Democratic Critique

least because they have not been shy to claim the credit.[12] There has, however, been much debate about the precise contribution made by policing to the crime drop of the 1990s. Many analysts point out that the timing of the drop did not tally with the policing changes, that substantial (although smaller) crime reductions were achieved in many parts of the USA and the rest of the world that had not adopted similar policing tactics, and that other economic, social and criminal justice changes also played a large part[13] (Bowling, 1999; Karmen, 2000; Levitt, 2004; Zimring, 2007).

The crucial problem with traditional policing tactics ('random' uniform patrol and after-the-event investigation) is that they are spread too thinly over the multitude of potential victims and offenders to be able to achieve much preventive cover or detection. The innovative tactics that have produced some improvements in police performance are directed at remedying aspect(s) of this. 'Smart', intelligence-led analysis helps identify and target crime hot spots and prolific offenders. 'Problem-solving' may identify and remove risks. 'Community policing' may improve the flow of information and public cooperation that is crucial for investigation. 'Zero tolerance' order maintenance blitzes can create false impressions of police omnipresence and omnipotence that may deter potential offenders and reassure others. All these are examples of the kind of risk-oriented strategies that the new policing theorists attribute to the influence of the commercial private security industry. 'Through community policing and order-maintenance policing, the public police are developing strategies for reducing disorder and the opportunities for crime that are similar to the practices readily accepted by commercial and informal communities from private police' (Bayley and Shearing, 1996 in Newburn, 2005: 721). But they are more plausibly interpreted as formalizations of tactics that were deeply engrained in traditional public policing. Cultivating public cooperation was central to the Peelian model from the outset, especially because of the deep and wide hostility to the creation of the New Police in 1829, and many

[12] 'Crime is down, blame the police' wrote ex-NYPD Chief Bratton, whose 1998 memoirs bear the modest title *Turnaround: How America's Top Cop Reversed the Crime Epidemic* (Bratton, 1998a and b).

[13] There is also some dispute about the relative importance of the various policing changes—'zero tolerance', Compstat, increasing numbers for example—as well as their influence elsewhere (Weisburd *et al*, 2003; Moore, 2003; Dixon and Maher, 2005; Jones and Newburn, 2007).

measures were adopted to secure consent (Reiner, 2000: ch 2). Community policing, spreading out from John Alderson's pioneering vision in Devon and Cornwall in the 1970s to become a worldwide vogue, was a bid to recapture the popular support that had been built up between the mid-nineteenth and twentieth centuries but was threatened by social and economic change (Brogden, 1999; Brogden and Nijhar, 2005; Savage, 2007: 75–8, 131–5). The only sense in which it was inspired by private sector examples is that it has parallels with the heritage industry developing in the same period as a response to similar stresses. Its consumerist phase, at its height in the early 90s as 'businesslike' management began to be the new Gospel and even prisoners were rebranded as 'customers', was modelled on the private sector but has had scant positive results. The careful cultivation and use of information was a staple tool, exemplified in studies of criminal investigation before and after the creation of the New Police (eg Styles, 1982, 1983; Rock, 1983; Davey, 1983; Maguire and Norris, 1992; Maguire and John, 1996; Norris and Dunnighan, 2000). Appraising situations and people to assess risk and danger was a repeatedly noted trope of traditional police culture (Banton, 1964; Skolnick, 1966). These are not aspects of a new risk-oriented, actuarial mentality, although they are of course greatly enhanced by recent technological developments (Tilley, 2008; Cope, 2008; Maguire, 2008).

What has undoubtedly been imported from private sector models, largely but not only at the behest of neo-liberal governments, is the 'New Public Management' (NPM) with its focus on central government 'ruling at a distance' by devolving responsibility to local levels of service delivery, 'steering' the local 'rowers' by target-setting, performance measurement, league tables, competition, 'best value', and financial and other instrumental sanctions. The new police theorists take over an enthusiasm for these tactics from the neo-liberal belief that private enterprise and market models work best, and attribute the improvements in tactics largely to NPM pressures (O'Malley, 1997 in Newburn, 2005: 701–10; Johnston and Shearing, 2003: ch 5; McLaughlin, 2007: 96–7, 182–7). But such faith is largely *a priori*, with little evidence that the new managerial models have the intended benign effects on practice, except in cases where there were particular pathologies in unequivocally underperforming units (which may include the NYPD before the reforms of the 90s). Indeed, even right-of-centre, market-oriented think-tanks have questioned the way NPM has

160   New Theories of Policing: A Social Democratic Critique

been implemented, with the likelihood of perverse incentives that may direct police activity away from the important but hard to the trivial but achievable (Loveday, McClory, and Lockhart, 2007: 16–19).

The claim that pluralization improves the achievement of policing functions is fundamentally questionable, however, not only empirically but as a category error. It presupposes that policing is best thought of in terms of the achievement of macro-functions such as crime control, law enforcement, maintaining public order and security. The problems are not only the thorny practical ones of measurement of the achievement of such functions and identifying the policing contribution towards this. As suggested earlier, it misidentifies the bulk of policing activity which is not related directly to any of these supposed functions but is an emergency response to a myriad of problems for which policing can at best provide only an interim solution. Tank Waddington expressed this most succinctly: 'The police are the social equivalent of the AA or RAC patrolmen, who intervene when things go unpredictably wrong and secure a provisional solution.' (Waddington, 1983: 34). To switch to a medical metaphor, they are analogous to paramedics or A and E doctors, delivering first-aid relief but generally unable to cure the basic problems.[14] Their contribution may well be enhanced by the kind of partnerships with other local agencies that are mandated by the Crime and Disorder Act 1998, which the new theorists celebrate rightly at least in principle as an illustration of the nodal governance mentality (Johnston and Shearing, 2003: ch7, McLaughlin, 2007: 126–30). But even this is often unlikely to be able to tackle the root causes of problems which lie outside the locality and require central government or even transnational support (such as unemployment, crunched credit to aid local enterprise, or public finance to develop infrastructure). This is a major lacuna of the nodal vision, indicating a necessary role for the state (Loader and Walker, 2001, 2006, 2007; Goldsmith, 2003; Marks and Goldsmith, 2006; Jones 2007, 859–61; Zedner, 2009: 161–7).

Policing cannot be seen primarily as satisfying grand social functions but rather as a Sisyphean labour of continuous partial

---

[14] 'Crime isn't a disease, it's a symptom. Cops are like a doctor that gives you aspirin for a brain tumour' as Raymond Chandler put it in his novel *The Long Goodbye*.

emergency alleviation of recurring problems. They should be judged by the quality of interaction in their case-work interventions, rather than by the results, by the process not the product, presenting thorny problems of assessment and accountability (Reiner, 1998). The statistical measures of performance that are the stock-in-trade of NPM and 'businesslike' models may be useful diagnostic tools, prompting questions about comparative results and reflexive analysis of why one sector's results are less favourable than a comparator's. But used as sanctions they are likely to lead to dissimulation of practices, distortion of statistics, and counterproductive diversion of activity to the measurable and easily achievable (Hough, 2007). To think of policing as capable of achieving the grand functions of order and security is a dangerous category error, but they can and often do bring balm to desperate suffering.

How does policing impact on different groups?

The above suggests that policing is indeed a socially valuable activity, although not in the way it is usually conceived as the achievement of a grand function like social peace. This is regularly vitiated, however, by inequality, injustice, and discrimination in the way policing impacts on different groups. Groups that are low in power and status, such as the poor and unemployed, ethnic minorities, young men (and underclass young women), gays and lesbians, become 'police property' (Lee, 1983), disproportionately likely to be treated as suspects at each stage of the criminal justice process: stop/search, arrest, detention, charge, prosecution (Reiner, 2000: 124–37; Bowling and Phillips, 2002; Fitzgerald et al, 2002; Bowling, Parmar, and Phillips, 2008; Heidensohn, 2008). This arises for a variety of reasons. The kinds of crime that the police in practice focus on: volume property offences, violence and disorder in public space, are more likely to be perpetrated by young, poor men (and certain ethnic minorities are disproportionately poor). These groups are more likely to spend time in public spaces, lacking the wherewithal to enter mass private property citadels of consumption. So they are more 'available' to become targets of suspicion (Waddington, Stenson, and Don, 2004). They are likely to fit stereotypes of suspiciousness, and have less power to challenge successfully (and hence deter) coercive police actions. These same groups are also disproportionately likely to be victimized by crime, and tend to receive less satisfactory police treatment (Bowling, 1999; Heidensohn and

162   New Theories of Policing: A Social Democratic Critique

Gelsthorpe, 2007; Phillips and Bowling, 2007; Hoyle and Zedner, 2007). They are also less often recruited into the police, and have often suffered discrimination internally in career terms (Brown and Heidensohn, 2000; Holdaway and Barron, 1997).

Discrimination and disparity in the treatment of different groups is a perennial problem of policing. They are violations of the public service mandate of the police, and contradict the principle of equality before the law, a vital element of notions of legality. The revelation of discrimination usually creates a major scandal, setting in train efforts to reform the police (Foster, Newburn, and Souhami, 2005; Savage, 2007: ch 1; McLaughlin, 2007: chs 6, 8). It is a violation of the public service mandate of the police, and a contradiction of the principle of equality before the law, a vital element of notions of legality.

This is in sharp contrast to private policing. Inequality of treatment and access is a barnacle on the boat of *soi disant* public service policing. But it is the hull of the corporate policing vessel. Private security firms have duties to their shareholders and to those they contract to provide services to. The consequences of their activities to other parties—those they police, and the public at large—are not even a formal concern of theirs. As Zedner argues cogently:

Although the practice of state policing never fulfilled its collectivist pretensions, it did profess, at least, to provide a public service available to all. To the extent that it failed to fulfil this idea, as fail it did, its failing could be measured, criticized and sanctioned. Private providers make no such claim but avowedly seek to protect the partisan interests (whether individual, communal or commercial) of those who pay. No surprise here: it is central to the logic of market societies that goods be distributed not according to need, but to the ability of the consumer to buy. (Zedner, 2006: 92).

The new policing theorists themselves have demonstrated how the growth of mass private property and corporate security creates security fortresses separated sharply from the surrounding society, and dubbed this a 'new feudalism' (Shearing and Stenning, 1983). This analysis of growing social division originally had sinister and critical tones, but as the transformation thesis has developed it has come to be represented positively as 'nodal governance', with the private sector supposedly setting an example to the public police with its actuarial mentality of risk prevention. But as argued above, the peace of security bubbles is achieved through exclusionary and coercive tactics derived from the powers of property ownership, rather than any superiority of personnel or strategy. Their success derives directly from their exclusive status as positional goods. As with private education or health, inequality of provision is the key to their desirability and functioning.

The new theorists recognize the problem of equity, and explore the possibilities of levelling-up security provision. They recognize difficulties in increasing the provision of police to poorer areas, fundamentally changing their strategy to a more effective one or communal self-help alone (Bayley and Shearing, 1996 in Newburn, 2005: 722–3). So their main hope is finding means 'to enable poor people to participate in markets for security' by vouchers or block grants (*op cit*: 730–1). 'In effect, communities would be given security budgets that they could spend on various mixtures of public and private policing' (*ibid*). This presupposes that the problems can be met by policing and that pluralization improves its efficacy—propositions that were questioned earlier. It also raises the issue of how the redistributive security budget is to gain political acceptance, as the theorists recognize:

Distributional problems between rich and poor might still arise, of course, particularly if the rich refused to pay. All policies that have any prospect of mitigating the growing class differences in public safety depend on the affluent segments of our societies recognising that security is indivisible. The well-to-do are paying for crime now; but they have not learned that they will save more by levelling up security than by ghettoising it (*ibid*: 730).

Achieving this consensus in support of redistribution presents a formidable challenge. But as safety depends on much wider social and economic justice than can be provided by security measures alone, tackling the 'root causes' of threat, the task is the even more daunting but necessary one of constructing a consensus for a broader alleviation of inequality and ghettoization. The new theorists offer impressive and inspirational examples of successful efforts to organize security in poor communities such as the South African township Zwelethemba (Johnston and Shearing, 2003: 151–60). But these are dependent on outside financial and other support (Marks and Goldsmith, 2006; Jones, 2007: 858–60). The state remains the necessary 'anchor' for security (Loader and Walker, 2006, 2007) to avert stark polarization between safe and dreadful enclosures.

By whom and how are the police themselves policed?

Who guards the guardians is of course one of the most ancient conundrums of governance. The issues of accountability remain

164   New Theories of Policing: A Social Democratic Critique

vexed in debates about policing. One of the reasons for this is the Janus-face of policing discussed earlier: policing usually involves conflict control, and is simultaneously a general and a partisan good. Thus the problem of accountability has a double aspect: achieving effective and efficient service delivery but also minimizing any abuse or injustice in the use of coercive powers. In the last two decades, with the dominance of the politics of law and order, the issue of accountability has shifted strongly towards emphasizing effective delivery of security with much lower priority given to the control of malpractice. Crime control has been declared as the overriding objective of policing, and a 'calculative and contractual' structure of monitoring and incentives is intended to achieve this (Reiner, 2000: ch 6). Police powers have been expanded at an accelerating rate whilst the safeguards attached by the Police and Criminal Evidence Act 1984 have been diluted (Cape and Young, 2008). The Human Rights Act 1998 and the introduction of the Independent Police Complaints Commission by the Police Reform Act 2002 are two significant counter-measures, but the dominant trend is clearly towards a relatively unregulated growth of police powers.

The transformation thesis claims that pluralization is making policing more accountable and responsive. Private security, they claim, is inherently so because of the contractual relationship between client and security firm, and between the latter and its employees which provides sanctions for performance failures. As far as the public sector is concerned, they welcome a more businesslike structure of accountability based on New Public Management principles (Johnston and Shearing, 2003: 26). In the endlessly cited nautical analogy of the NPM gurus Osborne and Gaebler, government should 'steer' but not 'row' public services like policing (Osborne and Gaebler, 1993). 'Rowing' must be devolved to local levels of delivery like police Basic Command Units, whose performance is steered by target setting, performance measurement, and corresponding sanctions. This brave new world of 'rule at a distance' is contrasted with a supposed sclerotic old regime of centralized command and control of state services. The latter is necessarily inefficient because of the Hayekian problem: 'top-down government does not permit entrepreneurship because those "at the top of the pyramid" do not have "enough information to make informed decisions" [Osborne and Gaebler, 1993: 15] about how to govern locally' (Shearing, 2006: 23). Such problems do not apply to the corporate sector, which is supposedly kept vibrant, responsive and efficient by market incentives.

This formulation misrepresents the past and current pattern of police governance. In Anglo-American policing it was never the case that the state 'rowed'. The British legal doctrine of constabulary independence explicitly sought to shield police officers from direct instruction by government, central or local (Lustgarten, 1986; Walker, 2000), although the operation of this in practice has always been more problematic (Reiner, 1991). In the USA until relatively recently with the politicization of law and order, the federal government role in local and state law policing was minimal. Sociological studies of policing in action have shown that decision-making is shaped largely by the rank-and-file officers on the street, who enjoy a considerable measure of discretion (Skolnick, 1966; Wilson, 1968; Muir, 1977; Smith, 1983). Paul Rock summed up the implications of early sociological research on policing thus: 'As inhibitors, transformers, translators and creators of reality . . . the police are considerably more than a simple instrument of legislative intentions.' (Rock, 1973: 200).

So Anglo-American policing has traditionally been governed 'at a distance' by the state (unless it is tautologically equated with it). This has been transformed in the last 20 years by the application of new 'calculative and contractual' modes of regulating policing which have given central government unprecedented formal and effective levers for penetrating 'constabulary independence', which is now an empty rhetorical formula (Reiner, 2000: ch 6; Savage, 2007: chs 3, 5; Jones, 2008). This creeping centralization of control over policing has been increasingly controversial, and in recent years both parties have pledged to bolster local input in a complicated and confusing variety of ways, but it is doubtful that this new localism will succeed in reversing the current central dominance (McLaughlin, 2007: ch 7; Newburn, 2007).

Legal and state regulation of private security is notoriously weak and patchy, and there have long been calls for its enhancement (Button, 2008: ch 5). However, the new policing theorists see private policing as more accountable and responsive because of commercial pressures. Inadequate performance by companies is sanctioned by the threat of contract termination, and individual officers are kept on their toes by fear for their jobs. 'Private police are more responsive than public police to the "bottom line" of safety. If safety is not increased, private police can be fired.' (Bayley

166   New Theories of Policing: A Social Democratic Critique

and Shearing, 1996 in Newburn, 2005: 721). How effective private security is in satisfying its customers is no doubt variable, but in principle it is acceptable to say *caveat emptor*.[15] But they have no responsibilities for *public* security apart from the limited sections allowed into their 'nodes'. It is hard to see how pluralization has enhanced accountability, either in the sense of responsiveness to public concerns about safety or malpractice.

How can the developing purposes and practices of policing be understood?

The transformation thesis is primarily presented as a description of trends and an analysis of their 'progressive' potential. Attempts to explain the changes are rather perfunctory, and by implication derived from broader theorizations of late or postmodernity, risk society, and shifts in governmentality.

The main explanatory theme is what can be called the 'truth will out' perspective: the new trends have emerged because they solve manifest problems with the old, supposedly state-dominated policing arrangements. This is summed up in the following passage:

Peel's aspiration to ensure prevention through the certainty of detection and punishment has remained unrealized during the two centuries since the inception of the new police. There are a number of reasons for this, some of which relate to shortcomings within policing, others to problems within the wider criminal justice system. For example, during most of the post-war period, steadily rising rates of crime have exposed the limits of the Peelian project. Added to that . . . the public's willingness to report offences cannot be taken for granted; the police's capacity to detect offences is limited; and the court's (sic) ability to secure convictions is restricted. (Johnston and Shearing, 2003: 67).

These claims distort the history of policing in a number of ways. Crime rates fell steadily after the 1850s as the Peelian police were rolled out across the country (following the 1856 County and Borough Police Act), remaining low until the First World War. As the historian Vic Gatrell summed up the Victorian and Edwardian

---

[15] The House of Lords in effect decided this in the 1980 case *Photo Production v Securicor* [1980] AC 827. A guard for Securicor caused £615,000 worth of damage to Photo Production, whose plant he was patrolling, when he deliberately tossed a lit match on some cartons. It was held that Securicor was not liable, as it had fulfilled its contractual obligations by supplying night patrol cover whatever the actual consequences for the safety of the plant.

recorded crime trends, 'the war against criminal disorder was palpably being won by the State, and contemporaries knew it.' (Gatrell, 1980: 240–1). Indeed the criminological question for conferences in the late nineteenth century to mull over was how to explain *falling* crime trends (Radzinowicz and Hood, 1985), a puzzle that was not to recur until the 1990s. Recent research has suggested that this decline was largely a statistical artefact conjured up by the police and Home Office to vindicate the new system, and to save Treasury resources (Taylor, 1998a, b; 1999). It is doubtful that the falling crime rates were primarily due to the policing changes, for reasons which have already been discussed. A much greater role was played by the long-term process of converting the 'dangerous classes' into the solid working class by incorporating them into the civil, political, and economic rights of citizenship (Reiner, 2000: 42–3, 58 9). But even if the falling crime rates were a political conjuring trick to promote the Bobbies it worked, and the myth of Scotland Yard's prowess ('always getting their man') became an international symbol of successful policing.

Although crime rates rose in the 1920s and 30s, they declined again in the first post-war decade, and the myth of the Bobby as an important aspect of British national pride reached its zenith in the 1940s and 50s. Recorded crime rates did begin to increase almost continuously after the mid-1950s, only falling briefly in the early 1990s and mid-2000s. The increase up to 1980 was largely a statistical illusion, as more property crime was reported to the police by victims owing to the spread of household insurance. The real explosion in crime came in the 1980s and early 90s, when the new British Crime Surveys confirmed the police recorded trend (Reiner, 2007: ch 3). The police certainly got some of the blame for this—but as unfairly as the credit they had received for the earlier fall. The main factor in the crime explosion was the advent of neo-liberal economic policy with its consequent effects of precipitously increasing inequality, long-term unemployment, and social exclusion, and a culture of ever expanding consumer aspirations and egoism (Reiner, 2007: ch 4; Hall *et al*, 2008). Faced with these huge crime increases, swamping their resources, the police were able to detect only a diminishing proportion of offences, further undermining public confidence in them.

But neither the crime trends nor the changing public standing of the police were primarily due to failures of the Peelian model. The real driver of the problematic crime and criminal justice

168   New Theories of Policing: A Social Democratic Critique

trends of recent years was the neo-liberal dominance that the new theorists see as bearing the seeds of a solution. But in the new policing theories neo-liberalism is discussed almost entirely as a rational set of programmes and ideas, curiously abstracted from its material effects and sources (Harvey, 2005 provides a succinct account of the economic and political sources and consequences of neo-liberalism). The rhetoric of neo-liberal advocates is presented as if it was how it worked in practice (eg O'Malley, 1997 in Newburn, 2005: 701–12), ignoring the now clear disastrously deleterious effects. There is an acceptance of neo-liberal claims about the possible pathologies of state institutions but no recognition of the pathologies of the market that were understood even by neo-classical economists of earlier generations such as Alfred Marshall and Pigou.

The new theorists' critique of the state is presented as developing out of the radical criminologies that flourished in the 1960s and early-70s:

Three decades ago cutting-edge criminological theory grappled with 'the problem of the state'. . . . While the state—through the law—presented itself as an independent adjudicator between competing interests and claimed to ensure that all individuals had equal access to justice, formal legal equality was, in reality, a sham. . . Thirty years ago the state was considered to be 'the problem', its capitalist character rendering it structurally incapable of representing general 'public interests' over particular private ones. (Johnston and Shearing, 2003: 33–4).

They then reflect on the 'strange paradox' that 'many of today's theorists' bemoan 'how neo-liberalism has disaggregated the state apparatus' (*ibid*). There is no paradox here. The nub of the critique of the state was that it was captured by the interests of capital, and the problem was how to make it deliver on its promise to represent the public good. As Tawney put it some 70 years ago, 'The question is not merely whether the State owns and controls the means of production. It is also who owns and controls the State.' (Tawney, 1935: 165). 'The reality behind the decorous drapery of political democracy' he argued is 'the economic power wielded by a few thousand—or . . . a few hundred thousand—bankers, industrialists, and landowners' (*op cit*: 60).

To espouse neo-liberalism, 'capitalism unleashed' (Glyn, 2006) from behind the ideological veil of the state, is jumping from the frying pan into the fire. The claim that there are 'possibilities for disaggregating neo-liberal strategies and practices, and rendering their often highly innovative developments available for appropriation and development by a "progressive" postwelfare politics' overlooks the inherent dysfunctional consequences of markets (O'Malley, 1997 in Newburn, 2005: 712). Markets have many unwelcome economic consequences unless states take countervailing measures: growing inequalities of power and wealth; allocation of resources tilted towards the desires of the rich (the democracy of the market is not one person one vote, but one pound one vote); insecurities caused by vicissitudes of health, age, natural disasters; and as we have relearned painfully, wild macroeconomic fluctuations (I have elaborated on these points in Reiner, 2007: 1–11). Market-dominated societies are associated with further social, ethical, political, and cultural problems: the financialization of all values, anomie produced by the stimulation of desires and aspirations beyond the possibility of achievement, egoism, corruption of democracy by the best politicians money can buy (Palast, 2004; Jacobs and Skocpol, 2005), authoritarianism as the 'strong state' wrestles to suppress resistance to the pathologies of the 'free market' (Polanyi, 1944; Gamble, 1994).

Specifically relevant to the concerns of this paper, there is now a host of research evidence showing that neo-liberalism—as contrasted with social democracy—is associated with higher risks of serious violent crime, *and* more punitive cultures and penal practices (Hall and Winlow, 2003; Dorling, 2004; Cavadino and Dignan, 2006; Reiner, 2007; Lacey, 2008; Hall and McLean, 2008; Wilkinson and Pickett, 2009), as a consequence of its economic, social, and cultural pathologies. The explanatory deficit of the new policing theories is a bracketing-out of the significance of political economy in shaping the context and problems that police organizations, cultures, and officers face. Explanations of changing programmes and practices, and their impacts—intended and unintended—require a multi-layered political economy of the macro-, intermediate, and immediate social processes and contexts that shape policing (Reiner, 2007b: 343–4), a perspective reminiscent of the eighteenth century 'science of police' which preceded the Peelian institution (*opcit,* 345–7).

Analysing the historical roots of the recent policing transformations through the lens of political economy suggests a very different diagnosis to the new policing theorists. The pluralization of policing and the application of NPM to the public police, are

170   New Theories of Policing: A Social Democratic Critique

symptoms of, not solutions to, the current predicament. As indicated earlier, the Peelian police were established in Britain (and the US) in the early-nineteenth century against wide and deep hostility especially from the then politically, socially, and economically excluded masses. The police were established not because of technical failures of the previous forms of citizen policing, but because these were all clearly under the control of the gentry and made manifest the class nature of governance and law (Silver, 1967). The big job facing the early police leaders was to gain public consent, and somewhat different strategies were followed in Britain and the US (Miller, 1977). The British route was a set of organizational policies seeking to represent the police as disciplined, apolitical, minimally armed, 'citizens in uniform' without special powers separating them from the public, enforcing an impartial law that benefitted all classes as well as providing emergency social services to those in need (Reiner, 2000: ch 2). These ultimately succeeded in dispelling hostility and winning a fragile legitimation of the police, but only because the policies were developed in a benign context of the general march of social, political, and economic citizenship (as classically spelled out by Marshall, 1950). This reduced the extent of crime and disorder confronting the police allowing them to consolidate the image of operating with minimum force and allowing room for the service role to be emphasized.

Police legitimacy was gradually undermined after the late-1960s but not because of defects in the policing model. The ultimate source was economic neo-liberalism, initially heralded in the 'Selsdon Man' manifesto on which the Heath government was elected in 1970 but defeated by trade union opposition, re-imposed on a reluctant Labour government by the IMF in 1976, enthusiastically espoused by the Thatcher Tories in 1979, and deeply embedded by New Labour's embrace of it in the 1990s. This set in train massive economic and social dislocation (especially large-scale long-term unemployment, inequality, and social exclusion) and an increasingly anomic and egoistic culture, which in the 1980s generated a crime explosion and public disorder on a scale not seen for a century. Mediated by the unintended reversal of the policing policies that had achieved legitimation, the result was a decline in public confidence in the police.

How to deal with this was politically controversial in the 1970s and 80s, and there appeared sharp politicization of the issue of law and order (Downes and Morgan, 2007; Reiner, 2007: ch 5). The Tories espoused a tough new law and order rhetoric, whilst

Labour clung to a social democratic analysis of the social roots of crime and disorder similar to the one suggested here. This was fundamentally changed in 1992 when the then Shadow Home Secretary Tony Blair's celebrated slogan 'tough on crime, tough on the causes of crime' heralded New Labour's conversion to the law and order approach, the first of several 'Clause 4' moments signifying its embrace of neo-liberalism.

For the police this meant calling a bluff that had been successful for 150 years. The police had been symbolically acclaimed as the guardians of the public against threats of crime and disorder, but the real work achieving this was an array of economic, social, and cultural processes that incorporated most sections of society into a common status of citizenship and held tensions and conflicts at bay. When neo-liberalism unravelled this complex of subtle, hidden controls, the thin blue line turned out to be a Maginot line. The 'sovereign state' myth (Garland, 1996) was unmasked, naked as Anderson's Emperor in his new clothes. As researchers had suggested all along, the police alone could not have much impact on crime and disorder. But the newly ascendant and unquestioned politics of law and order demanded that they do just that, indicated most explicitly by the 1993 White Paper on *Police Reform* which declared bluntly that the police task was simply 'catching criminals' vindicating a folkloric view that official statements from Peel to Scarman had been at pains to deny (Reiner, 2000: 209). This kick-started the NPM-inspired reforms of the 1990s and 2000s, from the quixotic hunt to extirpate extraneous tasks and free them for their core criminal-catching role, to the calculative and contractual businesslike management regime to keep them on their toes doing it (Savage, 2007: chs 3, 5). Meanwhile the 'new feudalism' also gathered pace, as those with the power built their exclusive bubbles of security. The transformation of policing stems not from the inherent deficiencies of old, state policing or the technical superiority of a new corporate mentality of pluralism combining private security and an NPM invigorated public sector. It results from the destabilizing and criminogenic effects of neo-liberalism, which is the problem not the solution.

Conclusion: For Social Democratic Policing

There have been many valuable analyses of the legal, constitutional, procedural, and organizational requirements for democratic and

172   New Theories of Policing: A Social Democratic Critique

legitimate policing (Lustgarten, 1986; Walker, 2000; Skogan, 2006; Tyler, 2007; Hough, 2007; Smith, 2007a and b; Sklansky, 2008). The above sketch of British policing history suggests that a further ingredient is needed: social democracy. The organizational elements of the legitimation of the police only succeeded because of the wider transformation of British society that culminated in the post-war Keynesian and welfare state settlement, incorporating all sections of society into a common status of citizenship. The political triumph of neo-liberalism since the 1970s and the ensuing 'death of the social' (Rose, 1996) eroded these conditions of peace and security.

The dire consequences of this in the economic arena have become manifest with the return of depression on a scale unprecedented since the 1930s. The holes in the neo-liberal model are widely acknowledged now even by erstwhile neo-liberal economists and policy-makers. The risk society and neo-liberal 'responsibilization' (O'Malley, 1992, 2004; Garland, 2001) were euphemisms for a massive 'risk shift' (Hacker, 2006) from government and corporations to the mass of the population who could not carry the burden.

When the Bush-Cheney administration proposed to replace Social Security with a system of individually accumulated, individually owned, and individually invested accounts, my first thought was that its goal was to take the Social out of Social Security. It took a few minutes longer to realize that it also intended to take the Security out of Social Security (Solow, 2008, reviewing Gosselin 2008).

The news does not seem to have penetrated most criminology as yet, but there is a growing sense amongst economic and political analysts that the state remains needed and indeed that social democracy is as necessary as the post-war generation felt it to be. The prospects for civilization depend 'on whether the social-democratic leaders of western Europe can breathe life into the dry bones of what seemed, until recently, a dead doctrine' (Bogdanor, 2009). Tawney's statement of social democratic principles, at the start of the last great depression, remains a valuable yardstick for democratic and ethical politics and policing:

its fundamental criticism of capitalism is not merely that it impoverishes the mass of mankind—poverty is an ancient evil—but that it makes riches a god. . . Socialism accepts. . . the principles which are the cornerstones of democracy, that authority, to justify its title, must rest on consent; that power is tolerable only so far as it is accountable to the public; and that differences of character and capacity between human beings, however important on their own plane, are of minor significance compared with the capital fact of their common humanity (Tawney, 1931: 197).

Contrary to popular mythology and indeed the new policing theorists, even the best policing (public and/or private) cannot provide the foundations of security. But if these are once more reproduced by inclusive economic and social policies then the police can offer what they are capable of: legitimate and effective first-aid responses to crime and emergencies. To stand the sentiment expressed in Psalm 127 on its head, if the Lord *is* with the city, the watch does *not* watch in vain.

References

Audit Commission (1996) *Streetwise: Effective Police Patrol*, London: HMSO.

Banton, M. (1964) *The Policeman in the Community*, London: Tavistock.

Bayley, D. (1985) *Patterns of Policing*, New Brunswick, NJ: Rutgers University Press.

—— (1994) *Police For the Future*, New York: Oxford University Press.

—— and Bittner, E. (1984) 'Learning the Skills of Policing', *Law and Contemporary Problems*, 47: 35–60.

—— and Shearing, C. (1996) 'The Future of Policing', *Law and Society Review*, 30/3: 586–606, as reprinted in T. Newburn (ed) (2005) *Policing—Key Readings*, Cullompton: Willan.

Bittner, E. (1970) *The Functions of the Police in Modern Society*, Chevy Chase, MD: National Institute of Mental Health.

—— (1974) 'Florence Nightingale in Pursuit of Willie Sutton: A Theory of the Police' in H. Jacob (ed) *The Potential for Reform of Criminal Justice*, Beverly Hills, CA: Sage.

Bogdanor, V. (2009) 'Loosening Labour's Golden Straitjacket', *New Statesman*, 19 March.

Bowling, B. (1999a) 'The Rise and Fall of New York Murder', *British Journal of Criminology*, 39/4: 531–54.

—— (1999b) *Violent Racism*, Oxford: Oxford University Press.

—— (2010) *Policing the Caribbean*, Oxford: Oxford University Press (forthcoming).

—— and Phillips, C. (2002) *Racism, Crime and Justice*, London: Longman.

—— Parmar, A, and Phillips, C. (2008) 'Policing Minority Ethnic Communities' in T. Newburn (ed) *Handbook of Policing*, Second Edition, Cullompton: Willan.

174   New Theories of Policing: A Social Democratic Critique

Braithwaite, J. (2000) 'The New Regulatory State and the Transformation of Criminology', *British Journal of Criminology*, 40/2: 222–38.

Bratton, W. (1998a) 'Crime is down: blame the police' in N. Dennis (ed), *Zero Tolerance: Policing a Free Society*, Second Edition, London: Institute of Economic Affairs, as reprinted in T. Newburn (ed) (2005) *Policing—Key Readings* Cullompton: Willan.

Bratton, W. (with Knobler, P.) (1998b) *Turnaround: How America's Top Cop Reversed the Crime Epidemic*, New York: Random House.

Brogden, M. (1999) 'Community Policing as Cherry Pie' in R. Mawby (ed) *Policing across the World*, London: UCL Press.

—— and Nijhar, P. (2005) *Community Policing: International Concepts and Practice*, Cullompton: Willan.

Brown, D. (1997) *PACE Ten Years On: A Review of the Research*, London: Home Office Research Study, 155.

Brown, J. and Heidensohn, F. (2000) *Gender and Policing: Comparative Perspectives*, London: Macmillan.

Button, M. (2002) *Private Policing*, Cullompton: Willan.

—— (2007) *Security Officers and Policing*, Aldershot: Avebury.

—— (2008) *Doing Security*, London: Macmillan.

Cain, M. (1973) *Society and the Policeman's Role*, London: Routledge.

Cape, E. and Young, R. (2008) (eds) *Regulating Policing: The Police and Criminal Evidence Act 1984: Past, Present and Future*, Oxford: Hart.

Cavadino, M. and Dignan, J. (2006) *Penal Systems: A Comparative Approach*, London: Sage.

Clarke, R. and Hough, M. (1984) *Crime and Police Effectiveness*, London: Home Office Research Unit.

Cooley, D. (2005) (ed) *Re-Imagining Policing in Canada*, Toronto: University of Toronto Press.

Cope, N. (2008) '"*Interpretation for Action?*": Definitions and Potential of Crime Analysis For Policing' in T. Newburn (ed) *Handbook of Policing*, Second Edition, Cullompton: Willan.

Crawford, A. (2006) 'Policing and Security as "Club Goods": the New Enclosures' in J. Wood and B. Dupont (eds) *Democracy, Society and the Governance of Security*, Cambridge: Cambridge University Press.

—— (2008) 'Plural Policing in the UK: Policing Beyond the Police' in T. Newburn (ed) *Handbook of Policing*, Second Edition, Cullompton: Willan.

Crawford, A. and Lister, S. (2004) *The Extended Policing Family*, York: Joseph Rowntree Foundation.

Crawford, A., Lister, S., Blackburn, S., and Burnett, J. (2005) *Plural Policing: The mixed economy of visible patrols in England and Wales*, Bristol: Policy Press.

Davey, B.J. (1983) *Lawless and Immoral: Policing a Country Town 1838–57*, Leicester: Leicester University Press/New York: St Martin's Press.

References   175

Davis, M. (1990) *City of Quartz*, London: Vintage.

De Lint, W. (1999) 'A Post-modern Turn in Policing: Policing as Pastiche?' *International Journal of the Sociology of Law*, 27/1: 127–52.

Di Tella, R. and Schargrodsky, E. (2004) 'Do Police Reduce Crime? Estimate Using the Allocation of Police Forces After a Terrorist Attack', *American Economic Review*, 94/1: 115–33.

Dixon, D. and Maher, L. (2005) 'Policing, crime and public health: lessons for Australia from the "New York miracle"', *Criminal Justice*, 5/1: 115–44.

Dorling, D. (2004) 'Prime Suspect: Murder in Britain' in P. Hillyard, C. Pantazis, S. Tombs, and D. Gordon (eds) *Beyond Criminology*, London: Pluto.

Downes, D. and Morgan, R. (2007) 'No Turning Back: The Politics of Law and Order into the Millennium' in M. Maguire, R. Morgan and R. Reiner (eds) *The Oxford Handbook of Criminology*, Fourth Edition, Oxford: Oxford University Press: 201–40.

Draca, M., Machin, S., and Witt, R. (2008)   *Panic on the Streets of London: Police, Crime and the July 2005 Terror Attacks*, London: LSE Centre for Economic Performance.

Dubber, M. (2005) *The Police Power*, New York: Columbia University Press.

—— and Valverde, M. (eds) (2006) *The New Police Science*, Stanford: Stanford University Press.

Ericson, R. (1982) *Reproducing Order: A Study of Police Patrol Work*, Toronto: University of Toronto Press.

—— and Haggerty, K. (1997) *Policing Risk Society*, Oxford: Oxford University Press.

—— (2002) 'The Policing of Risk' in T. Baker and J. Simon (eds) *Embracing Risk*, Chicago: Chicago University Press (as reprinted in T. Newburn (ed) (2005) *Policing—Key Readings* Cullompton: Willan 2005.

Fielding, N. (1995) *Community Policing*, Oxford: Oxford University Press.

—— (2002) 'Theorising Community Policing', *British Journal of Criminology*, 42/1: 47–63.

—— and Innes, M. (2006) 'Reassurance Policing, Community Policing and Measuring Police Performance', *Policing and Society*, 16/2: 127–45.

Fitzgerald, M., Hough, M., Joseph, I., and Quereshi, T. (2002) *Policing for London*, Cullompton: Willan.

Forst, B. and Manning, P. (1999) *The Privatization of Policing*, Washington, DC: Georgetown University Press.

Foster, J., Newburn, T. and Souhami, A. (2005) *Assessing the Impact of the Stephen Lawrence Enquiry*, London: Home Office.

Gamble, A., (1994) *The Free Economy and the Strong State*, London: Macmillan.

176   New Theories of Policing: A Social Democratic Critique

Garland, D. (1996) 'The Limits of the Sovereign State: Strategies of Crime Control in Contemporary Societies', *British Journal of Criminology*, 36/4: 1–27.

—— (2001) *The Culture of Control*, Oxford: Oxford University Press.

Gatrell, V. (1980) 'The Decline of Theft and Violence in Victorian and Edwardian England' in V. Gatrell, B. Lenman and G. Parker (eds) *Crime and the Law*, London: Europa.

Glyn, A., (2006) *Capitalism Unleashed*, Oxford: Oxford University Press.

Goldsmith, A. (2003) 'Policing Weak States: Citizen Safety and State Responsibility', *Policing and Society*, 13/1: 3–21.

Goold, B. (2004) *CCTV and Policing: Public Area Surveillance and Police Practices in Britain*, Oxford: Oxford University Press.

—— (2009) *Surveillance*, London: Routledge.

Gosselin, P. (2008) *High Wire: The Precarious Financial Lives of American Families*, New York: Basic Books.

Hacker, J. (2006) *The Great Risk Shift: The Assault on American Jobs, Families, Health Care and Retirement And How You Can Fight Back*, New York: Oxford University Press.

Hall, S. and McLean, C. (2009) 'A Tale of Two Capitalisms: A Preliminary Comparison of Murder Rates in Western European and Anglo-American Market Societies', *Theoretical Criminology*, forthcoming.

—— and Winlow, S., (2003) 'Rehabilitating Leviathan: Reflections on the State, Economic Regulation and Violence Reduction', *Theoretical Criminology*, 7/1: 139–62.

—— , Winlow, S. and Ancrum, C. (2008) *Criminal Identities and Consumer Culture*, Cullompton: Willan.

Harvey, D. (2005) *A Brief History of Neoliberalism*, Oxford: Oxford University Press.

Heidensohn, F. (2008) 'Gender and Policing', in Newburn, T. (ed) *Handbook of Policing*, Second Edition,. Cullompton: Willan.

—— and Gelsthorpe, L. (2007) 'Gender and Crime' in M. Maguire, R. Morgan, and R. Reiner (eds) *The Oxford Handbook of Criminology*, Fourth Edition, Oxford: Oxford University Press.

Henry, A. and Smith, D. (eds) (2007) *Transformations of Policing*, Aldershot: Ashgate.

Holdaway, S. and Barron, A-M. (1997) *Resigners—The Experience of Black and Asian Police Officers*, London: Macmillan.

Hope, T. (2000) 'Inequality and the Clubbing of Private Security' in T. Hope and R.Sparks (eds) *Crime, Risk and Insecurity*, London: Routledge.

Hough, M. (2007) 'Policing, new public management and legitimacy in Britain' in T. Tyler (ed) *Legitimacy and Criminal Justice*, New York: Russell Sage Foundation Press.

Hoyle, C. and Zedner, L. (2007) 'Victims, Victimisation, and Criminal Justice' in M. Maguire, R. Morgan and R. Reiner (eds) *The Oxford*

References   177

Handbook of Criminology, Fourth Edition, Oxford: Oxford University Press.

Innes, M. (ed) (2006) 'Reassurance and the "New" Community Policing', Special Issue, *Policing and Society*, 16/2.

Jacobs, L. and Skocpol, T. (eds) (2005) *Inequality and American Democracy*, New York: Russell Sage Foundation.

Johnston L. (1991) 'Privatisation and the Police Function: From "New Police" to "New Policing"' in R. Reiner and M. Cross (eds) *Beyond Law and Order: Criminal Justice Policy and Politics into the 1990s*, London: Macmillan.

—— (1992) *The Rebirth of Private Policing*, London: Routledge.

—— (2000) *Policing Britain: Risk, Security and Governance*, Harlow: Longman.

—— (2007a) 'The Trajectory of "Private Policing"' in A. Henry and D. Smith (eds) *Transformations of Policing*, Aldershot: Ashgate.

   (2007b) '"Keeping the family together". Police Community Support Officers and the "police extended family" in London', *Policing and Society*, 17, 2: 119–40.

Johnston, L. and Shearing, C. (2003) *Governing Security*, London: Routledge.

Jones, R. (2007) 'The Architecture of Policing: Towards a New theoretical Model of the Role of Constraint-Based Compliance in Policing' in A. Henry and D. Smith (eds) *Transformations of Policing*, Aldershot: Ashgate.

Jones, T. (2007) 'The Governance of security: Pluralisation, Privatisation, and Polarisation in Crime Control' in M. Maguire, R. Morgan and R. Reiner (eds) *The Oxford Handbook of Criminology*, Fourth Edition, Oxford: Oxford University Press.

—— (2008) 'The Accountability of Policing' in T. Newburn (ed) *Handbook of Policing*, Second Edition, Cullompton: Willan.

—— and Newburn, T. (1998) *Private Security and Public Policing*, Oxford: Oxford University Press.

—— (eds) (2006) *Policy Transfer and Criminal Justice*, Maidenhead: Open University Press.

—— (2002) 'The Transformation of Policing? Understanding Current Trends in Policing Systems', *British Journal of Criminology*, 42/1: 129–46.

—— (2006a) *Plural Policing: A Comparative Perspective*, London: Routledge.

—— (eds) (2006b) *Policy Transfer and Criminal Justice*, Maidenhead: Open University Press.

Karmen, A. (2000) *New York Murder Mystery*, New York: New York University Press.

Klick, J and Tabarrok, A. (2005) 'Using Terror Alert Levels to Estimate the Effect of Police on Crime', *The Journal of Law and Economics*, 48/2: 267–79.

178   New Theories of Policing: A Social Democratic Critique

Klockars, C. (1985) *The Idea of Police*, Beverly Hills, CA: Sage.

Lacey, N. (2008) *The Prisoners' Dilemma*, Cambridge: Cambridge University Press.

Lee J.A. (1981) 'Some Structural Aspects of Police Deviance in Relations with Minority Groups', in C. Shearing (ed) *Organizational Police Deviance*, Toronto: Butterworth.

Levitt, S. (2004) 'Understanding why crime fell in the 1990s: four factors that explain the decline and six that do not', *Journal of Economic Perspectives*, 18/1: 163–90.

Loader, I. (1997) 'Policing and the Social: Questions of Symbolic Power', *British Journal of Sociology*, 48/1: 1–18.

—— (1999) 'Consumer Culture and the Commodification of Crime and Security', *Sociology* 33: 373–92.

—— and Mulcahy, A. (2003) *Policing and the Condition of England*, Oxford: Oxford University Press.

Loader, I. and Walker, N. (2001) 'Policing as a Public Good: Reconstituting the Connections Between Policing and the State', *Theoretical Criminology*, 5/1: 9–35.

—— (2006) 'Necessary Virtues: the Legitimate Place of the State in the Production of Security' in J. Wood and B. Dupont (eds) *Democracy, Society and the Governance of Security*, Cambridge: Cambridge University Press.

—— (2007) *Civilising Security*, Cambridge: Cambridge University Press.

—— and Zedner, L. (2007) 'Police Beyond Law?', *New Criminal Law Review* 10/1: 142–52.

Loveday, B., McClory, J., and Lockhart, G. (2007) *Fitting the Bill: Local Policing for the 21st Century*, London: Policy Exchange.

Lustgarten, L. (1986) *The Governance of the Police*, London: Sweet & Maxwell.

Maguire, M. (2008) 'Criminal Investigation and Crime Control' in T. Newburn (ed) *Handbook of Policing*, Second Edition, Cullompton: Willan.

—— and John, T. (1996) *Intelligence, Surveillance and Informants*, London: Home Office.

——and Norris, C. (1992) *The Conduct and Supervision of Criminal Investigations*, London: HMSO.

Manning, P. (1977) *Police Work*, Cambridge, Mass.: MIT Press.

—— (2003) *Policing Contingencies*, Chicago: Chicago University Press.

Marenin, O. (1982) 'Parking Tickets and Class Repression: The Concept of Policing in Critical Theories of Criminal Justice', *Contemporary Crises*, 6/2: 241–66.

Marks, M. and Goldsmith, A. (2006) 'The State, the People and Democratic Policing: the Case of South Africa' in J. Wood and B. Dupont (eds) *Democracy, Society and the Governance of Security*, Cambridge: Cambridge University Press.

References   179

Marshall, T.H. (1950) *Citizenship and Social Class*, Cambridge: Cambridge University Press.

McLaughlin, E. (2007) *The New Policing*, London: Sage.

—— and Murji, K. (1998) 'Resistance Through Representation: "Storylines", Advertising and Police Federation Campaigns', *Policing and Society*, 8/4: 367–99.

—— (1999) 'The Postmodern Condition of the Police', *Liverpool Law Review*, 21: 217–40.

Michael, D. (1999) 'The Levels of Orientation Security Officers Have towards a Public Policing Function', *Security Journal*, 12/4: 33–42.

—— (2002) *A Sense of Security? The Ideology and Accountability of Private Security Officers*, PhD Thesis, London School of Economics.

Moore, M. (2003) 'Sizing up compstat: an important administrative innovation in policing', *Criminology and Public Policy*, 2: 469–94.

Muir, W.K. Jr., (1977) *Police: Streetcorner Politicians*, Chicago: Chicago University Press.

Neocleous, M. (2006) 'Theoretical Foundations of the "New Police Science"' in M. Dubber and M. Valverde (eds) *The New Police Science*, Stanford: Stanford University Press.

Newburn, T. (ed) (2005) *Policing—Key Readings*, Cullompton: Willan.

—— (2007) 'The Future of Policing in Britain' in A. Henry and D. Smith (eds) *Transformations of Policing*, Aldershot: Ashgate.

Norris, C. and Armstrong, G. (1999) *The Maximum Surveillance Society: The Rise of CCTV*, West Sussex: Berg.

—— and Dunnighan, C. (2000) 'Subterranean Blues: Conflict as an Unintended Consequence of the Police Use of Informers', *Policing and Society*, 9/1: 385–412.

O'Malley, P. (1992) 'Risk, power and crime prevention', *Economy and Society*, 21/3: 252–75.

—— (1997) 'Policing, Post-Modernism and Political Rationality', *Social and Legal Studies* 6/3: 363–81, as reprinted in T. Newburn (ed) (2005) *Policing—Key Readings*, Cullompton: Willan.

—— (2004) *Risk, Uncertainty and Government*, London: Glasshouse.

—— and Palmer, D. (1996) 'Post-Keynesian Policing', *Economy and Society*, 25/2: 137–55.

Osborne, D. and Gaebler, T. (1992) *Reinventing Government*, New York: Addison-Wesley.

Palast, G. (2004) *The Best Democracy Money Can Buy*, New York: Plume.

Phillips, C. and Bowling, B. (2007) 'Ethnicities, Racism, Crime, and Criminal Justice' in M. Maguire, R. Morgan and R. Reiner (eds) *The Oxford Handbook of Criminology*, Fourth Edition, Oxford: Oxford University Press.

Polanyi, K. (1944) *The Great Transformation*, Boston: Beacon, 2001 Edition.

180   New Theories of Policing: A Social Democratic Critique

Punch, M. (1979) 'The Secret Social Service' in S. Holdaway (ed) *The British Police*, London: Edward Arnold.

—— (2007) *Zero Tolerance Policing,* Bristol: Policy Press.

Radzinowicz, L. and Hood, R. (1986) *The Emergence of Penal Policy in Victorian and Edwardian England*, London: Stevens.

Rawlings, P. (1991) 'Creeping Privatisation? The Police, the Conservative Government and Policing in the Late 1980s', in R. Reiner and M. Cross (eds), *Beyond Law and Order: Criminal Justice Policy and Politics into the 1990s*, London: Macmillan.

Reiner, R. (1989) 'The Politics of Police Research', in M. Weatheritt (ed) *Police Research: Some Future Prospects*, Aldershot: Avebury.

—— (1991) *Chief Constables*, Oxford: Oxford University Press.

—— (1992a) 'Policing a Postmodern Society', *Modern Law Review*, 55/6: 761–81.

—— (1992b) 'Police Research in the United Kingdom: A Critical Review' in N. Morris and M. Tonry (eds) *Modern Policing*, Chicago: Chicago University Press.

—— (1998) 'Process or Product? Problems of Assessing Individual Police Performance' in J.P. Brodeur (ed) *How to Recognise Good Policing*, Thousand Oaks, CA: Sage.

—— (2000) *The Politics of the Police*, Third Edition, Oxford: Oxford University Press.

—— (2007a) *Law and Order: An Honest Citizen's Guide to Crime and Control*, Cambridge: Polity.

—— (2007b) 'Political economy, crime and criminal justice' in M. Maguire, R. Morgan and R. Reiner (eds) *The Oxford Handbook of Criminology*, Fourth Edition, Oxford: Oxford University Press.

—— (2008) 'Policing and the Media' in T. Newburn (ed) *Handbook of Policing*, Second Edition, Cullompton: Willan.

—— and Newburn, T. (2006) 'Police Research' in R. King and E. Wincup (eds) *Doing Research on Crime and Justice*, Second Edition, Oxford: Oxford University Press.

Rikagos, G. (2005) 'Beyond Public-Private: Towards a New Typology of Policing' in D. Cooley (ed) *Re-Imagining Policing in Canada*, Toronto: University of Toronto Press.

Rock, P. (1973) *Deviant Behaviour*, London: Hutchinson.

—— (1977) 'Law, Order and Power in Late Seventeenth and Early Eighteenth-century England', *International Annals of Criminology*, 16, as reprinted in S. Cohen and A. Scull (eds) (1983) *Social Control and the State*, Oxford: Martin Robertson.

—— (2005) 'Chronocentrism and British Criminology', *British Journal of Sociology*, 56/3: 473–91.

Rose, N. (1996) 'The death of the social?', *Economy and Society*, 25/3: 327–56.

Savage, S. (2007) *Police Reform*, Oxford: Oxford University Press.

References   181

Shearing, C. (1984) *Dial-A-Cop: A Study of Police Mobilisation*, Toronto: University of Toronto Centre of Criminology.

—— (2006) 'Reflections on the Refusal to Acknowledge Private Governments' in J. Wood and B. Dupont (eds) *Democracy, Society and the Governance of Security*, Cambridge: Cambridge University Press.

—— (2007) 'Policing Our Future' in A. Henry and D. Smith (eds) *Transformations of Policing*, Aldershot: Ashgate.

Shearing, C. and Stenning, P. (1983) 'Private Security: Implications for Social Control', *Social Problems*, 30/5: 493–506.

—— (eds) (1987a) *Private Policing*, Beverly Hills, CA: Sage.

—— (1987b) '"Say cheese!" The Disney order that's not so Mickey Mouse', in C. Shearing and P. Stenning (eds), *Private Policing*, Beverly Hills: Sage.

Sheptycki, J. (2000a) 'Surveillance, Closed Circuit Television and Social Control', *Policing and Society*, 9/4: 429-34.

Sheptycki, J. (2000a) 'Surveillance, Closed Television and Social.

—— (ed) (2000b) *Issues in Transnational Policing*, London: Routledge.

—— (2002) *In Search of Transnational Policing*, Aldershot: Ashgate.

Sheptycki, J. and Wardak, A. (eds) (2005) *Transnational and Comparative Criminology*, London: Glasshouse.

Silver, A. (1967) 'The Demand for Order in Civil Society' in D. Bordua (ed), *The Police*, New York: Wiley.

Sklansky, D. (2008) *Democracy and the Police*, Stanford: Stanford University Press.

Skogan, W. (2006) 'Asymmetry in the Impact of Encounters With the Police' *Policing and Society*, 16/2: 99–126.

Skolnick, J. (1966) *Justice without Trial*, New York: Wiley.

Smith, D. (2007a) 'New Challenges to Police Legitimacy' in A. Henry and D. Smith (eds) *Transformations of Policing*, Aldershot: Ashgate.

—— (2007b) 'The Foundations of Legitimacy' in T. Tyler (ed) *Legitimacy and Criminal Justice*, New York: Russell Sage Foundation Press.

Smith, D., Small, S., and Gray, J. (1983) *Police and People in London*, London: PSI.

Solow, R. (2008) 'Trapped in the New "You're on Your Own" World', *New York Review of Books*, 55/18: 20 November.

South, N. (1988) *Policing for Profit*, London: Sage.

Spitzer, S. and Scull, A. (1977) 'Privatisation and Social Control', *Social Problems*, 25/1: 18–29.

Stenning, P. (2000) 'Powers and Accountability of the Private Police', *European Journal on Criminal Policy and Research*, 8: 325–52.

Styles, J. (1982) 'An 18th Century Magistrate as Detective', *Bradford Antiquary*, 47.

—— (1983) 'Sir John Fielding and the Problem of Criminal Investigation in 18th century England', *Transactions of the Royal Historical Society*, 33.

Tawney, R.H. (1931) *Equality*, London: Unwin, 1964 reprint.

182   New Theories of Policing: A Social Democratic Critique

—— (1935/1981) *The Attack and Other Papers*, Nottingham: Spokesman.

Taylor, H. (1998a) 'The Politics of the Rising Crime Statistics of England and Wales 1914–1960', *Crime, History and Societies*, 2/1: 5–28.

—— (1998b) 'Rising Crime: The Political Economy of Criminal Statistics since the 1850s', *Economic History Review*, 51: 569–90.

—— (1999) 'Forging the Job: A Crisis of "Modernisation" or Redundancy for the Police in England and Wales 1900–39', *British Journal of Criminology*, 39/1: 113–35.

Tilley, N. (2008) 'Modern Approaches to Policing: Community, Problem-Oriented and Intelligence-led' in T. Newburn (ed) *Handbook of Policing*, Second Edition, Cullompton: Willan.

Tyler, T. (ed) (2007) *Legitimacy and Criminal Justice*, New York: Russell Sage Foundation Press.

Waddington, P.A.J. (1983) 'Beware the Community Trap', *Police*, March: 34.

—— Stenson, K. and Don, D. (2004) 'In Proportion: Race and Police Stop and Search', *British Journal of Criminology*, 44, 889–914.

Wakefield, A. (2003) *Selling Security: The private policing of public space*, Cullompton: Willan.

Walker, N. (1996) 'Defining Core Police Tasks: The Neglect of the Symbolic Dimension', *Policing and Society*, 6/1: 53–71.

—— (2000) *Policing in a Changing Constitutional Order*, London: Sweet and Maxwell.

—— (2008) 'The Pattern of Transnational Policing' in T. Newburn (ed) *Handbook of Policing*, Second Edition, Cullompton: Willan.

Weisburd, D., Mastrofski, S., McNally, A., Greenspan, R., and Willis, J. (2003) 'Reforming to Preserve: Compstat and Strategic Problem Solving in American Policing', *Criminology and Public Policy*, 2/3: 421–56.

Wilkinson, R. and Pickett, K. (2009) *The Spirit Level: Why More Equal Societies Almost Always Do Better*, London: Allen Lane.

Wilson, J.Q. (1968) *Varieties of Police Behavior*, Cambridge, MA: Harvard University Press.

Wood, J. and Dupont, B. (2006) eds. *Democracy, Society and the Governance of Security* Cambridge: Cambridge University Press.

—— and Shearing, C. (2007) *Imagining Security*, Cullompton: Willan.

Zedner, L. (2006) 'Policing Before the Police', *British Journal of Criminology*, 46/1: 78–96.

—— (2009) *Security*, London: Routledge.

Zimring, F. (2007) *The Great American Crime Decline*, New York: Oxford University Press.

Part II
Popular Culture and Crime

[9]
The New Blue Films

A man's gotta do what a man's gotta do. But why?
The new cop movies feature knight-errants with nowhere to go.

Joseph Wambaugh has almost single-handedly created a new popular genre, the cop as hero. The latest example of this, *The Choirboys*, has now hit our screens.

Policemen themselves often attribute success in the force to 'being in the right place at the right time'. Wambaugh, then a 34 year old Los Angeles police sergeant and night-school graduate in English Literature, was well placed to write the 1971 hit novel *The New Centurions,* which established the cop as the new American hero. The film spin-offs of Wambaugh's novels have ranged from the pleasing (*The New Centurions – Precinct 45, Los Angeles Police* in Britain), through the satisfactory (*The Blue Knight*), to the downright disaster of *The Choirboys*. This last film is essentially a series of scatological jokes strung together around 'choir practices' – the Los Angeles police term for their tension-releasing, after-work orgies in McArthur Park, where their needs are catered for by cop-groupies like Ora Lee Tongle. But whatever their aesthetic merits, Wambaugh's books provide an important insight into the police mind, and the public mood of the cynical seventies.

Wambaugh's world is divided into two kinds of people. At its centre are blue-coated knights riding their black-and-white patrol cars through a concrete jungle of 'ass-holes' – that's you, me and everyone else without the savvy of the street-wise cop. In *The Choirboys*, Roscoe Rules, most foul-mouthed and bigoted of the bunch, declares that this traditional anal label for civilians is too flattering. The sadistic and racist Rules is scorned by the other cops, but his view of civilians is only an exaggerated version of the general one.

Not all the boys in blue are OK either, only the patrolmen and the occasional sergeant or detective. Senior officers are dishonest dictators who have grafted their way to the top, like Lieutenant Hardass Grimsley, or incompetent and naive penpushers like Lieutenant Finque – promoted for answering irrelevant questions in exams, not thier police competence. They hamstring the work of the street cops by emphasising spit, polish and the rule book, or by dreaming up harebrained schemes to 'prevent' crime.

However, this underlines one of Wambaugh's key themes – namely that cops are human, only more so. This distinguishes his treatment from earlier fictional images of the police. Until the late 1960s, a professional policeman was rarely the hero of a film. In the early days of Hollywood, the Keystone Cops were portrayed as clumsy buffoons, causing much protest from the law-enforcement establishment about this imbecilic image. At the 1913 convention of the International Association of Chiefs of Police, a resolution was passed to stop such movie misrepresentation.

In the same period in England, fictional police were not generally credited with a greater endowment of little grey cells. During the heyday of the classic English detective novel, the professional policeman was only the foil for emphasising the intellectual pyrotechnics of the amateur her – like Inspector Lestrade of the Holmes series. Only Freeman Wills Croft and Ngaio Marsh used professional police heroes. The one story where a policeman *did* play a crucial part, Thomas Burke's 1912 *The Hands of Mr Ottermole* merely brings home the point. The patrolling bobby was the strangler unnoticed by any witness, for his very familiarity made him inconspicuous. Society took its law and order for granted: fictional murder was a storm among the teacups, a cosy country-house weekend recreation for the Drones set.

In America, the early 1930s saw the gangster emerge as folk-hero. James Cagney, Edward G. Robinson and George Raft acted out rags-to-riches fables for Deperession victims, but taught them that crime comes before a fall. Despite the cautionary endings, the apparent glorification of the gangster was deplored by the police, as well as priggish custodians of public morals. While the gangster film no longer portrayed the cop as either thick or comic, he was still an unglamorous figure, far from the limelight. This was implied clearly by the type of women the policemen were involved with, a sensitive indicator of their social standing. While Cagney had Jean Harlow, the cop was stuck with cooks or domestics. After much flak from civic groups, Hollywood did allow plain-clothes policemen to be leads in some later 1930s gangster films, like *G-Men*, but by then the genre was past the peak of popularity.

The private eye was the hero of the early 1940s crime film, spearheaded by Philip Marlowe and Sam Spade. The public law-enforcers were seen as less caring or competent, or actively corrupt. It was the individual, private knight-errant whos sought to preserve honour in the city's mean streets.

Only in the late 1940s did professional police begin to appear frequently in lead roles, in films purporting to give a realistic, deglamourised portrait of police procedure, starting with Jules Dassin's 1948 *Naked City*. For all its pretensions to be telling it like it is, *Naked City* was essentially a conventional murder story, with the gimmick of a documentary presentation. But the cycle of police procedure films marked a new high for police status in the movies, appreciated by real-life cops.

But the film image of the police did not remain long untarnished. The 1950s penchant for injecting 'adult', psychological undertones into action genres spread to the police film. The flatfoot image gave way to the Freudian fuzz. In the earliest example of this, William Wyler's 1951 *Detective Story*, Kirk Douglas's strong-arm technigue is explained in Oedipal terms: his nasty father drove his mother mad. The 1950s also emphasised the corrupt cop character, as in Joseph Losey's *The Prowler*, and *Rogue Cop*.

The year 1968, was, of course, also the year in which Nixon was elected President, not least because of the vicious law and order campaign mounted by John Mitchell against LBJ's decent and humane Attorney General Ramsay Clark, who was accused of being soft on crime and batting against the police. Not coincidentally, it was this year which also saw a flurry of films with police heroes. One of the first examples was the liberally minded *In the Heat of the Night* (1967). But the uniformed police character played by Rod Steiger was a racist bigot, and the film's hero, the detective played by Sidney Poitier, probably reflected the cult of black supermen sparked off by the the civil rights movement rather than the coming cop cycle. 1968 saw Frank Sinatra as *The Detective,* Richard Widmark as *Madigan*, Steve McQueen as *Bullitt*, Clint Eastwood as the eponymous hero of *Coogan's Bluff,* George Segal as a Portnoyish policeman in *No Way to Treat a Lady*, and Henry Fonda and George Kennedy hunting *The Boston Strangler* in a *Naked City* style depiciton of detailed police prodedure.

Not only did these films all reflect an interest in the work of the professional police, but most of them showed a concern with the impact of police work on the cop's personality and home-life. This was not altogether new. The psychological style of the 1950s had put the policeman on the couch, and taken us inside his home. *The FBI Story* of 1959, for example, had devoted much attention to problems James Stewart faced in his marriage. But generally these films simply applied the standard analyses of soap-opera to the police. The post-1968 cycle was much more concerned with clarifying the *specific* character of the cop. As Sinatara explains in *The Detective*, he's a cop because his father and grandfather were. 'It's the most useful thing I can be.' The cop's higher social standing was reflected in his feamale companions: usually rich or professional career women.

Perhaps the most significant departure in the new wave is the prominence given to *internal* relations in the police department. The drama of *Madigan*, for example, is much more about the conflict between the rough and ready street-wise methods of Widmark, and the rule-book procedures of Henry Fonda as the commissioner, than it is about the pursuit of the escaped criminal which provides the plot's ostensible purpose.

Don Siegel's *Dirty Harry* is significant for clearly taking up the perspective of the lower-level cop *against* the organisational hierarchy and the rest of the criminal justice system. *Harry* was the first film to echo the rank-and-file cops' complaint about the way legal restraints on police power crippled law enforcement.

Not all the police films of the 1970s were rightist in their politics. *Electra Glide in Blue* probed the roots of police machismo and paranoia, while *Serpico* had a hippie cop exposing corruption in the force. The sequel to *Dirty Harry*, *Magnum Force*, had Eastwood tracking down a secret vigilante group of policemen (including David Soul, TV's clean-cut Hutch) who take the law into their own hands, in a way apparently indistinguishable from Harry's vendetta in the earlier film. In his latest directorial effort, *The Gauntlet*, Eastwood further questions the police power mythology he had helped to create. But most of the 1970s police films carried on the law and order tradition: *Walking Tall* (based on the exploits of real-life Sheriff Buford Pusser), *Badge 373* (derived from the exploits of Eddie Egan, the original of *The French Connection*'s Popeye Doyle), John Wayne's *McQ*, and *The Enforcer*, last of the Dirty Harry series.

At one level, Wambaugh's novels and their film derivatives simply reflect this cycle. But unlike the others, they are not crime stories. Most recent cop films have basically been in the thriller tradition, with the novelty of a professional police hero. The policeman's image is of a crime-fighter. The hero fits the Hollywood machismo mould, a virtuoso of violence. In many respects, he is really the traditional western hero. The most obvious western parallels are in *Coogan's Bluff*, where Clint Eastwood actually plays an Arizona sheriff come east to get his man, with much banter about the contrast between his hick ways and those of the seedy urban milieu of his prey. At the end of *Dirty Harry*, Eastwood disgustedly throws his star away, a gesture clearly refering to Gary Cooper's similar action in *High Noon*. Many of the police films are urbanised equivalents of the *Town Tamer* western, in which the *Frontier Marshal* brings *Law and Order to Dodge City*, *Virginia City* or *Wichita*.

The Wambaugh stories are quite different. They show the real-life police chores, including being 'philosopher, guide and friend' to people in trouble, rounding up prostitutes or spying on gays, or coming across a robbery in progress. This picture of all-round policing is reminiscent of the English PC, George Dixon. But the cynical, foul-mouthed Los Angeles policemen of Wambaugh's creation are a far cry from the avuncular Jack Warner; and the beat of massage parlours, skid rows adult-movie houses and gay bars which they patrol is a world apart from the cosy pubs of Dock Green. It's interesting, though, that the traditional English bobby has now been replaced by the tougher law-enforcers of *The Sweeney* and *Target*.

Wambaugh is not the first to deglamourise the police task. But in earlier police procedure films like *Naked City*, the routines were still concerned with crime detection. Wambaugh's work does not have a crtime story as its centre. His novels are picaresque narratives involving the whole gamut of police duties, held together by developments in the lives of the cop heroes. In so far as there is a central plot, it is the moral progression or decay of the police characters – the 'greening' of the three rookies in *The New Centurions*, the ultimately unsuccessful struggle of the ageing Bumper Morgan to free himself from the job to which he has become wedded in *The Blue Knight*; *The Choirboys'* vain attempts to retain some tattered pride and sanity through their orgiastic 'choir practices'.

The fact that Wambaugh was a cop (until 1974, when he claims the pressure of his dual role made him quit), is a necessary but not sufficient explanation of his work. Many other recent cop films derive from the real-life exploits of policemen who often served as 'consultants' to the movies: *The French Connection, Badge 373, Walking Tall, Serpico, The Super Cops*. But these are varieties of the old 'Nipper of the Yard Tells How He Caught The Wigan Wildcats' sagas. Only in Wambaugh does the emphasis shift from the crime to the policeman.

The emergence of the cop as hero cannot be simply explained by growing fear of crime in the streets and public preoccupation with law and order, as Andrew Weiner implied in his article 'Crime wave – the TV cops' (NEW SOCIETY, 12 DECEMBER 1974). I think the new blue-coated heroes signify a growing *doubt* about the meaning and possibility of 'law and order'. In private-eye or police procedure films, the one-off crimes which stimulate the hunt used not to threaten society itself, but individual victims. 'Law and order' as such was at issue only in the classic western, which traced the building-up of civilised communities against outlaws who threatened the very basis of a peaceful, ordered existence. But these films ended optimistically with the sheriff saving the town for the decent folk.

In the recent cop films, this optimism has gone. But the reason is not just that the sheer volume of crime has increased. What actually prevents the crime being cleared up in the first reel are own-goals scored against the hero by people nominally on his team. In the conservative kind of police movie, like *Dirty Harry*, the people who shackle the cop are liberal do-gooders who care 'more for the criminal than the victim'. In the liberal variety, like *Serpico* or *The Gauntlet*, the problem is corruption within the police department, or fatal flaws within the cop personality, as in *Electra Glide in Blue*. Both kinds reflect the breakdown of the simple moral values of the old western and crime movies where the source of villainy was clearly outside the community, and limited to evil individuals.

The conservative still reveres the old verities. But he sees them threatened not so much by psychopathic killers and greedy robbers as the misguided liberals, ostensibly on the right side of the law, who prevent the necessary crackdown. The *liberal* begins to fear the police more than their prey, who are seen as victims of society, or people 'doing their own thing' harassed by puritanical pigs (*The Strawberry Statement, Electra Glide in Blue*). They begin to doubt the validity of a war against crime when the state commits greater crimes, legally (Vietnam) or illegally (Watergate).

Wambaugh takes these doubts a stage further. There is no question in his work of actually containing the crime or misery the cop sees all around him. The struggle is to preserve some minimum integrity and decency in an irredeemably savage and amoral world. Will the cop be able to mature and develop as a man, despite the degredation he is immersed in, as *The New Centurions* do, or will he surrender to the vicious cynicism of a Roscoe Rules? As Wambaugh himself has emphasised, the danger to the policeman is not so much physical as spiritual. His cops *do* risk violent attack. But as Wambaugh stresses, many occupations are *more* exposed to physical risk than the police. In all these stories, the real threat is to the policeman's humanity of spirit, the tip of the iceberg being the high suicide, mental and marital breakdown rates of the police. What the policeman must come to terms with is the futility of his job. The bad policeman, like Roscoe Rules, resorts to violence in a futile endeavour to control crime. Good policemen try to reconcile themselves to being caretakers of a civilisation that relentlessly breeds misery and degradation. Wambaugh's ideology cannot readily be classified as either conservative or liberal. He is certainly not in the law and order camp, but at the same time his deep pessimism precludes any hope of social change.

The Choirboys reaches a new depth of blackness and despair. *The New Centurions* and *The Blue Knight* ended with the death of a leading character – but the ethical purity of the cop's tragic world-view remained unsullied. In *The Choirboys*, the choristers survive physically, but they are morally destroyed, none more so than the leader, Spermwhale Whalen, who is forced to testify against his buddies to save his pension. (The film serves Wambaugh badly, and he has dissociated himself from it. The producers have tacked on an unconvincing 'happy' ending.)

The end of the novel, *The Choirboys*, implies that the project of saving the individual's integrity is doomed. Wambaugh finally succumbs to the view that 'the heart of man is incurably evil' (as Enoch Powell once put it at a Police Federation seminar). A man's gotta do what a man's gotta do – but for what he no longer knows.

[10]
True Lies: Changing Images of Crime in British Postwar Cinema

ABSTRACT

■ Academic and public attention has long focused on media images of crime. Crime media create and reproduce cultural narratives about social and moral order, and the putative links between such images and their effects on society have been much debated. While acknowledging the complexity of the relationship between media representations and social influence, this article argues that the assumptions concerning actual trends in crime media which underlie and inform these debates have received little empirical investigation. Particularly neglected has been research on the cinema, and little research has adopted the historical perspective necessary to make claims regarding long-term trends. As part of a larger project, we report a quantitative and qualitative content analysis of popular crime films in Britain released between 1945 and 1991. Despite common beliefs, we find no overall increase in the number of crime films. However, the nature of representations of crime and social order shows a variety of significant shifts over this time. In brief, the nature of crime changes, the violence and threat of crime increases, as does the portrayed suffering of victims. To combat this, police officers increasingly assume the hero role and they increasingly use vigilante, even corrupt, tactics to achieve their goals, although their chances of bringing criminals to justice actually decrease. Such findings lead us to propose a three-stage periodization for crime films. ■

Key Words content analysis, crime, film, historical comparison, media

Jessica Allen is Research Officer, Sonia Livingstone is Senior Lecturer in Social Psychology and Robert Reiner is Professor of Criminology at the London School of Economics and Political Science, Houghton St, London WC2 2AE, UK. [email: s.livingstone@lse.ac.uk]

EUROPEAN JOURNAL OF COMMUNICATION 13(1)

Media made criminality: moral panic or legitimate concern?

Concerns about the harmful consequences of the mass media for law, order and morality are as old as the media themselves. The 18th century magistrate, political economist and pioneer of modern policing Patrick Colquhoun was one of many respectable commentators of his time worrying that 'the morals and habits of the lower ranks in society are growing progressively worse' (cited in Radzinowicz, 1956: 275). He blamed this on a variety of more or less familiar causes, from the decline in religion and the inadequacy of contemporary policing arrangements, to the growth of indigence and the rising price of pickled salmon. Among his litany of criminogenic cultural trends he bemoaned a supposed wave of 'bawdy ballad singers' who went around the pubs debauching the morals of the masses with their salacious lyrics. Unlike his counterparts today, however, he did not advocate censorship, which he saw as counterproductive. Instead he wanted the Government to form rival groups of wholesome ballad singers, confident that the uplifting lyrics of the 18th century precursors of Sir Cliff Richard and Dame Vera Lynn would soon supplant the prophets of sex, gin and rock 'n' roll in popular affection.

Each new mass medium has attracted its own wave of moral panic about prospective insidious effects on crime and order (Pearson, 1983). Until the advent of television, probably the most vigorous and protracted debate was about the cinema, the dominant popular entertainment in the first half of this century, and still prominent ever since. Authority figures had no doubts about the baleful consequences of large groups of young people huddled together in the dark to see huge, graphic images of law-breaking and lewdness projected onto a silver screen. 'The cinema is partly responsible for the increase in crime committed by juveniles', declared one John Perceval, chief constable of Wigan, in 1917 as part of his 'evidence' to the so-called 'National Council of Morals' (Mathews, 1994: 27). The same year he joined with his fellow chief constables in stating that 'the establishment of a central censor of cinematograph films is essential and will conduce to the reduction of juvenile crime in the country' (Mathews, 1994: 26). Concern about harmful effects of the mass media have not been confined to conservatives. Radical analyses have portrayed the media as one of the sources of the hegemony of ruling-class ideology and representations of crime and criminal justice figure prominently in these arguments (Sparks, 1992). Where conservatives have worried about what they perceive as celebrations of deviance, radicals have seen the whipping up of popular anxieties about crime as a means of bolstering support for repressive state measures of control (Hall, 1979).

Both sets of concerns, but especially the conservative fears of criminogenic consequences of media representations, have generated an industry of research attempting to assess the impact of the media on crime and violence. A recent overview found that 'since the 1920s thousands of studies of mass media effects have been conducted' (Livingstone, 1996: 306), and yet the results of this vast body of disparate research are far from clear or consistent. The fairly meagre payoff from countless research hours and dollars stems in part from the focus on testing the implausible, though still prevalent, notion of a pure media effect. The implicit model underlying popular anxieties, imported straightforwardly into much research, is of the media as an ideological hypodermic syringe injecting noxious emotions and values into a passive audience of cultural dopes. These 'dopes' then imitate in reality the thrilling crimes and deviant acts committed in fantasy by their screen idols.

Clearly this mechanistic model of the causal relationship between media messages and subsequent deviant behaviour should be rejected. Media images may be as much a reflection as a cause of developing patterns of culture and practices. Moreover, viewers and readers are active interpreters, bringing to bear a variety of perspectives derived from their particular social experiences and positions. In short, there is a complex relationship between changing media representations and wider social practices (Dahlgren, 1988; Gerbner et al., 1986; Sparks, 1992; Quart and Auster, 1984). As suggested elsewhere:

> ... maybe it is time to accept that violent images, for example, have in general little direct effect on viewers' actions, and time for more research on the enculturating role of the media. ... The study of enculturation processes which work over long time periods, and which are integral to rather than separate from other forms of social determination, would not ask how the media make us act or think, but rather how the media contribute to making us who we are. (Livingstone, 1996: 321)

In short, this more interactive and complex conception of the inter-relationship between media and society suggests that the pursuit of a pure media effect by traditional experimental research is chimerical. On the other hand, one must also question the automatic instinct of liberals, concerned about the dangers of censorship, who have tended to rely on the difficulties of proving a straightforward causal link between media, crime and violence as a rather implausible way of denying any such relationship at all.

EUROPEAN JOURNAL OF COMMUNICATION 13(1)

More important for the present article is our argument that claims for media effects, whether originating in academic research or public debate, inevitably rest upon implicit or explicit claims about the contents of media texts. These claims take various, sometimes contradictory forms. For example, it may be argued that rising crime statistics are related to increasingly permissive and glamorized representations of film crime, or that increasingly serious and graphic film violence bears some responsibility for the levels of fear of crime in society. In other words, whatever the existence, direction and contextualization of the link between images of crime and actual crime in society, the prior question of media contents requires consideration. Such consideration must be explicit if debates over crime, media and society are to develop beyond implicit speculation about, for example, whether certain media contain more crime images or crime images of a different nature compared with those of earlier periods. In any case, academic theories of media effects are rarely pitched at the most general level of presuming 'more effects' for 'worse' crime representations; rather they hypothesize more specific links between particular patterns or processes of media effect in relation to the particular nature of crime representations. It matters, therefore, not only whether crime is up or down in the cinema or press, but whether crime is seen to pay, whether villains are portrayed as glamorous, whether endings are conclusive or ambiguous, and so forth (Bryant and Zillman, 1993; Gerbner et al., 1986; Gunter, 1985; Hearold, 1986).

Crime and the cinema since the Second World War: aims and methods of the study

The present research was conducted within such an enculturation framework as part of a major research programme in Britain on 'Crime and Social Order', which aims to understand changes since the Second World War. Our project, 'Discipline or Desubordination? Changing Media Images of Crime Since the Second World War', seeks to analyse how media images of crime and criminal justice may have shifted over the past half century, and how audiences have interpreted these shifts. We have conducted an historical content analysis of changing representations of crime in film, newspapers and television, together with focus group discussions with viewers differentiated particularly according to age/generation. This is the first time a comparative analysis of the crime content of media has been conducted over such a lengthy period or across three types of media (Garofalo, 1981). While a number of studies have focused on crime in newspapers, fewer have systematically examined the crime content of television or film.[1] Yet, one cannot assume that all media represent crime similarly, or that analysis of one medium (most commonly, the press) necessarily tells us about crime representations in other media (particularly when extrapolating from factual reporting to fictional genres). Nor can one assume that crime representations are unchanging over time (thus making historical content analysis unnecessary) or, equally simplistically, that crime representations are just 'getting worse', as is often popularly assumed based on a nostalgic view of the past. Different media and different time-periods are subject to varying conditions, conventions and concerns; only following comparative analysis can the constancies and changes be identified.

The purpose of conducting an historical content analysis of representations of crime in the cinema is to provide data which may inform the wider debates outlined above concerning the relation between crime media and society/social influences. Of course, many other factors not considered here are also relevant, making straightforward conclusions difficult; yet some attempt to survey the shifts, or constancies, in crime representations over time can only be informative. Our historical content analysis of changes in the representation of crime in cinema films falls into two related parts, using quantitative and qualitative methods. The quantitative aspect involved a preliminary calculation of shifts in the degree to which films concerned themselves with crime at all: is there some basis to the common assumption in political and public debate that the media are more than ever saturated with crime stories? The more detailed qualitative analysis begins with a broad definition of the crime film, and within this category attempts to look at the changing moral and social frameworks which inform cinema narratives about crime: to the extent that changes in crime representations can be identified, what specific changes have or have not occurred and when?

In terms of method, it may be appropriate to comment on our use of content analysis for analysing trends in crime films, particularly given the critical attention which this method has received. Our aim is to offer a general overview of changes in representations of crime and the criminal justice system since 1945. Following Thomas's (1994) defence of content analysis, we attend to infrequent as well as frequent themes and incorporate some assessment of context in framing our categories for coding. Inevitably, the changes we discuss depend on theoretically informed judgements about aspects of crime films we first consider important and, second, were able to categorize. Despite the limitations to this style of content analysis, the method offers the benefit of enabling summaries of changes over a lengthy time-period. Basing such an

EUROPEAN JOURNAL OF COMMUNICATION 13(1)

historical overview on a careful consideration of the sizeable body of films released over, say, the past half century seemed to us especially pressing. For most film studies concentrate on in-depth analyses of only a few selected films, resulting in a problematic potential for distortion in our appreciation of overall trends, especially given the tendency to select films primarily for their critical or aesthetic particularity. However, in acknowledging the insights which often result from such in-depth analyses, the present study is intended to be complementary, offering different advantages and disadvantages to enrich our understanding of shifts in crime films over time.

Celluloid crime waves?

Our broader quantitative analysis asked whether the degree of cinematic preoccupation with crime in a broad sense had changed since 1945 (see also Allen et al., 1997). We addressed two related issues here: (1) has there been a change in the proportion of all films which are predominantly concerned with crime; and (2) has the crime content of films in other genres altered?

Crime films as a genre

Many historical and critical accounts of crime films as a specific genre have been published (e.g. Clarens, 1980; McArthur, 1972; Rosow, 1978; Shadoian, 1977). As with other genres there is room for considerable debate about the definitions of the crime film (Cook, 1985; Kaminsky, 1974; Mast and Cohen, 1979; Nichols, 1976; Schatz, 1981). Our category of the 'crime film' is not based on genre theory; instead we developed a straightforwardly operational definition, derived from the categories of the law and the criminal justice system of the period. The question of what genre and typical narrative structures exist within the broad terrain of films which are primarily concerned with crime is central to our research agenda. This does mean that our category of crime films is very broad, but the intention was to encompass all those films in which crime features as a major concern, whatever their precise generic characteristics. We classify a film as a 'crime film' if (1) the central focus of the narrative is the commission and/or the investigation of a crime and/ or (2) the principal protagonist is either an offender or a professional working in the criminal justice system. Thus a crime film for us might have an amateur type of crime investigator (e.g. Agatha Christie's Miss

Marple) or a professional criminal justice employee as its protagonist, and would also include films whose central focus is on the protagonist's personal problems or social milieu rather than on the commission or investigation of a crime. The category also does not imply any judgements of aesthetic quality or intent: *Crime and Punishment, Les Miserables* or *An Inspector Calls* would be as much crime films as a standard formulaic Hollywood assembly-line product.

To measure the trends in crime in film accurately would ideally require viewing every film released in Britain since 1945. This is clearly not practical, because of both the time involved and the unavailability of many films. Although the number released each year has declined considerably over the last 50 years, from around 400 to about 200, the total since the Second World War approaches 15,000. Clearly we could not view all of these and our estimates of trends are based inevitably on cruder procedures. Our prime source of data on trends in the proportion of crime films was F. Maurice Speed's *Film Review Annual*. This has been published annually since 1944 and each year provides a comprehensive list of all films released in Britain, together with synopses and credits. From this we obtained a 20 percent random sample of the films listed every second year (i.e. 10 percent sample of the total number of films), amounting to a sample of 1461 films released between 1945 and 1991.

Using the synopses we then calculated the proportion of films each year which were in the crime genre, as defined above, based on the assumption that genre is clearly indicated even by a brief synopsis. While crime and/or criminal justice are by definition central narrative concerns of films in the crime genre, it is also the case that there are many representations of crime outside the genre itself. Almost any film, in any genre, will involve some references to crime or criminal justice, even if it is as fleeting as the beat cop giving Gene Kelly an enquiring look in the title sequence of *Singin' in the Rain*. This is what we refer to as the *crime content* of non-crime films, and we estimated this also insofar as the crime content could be described as central to the film. Our assumption, in short, was that the synopses allow us to identify those films where crime is sufficiently prominent to figure even in a brief account of the narrative, even though it is not central enough to make the film a 'crime film'. Following initial training on a pilot sample of film synopses, the main sample was coded by two independent coders, with eight of the 23 years being dual coded. Reliability between coders was quite high, with an average of 95 percent agreement for crime content and 73 percent for allocations to one of 10 genres. Where the two main coders disagreed, the

EUROPEAN JOURNAL OF COMMUNICATION 13(1)

disputed or borderline cases were resolved by a third researcher drawing upon a wider range of reference sources.

Our confidence that this methodology does provide a sufficiently accurate account of trends in different genres is bolstered by applying it to other genres where the trends are well known. Our estimates indicate very clear trends in the genres where these would be expected. For example, our figures chart the virtual disappearance of the western by the 1980s (its subsequent tentative revival occurs only after 1991, after our period for analysis), and a similar trend is revealed for romance films. War films decline after the early 1950s apart from a couple of Vietnam-related films in the early 1980s, and our data clearly indicate the rise of sex-centred films in the 1960s and early 1970s as permissiveness first hits the cinema, followed by their relative decline as a much more explicit sex content becomes normalized in all other genres (Allen et al., 1997). While our methods do reveal trends in other genres, this is not so for crime films, as discussed below.

Crime content of postwar movies

As Figure 1 shows, since 1945 there is no clear trend for the proportion of films falling in the crime genre, or for significant crime content, although there are many sharp fluctuations in individual years around this basic steady state. Clearly, crime has been a significant concern of the cinema throughout the postwar period (and probably before that as well). In Figure 1, the top line represents the total percentage of crime content for all films, the area between the two lines represents films which contain significant amounts of crime but are not crime films, while crime films proper are represented by the lower line. In most years around 20 percent of all films in our sample are crime films. The proportion only dips below 10 percent in one year (1965). There are no discernible trends up or down over the 50 years as a whole, although there are sharp rises and falls in particular years. The apparent decline in the mid-1950s from postwar highs may be attributable to the decline of *film noir*.

The representation of crime content in other genres also does not show any clear long-term trends, up or down, as Figure 1 shows. Crime content does vary across genres, being highest in westerns and adventure films which are essentially crime stories set in times and places other than contemporary urban societies (as well as 100 percent in crime films of course). However, there appears to be no overall trend towards a

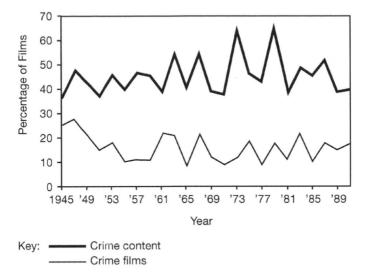

Figure 1 Percentage of crime films and crime content for all films

quantitatively greater representation of crime in films since the Second World War. This constancy of cinematic concern with crime is not altogether surprising: it is parallelled in publishing (about 25 percent of all fiction has been crime fiction over the same period), newspaper reporting (Graber, 1980) and prime-time television shows (Dominick, 1978); although it should be noted that these content analyses cover more limited time-periods. Available estimates for other media thus concur with the present findings that about a fifth to a third of the output of each medium are crime stories, whether fictional or factual, although most have some crime content.

Thus contrary to general beliefs about increasing crime content of the media (as in 'Watchdog Attacks ITV Over Glut of Crime Programmes'[2]), our data show a constant rate of representation, at least in the cinema, over 50 years. This by itself does not demolish claims that media images may be a contributory factor in the rise in crime rates over the same period. It is entirely possible that qualitative changes in the mode and manner of representation have occurred within a constant quantity, and that these could possibly have had criminogenic consequences or that these might reflect sociocultural shifts over the period. The rest of this article reports on our detailed qualitative analysis of crime films to cast light on this.

Table 1 Most popular crime films in the UK, 1945–91

1991	*Silence of the Lambs,* Sleeping with the Enemy, The Naked Gun 21/2,* Kindergarten Cop, Backdraft, Misery,* Home Alone*
1990	*Ghost**
1989	*The Naked Gun,* Lethal Weapon 2, Who Framed Roger Rabbit?, Batman, Twins*
1988	*Fatal Attraction,* Buster, Police Academy 5, Robocop,* Wall Street, Crocodile Dundee II, The Running Man*
1987	*The Untouchables,* Lethal Weapon, Beverly Hills Cop II,* Police Academy IV*
1986	*Mona Lisa,* Cobra, Jagged Edge,* Police Academy III*
1985	*Beverly Hills Cop,* Witness,* Police Academy 2**
1984	*Police Academy, Sudden Impact,* Scarface**
1983	*Superman III**
1982	*Death Wish II, Who Dares Wins, Mad Max 2**
1981	*The Postman Always Rings Twice,* Superman II*
1980	*Escape from Alcatraz,* McVicar, Friday 13th*
1979	*Midnight Express, The Warriors, Death on the Nile,* Superman, Porridge, The Bitch*
1978	*The Gauntlet,* Convoy, Ruby/Satan's Slave, The Choirboys, Assault in Precinct 13,* Candleshoe*
1977	*The Enforcer,* Sweeny,* Bugsy Malone, The Pink Panther Strikes Again*
1976	*All the Presidents Men, One Flew Over the Cuckoo's Nest, The Return of the Pink Panther*
1975	*Murder on the Orient Express, Papillon, Death Wish,* Freebie and the Bean**
1974	*The Sting, Papillon, Chinatown,* The Way of the Dragon, Don't Look Now*
1973	*The Godfather, A Clockwork Orange*
1972	*The Godfather, The French Connection,* Dirty Harry,* A Clockwork Orange, Straw Dogs, Shaft,* Klute**
1971	*Get Carter*
1970	–
1969	*Bulitt,* The Italian Job**
1968	*Robbery*
1967	*Bonnie and Clyde**
1966	*The Great St Trinian's Train Robbery*
1965	*A Shot in the Dark,* The Big Job, How to Murder Your Wife,* Repulsion, Hush. . .Hush, Sweet Charlotte, Topkapi,* What's New Pussycat?*
1964	*Charade,* The Prize, Marnie, Woman of Straw, Yesterday, Today and Tomorrow, The Pink Panther, Robin and the 7 Hoods, Goldfinger**
1963	*Cape Fear, The Cracksman, On the Beat, The Wrong Arm of the Law**

Table 1 *Continued*

1962	*The Boys, Dr No**
1961	*Victim, A Taste of Fear*
1960	*Anatomy of a Murder,* The League of Gentlemen,* Ocean's Eleven,* The Rise and Fall of Legs Diamond,* Two Way Stretch,* Psycho, A Touch of Larceny, The Trials of Oscar Wilde,* Carry on Constable**
1959	*The 39 Steps**
1958	*The Defiant Ones, Tread Softly Stranger, Witness for the Prosecution**
1957	*The Girl Can't Help It,* Brothers in Law, These Dangerous Years*
1956	*The Bad Seed, The Ladykillers,* The Man Who Knew Too Much,* Yield to the Night*
1955	*Black Widow, Cast a Dark Shadow, Footsteps in the Fog, We're No Angels, Blackboard Jungle, Love Me or Leave Me*
1954	*Dial M For Murder, Father Brown,* The Green Scarf, Rear Window,* Riot in Cell Block 11,* The Sleeping Tiger, The Weak and the Wicked, On the Waterfront**
1953	*Turn the Key Softly, Scared Stiff, The Intruder*
1952	*Affair in Trinidad,* Hunted, Murder Inc.,* Sudden Fear*
1951	*The Lavender Hill Mob,* Pool of London, The Lemon Drop Kid, Detective Story,* Strangers on a Train,* Highway 301*
1950	*The Blue Lamp,* The Red Light,* Stage Fright,* White Heat**
1949	*The Paradine Case,* Knock on any Door,* Street with No Name, Third Man**
1948	*Monsieur Verdoux,* Possessed, Brighton Rock,* The Unfaithful, Blanche Fury, Good Time Girl, London Belongs to Me,* Kiss of Death, Noose, Killer McCoy, Saigon*
1947	*Odd Man Out,* Holiday Camp, Calcutta,* My Favourite Brunette,* Hue and Cry,* The Upturned Glass, They Made Me a Fugitive,* The Two Mrs Carrolls, October Man, A Man about the House, White Unicorn, Desert Fury*
1946	*Gilda,* Blue Dahlia,* Bedelia, Spellbound,* Mildred Pierce**
1945	*Arsenic and Old Lace,* Conflict*

Note: The sample coded comprises all films marked with an asterix (*).

Consensus to chaos? Shifting moral paradigms in postwar crime movies

We examined the changes in moral and social perspectives which frame cinema narratives about crime through a detailed analysis of some of the most popular crime films since 1945. Our general methodological approach is informed by that of Will Wright's study of the western genre (Wright, 1975). This study stands out as one of the most systematic sociological analyses of a cinema genre. Instead of concentrating on a few

EUROPEAN JOURNAL OF COMMUNICATION 13(1)

examples of the genre based on personal preference or critical consensus, Wright constructs a sample of the most generally influential films of the period judged by box office success, in order to analyse those films which had the widest resonance with popular consciousness. We have proceeded in a similar way. Looking at box office hits, rather than critical successes, seemed congruent with our interest in what was watched by audiences.[3] For our primary concern is not an aesthetic or production-oriented analysis of shifts in media forms, but an audience-oriented analysis of media which are available, popularly attended and responded to as part of the circulation of meanings in everyday life.

We first identified those crime films (as defined above) which figured in the lists of top box office successes in the UK since 1945. The resulting 150 or so films are thus the most commercially successful crime films (see Table 1). Of these we have viewed and analysed just over half (the 80 films asterisked in Table 1). The selection of films to watch was based on availability and an attempt to draw the sample evenly across the whole period.

During the viewing of these films, we took detailed notes on the narratives, focusing on diverse aspects of the representation of crime and criminal justice. After each viewing we completed a detailed content analysis of the film, seeking to record systematically diverse aspects of the images and narrative. As the vast majority of films were organized according to some variant of the classic Hollywood narrative (Grant, 1986; Kaminsky, 1974), our analytic categories were constructed according to both narrative structure (protagonist, opponent, setting, central events, narrative resolution, moral coda, etc.) as well as categories concerned with crime (nature and severity of crime, representations of police, villains, etc.). In addition to relatively concrete features of the images of crime, criminals and criminal justice, we attempted to assess the more general moral and social perspectives suggested by the films. We offer a preliminary view of these results in the rest of the article. First we describe the changes in some specific aspects, and then venture a tentative overall analysis.

The movie crimes

We distinguished four ways in which crimes could feature in crime movies. First, in most crime movies the central theme of the narrative is the commission and/or investigation of a crime, by definition. Adapting Hitchcock's usage we have called the primary crime which animates the narrative the 'MacGuffin'; Hitchcock used this term to refer to the object whose pursuit provides the driving force of the narrative. By our definition of a crime film this is always the commission and/or investigation of a crime, although identifying the MacGuffin crime is not always straightforward. The first crime shown may well not be the MacGuffin. For example, Brian de Palma's *The Untouchables* begins with the bombing of a tavern by Al Capone's mob, during which a child is blown up. This serves to kick-start our horror of Capone, but the crime which animates the narrative is really his continuous operation of a criminal empire which generates other crimes, many of them more serious than the MacGuffin, such as the murder with which the film opens. We label those crimes which are committed in the course of, or in order to cover up the MacGuffin, 'consequential crimes'. Crimes committed by the central criminals, but not directly related to the MacGuffin, we have labelled 'collateral crimes'. Finally in many crime movies we see crimes committed which are unrelated to the MacGuffin but portray aspects of the wider society and we call these 'contextual crimes'.

The distinction between these four categories can be illustrated by Don Siegel's *Dirty Harry*. The MacGuffin is the serial murder campaign waged by Scorpio in order to hold the city to ransom (an example of which opens the film). In seeking to evade capture, Scorpio commits several other crimes from kidnapping to assault and murder. These are consequential crimes. In addition to Scorpio's crimes, which are central to the narrative, we see many contextual crimes, such as the celebrated bank robbery which interrupts the eponymous hero's hamburger lunch and prompts the first version of his catch-phrase 'Do you feel lucky, punk?' The contextual crimes serve both to develop Harry's character and to convey the sense of the city as urban jungle which functions to justify his 'dirtiness'. A clear example of a collateral crime is in the *League of Gentlemen* at the start of the film where we see the central characters' criminal credentials established.

Homicide is by far the most common MacGuffin crime throughout the period: 48 percent of our sample films had a homicide MacGuffin. This does of course convey a very different picture from official crime statistics, where some 90 percent of recorded offences are property crimes like burglary or car theft. There are, however, some interesting variations in the other MacGuffin crimes. Up to 1967 property crimes featured more often as the MacGuffin than thereafter. On the other hand, sexual and other assaults, together with drug offences, only begin to appear as MacGuffins after 1968.

EUROPEAN JOURNAL OF COMMUNICATION 13(1)

Perhaps the most interesting changes occur in the contextual crimes. Before 1964 many films did not portray any crimes which were not directly related to the MacGuffin. Thereafter contextual offences began to proliferate. This is significant because it is contextual crimes perhaps even more than the MacGuffin which create a sense of society as a whole being threatened by crime. Before the mid-1960s crime is more often portrayed as an abnormal, one-off intrusion into a stable social order. Afterwards representations of an all-pervasive, routinized threat of crime begins to become common, Indeed, before 1970, only 20 percent of films show crime as ubiquitous, while after 1970 portrayals of ubiquitous crime are shown in 69 percent of films. This change is linked to another change: the increasing predominance of police heroes rather than amateur sleuths. As crime is increasingly portrayed as endemic to society, it justifies the employment of a large bureaucracy, with police heroes leading the narrative, but also with increasing prominence accorded to the organization, and organizational pressures and problems which lie behind their activities. Thus following this shift, crime is rarely portrayed as just a diversion for enthusiastic amateurs.

Among the contextual crimes there are also interesting changes. Essentially they become more professional and more serious. From the early 1960s sexual and drug offences become more common contextual crimes, as does homicide. Before that when contextual crimes were indicated they were more often assaults and more rarely homicides.

The violence of the crimes

There is a clear trend towards an increasingly graphic representation of violence in the portrayal of crime. Interestingly this is more marked in the representation of consequential and contextual than MacGuffin crimes. As already noted most MacGuffins have always been murder, the ultimate crime of violence. Before 1974 only one film in our sample displayed a significant degree of violence in its depiction of the MacGuffin (*London Belongs to Me*). Almost all had only minor or no representation of pain or damage beyond the fact of the murder itself. After 1974 this continues to be the case usually, but there are an increasing number of films with significant degrees of violence in the MacGuffin. There are clearer changes in the representation of consequential, collateral and contextual crimes.[4] Before 1974 only a few of these portrayed a significant amount of graphic violence, and most none or a small amount. After 1974 a significant degree of violence predominates in representations of these crimes (although see Cumberbatch et al., 1995 for differing conclusions about levels of violence in the news).

This increase in violence is linked to a change in the representation of both the leading and other criminals. After 1974 no films had non-violent central offenders, although they were common in the 1940s and 1950s. Up to the end of the 1950s, where the leading offenders did engage in violence this was usually portrayed as a necessary means of achieving their objectives, rather than as gratuitous or sadistic. After 1974 the proportion of sadistic or gratuitously violent chief offenders increases, and after 1985 there are none represented in any other way. Similar trends appear for supporting offenders. After 1974 these are mainly portrayed as sadistic and gratuitously violent. While there had been some sadistic or gratuitously violent criminals in the 1940s and 1950s too, 43 percent of films showed non-violent offenders or offenders who were only violent to the extent necessary to achieve their criminal objectives.

Following from this the impact of crime on the victims is increasingly presented as traumatic. Before the mid-1970s while 25 percent of films showed victims as traumatized, many were not. In the 1980s they were overwhelmingly represented as suffering extreme trauma, indeed from 1977 63 percent of victims are visibly traumatized. This perhaps surprising ambivalence or even indifference towards victims in the earlier years may have interesting repercussions. By positioning the audience as sympathetic to the victims, revealing the effects and consequences of violent crime, later films may in fact make the audience more inclined to abhor violence and crime in general (Schlesinger et al., 1992).

The nature of protagonists

There have been congruent changes in who the protagonists of crime films are, and how they are portrayed. As noted earlier, perhaps the main change is the increasing prevalence of professional police heroes, especially after the late 1960s. The only other type of law enforcer featuring to any significant extent after the early 1970s is the professional private investigator. Amateur sleuths, ordinary people who become involved in investigating a crime, or other criminal justice related occupations such as lawyers or crime reporters were frequently heroes of crime movies up to the mid-1960s but declined after that. Offenders,

EUROPEAN JOURNAL OF COMMUNICATION 13(1)

however, become the protagonists of movies with increasing frequency, although there have always been a few. Nevertheless, criminals remain far less common as heroes compared with the police.

How have these 'police heroes' been portrayed? Before the mid-1960s only 11 percent of police were vigilante cops: most abided by the due process of law in their apprehension of criminals. By contrast, since 1964 only four films in our sample featured due process police heroes — the rest (i.e. 80 percent of police heroes) all used vigilante tactics to a greater or lesser extent. Police representations in the second half of the period were not restricted to vigilantism: what Sir Paul Condon, Chief Constable for the Metropolitan Police, has dubbed 'noble cause corruption'. While most police continue to be portrayed as personally honest, all the cases of police corruption in our sample are concentrated in post-1964 movies.

Despite, or perhaps because of their declining respect for the rule of law, the police and the criminal justice system appear less successful in later films (corresponding to declining clear-up rates in reality). Up to 1952 no film showed criminals getting away with their crimes. This remained rare up to the early 1970s but then occurs in a substantial minority of films. Whereas between a third and a half of the films up to the early 1960s show the criminal justice system as usually successful, virtually none do thereafter. Indeed, over half the post-1960s films represent the system as highly incompetent. When criminal justice agents do succeed in defeating criminals they are increasingly likely to do this outside the law. Thus, while up to 1967 around half of all MacGuffin criminals were brought to justice, after that this happened in only three of the sample films. Conversely, before 1959 there were only two films where crimes were cleared up by the offender being killed by the cops, while after that, this becomes a common pattern. The criminal justice system is therefore seen as increasingly impotent: the only way to get criminals, and so to conclude the film, is to kill them.

Overall the extent to which police officers are portrayed as sympathetic human beings shows a U-shaped rather than linear trend. Up to the 1950s they were mainly represented as caring and socially responsible. Afterwards, negative portraits of corrupt, driven and violent cops or the opposite — purely instrumental 'uniform-carriers' or bumbling, buffoon-like cops — proliferated. However, during the 1980s there is a clear resurgence of the caring, socially responsible police image, although there are also a number of films which portray the police as idiotic, but good natured fools — such as the *Police Academy* series.

The threat of crime

Related to the changing representation of protagonists, crimes, victims and violence is the overall sense of crime as increasingly a serious, all-pervasive threat to the social order. This is not a straightforward linear increase but a curvilinear pattern. Up to the mid-1960s there was a roughly equal balance between films in which crime appears as a one-off occurrence and those where it is a more widespread threat. After 1964 the representation of crime as a common threat begins to predominate; in the mid-1980s the pattern changes again with about half of the films in the sample presenting one-off crimes. Often, however, these are seen as emblematic of wider issues, as in *The Accused* or *Basic Instinct*, where the rapes or murders raise questions of a more general kind about gender relations (albeit from widely contrasting viewpoints).

A related shift is the representation of crime as having wider social roots. Up to the mid-1960s the sources of crime were typically individual moral failings. One-off crimes were motivated by exceptional lust — for money, sex, power or all three. Occasionally they were the product of individual psychopathology. When crime was represented as a more general threat from organized gangland, this underworld was itself the creation of greedy individuals, as in *The Rise and Fall of Legs Diamond*, or even of psychopaths as in *White Heat*. After the mid-1960s there is an increasing number of films where the threat of crime has social origins. Gangland becomes the ghetto: even more violent and threatening, but a clear product of historic patterns of institutionalized oppression and injustice, as in *Shaft*. Or gangland becomes the 'family': an alternative moral universe and opportunity structure for those excluded from established hierarchies by their ethnic roots, as with the *Godfather* series. While this sense of the socially structured contours of crime causation remains common after the early 1980s there is also a re-emergence of films where gangland is once more the simple product of amoral and overweening greed, without any broader dimension. Only it is now even more ruthless and violent than before: an enemy to be extirpated in no-holds-barred all-out war by superhero cops like Stallone or Schwarzenegger.

Representations of social and moral order

The clearest changes of all are in the broader representations of social and moral order and authority in general. After the mid-1960s there is an increasing representation of society riven by inequalities and tensions which are a source of conflict and instability, with society increasingly

EUROPEAN JOURNAL OF COMMUNICATION 13(1)

fragmented rather than united (73 percent of films after 1966 compared with 33 percent pre-1966). Up until then, insofar as social divisions are portrayed at all they are represented as essentially fair and accepted by everyone. From the late 1950s an increasing number of crime films present racial divisions as a source of conflict and crime, and more recently this is also true of gender. Class divisions are frequently presented throughout the period but seem to be a source of tension only after the early 1960s. Up to the mid-1960s society is predominantly represented as consensual on moral issues albeit socially stratified; thereafter conflict figures prominently, although consensus portraits continue, and indeed seem to be increasingly common again towards the later 1980s. Perhaps related to this is increasing numbers of films portraying society as unstable, especially from 1966 onwards, though during the 1980s this reverts to half portraying society as stable and half as unstable. Following a similar periodization, depictions of moral certainty collapse around the mid-1960s, and films thereafter depict moral conflict and uncertainty as commonplace.

Related to the collapse of moral certainties, is an increasing prevalence of films with no moral resolution of the issues or problems raised by the narrative. Up to the mid-1960s most of the crime films which were successful at the box office (which excludes most of the *films noirs* which critics and historians concentrate on) had 'feel-good' endings. After that, disturbing, ambivalent, downbeat endings begin to predominate. However, this has been reversed since the mid-1980s: the feel-good factor has fought back successfully, at least in films. There is a bifurcation between those where the plot problems are resolved at the end, and those leaving questions and fears unsettled.

To hell and back? The dialectic of postwar crime films

The variables we have analysed in our viewing of the most commercially successful crime movies released in Britain since 1945 seem to change according to three different patterns. Some rise or fall in a straightforward linear fashion; others go through a curvilinear path; for yet others there appear to be qualitative changes at some point which have not been reversed. The graphic representation of violence, for example, seems to increase steadily throughout the period. The integrity of the police changes in a U-shape: falling after the early 1960s but rallying a little in the 1980s. The movement of the police into the forefront as hero figures happens in a once-and-for-all way at the end of the 1960s. In other words, contrasting the picture of crime and society in films of the late 1940s and early 1950s with those of today suggests many clear changes. However, these have not occurred either continuously, at one sharp break point, or without any reversals. The processes of change are clearly complex, and are intertwined with broader patterns of cultural and social development in the postwar world.

We suggest a rough periodization which can be stated in terms of three ideal-type patterns of representation of crime. The first decade after the end of the Second World War is generally seen as a period of relative domestic consensus and social harmony on both sides of the Atlantic. No doubt part of this is nostalgic hindsight, and there were of course many sites of political and social tension and conflict: the fall-out from the Cold War and the advent of nuclear weapons for example. Nonetheless compared to what went before and was to come after, these years were relatively devoid of major political conflict. This consensus mood is reflected clearly in the popular crime films of the period, such as *The Blue Lamp*, *Hue and Cry*, and *Father Brown*. Other crime films of the period which were commercially less successful, notably the critically much loved and analysed *films noirs* such as *Double Indemnity*, *Kiss Me Deadly* or *The Asphalt Jungle* offered much bleaker pictures of social relationships, indicating subterranean tensions of various kinds.

However, in this consensus period crime films — though not monolithic — broadly presented an image of society as largely based on shared values and a clear but accepted and just hierarchy of status and authority. The traditional family provided a flourishing, generally fulfilling, foundation for social order. Crime was the product of individual greed for styles of life — material, sexual and in terms of power — which were not available legitimately. It did not reflect or create any wider tensions in society or culture. While sometimes attractive on the surface, criminals were unequivocally evil; when this was revealed all healthy consciences unite, in Durkheimian style to root them out. In many films, for example, *The Blue Lamp* or *The Wrong Arm of the Law*, even the underworld turn on the narrative's MacGuffin criminals who have committed crimes which place them beyond the pale. Criminals were normally brought to justice. In the movies crime *never* paid as the crack forces of the law, whether Scotland Yard, the FBI or the Mounties, *always* got their man. The criminal justice system was almost invariably represented as righteous, dedicated and efficient agents of the common good (though there might be the occasional individual rotten apple, or bumbling fool as the exceptions which prove the rule).

EUROPEAN JOURNAL OF COMMUNICATION 13(1)

Although occasional depictions of consensus continued to appear, during the mid-1960s the dominant mode of representation of crime and justice became increasingly questioning of the values and integrity of authority. Doubts about the justice and the effectiveness of criminal justice proliferated. Criminals came to be portrayed increasingly in ambivalent or even sympathetic terms. Instead of a consensus on values and hierarchy, increasing prominence was given to social conflict: between ethnic groups, men and women, social classes, and even within the police and other criminal justice organizations, between the management levels (often depicted as ineffectual and/or corrupt) and the crusading vigilantes at street level. Street cops became increasingly common as protagonists, but in most films they were morally tarnished heroes — 'Dirty' like Harry not overgrown boy-scouts like Dixon — with growing frequency they were even the narrative's villains.

During this period of conflict, crime movies increasingly question the cosy assumptions of earlier years, but they do so from a variety of alternative moral standpoints which inform the critique of established institutions. This includes a liberal position questioning institutionalized discrimination in civil rights films like *In the Heat of the Night*, and an anti-liberal perspective criticizing the excessively liberal due process constraints imposed on the police in the 1960s as in *Dirty Harry*. Thus the films of this critical period questioned the dominant values and institutions because they were championing some alternative (*Shaft, Death Wish*).

Since the late 1970s or early 1980s there seems to have been another shift, to a post-critical era. This is bifurcated by contrasting narrative patterns. On the one hand, there are counter-critical films, attempting to restore some of the values of the consensus stage, such as respect for the integrity and public spirit of criminal justice agents like *The Untouchables*, while incorporating some earlier changes like more explicit levels of violence and sex. On the other hand, there are narratives which move from positive critique to a nihilistic and Hobbesian universe in which might — or more precisely — cool prevails, as in the world of Tarantino or *The Last Seduction*. In between there are conventional crime-fighting stories in which the heroes win not because they are more virtuous and law abiding as in the consensus stage, but because they are either the epitome of cool (Eddie Murphy), or possessed of virtually (or actually) superhuman strength (Superman, Batman). Even though criminals still usually (but no longer invariably) lose out, this is no longer a triumph for the rule of law or order let alone social justice.

Conclusions

While quantitatively there is no major change in the amount of crime in crime films since 1945, there have been major changes in depictions of violence, crime, protagonists, the criminal justice system and, more broadly, the relation between crime and society. These changes are complex but seem to conform roughly to a three-stage model; stages we describe as 'consensual', 'conflictual' and 'post-critical'. Inevitably there are problems with such periodizations, but it seems a useful way of summarizing changes in film depictions of crime, criminality and the criminal justice system since 1945, particularly as this is the first study we are aware of which attempts a broad sweep analysis of numerous, popular films over 50 years.

The present findings allow us to reject any argument which proposes that the media increasingly contain representations of crime, whether this increase is suggested as a cause or a reflection of increased levels of crime in society (this being itself a controversial issue). They also allow us, however, to reject any argument which proposes that crime representations are unchanging over time, for while there is no simple overall trend towards increasing crime images, a variety of complex changes in crime images have been identified. The present findings cannot help in determining whether the changes identified reflect wider social changes (e.g. a questioning of authority or a greater acceptability of police vigilantism). There are a number of plausible explanations of the changing patterns we have discerned. These include: the increase in proportion of films which were produced in Hollywood as opposed to Britain, the waning of old censorship codes, and the demography of the audience (now overwhelmingly young people).

Whatever the explanation of the changing patterns, they do provide a firm grounding for those who wish to propose certain theories of the relations between media representations, public attitudes and actual occurrence of crime. For example, if the moral resolution of a film is considered important to the mitigation of effects of viewing crime (whether effects of aggression or of fear of crime), then the modest but discernible rise in films without clear endings, plus the considerable shift from resolutions effected by the criminal justice system towards those dependent on violence, albeit legitimate, by the police, may be of concern. As regards a more constructivist account of the importance of crime representations, the present findings raise a number of interesting issues. For example, the clear shift from crime as a moral problem for individuals towards crime as a bureaucratic and political problem for

EUROPEAN JOURNAL OF COMMUNICATION 13(1)

organizations raises a number of questions about the social explanation of crime, morality and social order. Finally, the findings raise a series of questions for future studies of audience reception and effects, particularly as film representations of crime appear at times to suggest contradictory kinds of messages, such as trends towards increased confidence in authority and, simultaneously, towards increased uncertainty about authority and sympathy for criminals.

Notes

The authors thank an anonymous referee for their very helpful comments. The research reported in this article was supported by a grant from the Economic and Social Research Council (Great Britain), No. L/210/25/2029.

1. This is particularly true in Britain (see Dale, 1935 and Lichter et al., 1991 for American studies).
2. This not uncommon headline comes from *The Times* (25 April 1996: 6).
3. Box office hits were identified using *Kine Weekly* until 1965, based around Josh Billings's identification of hits on the screen, in conjunction with *Motion Picture Herald* from 1957 to 1975, and thereafter *Screen International*.
4. Before 1974 only 5 percent of films showed violent consequential crimes, 5 percent violent contextual crimes and 7 percent violent collateral crimes. After 1974 these depictions of violence increase to 52 percent for consequential crimes, 26 percent for contextual crimes and 41 percent for collateral crimes.

References

Allen, J., S. Livingstone and R. Reiner (1997) 'The Changing Generic Location of Crime in Film: A Content Analysis of Film Synopses, 1945–9', *Journal of Communication* 47(4): 1–13.

Bryant, J. and D. Zillman (eds) (1993) *Media Effects: Advances in Theory and Research*. Hillsdale, NJ: Lawrence Erlbaum.

Clarens, C. (1980) *Crime Movies*. New York: Norton.

Cook, P. (ed.) (1985) *The Cinema Book*. London: British Film Institute.

Cumberbatch, G., S. Woods and A. Maguire (1995) *Crime in the News: Television, Radio and Newspapers*. Birmingham: Communications Research Group, Aston University.

Dahlgren, P. (1988) 'Crime News: The Fascination of the Mundane', *European Journal of Communication* 3(2): 189–206.

Dale, E. (1935) *The Content of Motion Pictures*. New York: Macmillan.

Dominick, J. (1978) 'Crime and Law Enforcement in the Mass Media,' pp. 105–28 in J. Winick (ed.) *Deviance and Mass Media*. Beverly Hills, CA: Sage.

Garofalo, J. (1981) 'Crime and the Mass Media: A Selective View of Research,' *Journal of Research in Crime and Delinquency* 18 July: 319–50.

Gerbner, G., L. Gross, M. Morgan and N. Signorielli (1986) 'Living with Television: The Dynamics of the Cultivation Process,' pp. 17–40 in J. Bryant and D. Zillman (eds) *Perspectives on Media Effects*. Hillsdale, NJ: Lawrence Erlbaum.

Graber, D. (1980) *Crime News and the Public*. New York: Praeger.

Grant, B. (ed.) (1986) *Film Genre Reader*. Austin: University of Texas Press.

Gunter, B. (1985) *Dimensions of Television Violence*. London: Gower.

Hall, S., C. Critchley, T. Jefferson and J. Clarke (1979) *Policing the Crisis: Mugging, the State and Law and Order*. London: Macmillan.

Hearold, S. (1986) 'A Synthesis of 1043 Effects of Television on Social Behaviour', pp. 65–133 in G. Comstock (ed.) *Public Communications and Behaviour*, Vol. 1. New York: Academic Press.

Kaminsky, S. (1974) *American Film Genres*. Dayton, OH: Pflaum.

Lichter, L., S. Lichter and S. Rothman (1991) *Watching America*. New York: Prentice-Hall.

Livingstone, S. (1996) 'On the Continuing Problem of Media Effects', pp. 305–24 in J. Curran and M. Gurevitch (eds) *Mass Media and Society*, 2nd edn. London: Edward Arnold.

McArthur, C. (1972) *Underworld USA*. London: Secker and Warburg.

Mast, G. and M. Cohen (eds) (1979) *Film Theory and Criticism*. New York: Oxford University Press.

Mathews, T. (1994) *Censored*. London: Chatto.

Nichols, B. (ed.) (1976) *Movies and Methods*. Berkeley: University of California Press.

Pearson, G. (1983) *Hooligan: A History of Respectable Fears*. London: Macmillan.

Quart, L. and A. Auster (1984) *American Film and Society Since 1945*. London: Macmillan.

Radzinowicz, L. (1956) *A History of English Criminal Law*, Vol. II. London: Stevens.

Rosow, E. (1978) *Born to Lose*. New York: Oxford University Press.

Schatz, T. (1981) *Hollywood Genres*. New York: Random House.

Schlesinger, P., R.E. Dobash, R. Dobash and K. Weaver (1992) *Women Viewing Violence*. London: British Film Institute.

Shadoian, J. (1977) *Dreams and Dead Ends*. Cambridge, MA: MIT Press.

Sparks, R. (1992) *Television and the Drama of Crime: Moral Tales and the Place of Crime in Public Life*. Milton Keynes: Open University Press.

Thomas, S. (1994) 'Artifactual Study in the Analysis of Culture: A Defence of Content Analysis in a Postmodern Age', *Communication Research* 21(6): 683–97.

Wright, W. (1975) *Sixguns and Society*. Berkeley: University of California Press.

[11]
Media, Crime, Law and Order

Introduction

On the 24th April 2006 the then Home Secretary Charles Clarke delivered a much publicised lecture at the LSE on 'The Media and Civil Liberties'. This castigated the media for undermining the forces of law and order because of a misplaced emphasis on civil liberties. The following week Mr Clarke lost his post in the wake of a media furore concerning the Home Office's failure to consider the deportation of prisoners from overseas when they were released at the end of their sentences.

At the end of January 2006 the Metropolitan Police Commissioner Sir Ian Blair faced a chorus of calls for his resignation from conservative politicians and newspapers following remarks about the media coverage of crime that he had made at a meeting of the Metropolitan Police Authority. Sir Ian had accused the media of 'institutional racism' for giving less prominence to reporting murders of minority ethnic victims, and expressed puzzlement over the huge attention paid to the Soham murders by contrast.

These recent incidents illustrate concerns about media representations of crime and criminal justice that have very long histories. Do the media undermine authority and order? Do they exaggerate and misrepresent the risks of crime, fanning fear and encouraging support for authoritarian solutions? Such anxieties have stimulated not only endless argument but also substantial social science research industries. This article will briefly summarise the huge literature on these topics, which has sought to analyse the content, consequences, and causes of media representations. It will then report on a historical study of changing media representations of crime since the Second World War. It will conclude that there have been fundamental transformations in media discourse about crime in the course of the last thirty years, corresponding to wider changes in political economy, social structure, and culture, crystallised in the rise of the politics of law and order.

The Media-crime debate

There is a centuries-long history of anxiety about criminogenic consequences of the mass media, a central part of perennial 'respectable fears' about supposedly declining moral standards that Geoffrey Pearson has traced back over the last few centuries (Pearson, 1983). We can call this the 'desubordination' thesis: the media tend to represent crime and criminal justice in ways that undermine authority and encourage deviance.

There is also a long-standing liberal/radical concern about media representations of crime. In this view the media exaggerate and distort the threat of crime, thus bolstering fear and stimulating public support for authoritarian solutions. We can call this the 'discipline' thesis.

A more complex view can also be distinguished: the media are an arena of contestation between different interests, pressures and perspectives, and cannot be seen monolithically as either desubordinating or disciplining. This approach has been called 'liberal pluralism' (Greer, 2003), and it tends to be supported by research, especially on 'effects' and on production processes, which portray a messy world of conflicting influences.

The Content of Media Representations

'Content analysis' usually refers to statistical studies within a positivist paradigm, that – in the words of one practitioner – provide an 'objective and quantitative estimate of certain message attributes' (Dominick, 1978: 106). There are many problems with this claim however (Sparks, 1992). The categories for counting categories reflect the researcher's theoretical conceptions of significance, not intrinsic characteristics of an objective structure of meaning in the text itself. Items deemed as identical by the analyst may have very different meanings to different audiences. It is not possible to read off the significance of media narratives from their content, even though such inferences are frequently made. Because of these problems analyses of content must be interpreted reflexively and cautiously. Nonetheless it is noteworthy that the many studies of the content of mass media representations of crime and criminal justice, at different places and times, whether the focus is on purportedly 'factual' representations (news, documentaries) or fictional, tend to concur on certain fundamental themes (Reiner, 2002 is a detailed summary).

A broad convergence of results of content analyses can be discerned, that can be called the 'established model'. The following are its key features: There is first of all the prominence of crime stories. News and fiction crime stories are prominent in all media. There are, however, significant variations according to medium, market, methods of research, historical period and cross-culturally. There is also what has been called the 'law of opposites'

(Surette, 1998). The pattern of representation of crime and criminal justice is in many respects the reverse of that portrayed by official statistics. Media representations are characterised by these features:

- An overwhelming overemphasis on serious violent crime against individuals;
- The risks of crime are exaggerated quantitatively and qualitatively, though property crime is relatively downplayed;
- There is a concentration on older, higher status victims and offenders;
- There is a generally positive image of the effectiveness and integrity of policing and criminal justice (e.g. most cases are cleared-up) and there is little focus on corruption or abuse;
- Most stories are about individual cases, not trends, analysis or policy.

Consequences of media representations

There is a huge volume of research seeking to measure the 'effects' of media representations of crime (Reiner, 2002 offers a more detailed summary). The longest standing concern has been with testing possible consequences of media representations of crime for offending and violence. More recently there has also been considerable work on the impact of the media on fear of crime (Sparks, 1992; Ditton and Farrall, 2000).

As with content analysis, the bulk of this work has been conducted within a positivist paradigm. A typical approach has used social psychological laboratory research: an experimental and a control group are exposed to some media content, and measured before and after this to ascertain the 'effects' on behaviour or attitudes. This vast body of research has yielded little for the enormous expenditure and effort involved. The following masterpiece of agnosticism is typical of the findings: 'for some children, under some conditions, some television is harmful. For some children under the same conditions, or for the same children under other conditions, it may be beneficial. For most children, under most conditions, most television is probably neither particularly harmful nor particularly beneficial' (Schramm, *et al.*, **1961**).

This is not to say that the media have little or no consequences for crime. Some criminogenic effects are likely. The media figure in most theoretical accounts of crime, and 'field' studies of the introduction of new media in practice do suggest effects on crime rates (e.g. Hennigan, *et al.,* 1982, an econometric study of the spread of television in the USA in the early

1950s). But the measurable *direct* effects of media on crime are small. This is because the predominant social psychological research paradigm is geared to testing a most implausible hypothesis, that media representations have immediate effects of a uniform kind immediately. A more plausible approach is that the media are an important dimension of cultural formation, but working interdependently with other processes, differently for different sections of audiences, and slowly over time. 'The study of enculturation processes, which work over long time periods, and which are integral to rather than separate from other forms of social determination, would not ask how the media make us act or think, but rather how the media contribute to making us who we are' (Livingstone, 1996: 31-2). This model is hard to test, of course, and certainly cannot be the subject of laboratory experiments!

The media's exaggeration of the threat of serious violent and sexual crime has often been seen as leading to unrealistic, disproportionate, 'irrational' fear of crime (Gerbner, 1995). As with the research on the criminogenic effects of the media, studies of the relationship between media and fear of crime are equivocal about the strength, direction, or even the existence of a causal relationship between media consumption and anxiety (Ditton and Farrall, 2000; Jackson, 2004; Ditton *et al.*, 2004; Farrell and Gadd, 2004; Chadee and Ditton, 2005).

Even if though the media are not a straightforward cause of 'fear of crime', media representations are important in framing public discourse about crime, and have played an important part in the rise of the 'politics of law and order'. They are the principal source of information about crime and criminal justice for most people who have little or no direct experience of offending or victimisation. The media frame debate about 'law and order', in conjunction with politicians' campaigning and broader shifts in culture, social structure, and political economy. It has been shown that fluctuations in public concern *follow* media and political campaigns (Beckett, 1997), not statistical crime trends. The media played a central role in the politicisation of law and order, by Richard Nixon in the1968 US Presidential election, and by Margaret Thatcher in Britain in the 1970s. They undoubtedly are an important explanation of what the Home Office and police leaders have referred to recently as the 'reassurance gap': the failure of public confidence to respond to the crime drop since the mid-1990s (Hough, 2003; Roberts and Hough, 2005).

Causes of media representation

The pattern of media representation of crime can only be explained to a limited extent as a direct reflection of the ideologies of media owners, producers or

8

reporters. It is true that most media organisations are large corporations, and their owners predominantly c(C?)onservative. Specialist crime reporters in the past tended to be self-consciously police groupies (Chibnall, 1977), working closely with detectives, but this is much less true of the current breed of home affairs, legal or even crime correspondents, who often have an explicitly civil libertarian or human rights perspective (Schlesinger and Tumber, 1994). Even the old-fashioned crime reporters who had a close relationship with the police shared a 'watchdog' ethic, and would be keen to hound out wrongdoing (they would certainly be alert to the news interest of stories of police or other official corruption).

Much research on the work of reporters has emphasised the importance of the professional sense of 'newsworthiness', the values that are seen as making a good story. As classically formulated by Chibnall, these are: 'dramatisation, personalisation, titillation, novelty' (Chibnall, 1977; Jewkes, 2004, chapter two, offers an up-dated expansion of this list). Crime stories similarly offer the narrative virtues of clarity and closure, as well as the thrills of vicarious danger and 'edgework', making them popular as fictional entertainment.

The underlying structural pressures of news production are a fundamental basis of the pattern of representation of crime and criminal justice. The police and courts are reliable story suppliers. The economic pressures governing the allocation of scarce journalistic resources leads to a concentration on such predictable sources. The police in particular become 'primary definers' of crime news. Safety and other constraints also lead to reporters or broadcasters of crime news becoming 'embedded' with the police.

Changing Content Since 1945

In earlier sections the predominant pattern of media representation of crime, the 'established model', has been analysed. This section addresses the question of whether this has changed over time, and if so, how? It reports some results of a historical content analysis of cinema crime films and news stories about crime (Allen *et al.* 1997, 1998; Reiner *et al.* 2000, 2001, 2003). The study analysed in detail a random sample of 84 out of the 196 crime movies released in Britain between 1945-1991 that featured in lists of the annual box office hits, and also estimated the shifting proportion of crime films overall by examining a 10% random sample of all films. The news analysis was based on a 10% random sample of home news stories in the *Times* and the *Mirror* between 1945 and1991, and a closer qualitative reading of a smaller sample of the crime news stories published on a randomly selected 10 days in every second year over that period.

The quantitative analysis of both the films and the news stories suggests that most features of the 'established model' were found throughout the period, but with an intensification of the 'law of opposites' (Surette 1998): the focus on serious violent crime grew stronger. The criminal justice system became more controversial, however, with more negative representations of the integrity and effectiveness of the police in particular (the police are overwhelmingly the most commonly depicted part of criminal justice).

There was no clear trend in the proportion of films released since 1945 that were primarily crime stories (Allen *et al.* 1997). There were fluctuations from year to year, but generally about 20% of films released could be classified as crime movies. There was, however, an increase in the prominence of crime news after the mid-1960s. Until then the overall percentage of home news stories that were primarily about crime averaged about 10% in both the *Times* and the *Mirror*. Since the late 1960s this has doubled to around 20%. The proportion of stories about the criminal justice system also increased after the late 1960s in both papers (from around 3% to 8%), corresponding to the politicisation of law and order in that period (Downes and Morgan 2002).

The pattern of representation of crime has changed since World War II in ways that can broadly be described as a reinforcement of the 'established model' i.e. the disproportionate focus on the threat of serious violent crime has intensified. This is indicated by several statistical trends.

Table 1: Principal Crimes in Newspaper Stories

THE MIRROR

%	1945-64	1965-79	1980-91
Homicide	29	28	31
Violence	24	28	24
Property	16	8	9
Fraud	5	2	4
Against State	10	7	6
Public Order	5	6	4
Drugs	-	4	8
Sex	7	4	8
Traffic	-	5	5
	N=112	=166	N=140

10

THE TIMES

%	1945-64	1965-79	1980-91
Homicide	44	29	37
Violence	16	38	25
Property	21	5	5
Fraud	10	22	8
Against State	13	4	3
Public Order	6	6	5
Drugs	-	3	3
Sex	3	1	6
Traffic	4	-	1
	N=99	N=77	N=63

Table 1 shows the principal crimes that are the focus of the newspaper stories in our sample. In both newspapers, homicide and violent crime constitute the largest category by far in all three sub-periods, but to a slightly increasing extent. The reporting of 'volume' property crimes in which there is no element of violence diminishes considerably over the period.

This is also true of cinema films as Table 2 shows. The majority of films feature homicide or sex crimes as the principal offence animating the plot. Property crimes have almost disappeared as central to narratives. This table also shows that the degree of violence depicted has intensified considerably.

Table 2: Cinema Crime Films, 1945-91

	(%)		
	1945-64	1965-79	1979-91
Principal Crime			
Homicide	50	35	45
Property	32	20	5
Sex crime	3	10	15
Drugs	2	10	5
Intense pain/ suffering of victim	2	20	40

News and fictional stories also feature an increasing number of crimes in addition to the central one animating the narrative. Some of these are 'consequential' offences: other crimes committed as a result of the primary one (for example to cover it up). Others are 'contextual': crimes that have no relationship to the primary one but are still featured in the story (for example the robbery in progress encountered by Clint Eastwood as 'Dirty Harry' when he goes for a hamburger). These 'contextual' crimes in particular signify a world permeated by a threat of crime. An increasing proportion of news stories feature such secondary offences, as Table 3 shows. Cinema films exhibit a similar trend (Reiner *et al.* 2001: 184).

Table 3: Multiple Crime News Stories

Consequential Crimes (as % of all principal crime reports)

1945-64	1965-79	1981-91
16	22	22

Contextual Crimes (as % of all principal crime reports)

1945-64	1965-79	1981-91
19	32	44
(N=211)	(N=243)	(N=203)

These tables suggest that both news and fiction stories are increasingly depicting crime as a serious and pervasive threat. They are also representing the police as less reliable and successful as a protection for potential victims, although they still portray the police as usually successful in clearing-up crime. Tables 4 and 5 show an increase in the proportion of both news and fiction films that question the integrity and the effectiveness of policing. In both news and fiction stories the police are overwhelmingly the most common part of the criminal justice system to be represented at all. Table 5 also shows that there is a marked trend for the police to become the protagonists of fictional films, displacing other types of hero figure that used to be more prominent.

12

Table 4: Police Success and Integrity Newspaper Stories (1945-91)

CLEARING-UP CRIME
% of principal crimes reported as cleared-up

1945-64	1965-79	1981-9
73	63	51

POLICE DEVIANCE IN NEWSPAPERS 1945-91
% of all crime stories primarily concerning police deviance

1945-64	1965-79	1981-91
10	12	19

Table 5: Police Legitimacy in Cinema Films, 1945-91

	Protagonist		
Police	9	50	40
Amateur/PI	36	5	-
Victim	13	-	25
	Police		
Violate due process	11	80	67
Excessive force	3	44	25
Honest	89	67	77

Quantitative content analysis thus shows a clear trend in the last half century for crime to be represented as an increasingly fearful and common threat. The police (the primary symbols of social control in general) are seen more negatively, both in terms of their effectiveness in providing security, and their integrity and adherence to the rule of law – although they are still portrayed predominantly in a favourable light. Qualitative analysis of news and cinema crime stories suggests even more fundamental shifts in popular media discourse about crime and justice.

The Changing Discourse of Crime Stories

The quantitative changes indicate a deeper qualitative transformation in public discourse about crime. Crime news is almost by definition bad news: it reports the occurrence of officially proscribed activity, although this may be depicted as isolated unfortunate incidents. From the late 1960s, however, crime is presented as increasingly threatening and out of control – as symptomatic of wider social crisis, and ever more serious and pervasive in its impact on ordinary people with whom the audience is invited to identify. Three principal themes can be discerned in this new law and order discourse:

1. *Accentuate the negative*

News stories increasingly represent developments in a negative way, emphasising crime as an ever more menacing problem. One striking example is a pair of stories reporting essentially similar changes in the official crime statistics. Both are from the *Daily Mirror*, the first on May 2 1961 (p.7), the second August 26 1977 (p.4). The 1961 story was the first report of the annual crime statistics that we found in our sample (although the publication of crime statistics now always attracts much attention and concern, reflecting the politicisation of law and order). It was headlined 'Fewer Sex Crimes', and reported that there had been a 'slight' fall in the recorded number of sex crimes since 1959. This was contrasted with a rise of 10% in indictable offences known to the police, including a 14% increase in violence. What is remarkable in retrospect is the emphasis on the *good* news, the 'slight' drop in sex offences, highlighted in the headline and the first paragraph, but the downplaying of the fairly large rise in violent and other offences. The story is written entirely without any emotional or evaluative expressions, as a straightforward report of new data.

This is in stark contrast to a report in 1977, headlined 'Crime soars to new peak'. It is of course a story from a period in which law and order was beginning to be politicised, emerging as a leading issue with which the Conservatives under Margaret Thatcher were attacking the Labour government (Downes and Morgan, 2002). What is really striking is that the changes in the crime figures reported are mainly worse than the 1959 ones. This time, however, every bit of bad news is stressed. The overall rise in recorded crime was 1% (by contrast with the 10% of 1959). 'The grim Home Office figures show' a 10% rise in violent crime, a 24% increase in firearms offences, a 9% rise in homicide, and a 15% increase in muggings (mainly because of a 24% increase in London – the rest of England and Wales reported an 11% decline). Tucked away at the end the story reports that 'there were 1500 fewer sexual offences' recorded.

In short, the statistical changes reported are very similar. But whereas in 1961 the emphasis was on the good news, and the writing style restrained and

14

descriptive, the 1977 story spotlights the bad news in a tone of panic. The contrast illustrates a number of basic trends in the reporting of crime news. Above all it indicates the construction of crime as a major problem posing an increasing threat both in extent and seriousness. It shows the news expressing and reinforcing the emergence of law and order as a public concern and a political issue. 'Bad news' and sensationalism have become core news values.

2. Victim culture: crime as a zero-sum game

Both news and fiction crime stories have become increasingly centred on the victim as the focus of the narrative. There has been a profound change in the characterisation of victims and their role within crime stories. Increasingly the harm done by crime is equated with the suffering and distress of individual victims, as well as the potential threat of victimisation to readers who are invited to identify with the victims through portrayals of their ordinariness, innocence and vulnerability. Whereas in the earlier part of the period studied there was also often a measure of concern for offenders, both to understand and if possible rehabilitate them, increasingly the victim/perpetrator relationship is presented as zero-sum: compassion for the offender is represented as callous and unjust to victims. Two contrasting pairs of news stories can be taken as examples. The first pair both concern violence against a child, the second pair both involve a marital triangle.

On February 27 1945 the *Daily Mirror* front page prominently featured a photo of a two year old girl, looking sad and in pain, headlined 'Another cruelty victim'. Even in a murky photocopy, even after more than half a century, the child's pitiful, anguished face cries out for comfort. The story is the main home news of the day. One paragraph details the poor girl's injuries: black eye, bruises, 'Red weal marks extended over her temple and across her cheeks.' Beyond this clinical detail there is no attempt to spell out the trauma and suffering of the victim, or the evil of the assault. Approximately two thirds of the story focuses on the offender, a 26 year old Birkenhead man who lived with the girl's mother, and was sentenced to six months with hard labour. The last part of the story concentrates on his account of his own actions. He claimed 'the child's crying got on his nerves and that he "couldn't help himself." This was explained by the fact that 'he had been torpedoed three times and that his nerves were very bad.' What is noteworthy is the absence of demonisation of the perpetrator, and the concern to understand how he could have carried out such an act from *his* point of view. Attempting to understand the offender is not seen as incompatible with the greatest concern for the victim, and condemnation of the act is taken for granted.

This can be contrasted with the way the *Times* reported a child murder case on November 25 1989 (p.3). This is of course a much more serious offence: murder rather than assault. Nonetheless the presentation of the story suggests a fundamental transformation in discourse about serious crime since 1945. The story is the lead story on the main home news page. A banner headline reads 'Martial arts fanatic gets life for killing daughter aged five' and a smaller headline above it tells us that the 'Girl died from a combination of pain, shock and exhaustion after vengeful beating'. A sub-headline says that 'Social workers held many case conferences but she slipped through the safety net'. Three pictures illustrate the story: a large one of the unfortunate victim, happy and smiling; her mother weeping; and her father, the killer, looking dishevelled and menacing. All are Afro-Caribbean. The most immediately noticeable contrast with the 1945 story is the use of much more emotionally charged language to emphasise the victim's suffering and the perpetrator's evil – not only in his actions but his essence. The assault leading to the girl's death is elaborated in brutal detail, and the victim's pain and fear are stressed. Hammond is portrayed as essentially violent behind a façade of respectability and concern for his children. 'Outwardly he was a doting father, proud of his children and anxious that they should do well at school, but inwardly he was a moody fitness fanatic' and martial arts expert. His 'three children were placed on the at-risk register following incidents in which Sukina and her three year old sister were taken to hospital with broken limbs.' The only glimpse at the defendant's perspective offered, reporting his admission that 'he lost control and did not realise what he was doing', is undercut by its placement in the middle of a detailed, gruesome account of his actions. The only comment showing any sympathy towards him comes from the mother: 'Whatever they do to David will never bring my daughter back to me. I have got no feelings whatever towards him. But I cannot condemn him as he was a good father in a loving way. He just had a bad temper that he would not control.' This is immediately contradicted by the Detective Superintendent in charge of the case, who tells us that the perpetrator had previous convictions. The killer is not the only character in the story who is blamed, however. Considerable attention is given to the failure of social services to protect the child adequately despite repeated warnings.

The presentation of these stories is radically different in a number of ways. The 1945 *Mirror* story describes a tragic situation in which a child is assaulted by a man who is presented as himself a victim rather than an essentially evil person. The injury suffered is presented in degree zero clinical language, and no emotional or evaluative adjectives are used to colour the report. The 1989 *Times* story by contrast is replete with adjectives stressing the victim's anguish and the perpetrator's pathologically violent character. It is noteworthy that by 1989 the *Times* is using more emotive styles of reporting than a tabloid had forty five years earlier. The stories illustrate a profound change in discourse about crime. By 1989 it has become a zero-sum game in which only the victim is represented as a suffering human being. Her plight is caused by two villains. A demonised brute who attacks her, and a negligent authority that fails to protect her. Instead of a complex human tragedy we have a one-dimensional battle of good vs. evil.

This illustrated further by the following two cases of violence in the context of a marital triangle. On December 13 1945 the *Mirror* published a story on its front page under the headline 'Three years for "savage" cripple who branded rival'. The story continued on the back page, under another headline, 'Cripple and branded woman "in a fervour"'. Nearly all the front and back page stories concerned crime, but this was the most prominent. It concerned a crippled woman who had branded another woman that her husband had 'associated' with whilst his wife was in hospital. The story highlights the judge's comments whilst sentencing her to three years for the 'savage' offence. His emphasis is not so much on the brutality of her attack *per se* as that she took 'the law into her own hands' and used a punishment – branding – that 'our laws' now regarded as 'too revolting to the civilised mind to be inflicted for any offence whatsoever'. The bulk of the story concerns the anguished expressions of guilt by all three parties in this triangle. The husband pleads for mercy for his wife, whilst the victim is described as having accepted the branding as a deserved punishment after confessing to the 'association'. Both the victim and the husband seemed to accept the primary responsibility for what had occurred. Altogether this is presented as a tragic human situation, with no innocent parties, in which all are victims of their own wrongful actions, and filled with remorse. The punishment is necessary to maintain the integrity of the law rather than to avenge harm done, to placate the victim's pain, or to incapacitate or deter an evil perpetrator.

On 6 July 1991 both the *Mirror* and the *Times* reported another case arising from a marital triangle. The *Times* covered it on the front page with a photo spread, and more fully on an inside home news page. The *Mirror* spread it over two full pages (2/3), with many photos. The case involved an armed man who held his ex-wife's lover hostage in a car for 29 hours, surrounded by armed police. The kidnapper had been alarmed that his children were to be taken into care - apparently a mistake as they were to stay with his ex-wife. The pictures in both papers exhibit much of the iconography of thriller movies: the surrounded car, police marksmen in bullet-proof vests, the hostage emerging with blood pouring from his left arm where he'd been shot, the hand-cuffed offender with face blacked out being led away. No doubt the prominence given the story owed much to the availability of this dramatic visual material.

There is a sharp contrast with the 1945 story, as the narrative is constructed with a clear hero/victim and villain/perpetrator. Although the incident is referred to as tragic, the sympathies expressed are entirely one-sided. The violence is emphasised: the victim was threatened with a noose, the perpetrator was armed with a crossbow and gun and shot the victim in the arm as police converged on the car. The perpetrator is continuously described in one-dimensionally villainous terms as 'the gunman', and we are told that he had been involved in a 'tug of love drama' 20 years previously in Australia. His arsenal of weapons is described in detail. By contrast the victim is extolled in heroic terms: 'Hero is Mr Cool' reads a sub-headline, and the police credit him with 'remarkable resilience and patience'. What could be read as a tragic personal conflict in which everyone was a victim (as the 1945 story had been constructed) is transformed into a straightforward fight of good vs. bad.

These pairs of stories illustrate the key change in the discourse of crime news reporting since the Second World War. The narratives have become personalised and sensationalised. What drives them is a battle against one-dimensionally evil villains who inflict dramatic and frightening suffering on individual victims. This pattern is also found increasingly in crime fiction (Reiner, *et al.*, 2000, 2001).

3. It's Not Business, It's Personal

In quantitative terms many aspects of the pattern of crime news stories remain constant in the half century after the Second World War, and confirm the 'law of opposites'. In particular there is disproportionate reporting of violent crime, and of older and higher status victims and offenders. Nonetheless even in terms of the quantitative analysis much has changed. Property crime without violence has dropped out of the news picture, unless there is a celebrity angle. Victims increasingly feature prominently, and often occupy the subject positions of crime stories. The police are represented in a much more negative way both in terms of effectiveness and integrity, although the predominant portrayal of them remains positive.

Crime is now portrayed as a much greater risk than before, not just because it is more common, but because it is represented in much more highly charged emotional terms as a serious threat to ordinary people. There is much greater individualism underlying the narratives. Crime is seen as problematic not because it violates the law or other moral reference points, but because it hurts individual victims with whom the audience is led to sympathise or empathise. Offenders are portrayed not as parts of social relations or structures that the victims and the public are also embedded in, but as pathologically evil individuals. Any attempt to understand them, let alone any concern for their point of view or their rehabilitation, is seen as insensitive to the suffering of their victims. These features also testify to a decline of deference. Crime is seen as wrong not because of acceptance of legality as a benchmark of how people should behave but because it causes personal harm to individuals we identify with. The police and other authorities are themselves portrayed as increasingly immoral or irrelevant.

Conclusion

The changing discourse of crime news and fiction stories is part and parcel of those broader developments in the politics of crime and criminal justice policy that Garland has called the 'culture of control' (Garland, 2001). Clearly they can only be understood as aspects of much broader transformations of political economy and culture, above all the hegemony of neo-liberalism, the combination of free market economics and cultural individualism that has become dominant since the 1970s. A less deferential, consumerist society conceives of crime and policing not as the breaking and enforcement of generally respected laws, but as the violation of sympathetic and vulnerable individual victims. Each narrative has to construct its own moral universe in these terms: identification of characters as good or bad cannot be read off from their legal status. This contrasts sharply with the earlier narratives in which the legitimacy of law and the evil of breaking it could be taken for granted. Perpetrators and victims shared a common humanity, and the interest of stories often turned on understanding offenders' motivations, not simply demonising them. Following the politicisation of law and order crime stories have increasingly become an orchestration of hate and vengefulness against individual offenders, supposedly on behalf of their victims, in what sometimes amount to virtual lynch-mobs.

References

ALLEN, J., LIVINGSTONE, S., and REINER, R. (1997), 'The Changing Generic Location of Crime in Film', *Journal of Communication*, 47 (4): 1–13.

ALLEN, J., LIVINGSTONE, S., and REINER, R. (1998), 'True Lies: Changing Images of Crime in British Postwar Cinema', *European Journal of Communication*, 13 (1): 53–75.

BECKETT, K. (1997), *Making Crime Pay*, New York: Oxford University Press.

CHADEE, D. and DITTON, J. (2005) 'Fear of Crime and the Media: Assessing the Lack of Relationship' *Crime, Media, Culture* 1 (3): 322-32.

CHIBNALL, S. (1977), *Law and Order News*, London: Tavistock.

DITTON, J. and FARRALL, S. (eds) (2000), *The Fear of Crime*, Aldershot: Dartmouth.

DITTON, J, CHADEE, D., FARRALL,S., GILCHRIST, E. and BANNISTER, J. (2004) 'From Imitation to Intimidation: A Note on the Curious and Changing Relationship Between the Media, Crime and Fear of Crime' *British Journal of Criminology* 44 (4): 595-610.

DOMINICK, J. (1978), 'Crime and Law Enforcement in the Mass Media', in C. Winick (ed.), *Deviance and Mass Media*, 105–28, Beverly Hills, Cal.: Sage.

DOWNES, D. and MORGAN, R. (2002), 'The Skeletons in the Cupboard: The Politics of Law and Order at the Turn of the Millennium' in M. Maguire, R. Morgan and R. Reiner (eds.) *The Oxford Handbook of Criminology* 3rd Ed., Oxford: Oxford University Press.

FARRALL, S. and GADD, D. (2004) 'The Frequency of the Fear of Crime' *British Journal of Criminology* 44 (1): 127-32.

GARLAND, D. (2001), *The Culture of Control*, Oxford: Oxford University Press.

GERBNER, G. (1995), 'Television Violence: The Power and the Peril', in G. Dines and J. Humez (eds), *Gender, Race and Class in the Media*, 547–57, Thousand Oaks, Cal.: Sage.

HENNIGAN, K.M., DELROSARIO, M.L., HEATH, L., COOK, J.D., and CALDER, B.J. (1982), 'Impact of the Introduction of Television Crime in the United States: Empirical Findings and Theoretical Implications', *Journal of Personality and Social Psychology*, 42 (3): 461–77.

HOUGH, M. (2003) 'Modernisation and Public Opinion: Some Criminal Justice Paradoxes' *Contemporary Politics*, 9: 143-55.

JACKSON, J. (2004), 'An Analysis of a Construct and Debate: The Fear of Crime' in H-J. Albrecht, T. Serassis and H. Kania (eds.) *Images of Crime II*, 35-64, Freiburg: Max Planck Institute.

JEWKES, Y. (2004), *Media and Crime*, London: Sage.

20

LIVINGSTONE, S. (1996), 'On the Continuing Problem of Media Effects', in J. Curran and M. Gurevitch (eds), *Mass Media and Society*, 305–24, London: Arnold.

PEARSON, G. (1983), *Hooligan: A History of Respectable Fears*, London: Macmillan.

REINER, R. (2002), 'Media Made Criminality' in M. Maguire, R. Morgan and R. Reiner (eds.) *The Oxford Handbook of Criminology* 3rd Ed., Oxford: Oxford University Press.

REINER, R., LIVINGSTONE, S., and ALLEN, J. (2000), 'No More Happy Endings? The Media and Popular Concern About Crime Since the Second World War', in T. Hope and R. Sparks (eds), *Crime, Risk and Insecurity*, 107–25, London: Routledge.

REINER, R., LIVINGSTONE, S., and ALLEN, J., 'Casino Culture: Media and Crime in a Winner-Loser Society', in K. Stenson and R. Sullivan (eds), *Crime, Risk and Justice*, 175–93, Cullompton: Willan.

REINER, R., LIVINGSTONE, S., and ALLEN, J., (2003), 'From Law and Order to Lynch Mobs: Crime News Since the Second World War' in P. Mason (ed.), *Criminal Visions*, 13-32, Cullompton: Willan.

ROBERTS, J. and HOUGH, M. (2005), *Understanding Public Attitudes to Criminal Justice*, Maidenhead: Open University Press.

SCHLESINGER, P. and TUMBER, H. (1994), *Reporting Crime*, Oxford: Oxford University Press.

SCHRAMM, W., LYLE, J. and PARKER, E. (1961), *Television in the Lives of Our Children*, Stanford, Cal.: Stanford University Press.

SPARKS, R. (1992), *Television and the Drama of Crime*, Buckingham: Open University Press.

SURETTE, R. (1998), *Media, Crime and Criminal Justice: Images and Realities*, 2nd edn, Belmont: Wadsworth.

Part III
Political Economy of
Crime and Control

[12]
British Criminology and The State

"So we beat on, boats against the current, borne back ceaselessly into the past."
F. Scott Fitzgerald: *The Great Gatsby*

The standard legal textbook definition of a crime is "an illegal act, omission or event.... the principal consequence of which is that the offender, if he is detected and it is decided to prosecute, is prosecuted by or in the name of the State " (Cross and Jones, 1984, 1). All the current criminal law texts concur in the view that the only consistent distinguishing feature of a crime is that it "is a legal wrong that can be followed by criminal proceedings which may result in punishment" (Glanville Williams, 1983, 27).

The labelling-theory insight that "deviance is *not* a quality of the act the person commits, but rather a consequence of the application by others of rules and sanctions" (Becker, 1963, 5), may have been news to criminology, but it was platitudinous to criminal lawyers.[1] Lest it be thought that the definitions quoted mark some recent departure from a former legal absolutism, the text-books all draw on a 1931 case in which Lord Atkin declared: "The domain of criminal jurisprudence can only be ascertained by examining what acts at any particular period are declared by the State to be crimes, and the only common nature they will be found to possess is that they are prohibited by the State." (*Proprietary Articles Trade Assn.* v. *Att. Gen. for Canada* [1931] AC at 324).

It would seem to follow that the concept of "the state" would be at the heart of criminology.[2] For as Hermann Mannheim puts it at the start of his 1965 textbook *Comparative Criminology,* "criminology.... means the study of crime", and crime, we have just seen, is a legal domain demarcated by the state. But Mannheim makes it clear that he is using criminology in a "narrower" sense, the study of criminal behaviour and criminals, not the "wider" sense which would encompass in addition issues of penology and prevention (Mannheim, 1965, 3).

The "science of criminology", as it sought to establish itself in the latter part of the nineteenth century as an independent and objective discipline, demarcated a distinctive object of knowledge: "what in fact *is* the criminal?" (Garland, 1985b, 122). Whereas the law denied any absolute basis for

---

[1] Indeed the concept of "crime" as an entity distinct from other wrongs develops only with the evolution of the modern, centralised, capitalist state (Jeudwine, 1917; Jeffrey, 1957; Kennedy, 1970; Lenman and Parker, 1980).

[2] These legal citations only establish a relationship between crime and the state in a descriptive, nominal way. It does not follow that the state is central to understanding or explaining the phenomena of crime and its control (Young, 1983, 87–9). The utility of notions of "the state" to criminology is the subject-matter of this essay, and is an open question unless one forecloses it by adopting a *functional* definition of the state, identifying it with particular purposes or consequences (Dunleavy and O'Leary, 1987, 3–4). Here I adopt an *organisational* definition, identifying the state with a specific configuration of governmental institutions, of relatively recent historical origin, marked by a separation of a "public", bureaucratic constellation of institutions claiming sovereignty and authority over a given territory (ibid., 1–3).

delineating the category of crime, criminology as the naturalistic science of "the criminal" *could* discern that he was "a being apart" (Marro, cited in Garland, op. cit., 124). Thus "the criminological positivists succeeded in what would seem the impossible, they separated the study of crime from the work-ings and theory of the state." (Matza, 1969, 143). As Matza goes on to suggest, the "lofty subject" of the role of the state, "unrelated to so seamy a matter as deviation', was implicitly demarcated by criminologists as the province of *political* science.

However, a parallel blindness occurred on the side of political theory. The "law and order" or "watchman" function of the state is seen by all political philosophies as its bedrock role (Held *et al.*, 1983, Part 1). Weber's definition of the state, probably the most influential in contemporary social science, points this way (even though it is explicitly couched as a statement of the *means* peculiar to the modern state, not the ends it pursues): "a state is a human community that (successfully) claims the *monopoly of the legitimate use of physical force* within a given territory" (Weber, 1919, 77). On the political left, whatever arguments there may be about the boundaries of the state, the Althusserian "repressive state apparatus" of army, police and prisons are pradigmatically within them (Althusser, 1971). Even on the libertarian right, Nozick's utopian "minimal state" would be a "protective agency" against force, theft, and fraud. (As well as the violation of contracts. Nozick, 1974, IX).

Yet until recently questions of law, order, crime and policing were never addressed in any detail in politics books (though nowadays no self-respecting text would be without a section on this area: Norton, 1984; Dearlove and Saunders, 1984; Drucker *et al.*, 1986). Indeed, in the heyday of its scientistic pretensions, political sociology (like criminology) eschewed any concern with the state (King, 1986, 2–3).

This paper will document and analyse British criminology's conceptualis-ation of, and relationship to, the state. For the century or so during which the positivistic conception of criminal science held sway, the exploration of its notion of the state matches Sherlock Holmes' celebrated non-barking dog (in *Silver Blaze*): how to interpret an absence.

An increasing concern with the state and the politics of crime was a keynote of the varieties of "new", "critical", "radical" and Marxist criminologies which began to flourish in the 1960s. Although these were often seen as totally fresh departures, consideration of crime in relation to wider questions of the state, legal order and political economy was commonplace before the blinkers of a specialised and technical criminal science rendered invisible what (with hindsight's 20:20 vision) seem obvious connections. For before this, during the late eighteenth and early nineteenth centuries, there had flourished on the Continent and in Britain "a science of police" (with connotations far broader than the present meaning of the term). This comprised a variety of projects for regulating crime and maintaining order which were part of the context within which what is characterised by histories of criminology as the "classical" school flourished. However this "science of police" is neglected in all the histories of criminological thought, with the sole exception of Radzinowicz's

BJC/270 ROBERT REINER

encyclopedic *History of English Criminal Law*, the third volume of which is largely taken up with an account of it. The work of this "police science", especially that of its foremost British exponent Patrick Colquhoun, is important for a proper understanding of "classical" criminology, and because it prefigures the broader conceptualisation of the problems of crime, order and justice which became the concern of radical criminology after the 1960s, (and most recently also of a notable revival of interest in criminal justice issues from the perspective of mainstream political thought: Dahrendorf, 1985; Berki, 1983; 1986; Norton, 1987).

The Science of "Police"

If we take "criminology" as a coterminous with self-avowed criminologists then, of course, it dates back only to the 1870s (Mannheim, 1960, 1). Similarly, if we restrict our concern not to the label, but to that particular conception of the domain of criminology derived from the naturalistic "human sciences" of the later nineteenth century. Indeed "to call the work of writers such as Beccaria, Voltaire, Bentham and Blackstone a 'criminology' is altogether misleading" (Garland, 1985, 14–15), and *a fortiori* to see them as "classical criminology". But this is to accept the perspective of the latter positivistic criminological "science" and its casting of its "metaphysical" ancestors into mere prehistory.

The main reason advanced for seeing the work of the earlier writers as not really a "criminology" is that they do not concern themselves with aetiological questions in an empirical way, (Vold, 1958, 23). Rather they take over from utilitarian psychology and mainstream jurisprudence a "voluntarist and rationalist theory of action" (Garland op. cit., ibid. 14–15.)[3] This picture comes from identifying a "classical criminology" what is only one strand in the spectrum of discourse about crime, order and control in the eighteenth and early nineteenth centuries. It arises from taking as paradigmatic Beccaria's *Dei Delitti e Delle Pene*, and its influence on Blackstone, Bentham and the movement for reform of the substantitive criminal law and punishment. The latter reforms are, of course, widely recognised to be only part of a set of profound changes in the field of crime control, concompassing also the system of policing, the administration of justice, and more diffuse measures of "social control" (Donajgrodski, 1977; Phillips, 1980; Cohen and Scull, 1983). Although there is an extensive and sophisticated historical literature on the development of policing in this period (which I have summarised in Reiner, 1985a, Chapter 1), there has been virtually no consideration of it in writings on punishment or, more broadly, "penality" (Garland and Young, 1983)—nor vice versa in the police literature. This mutual blindness not only impoverishes our understanding of the complexity and range of different

[3] An apparently contradictory criticism is offered by Taylor, Walton and Young, 1973, 6–7, in relation to the "classical" explanation of the crime of the depraved poor as "the result of factors militating against the free exercise of rational choice". But this is only conceded as an exception to the over-arching conception of rational criminal man, and Taylor, Walton and Young's main line of attack on classicism is that "detailed discussion of the nature of criminal motivation is ... avoided in most classical writings" (ibid., 5).

positions in the debate about crime and control. It also has led to the eclipse of an important body of thought, the "science of police", which had a close if ambiguous relationship to what is commonly called "classical criminology". When this array of partly competing, partly complementary discourses is excavated, it becomes clearer that while it advanced understanding by fore-grounding questions of causation, positivism simultaneously excluded a set of broader issues which have only resurfaced recently.[4] In this sence the development of "criminology" bears the same relation to "police science" as "neo-classical economics" to "political economy" (Robbins, 1981).[5]

The "science of police" was a much broader intellectual enterprise than what has come to be understood as "classical criminology".[6] When the term "police" was introduced into England early in the eighteenth century it was viewed, usually with distaste, as a sinister and Continental, primarily French, conception (Radzinowicz, 1956, 1–8). The term had a much wider sense than the present-day one, Adam Smith defined "police" in 1763 as "the second general division of jurisprudence. The name is French, and is originally derived from the Greek 'politeia' which properly signified the policy of civil government, but now it only means the regulation of the inferior parts of government, viz: cleanliness, security and cheapness of plenty." (Smith, *Lectures on Justice, Police, Revenue and Arms*, cited in Radzinowicz, op. cit., 421.)

The "science of police" which flourished in Europe during the eighteenth century was a vast body of work[7] which encompassed the whole art of govern-ment in the sense of the regulation, management and maintenance of popu-lation, what Foucault has called "governmentality" (Foucault, 1979). In the eighteenth century the various discourses on government took the form of a science of police, the latter being a reference to the development and pro-motion of "happiness" or the "public good", rather than to the suppression of disorder, the surveillance of public space or the protection of private property, which is its contemporary reference." (Smart, 1983, 80). This narrower definition only begins to appear later in the eighteenth century in England (following the inspiration of the Fieldings) and on the Continent (Radzinowicz, 1956, 4; Pasquico, 1978, 45). Even then, the main English exponents—Bentham, Colquhoun; Chadwick all used the term in a much broader sense than the present day one, as did their European counterparts. As late as 1885 we find Maitland defining police as "such part of social organisation as is concerned immediately with the maintenance of good order, or the prevention or detection of offences," (Maitland, 1885, 105)—a usage connoting much more than stout men in blue coats.

---

[4] Interestingly Dahrendorf refers to himself in the Foreword to his lectures on *Law and Order* as "an unreconstructed eighteenth-century liberal" (Dahrendorf, 1985, xi). Beccaria was appointed to a Chair of "Political Economy and Science of Police" at Milan. In his lectures on *Elements of Political Economy* 1769 he included "police" as the "fifth and last object of political economy". (Cited in Pasquino, 1978, 45.)

[5] Let alone what is currently called "police science" i.e. the technical aspects of practical crime investigation (Walsh, 1985).

[6] Pasquino cites a bibliography which lists "for German–speaking lands alone and within the period from the start of the 17th century to the end of the 18th, no fewer than 3,215 titles under the heading of 'Science of police in the strict sense' ". (Pasquino, 1978, 48).

[7] Pasquino cites a 1760 book by Von Justi: *Foundations of the Power and Happiness of States, or an Exhaustive Presentation of the Science of Public Police (op. cit.,* 44).

BJC/272 ROBERT REINER

This whole corpus of work, and especially the contribution of Colquhoun, merits attention as a precursor of criminology, especially in its latter-day newly rediscovered relationship with political economy and the state. It highlights the fact that what is taken to be "classical criminology" (the Beccaria tradition) represented only one pole in a complex network of debate about law, crime, order, punishment, control, the state, morals and "happiness". Beccaria and Von Humboldt were suspicious of strategies seeking to control crime through expansions of state power or police activity. In England an array of liberal and conservative opinion including Burke, Blackstone, Adam Smith and Paley all opposed the apostles of "police science". The Benthamite Utilitarian position which attempted to combine Beccaria's advocacy of reform of law and punishment, with a more positive strategy of prevention by policing and other interventionist social policies, was anything but predominant, and always faced considerable opposition and uneven political successes in such compromise measures as the 1839 or 1856 Police Acts.

The work of Colquhoun in particular is worthy of attention for a number of reasons.[8] He maps out his proposals for the prevention and control of crime on the basis of an attempt to investigate empirically and thereby to explain the pattern of crime.[9] But the phenomena of crime and criminal justice are not seen as independent realms which can be considered in isolation from a broader analysis of the social and economic structure. Like all his contemporaries, Colquhoun saw himself as engaged in political economy, not some specialist "criminology" asbstracted from the total project of governing (or "police"), yet Colquhoun was also very much alive to the symbolic as well as the instrumental aspects of policing.

This is not to suggest Colquhoun as a model for us. His staunch conservatism and lack of regard for civil liberties is unlikely to endear him to most present-day criminologists.[10] He did accept much of the "classical" argument for restricting the scope and severity of criminal sanctions on both humanitarian and instrumental grounds, and was an ardent advocate of after-care (Radzinowicz, 1956, 255–7). But he was an unsqueamish upholder of the political *status quo,* and as a magistrate "endeavoured with unflinching firmness to put down popular manifestations and disturbances" (Ibid, 213–4).

Colquhoun's criminology was one which located the ultimate causes of crime in the overall structure of economy and society. In addition to his better-known *Treatise on the Police of the Metropolis* and *Treatise on the Commerce*

[8] It has also been almost entirely neglected. The only lengthy consideration of this prolific writer's corpus of work is in Radzinowicz, 1956, 211–312. Apart from one article (Stead, 1977), he appears fleetingly in footnotes in most histories of the police, and virtually nowhere else. His contribution to the development of the police is underestimated, possibly because Peel slighted him (Radzinowicz, 1956, 230–1), but it was significant and acknowledged by many others (ibid.). But the importance of his work to criminology more generally is overlooked, perhaps because of an erroneous impression that it only concerned police reform.

[9] In his attempt to map quantitatively the contours of crime and social structure Colquhoun anticipates (albeit at a crude level) the French "moral statisticians" Quetelet and Guerry, and their more sociological approach, which was itself largely submerged later in the nineteenth century by individualistic criminal science (Morris, 1957, 44–8). The etymology of "statistics" as the "science of the state" ("political arithmetic" in Petty's usage) is worth noting (Pasquino, 1978, 50; Smart, 1983 79.)

[10] Or to some contemporaries. An anonymous pamphlet of 1800 spoke of his scheme as "a new engine of Power and Authority so enormous and extensive as to threaten a species of despotism" (Cited in Philips, 1980, 155.)

and Police of the River Thames, Colquhoun was the author of *A Treatise on Indigence* and numerous other works on political economy and the relief of poverty. Indigence was related to crime in a relationship of mutual interdependence,[11] and Colquhoun devoted much effort to mapping and measuring the class structure (primarily in *Treatise on the Wealth, Power, and Resources of the British Empire*). But Colquhoun's analysis was not a simple or reductionist economic determinism. The link between indigence and crime was "the character of the labouring people" (*Treatise on Indigenence,* 239). Poverty exerted a structural pressure to crime—"from a state of indigence, wretchedness and despair, the transition is easy to criminal offences"—and hence the relief of poverty was integrally related to the prevention of crime. But there were many links between objective structural condition and criminality, social and cultural processes which required specific analysis. The precise availability of legitimate opportunities had to be discovered.[12]

The link between ethnicity and crime, for example, was explored in these terms. Colquhoun addressed what he saw as the "system of fraud and depradation" among Jews of German–Dutch extraction. This was not a racial issue—it was not due to "any actual disposition on their parts to pursue these nefarious practices," a point evident in the contrast with the respectable Portuguese Jewish community. It was "generated in a greater degree by their peculiar situation in respect to society", in particular lack of training. The remedy was utilising internal community resources: better integration with the Portuguese Jews and the influence of the synagogues, with state intervention (in the form of compulsory apprenticeship) only as a last resort (Radzinowicz, 1956, 273–4).

Overall, though the link between structural economic conditions and crime was constituted by a variety of factors which in modern jargon would be seen as aspects of "control theory" (Downes and Rock, 1982, Ch. 9). The basic problem was that "the morals and habits of the lower ranks in society are growing progressively worse". This was the product of the erosion of positive influences such as religion, and the flourishing of malign influences, such as bawdy ballad-singers and pubs. Rather than prohibiting such leisure pursuits, they should be turned to good effect, for example by distributing uplifting literature for the use of ballad-singers (Radzinowicz, op. cit., 275). In addition, there was invoked a free-floating variable of "the thoughtless improvidence of this class of labouring people, that they are generally the first who indulge themselves by eating oysters, lobsters and pickled salmon etc., when first in season, and long before these luxuries are considered accessible to the middle ranks of the community; whose manners are generally as virtuous as the others are depraved". (Ibid., 235.)

Formal and negative social control in the specific sense of criminal justice and punishment was only a relatively minor element in the reduction of crime,

[11] The *Treatise on Indigence* was subtitled *Ameliorating the Condition of the Poor. . . .by the Diminution of Moral and Penal Offences, and the Future Prevention of Crimes.*

[12] Illegitimate opportunities and the sheer volume of goods available to steal were also relevant: crime was "the constant and never-failing attendant on the accumulation of wealth" (*Treatise on the Commerce and Police of the River Thames,* 155–6).

BJC/274 ROBERT REINER

and their role was conceived more in terms of prevention through the restriction of temptations and the bolstering of mortality than through deterrence and fear (though these were important for the hard-core delinquent). Colquhoun's distinctive advocacy of a professional police force must be located within this overall analysis and strategy, but its role was to be much broader than merely enhancing the certainty of detection (and thus the deterrent efficacy of the precisely calculated penalties of the classical criminological schema). The explanation of crime was not in terms of a classical "rational man" model, nor even "the rational choice within social constraints" model attributed to the "moral statisticians" (Garland, 1985a, 110). For all its crudity and bourgeois snobbery, it was a complex (if sometimes unsubtle) unravelling of a network of cultural and social processes and influences interplaying with moral choice. The answer lay more in the field of welfare than penality, and even the police were conceived primarily in these terms. A more effective police would not only benefit the respectable, but "all those whose vices and enormities it tends to restrain". Its terrain of operation was to be "upon the broad scale of General Prevention—mild in its operations—effective in its results; having justice and humanity for its basis, and the general security of the State and Individuals for its ultimate object". (*Treatise on the Commerce and Police of the River Thames*, 38.)

This brief consideration of the late eighteenth early nineteenth century "science of police" has demonstrated that alongside the "classical" school of criminology there flourished, in Britain as well as Europe, a conception of crime, order and control which was more alive to the interpretation of politics, law and social justice with criminality than was the later science of the criminal. It also operated with a more sociological notion of the aetiology of crime than the standard picture of classical criminology's "economic man". For all the gains of the later positivist school in the direction of understanding criminal psychology (cf. West's essay in this volume), it eclipsed the relationship between state, social and legal order which has only been re-addressed in the last three decades.

Positivist Criminology

The content, conditions of existence and implications of the programme of positivist criminology have been so definitively analysed recently (Garland, 1985a and b; Radzinowicz and Hood, 1986) that no more is needed here than a brief summary of its relationship to the state.

Garland identifies as "the heart of the criminological enterprise ... the dual concepts of *individualisation* and *differentiation*" (Garland, 1985b, 115). The individualism of "classical criminology" insisted "that all men are equal, free and rational" and this liberal humanism "put definite limits upon the operation and presentation of regulatory forms" (ibid, 130). The location of crime in particular social classes—the indigent or the dangerous—by Colquhoun and the "science of police" laid bare the links between crime, politics and morality. It led either to demands for social reform or outright clashes between class cultures or both. What scientific criminology offered was relief of this "legitimatory deficit" . . . The existence of a class which was constantly criminalised—indeed the very existence of an impoverished sector of the population—could now be explained by reference to the natural, constitutional propensities of these individuals, thereby excluding all reference to the character of the law, of politics or of social relations." (Ibid., 131.)

While the analytic relationship between the state and crime slipped out of the frame, underlying the project of scientific criminology was "the constant figure of the State as the presumed subject of this enterprise. . . criminology's arguments were explicitly directed towards an increased interventionism on the part of the State . . . But this assumption that the central State is indeed the proper subject of this process (and not private organisations, or more localised administrations), and the political arguments and ideologies which might justify such a position, are so entrenched in this programme that they go mostly unspoken . . . the issue is passed over in the silence of self-evidence. However . . .not only the politics but also the practical ambitions of criminology necessitate the State as their subject." (Ibid., 129–30.) Thus criminological science, while dropping the relationship of crime and the state from its field of vision, nonetheless promoted "an extended statism" (ibid., 134) through demands for public support of the caring and controlling professions who delivered the new scientific expertise and policies.

The changing conceptions of the state and its strategies for social regulation within which criminology was embedded are usually interpreted as a response to "crisis" (Garland, 1985a, 59–66). It is important, however, to recognise exactly what constituted the sense of crisis in this period. Crime in general was *falling* not rising in the latter part of the nineteenth century (Gatrell, 1980), and this was widely recognised by contemporaries who puzzled about the causes of this "English miracle" (Radzinowicz and Hood, 1986, Ch. 5).[13] The Metropolitan Police Commissioner's Report for 1882 spoke of London as "the safest capital for life and property in the world", while the criminal statistics at the dawn of the new century were said to exhibit our "exceptional immunity from crime" (ibid., 116–7). The last quarter of the nineteenth century was "a period of unfaltering optimism" concerning crime, following on the mid-century decades of "qualified optimism"—and a far cry from the "unrelieved pessimism" of the first four decades of the nineteenth century (ibid., 113–5).

Where then was the "social and penal crisis of the 1890s' which is often seen as a precondition of the criminological programme? (Garland, 1985b, 117). The fundamental root of the feeling of anxiety which many commentators have identified in the last two decades of the nineteenth century was Britain's reduced and threatened economic dominance, undermining confidence in the old liberal notions of self-adjusting social equilibrium. "Confidence waned and prospects clouded over, as the last quarter of the nineteenth-century saw Britain slipping from the sunny uplands of mid-Victorian liberal capitalism towards the valley of the shadow of socialism and war." (Porter, 1987, 13.) The response of the governing classes was divided. Some saw the remedy in a

---

[13] At the same time there were panics about specific kinds of crime, for example a supposedly new strain of juvenile violence (Pearson, 1983).

BJC/276   ROBERT REINER

tougher marshalling of the state's forces of order. Others advocated increasing state intervention in the economic and social arena to secure the long-term allegiance of the working-class as the necessary precondition for safeguarding the core of the free-enterprise system and the rights of property. (Ibid., 20–1). Unevenly and patchily to be sure, but nonetheless steadily, it was the latter position which prevailed. The consequences for the state's "repressive apparatuses" of the long-term strategy of stability through incorporation and winning the consent of the mass of the working-class were complex. Deprivation, crime, public order and political subversion were separated out into differentiated problems for state policy, not the integrated image of the indigence/dangerousness couplet which had been perceived by the "science of police". The coincidence of wider social anxiety with the growth of Fenian and anarchist terrorist incidents was the precondition for the radical departure from British tradition of establishing the Special Branch in the 1880s as the first specifically political police (Porter, 1987). The continuing concern with demarcating and elucidating the political as distinct from the ordinary (i.e. abnormal) offender, although it had a long history in England, was sharpened and accentuated in this period, (Radzinowicz and Hood, 1986, Ch. 13; Bottomley, 1979, 10–20).

The latter part of the nineteenth century saw many disturbances and riots, arising out of industrial or political conflict. (Stevenson, 1979; Richter, 1981). However the conception of these, and the strategy for dealing with them, altered as mid-Victorian ruling-class confidence receded. The police had been established in part as a way of supplanting brute coercion with a more complex combination of moral co-option and surveillance of the masses, with finely-tuned delivery of legitimate "minimum force" as the ultimate back-up (Silver, 1967). This became accentuated with the rise of the more inter-ventionist state towards the end of the nineteenth century. By the early years of this century the police had almost completely taken over from the army for purposes of riot control. Police strategy itself became part of a virtuous circle of declining levels of violence as the state and those involved in political or industial conflict accepted constitutional parameters for resolving disputes and the prime battle became one over public opinion rather than immediate physical control of particular spaces, (Geary, 1985). This more subtle strategy for controlling disorder went hand-in-hand with the growing involvement of the central state, concerned more with long-run social stability than short-term suppression (Reiner, 1985b; 140; Geary, 1985, Chs. 3, 4, 6). Police ability to tread the tightrope between premature or excessive shows of force and the threat of being overwhelmed due to inadequate preparation was crucially dependent on adequate political intelligence, gathered through the political police whose birth had been contested for so long (Porter, 1987; Khan et al., 1983, 94–5).

As far as mundane crime is concerned the twin themes of individualisation and differentiation which Garland has identified as the core of positivist criminological science continued to underpin theory, research and penal policy throughout the first five decades of this century. Criminals were dis-tinguished not only from "normal" conformists or political dissidents, but in increasingly complex ways from each other. Distinctions between habituals, the feeble-minded, vagrants, drunkards, juveniles, and young adults proliferated in penal theory and practice (Radzinowicz and Hood, 1986). Right down to the post-Second World War "Welfare State" penal policy developed as one aspect of an increasingly interventionist state. The state's task was seen stretching beyond negative crime-control measures to a broader responsibility for reducing criminogenic features of the social structure by a panoply of social and welfare policies. Offenders, especially juvenile ones, were hopefully to be reclaimed by rehabilitative interventions shaped by scientific research and advice (Bailey, 1987). This approach also underlay the state's sponsorship of criminological research, falteringly in the inter-war years, but with a strong institutional base after the 1957 creation of the Home Office Research Unit and the establishment of the Cambridge Institute of Criminology two years later. These developments were made possible by s.77 of the Criminal Justice Act 1948 which authorised the Home Secretary to conduct, or support financially, research into "the causes of delinquency and the treatment of offenders, and matters connected therewith". (See papers by Morris and Martin in this volume. Also: Butler,1974; Lodge, 1974; Sparks, 1983; Clarke and Cornish, 1983; Bottoms, 1987; Hood, 1987). Thus in the century after the birth of a self-conscious and self-labelled criminological movement, the state became increasingly involved in sponsoring it, as well as supporting a panoply of experts in penal treatment. This was all part-and-parcel of the generally more interventionist state, promoting an array of social and welfare policies and responsible for economic management, partly, although by no means only, as a way of sustaining the preconditions of order and conformity. Down to the 1950s this programme was broadly successful in achieving a more crime-free, orderly and integrated society. The project of the original "science of police" as an interrelated set of policing, legal and social measures, was implemented, even though the criminal science that replaced it in theory blocked out overt recognition of the role of the state which nourished it. The state only came back into criminological awareness following the "epistemological break" engendered by the variety of radical criminologies which flourished after the 1960s.

Radical criminology and the state

During the late 1960s British criminology began to experience a proliferating babble of critiques and proposed new programmes for theory and research. As one commentator remarked: "The danger of experiencing too great a succession of so-called paradigmatic revolutions, without any concomitant intervals of normal science, is a sense of toppling into a metaphysical swamp." (Downes, 1978, 498.) At first the National Deviancy Conference constituted a kind of organisational umbrella.Mutual opposition to "establishment criminology" and its institutional denizens the Home Office Research Unit and the Cambridge Institute (both barely ten years old despite being perceived as hoary monoliths) provided some ideological glue. But by the early 1970s theoretical and political schisms began to proliferate, and by

BJC/278   ROBERT REINER

1976 it was necessary to speak of "the new criminolog*ies*" (Wiles, 1976). The history of these developments and controversies has been well documented elsewhere (for example in Cohen, 1971, 1983; Rock and Mackintosh, 1974; Sparks, 1980, 1983). Consequently I will restrict myself to the way that the new departures all involved a rediscovery of the state. Indeed one of the key unifying themes was a generally oppositional stance to the state and its works, for all the divergent ways in which these might be analysed. Roughly we can distinguish three main stages in the treatment of the state in recent radical British criminology.

(a) Radical conflict theory

One of the key British works of Marxist criminology has claimed that: "Most criminological theories—including much of 'radical criminology'—have no concept or theory of the state." (Hall *et al.*, 1978, 194). It is true that, in so far as they used the term at all, the new criminologies of the late 1960s and early 1970s operated with a hazy and amorphous image of the state as "Leviathan" (Matza, 1969).[14] Mostly they did not use the concept of the state explicitly in referring to the collectivity of official control institutions. These were given some vaguer label, such as "societal control culture" (Lemert, 1951) or "social reaction" (Taylor, Walton and Young, 1973).

The official control institutions of the state became problematic for British criminologists in a variety of ways. "Labelling theory" emphasised that the origins and application of deviant labels required analysis, both because these constituted the categories of deviance, and because they were able causally implicated in "secondary deviation", which was supposedly more significant socially than initial "primary" deviant acts (Becker, 1963; Lemert, 1967).[15] Control institutions were also morally and politically problematic for the "new" criminologists' "underdog" sympathies (Becker, 1967). Gouldner's influential 1968 critique of Becker pointed the way towards a more macro-structural analysis of the operation of control institutions.

The culmination of this plea was Taylor, Walton and Young's 1973 *The New Criminology*, which was both the most controversial and the most seminal work of radical criminology in this period. What is striking in the light of the subsequent development of radical criminology is the virtually complete absence of discussion of the state. In their sketch of the "formal requirements" of "a fully social theory" of deviance, the state figures fleetingly in the call for analysis of how "the political economy of the state" must play a part in elucidating the "wider origins of deviant reaction" (pp. 273–4). *The New Criminology* has a problematic relationship to Marxist theory, as the authors' well-known debate with Hirst indicated (Taylor, Walton and Young, 1975, Chs. 8–10).[16]

[14] "Matza's discussion is so abstract and ahistorical as to provide little guidance to understanding the operation of the state in a particular society at some given historical moment." (Pearce, 1976, 48).

[15] Studying the development of categories of crime as well as of criminal behaviour had already been urged by some writers within a more conventional criminological framework e.g. Jeffery, 1960.

[16] Though a debate about whether there could be an authentically Marxist theory of law and crime was to appear ironic a few years later when the issue had become rather "whether a Marxist framework can and should replace all others" (Nelken, 1980, 197).

The absence of an elaborated analysis of the role of the state is a key to what is probably the central weakness of *The New Criminology* (and the radical criminologies of which it is the ultimate embodiment): its totally oppositional stance. This was pin-pointed not only by mainstream "bourgeois" critiques (e.g. Inciardi, 1980; Sparks, 1980) but also by more explicitly Marxist writers. Their castigation of the "correctionalism" of traditional criminology meant a failure to "distinguish the destructive or demoralising aspects of some kinds of deviance from the potentially liberating ones. . . . An approach to deviance that can't distinguish between politically progressive and politically retrogressive forms of deviance doesn't provide much of a basis for real understanding or political action". (Currie, 1974, 112). This would require "a political philosophy and a theory of history within which to assess the deviant act" (ibid., 111). That is, a more articulated and rounded notion of the state and its functions is needed. Hirst makes this explicit: "The operation of law or custom, however much it may be associated in some societies with injustice and oppression, is a necessary condition of existence of any social formation. Whether the social formation has a State or not, whether it is communist or not, it will control and coerce in certain ways the acts of its members. . . One cannot imagine the absence of the control of traffic or the absence of the suppression of theft and murder, nor can one consider these controls as purely oppressive." (In Taylor, Walton and Young, 1975, 240). A similar conclusion about the one-sided, simplistically oppositional treatment of moral and political issues by the "new" deviance theory was also reached through a different route, via symbolic interactionism. "Rather than convey a model of moral life as densely textured and intricate, they have constructed a kind of sociological Flatland. . . . Not only is there a denial of complexity and ambiguity, there is a failure to differentiate between *kinds* of value. It seems to be assumed that notions concerning, say, murder, clothing, marihuana and chocolate are all interchangeable analytic units." (Rock, 1974, 154–6).

The central weakness in the radical criminologies culminating in *The New Criminology* was this absence of a systematic analysis of the concepts of the state, law and order (political and moral). In the years after *The New Criminology*, three reactions are discernible. Business as usual continued for conventional "mainstream" work, side-stepping the issues posed by the new theoretical critique (Sparks, 1983, 89). Theoretical analysis moved predominantly into some kind of Marxist direction, explicitly foregrounding the concepts of law and state. At the same time, problems with Marxist approaches were broached by critiques from a number of other theoretical traditions (notably in Downes and Rock, 1979).

(b) Marxist criminology and the state

The first phase of an overtly Marxist criminology primarily involved erstwhile radical conflict theorists altering the language and tone, rather than the conceptual structure of their theories. This is vividly shown in an American example by a detailed comparison of two versions of Chambliss' article on the law of vagrancy (Klockars, 1980, 100–2). The jargon of pluralist conflict

BJC/280   ROBERT REINER

theory is consistently swapped for Marxist terms in the later version but the structure remains the same. (E.g. in "The Statutes served a new and equally important function for the social order" the word "ruling class' replaces "social order.") An English example is Taylor, Walton and Young's more explicitly Marxist reworking of *The New Criminology*, the 1975 collection *Critical Criminology*. The former book's advocacy of "human diversity" which would not be subject to control in socialist society should have been discussed in terms of "the withering away of the state" according to the later book (Taylor, Walton and Young, 1975, 20). The result of these changes in the development of a criminology built around an *instrumentalist* theory of law and state as straightforward tools of ruling-class interests. (E.g. Pearce, 1976, 58–66.) As Young put it: "Radical criminological strategy is not to argue for legality and the rule of law but it is to show up the law, in its true colour, as the instrument of a ruling class, and *tactically* to demonstrate that the State will break its own laws, that its legitimacy is a sham, and that the rule-makers are also the greatest of rule-breakers." (Young, 1975, 89).[17] This is a succinct instance of what Young in his later "realist" incarnation would call "left idealism".

The instrumentalist notion of law and state has many obvious problems. Above all it cannot readily or plausibly interpret laws which on the face of it operate to control members of the ruling-class or to advance the welfare of the working-class. Nor can it explain why there is clear cross-class consensus about the most central aspects of criminal law and criminal justice (Levi, 1987, Ch. 3). A reading of Marx on the origins of the Factory Acts in *Capital* (Vol. 1, Ch. 10) shows clearly that Marx's own analysis of the relationship between class, law and state was not an instrumentalist one.

The reaction to the perceived inadequacies of instrumentalism amongst many Marxist criminologists was "back to the classics". Nor so much to Marx himself because of the lack of an elaborated theory of law and the state in his mature work, as to later Marxist theorists. Thus in the joint National Deviancy Conference/Conference of Socialist Economists' 1979 *Capitalism and the Rule of Law: From Deviancy Theory to Marxism*, there are papers exploring the possibilities of such early twentieth century Marxists as Renner or Pashukanis.

The apogee of the attempt to develop an analysis of law, crime and the state within the Marxist tradition is the ambitious and complex 1978 book *Policing the Crisis* by Stuart Hall *et al*. This is an impressive marriage of concepts derived from "new" deviance theory (moral panic, folk-devils, deviance amplification, labelling) with modern Marxist theory of the state, particularly as developed by Gramsci, Althusser and Poulantzas. Starting with the analysis of the "mugging" scare of 1972–3 (and in particular one particular

[17] In so far as it argues that dominant state-defined conceptions of crime neglect much anti-social behaviour, Box's claim that "there is more to crime and criminals than the state reveals" (Box, 1983, 15) is a recent example of this position. It is not clear what is gained by encompassing all evils under an amorphous category of "crime" (Bottomley, 1979, 10). Box's book does, however, valuably underline most criminology's neglect of offending (against ordinary rules of criminal law) by agents of the state itself and "the powerful" more generally.

robbery in Handsworth in 1972), the authors "go behind the label to the contradictory social content which is mystifyingly reflected in it" (Hall *et al.*, 1978, vii). From the study of the "mugging" panic the authors are led to analyse "the general 'crisis of hegemony' in the Britain of the 1970s". This involves both the elaboration of a theoretical framework for understanding crime, law and state, and a breakdown of post-war British social history, centring on how economic and political crises pave the way for the mobilisation of fears and anxieties, and legitimate the development of an exceptional form of authoritarian "strong state" and "law and order society".

Policing the Crisis is undoubtedly an intellectual *tour de force* in its bold attempt to synthesise a diversity of approaches, and gives a fascinating spectacle of "the epistemological dilution of structuralist Marxism through its confrontation with the nasty business of empirical reality" (Sumner, 1981, 277–8). The complex theoretical edifice seems, however, to be built on a rather cursory brush with this "nasty business".

Two critiques, from opposing ideological positions (and different perceptions of "empirical reality"), have converged on the problem of identifying the central concept of moral panic. When is concern, and public policy directed towards it, to be analysed as a "panic", as distinct from a reasonable response to a problem? Hall *et al.* speak of "panic" when "the official reaction to a person, groups of persons or series of events is *out of all proportion* to the actual threat offered"? (p. 16). But this reference to "proportion" makes the concept an arbitrary value judgement unless it is solidly anchored in both agreed criteria of proportionality and convincing evidence about the scale of "the threat". Subsequent research has shown that contrary to the implication of Hall *et al.* the mugging scare was preceded by substantial increases in crime in general, as well as crimes of violence and "robbery and assault with intent to rob" more specifically (Pratt, 1980; Waddington, 1986). From an opposing perspective, it has been pointed out that the evidence for a general public panic about mugging in 1972–3 is itself flimsy (Sumner, 1981, 281–5). It is inferred from a top-down reading of the state's reaction to mugging, with the only direct evidence about *public* opinion being dubiously representative "letters to the editor". The more general point is the lack of grounding of even more sophisticated Marxist analyses of state and crime in empirical research, especially on the inside workings of state institutions.[18] (The sole exception is a recently published volume on the police by members of the *Policing the Crisis* team: Grimshaw and Jefferson, 1987. Although primarily focused on patrol work this does mark an important advance in giving some empirical data on the decision-making process within a police force.) There are still no criteria developed for demarcating the oppressive from other aspects of the functioning of the state, as is indicated by the unanalysed notion of the "proportionality" of "panic" to "problem".[19]

---

[18] A partial exception to this is the burgeoning "revisionist" historical literature on policing and punishment (Brogden, 1982; Philips, 1983; Ignatieff, 1981; Reiner, 1985: Ch. 1). This is mostly "bottom-up" history, however, revealing little about state institutions from the inside.

[19] One exception is Jefferson and Grimshaw, 1984 and its discussion of "socialist justice" principles.

BJC/282   ROBERT REINER

Post-Marxist criminology and the state

In recent years a number of strands of criminological discussion have emerged which recognise the political context of crime and law but reject or qualify a Marxist approach. There are two primary roots of these developments. The first is the magnitude of the crime problem as a public issue, and the reappearance of public disorder with clear political implications, both after a century of apparent decline (Reiner, 1985c; Gatrell, 1987; Lea *et al.*, 1987; Dunning *et al.*, 1987). The second is the fragmentation of the class context for radical perceptions of crime and disorder, and the growing salience of other dimensions: race, gender, age, generation and location.

Three main post-Marxist strands can be discerned in current debate about the state, law, order, crime and politics. The first reflects the influence of Foucault, in particular his seminal work on the history of punishment (Foucault, 1977, 1979). This has sensitised many British criminologists to the integral links of power and knowledge, the complex and subtle weaving of relations of power throughout the social sphere as distinct from a concentrated locus of state power, and the disciplinary face of apparently liberating movements towards relaxing formal social controls (Cohen, 1979, 1984, 1985; Abel, 1982; Garland and Young, 1983; Scull, 1979; Cohen and Scull, 1983). The price of this analytic subtlety is a lack of clear implications for policy or politics, beyond rather vague gestures towards "anarchism" or "progressive penal politics", which indicate little more than one's heart is in the right (or left?) place (Young, 1983, 100; Garland, 1985; 262; Cohen, 1985, 272).

The second strand is the development of what Young calls a new "left realism" (Young, 1979, 1986; Lea and Young, 1984; Kinsey, Lea and Young, 1986; Taylor, 1981). This starts from the recognition that crime ought to be an important political issue for the left, but that hitherto the right has succeded in "stealing" it to their political advantage (Downes, 1983). Victimisation surveys, especially those conducted on a local basis, reveal that crime is a major problem in reality precisely for the most socially deprived and vulnerable sections of the population, the left's traditional heartland (Kinsley, 1985; Jones *et al.*, 1986). Viable policies for preventing or alleviating crime can be pursued as immediately practical reforms, without waiting for a socialist millenium or succumbing to the tough "law and order" placebos of the right (Morison, 1987). At the same time these policies would be compatible with, if not presuppose, a wider agenda of progressive democratisation of local and central state structures and an empowerment of the deprived. This analysis has been subject to severe criticism, questioning its realism and its socialism (Scraton, 1985; Gilroy and Sim, 1985). But it has been widely welcomed for taking the issue of crime seriously while still recognising its broader political dimensions, (and it influenced Labour's 1987 General Election Campaign (Reiner, 1987b). The analytic side of "left realism" has not developed in pace with its empirical research and policy recommendations. In particular there has been little discussion of the concept of, and relationship to, the state. (Apart from some parts of Taylor,

1981).[20] Interestingly the empirical research by "left realists" has been sponsored by parts of the "local state", radical councils such as Merseyside or Islington (Reiner, 1987a).

The final strand of recent work on crime and the state, perhaps the most noteworthy of all, is the appearance of liberal and conservative analysis of "law and order" which recognise its political aspects. In a sense this returns to the problematic of "the science of police", locating the crime and order issue within the broader project of governance.[21] Traditionally the liberal and conservative stance has been to see problems of crime control as merely technical matters, or as straightforward moral confrontations of good and evil. But in recent years a number of important works have appeared, developing sophisticated analysis of "law and order" from within the traditions of liberal or conservative political philosophy (Berki, 1983, 1986; Dahrendorf, 1985; Norton, 1985, 1987).

One of the key aspects of this has been the attempt to distinguish between different facets of state activity. This has also been a keynote of a significant American contribution to Marxist analysis of crime and the state, which could potentially provide a theoretical underpinning to "left realism" (Marenin, 1982, 1985). This distinguishes between the role of the state in preserving "general order, the interests of all in regularity", from "specific order, that is the use of state power to promote particular interests" (Marenin, 1982, 258–9). This points to a theoretical rationale for the "left realist" stance of perceiving the issue of crime and order at least partly from *within* the state, as contrasted with radical criminology's erstwhile totally oppositional perspective. There is here the prospect of some convergence of hitherto conflicting positions, with a measure of consensus stemming from a more complex analysis of the state's functioning. One novel fall-out from this might be the development of empirical research on, and a more grounded understanding of, the working's of the state's institutions for crime control.[22] The state would thus become not only part of criminology's conceptual field but also of its research agenda.

REFERENCES

ABEL, R. (ed.) (1982). *The Politics of Informal Justice*. New York, Academic Press.
ALTHUSSER, L. (1971). "Ideology and ideological state apparatuses," in *Lenin and Philosophy*. London, New Left Books.

[20] This has been facilitated partly by left realism's implicit conception of the "law and order" issue in terms of mundane property and personal crime, as distinct from questions of public disorder, large-scale professional crime, or white-collar offences. There is a parallel with the way that labelling theory's concentration on "nuts, sluts and perverts" permitted the flourishing of sympathy with the deviant and hostility to social control.

[21] Significantly the Home Office Research Unit's work is now much more concerned with studies of the police and other aspects of the state, as distinct from its earlier concentration on penal technique (Reiner, 1987a).

[22] Empirical research on state control apparatuses has hitherto been restricted to the lower-levels of police organisations or the under-life of prisons. Work on the more overtly political and policy levels has been mainly within a public law framework, focusing on the accountability issue, (Lustgarten, 1986; Maguire, Vagg and Morgan, 1985). What empirical research there has been on higher-level functioning has been either historical or based on official statistics. It is only recently that empirical field-work on higher levels of state control organisations has been attempted, as by Rock, 1987 (and forthcoming) on the development of victim policy in Canada and the U.K., and my own current research on chief constables.

BJC/284   ROBERT REINER

BAILEY, V. (1987). *Delinquency and Citizenship*. Oxford, Oxford University Press.

BECKER, H. (1963). *Outsiders*. New York, Free Press.

BECKER, H. (1967). "Whose side are we on?". *Social Problems*, **14**, 239–247.

BERKI, R. (1983). *Considerations on Law and Order*. Hull Papers in Politics 35, University of Hull.

BERKI, R. (1986). *Security and Society: Reflections on Law, Order and Politics*. London, Dent.

BOTTOMLEY, A. K. (1979). *Criminology in Focus*. Oxford, Martin Robertson.

BOTTOMS, A. E. (1987). "Reflections on the Criminological Enterprise". *Cambridge Law Journal*, 240–263.

BOX, S. (1983). *Power, Crime and Mystification*. London, Tavistock.

BROGDEN, M. (1982). *The Police: Autonomy and Consent*. London, Academic Press.

BUTLER, Lord R. A. B. (1974) "The Foundation of the Institute of Criminology in Cambridge", in Hood, R. (1974), 1–11.

CLARKE, R. and CORNISH, D. (1983). *Crime Control in Britain*. Albany, State University of New York Press.

COHEN, (ed.) (1971). *Images of Deviance*. London, Penguin.

COHEN, S. (1974). "Criminology and the sociology of deviance in Great Britain," in Rock, P. and Mackintosh, M. (1974), 1–40.

COHEN, S. (1979). "The Punitive City". *Contemporary Crises*, **3**, 339–363.

COHEN, S. (1981). "Footprints in the sand," in Fitzgerald, M. *et al.* (1981), 220–247.

COHEN, S. (1984). "The deeper structures of the law or 'Beware the rulers bearing justice' ". *Contemporary Crises*, **8**, 83–93.

COHEN, S. (1985). *Visions of Social Control*. Cambridge, Polity Press.

COHEN, S. and SCULL, A. (eds.) (1983). *Social Control and the State*. Oxford, Martin Robertson.

COLQUHOUN, P. (1797). *Treatise on the Police of the Metropolis* 4th ed.

COLQUHOUN, P. (1800). *Treatise on the Commerce and Police of the River Thames*.

COLQUHOUN, P. (1806). *Treatise on Indigence*.

COLQUHOUN, P. (1814). *Treatise on the Wealth, Power and Resources of the British Empire*.

CROSS, R. and JONES P. (1984). *Introduction to Criminal Law*, 10th ed. by R. Card. London, Butterworth.

CURRIE, E. (1974). "The New Criminology". *Crime and Social Justice*, 109–113.

DAHRENDORF, R. (1985). *Law and Order*. London, Stevens.

DEARLOVE, J. and SAUNDERS, P. (1984). *Introduction to British Politics*. Cambridge, Polity Press.

DONAJGRODSKI, A. P. (ed.) (1977). *Social Control in Nineteenth Century Britain*. London, Croom Helm.

DOWNES, D. (1978). "Promise and performance in British Criminology". *British Journal of Sociology*, 483–502.

DOWNES, D. (1983). *Law and Order: Theft of an Issue*. Fabian Society/Labour Campaign for Criminal Justice.

DOWNES, D. and ROCK, F. (eds.) (1979). *Deviant Interpretations*. Oxford, Martin Robertson.

DOWNES, D. and ROCK, P. (1982). *Understanding Deviance*. Oxford, Oxford University Press.

DUCKER, H., *et al.* (eds.) (1986). *Developments in British Politics 2*. London, Macmillan.

DUNLEAVY, P. and O'LEARY, B. (1987). *Theories of the State*. London, MacMillan.

DUNNING, E., *et al.* (1987). "Violent disorders in twentieth century Britain," in Gaskell, G. and Benewick, R. (eds.) *The Crowd in Contemporary Britain*. London, Sage, 19–75.

FOUCAULT, M. (1977). *Discipline and Punish*. London, Allen Lane.

FOUCAULT, M. (1979). "On governmentality". *Ideology and Consciousness*, **6**, 5–23.

FOUCAULT, M. (1980). "Prison talk", in Gordon C. (ed.) *Michel Foucault: Power/ Knowledge*. Brighton Harvester.

GARLAND, D. (1985a). *Punishment and Welfare*. Aldershot, Gower.

GARLAND, D. (1985b). "The criminal and his science". *British Journal of Criminology*, **25**, 109–137.

GARLAND, D. and YOUNG, P. (eds.) (1983). *The Power to Punish*. London, Heinemann.

GATRELL, V. (1980). "The decline of theft and violence in Victoria and Edwardian England", in Gatrell, V., *et al.* (1980); 238–338.

GATRELL, V. (1987). "Crime, Authority and the Policeman—State 1750–1950," in Thompson, F. (ed.) *The Cambridge Social History of Britain 1750–1950*. Cambridge, Cambridge University Press.

GATRELL, V., LENMAN, B. and PARKER, G. (eds.) (1980). *Crime and the Law*. London, Europa.

GEARY, R. (1985). *Policing Industrial Disputes 1893–1985*. Cambridge, Cambridge University Press.

GILROY, P. and SIM, J. (1985). "Law, Order and the State of the Left". *Capital and Class*, **25**, 15–55.

GOULDNER, A. (1968). "The sociologist as partisan: sociology and the welfare state". *The American Sociologist*, 103–116.

GRIMSHAW, R. and JEFFERSON, T. (1987). *Interpreting Policework*. London, Allen and Unwin.

HALL, S., *et al.* (1978). *Policing the Crisis*. London, Macmillan.

HELD, D., *et al.* (eds.) (1983). *States and Societies*. Oxford, Martin Robertson.

HIRST, P. Q. (1985). "Marx and Engels on law, crime and morality," in Taylor, I., Walton, P. and Young, J. (1985), 203–244.

HOOD, R. (ed.) (1974). *Crime, Criminology and Public Policy*. London, Heinemann.

HOOD, R. (1987). "Some reflections on the role of criminology in public policy", *Criminal Law Review*, 527–538.

IGNATIEFF, M. (1981). "State, Civil Society and Total Institutions: A critique of recent social histories of punishment," in Cohen, S. and Scull, A. (1983), 75–105.

INCIARDI, J. (ed.) (1980). *Radical Criminology: The Coming Crises*. Beverly Hills, Sage.

JEFFERSON, J. and GRIMSHAW, R. (1985). *Controlling the Constable*. London, Muller.

JEFFERY, C. R. (1957). "The development of crime in early English Society". *Journal of Criminal Law, Criminology and Police Service*, **47**, 647–666.

JEFFERY, C. R. (1960). "Historical development of criminology," in Mannheim, H. (1960), 364–394.

JEUDWINE, J. W. (1917). *Tort, Crime and Police in Medieval Britain*. London, Williams and Norgate.

JONES, T., MACLEAN, B. and YOUNG, J. (1986). *The Islington Crime Survey*. Aldershot, Gower.

KAHN, P., LEWIS, N., LIVOCK, P. and WILES, P. (1983). *Picketing*. London, Routledge.

BJC/286   ROBERT REINER

KENNEDY, M. (1970). "Beyond Incrimination". *Catalyst,* reprinted in Chambliss, W. and Mankoff, M. (eds.) (1976) *Whose Law, What Order?* New York, Wiley, 34–64.

KING, R. (1986). *The State in Modern Society.* London, Macmillan.

KINSEY, R. (1985). *Merseyside Crime Survey.* Liverpool, Merseyside County Council.

KINSEY, R., LEA, J. and YOUNG, J. (1986). *Losing the Fight Against Crime.* Oxford, Blackwell.

KLOCKARS, C. (1980). "The contemporary crises of Marxist criminology," in Inciardi, J. (1980), 92–123.

LEA, J. and YOUNG, J. (1984). *What is to be done about law and order?* London, Penguin.

LEA, J., MATTHEWS, R. and YOUNG, J. J. (1987). *Law and Order: Five years On.* London, Middlesex Polytechnic.

LEMERT, E. (1951). *Social Pathology.* New York, McGraw-Hill.

LEMERT, E. (1967). *Human Deviance, Social Problems and Social Control.* Englewood Cliffs, Prentice-Hall.

LENMAN, B. and PARKER, G. (1980). "The State, the community and the criminal law in early modern Europe," in Gatrell, V., *et al.* (1980), 11–48.

LEVI, M. (1987). *Regulating Fraud.* London, Tavistock.

LODGE, T. (1974). "The founding of the Home Office Research Unit," in Hood, R. (1974), 11–24.

LUSTGARTEN, L. (1986). *The Governance of the Police.* London, Sweet and Maxwell.

MAGUIRE, M., VAGG, J. and MORGAN, R. (eds.) (1985). *Accountability and Prisons.* London, Tavistock.

MAITLAND, R. (1985). *Justice and Police.* London, Macmillan.

MANNHEIM, H. (ed.) (1960). *Pioneers in Criminology.* London, Stevens.

MANNHEIM, H. (1965). *Comparative Criminology.* London, Routledge and Kegan Paul.

MARENIN, O. (1982). "Parking Tickets and Class Repression: The Concept of Policing in Critical Theories of Criminal Justice". *Contemporary Crises,* **6,** 241–266.

MARENIN, O. (1985). "Police Performance and State Rule". *Comparative Politics,* 101–122.

MATZA, D. (1969). *Becoming Deviant.* Englewood Cliffs, Prentice-Hall.

MORRISON, J. (1987). "New strategies in the politics of law and order". *Howard Journal of Criminal Justice,* 203–216.

MORRIS, T. (1957). *The Criminal Area.* London, Routledge and Kegan Paul.

NATIONAL DEVIANCY CONFERENCE/CONFERENCE OF SOCIALIST ECONOMISTS (1979). *Capitalism and the Rule of Law.* London, Hutchinson.

NELKEN, D. (1980). "Capitalism and the Rule of Law: Review Article". *International Journal of the Sociology of Law,* **8,** 193–199.

NORTON, P. (1984). *The British Polity.* London, Longmans.

NORTON, P. (ed.) (1985). *Law and Order and British Politics.* Aldershot, Gower.

NORTON, P. (1987). " 'Law and Order' in Perspective", paper to British Society of Criminology, May.

NOZICK, R. (1974). *Anarchy, State and Utopia.* Oxford, Blackwell.

PASQUINO, P. (1978). "Theatrum politicum: the genealogy of capital, police and the state of prosperity". *Ideology and Consciousness,* 41–54.

PEARCE, F. (1976). *Crimes of the Powerful.* London, Pluto.

PEARSON, G. (1983). *Hooligan*. London, Macmillan.

PHILIPS, D. (1980). "A new engine of power and authority," in Gatrell, V., *et al.* (1980), 155–189.

PHILIPS, D. (1983). "A just measure of crime, authority, hunters and blue locusts," in Cohen, S. and Scull, A. (1983), 50–74.

PORTER, B. (1987). *The Origins of the Vigilant State*. London, Weidenfeld.

PRATT, M. (1980). *Mugging As A Social Problem*. London, Routledge and Kegan Paul.

RADZINOWICZ, L. (1956). *History of the English Criminal Law*, Vol. 3. London, Stevens.

RADZINOWICZ, L. and HOOD, R. (1986). *History of the English Criminal Law*, Vol. 4. London, Stevens.

REINER, R. (1985a). *The Politics of the Police*. Brighton, Wheatsheaf.

REINER, R. (1985b). "Policing strikes". *Policing*, 138–148.

REINER, R. (1985c). "Policing, Order and Legitimacy," in Spitzer, S. and Scull, A. (eds.) *Research in Law, Deviance and Social Control 1:8*. Greenwich, Connecticut, JAI Press.

REINER, R. (1987a). "The Politics of Police Research," in Weatheritt, M. (ed.) *Police Research*. London, Croom Helm.

REINER, R. (1987b). "Law and Order," in *Channel 4 Election Brief*, 17.

RICHTER, D. (1981). *Riotous Victorians*. Ohio University Press.

ROBBINS, L. (1981). "Economics and Political Economy". *American Economic Review*, reprinted in *Essay on the Nature and Significance of Economic Science 3rd. ed*. London, Macmillan, xi–xxxiii.

ROCK, P. (1974). "The sociology of deviancy and conceptions of moral order". *British Journal of Criminology*, reprinted in Wiles, P. (1976) 145–158.

ROCK, P. (1987). *A View From the Shadows: The Ministry of the Solicitor General of Canada and the Justice for Victims of Crime Initiative*. Oxford, Oxford University Press.

ROCK, P. and MACKINTOSH, M. (eds.) (1974). *Deviance and Social Control*. London, Tavistock.

SCRATON, P. (1985). *The State of the Police*. London, Pluto.

SCULL, A. (1977). *Decarceration*. Oxford, Martin Robertson.

SILVER, A. (1967). "The demand for order in civil society," in Bordus, D. (ed.) *The Police*. New York, Wiley.

SMART, B. (1983). "On discipline and social regulation," in Garland, D. and Young, P. (1983), 62–83.

SMITH, A. (1763). *Lectures on Justice, Police, Revenue and Arms*. (Published as *Lectures on Jurisprudence*, Oxford University Press, 1978).

SPARKS, R. (1980). "A critique of Marxist criminology," in Morris, N. and Tonry, M. (eds.) *Crime and Justice 2*. Chicago University Press, 159–210.

SPARKS, R. (1983). "Britain," in Johnson, (ed.) *International Handbook of Contemporary Developments in Criminology Vol. 2*. Westport, Conn., Greenwood Press, 79–105.

STEAD, P. J. (1977). "Patrick Colquhoun" in Stead, P. J. (ed.) *Pioneers in Policing*. New Jersey, Patterson Smith, 48–63.

STEVENSON, J. (1979). *Popular Disturbances in England 1700–1870*. London, Longman.

SUMNER, C. (1981). "Race, crime and hegemony". *Contemporary Crises*, **5,** 277–291.

TAYLOR, I. (1981). *Law and Order: Arguments for Socialism*. London, Macmillan.

TAYLOR, I., WALTON, P. and YOUNG, J. (1973). *The New Criminology*. London, Routledge and Kegan Paul.

BJC/288   ROBERT REINER

TAYLOR, I., WALTON, P. and YOUNG, J. (1975). *Critical Criminology*. London, Routledge and Kegan Paul.

VOLD, G. (1958). *Theoretical Criminology*. New York, Oxford University Press.

WADDINGTON, P. A. J. (1986). "Mugging as a moral panic". *British Journal of Sociology*, 245–259.

WALSH, D. (1985). *A Dictionary of Criminology*. London, Routledge and Kegan Paul.

WEBER, M. (1919). "Politics as a vocation," in Gerth, H. and Mills, C. W. (eds.) *From Max Weber*. London, Routledge and Kegan Paul, 1970.

WILES, P. (ed.) (1976). *The Sociology of Crime and Delinquency in Britain; Vol. 2: The New Criminologies*. Oxford, Martin Robertson.

WILLIAMS, GLANVILLE (1983). *Textbook of Criminal Law*. London, Stevens.

[13]
Crime and Control in Britain

ABSTRACT This paper explores the possible patterns of crime and control in the twenty-first century, drawing on an analysis of current and recent developments. These suggest a dystopian prospect of permanently high crime rates, and control strategies that reinforce social division and exclusion. Current 'third way' policies for crime reduction may achieve modest success, in part because they indirectly encourage agencies to manipulate statistically recorded outcomes to their advantage. They do not however tackle the underlying sources of crime in the political economy and culture of global capitalism, offering only actuarial analyses of risk variation, and pragmatic preventive interventions to reduce these. In the absence of any broader changes to the social patterns which generate high-crime societies the prospect is of marginal palliatives for crime, which themselves have the dysfunctional consequences of increasing segregation, distrust and anxiety.

KEYWORDS control, crime, crime statistics, criminal justice policy, policing, politics of law and order.

A century ago Durkheim proposed the avowedly paradoxical argument that crime, by his own definition behaviour that shocked all healthy consciences, was none the less a normal not a pathological phenomenon (Durkheim 1964). What was then a theoretical claim about the necessary features of any conceivable social order has become an almost taken for granted aspect of the everyday experience of late or post-modern societies at the turn of the second millennium. Government policies, popular culture and the pragmatic preventive routines of citizens testify to a *de facto* acceptance that we are living in a high-crime society (Garland 1995). It is not just that criminal activity, victimisation and fear have become commonplace. In pluralistic, rapidly changing cultures that celebrate diversity and choice there is increasing ambiguity about what constitutes deviance (Young 1999). As the shifting pieces of a collage of life-styles gain or seek acceptance as legitimate alternatives, it is the concept of an absolutist, dominant moral order that has become deviant. Despite the normalisation of deviance, political and popular concern about crime has become ever more prominent, generating punitive and exclusionary control policies.

This paper seeks to consider the likely trajectory of crime and control over the next quarter century. For this it is necessary to probe the dynamics of current and recent trends and patterns, in order to extrapolate tentatively the future they imply. This is a conditional prediction not a prophecy. What is offered is a possible history of the future. But it is so dystopian that I very much hope it might be averted by a wider realisation of the divisive, crime and conflict-generating implications of present patterns and policies.

The paper begins with an account of the recent emergence of crime and fear of crime as key political and social issues. It then considers how far they are rooted in the reality of crime as – notoriously problematically – indicated by official statistics. This is followed by a discussion of alternative explanations of the rising rate of recorded crime, and an assessment of alternative control strategies. On the basis of this analysis of the recent past and the present, possible crime and control scenarios for the first twenty-five years of the next millennium are then considered.

Criminology has generally been a 'can-do' rather than a dismal science. Its main theoretical paradigms – classicism and positivism – intended to inform effective crime control strategies, whilst the social constructionist approaches which grew out of labelling theory in the 1960s sought to deconstruct the apparent problem of crime and the apparatus of control. Current government policies, drawing on situational and rational choice perspectives, are more optimistic than ever about the prospects for effective crime reduction. This is believed to be attainable without the major social reforms implied by sociological analyses of the 'root causes' of crime so scathingly dismissed by the arch-prophet of pragmatic realism, James Q. Wilson (Wilson 1985:6). The analysis I offer below harks back to the macro perspectives of critical criminology and classical sociology, implying pessimism about the prospects of success for current policies in the absence of wider social reforms directed at the roots of rising crime. Without this there will be an accentuation of the social divisions which both generate and are reinforced by crime.

Crime is a topic of perennial popular fascination, as indicated by its centrality as a theme in the mass media (Ericson *et al.* 1991; Sparks 1992; Reiner 1997a; Allen *et al.* 1998). Representations of crime and punishment offer, in varying measure, titillating glimpses of the seductions of deviance, moral boundary maintenance, and an anxiety arousing *frisson* of fear. However, in popular discourse, criminal statistics and most policy debates, crime is identified with only a narrow range of all offences against criminal law (let alone any wider sense of harmful or unethical behaviour), predatory offending by individuals against the property or person of others. Policy debates and public anxieties primarily concern street crime not suite crime, although critical criminologists have rightly emphasised that the harm done by the latter in many respects exceeds the former (Nelken 1997; Slapper and Tombs 1999).

The Politics of Law and Order

Despite the centrality of crime as a matter of popular interest it only became a political issue in Britain some thirty years ago. Election campaigns did not mention crime until 1970 (Downes and Morgan 1997). It was only after Margaret Thatcher became Conservative leader that law and order developed into a major arena of ideological conflict. Many of Labour's traditional values and associations were 'hostages to fortune' (Downes and Morgan 1997:102) in the face of Conservative attack. In particular, Labour's defining commitment to alleviating the extreme effects of inequality associated it with those sections of society that came to be castigated by the Right as the 'underclass', whose supposed fecklessness were represented as the source of many social ills, including crime. In the 1979 general election the Conservatives successfully 'stole' the issue of law and order (Downes 1983), making it one of their key election assets and successfully branding Labour as 'soft' on crime.

In practice, however, the criminal justice policies developed during the years in which Douglas Hurd was Home Secretary were much more sophisticated than Mrs Thatcher's tough talk (Reiner and Cross 1991). The Police and Criminal Evidence Act of 1984 enhanced police powers, but also introduced new safeguards for suspects which arguably protect them better (Brown 1997; Reiner 1997b:1025–8. For a more critical view see McConville et al. 1991; Sanders 1997). In the late 1980s, as crime rates rose despite the law and order medicine, the Home Office emphasised crime prevention rather than tough punishment (King 1989; Bottoms 1990; Pease 1997; Gilling 1997; Crawford 1998; Hughes 1998). The 1991 Criminal Justice Act, the culmination of years of research and consultation by Home Office civil servants, based sentencing on a 'just deserts' rather than retributive model, emphasised community sanctions rather than imprisonment, and aimed at reintegration not reinforced exclusion of offenders (Lacey 1994; Ashworth 1995, 1997; Mair 1997).

The carefully crafted package of the Criminal Justice Act 1991 was rejected by Home Secretary Kenneth Clarke, in one of the most rapid and complete U-turns in political history (Cavadino and Dignan 1997; Dunbar and Langdon 1998). His successor Michael Howard rejected the advice of his own civil servants and researchers, declaring without equivocation that 'prison works', and initiating a record expansion of the prison population (Morgan 1997). He also continued Clarke's reforms of the police, which were premised on a 'businesslike' model seeking market incentives to enhance police efficiency in catching criminals (Leishman et al. 1996; Reiner 1997b:1030–4).

New Labour, New Criminology

Labour only succeeded in shedding its electorally damaging image as 'soft' on law and order after Tony Blair became Shadow Home Secretary. Labour's new approach was summed up in the celebrated sound-bite 'tough on crime, tough on the causes of crime'. This seemed to synthesise Labour's traditional concern to alleviate the causes of crime with a new realist awareness of the need to address criminal behaviour through adequately 'tough' penal measures to assuage public anxiety and punitiveness. The message proved electorally popular, and drove the Tories into escalating the toughness of their own policies, resulting in a penal auction in the run-up to the 1997 general election.

In office Labour Home Secretary Jack Straw has introduced a highly innovative package of crime control policies, notably in the Crime and Disorder Act of 1998. It encourages a co-ordinated ('joined-up') approach to crime reduction based on partnership between local authorities, the police and other criminal justice agencies. These organisations are expected to target specific crime and disorder problems based on detailed analysis of the local situation, and regularly monitor the effectiveness of their strategies, adjusting them according to the outcome of these evaluations. The strategy is remarkable for its grounding in policy research (Nuttall *et al.* 1998), and its reflexive approach in which rigorous evaluation is intended to be an integral part of the policy development process. A very substantial part (£250 million) of the Home Office budget has been directed at the Crime Reduction Programme, of which 10 per cent has been set aside specifically for evaluative research (Home Office 1998a). All of this is faithful in a narrow sense to the 'tough on crime, tough on the causes of crime' formula, but any conception of crime's causes being found in wider social and economic policies seems to have disappeared, whilst the tough penal policy remains undiluted.

Fear of Crime

The politicisation of law and order both reflected and encouraged public concern about crime. Although popular anxiety (and fascination) with crime are perennial (Pearson 1983), 'fear of crime' only came to be analysed and addressed as a public issue in its own right in the early 1980s. Identification of 'fear of crime' as a distinct problem resulted primarily from the development of victim surveys in this country (following similar developments in the United States a decade earlier), notably the Home Office's British Crime Surveys (BCS). The apparent discrepancy between people's risks of victimisation and their 'fear' of crime as measured by the BCS was used by governments to suggest that much concern about crime was not rational. This position has been extensively criticised, notably by the 'left realists' on the basis of their own local crime surveys (Jones *et al.* 1986; Kinsey *et al.* 1986). Given the deep, complex and ambivalent meanings of crime the notion of assessing the 'rationality' of fear is in any case largely misplaced (Sparks 1992; Taylor 1996, 1997a; Hollway and Jefferson 1997; Walklate 1997, 1998).

None the less by the late 1980s the official line was that fear of crime was a problem in its own right. In 1989 a Home Office Working Party declared that fear of crime as an 'issue of social concern . . . has to be taken as seriously as . . . crime prevention and reduction' (Home Office 1989:ii). To a large extent this attempt to play down the rationality of fear was a response to the Thatcher Government's apparent inability in the 1980s and early 1990s to tackle crime despite its promises in the 1979 election. Although the policy emphasis shifted back to crime control in the early 1990s, fear of crime remains a prominent issue.

Trends in Recorded Crime in Contemporary Britain

The trends in crime indicated by official crime statistics are clear and dramatic, and appear amply to justify public and political concern about law and order. From the 1870s to the early 1920s crime rates remained on a plateau of under 100,000 offences recorded by the police per annum. Thereafter recorded crime rates began a rise that has proved remorseless for nearly three-quarters of a century, albeit punctuated by brief periods of slight decline. Since the early 1920s the average increase in the crime rate has been consistently around 5 per cent (Home Office 1995:3). By 1950 the police were recording half a million crimes per year. Although this fell slightly in the early 1950s, from 1955 the statistics began to record increases almost every year until the 1990s.

The rate of recorded crimes grew to unprecedented levels. By 1971 the annual total was 1.6 million, in 1980 2.5 million, and in 1992 it was 5.4 million. This has been followed by a period of respite. The recorded crime rate has fallen in each of the last four years, from 5.4 million in 1993/4 to 4.5 million in 1997/8 (Home Office 1998b).

Rising crime rates are not an inevitable or universal phenomenon, but almost everyone alive today will never have known a time when crime rates were not getting worse. Not only has total recorded crime increased, but the proportion of violent offences which cause the greatest anxiety has grown, although still relatively small compared to property crime. Recorded violence has increased in each of the years of falling overall crime, bringing it up from 5 per cent to 8 per cent between 1993 and 1998. The recorded crime figures thus offer a rational kernel for the increasing public and political concern about law and order described above.

The Limitations of Crime Statistics

Official crime statistics are, however, notoriously problematic (Walker 1995; Coleman and Moynihan 1996; Reiner 1996; Maguire 1997). For obvious reasons perpetrators of deviant and criminal acts wish to hide their behaviour, and usually conduct themselves with stealth and disguise, adding to the plethora of problems which plague most official statistics (Levitas and Guy 1996). Criminology has been haunted by the so-called 'dark figure' of unrecorded crime. What is commonly called the crime rate is labelled more accurately in the Home Office statistics as 'notifiable offences recorded by the police'. This they are by definition as they are based on police reports, but the problem is that they have usually been treated as if they were a measure of all criminal behaviour. However, many, probably most, offences are only known to their perpetrators or willing associates, and victims frequently do not report offences to the police. Thus many crimes do not come to be known to the police.

Police Massaging of Crime Trends

A less frequently discussed leakage from the crime statistics is that many crimes which are known to the police are not recorded by them, or are recorded in different ways from the victim's or perpetrator's perception. In practice, the police enjoy considerable discretion in recording offences, despite Home Office promulgation of standardised counting rules (McCabe and Sutcliffe 1978; Bottomley and Coleman 1981, 1995). To a large extent the better name for 'crimes recorded by the police' might be 'crimes which the police wish to make known'.

Manipulation of the crime figures to suit police and Home Office interests has been common practice, and arguably still is. There have been occasional scandals about data rigging by the police, most notoriously in the late 1980s in Kent, and recently in Nottinghamshire (Davies 1999). Observational studies of police work have also demonstrated that this is a common practice (notably Young, M. 1991). A recent historical study indicates extensive Home Office and police machinations to achieve the crime rates that suited their changing agendas (Taylor, H. 1998a and b; 1999). The stability of rates in the late nineteenth and early twentieth century was congenial both to Home Office parsimony and to the police who were seen as keeping crime and disorder under control. The increase thereafter was driven by the police in an attempt to fight off budget cuts, as they forged a new role as specialist crime-fighters. This supply-side determination of the crime figures sheds light on the long-term pattern of roughly steady levels over three-quarters of a century up to the early 1920s, succeeded by roughly constant rates of increase in the next three-quarters of a century. This is otherwise inexplicable in the light of the massive social and cultural upheavals during this period that would be expected to have had a profound effect on rates of offending.

In the last thirty years there have been important developments in criminological research methods aimed at probing the 'dark figure' of unrecorded crime, and find supplementary estimates to the dubious official statistics. Self-report studies based on interviews with offenders shed much light on the characteristics of those who commit crime (Coleman and Moynihan 1996:chap. 3). The development of victimisation studies has been even more significant (Hough and Mayhew 1983, 1985; Mayhew et al. 1989; Mayhew and Mirrlees-Black 1993; Mirrlees-Black et al. 1996, 1998; Coleman and Moynihan 1996:chap. 4; Reiner 1996; Maguire 1997). For crimes with individual victims the regular British Crime Surveys provide an estimate of the extent of victimisation that can be compared with the police recorded figures to assess change over time.

The BCS itself does not give us the 'true' crime rate (a figure known only to Mephistopheles). Like any survey it is subject to all sorts of sampling, interviewing and other methodological problems. None the less the triangulation of data between the BCS, self-report studies and the police figures means more confidence can be placed in judgements about overall trends after judicious sifting of the different sources. The BCS, for example, sheds much light on the factors affecting victims' decisions about whether or not to report offences. It also gives some estimate of the second aspect of the 'dark figure', police failure to record crimes reported to them.

Recent British Crime Trends

The implications of the new data sources for the validity of the picture given by official statistics is mixed. With regard to the overall increase in recorded crime since the early 1980s the BCS suggests an ambivalent conclusion: the glass can with equal justification be described as half full or half empty. Between 1981 and 1992 recorded crime more than doubled, but has since fallen to just under double the level of the early 1980s. By contrast BCS crimes increased by 49 per cent between 1981 and 1997 (Mirrlees-Black *et al.* 1998:10). The bottom line thus seems to be that the recorded increase was in equal measure attributable to an increase in criminal offending and victimisation, *and* an increase in the proportion of crimes recorded by the police.

The picture becomes more complicated when variations between different kinds of offence, and different sub-periods, are analysed. The most extensive data about victimisation concerns burglary, as the General Household Survey (GHS) began to ask questions about this in 1972. This showed that the doubling of burglaries recorded by the police during the 1970s was mainly a recording phenomenon: victimisation only increased by 20 per cent according to the GHS. There was a huge rise in the proportion of burglary victims who reported the crime to the police, mainly because of the spread of household insurance which increased the incentive to report, thus diminishing the 'dark figure'. By the early 1980s when the BCS was launched the proportion of the most common property crimes reported to the police by victims was virtually at saturation point, largely eliminating the possibility of further rises through reducing the 'dark figure'. Consequently, during the 1980s the increase in recorded property crime grew in step with BCS estimates of victimisation: both doubled.

Yet, although violent crime measured by the BCS went up substantially (21 per cent), this was much less than the recorded increase of nearly 100 per cent. This suggests that much of the recorded increase in violence was really a shrinking of the 'dark figure'. More victims reported attacks to the police and the police recorded more of these offences (a reflection of extensive reforms in the handling of victims of domestic violence and rape; cf. Blair 1985; Hoyle 1998; Gregory and Lees 1999). There was also a huge rise in the proportion of criminal damage cases recorded by the police in the 1980s, increasing the discrepancy with the victimisation data.

Overall it seems that much of the rise in recorded crime before the early 1980s was a recording phenomenon: greater reporting diminished the 'dark figure'. However, during the 1980s the rise in recorded crime mainly reflected increasing victimisation, especially in the predominant category of property offences.

The Mystery of the Disappearing Crimes

During the 1990s there has been a drop in recorded crime for four consecutive years, a phenomenon without precedent for most of this century. Both Conservative and Labour governments have not hesitated to claim the credit for this as a vindication of their law and order policies.

However, the implications of other data sources are more ambiguous. The 1991, 1993 and 1995 BCS results showed the level of victimisation as continuing to rise. Only the 1997 BCS shows a fall: 14 per cent since 1995, roughly paralleling the decrease in the recorded crime rate in those years. During the 1990s as a whole the decline in recorded crime figures is primarily the result of recording changes, not a fall in crime. The 'dark figure', which fell throughout the 1970s and 1980s, exaggerating the increase in crime, now began to rise again, creating a misleading picture of declining crime. Throughout the 1990s the BCS indicates a falling proportion of crimes being reported to the police by victims, declining from 49 per cent in 1991 to 44 per cent in 1997. This itself is attributable to the paradoxical effects of a high rate of crime, which generates disincentives for victims to report offences: for example, adverse effects on their insurance, such as higher premiums or more onerous reinsurance conditions.

The proportion of crimes which the police choose to record has also fallen according to the BCS: from 62 per cent in 1981 to a low of 50 per cent in 1995, with a rise to 54 per cent in 1997 (Mirrlees-Black *et al.* 1998: 22–3). A plausible explanation is that the police are increasingly pressured by the new regime of 'businesslike', performance-indicator-driven policing to present falling crime levels and higher clear-up rates (Reiner 1996; Davies 1999). It is not quite what they promised, but the government has certainly got tough on the causes of *recording* crime.

Who Commits Crime?

The official crime statistics are not merely problematic as a guide to trends in crime levels. They also present a dubious picture of who commits crime. Analysis of the characteristics of the prison population, or of people stopped and/or arrested by the police, suggests that they are a highly unrepresentative sample of the population. They are overwhelmingly young, male, economically and socially marginal, and black (Coleman and Moynihan 1996:chap. 5; Maguire 1997:172–81). In a nutshell, the 'rich get richer and the poor get prison' (Reiman 1990).

It is extremely unlikely that this fully mirrors the characteristics of those who commit crime, as opposed to the institutional biases of the criminal justice process (with the exception that most offenders probably are male). The Home Office regularly produces statistics on what it calls the 'attrition' rate, showing that of all offences measured by the BCS only about 2 per cent result in the conviction of an offender, and just under another 1 per cent lead to a caution (Home Office 1995: 25). Thus in nearly 98 per cent of crimes the offender is not known (or at any rate not officially identified). This bleak statistic itself overlooks the vast array of offences with no individual victim, which cannot by definition feature in a victimisation survey like the BCS. Since this includes most 'white-collar' crimes, as well as vice offences which are probably engaged in by a wider range of people than the 'usual suspects', the official data omits almost all the offending perpetrated by people higher up the social scale.

Explaining Crime Trends

Criminal behaviour can only occur if five necessary conditions are satisfied. There must be: *labelling* of the behaviour as criminal; at least one *motivated* offender; the *means* for the offender to commit the crime; criminal *opportunities*; and the absence of effective *controls*, both formal and informal. By definition if any one of these factors is absent a crime cannot occur. All the major criminological theories (cf. Taylor *et al.* 1973; Downes and Rock 1995; Morrison 1995; Rock 1997; Jones 1998) can be seen as attempts to explain the conditions of existence of one or more of these elements.

The politicisation of the debate about law and order has meant that different positions focus on only one or two of these elements, ignoring or denying the relevance of the others. Conservative accounts claim there has been a weakening of formal and informal social controls, with rational choice, or individualistic accounts of pathology as their explanation of criminal motivation. Radicals stress either the importance of labelling processes in creating or exaggerating state-defined deviance, or see 'strains' and injustices in the social structure as generating pressures on excluded groups to offend. Policy-makers and analysts have concentrated on the means and opportunities to commit crime, and on administrative solutions to prevent these arising, such as target-hardening or improved police effectiveness. However, any adequate account of the development of rising crime rates in the period since the Second World War requires a complex synthesis of these elements, rather than their ideological separation (Young 1997, 1999).

Understanding recent changes in levels and patterns of crime involves accounting for the impact of social, economic, political and cultural developments on the ingredients of crime. How have these wider processes impacted upon legal and popular definitions of deviance, structured the circumstances in which potential offenders act and their experience of these as pressures and temptations to commit crimes, shifted the availability of means and opportunities to offend, and strengthened or weakened social controls? Clearly, such an account can only be sketched here. It will be argued that significant cultural and socio-economic changes have interacted to produce the upward movement of recorded crime rates.

Around this long-term increasing trend, fluctuations have been related to economic cycles that affect the pressures, opportunities and controls leading to or preventing crime. Recorded property crime rates are inversely related to economic cycles (as recession generates more pressures to acquire goods illicitly), whilst violent crime levels are positively associated with rising prosperity – which involves more socialising and alcohol consumption, thus increasing the opportunities for and lowering inhibitions against violent conflict (Field 1990).

Permissiveness and Crime

During the period since the Second World War long-term changes have occurred sequentially which generate more offending as well as more recording. Each new development has added to the pressures already created by the earlier factors. Many analysts (mainly conservative ones) have emphasised the long historical process that is often referred to as the growth of 'permissiveness' as a source of crime. It has been argued that during the twentieth century there has occurred a kind of democratisation, a spread to the masses, of the values of Enlightenment liberalism such as individual autonomy, self-realisation and scepticism about claims of authority (Wilson and Herrnstein 1985). The effect of this is said to have become precipitous since the 1960s, commonly seen as a critical watershed (Dennis 1997). The criminogenic consequence has been an undermining of the informal social controls and internalised inhibitions that once held deviant impulses in check. Many liberal and radical commentators would agree that there has been a long-term trend towards greater individual autonomy and 'desubordination' (Miliband 1978; Dahrendorf 1985). Indeed, this is a view commonly found in popular discourse and media representations, although with varying evaluations of whether it is desirable or not (Reiner *et al.* 1998:19–25).

The legal and policy changes that are often referred to as promoting 'permissiveness', however, represent a restructuring rather simple weakening of social control (National Deviancy Conference 1980; Newburn 1992). A clear example is drugs policy, which has toughened into a 'war on drugs' despite growing consumption of illegal drugs indicating wider popular acceptance (South 1997b). In any event, whilst liberalisation offers the potential for crime to rise if pressures or temptations increase, by itself it is no more an explanation of rising crime than failing brakes explain a car's forward motion. Changes in informal control and attitudes to authority make sense of increasing crime rates only in a context where other factors generate social strains and opportunities conducive to offending.

The inexorable rise in recorded crime that began in the late 1950s was kick-started by a number of consequences of the development of a mass consumerist 'affluent society'. This had several implications for the growth of property crime, which constitutes the bulk of offending, as well as making the reporting of and recording of such crime more likely. Perhaps the most obvious effect was the creation and dispersion of attractive and vulnerable criminal targets in the shape of new, widely available consumer goods. The car and its equipment, the most common 'victim' of an offence, proliferated. Mass-produced consumer durables were not only tempting to steal, but relatively anonymous and untraceable and hence easier to dispose of without fear of identification. The spread of insurance cover for these expensive items also made it much more likely that their theft would be recorded and reported. The proliferation of such consumer goods also heightened a sense of relative deprivation amongst those who were excluded from the new 'affluence' (Merton 1957). It was also associated with the development of a more materialistic and acquisitive culture, stimulated by commercial television with its advertising and game shows (it is perhaps no coincidence that the onset of the crime boom in Britain coincides with the advent of ITV). Finally the growth of a more autonomous teenage market was associated with the emergence of youth cultures whose styles of dress, music and behaviour were the subject of successive 'moral panics' about youthful deviance (Rock and Cohen 1970; Cohen 1972). These intertwined processes drove up both the occurrence and the labelling of offending.

The Political Economy of Crime

The increases in recorded crime levels were fuelled further after the mid-1970s by the consequences of the fundamental shift in the political economy represented by the return of free-market economics, and the deregulation of increasingly globalised markets. Whether or not this amounts to a fundamental and qualitative break to a new kind of post-modern social order with its own novel dynamic can be debated (Callinicos 1989; Giddens 1994; Bauman 1997, 1998; Castells 1996–98; Hirst and Thompson 1996; Panitch and Leys 1999). But it does amount to a reversal of the long process, of nearly two centuries duration, of gradually increasing incorporation of all sections of society into a common status of citizenship, albeit with considerable – but diminishing – inequalities (Marshall 1950; Bulmer and Rees 1996).

The consequences for crime and social cohesion are enormous, above all because of the widening of social divisions and growth of social exclusion (Hutton 1995; Levitas 1998). In many parts of the world 'lawlessness and crime have so destroyed the social fabric that the State itself has withdrawn' (Cohen 1997a:234). Whilst not threatened by such extremes of social meltdown, Britain and other industrial societies are experiencing profound shifts in the modalities of social control (Hudson 1997; Bergalli and Sumner 1997).

As social exclusion, economic insecurity and inequality grow so the motives and opportunities for crime multiply, and the restraining effects of both formal and informal social controls are eroded. The consequences for crime and order of this social earthquake are profound and intertwined (Young 1997, 1998a and b, 1999; Taylor, I. 1997b, 1998a and b, 1999; Currie 1998a and b; Davies 1998). There is long-standing debate about the relationship between crime, unemployment and inequality (Farrington *et al.* 1986; Box 1987; Field 1990; Downes 1993, 1998:193–4; Dickinson 1994; Pyle and Deadman 1994; Wells 1995; Coleman and Moynihan 1996:chap. 6; Hale 1998; Witt *et al.* 1999). This debate has been inconclusive in part because of a failure to recognise that unemployment and inequality have different social meanings and implications in different periods and contexts, so that a given statistical rate is unlikely to have constant effects on crime or any other variable. Unemployment in the last twenty-five years has quite different implications from those that it had in the earlier post-war period, as it is much more likely to be related to complete and permanent social exclusion: in effect to be never-employment, not a transitional phase. Growing exclusion and immiseration – and the perceived hope-lessness of its reversal by legitimate means – not only increases pressures to offend, it undermines the informal social controls of family, education, work and community, and encourages a neo-Social Darwinist culture of survival of the fittest. The delegitimation of public expenditure and collective provision by the ethos of the market weakens the state's capacity to provide either the 'soft' controls of welfare provision or effective public policing. Inequalities in access to security widen, as a burgeoning private market in policing develops (Shearing and Stenning 1983, 1987; South 1988; Johnston 1992; Jones and Newburn 1998).

During the 1980s, the heyday of free market triumphalism, recorded crime rates rocketed. As noted earlier, the evidence of victim surveys suggests that in this period they corresponded closely to genuine increases in victimisation, especially by property crime, rather than shifts in reporting and recording practices. However, the downturn in recorded crime rates during the 1990s is largely a recording phenomenon. The BCS suggests that until 1995–77 victimisation rates continued to rise. The fall in reporting and recording of crime were paradoxical consequences of the high levels of offending. On the one hand, victims were deterred from reporting because of concern about their insurance policies. On the other hand, the police were under pressure to reduce the proportion of crimes they recorded because of the new managerialist policing-by-numbers regime introduced to enhance their crime-fighting efficiency. It is only in the last couple of years that the survey confirms the downward trend of the official statistics, and it remains to be seen how long this will last.

Crime-control Policies

For most of the twentieth century a bipartisan consensus around a reformist and welfarist approach to crime prevailed (Garland 1985; Bailey 1987; Wiener 1990; Emsley 1997:81–2). Crime was perceived as the product of various pathologies, individual and/or social, and its control required the correction of these. This was to be achieved through rehabilitative penal measures in the first instance, but more broadly by social amelioration to remove the ultimate causes of offending – though there were fierce partisan debates about the deterrent value of capital and corporal punishment (Morris 1989).

In the 1970s as law and order became politicised this consensus fell apart. A self-proclaimed 'realism' became widespread, which was sceptical about talk of 'root causes' of crime. These were held to be variously non-existent or unfathomable, but at any rate irrelevant to the time-scale for hard-headed policy intervention (Wilson 1985; Young 1986). Martinson and others' seminal evaluations of 'what works' in penal treatment (Martinson *et al.* 1974; Brody 1975) were rapidly misread as 'nothing works' (Ashworth 1997:1098–9). So too were contemporaneous assessments of police effectiveness (Kelling *et al.* 1974; Clarke and Hough 1980, 1984; Morris and Heal 1981). However unwarranted by the research evidence itself, it rapidly became an article of faith that neither social reform, rehabilitation in penal policy, nor traditional policing methods worked effectively to control crime (Cohen 1997b).

The Conservatives were first into this policy vacuum. Margaret Thatcher promised a suitably stern mix of tough punishment and policing, plus the moral rearmament of 'Victorian values', as the remedy. Nothing works became nothing *liberal* works in penal policy (unlike the economy). During the 1980s as the medicine palpably failed to deliver crime reduction a third element was added: prevention. Crime prevention Tory-style meant primarily target-hardening and opportunity reduction, rather than any attempt to grapple with crime-generating causes in that unutterable non-entity, 'society' (King 1989). None the less, over time an element of 'community' crime prevention entered the picture too, based on notions of resuscitating citizenly responsibility and virtue as the prophylactic against offending (Nelken 1985).

Tough on Crime?

It was only in the early 1990s that Labour was able to make an impact on the law and order issue, with Tony Blair's successful promotion of the 'tough on crime, tough on the causes of crime' formula. The Conservatives retaliated with Michael Howard's mantra 'prison works'. To his manifest satisfaction, crime rates fell in the years following his crackdown. Conservatives were also buoyed by the much-trumpeted decline of crime in New York City and other American cities supposedly as a result of 'zero-tolerance' policing and a huge rise in the prison population. The tabloid press was jubilant: something worked at last – given his head Dirty Harry could deliver. In fact the American experience is much more complicated than a simple vindication of police and penal toughness (Bowling 1996; Young 1999:chap. 5). Policing reform in New York was more subtle and complex than implied by the zero-tolerance label, which was a media concoction disowned by its supposed practitioners like former NYPD Chief Bratton (Weatheritt 1998). In any event the pattern of change in crime rates in American cities as a whole bears no discernible relationship to the policing styles they espouse (Massing 1998). It is likely that the mass incarceration that has been the recent American experience has reduced crime somewhat, if only as a result of the huge impact on unemployment levels resulting from the removal of so many economically marginal men from the labour market (Downes 1998:194). But the price is the crippling of other public services, notably education, with hugely detrimental future consequences for crime. In any event, many European countries have also experienced falling crime rates in the 1990s, without resorting to such punitiveness.

There are also other, more plausible explanations than 'prison works' of the fall in crime rates in this country during the 1990s. It was noted earlier that much of the fall is a recording phenomenon, not a decline in offending. High crime rates para-doxically generated a set of perverse incentives leading victims to report less and the police to record fewer crimes. Subjected to a tighter regime of performance indica-tors, some police at any rate cracked down on crime statistics rather than crime (Davies 1999). None the less the BCS does suggest that there has also been some reduction in offending. However, this is likely to be due in very small part at best to the rise in imprisonment. The Home Office's own calculation is that in order to obtain a 1 per cent fall in crime the prison population has to go up by 25 per cent (Tarling 1994). In so far as the reduction in crime is due to criminal justice policy at all, it is probably the result of much more sophisticated, intelligence-based strategies of policing and crime prevention bearing some fruit (Nuttall et al. 1998). More important is the unintended consequence of Britain's forced departure from the European Exchange Rate Mechanism in 1992. As devaluation of the pound and falling interest rates had the predictable consequence of some economic growth and reductions in unemployment, the crime rate fell, in line with the Home Office's own modelling of the relationship between recorded crime and the business cycle (Field 1990). Paradoxically, no party could claim responsibility for this achievement. The Conservatives were inhibited by a decade of denial of any relationship between crime and economic conditions. Labour, newly benefiting from a tougher line on crime, could not revert to the old social democratic analysis that had been so electorally costly in the 1980s.

'Third Way' Penal Policy

In its first two years in office the new Labour government has developed a set of criminal justice policies which appear to be a penal 'third way' (Downes 1998). On the one hand, they have introduced some civil libertarian reforms that would have been unlikely under the Conservatives, such as reinstating trade-union rights at GCHQ, accepting the European Convention on Human Rights (Walker 1993), establishing the Stephen Lawrence Inquiry and accepting most of its recommendations. On the other hand, they have continued much of the 'tough on crime' rhetoric as well as practice, for example activating the minimum mandatory sentencing provisions of the 1997 Crime (Sentencing) Act, and by continuing the prison privatisation programme.

However, the main thrust of their policy, embodied in the Crime and Disorder Act 1998 and the Crime Reduction Programme, has been a departure from traditional Conservative or Labour policies. As many critics have pointed out the Act does contain provisions (notably the Anti-Social Behaviour Orders) which are potentially oppressive for human rights and counter-productive (Ashworth *et al.* 1998). Its main strategy, none the less, is novel and cannot be dismissed as either simply punitive or liberal. It is based on an intelligence-led, problem-solving approach, with systematic analysis and reflexive monitoring built into policy development. Its intellectual basis is a thorough review of the evidence concerning the effectiveness, costs and benefits of the main strategies for dealing with offending: preventing the development of criminality by early childhood intervention and education, situational and community crime prevention, policing, sentencing and alternative penal techniques (Nuttall *et al.* 1998). The Crime and Disorder Act (s.6) requires local authorities and the police in partnership to audit local crime and disorder problems, identify their sources, and develop appropriate strategies for reducing these, with regular research evaluations of effectiveness. The Crime Reduction Programme has devoted a substantial part of its budget to on-going research evaluation. In principle this *is* tough on the causes of crime, and not just (as the Tories were) tough on the few lottery losers of the criminal justice system who are convicted. The problem with the approach, however, lies in its place within the overall strategy of new Labour, many other aspects of which threaten the possible success of the crime reduction programme. Most obviously, the commitment to keep within Conservative spending plans undermines the capacity of the police, probation, education and other social services to perform as intended, whilst exacerbating the pressures leading young people into crime, such as school exclusions and truancy (Downes 1998:196–7). More generally the criminogenic consequences of failure to bring unemployment down by the New Deal and through macro-economic policy would vastly outweigh any crime-reducing effects of the Home Office programme. New

Labour's commitment to old Tory economic policy is its new hostage to fortune in the crime control policy area.

The Politics of Law and Order 2025

Only a criminological Mystic Meg could forecast what is going to happen to crime and criminal justice in the next century. But the above analysis of trends in crime and control does suggest a few conditional predictions.

Will the 'third way' work in crime reduction? 'Nothing works' was far too bleak and demoralising a conclusion to draw from evaluation studies of criminal justice practice. There are enough well-researched examples of targeted policing and crime-prevention innovations, for example, to suggest that these can have a significant, if modest, effect on crime and fear (Sherman 1992; Pease 1997; Ekblom 1998; Hope 1998; Jordan 1998). However, the burden placed on these by the Crime Reduction Programme is excessive. The kind of reductions which have been experienced or are envisaged – whilst welcome, and cost-effective compared to either more crime or mass imprisonment – would go nowhere near reversing the increases of the last quarter century. For example, Home Office research suggests that targeting higher-risk areas (about one-tenth of households) with Safer Cities-style burglary prevention programmes would reduce national burglary rates by 5.5 per cent, and if this was extended to half the country's households the reduction would be just under one-eighth (Ekblom 1998:35). Extensive delivery of crime and criminality reduction programmes to the most vulnerable, whilst justifiable even in cost–benefit terms, would involve significant amounts of public expenditure. This would breach current fiscal policies, and amount to a significant redistribution of resources to the poorer sections of society.

A substantial return to earlier levels of crime is simply not possible without major changes in the conditions that generated the rise in the first place. The 'realist' exploration of what works more immediately is worth while, but at best can have modest results unless it becomes a wedge for broader reforms. It may be that the 'social' is indeed dead (Rose 1996), and that a return to Keynesian style economic policies aimed at stabilisation and solidarity are no longer feasible, because of globalisation and changes in popular values. But there is a price to be paid: living with a high-crime society permanently.

David Garland has cogently argued that states have already adjusted their policies and rhetoric in recognition of the limits to their sovereignty in terms of crime control (Garland 1995). There has been a bifurcation between two levels of crime control policy and discourse. On the one hand, there is promulgation of detailed policies to implement best practice in crime prevention – what he calls the 'criminologies of everyday life' – as in Labour's Crime Reduction Programme. Such discourses are largely stripped of moral condemnation, but treat crime pragmatic-ally, as an actuarial risk to be calculated and minimised (Feeley and Simon 1994). On the other hand, there are regular moral panics about especially horrific crimes (such as the murder of Jamie Bulger or the Dunblane massacre), which become occasions for orgies of punitiveness and anguished Jeremiads about moral decline. The explosions of punitiveness prompted by the relatively rare, spectacular, exceptionally fear-provoking crimes symbolically assuage popular anxiety and frustration, whilst the 'criminologies of everyday life' are geared to provide as much limited pragmatic protection as possible against more mundane offences.

However, a continuation of high rates of routine crime, and the variety of security and control measures adopted to contain or reduce them, offers a highly dystopian image of the future. We are already getting accustomed to everyday routines geared around crime prevention, with varying tactics and success depending on social location. In essence there is a vicious circle of interdependence between social divisions and exclusion, crime and crime-control strategy. Growing social divisions fuel rising crime, which in turn generates control strategies that accentuate social exclusion. In a variety of interlocking ways crime and reactions to crime both exacerbate the social divisions that generated them.

The clearest example is the social bifurcation that produces and is in turn reinforced by the flourishing market in private security, heralding a global 'mixed economy of control' (South 1997a:104–9). This has aptly been described as a 'new feudalism' (Shearing and Stenning 1983). The more privileged sections of society increasingly protect themselves from the burgeoning 'dangerous classes' of the socially excluded by a variety of environmental, spatial, architectural and techno-logical segregation devices such as the increasingly ubiquitous closed-circuit television cameras (Norris and Armstrong 1999). Together with private policing personnel, these provide the 'moats' seeking to secure the castles of consumerism. The wealthy flit between 'security bubbles' in 'cities of quartz' guarded not so much by police (public or private) as by more or less subtle physical and social barriers (Davis 1990, 1998:chap. 7; Bottoms and Wiles 1997:349–54). Inequalities in exposure to crime and disorder are exacerbated as policing and security increasingly become strategies of border control between the dreadful enclosures of the excluded and the gated denizens of the wealthy, between and within different countries.

On an international scale there has been much talk of globalisation stimulating a growth of international organised and professional crime, especially in the form of drug-trafficking (Dorn *et al.* 1992; Ruggiero and South 1995; South 1997b). Mafiosi from the former Soviet Union and elsewhere are feared to be exploiting improve-ments in communications and the growth in cross-border trade and transport to enhance their markets and power. The accuracy of such images of global criminal conspiracies is debatable (Backman 1998; Rawlinson 1998). But they have certainly resulted in an unprecedented degree of international police co-operation and organisation (Mawby 1999; Sheptycki 1995, 1997; Anderson 1989; Anderson *et al.* 1995). The mundane reality of international policing, however, is that it is in practice focused more on border control of refugees and migrants than on the criminal conspiracies that purport to justify it. The overwhelming majority of reports filed in the Schengen Information System concern aliens rather than the investigation of crime (Dumortier 1997).

Unable or unwilling to tackle the sources of rising crime, states and citizens react punitively on the hapless minority of criminals they encounter or apprehend. Tough new sentencing policies on the 'three strikes and out' model have swelled the prison populations of the United States, Britain, and other countries which have increasingly followed this example, to unprecedented levels (Morgan 1997; Young 1999:chap. 5). This is despite little evidence that this can cut crime to any substantial extent (Moxon 1998) None the less current policies will result in further huge growth of the penal empire, if only as an expression of impotent rage at the losers of the criminal justice lottery. An apparent rise in vigilante activity is the citizen counterpart of the increase in official punitiveness, striking at those suspected offenders who are at hand as an expression of impotence in the face of crime and insecurity (Johnston 1996; Abrahams 1998).

This image of a society polarised between a gilded but insecure elite and a threatening, temporarily subjugated mass haunted dystopian visions of the future at the turn of the last century, such as H.G. Wells's *The Time Machine*. They have returned with a vengeance in the last quarter of this century not because of some inevitable *fin de siècle* phobia, but because of the rapid reversal of the slow march of social inclusion (Hobsbawm 1995; Young 1999). The proliferation of *Blade Runner* style imaginings of the revolt of the repressed (Davis 1998:chaps. 6, 7) testify to a scarcely subconscious anxiety that the burgeoning panoply of sophisticated surveillance and control cannot indefinitely hold the lid down on the expanding excluded classes. It is hard to see how order of any kind can be maintained as we head towards the '20:80' society of four-fifths excluded from legitimate work projected by some analysts of globalisation (Martin and Schumann 1997:chap. 1). There are of course already many parts of the world where functioning states and civil society have weakened to an extent that a 'new barbarism' prevails (Hobsbawm 1994:53). In such places the tenuous modern distinction between crime and politics ceases to be useful as 'low intensity warfare runs into high intensity crime' (Cohen 1997a:243). At present the new 'mixed economy' of control (South 1997a) has prevented such 'degree zero' collapses of order in most advanced industrial societies (Reiner 1999). However, given the huge increases in crime and disorder in our current two-thirds/one-third societies, it is hard to be optimistic about the consequences of even more precipitous inequality and exclusion.

Whether this will be the shape of law and order 2025 is anyone's guess. But the prospects can be summed up by a paraphrase of Rosa Luxemburg. The choice is some form of social democracy or at best the barbarism of high crime rates, and a fortified society. There is no other third way.

REFERENCES

Abrahams, R. 1998. *Vigilant Citizens*. Cambridge: Polity Press.

Allen, J., Livingstone, S. and Reiner. R. 1998. 'True Lies: Changing Images of Crime in Postwar British Cinema'. *European Journal of Communication* 13:53–75.

Anderson, M. 1989. *Policing the World*. Oxford: Oxford University Press.

Anderson, M., Cullen, P., Gilmore, W., Raab, C. and Walker, N. 1995. *Policing the European Union*. Oxford: Oxford University Press.

Ashworth, A. 1995. *Sentencing and Criminal Justice*. London: Weidenfeld.

Ashworth, A. 1997. 'Sentencing'. In M. Maguire, R. Morgan and R. Reiner (eds.), *The Oxford Handbook of Criminology*. Oxford: Oxford University Press.

Ashworth, A., Gardner, J., Morgan, R., Smith, A.T.H., von Hirsch, A. and Wasik, M. 1998. 'Neighbouring on the Oppressive: The Government's "Anti-Social Behaviour Order" Proposals'. *Criminal Justice* 16: 7–14.

Backman, J. 1998. *The Inflation of Crime in Russia*. Helsinki: National Research Institute of Legal Policy.

Bailey, V. 1987. *Delinquency and Citizenship: Reclaiming the Young Offender 1914–48*. Oxford: Oxford University Press.

Bauman, Z. 1997. *Postmodernity and Its Discontents*. Cambridge: Polity.

Bauman, Z. 1998. *Globalization: The Human Consequences*. Cambridge: Polity.

Bergalli, R. and Sumner, C. (eds.) 1997. *Social Control and Political Order*. London: Sage.

Blair, I. 1985. *Investigating Rape*. London: Croom Helm.

Bottomley, A. K. and Coleman, C. 1981. *Understanding Crime Rates*. Farnborough: Gower.

Bottomley, A. K. and Coleman, C. 1995. 'The Police'. In M. A. Walker (ed.), *Interpreting Crime Statistics*. Oxford: Oxford University Press.

Bottoms, A. E. 1990. 'Crime Prevention Facing the 1990s'. *Policing and Society* 1:3–22.

Bottoms, A. E. and Wiles, P. 1997. 'Environmental Criminology'. In M. Maguire, R. Morgan and R. Reiner (eds.), *The Oxford Handbook of Criminology*. Oxford: Oxford University Press.

Bowling, B. 1996. 'Zero Tolerance'. *Criminal Justice Matters* 25:11–12.

Box, S. 1987. *Recession, Crime and Punishment*. London: Macmillan.

Brody, S. 1975. *The Effectiveness of Sentencing*. Home Office Research Study 64. London: HMSO.

Brown, D. 1997. *PACE Ten Years On: A Review of the Research*. London: Home Office.

Bulmer, M. and Rees, A. M. (eds.) 1996. *Citizenship Today: The Contemporary Relevance of T. H. Marshall*. London: UCL Press.

Callinicos, A. 1989. *Against Postmodernism*. Cambridge: Polity.

Castells, M. 1996–8. *The Information Age, Vols. I–III*. Oxford: Blackwell.

Cavadino, M. and Dignan, P. 1997. *The Penal System*. London: Sage.

Clarke, R. and Hough, M. (eds.) 1980. *The Effectiveness of Policing*. Farnborough: Gower.

Clarke, R. and Hough, M. 1984. *Crime and Police Effectiveness*. London: Home Office Research Unit.

Cohen, S. 1972. *Folk Devils and Moral Panics*. London: Paladin.

Cohen, S. 1997a. 'Crime and Politics: Spot the Difference'. In R. Rawlings (ed.), *Law, Society and Economy*. Oxford: Oxford University Press.

Cohen, S. 1997b. 'The Revenge of the Null Hypothesis: Evaluating Crime Control Policies'. *Critical Criminologist* 8: 21–5.

Coleman, C. and Moynihan, J. 1996. *Understanding Crime Data*. Buckingham: Open University Press.

Crawford, A. 1997. *The Local Governance of Crime: Appeals to Community and Partnerships.* Oxford: Oxford University Press.

Crawford, A. 1998. *Crime Prevention and Community Safety.* London: Longman.

Currie, E. 1998a. *Crime and Punishment in America.* New York: Holt.

Currie, E. 1998b. 'Crime and Market Society: Lessons From the United States'. In P. Walton and J. Young (eds.), *The New Criminology Revisited.* London: Macmillan.

Dahrendorf, R. 1985. *Law and Order.* London: Sweet and Maxwell.

Davies, N. 1998. *Dark Heart.* London: Verso.

Davies, N. 1999. 'Watching the detectives: how the police cheat in the fight against crime'. *The Guardian*, 18 March, p. 12.

Davis, M. 1990. *City of Quartz.* London: Vintage.

Davis, M. 1998. *Ecology of Fear.* New York: Metropolitan Books.

Dennis, N. 1997. 'Editor's Introduction'. In N. Dennis (ed.), *Zero Tolerance Policing.* London: Institute of Economic Affairs.

Dickinson, D. 1994. 'Criminal benefits'. *New Statesman*, 14 January.

Dorn, N., Murji, K. and South, N. 1992. *Traffickers.* London: Routledge.

Downes, D. 1983. *Law and Order: Theft of an Issue.* London: Fabian Society/Labour Campaign for Criminal Justice.

Downes, D. 1993. *Employment Opportunities for Offenders.* London: Home Office.

Downes, D. 1998. 'Toughing It Out: From Labour Opposition to Labour Government'. *Policy Studies* 19:191–8.

Downes, D. and Morgan, R. 1997. 'Dumping the "Hostages to Fortune": The Politics of Law and Order'. In M. Maguire, R. Morgan and R. Reiner (eds.), *The Oxford Handbook of Criminology.* Oxford: Oxford University Press.

Downes, D. and Rock, P. 1995. *Understanding Deviance.* Oxford: Oxford University Press.

Dumortier, J. 1997. 'The Protection of Personal Data in the Schengen Convention'. *International Review of Law, Computers and Technology* 11:93–106.

Dunbar, I. and Langdon, A. 1998. *Tough Justice: Sentencing and Penal Policies in the 1990s.* London: Blackstone Press.

Durkheim, E. 1964 [original edn. 1895]. *The Rules of Sociological Method.* New York: Free Press.

Ekblom, P. 1998. 'Situational Crime Prevention'. In C. Nuttall, P. Goldblatt and C. Lewis (eds.), *Reducing Offending.* Home Office Research Study 187. London: Home Office Research and Statistics Directorate.

Emsley, C. 1997. 'The History of Crime and Crime Control Institutions'. In M. Maguire, R. Morgan and R. Reiner (eds.), *The Oxford Handbook of Criminology.* Oxford: Oxford University Press.

Ericson, R., Baranek, P. and Chan, J. 1991. *Representing Order.* Milton Keynes: Open University Press.

Farrington, D., Gallagher, B., Morley, L., St Ledger, R. and West, D. J. 1986. 'Unemployment, School Leaving and Crime'. *British Journal of Criminology* 26:335–56.

Feeley, M. and Simon, J. 1994. 'Actuarial Justice: The Emerging New Criminal Law'. In D. Nelken(ed.), *The Futures of Criminology.* London: Sage.

Field, S. 1990. *Trends in Crime and Their Interpretation: A Study of Recorded Crime in Post-War England and Wales.* Home Office Research Study 119. London: HMSO.

Garland, D. 1985. *Punishment and Welfare.* Aldershot: Gower.

Garland, D. 1995. 'The Limits of the Sovereign State: Strategies of Crime Control in Contemporary Society'. *British Journal of Criminology* 36:1–27.

Giddens, A. 1994. *Beyond Left and Right.* Cambridge: Polity.

Gilling, D. 1997. *Crime Prevention: Theory, Practice and Politics.* London: UCL Press.

Gregory, J. and Lees, S. 1999. *Policing Sexual Assault.* London: Routledge.

Hale, C. 1998. 'Crime and the Business Cycle in Post-War Britain Revisited'. *British Journal of Criminology* 38:681–98.

Hirst, P. and Thompson, G. 1996. *Globalisation in Question*. London: Polity.

Hobsbawm, E. 1994. 'Barbarism: A User's Guide'. *New Left Review* 206:44–54.

Hobsbawm, E. 1995. *The Age of Extremes*. London: Abacus.

Hollway, W. and Jefferson, T. 1997. 'The Risk Society in an Age of Anxiety: Situating Fear of Crime'. *British Journal of Sociology* 48:255–65.

Home Office 1989. *Report of the Working Group on Fear of Crime*. London: HMSO.

Home Office 1995. *Information on the Criminal Justice System in England and Wales: Digest 3*. Home Office: Research and Statistics Department.

Home Office 1998a. *Crime Reduction Strategy: News Release 282/98*, 21 July. London: Home Office.

Home Office 1998b. *Notifiable Offences England and Wales*. Statistical Bulletin 22/98, 13 October. London: Home Office Research, Development and Statistics Directorate.

Hope, T. 1998. 'Community Crime Prevention'. In C. Nuttall, P. Goldblatt and C. Lewis (eds.), *Reducing Offending*. Home Office Research Study 187. London: Home Office Research and Statistics Directorate.

Hough, M. and Mayhew, P. 1983. *The British Crime Survey*. Home Office Research Study 76. London: HMSO.

Hough, M. and Mayhew, P. 1985. *Taking Account of Crime: Findings From the 1984 British Crime Survey*. Home Office Research Study 85. London: HMSO.

Hoyle, C. 1998. *Negotiating Domestic Violence*. Oxford: Oxford University Press.

Hudson, B. 1997. 'Social Control'. In M. Maguire, R. Morgan and R. Reiner (eds.), *The Oxford Handbook of Criminology*. Oxford: Oxford University Press.

Hughes, G. 1998. *Understanding Crime Prevention: Social Control, Risk and Late Modernity*. Buckingham: Open University Press.

Hutton, W. 1995. *The State We're In*. London: Vintage.

Johnston, L. 1992. *The Rebirth of Private Policing*. London: Routledge.

Johnston, L. 1996. 'What Is Vigilantism?' *British Journal of Criminology* 36:220–36.

Jones, S. 1998. *Criminology*. London: Butterworths.

Jones, T., MacLean, B. and Young, J. 1986. *The Islington Crime Survey*. Aldershot: Gower.

Jones, T. and Newburn, T. 1998. *Private Security and Public Policing*. Oxford: Oxford University Press.

Jordan, P. 1998. 'Effective Policing Strategies for Reducing Crime'. In C. Nuttall, P. Goldblatt and C. Lewis (eds.), *Reducing Offending*. Home Office Research Study 187. London: Home Office Research and Statistics Directorate.

Kelling, G., Pate, A., Dieckman, D. and Brown, C. 1974. *The Kansas City Preventive Patrol Experiment*. Washington, DC: Police Foundation.

King, M. 1989. 'Social Crime Prevention à la Thatcher'. *Howard Journal* 28:291–312.

Kinsey, R., Lea, J. and Young, J. 1986. *Losing the Fight Against Crime*. Oxford: Blackwell.

Lacey, N. 1994. 'Government As Manager, Citizen As Consumer: The Case of the Criminal Justice Act 1991'. *Modern Law Review* 54:534–54.

Leishman, F., Loveday, B. and Savage, S. (eds.) 1996. *Core Issues in Policing*. London: Longman.

Levitas, R. 1998. *The Inclusive Society?* London: Macmillan.

Levitas, R. and Guy, W. 1996. *Interpreting Official Statistics*. London: Routledge.

Maguire, M. 1997. 'Crime Statistics, Patterns and Trends: Changing Perceptions and their Implications'. In M. Maguire, R. Morgan and R. Reiner (eds.), *The Oxford Handbook of Criminology*. Oxford: Oxford University Press.

Mair, G. 1997. 'Community Penalties and the Probation Service'. In M. Maguire, R. Morgan and R. Reiner (eds.), *The Oxford Handbook of Criminology*. Oxford: Oxford University Press.

Marshall, T. H. 1950. *Citizenship and Social Class.* Cambridge: Cambridge University Press.

Martin, H-P. and Schumann, H. 1997. *The Global Trap.* London: Zed Books.

Martinson, R., Lipton, D. and Wilks, J. 1974. 'What Works? Questions and Answers about Penal Reform'. *Public Interest* 35:22–54.

Massing, M. 1998. 'The Blue Revolution'. *New York Review of Books,* 19 November, pp. 32–6.

Mawby, R. 1999. *Policing Across the World: Issues for the Twenty-First Century.* London: UCL Press.

Mayhew, P., Aye Maung, N. and Mirrlees-Black, C. 1993. *The 1992 British Crime Survey.* Home Office Research Study 132. London: HMSO.

Mayhew, P., Elliott, D. and Dowds, L. 1989. *The 1988 British Crime Survey.* Home Office Research Study 111. London: HMSO.

McCabe, S. and Sutcliffe, F. 1978. *Defining Crime.* Oxford: Blackwell.

McConville, M., Sanders, A. and Leng, R. 1991. *The Case for the Prosecution.* London: Routledge.

Merton , R. 1957. *Social Theory and Social Structure.* Glencoe: Free Press.

Miliband, R. 1978. 'A State of De-subordination?' *British Journal of Sociology* 4:399–409.

Mirrlees-Black, C., Mayhew, P. and Percy, A. 1996. *The 1996 British Crime Survey.* Home Office Statistical Bulletin 19/96. London: Home Office.

Mirrlees-Black, C., Budd, T., Partridge, S. and Mayhew, P. 1998. *The 1998 British Crime Survey.* Home Office Statistical Bulletin 21/98. London: Home Office.

Morgan, R. 1997. 'Imprisonment'. In M. Maguire, R. Morgan and R. Reiner (eds.), *The Oxford Handbook of Criminology.* Oxford: Oxford University Press.

Morris, P. and Heal, K. 1981. *Crime Control and the Police.* London: Home Office Research Unit.

Morris, T. 1989. *Crime and Criminal Justice Since 1945.* Oxford: Blackwell.

Morrison, W. 1995. *Theoretical Criminology.* London: Cavendish.

Moxon, D. 1998. 'The Role of Sentencing Policy'. In C. Nuttall, P. Goldblatt and C. Lewis (eds.), *Reducing Offending.* London: Home Office.

National Deviancy Conference (ed.) 1980. *Permissiveness and Control.* London: Macmillan.

Nelken, D. 1985. 'Community Involvement in Crime Control'. *Current Legal Problems* 85:259–67.

Nelken, D. 1997. 'White-Collar Crime'. In M. Maguire, R. Morgan and R. Reiner (eds.), *The Oxford Handbook of Criminology.* Oxford: Oxford University Press.

Newburn, T. 1992. *Permissiveness and Regulation.* London: Routledge.

Norris, C. and Armstrong, G. 1999. *The Maximum Surveillance Society: The Rise of CCTV.* West Sussex: Berg.

Nuttall, C., Goldblatt, P. and Lewis, C. (eds.) 1998. *Reducing Offending.* Home Office Research Study 187. London: Home Office.

Panitch, L. and Leys, C. (eds.) 1999. *Global Capitalism versus Democracy: Socialist Register 1999.* Rendlesham: Merlin Press.

Pearson, G. 1983. *Hooligan.* London: Macmillan.

Pease, K. 1997. 'Crime Prevention'. In M. Maguire, R. Morgan and R. Reiner (eds.), *The Oxford Handbook of Criminology.* Oxford: Oxford University Press.

Pyle, P. J. and Deadman, D. F. 1994. 'Crime and the Business Cycle in Post-War Britain'. *British Journal of Criminology* 34: 339–57.

Rawlinson, P. 1998. 'Mafia, Media and Myth: Representations of Russian Organised Crime'. *Howard Journal of Criminal Justice* 37: 346–58.

Reiman, J. 1990. *The Rich Get Richer and the Poor Get Prison.* New York: Macmillan.

Reiner, R. 1996. 'The Case of the Missing Crimes'. In R. Levitas and W. Guy (eds.), *Interpreting Official Statistics.* London: Routledge.

Reiner, R. 1997a. 'Media Made Criminality'. In M. Maguire, R. Morgan and R. Reiner (eds.), *The Oxford Handbook of Criminology.* Oxford: Oxford University Press.

Reiner, R. 1997b. 'Policing and the Police'. In M. Maguire, R. Morgan and R. Reiner (eds.), *The Oxford Handbook of Criminology*. Oxford: Oxford University Press.

Reiner, R. 1999. 'Order and Discipline'. In I. Holliday, A. Gamble and G. Parry (eds.), *Fundamentals in British Politics*. London: Macmillan.

Reiner, R. and Cross, M. (eds.) 1991. *Beyond Law and Order*. London: Macmillan.

Reiner, R., Livingstone, S. and Allen, J. 1998. 'Discipline or Desubordination? Changing Images of Crime in the Media Since World War II'. Paper presented to the International Sociological Association World Congress, Montreal.

Rock, P. and Cohen, S. 1970. 'The Teddy Boy'. In V. Bogdanor and R. Skidelsky (eds.), *The Age of Affluence 1951–64*. London: Macmillan.

Rock, P. 1997. 'Sociological Theories of Crime'. In M. Maguire, R. Morgan and R. Reiner (eds.), *The Oxford Handbook of Criminology*. Oxford: Oxford University Press.

Rose, N. 1996. 'The Death of the Social? Refiguring the Territory of Government'. *Economy and Society* 25:321–56.

Ruggiero, V. and South, N. 1995. *Eurodrugs*. London: UCL Press.

Sanders, A. 1997. 'From Suspect to Trial'. In M. Maguire, R. Morgan and R. Reiner (eds.), *The Oxford Handbook of Criminology*. Oxford: Oxford University Press.

Shearing, C. and Stenning, P. 1983. 'Private Security: Implications for Social Control'. *Social Problems* 30:493–506.

Shearing, C. and Stenning, P. (eds.) 1987. *Private Policing*. Beverly Hills: Sage.

Sheptycki, J. 1995. 'Transnational Policing and the Makings of a Postmodern State'. *British Journal of Criminology* 35:613–35.

Sheptycki, J. 1997. 'Insecurity, Risk Suppression and Segregation: Some Reflections on Policing in the Transnational Age'. *Theoretical Criminology* 1:303–14.

Sherman, L. 1992. 'Police and Crime Control'. In M. Tonry and N. Morris (eds.), *Modern Policing*. Chicago: Chicago University Press.

Slapper, G. and Tombs, S. 1999. *Corporate Crime*. London: Longman.

South, N. 1988. *Policing for Profit*. London: Sage.

South, N. 1997a. 'Control, Crime and "End of Century" Criminology' In P. Francis, P. Davies and V. Jupp (eds.), *Policing Futures*. London: Macmillan.

South, N. 1997b. 'Drugs: Use, Crime and Control'. In M. Maguire, R. Morgan and R. Reiner (eds.), *The Oxford Handbook of Criminology*. Oxford: Oxford University Press.

Sparks, R. 1992. *Television and the Drama of Crime*. Buckingham: Open University Press.

Tarling, R. 1994. *Analysing Offending*. London: HMSO.

Taylor, H. 1998a. 'The Politics of the Rising Crime Statistics of England and Wales 1914–1960'. *Crime, History and Societies* 2:5–28.

Taylor, H. 1998b. 'Rising Crime: The Political Economy of Criminal Statistics Since the 1850s'. *Economic History Review* 51: 569–90.

Taylor, H. 1999. 'Forging the Job: A Crisis of "Modernisation" or Redundancy for the Police in England and Wales 1900–39'. *British Journal of Criminology* 39: 113–35.

Taylor, I. 1996. 'Fear of Crime, Urban Fortunes and Suburban Social Movements'. *Sociology* 30: 317–37.

Taylor, I. 1997a. 'Crime, Anxiety and Locality: Responding to the "Condition of England" at the End of the Century'. *Theoretical Criminology* 1:53–76.

Taylor, I. 1997b. 'The Political Economy of Crime'. In M. Maguire, R. Morgan and R. Reiner (eds.), *The Oxford Handbook of Criminology*. Oxford: Oxford University Press.

Taylor, I. 1998a. 'Crime, Market-Liberalism and the European Idea'. In V. Ruggiero, N. South and I. Taylor (eds.), *The New European Criminology*. London: Routledge.

94   ROBERT REINER

Taylor, I. 1998b. 'Free Markets and the Costs of Crime: An Audit for England and Wales'. In P. Walton and J. Young (eds.), *The New Criminology Revisited*. London: Macmillan.

Taylor, I. 1999. *Crime in Context: A Critical Criminology of Market Societies*. Cambridge: Polity.

Taylor, I., Walton, P. and Young, J. 1973. *The New Criminology*. London: Routledge.

Walker, M. (ed.) 1995. *Interpreting Crime Statistics*. Oxford: Oxford University Press.

Walker, N. 1993. 'The International Dimension'. In R. Reiner and S. Spencer (eds.), *Accountable Policing*. London: Institute for Public Policy Research.

Walklate, S. 1997. 'Risk and Criminal Victimisation: A Modernist Dilemma'. *British Journal of Criminology* 37:35–46.

Walklate, S. 1998. 'Excavating the Fear of Crime'. *Theoretical Criminology* 2:403–18.

Weatheritt, M. (ed.) 1998. *Zero Tolerance*. London: Police Foundation.

Wells, J. 1995. *Crime and Unemployment*. London: Employment Policy Institute.

Wiener, M. 1990. *Reconstructing the Criminal: Culture, Law and Policy in England 1830–1914*. Cambridge: Cambridge University Press.

Wilson, J. Q. 1985, 2nd edn. *Thinking About Crime*. New York: Vintage.

Wilson, J. Q. and Herrnstein, R. 1985. *Crime and Human Nature*. New York: Simon and Schuster.

Witt, R., Clarke, A. and Fielding, N. 1999. 'Crime and Economic Activity: A Panel Data Approach'. *British Journal of Criminology* 39:391–400.

Young, J. 1986. 'The Failure of Criminology: The Need for a Radical Realism'. In R. Matthews and J. Young (eds.), *Confronting Crime*. London: Sage.

Young, J. 1997. 'Left Realist Criminology' in M. Maguire, R. Morgan and R. Reiner (eds.), *The Oxford Handbook of Criminology*. Oxford: Oxford University Press.

Young, J. 1998a. *The Criminology of Intolerance*. Middlesex University: Centre for Criminology.

Young, J. 1998b. 'From Inclusive to Exclusive Society: Nightmares in the European Dream'. In V. Ruggiero, N. South and I. Taylor (eds.), *The New European Criminology*. London: Routledge.

Young, J. 1999. *The Exclusive Society: Social Exclusion, Crime and Difference in Late Modernity*. London: Sage.

Young, M. 1991. *An Inside Job*. Oxford: Oxford University Press.

Biographical note: ROBERT REINER is Professor of Criminology in the Law Department, London School of Economics. He was formerly Reader in Criminology at the University of Bristol, and at Brunel University. He has a BA in Economics from Cambridge University (1967), an MSc in Sociology (with Distinction) from the London School of Economics (1968), a PhD in Sociology from Bristol University (1976), and a Postgraduate Diploma in Law (with Distinction) from City University, London (1985). He is author of *The Blue-Coated Worker* (Cambridge University Press, 1978), *The Politics of the Police* (Wheatsheaf, 1985; 2nd edn 1992), *Chief Constables* (Oxford University Press, 1991), and editor of (with M. Cross) *Beyond Law and Order* (Macmillan, 1991), (with S. Spencer) *Accountable Policing* (Institute for Public Policy Research, 1993), *Policing* (Dartmouth, 1996), and (with M. Maguire and R. Morgan) *The Oxford Handbook of Criminology* (Oxford University Press, 1994; 2nd edn 1997). He has published nearly one hundred papers on policing and criminal justice topics. He was Editor (with Rod Morgan) of *Policing and Society: An International Journal of Research and Policy*, 1989–98, and review editor of *The British Journal of Criminology*, 1986–88. He was President of the British Society of Criminology, 1993–96. His current research is a study financed by the Economic and Social Research Council analysing changing media representations of crime and criminal justice since the Second World War.

Address: Law Department, The London School of Economics and Political Science, Houghton Street, London WC2A 2AE.

[14]
Beyond Risk: A Lament for Social Democratic Criminology

Introduction

This chapter will examine one aspect of the profound changes in crime, control and criminal justice over the last thirty years, the mysterious disappearance of social democratic criminology. This was a way of understanding and responding to crime that was widespread, perhaps dominant, for much of the twentieth century. Was its disappearance due to death by suicide, murder, or natural causes—or is it still alive and capable of returning?

In the next section I will define what I mean by 'social democratic' criminology. I shall then chart and analyse its virtually complete replacement by a variety of perspectives to which I shall give the general label 'contrology'.[1] The conclusion will argue that without a return to social democracy—however remote this may seem—the future directions of crime and control are grim.

Social Democratic Criminology

The term social democratic criminology has been used before (e.g. Taylor 1981 ch. 2), but it has never been a self-espoused label. What I mean by it is a set of assumptions about the nature

---

[1] The term 'controlology' was coined by Jason Ditton in his book with that title (Ditton 1979). He used it to refer to a thorough-going formulation of 'labelling' theory, seeing crime as shaped by control. I have not only slightly shortened the word, but am using it in almost the opposite way. By 'contrology' I mean the variety of fundamentally conservative criminologies that are concerned with the pursuit of direct crime control rather than analysing causes of crime or criticizing criminal justice.

8 Robert Reiner

of human action, ethics, and political economy that broadly correspond to the most common meaning of the term 'social democratic'.

Social Democracy

'Social democracy' has been used as a badge by many very different political movements. In the late nineteenth and early twentieth centuries the label 'Social Democratic' was espoused by Marxist parties, such as Hyndman's Social Democratic Federation in England and Kautsky's German Social Democratic Party (Sassoon 1996: ch. 1). Trotsky once declared that his nationality was 'Social Democratic' (Figes 2005: 10).

After the First World War, with the establishment of Bolshevik government in the Soviet Union, the term social democracy came to be contrasted with communism. Social democracy signified at the very least a distinction of means from Bolshevism—the parliamentary road to socialism—and for many a change of ends too, reform of capitalism rather than its overthrow. Perhaps the culmination of this evolution was the founding of the British Social Democratic Party in 1981 as a breakaway from what was perceived as an unacceptably militant Labour Party. But for most of the twentieth century 'social democratic' referred to a wide variety of socialist viewpoints distinguished from, on the left border, Soviet communism, and on the right, the 'new' liberalism inspired by T.H.Green and his disciples in the late nineteenth and early twentieth centuries (Clarke 1978).

Its intellectual centre of gravity was the English tradition of ethical socialism (Dennis and Halsey 1988), the quintessential exemplar of which was R.H.Tawney but which also included such thinkers as Graham Wallas, Hobhouse, and T.H.Marshall. The 1990s' 'third way' of the two Tonies, Blair and Giddens, explicitly sought to triangulate this 'social democracy' and neo-liberalism. 'Social democracy' was always a species of socialism, but it was itself a 'third way' between two poles, communism and liberalism. It was not, however, a presentational splitting of the difference, but an anguished and internally contested terrain, an intellectual and moral Buridan's ass, torn between the powerful pulls of justice and liberty. There were of course many attempts to synthesize the two poles. The most fully developed of these, John Rawls' magisterial *Theory of Justice* (Rawls 1971),

Beyond Risk: A Lament for Social Democratic Criminology   9

appeared just as the political and social influence of social democracy was about to dip below the horizon, a paradigm example of Hegel's owl of Minerva spreading its wings at dusk.[2]

'Social democracy' as an intellectual discourse, and *a fortiori* actually existing social democratic parties and governments, encompassed a wide variety of viewpoints and programmes. In the middle of the twentieth century, the heyday of European mixed economy welfare states and the Rooseveltian New Deal in the United States, it stood for a broad consensus, albeit with vigorous opposition from unreconciled free marketeers, old conservative nostalgists, and most Marxists.

This consensus also tacitly underpinned the analyses of crime and strategies for reform developed by most criminologists (Garland and Sparks 2000: 195), despite sharp conflicts over specific issues, notably capital punishment (Ryan 1983; Morris 1989: 32, 77-85). The quintessential expression of social democratic criminology is Robert Merton's seminal formulation of anomie theory (Merton 1938), probably the most quoted article in criminology, and arguably one of the most misrepresented (Reiner 1984: 186–94). In Britain its clearest exponent was Hermann Mannheim. But beyond specific exemplars there was a deep structure of shared assumptions that could be characterized as social democratic. This was shown by the quiet confidence of policy-makers that, for all the problems of wartime and post-war crime, social progress would resolve these (Morris 1989: Chs. 2, 3, 6; Bottoms and Stevenson 1992). Social democratic criminology as an ideal-type can, I believe, be characterized by the following ten dimensions incorporating the key themes of social democracy in general.

Social democratic criminology: an ideal-type

The problem of crime

Social democratic criminologists were well aware of the difficulties in conceptualizing crime,[3] and did not simply take for

---

[2] Rawls is normally seen as a liberal theory, but its arguments for principles that balance liberty and equality offer a powerful case for the values underpinning social democracy.

[3] Henry and Lanier 2001; Lacey *et al.* 2003: Chs. 1, 2; Zedner 2004; Chs. 1, 2; Hillyard *et al.* 2004; Morrison 2005 are recent analyses of the vexed issues in conceptualizing crime.

10   Robert Reiner

granted the categories of criminal law. Legal definitions of crime embodied power rather than morality, so they inadequately reflected the gravity of different forms of anti-social or harmful behaviour.[4] Mannheim's *Criminal Justice and Social Reconstruction*, for example, offered a critical analysis of criminal law, assessing its appropriateness for curbing the most harmful forms of antisocial behaviour in the post-war period. It was particularly concerned about the inadequate definition and enforcement of the law against dishonest and harmful business practices. Weak policing of white-collar crime was not only problematic in itself—it called into question the moral integrity of criminal justice and undermined its ability to deal with routine crimes such as theft and burglary (Mannheim 1946: 119). In the United States, Sutherland had launched his pioneering attempt to bring white-collar crime within the ambit of criminological concern in 1939 (Sutherland 1983), for which Mannheim thought he deserved a Nobel prize (Nelken 2002: 848). Merton's pivotal theory of anomie was explicitly intended as an analysis of deviance, not limited to legal or criminal justice categories (Merton 1938). It is commonly criticized for adopting the official picture of crime as primarily a lower class phenomenon, ignoring white-collar crime. However Merton began with an analysis of how a culture that defines success in purely financial terms is prone to anomie at all levels, because there is no inherent end-point to the goal of monetary gain. He explicitly applied this to crime in the suites as well as the streets (Merton and Ross 1957: 131–44).

Social democratic criminologists realized that the powerful and privileged often perpetrated far greater harms than did ordinary crime, usually escaping criminal labelling or even its possibility.[5] Nonetheless, like subsequent 'left realism' in the

---

[4] Social democratic definitions of crime sought to combine the two elements of harm and official enforcement. An example is Bonger's definition of crime as 'a serious antisocial act to which the State reacts consciously by inflicting pain' (Bonger 1936: 5).

[5] Expressed in Anatole France's much quoted aphorism about 'the majestic impartiality of the law, which forbids the rich as well as the poor to sleep under bridges, to beg in the streets, and to steal bread' (*Le Lys Rouge* Paris1894). Jock Young's recent reformulation of the golden rule puts this even more pithily: 'it is the people with the gold who make the rules' (Young 2005: vi).

Beyond Risk: A Lament for Social Democratic Criminology   11

1980s (Lea and Young 1984), social democrats viewed routine crime as harmful and problematic—especially to the most vulnerable in society—however much they may have been sympathetic to the plight of offenders. Social democratic criminology (like all criminology prior to the paradigm shift associated with the 'labelling' perspective of the 1960s) was primarily concerned with developing causal explanations of crime, with a correctionalist ambition of reducing offending.

Primacy of the ethical
In current political debate the language of morality has been captured by the religious Right in the United States, and by *Daily Mail* reading or fearing circles in the United Kingdom, restricting it to an extremely narrow conception of 'traditional family values'. This blots out much broader conceptions of the moral, governing all spheres of human activity, that used to be the focus of both religious and secular philosophies, on the left as much as the right of politics. As Michael Walzer put it recently 'For right-wing intellectuals and activists, values seem to be about sex and almost nothing else; vast areas of social life are left to the radically amoral play of market forces. And yet they "have" values, and we [the liberal left] don't' (Walzer 2005: 37). Especially in the wake of George W. Bush's second Presidential election victory,[6] attributed by many analysts to the 'values' issue above all (Frank 2004), there has been much discussion of the need for the left to recapture the language of ethics and passionate commitment to justice.

The left has often been uncomfortable with discussions of morality. Marx is said to have roared with laughter when he heard talk about morality (Lukes 1985: 27). He and Engels castigated ethically derived versions of socialism as 'utopian', rejecting them for a 'scientific' materialism (Marx and Engels 1848 [1998]: 72–5; Engels 1880). This 'obstretric' view of history, in which socialists act merely as the midwives of communism that will inevitably be born after the revolution generated by the contradictions of capitalism, has been a deadly illusion (G. Cohen 2000). It fatally underestimated the huge moral transformation that

---

[6] Perhaps 2004 should be called his first election victory in the light of the still contested legitimacy of the 2000 result (Palast 2004).

12   Robert Reiner

needs to anticipate and accompany political and economic change if it is to not to produce new forms of tyranny in the guise of liberation. It is also arguably a misreading of the depth of Marx and Engels' own moral sensitivity to the evils of industrial capitalism, which paradoxically underlay their rejection of moralism in favour of the wishful thinking of an inevitable progression to communism.

The non-Marxist left has always been clearly driven by moral concerns. Social democracy, in particular, was fundamentally idealist. The ends that social democratic political action aimed at, and the means adopted for their pursuit, were derived from and subject to explicitly espoused ethical values. Secular or religious, social democrats espoused the fundamental equality of value of individuals, the ancient Golden Rule embodied in the Biblical injunction to love your neighbour as yourself (Leviticus XIX: 18). Shorn of its religious cloak, this principle continued to underlie most modern (and arguably some post-modern) conceptions of morality and justice. This is most evident in Kantian formulations of the ethical as the universalisable (Kant 1785). But it is also implied in utilitarianism, usually regarded as a fundamentally opposed perspective, which at least as a starting point treats every individual's utilities as equal inputs into the felicific calculus.[7]

Nietzsche in the late nineteenth century, and some post-modernist and Foucauldian approaches in the late twentieth century, expressly reject both traditional religious and Enlightenment versions of universalist ethics as restrictions on human autonomy and diversity, advocating instead an aesthetic ethics and politics (Nietzsche 1885; Rose 1999: 282–4). However, rejecting the claims of transcendental moral codes, and of any absolute epistemological foundations for ethics, does not entail the rejection of the value of the Golden Rule. Several attempts at developing post-foundational ethics—for all their differences—nonetheless seem to echo the principle of what Dworkin calls 'equal respect and concern for

---

[7] Kantians stress that utilitarianism does not respect the specificity of persons, so is compatible with outcomes that sacrifice individuals for the greater good of the majority (Rawls 1971; Hudson 2003: 19). This tyranny of the majority problem was recognized by utilitarians like John Stuart Mill early on, and their more sophisticated formulations attempt to cope with it (Reiner 2002).

Beyond Risk: A Lament for Social Democratic Criminology   13

others' (Dworkin 2000). Boutellier has made an impressive attempt to develop criminal justice ethics from Rorty's pragmatic conception of liberal irony (Rorty 1989, 1999; Boutellier 2000: ch. 6). Rorty argues that the ironist, who recognizes the contingency of her convictions, can still be a 'liberal', including among their 'ungroundable desires their own hope that suffering will be diminished, that the humiliation of human beings by other human beings may cease' (Rorty 1989: xv). This is paralleled by Bauman's attempt to develop a post-modern 'morality without ethics', 'resurrecting the consideration of the Other temporarily . . . suspended by the obedience to the norm' (Baumann 1995:7). This also recalls Levinas' notion of the ethical as the obverse of 'egology'—the assertion of the primacy of the self. 'We name the calling into question of my spontaneity by the presence of the other ethics' (Levinas 1969: 33).

Some liberals and social democrats may have thought their values were grounded in the self-evidence of intuition, scientific knowledge, the ineluctable march of history, or the will of God. But for many it was clear that there are no indubitable Archimedean points on which to ground ethical commitments in an objective, unanswerable way. This does not mean, however, that the values espoused by social democrats—liberty, equality, fraternity, in the now hallowed formula of the French and other democratic revolutions—were unreasonable or that there were not arguments that could be marshalled for them. But these arguments were always essentially contested and potentially endless.

Ethics were also primary for social democrats in considering legitimate means. Good ends did not justify dirty hands (Sartre 1948). Violence in particular could not be adopted as a tactic of choice, however noble the cause pursued, but only defensively, of necessity, and proportionately. The use of morally dirty means was not only wrong in itself but also counter-productive. It corrupted the users and frustrated the achievement of ethically desirable goals.

Social democratic criminology is often associated with explanations of crime in terms of economic factors (poverty, inequality, unemployment). But it was much more than just criminological Clintonism ('it's the economy, stupid'). Social democratic criminology was primarily concerned with ethical

14   Robert Reiner

issues, not least in its attempts to explain crime. In the first place crime, criminal justice, punishment, and anti-social behaviours (at all levels of the social hierarchy) were problematic because they were sources of harm and suffering. Not only victims of crime but also perpetrators and the social conditions that ultimately underlay crime were all matters for ethical concern.

More specifically it is important to stress that economic factors like poverty, inequality, or unemployment were seen as leading to crime primarily because they weakened support (in general and in potential offenders) for morality, in the sense of concern and respect for others. Bonger's work, for example, is usually characterized as the most thorough-going example of Marxist economic determinism applied to crime (Taylor, Walton and Young 1973). But Bonger analyses the inequities of capitalism as criminogenic not in themselves but because they stimulate a culture of egoism.

Merton's anomie theory, the paradigm social democratic account of crime, is often reduced to a simplistic explanation in terms of structural inequalities in legitimate opportunities. But moral factors are basic to Merton's analysis. Merton stresses that a materialistic culture, in which success is primarily defined in money terms, encourages deviance at all levels of society. This is because monetary aspirations are inherently unlimited and prone to anomie. The materialist ethos also prioritizes goal attainment over the legitimacy of means, and in itself erodes social and ethical controls. Merton's central typology of deviant reactions to anomie does indeed stress the significance of an unequal structural distribution of legitimate opportunities. However, this produces a strain towards deviance in cultures (like that of the United States) which stress an ideal of equal opportunities. The key variable is the ethic of meritocracy, rather than inequality of opportunities *per se*. Mannheim's analysis of how wartime and post-war conditions generated crime, inextricably mixed together economic and moral issues (Taylor 1981: 45). The 1964 Labour Party study group document *Crime: A Challenge For Us All*, which informed the Wilson government's criminal justice agenda, adopted Tawney's analysis of the 'acquisitive society' to explain how Conservative economic policies had emphasized individual economic success thus 'weakening the moral fibre of individuals' (Labour Party 1964: 5).

Critique of capitalism

Social democrats saw capitalism as having systemic flaws that could be mitigated but were intrinsic to it. Its productive capacities were of course recognized. To ethical socialists like Tawney, however, economic growth was a means to desirable ends such as the relief of poverty, not an end in itself. Indeed material affluence posed moral dangers as it stimulated acquisitiveness and egoism (Tawney 1921).

Whatever its virtues, however, capitalism had several fundamental problems. Whilst differing from Marx's diagnosis of possible end states and how to achieve them, social democrats largely endorsed his critique of the pernicious consequences of market anarchy. The operation of unregulated markets inexorably generated inequality. Whilst growth offered increasing capacity to alleviate poverty there was no automatic trickle-down. Indeed the market price valuations that underpinned measures of economic growth reflected differential economic power. Price was determined by effective demand (desire backed by the ability to pay) not social need.[8] Capitalists' pursuit of their own economic rationality could produce external diseconomies, wider social costs such as pollution, which did not figure in their own private calculations of efficient productive methods. The neo-classical economists, such as Marshall and Pigou, who demonstrated that free market systems led to 'Pareto-optimal' allocation of resources in which (in the language of welfare economics) the 'gainers could over-compensate the losers', agreed with these criticisms. They endorsed political action to correct market dysfunctions. Capitalism also suffered from macro-economic fluctuations, the cycle of depression and boom, which, following Keynes' arguments in the 1930s, required government regulation to alleviate the ensuing misery. Social democrats' criticisms of capitalism were not only aimed at its economic consequences but also the culture of amoral and possessive individualism that it accentuated.

---

[8] It is this point that has stimulated the New Economics Foundation and others to explore alternative measures of economic welfare and growth, building in estimates for social costs of conventional economic activity, and forms of wellbeing that do not command an adequate market price (Jackson 2004).

16   Robert Reiner

The economic dysfunctions of capitalism that social democracy identified were seen by criminologists as leading to crime,
albeit not straightforwardly but mediated by intervening factors
(such as their effects on morality, family life, and informal
social controls). This has produced a plethora of research on the
possible links between economic factors and crime, which will
be considered later in the chapter. The results of this research
are complex, but there can be no doubt that the political economy plays a significant, if not straightforward, part in the
explanation of crime. Certainly the turbo-capitalism of the
Thatcher–Reagan years has been a major causal factor in
rocketing crime rates, and its slight attenuation under New
Labour has contributed to recent falls in crime (Downes 2004;
Hale 2005a).

Gradualism
Despite the critique of capitalism offered by social democrats
they did not advocate its overthrow. Specific reforms aimed at
alleviating particular problems were to be argued for through
the democratic process, and implemented gradually. For many
social democrats the accumulation of such reforms was intended
to result ultimately in a qualitatively different social order,
socialism. But for many social democrats capitalism was seen as
beneficial, or at any rate inevitable, so that perpetual struggle
was required to alleviate its egregious failings. Gradualism was
favoured in part to ensure by cautious experimentation that
reforms worked without unintended negative consequences. But
most fundamentally it was the necessary price of seeking to pro-
ceed democratically, by building consent, rather than through
coercion.

The psychic cost of gradualism was living with a world of
injustice and suffering, albeit one that was improving in stages. This
required patience, fortitude, stoicism in the face of indefensible evil.
Piecemeal reform aimed at little dollops of jam today, rather than
vats of it after the Revolution. Social democracy sought gradual
improvement in a forever messy and conflict-ridden world. As
Kolakowski once put it: 'The trouble with the social democratic
idea is that it does not . . . sell any of the exciting commodities which
various totalitarian movements . . . offer dream-hungry youth . . . It
has no prescription for the total salvation of mankind . . . It believes
in no final easy victory over evil. It requires, in addition to

commitment to a number of basic values, hard knowledge and rational calculation . . . It is an obstinate will to erode by inches the conditions which produce avoidable suffering, oppression, hunger, wars, racial and national hatred, insatiable greed and vindictive envy.' (quoted in Jenkins 1989: 142).

Social democratic criminologists sought not only to understand and reverse the macro causes of crime through economic and social policy. They were extensively involved in research and reform interventions aimed at effective (but humane) penal practice. The charge levelled both by Conservatives and by Left Realists in the 1980s that radical criminology was preoccupied with ultimate causes, not practical interventions to control crime, may have been true of the 'left idealism' of the 1970s. But it was certainly not true of social democratic criminologists, although they were concerned as much with the humanity and fairness of penal intervention as with 'what works?'.

Equality *AND* democracy

Social democracy sought equality through democratic means. There are of course extensive debates about how to interpret equality and democracy. But most social democrats subscribed to a fundamental principle of treating everyone with 'equal concern and respect' (Dworkin 2000). Rawls' two principles of justice—equality of basic liberties, and equality of material distribution (subject only to departures if they raise the position of the least well-off, the 'difference' principle)—expressed most explicitly the values of most social democrats.

Social democracy saw equality and liberal democracy as mutually reinforcing rather than in tension. In societies split by hierarchies of class (and gender, and ethnicity), equality was in the interest of the majority, so that ultimately the democratic process would produce a consensus for egalitarian measures. Conversely, in a highly unequal society, it was only possible to have the 'best democracy money could buy' (Palast 2004). Substantive democracy is incompatible with gross inequalities.

Social democrats certainly believed that the slow incorporation of all sections of society into civil, political and social citizenship (Marshall 1950) would achieve social order. The experience of the second half of the nineteenth century, during which recorded crime rates declined and then remained stable until after

18   Robert Reiner

the First World War, seemed to confirm this (Gatrell 1980; Radzinowicz and Hood 1985). The 'dangerous classes' of the early Victorian period were progressively disciplined by the physically gentler, quotidien 'dull compulsion of economic relations' (Marx 1867: 737). Formal social control in the early twentieth century moved towards a more individualized, reform-oriented penal/welfare complex, informed by criminological research on the causation of offending and the requirements of rehabilitation (Garland 1985).

Quiet optimism
Until the early 1970s social democrats shared a tacit Whig theory of history. Without postulating any iron laws, there was a sense of continuing, if sometimes broken and tentative, progress towards equality, liberty and democracy. This rested implicitly on a sense that there was a substantive historical agent, the working class, who constituted the majority of society and were receptive (if initially for self-interested reasons) to the ideals of social democracy.

Social democratic criminology shared this quiet optimism. However, this was challenged by the increase in recorded crime in the late 1950s. The rise in crime rates during a period of unprecedented mass affluence seemed to refute the expectation that crime would reduce with better social conditions. Jock Young famously called this an 'aetiological crisis' for social democratic criminology (Young 1986). But it is important to stress that social democratic criminology did not postulate a simple relationship between economic conditions and crime. This is not just reinterpretation with the benefit of hindsight. There are many examples of predictions by social democratic criminologists in the early 1960s of rising crime rates, due to the acquisitiveness, anomie and relative deprivation sparked by the new consumerist culture (Labour Party 1964: 5; Downes 1966, 1988: 103–9).

Dimensions of justice
Essentially creatures of their time, most social democrats did not speak of other dimensions of inequality or oppression, such as gender, ethnicity, or sexual preference. There were isolated examples who did of course. John Stuart Mill (a liberal but with views that became close to social democracy) was a famous early champion of the rights of women. As criminologists we can be

proud of the example of Willem Bonger, the Dutch Marxist, Social Democratic Party activist, and academic criminologist, who championed the rights of gay people, and in the 1930s of Jews, ultimately committing suicide in despair when the Nazis invaded Holland (Bemmelen 1960; S. Cohen 1998). Certainly the principles of social democracy demanded justice for all forms of oppression, not just economic.

Social democratic criminologists primarily thought of issues of crime and justice in terms of class. The hope was that the gradual emancipation of the working class would alleviate progressively the problems of criminal justice. There was certainly recognition of the age dimension, and much work on juvenile delinquency. But differences of gender, race and sexual preference were largely outside their attention until the 1970s. However, the general principle of equal concern and respect underpinning social democracy certainly lends itself to incorporating these dimensions of inequality and injustice into the analysis of crime, victimization and criminal justice. It is also important not to neglect the continuing importance of class and economic inequality, not only in itself, but also as an underlying element in racial differences in crime and criminalization (Fitzgerald 2004).

The state as instrument of justice

Social democrats saw the democratic state as the primary means of achieving greater equality and justice. This is not to say that they were not acutely aware of the dangers of state power. The two most widely celebrated novels about the dangers of totalitarianism, *Animal Farm* and *1984*, were written by a social democrat (however idiosyncratic), George Orwell. There were always currents in social democracy that espoused non-state forms to achieve justice, such as the co-operative movement, the Friendly Societies, and versions of syndicalism and communitarianism. The 'local state' was also, in theory and in practice, an important agent of social democracy. Social democratic criminology saw the liberal democratic state's criminal justice agencies as fundamentally benign, although there was an agenda of reform to make them representative of, and responsive to, working class concerns. But it was only from the mid-1960s that empirical socio-legal and criminological research began to focus on the way that policing and other parts of the criminal justice

20   Robert Reiner

system discriminated in terms of class, age, gender, race and sexuality (Heidensohn 2002; Gelsthorpe 2002; Bowling and Phillips 2002). The state centred character of social democratic criminology has been called into question more recently by the proliferation of non-state modes of control (Jones and Newburn 1998), and of theoretical perspectives critical of state domination of criminal justice (Johnston and Shearing 2003).

Science

Social democrats viewed science as a positive force. Physical science offered the prospect of reducing the economic pressures underlying human drudgery and servitude. Piecemeal social engineering and the regulation of markets required social science to analyse problems systematically, and to predict the probable consequences of policies.

This did not entail the simplistic positivism that has become a crude term of abuse by many contemporary sociologists. Social democrats recognized that observations were theory-laden, that values affected the choice of study and the application of results, and indeed were hard to separate from the process of research. For the most part they saw human behaviour as a dialectical outcome of structure and action, people making their own histories but not under conditions of their own choosing. But they would also have accepted that there are regularities that can be discerned in social interaction, even if these are probabilistic and not the product of iron determinism. Knowing and understanding as much as possible about these was necessary to guide practical reform. Whilst a vital element of the liberal democracy that social democrats believed in was tolerance, this did not entail relativism with regard to either 'facts' or values.

There can be no question that social democratic criminology was broadly 'positivist' in its approach to social science, in that it felt it important to research as rigorously as possible the causes of crime and the effectiveness, humanity and justice of crime control policies. Occasionally they even used numbers in their analyses! But for the most part they would not have been guilty of the accusations routinely hurled at a straw person version of positivism by subsequent critics. They did not think that social science results could be regarded as absolute truth, completely objective representations of reality, or that they could resolve all issues. Most would have accepted Weber's analysis of the problems, limitations, ultimate impossibility and yet importance and desirability as an ideal of value-freedom in science (Weber 1918).

Whilst they regarded it as useful to formulate and test empirical generalizations, few saw these as laws that determined individual behaviour. Merton's analysis of deviant reactions to anomie has been criticized as a deterministic account that gives no space to individual interpretation of meaning and autonomy (Taylor *et al.* (1973): 108). However, it intended only to suggest probabilities not certainties (Merton 1995), and raises rather than forecloses exploration of why people in similar structural situations develop different reactions (Reiner 1984: 191–2).

Modernism

The values of justice and liberty, central to social democracy, have ancient origins. Many perceived a long chain of inspiration going back to antiquity—the Hebrew Prophets, Socrates, Jesus, Spartacus. The chain continued through the Middle Ages and early modernity—John Ball ('When Adam delved and Eve span who was then the gentleman?'), Wat Tyler, Jack Straw and other leaders of the Peasants' Revolt, Thomas More's Utopia, the Levellers.

The distinctly modern element in social democracy was the belief that these values were not a millenarian dream, but capable of implementation as a practical political project. This was not necessarily part of a modernist 'grand narrative', though it was often tied to a view of history as (probably) progressive.

Social democratic criminology, and its penological counterpart the rehabilitative ideal, were quintessential elements of 'penal modernism' (Garland 2001). However, the label 'modern' implies that they are discredited, dead, in an era of 'post' or 'late' modernity. The rest of this paper will be concerned to examine this, by analysing the eclipse of social democratic criminology, and assessing the possibility and desirability of resurrecting its core elements.

The Rise of Contrology

This section will analyse the displacement of the social democratic perspective. It will focus on six dimensions of the complex patterns of change:

22   Robert Reiner

Trends in crime and disorder

During the last quarter of the twentieth century crime and disorder increased to unprecedented levels. In the early 1950s the police recorded less than half a million offences per annum. By the mid 1960s this had increased to around 1 million, and by the mid 1970s 2 million. The 1980s showed even more staggering rises, with recorded crime peaking in 1992 at over 5.5 million— a tenfold increase in just under four decades (Barclay and Tavares 1999: 2). By 1997 recorded crime had fallen back to 4.5 million. Counting rule changes introduced in 1998 and 2002 make comparison of the subsequent figures especially fraught, but on the new rules (which undoubtedly exaggerate the increase) just under 6 million offences were recorded by the police for 2003/04 (Dodd *et al.* 2004).

There are of course enormous problems in interpreting recorded trends in crime (Maguire 2002; Hope 2005). It is impossible to determine with certainty how far the statistics track changes in offending, as distinct from shifts in reporting and recording practices by victims and police, and alterations in counting rules. The introduction of the British Crime Survey in 1981 does, however, cast light on a major aspect of the problems, variations in the propensity of victims to report crimes and of the police to record them. The General Household Survey in the 1970s had included questions on burglary victimization, so we also have some insight into reporting and recording changes in that crucial decade. During the 1970s a substantial proportion, but certainly not all, of the rise in recorded crime was due to increased reporting by victims. This was probably driven in large part by the spread of household contents insurance. Extrapolating back, the same may well be true of the 1960s.

However, during the 1980s police and survey recorded crime rose roughly in parallel. In the mid-1990s the two series diverged, with the police statistics registering falls. The British Crime Survey (BCS) by contrast found that victimization was still rising, but that the reporting and recording of crimes were falling. Since 1997 precisely the opposite has occurred. Above all because of counting rule changes, the police recorded statistics have recently started to rise again, whilst the BCS continues to record a decline in victimization[9] (Dodd *et al.* 2004). Recorded crime has for the last quarter of a century been at the highest levels since national statistics began to be collected in the 1850s. Victimization has become a normal phenomenon that most people have experienced.

Public disorder has also become a significant issue in a way it had not been at least since the 1930s. There was a clear resurgence of violent disorder and of militaristic policing in political and industrial conflict during the 1970s and 1980s, and in a variety of leisure contexts (Jefferson 1990; D. Waddington 1992; P.A.J. Waddington 2003 offer contrasting accounts).

Politicization of law and order

In the last quarter of the twentieth century the issue of law and order achieved an unprecedented prominence in Britain, following a similar politicization in the United States (Downes and Morgan 2002; Beckett 1997; Hale 2005b). A break becomes apparent around 1970, as shown most clearly by Downes and Morgan's analyses of election manifestos (Downes and Morgan 2002). Until then, crime and criminal justice had not been party political issues.

During the 1970s and 1980s partisan conflict on law and order became intensely heated. Margaret Thatcher's 1979 election victory owed much to the prominence she gave to the issue, and for most of the 1980s the Conservatives attacked Labour relentlessly on crime, gaining considerable electoral advantage (Downes 1983). The parties began to converge in the late 1980s. The Conservatives, embarrassed by the huge rise in recorded crime, moved to a more nuanced approach. This emphasized community crime prevention, and sought to reduce rising imprisonment in the 1991 Criminal Justice Act (Reiner and Cross 1991). Labour for its part began to distance itself from the

---

[9] This has made for an interesting politicization of the debate about crime statistics, especially in the context of the 2005 General Election. The police recorded statistics make Michael Howard's period as Home Secretary in the mid-1990s appear a success, and the post-1997 Labour government look bad. Conversely the BCS punctures the apparent Conservative success, and suggests that Labour has presided over a record fall in crime. So each party's electioneering focused on the deficiencies of the statistics that flattered the other.

24   Robert Reiner

image of being 'soft' on law and order (Downes and Morgan 2002: 290).

1993 marked a new watershed in law and order politics, with the advent of Michael Howard as Home Secretary and Tony Blair as his Shadow. A new 'second order' consensus on law and order emerged, based on a shared commitment to toughness (Downes and Morgan 2002: 295–7, 317–18; Ryan 2003). Subtle differences remain, and opportunism has brought about some odd temporary reversals. Labour retains more of an interest in being tough on the causes of crime, not just its perpetrators. But this is now limited primarily to encouraging local interventions in the immediate contexts of crime, supply side interventions to reduce unemployment, and highly focused attacks on family poverty (Newburn 2003; Matthews and Young 2003; Stenson and Edwards 2004). Added to this are attacks on permissiveness, blamed on the '60s', that seem to be plagiarized from the *Daily Mail*. Completely absent are the old concerns of social demo-cratic criminology, the structural sources of crime, such as inequality and unemployment (Downes 2004). The Tories primarily seem to be concerned to up the ante on toughness so as to regain the ground they lost in the 1990s, paradoxically combined with occasional attacks on some aspects of Labour policy from a civil libertarian direction, such as on identity cards. Thus law and order remains highly politicized, but in terms of a bidding war on effectiveness and toughness, not any fundamental differences of value or strategy.

Public discourse
The politicization of law and order is clearly related to broader changes in public discourse about crime and control. Opinion surveys broadly confirm the increasing salience of law and order concerns and generalized 'fear of crime' since the 1970s (Roberts and Stalans 2000; Hope and Sparks 2000; Roberts and Hough 2002; Nicholas and Walker 2004). There is also evidence of an increasing taste for 'cruelty' or 'punitiveness' in punishment (Simon 2001; Pratt *et al.* 2005).[10] This is bolstered by stereo-types of offending taken from media reports which, following a

---

[10] Matthews (2005) questions how far this has affected penal practice as distinct from rhetoric.

'law of opposites' (Surette 1998; Reiner 2002; Jewkes 2004), focus on the most atypical and grotesque crimes of violence. Although during the 1980s polls suggested a trend of declining police legitimacy, this has been reversed since the early 1990s, and the police remain a key security blanket in public imagery (Reiner 2000a: 11, 47; Loader and Mulcahy 2003).

Media discourse has moved increasingly to a law and order frame since the 1970s. In both fictional and news stories crime is represented as an ever greater threat. In the 1960s and 1970s there was a counter-trend, with an increasing minority of stories questioning the effectiveness and the legality of criminal justice agents (Reiner, Livingstone and Allen 2000, 2001). In the 1990s, however, this returned to overwhelming support of the police (Leishman and Mason 2003; Reiner 2003). Media stories increasingly dramatize the sufferings of individual victims as a means of demonizing offenders, orchestrating a vigilante discourse whereby cruelty inflicted on offenders is the only way of expressing sympathy for victims. This zero sum perspective was absent from media stories of the 1940s and 1950s, when concern to understand and rehabilitate offenders was presented as compatible with—if not a precondition of—helping victims (Reiner, Livingstone and Allen 2003).

Policy shifts

Criminal justice policy has shifted clearly, but not unambiguously, in a control oriented direction in the last three decades. The style of policy-making has also altered. In the pre-1970s consensus era, criminal justice policy was characterized by calm, expert-led decision-making, exemplified by the Royal Commission. The post-Thatcher style is a combination of internal government inquiries, with input from business people and the police rather than lawyers, the judiciary or academics, and relatively little if any public consultation. However there is also greater responsiveness to public opinion, as expressed in the popular media and populist campaigning (Ryan 2003, 2004).

During the Thatcher years the fierce rhetoric of statements on law and order was not matched by an unequivocal move towards tougher policing or punishment. Police expenditure did rise substantially in the first half of the 1980s as they performed their role in weakening the trade union movement and its

26   Robert Reiner

resistance to de-industrialization, as well as keeping the lid on the resulting pressures in the inner cities. But once this job was done, the police became subject increasingly to the new regimes for ensuring economy, efficiency and effectiveness in public services (Weatheritt 1993; McLaughlin and Murji 2000; Long 2003). The controversial Police and Criminal Evidence Act 1984 expanded police powers considerably, but was mitigated by accompanying safeguards (Reiner 2000a: ch. 6). In the late 1980s there was an attempt to move penal policy away from custodial sentencing, culminating in the Criminal Justice Act 1991 (Newburn 2003: 167–72).

During Michael Howard's period as Home Secretary policy shifted unequivocally in a tough law and order direction, as 'New' Labour attacked the record crime rises under the Tories, promising to be 'tough on crime, tough on the causes of crime'. 'Prison works' became Michael Howard's slogan to counter Labour's new toughness (Newburn 2003: 172–7). The police role was defined explicitly in narrow crime fighting terms, with managerial accountability to ensure 'businesslike' performance (Jones 2003).

Under the New Labour government since 1997 there has been a schizophrenic approach—pragmatic policies embodying the 'criminologies of everyday life', and demonstrative spasms of harsh control in response to moral panics about spectacularly shocking crimes (Garland 1996, 2001). The flagship Crime and Disorder Act 1998 embodied both elements (Newburn 2003: 92–4, 117–23, 206–3). On the one hand, it introduced a variety of measures reflecting a commitment to 'evidence-led', 'joined-up' policy. The Act required local authorities to form partnerships with the police and other agencies to develop strategies for reducing crime and disorder. It established a central Youth Justice Board and local Youth Offending Teams to co-ordinate, implement and monitor work with juveniles. It instituted a £400 million Crime Reduction Strategy to research, spread and evaluate best practice, which has been eviscerated by short-term electoral pressures (Maguire 2004; Hough 2004). The Crime and Disorder Act 1998 also included tougher measures, such as new minimum mandatory sentences for various offences, curfews for juveniles, the ending of the presumption that a child between ten and thirteen is incapable of committing a crime (*doli incapax*), and the introduction of anti-social behaviour orders (ASBOs).

Beyond Risk: A Lament for Social Democratic Criminology   27

Since 1998 legislation and policies have shifted the balance towards the demonstratively tough, and away from the pragmatic and evidence-led (Downes 2004). This has been embodied in a stream of new police powers (without balancing safeguards), and tougher sentencing laws (Tonry 2003). There has also been flirtation with the 'zero tolerance' policing that has been credited with the achievement of huge reductions in serious violent crime in New York City by its celebrants (Dennis 1998), although the crime falls are most likely to be the result of wider social factors and smarter rather than tougher policing (Eck and Maguire 2000; Karmen 2001).

Socio-economic and cultural change

Developments in crime and criminal justice are intertwined with the profound socio-economic and cultural changes that have occurred in the last four decades (Garland 2001; Taylor 1999; Young 1999). The economic consequences of globalization, and the shift from Keynesian to neo-liberal strategies of economic management, have generated pressures that drive crime upwards. The proliferation of consumer goods creates tempting targets for crime whilst consumer culture heightens expectations (Hayward 2004). Labour market changes generate higher unemployment and a shift to low paid part-time jobs, increasing poverty and inequality—which are exacerbated by the erosion of welfare state expenditure and less progressive taxation. The decline of deference, a more liberal culture, and changes in family life imply weaker informal social controls—conservatives' favourite explanation of rising crime.

Whilst criminogenic pressures have clearly increased in the last four decades, reflected in the large rise in recorded crime since the 1950s (paralleled in most Western countries although with some differences in timing), crime rates have been declining more recently. There is much debate about the relative parts played in the recent decline in crime rates by new modes of crime control ('smart' or 'tough'), and wider socio-economic change (Blumstein and Wallman 2000; Tonry 2004).

From criminology to contrology

Criminological paradigms have shifted in the last forty years, in interaction with these changes. Up to the mid-1960s criminology

28   Robert Reiner

had for nearly a century consisted primarily of research on causes of crime, with sociological approaches increasingly predominant over individualistic biological or psychological explanations (Rock 1988, 2002). Although the political commitments of criminological researchers varied, most tacitly accepted a broadly social democratic perspective on crime, seeing it as shaped by social deprivation and inequality. Dealing with crime required a combination of immediate penal interventions, primarily aimed at rehabilitation, and the broader social and economic amelioration that Keynesianism and the Welfare State were expected to deliver.

The first chink in this consensus came from the left. In the mid-1960s a variety of radical critiques developed (S. Cohen 1988). The 'labelling' perspective turned a critical spotlight on criminal justice, which came to be seen as constructing crime in discriminatory and oppressive ways. Although not a monolithic movement, most labelling theorists were associated with the libertarian and radical counterculture of the 1960s, taking the standpoint of deviants against social control agencies (Becker 1967).

The 'rehabilitative ideal' came under increasing attack from liberals and radicals (Allen 1981), primarily because the indeterminate sentencing implied by a therapeutic rather than just desserts rationale for penal intervention often meant longer incarceration and diminished prisoners' rights. This was joined with a growing body of research questioning the success of rehabilitative approaches in their own terms (Garland 2001: ch. 3). The positivist paradigm of research on causes of crime was criticized for being over-deterministic and taking the legitimacy of conventional definitions of deviance for granted, thus denying the meanings and autonomy of those labelled deviant.

These radical critiques did not for the most part question the political economy of crime suggested by social democratic criminology. They also saw crime as fundamentally rooted in the negative consequences of free market capitalism. The Marxist strand of critical criminology criticized social democrats for their lack of revolutionary zeal—*The New Criminology* castigated Merton as 'the cautious rebel' (Taylor, Walton and Young 1973)—but this was more a matter of attitude than analysis. *The New Criminology*'s concluding account of the ingredients of a 'fully social theory of deviance' is a sketch of what social democrats would also see as the categories for analysing crime and control. Social democrats would, however, question the prospects for a crime-free socialist society sketched in the last few pages as utopian and idealist—exactly as the authors themselves were to in the 1980s as they developed 'Left Realism' (Taylor 1981; Lea and Young 1984).

The fundamental assumptions of social democratic criminology were explicitly attacked with the advent of realism, in its initial right-wing guise, in the mid-1970s. The pivotal moment was James Q. Wilson's head-on assault on the idea of 'root causes' of crime (Wilson 1975). Of course what he meant was *social* causes of crime; after all ten years later he co-authored a 700-page tome on the causes of crime–individual biological and psychological causes (Wilson and Herrnstein 1985).[11] At the same time the resurgent rational choice theories, both in the guise of neo-classical economic theories (Becker 1968), and in the form of situational prevention (Cornish and Clarke 1986) and routine activities (Felson 2002) theories, explicitly rejected the notion of crime having any special causes at all. Crime was normal profit maximizing behaviour. It resulted from the open windows of opportunity left by irresponsible citizens, and from life-patterns that reduced informal guardianship, which enterprising individuals could profit from by offending. As Felson and Clarke put it explicitly, 'opportunity makes the thief' (Felson and Clarke 1998).

Left realism in the 1980s incorporated a political economy of crime that was very close to the mainstream of social democratic criminology. In their seminal book *What Is To Be Done About Law and Order?* Lea and Young offer an account of trends in crime and disorder in terms of relative deprivation[12] (Lea and Young 1984) that is very similar to Merton's anomie analysis.

Nonetheless, Jock Young explicitly sought to distance left realism from older social democratic criminology. This was

---

[11] This represents a broader resurgence of individualist theories of crime, biological and psychological (Fishbein 1990; Rose 2000; Hollin 2002).

[12] The concept of relative deprivation figured prominently in Merton's work (Merton and Rossi 1957) but strangely was not related by him to his parallel analysis of anomie.

30   Robert Reiner

primarily by his account of a supposed 'aetiological crisis' in social democratic criminology. 'The central problem for social democratic or Fabian positivism was that a wholesale improvement in social conditions resulted, not in a drop in crime, but the reverse' (Young 1988: 159). This misrepresents social democratic criminology as positing that poor social conditions directly cause crime, a view that may be dubbed 'vulgar' social democracy. As argued earlier, social democrats like Mannheim or Merton did not suggest any simple link between poverty and crime. In so far as they had a theory of causal connections between deprivation and offending this was in terms of relative not absolute deprivation (precisely the left realist account of aetiology). They also saw the acquisitive and anomic culture produced by consumerism and materialism as demoralizing and criminogenic. Thus several social democratic commentators anticipated that the new mass affluence after the late 1950s would exacerbate delinquency (Labour Party 1964: 5; Downes 1966; 1988: 103–9).

Whatever Happened to Social Democratic Criminology?

From right and wrong to risk

Clear shifts in crime control have thus developed in recent years, most apparently 'the new punitiveness' (Pratt *et al.* 2005), best interpreted as a form of 'acting out' (Garland 2001: 131–5). The key theme of practical crime control has become 'smartness': evidence and intelligence-led analysis of how to identify and neutralize risky places and people. Criminal justice is said to have become actuarial, concerned with calculating and minimizing risks through analysis of potential offenders and crime-prone situational contexts, rather than justice or reform (Feeley and Simon 1994; Ericson and Haggerty 1997; Rose 1999; Stenson and Sullivan 2000; Hope and Sparks 2000; Hudson 2003; O'Malley 2004).

This of course reflects a wider social and cultural turn identified by theorists of 'risk society' (Beck 1992). Whilst the terminology of 'risk' has become ubiquitous, it has been used in a variety of divergent ways. As Garland opens his comprehensive analysis of these: 'Risk is a calculation. Risk is a commodity. Risk is a capital. Risk is a technique of government. Risk is objective and scientifically knowable. Risk is subjective and socially constructed. Risk is a problem, a threat, a source of insecurity. Risk is a pleasure, a thrill, a source of profit and freedom. Risk is the means whereby we colonise and control the future. "Risk society" is our late modern world spinning out of control.' (Garland 2003: 49).

In relation to crime and control the rise of 'risk' seems to have two main dimensions: (a) increasing public and policy concern with risks of crime, problematically related to 'objective' patterns of risk of victimization; (b) new 'actuarial' ways of thinking about and responding to crime in terms of analysis of risky people, places, pursuits etc. The essence of risk-based approaches is usually seen as their instrumentalism, replacing attribution of blame, rehabilitating offenders or meting out retributive justice with pragmatic, business-like calculations of what works in terms of cost-effective harm reduction.

Giddens has claimed that the ascendancy of abstract systems of risk calculation in general spells the 'evaporation of morality . . . moral principles run counter to the concept of risk and to the mobilising dynamics of control' (Giddens 1991: 145). Ericson and Doyle challenge these arguments, pointing out that identifying phenomena as dangerous or risky 'is based on judgements about "goodness" and "badness" and distinctions between right and wrong' (Ericson and Doyle 2003: 2). Indeed risk perspectives, they argue, extend moral responsibility in that people who might once have been seen as innocent victims (whether of crime or accidents, disease or other suffering) are now often seen as at least partly culpable (ibid.: 4–9). This interpretation seems to make any evaluation, and any attribution of causal responsibility, a 'moral' judgement. However the term 'morality' is usually taken to be something much more specific, at the very least evaluation of behaviour with some degree of intentionality. I experience as 'bad' my window breaking in a storm. I also see it as 'bad' if someone smashes a brick through it. But it is only the latter that would normally be discussed in terms of *moral* badness.

Risk-based approaches differ fundamentally from older criminological perspectives in a number of other ways. Like the 'correctionalism' that was a prime target of 1960s and 1970s radical criminology, actuarialism takes for granted the legitimacy and purposes of crime control. However, unlike correctionalist approaches, it is not interested in the causes of offending other than as diagnostic indicators of risk (Metcalf and Stenson 2004).

Why has the social democratic criminology outlined earlier been displaced by the amoral and limited pragmatism of risk-based approaches? Most accounts of contemporary criminal justice assume that social democracy is dead, and security can only be found in smarter risk assessment and neutralization. But the explanations of why this perspective, all pervasive until some three decades ago, has withered or died seem somewhat perfunctory, taken for granted as what everyone already knows. The 'social' has been buried without much of an inquest on why or how it died, or indeed whether it is really dead or just dormant. The death certificate for social democracy is hastily read, and then the analysis moves on to detailed accounts of the implications for crime and criminal justice, and the emerging contours of new modes of control and governance.

There can be little doubt that a fundamental shift in political economy, social relations and culture has occurred during the last quarter of the twentieth century, with profound implications for crime and control. As outlined above, there has been a massive rise in crime rates (albeit with some attenuation recently). Concern about crime has become central in contemporary culture and politics. Responses have bifurcated between smart, fine-tuned, analytically based attempts to reduce risk, and cathartic emotional spasms of vindictiveness and cruelty against some identified offenders, in the name of justice to victims. In so far as causes of crime are considered at all they are seen in terms of individual or localized pathologies, or simply as radical evil. What has been eclipsed is the social democratic focus on analysing broader causes of crime and their amelioration through social reform.

Why has this happened, and what are its implications? There are at least three possible accounts:

Was the social democratic analysis of crime proven wrong?

The claim that the social democratic analysis of crime has been refuted is presented primarily in terms of what Jock Young referred to as the 'aetiological crisis'. As argued earlier, this attacked a straw person version of social democratic criminology— that crime is caused by absolute poverty. In its strongest forms

Beyond Risk: A Lament for Social Democratic Criminology   33

social democratic criminology did not postulate any mechanical relationship between economic conditions and crime. Whether economic circumstances were criminogenic depended on how they were experienced, and their consequences for morality and aspirations. Social democrats would expect crime to rise in a culture that is increasingly governed by economic success as the touchstone of all values, especially when this is coupled with an increasingly unequal social structure. Indeed Jock Young's analysis of the 'bulimia' of our contemporary culture itself shows this persuasively (Young 1999, 2003).

Such arguments can only be loosely tested by econometric studies of the relationship between economic variables and crime. Measures of poverty do not tap the meaning of it to those who are defined as poor. Indices of inequality cannot capture the concepts of anomie or relative deprivation, or a sense of injustice that could act as a 'technique of neutralisation' legitimating offending (Sykes and Matza 1957). Proportions of the population registering as unemployed cannot be translated straightforwardly into measures of deprivation, criminal opportunity, or the absence of the disciplining effects of work.

Nonetheless, on balance econometric studies *do* support the predictions of social democratic criminology about the crucial importance of the political economy for crime trends and patterns. Box's seminal 1987 review of the literature showed that even then a majority of studies found higher inequality and unemployment was related to more crime (Box 1987). Many of the studies he analysed were conducted during the post-war full employment decades when unemployment was primarily transitional and voluntary, without the criminogenic consequences of the growth of long-term exclusion of young people from the labour market since the 1970s.

The evidence of the significant links between political economy and crime is much clearer from later studies (Fielding, Clarke and Witt 2000; Marris 2003; Hale 2005a). Economic prosperity, as measured by levels of consumption or GDP for example, has a complex relationship to crime trends (Field 1990, 1999; Pyle and Deadman 1994; Hale 1998; Dhiri *et al.* 1999). In the long run it is positively related to overall recorded crime (which is predominantly property crime), probably above all because of the expansion of criminal opportunities. In the short

34   Robert Reiner

run, however, the relationship is negative, that is, recorded crime increases with economic downturns—possibly because of an increase in relative deprivation as incomes suddenly fall. Violent crime is positively related to short-term cyclical fluctuations, increasing with economic up-turns, possibly because of increasing alcohol consumption and socializing (Field 1990, 1999). The labour market is related to crime levels in part because of evidence that crime increases when unemployment is higher (Farrington *et al.* 1986; Witt, Clarke and Fielding 1999). The long-term shift to the predominance of part-time, insecure 'Mcjobs' in the service sector also is related to higher crime rates (Freeman 1995; Hale 1999; Grogger 2000). There also continues to be a plethora of evidence about the links between economic inequality and crime (Hale 2005a: 334–43). In short, there is plentiful evidence to confirm that the economic consequences of the neo-liberal economic policies pursued since the mid-1970s have had disastrous consequences for crime, exactly as social democratic criminology would predict (Davies 1998; Dorling 2004; Downes 2004; Garside 2004b; Hale 2005a).

Was social democratic criminology defeated by political campaigns?

During the heyday of the dominance of social democracy there was a relentless campaign against it mounted by business and free-market pressure groups (Fones-Wolf 1994; Frank 2001). They promoted a stream of publications and advertisements promoting the virtues of free markets (both in terms of efficiency and ethics) against the then dominant Keynesian, mixed economy, welfare state consensus.

In the crime control field too there were always powerful voices against the dominance of penal welfarism and social democratic criminology. These were found for example in the judiciary and the Conservative Party, most of whose members and backbenchers championed tougher punishments and greater social discipline (Ryan 1983; Morris 1989). During the late 1970s law and order became central to the Conservative Party's campaigning in the build-up to Margaret Thatcher's 1979 victory. They were aided in this by the emergence from the early 1970s of a vocal law and order lobby spearheaded by the Police Federation and some police chiefs (Reiner 1980; McLaughlin and Murji 1998; Loader and Mulcahy

2003). The mass media were also changing in their portrayal of crime, constructing law and order as a major issue with a growing focus on the (graphically represented) suffering of victims at the hands of demonized and feral offenders (Reiner, Livingstone and Allen 2000, 2001, 2003). The shift in discourse and practice about crime and control cannot be attributed solely to political and media campaigning (Ryan 2004). Nonetheless the campaigning was successful, because it resonated with profound changes in culture and political economy with which law and order perspectives had an elective affinity.

Was social democratic criminology politically defeated by 'New Times'?

An interlocking and mutually reinforcing set of changes from the late 1960s made law and order approaches to crime and control more congruent with emerging social and cultural patterns. Some of these were deep structural transformations, others were contingent policy choices—but once these had been made they set in train processes that embedded them and made reversal hard if not impossible.

The huge long-term rise in recorded crime described earlier was pivotal. In Jock Young's analysis it was 'the central motor of change' in post-war criminal justice and crime control (Young 1999: 35), and it is important in all accounts (Garland 2001: ch. 6; Loader and Sparks 2002: 85). However, this raises two more fundamental questions. What underlay the rise in recorded crime itself? Why did responses to rising crime rates take the law and order form? The answers to both questions lie in the package of wider social and cultural transformations.

The initial rise in recorded crime from the late 1950s is most plausibly explained by mass consumerism. This multiplied tempting targets for crime, and enhanced anomie throughout the social structure, fuelling motivations to acquire desired objects by whatever means were available. Consumerism also made it more likely that thefts would be reported, not least because of the spread of household insurance, increasing recorded crime rates much faster than crime itself. However the huge increases in recorded crime, and in political and industrial disorder, in the 1980s almost certainly reflect real increases in offending, as victimization studies confirm.

36   Robert Reiner

Rising crime and disorder was in large part explicable by the economic and social consequences of the adoption of neo-liberal economic policies after the mid-1970s. These hugely increased unemployment—largely in the shape of permanent never-employment for swathes of the young, especially amongst ethnic minorities in inner city areas. Many areas suffered economic and cultural devastation as they lost the industries that were the basis of their whole way of life (Davies 1998). Inequality rapidly increased, reversing nearly two centuries of slow progress towards greater social solidarity and inclusive citizenship. The result was literally murder. 'Behind the man with the knife is the man who sold him the knife, the man who did not give him a job, the man who decided that his school did not need funding, the man who closed down the branch plant where he could have worked, the man who decided to reduce benefit levels so that a black economy grew, all the way back to the woman who only noticed "those inner cities" some six years after the summer of 1981, and the people who voted to keep her in office ... Those who perpetrated the social violence that was done to the lives of young men starting some 20 years ago are the prime suspects for most of the murders in Britain' (Dorling 2004: 191).

There is of course another story. In July 2004 Tony Blair announced a new Home Office Strategic Plan which 'marks the end of the 1960s liberal, social consensus on law and order'. He explicitly blamed the '1960s revolution' for encouraging 'freedom without responsibility', when 'a society of different lifestyles spawned a group of young people who were brought up without parental discipline, without proper role models and without any sense of responsibility to or for others' (Blair 2004: 1). This embodies the quintessential conservative analysis of rising crime. In this view, the 'permissiveness' of the 1960s represented a dangerous democratization of the Enlightenment values of personal liberty, autonomy and self-realization. As it spread to the masses it brought the destruction of family, responsibility and self control—the bulwarks of civilisation (Wilson and Herrnstein 1985; Dennis and Erdos 2005). This line of argument cannot explain why tolerant and liberal cultures like those of Holland and the Scandinavian countries are not racked by crime, violence and law and order politics (Downes 1988; Tham 2001; Bondeson 2005)—though these are emerging with the impact of neo-liberalism and erosion of social democracy since the 1980s.

This is not to suggest that crime is a direct reflection of economic factors. Cultural and moral issues are crucial to explaining or understanding crime trends. What the conservative analysis completely ignores is that neo-liberal economic policies undermine informal control institutions and morality, producing cultures in which there is no restraint on egoism. The formation and stability of families, for example, has been undermined not by liberal ethics but by the erosion of secure and adequately paid employment, especially for men lower in the social scale (Campbell 1993; Currie 1998; Taylor 1999; Hale 1999). Exactly as forecast by Tawney eight decades ago,[13] the acquisitive society encouraged by free market liberalism has washed away the ethical values of responsibility for others and for 'society' (Tawney 1921). The character of the corporation director enjoined by company law (which 'dedicates the corporation to the pursuit of its own self-interest' Bakan 2004: 34–9) precisely fits the psychiatric model of the psychopath (ibid.: 56–7). The same is true of the 'responsibilized' citizen encouraged by neo-liberal strategies of governance–responsible, but only for oneself. In this culture of encouraged egoism the values of mutual concern and respect that animated social democracy seem to have no purchase, almost to have no meaning (as has been said of ethics more generally in the haunting opening of Macintyre 1981).

Conclusion: Barbarism or Social Democracy?

I have tried to show that social democratic criminology can provide an analysis of the changes in crime and control in the decades since it ceased to be the dominant paradigm, despite all the talk of its aetiological crisis. As represented by such figures as Merton, Mannheim or more recently David Downes (and outside criminology, Tawney), its primary emphasis was not a

---

[13] And indeed as Marx and Engels anticipated 150 years ago, when they famously declared: 'the bourgeois epoch...has torn away from the family its sentimental veil...All fixed, fast-frozen relations, with their train of ancient and venerable prejudices and opinions, are swept away...All that is solid melts into air, all that is holy is profaned' (Marx and Engels 1848 [1998]: 38).

38   Robert Reiner

mechanical relation between absolute poverty and crime—
although economic factors are in fact an important part of
explaining crime. Social democracy's focus was on the moral
forces emphasizing the importance of legitimate means above
goal attainment at any price, and shaping the aspirations that
underlie the experience of deprivation and unfairness. The
acquisitiveness of the consumerist society that developed from
the late 1950s would have been—and was—predicted to fan the
flames of crime, especially when it was coupled with the
increasing social injustice brought by neo-liberalism.

The problem is that neo-liberalism has not only exacerbated
the pressures leading to crime, and undermined the legal and
ethical constraints aimed at holding individuals and corporations to socially responsible practices. It has relinquished the
tools available to social democratic states to try and remedy this.
For example greater mobility of capital flows, partly because of
technological and cultural changes associated with globalization, but crucially because of liberalization of controls over
financial movements, has weakened the regulatory and taxation
capacity of individual governments in relation to corporations.
However the extent to which this has systematically and irretrievably weakened governments' abilities to tax for redistributive and welfare purposes is debatable, and the position
still varies considerably between different countries (Held 2004:
22–33). In any event, to the extent that the regulative capacity of
states to achieve social democratic ends has been undermined
this could be seen as a challenge not a fatal conclusion. The
social democratic deficit of states could lead to a search to
develop 'collaborative mechanisms of governance at supranational and global levels' (ibid.: 15).

If no attack on the fundamental causes of crime is mounted
then recorded crime will be likely to resume its upward march,
especially if economic conditions become more adverse. Beyond
this, the morally if not legally 'criminal' activities of corporations
and states, inflicting far greater harms and cruelties—as
'zemiologists' rightly argue (Hillyard *et al.* 2004)—will multiply.
Amongst these are the crime control practices documented by
many penal analysts: increasingly cruel punishment for apprehended offenders (Garland 2001; Simon 2001; Pratt *et al.* 2005).
Coupled with this is the 'responsibilized' self-protection enjoined

on the majority of citizens, producing ever greater social division and exclusion (Davis 1990; Young 1999; Taylor 1999; Reiner 2000b: 86–9). Paraphrasing Rosa Luxemberg, on present trends the choice is social democracy or barbarism.

Optimists and Blairites may say this flies in the face of the recent trend for crime rates to fall. Most analysts accept that crime has indeed decreased—although it is possible to debate this (cf. Garside 2004a and Dennis and Erdos 2005 from very different perspectives). But crime reduction has certainly not yet taken us away from what are still 'high crime' societies. There is also considerable debate about the sources of the trend to falling crime rates (Blumstein and Wallman 2000; Tonry 2004). The evidence suggests it is in *very* small part a product of greater toughness on crime (the huge increases in imprisonment above all, rather than the much vaunted 'zero tolerance' policing), and in greater measure increased smartness: more analytically based crime prevention and policing.

The more significant factors, however, have been nothing to do with criminal justice policy. Demographic trends have been important—declining proportions in the age-groups most prone to ordinary crime. The declines have also been to do with favourable economic trends: lower unemployment, and a partially successful attack on family poverty (Downes 2004)—a taste of social democracy by stealth. But because of its anxiety not to alienate *Daily Mail* reading circles by seeming to return to old Labourism, the government has had to disclaim those aspects of its policies that probably have the greatest impact on crime.

There is, however, some potential for a more overt espousal of social democratic criminology. Despite decades of propagandizing against it, there is evidence of latent public support for elements of the social democratic analysis of crime, hidden behind the more overt punitiveness revealed in surveys (Hart Research 2002; Allen 2004). In one recent study 65 per cent of Americans saw tackling causes as the key to controlling crime, compared to only 32 per cent favouring greater toughness–a substantial increase since a 1994 study when the respective proportions were 48 per cent and 42 per cent (Hart Research ibid.: 1–2). There is also growing, though of course still very tentative, discussion of social democracy in political and economic analysis

40   Robert Reiner

(Held 2004, Bakan 2004). This has been largely absent in criminology, but without it the future is bleak. Criminologists of the world unite, you have nothing to lose but your research grants.

Bibliography

Allen, F.A. (1981) *The Decline of the Rehabilitative Ideal* (Yale University Press: New Haven).

Allen, R. (2004) 'What Works in Changing Public Attitudes: Lessons From Rethinking Crime and Punishment' 1 *Journal for Crime, Conflict and the Media* 55–67.

Bakan, J. (2004) *The Corporation* (Constable: London).

Barclay, G. and Tavares, C. (1999) *Digest 4–Information on the Criminal Justice System in England and Wales* (Home Office: London).

Bauman, Z. (1995) *Life in Fragments* (Blackwell: Oxford).

Beck, U. (1992) *Risk Society* (Sage: London).

Becker, H. (1967) 'Whose Side Are We On?', 14 *Social Problems* 239–47.

Becker, G. (1968) 'Crime and Punishment: An Economic Approach', 76 *Journal of Political Economy* 175–209.

Beckett, K. (1997) *Making Crime Pay* (Oxford University Press: New York).

Bemmelen, J.M. (1960) 'Willem Adrian Bonger' in H. Mannheim (ed.), *Pioneers in Criminology* (Steven: London).

Blair, T. (2004) 'A New Consensus on Law and Order', Speech launching Home Office Strategic Plan for Criminal Justice, 19 July 2004 <www.labour.org.uk/news/tbcrimespeech>.

Blumstein, A. and Wallman, J. (eds.) (2000) *The Crime Drop in America* (Cambridge University Press: Cambridge).

Bondeson, U. (2005) 'Levels of Punitiveness in Scandinavia: description and explanations', in J. Pratt, D. Brown, M. Brown, S. Hallsworth, and W. Morrison (eds.), *The New Punitiveness* (Willan: Cullompton).

Bonger, W. (1936) *An Introduction to Criminology* (Methuen: London)

Bottoms, A.E. and Stevenson, S. (1992) 'What Went Wrong? Criminal Justice Policy in England and Wales 1945–70' in D. Downes (ed.), *Unravelling Criminal Justice* (Macmillan: London).

Boutellier, H. (2000) *Crime and Morality* (Kluwer: Dordrecht).

Bowling, B. and Phillips, C. (2002) *Racism, Crime and Justice* (Longman: London).

Box, S. (1987) *Recession, Crime and Punishment* (Macmillan: London).

Campbell, B. (1993) *Goliath: Britain's Dangerous Places* (Methuen: London).

Clarke, P. (1978) *Liberals and Social Democrats* (Cambridge University Press: Cambridge).

Cohen, G. (2000) *If You're An Egalitarian, How Come You're So Rich?* (Harvard University Press: Cambridge, Mass.).

Cohen, S. (1988) *Against Criminology* (Transaction: New Brunswick).

Cohen, S. (1998) 'Intellectual Scepticism and Political Commitment' in P. Walton and J. Young (eds.), *The New Criminology Revisited* (Macmillan: London).

Cornish, D. and Clarke, R. (eds.) (1986) *The Reasoning Criminal* (Springer-Verlag: New York).

Currie, E. (1998) *Crime and Punishment in America* (Holt: New York).

Currie, E. (2000) 'Reflections on Crime and Criminology at the Millennium', 2 *Western Criminology Review* 1–15.

Davies, N. (1998) *Dark Heart* (Verso: London).

Davis, M. (1990) *City of Quartz* (Vintage: London).

Dennis, N. (ed.) (1998) *Zero Tolerance* (IEA: London).

Dennis, N. and Erdos, G. (2005) *Cultures and Crimes* (Civitas: London).

Dennis, N. and Halsey, A.H. (1988) *English Ethical Socialism* (Oxford University Press: Oxford).

Dhiri, S., Brand, S. Harries, R. and Price, R. (1999) *Modelling and Predicting Property Crime Trends* (Home Office: London).

Ditton, J. (1979) *Controlology* (Macmillan: London).

Dodd, T., Nicholas, S., Povey, D. and Walker, A. (2004) *Crime in England and Wales 2003/4* (Home Office: London).

Dorling, D. (2004) 'Prime Suspect: Murder in Britain' in P. Hillyard, C. Pantazis, S. Tombs and D. Gordon (eds.), *Beyond Criminology* (Pluto: London).

Downes, D. (1966) *The Delinquent Solution* (Routledge: London).

Downes, D. (1983) *Law and Order—Theft of an Issue* (Fabian Society/ Labour Campaign for Criminal Justice: London).

Downes, D. (1988) *Contrasts in Tolerance* (Oxford University Press: Oxford).

Downes, D. (2004) 'New Labour and the Lost Causes of Crime' 55 *Criminal Justice Matters* 4–5.

Downes, D. and Morgan, R. (2002) 'The Skeletons in the Cupboard: the Politics of Law and Order at the Turn of the Millennium' in M. Maguire, R. Morgan and R. Reiner (eds.), *The Oxford Handbook of Criminology* (3rd edn., Oxford University Press: Oxford).

Dworkin, R. (2000) *Sovereign Virtue* (Harvard University Press: Cambridge, Mass).

Eck, J. and Maguire, E. (2000) 'Have Changes in Policing Reduced Violent Crime? A Review of the Evidence' in A. Blumstein and

42   Robert Reiner

J. Wallman (eds.), *The Crime Drop in America* (Cambridge University Press: Cambridge).

Engels, F. (1880) *Socialism: Utopian and Scientific* in *Marx and Engels—Selected Works* (Lawrence and Wishart: London [1968]: 375–428).

Ericson, R. and Doyle, A. (eds.) (2003) *Risk and Morality* (University of Toronto Press: Toronto).

Ericson, R. and Haggerty, K. (1997) *Policing Risk Society* (Oxford University Press: Oxford).

Farrington, D., Galagher, B. Morley, L. St. Ledger, R.J. and West, D.J. (1986) 'Unemployment, School Leaving and Crime' 26 *British Journal of Criminology* 335–56.

Feeley, M. and Simon, J. (1994) 'Actuarial Justice: The Emerging New Criminal Law' in D. Nelken (ed.), *The Futures of Criminology* (Sage: London).

Felson, M. (2002) *Crime and Everyday Life* (3rd edn., Pine Forge: London).

Felson, M. and Clarke, R. (1998) *Opportunity Makes the Thief: Practical Theory for Crime Prevention* (Home Office: London).

Field, S. (1990) *Trends in Crime and their Interpretation* (HMSO: London).

Field, S. (1999) *Trends in Crime Revisited* (Home Office: London).

Fielding, N., Clarke, A. and Witt, R. (eds.) (2000) *The Economic Dimensions of Crime* (Macmillan: London).

Figes, O. (2005) 'The Fiddler's Children' 52 *New York Review of Books* no 10, 8–12.

Fishbein, D.H. (1990) 'Biological Perspectives in Criminology' 28 *Criminology* 27–72.

Fitzgerald, M. (2004) 'Understanding Ethnic Differences in Crime Statistics' 55 *Criminal Justice Matters* 22–3.

Fones-Wolf, E. (1994) *Selling Free Enterprise: The Business Assault on Labour and Liberalism, 1945–1960* (University of Illinois Press: Urbana).

France, A. (1992) *Le Lys Rouge* (Flammarion: Paris).

Frank, T. (2001) *One Market Under God* (Secker and Warburg: London).

Frank, T. (2004) *What's the Matter With America?* (Secker and Warburg: London).

Freeman, R.B. (1995) 'Crime and the Labour Market' in J.Q. Wilson and J. Petersilia (eds.), *Crime* (ICS Press: SanFrancisco).

Garland, D. (1985) *Punishment and Welfare* (Gower: Aldershot).

Garland, D. (1996) 'The Limits of the Sovereign State: Strategies of Crime Control in Contemporary Societies' 36 *British Journal of Criminology* no 4: 1–27.

Beyond Risk: A Lament for Social Democratic Criminology   43

Garland, D. (2001) *The Culture of Control* (Oxford University Press: Oxford).

Garland, D. (2003) 'The Rise of Risk' in R. Ericson and A. Doyle (eds.), *Risk and Morality* (University of Toronto Press: Toronto).

Garland, D. and Sparks, R. (2000) 'Criminology, Social Theory and the Challenge of Our Times' 40 *British Journal of Criminology* 189–204.

Garside, R. (2004a) *Crime, Persistent Offenders and the Justice Gap* (Crime and Society Foundation: London).

Garside, R. (2004b) 'Is It The Economy?' 55 *Criminal Justice Matters* 32–3.

Gatrell, V. (1980) 'The Decline of Theft and Violence in Victorian and Edwardian England' in V. Gatrell, B. Lenman and G. Parker (eds.), *Crime and the Law* (Europa: London).

Gelsthorpe, L. (2002) 'Feminism and Criminology' in M. Maguire, R. Morgan and R. Reiner (eds.), *The Oxford Handbook of* (3rd edn., Oxford University Press: Oxford).

Giddens, A. (1991) *Modernity and Self Identity* (Polity: Cambridge).

Grogger, J. (2000) 'An Economic Model of Recent Trends in Violence' in A. Blumstein and J. Wallman (eds.), *The Crime Drop in America* (Cambridge University Press: Cambridge).

Hale, C. (1998) 'Crime and the Business Cycle in Post-war Britain Revisited' 38 *British Journal of Criminology* 681–98.

Hale, C. (1999) 'The Labour Market and Post-war Crime Trends in England and Wales' in P. Carlen and R. Morgan (eds.), *Crime Unlimited* (Macmillan: Basingstoke).

Hale, C. (2005a) 'Economic Marginalisation and Social Exclusion' in C. Hale, K. Hayward, A. Wahidin and E. Wincup (eds.), *Criminology* (Oxford University Press: Oxford).

Hale, C. (2005b) 'The Politics of Law and Order' in C. Hale, K. Hayward, A. Wahidin and E. Wincup (eds.), *Criminology* (Oxford University Press: Oxford).

Hart Research (2002) *Changing Public Attitudes Toward the Criminal Justice System* (Peter D. Hart Research Associates: Washington).

Hayward, K. (2004) *City Limits* (Glasshouse: London).

Heidensohn, F. (2002) 'Gender and Crime' in M. Maguire, R. Morgan and R. Reiner (eds.), *The Oxford Handbook of Criminology* (3rd edn., Oxford University Press: Oxford).

Held, D. (2004) *Global Covenant* (Polity: Cambridge).

Henry, S. and Lanier, M. (eds.) (2001) *What is Crime?* (Rowman and Littlefield: Lanham, MD).

Hillyard, P., Pantazis, C., Tombs, S. and Gordon, D. (eds.) (2004) *Beyond Criminology* (Pluto: London).

44   Robert Reiner

Hollin, C. (2002) 'Criminological Psychology' in M. Maguire, R. Morgan and R. Reiner (eds.), *The Oxford Handbook of Criminology* (3rd edn., Oxford University Press: Oxford).

Hope, T. (2005) 'What Do Crime Statistics Tell Us?' in C. Hale, K. Hayward, A. Wahidin and E. Winup (eds.), *Criminology* (Oxford University press: Oxford).

Hope, T. and Sparks, R. (eds.) (2000) *Crime, Risk and Insecurity* (Routledge: London).

Hough, M. (ed.) (2004) 'Evaluating the Crime Reduction Programme in England and Wales' 4 *Criminal Justice* no 3 (Special Issue).

Hudson, B. (2003) *Justice in the Risk Society* (Sage: London).

Jackson, T. (2004) *Chasing Progress: Beyond Economic Growth* (New Economics Foundation: London).

Jefferson, T. (1990) *The Case Against Paramilitary Policing* (Open University Press: Milton Keynes).

Jenkins, P. (1989) *Mrs Thatcher's Revolution* (Pan: London).

Jewkes, Y. (2004) *Media and Crime* (Sage: London).

Johnston, L. and Shearing, C. (2003) *Governing Security* (Routledge: London).

Jones, T. (2003) 'The Governance and Accountability of Policing' in T. Newburn (ed.), *Handbook of Policing* (Willan: Cullompton).

Jones, T. and Newburn, T. (1998) *Private Security and Public Policing* (Oxford University Press: Oxford).

Kant, I. (1785) *Groundwork of the Metaphysics of Morals* (Cambridge University Press: Cambridge, 1998).

Karmen, A. (2001) *New York Murder Mystery: The Story Behind the Crime Crash of the 1990s* (New York: New York University Press).

Labour Party (1964) *Crime: A Challenge to Us All* (London: Labour Party).

Lacey, N., Wells, C. and Quick, O. (2003) *Understanding Criminal Law* (London: Butterworths).

Lea, J. (2002) *Crime and Modernity* (London: Sage).

Lea, J. and Young, J. (1984) *What is to be Done About Law and Order?* (Harmondsworth: Penguin).

Leishman, F. and Mason, P. (2003) *Policing and the Media* (Willan: Cullompton).

Levinas, E. (1969) *Totality and Infinity* (Duquesne University Press: Pittsburgh).

Loader, I. and Mulcahy, A. (2003) *Policing and the Condition of England* (Oxford University Press: Oxford).

Loader, I. and Sparks, R. (2002) 'Contemporary Landscapes of Crime, Disorder and Control: Governance, Risk, and Globalisation' in M. Maguire, R. Morgan and R. Reiner (eds.), *The Oxford Handbook of Criminology* (3rd edn., Oxford University Press: Oxford).

Long, M. (2003) 'Leadership and Performance Management' in T. Newburn (ed.), *Handbook of Policing* (Willan: Cullompton).

Lukes, S. (1985) *Marxism and Morality* (Oxford University Press: Oxford).

Macintyre, A. (1981) *After Virtue* (Duckworth: London).

Maguire, M. (2002) 'Crime Statistics: The Data Explosion and its Implications' in M. Maguire, R. Morgan and R. Reiner (eds.), *The Oxford Handbook of Criminology* (3rd edn., Oxford University Press: Oxford).

Maguire, M. (2004) 'The Crime Reduction Programme in England and Wales', 4 *Criminal Justice* 213–38.

Mannheim, H. (1946) *Criminal Justice and Social Reconstruction* (Routledge: London).

Marris, R. (2003) *Survey of the Research Literature on the Economic and Criminological Factors Influencing Crime Trends* (Home Office: London).

Marshall, T.H. (1950) *Citizenship and Social Class* (Cambridge University Press: Cambridge).

Marx, K. (1867) *Capital Vol.1* (Lawrence and Wishart: London, 1970).

Marx, K. and Engels, F. (1848) *The Communist Manifesto* (Verso: London, 1998).

Matthews, R. (2005) 'The Myth of Punitiveness' 9 *Theoretical Criminology* 175–202.

Matthews, R. and Young, J. (eds.) (2003) *The New Politics of Crime and Punishment* (Willan: Cullompton).

McLaughlin, E. and Murji, K. (1998) 'Resistance Through Representation: "Storylines", Advertising and Police Federation Campaigns' 8 *Policing and Society* 367–400.

McLaughlin, E. and Murji, K. (2000) 'Lost Connections and New Directions: Neo-liberalism, New Public Managerialism and the "Modernisation" of the British Police' in K. Stenson and R. Sullivan (eds.), *Crime, Risk and Justice* (Willan: Cullompton).

Merton, R. (1938) 'Social Structure and Anomie' 3 *American Sociological Review* 672–82 (revised in R. Merton *Social Theory and Social Structure* (Free Press: London, 1957).

Merton, R. (1995) 'Opportunity Structure: The Emergence, Diffusion and Differentiation of a Sociological Concept, 1930s–1950s' in F. Adler and W.S. Laufer (eds.), *The Legacy of Anomie Theory* (Transaction: New Brunswick).

46   Robert Reiner

Merton, R. and Rossi, A. (1957) 'Contributions to the Theory of Reference Group Behaviour' in R. Merton, *Social Theory and Social Structure* ch.8 (originally 1950).

Metcalf, C. and Stenson, K. (2004) 'Managing Risk and the Causes of Crime' *Criminal 55 Justice Matters* 8–9.

Morris, T. (1989) *Crime and Criminal Justice Since 1945* (Blackwell: Oxford).

Morrison, W. (2005) 'What is Crime? Contrasting Definitions and Perspectives' in C. Hale, K. Hayward, A. Wahidin and E. Wincup (eds.), *Criminology* (Oxford University Press: Oxford).

Nelken, D. (2002) 'White-collar Crime' in M. Maguire, R. Morgan and R. Reiner (eds.), *The Oxford Handbook of Criminology* (Oxford University Press: Oxford).

Newburn, T. (2003) *Crime and Criminal Justice Policy* (2nd edn., Longman: London).

Nicholas, S. and Walker, A. (2004) *Crime, Disorder and the Criminal Justice System: Public Attitudes and Perceptions* (Home Office: London).

Nietzche, F. (1885) *Beyond Good and Evil* (New York: Random House: New York, 2000).

O'Malley, P. (2004) *Risk, Uncertainty and Government* (Glasshouse: London).

Palast, G. (2004) *The Best Democracy Money Can Buy* (Plume: New York).

Pratt, J., Brown, D., Brown, M., Hallsworth, S. and Morrison, W. (eds.) (2005) *The New Punitiveness* (Willan: Cullompton).

Pyle, D. and Deadman, D. (1994) 'Crime and the Business Cycle in Post-war Britain' 34 *British Journal of Criminology* 339–57.

Radzinowicz, L. and Hood, R. (1985) *A History of English Criminal Law vol. 5: The Emergence of Penal Policy in Victorian and Edwardian England* (Stevens: London).

Rawls, J. (1971) *A Theory of Justice* (Harvard University Press: Cambridge, Mass).

Reiner, R. (1980) 'Fuzzy Thoughts: The Police and Law and Order Politics' 28 *Sociological Review* 377–413.

Reiner, R. (1984) 'Crime, Law and Deviance: The Durkheim Legacy' in S. Fenton *Durkheim and Modern Sociology* (Cambridge University Press: Cambridge).

Reiner, R. (2000a) *The Politics of the Police* (3rd edn., Oxford University Press: Oxford).

Reiner, R. (2000b) 'Crime and Control in Britain' 34 *Sociology* 71–94.

Reiner, R. (2002) 'Justice' in Penner, J., Schiff, D. and Nobles, R. (eds.), *Introduction to Jurisprudence and Legal Theory* (Oxford University Press: Oxford).

Reiner, R. (2003) 'Policing and the Media' in T. Newburn (ed.), *Handbook of Policing* (Willan: Cullompton).

Reiner, R. and Cross, M. (eds.) (1991) *Beyond Law and Order* (London: Macmillan).

Reiner, R., Livingstone, S. and Allen, J. (2000) 'No More Happy Endings? The Media and Popular Concern About Crime Since the Second World War' in T. Hope and R. Sparks (eds.), *Crime, Risk and Insecurity* (Routledge: London).

Reiner, R., Livingstone, S. and Allen, J. (2001) 'Casino Culture: The Media and Crime in a Winner-Loser Society' in K. Stenson and R. Sullivan (eds.), *Crime and Risk Society* (Willan: Cullompton).

Reiner, R., Livingstone, S. and Allen, J. (2003) 'From Law and Order to Lynch Mobs: Crime News Since the Second World War' in P. Mason (ed.), *Criminal Visions* (Willan: Cullompton).

Roberts, J. and Stalans, L. (2000) *Public Opinion, Crime and Criminal Justice* (Westview: Boulder).

Roberts, J. and Hough, M. (eds.) (2002) *Changing Attitudes to Punishment* (Willan: Cullompton).

Rock, P. (ed.) (1988) *A History of British Criminology* (Oxford University Press: Oxford).

Rock, P. (2002) 'Sociological Theories of Crime' in M. Maguire, R. Morgan and R. Reiner (eds.), *The Oxford Handbook of Criminology* (3rd edn., Oxford University Press: Oxford).

Rorty, R. (1989) *Contingency, Irony and Solidarity* (Cambridge University Press: Cambridge).

Rorty, R. (1999) *Philosophy and Social Hope* (Penguin: London).

Rose, N. (1999) *Powers of Freedom* (Cambridge University Press: Cambridge).

Rose, N. (2000) 'The Biology of Culpability: Pathological Identities in a Biological Culture' 4 *Theoretical Criminology* 5–34.

Ryan, M. (1983) *The Politics of Penal Reform* (Longman: London).

Ryan, M. (2003) *Penal Policy and Political Culture in England and Wales* (Waterside: Winchester).

Ryan, M. (2004) 'Red Tops, Populists and the Irresistible Rise of the Public Voice(s)' 1 *Journal for Crime, Conflict and the Media* 1–14.

Sartre, J-P. (1948) *Les Mains Sales* (Routledge: London, 1985).

Sassoon, D. (1996) *One Hundred Years of Socialism* (New Press: New York).

Simon, J. (2001) ' "Entitlement to Cruelty?": Neo-liberalism and the Punitive Mentality in the United States' in K. Stenson and R. Sullivan (eds.), *Crime, Risk and Justice* (Willan: Cullompton).

Stenson, K. and Edwards, A. (2004) 'Policy Transfer in Local Crime Control: Beyond Naïve Emulation' in T. Newburn and R. Sparks (eds.), *Criminal Justice and Political Cultures* (Willan: Cullompton).

48   Robert Reiner

Stenson, K. and Sullivan, R. (eds.) (2001), *Crime, Risk and Justice* (Willan: Cullompton).

Surette, R. (1998) *Media, Crime and Criminal Justice* (2nd edn., Wadsworth: Belmont).

Sutherland, E. (1983) *White-Collar Crime: The Uncut Version* (New Haven: Yale University Press).

Sykes, G. and Matza, D. (1957) 'Techniques of Neutralisation' 33 *American Sociological Review* 46–62.

Tawney, R.H. (1921) *The Acquisitive Society* (Bell: London).

Taylor, I. (1981) *Law and Order: Arguments for Socialism* (Macmillan: London).

Taylor, I. (1999) *Crime in Context* (Polity: Cambridge).

Taylor, I., Walton, P. and Young, J. (1973) *The New Criminology* (Routledge: London).

Tham, H. (2001) 'Law and Order As A Leftist Project. The Case of Sweden' 3 *Punishment and Society* 409–26.

Tonry, M. (ed.) (2003) *Confronting Crime: Crime Control Under New Labour* (Willan: Cullompton).

Tonry, M. (2004) *Thinking About Crime* (Oxford University Press: New York).

Waddington, D. (1992) *Contemporary Issues in Public Disorder* (Routledge: London).

Waddington, P.A.J. (2003) 'Policing Public Order and Political Contention' in T. Newburn (ed.), *Handbook of Policing* (Willan: Cullompton).

Walzer, M. (2005) 'All God's Children Got Values' *Dissent* (Spring) 35–40.

Weatheritt, M. (1993) 'Measuring Police Performance: Accounting or Accountability?' in R. Reiner and S. Spencer (eds.), *Accountable Policing* (IPPR: London).

Weber, M. (1918) 'Science As A Vocation' and 'Politics As A Vocation', *The Vocation Lectures* (Indianapolis: Hackett: Indianapolis, 2004).

Wilson, J.Q. (1975) *Thinking About Crime* (Vintage: New York).

Wilson, J.Q. and Herrnstein, R. (1985) *Crime and Human Nature* (Simon and Schuster: New York).

Witt, R., Clarke, A. and Fielding, N. (1999) 'Crime and Economic Activity: a Panel Data Approach' 39 *British Journal of Criminology* 391–400.

Young, J. (1986) 'The Failure of Criminology: The Need for a Radical Realism' in R. Matthews and J. Young (eds.), *Confronting Crime* (Sage: London).

Young, J. (1988) 'Radical Criminology in Britain: The Emergence of a Competing Paradigm' 2 *Britsih Journal of Criminology* 289–313.

Beyond Risk: A Lament for Social Democratic Criminology   49

Young, J. (1999) *The Exclusive Society* (Sage: London).

Young, J. (2003) 'Merton With Energy, Katz With Structure: The Sociology of Vindictiveness and the Criminology of Transgression' 7 *Theoretical Criminology* 389–414.

Young, J. (2005) 'Foreword' in C. Hale, K. Hayward, A. Wahidin and E. Wincup (eds.), *Criminology* (Oxford University Press: Oxford).

Zedner, L. (2004) *Criminal Justice* (Oxford University Press: Oxford).

[15]
Law and Order—A 20:20 Vision

Introduction—Law and Order 1984–2020

Twenty-one years ago Michael Freeman gave a *Current Legal Problems* lecture called 'Law and Order in 1984'.[1] It was an impressively knowledgeable and accurate analysis of the rise of law and order politics in Britain in the run-up to the 1979 Conservative Party victory under Margaret Thatcher, and in the early years of her government. It detailed the truncheon-rattling rhetoric of the 'New Right', and the Thatcher government's budget bonanzas for expenditure on policing and prisons at the same time as it culled social spending. It offered a detailed analysis of the Police and Criminal Evidence Act 1984,[2] depicting it as 'the cornerstone of contemporary "law and order" politics'.[3] There was discussion of the restrictions on the powers of trade unions, new public order legislation, expanded powers against terrorism, tougher penal policy, and a transformation of policing towards a more proactive social control style based on information-led surveillance and targeting. Freeman concluded that the law and order policies of the New Right threatened our liberties and set us in the direction of George Orwell's dystopian *1984*. He ended with a call to 'fight against current law and order policies', in favour of more socially just ones that paid at least equal attention to the crimes of the powerful as they did to the crimes of the powerless.[4]

Freeman's paper was and is a state-of-the-art representation of liberal and Left thinking about law and order in the early 1980s. But it now reads nostalgically as a memento of a bygone age of comparative innocence. Inspired by Orwell's dystopian vision, it nonetheless failed to anticipate the enormity of the crime and control changes, and broader social transformation, that were to come. This is not a criticism of Freeman's failure to acquire the mantle of 'Mystic Michael'. No analyses at the time provided any inkling of how profoundly the whole context for

---

[1] M Freeman, 'Law and Order in 1984' (1984) *Current Legal Problems* 175–231.
[2] Hereafter 'PACE'.   [3] Freeman, n 1 above.   [4] ibid 220.

discussions of crime and criminal justice was to change over the last two decades of the twentieth century.

The vision of 2020 I am going to offer is an even more pessimistic one, with only the most tenuous prospect of amelioration. It is based on a reading of current trends, but I very much hope that it will be refuted by events and turn out to be myopic rather than 20:20 vision. The account I will give examines six issues: (1) the rise of law and order politics; (2) what is crime?; (3) what has actually happened to crime trends?; (4) the development of contemporary crime control policies; (5) the explanation of trends in crime; and (6) how to explain and assess the new punitiveness in crime control policies? It will then conclude with a discussion of possible futures.

The Rise of Law and Order Politics

Until the late 1960s criminal justice policy had not been a partisan policy issue, at least since the early nineteenth century. According to Downes and Morgan's definitive study it did not feature in any political party's election manifesto between the Second World War and 1970.[5] Nor was crime an important issue to the public until the 1970s, at least as registered by opinion polls, although it has been a favourite theme in all branches of popular entertainment for centuries.[6] Some specific aspects of criminal justice policy were politically controversial, notably capital punishment, and competing penal policy lobbies campaigned vigorously.[7] Particularly spectacular or salacious crimes have always been regular topics of popular fascination, part of a perennial tendency for middle-aged, respectable opinion to bewail the supposedly declining moral standards of young people, which seemed to sag in line with the belts of the lamenters.[8] But the overall state of crime was not a widespread cause of concern, nor was criminal justice policy subject to political controversy and conflict. For example, the publication of new crime statistics, which

---

[5] D Downes and R Morgan, 'The Skeletons in the Cupboard: The Politics of Law and Order at the Turn of the Millennium' in M Maguire, R Morgan, and R Reiner (eds), *The Oxford Handbook of Criminology* (3rd edn) (Oxford: Oxford University Press, 2002).

[6] R Reiner, 'Media Made Criminality: The Representation of Crime in the Mass Media' in Maguire *et al*, ibid.

[7] M Ryan, *The Acceptable Pressure Group* (Farnborough: Saxon House, 1978); M Ryan, *The Politics of Penal Reform* (London: Longman, 1983); T Morris, *Crime and Criminal Justice in Britain since 1945* (Oxford: Blackwell, 1989).

[8] G Pearson, *Hooligan* (London: Macmillan, 1983).

Law and Order   131

now are regularly a stimulus to 'shock-horror' news headlines, only began to feature in newspaper reports in the 1970s, and then in a minor way.[9]

'Law and order' had first become politicized in the USA in the 1960s.[10] 'Law and order' itself is an old phrase, traditionally invoked as if it represented some unproblematic, linked perfect partnership, like Laurel and Hardy or 'bangers and mash'. But as it came to be used as a political slogan it became impregnated with controversial meanings. Classical social theory of all kinds had been explicitly or implicitly sceptical about the law playing a significant part in social order.[11] Order was the product of complex processes of social interdependence and informal control,[12] or of ruling class interests,[13] or of different types of power and authority.[14] The law was the expression or product of order, not its source.

Like much of the current dominant Right-wing policies that prevail in the USA today, the law and order trail was blazed by Barry Goldwater in his abortive but prophetic Presidential bid in 1964. In the hands of the political Right, the demand for law and order condensed a number of specific meanings—above all, that law could and should produce order—but that it failed to do so because of weak formulation and enforcement. Law's purpose was crime control, but it was shackled by excessive due process restraints.[15] The law and its front-line troops, the police, should be unleashed to restore order. Law and order became a successful campaigning slogan for Richard Nixon in his 1968 election victory, becoming a codeword for race, culture, and generational backlash. As we now know Nixon, Spiro Agnew, and the rest of the elite Republican cadre

[9] R Reiner, S Livingstone, and J Allen, 'From Law and Order to Lynch Mobs: Crime News since the Second World War' in P Mason (ed), *Criminal Visions* (Cullompton: Willan, 2003), 25–6.

[10] K Beckett, *Making Crime Pay* (New York: Oxford University Press, 1997), ch 3.

[11] R Reiner, 'Classical Social Theory and Law' in J Penner, D Schiff, and R Nobles (eds) *Jurisprudence* (London: Butterworths, 2002).

[12] E Durkheim, *The Division of Labour in Society* (Glencoe: Free Press, 1973).

[13] K Marx, *Capital Vol 1* (London: Penguin, 1976), ch 10.

[14] M Weber, *Economy and Society Vol 1* (Berkeley: University of California Press, 1978), 217–20.

[15] The distinction between 'crime control' and 'due process' models of criminal justice was suggested by H Packer, *The Limits of the Criminal Sanction* (Stanford, Calif: Stanford University Press, 1968). For discussion of whether these values do conflict see D McBarnet, *Conviction* (London: Macmillan, 1981); M McConville, A Sanders, and R Leng, *The Case for the Prosecution* (London: Routledge, 1991); D Smith, 'Case Construction and the Goals of the Criminal Process' (1997) 37(3) *British Journal of Criminology* 319; M McConville, A Sanders, and R Leng, 'Descriptive or Critical Sociology?' (1997) 37(3) *British Journal of Criminology* 347; D Smith, 'Reform or Moral Outrage?' (1998) 38(4) *British Journal of Criminology* 616; A Ashworth and M Redmayne, *The Criminal Process* (3rd edn) (Oxford: Oxford University Press, 2005); A Sanders and R Young, *Criminal Justice* (3rd edn) (London: Butterworths, 2006).

of 1968 knew what they were talking about in relation to law and order, mostly ending up on the wrong side of the bars a few years later.

The politicization of law and order was heralded in Britain in the 1970 General Election, when the Conservative Party manifesto said that 'the Labour Government cannot entirely shrug off responsibility' for rising 'crime and violence'.[16] It also linked crime with industrial disputes as instances of 'the age of demonstration and disruption'.[17] The Labour manifesto replied by attacking the Conservatives' attempt 'to exploit for Party political ends the issue of crime and law enforcement'.[18]

It was under Margaret Thatcher's leadership of the Conservative Party that the politicization of law and order really accelerated. During the late 1970s, in the build-up to her election victory in 1979, Mrs Thatcher blamed the Labour government directly for rising crime and disorder, pledging a 'ring of steel' to protect people against lawlessness. She promised to boost the resources and powers of the police to prevent and clear up crime, and to sharply toughen penal policy, reversing the softness on crime that was attributed to Labour. The Tories' law and order campaign was greatly helped by the emergence of the police as a political lobby, backing up the Conservative's agenda in a series of advertisements and speeches.[19] The issue was a major factor in Thatcher's 1979 election victory, according to polls monitoring the shifts in public opinion.[20] The police were directly rewarded for their open support when the Conservatives implemented in full a recommended pay rise as one of their first acts in office.

The party political gulf on law and order reached its widest point in the mid-1980s. The key conflicts were over the policing of the urban disorders and of the Miners' Strike of 1984–5—both results of the economic and social dislocation engendered by the Thatcher government's monetarist policies—the Police and Criminal Evidence Act 1984, and the campaigns for democratic police accountability. On all these issues Labour took a civil libertarian stance, attacking the Conservative government for violating the principles of the rule of law. Labour also attacked Conservative law and order policies for being counter-productive in increasing social divisions, and aggravating rather than reforming the

---

[16] Downes and Morgan, n 5 above, 288.   [17] ibid.   [18] ibid 289.

[19] R Reiner, 'Fuzzy Thoughts: The Police and Law and Order Politics' (1980) 28(2) *Sociological Review* 377; E McLaughlin and K Murji, 'Resistance through Representation: "Storylines", Advertising and Police Federation Campaigns' (1998) 8(4) *Policing and Society* 367; I Loader and A Mulcahy, *Policing and the Condition of England* (Oxford: Oxford University Press, 2003), ch 7.

[20] D Butler and D Kavanagh, *The British General Election 1979* (London: Macmillan, 1980), 163.

root causes of crime in social inequality and relative deprivation. Whilst this position may have had the support of the majority of criminologists, it was an electoral liability for Labour. In the 1984 and 1987 General Elections the Tories attacked Labour for being 'soft' on crime because of its concerns about civil liberties, 'permissiveness', links with trade union-ism—associated with disorder—and failure to develop any short-term solutions to bolster public protection.

In the late 1980s signs appeared of a new cross-party consensus on law and order. The Conservatives began to offer a more nuanced approach, perhaps because of the apparent failure of toughness to stem rising crime. They began to emphasize crime prevention, proportionality in penal policy, and value-for-money—a major Thatcherite theme. The new tack culminated in the 1991 Criminal Justice Act. For its part, Labour began to try and repair some of the 'soft' law and order image that the Tories had successfully foisted on them, culminating in Tony Blair's legendary 1993 soundbite, 'tough on crime, tough on the causes of crime'.[21] This finely balanced the new realist recognition that crime really was a problem that needed short-run policies not just reliance on long-run reform, with a more traditional social democratic criminological concern with 'causes'. But the main departure was rhetorical: the double whammy of toughness packed into one short, sharp sentence.

Since 1993 there has developed a new 'second order' consensus on the fundamentals of law and order policy[22]—toughness, toughness, toughness—with frenzied partisan conflict on specifics—anything you can do, I can do tougher. Law and order politics has become a dominant discourse of the age: the 'culture of control'.[23] The reasons for this will be considered below.

What is Crime?

Crime and its control have become central concerns in public and polit-ical debate. The term 'crime' is usually tossed about as if its meaning is clear and unproblematic, yet many if not most arguments about it involve people talking past each other, with fundamentally different issues in mind.[24] At least the following five different constructions of crime and

---

[21] T Blair, 'Why Crime is a Socialist Issue' (1993) 29(12) *New Statesman* 27.
[22] D Downes and R Morgan, n 5 above, 287.
[23] D Garland, *The Culture of Control* (Oxford: Oxford University Press, 2001).
[24] S Henry and M Lanier (eds), *What is Crime?* (Lanham, Md: Rowman and Littlefield, 2001); N Lacey, C Wells, and O Quick, *Reconstructing Criminal Law* (3rd edn) (London:

134   *Robert Reiner*

the criminal can be distinguished, each itself signifying a complex web of concepts, practices, and values.

Legal Constructions

As Nicola Lacey has remarked, to 'anyone other than a specialist, the proposition that the intellectual concerns of criminology are intimately connected with those of criminal law would probably seem obvious to the point of banality'.[25] Probably most people would, if asked to define 'crime', invoke the criminal law as its basis. Yet there is considerable variation between legal and other social constructions of crime. There is also 'an enormous diversity among criminal laws: in terms of the style of their drafting; their scope; their construction of their subjects and objects; their assumptions about responsibility; their procedural requirements'.[26] Defining the scope of criminal law in substantive rather than formal or procedural ways is notoriously problematic because of the multitude of different kinds of function and character apparent in the vast, rapidly growing and shifting corpus of criminal law.[27]

Consequently, most criminal law texts define crime in a positivist, formal, and essentially circular way, following the arguments advanced fifty years ago in a celebrated *Current Legal Problems* lecture by Glanville Williams: 'crime is an act capable of being followed by criminal proceedings having a criminal outcome, and a proceeding or its outcome is criminal if it has certain characteristics which mark it as criminal'.[28] Article 6 of the European Convention for the Protection of Human Rights[29] on the right to a fair trial sets out various specific rights for those facing 'any criminal charge', notably the presumption of innocence, and adequate legal assistance with the preparation of a defence. There are further due process requirements specifically for criminal cases in Article 7

Lexis-Nexis, 2003), ch 1; L Zedner, *Criminal Justice* (Oxford: Oxford University Press, 2004), chs 1–2; P Hillyard, C Pantazis, S Tombs, and D Gordon (eds), *Beyond Criminology* (London: Pluto, 2004); W Morrison, 'What is Crime?' in C Hale, K Hayward, A Wahidin, and E Wincup (eds), *Criminology* (Oxford: Oxford University Press, 2005), are some recent discussions of the problems of defining crime.

[25] N Lacey, 'Legal Constructions of Crime' in Maguire *et al*, n 5 above, 264.
[26] ibid 281.
[27] L Farmer, 'The Obsession with Definition' (1996) 5(1) *Social and Legal Studies* 57; A Ashworth, 'Is the Criminal Law a Lost Cause?' (2000) 116(2) *Law Quarterly Review* 225; Lacey *et al*, n 24 above, 1–15; P Ramsay 'The Responsible Subject as Citizen: Criminal Law, Democracy and the Welfare State' (2006) 69(1) *Modern Law Review* 29.
[28] G Williams, 'The Definition of Crime' (1955) *Current Legal Problems* 107.
[29] Hereafter 'ECHR'.

and several Protocols. This has resulted in extensive ECHR jurisprudence on delineating the criminal/civil borderline.[30]

The leading case is *Engel,* [31] in which the Court formulated three criteria for determining whether proceedings are 'criminal'. These are: (i) the domestic classification of the offence; (ii) 'the very nature of the offence'; and (iii) the seriousness of the potential punishment. The ECHR has maintained an 'autonomous' definition of 'criminal', to ensure states cannot deny the rights necessary for a criminal trial by redefining the offence, so criterion (i) is asymmetric: an offence is criminal if it is so defined in domestic law, but it may also be held to be criminal even if not defined as such by a particular country. The second criterion, the substance of the offence, has not produced analysis of the principles characterizing behaviour as criminal. Rather, it has involved a set of essentially procedural issues: is there a punitive element to the sanction? Is the offence generally binding or restricted to a specific sub-group? Does the verdict require finding culpability? Are proceedings instituted by a public body? How are such matters defined in other jurisdictions? In most cases the third criterion, the severity of potential punishment, has proved decisive.[32] The ECHR case-law delineates the criminal/civil borderline in essentially formal and procedural terms, and does not offer a substantive theory of the nature of crime.

The issue of legal definitions of crime has become even more complex with the rise of hybrid offences whereby criminal sanctions attach to breach of orders that are initially determined by civil processes. The most significant of these is the Anti-Social Behaviour Order[33] that section 1 of the Crime and Disorder Act 1998 enables a magistrates' court to make in civil proceedings. Breach of this Order without reasonable excuse can attract a penalty of up to five years' imprisonment on indictment.[34] The ECHR principles outlined above would seem to suggest that this potentially severe penalty should make the proceedings as a whole, including the initial imposition of the Order, 'criminal', but against this the House of Lords has held that an ASBO is preventive not punitive in purpose.[35]

[30] These are reviewed in detail in B Emmerson and A Ashworth, *Human Rights and Criminal Justice* (London: Sweet and Maxwell, 2001), ch 4; S Treschel, *Human Rights in Criminal Proceedings* (Oxford: Oxford University Press, 2005), ch 2.

[31] *Engel v Netherlands* (1979–80) 1 European Human Rights Reports 647.

[32] Emmerson and Ashworth, n 30 above, 151–2.   [33] Hereafter 'ASBO'.

[34] A Ashworth, 'Social Control and "Anti-Social Behaviour": The Subversion of Human Rights' (2004) 120(2) *Law Quarterly Review* 263); P Ramsay, 'What is Anti-Social Behaviour?' (2004) *Criminal Law Review* 908.

[35] *Clingham v Royal Borough of Kensington and Chelsea; R v Crown Court at Manchester ex p McCann and others* [2003] 1 AC 787. For discussion, see S Macdonald, 'The Nature of the Anti-Social Behaviour Order' (2003) 66(4) *Modern Law Review* 630.

136 *Robert Reiner*

The imposition of an ASBO thus represents 'a position mid-way between the civil and the criminal paradigms',[36] in that the Lords have held it requires the criminal standard of proof because of the potential severity of penalties, but with the more relaxed civil rules of evidence, including hearsay. ASBOs have been controversial as an extension of criminal sanctions to vaguely defined behaviour, requiring judgements of value about what is 'reasonable' in specific contexts that are likely to vary according to the social position of the defendant,[37] and subject to procedures less rigorous than the criminal.

Andrew Ashworth has recently suggested that we can 'identify a principled core of criminal law',[38] comprising 'four interlinked principles'. The last three of these are procedural: equal treatment and proportionality in enforcement, the human rights protections of Article 6 of the ECHR for suspects, and proportionality in sentencing. The first, however, proposes a fundamental principle to delineate the ambit of criminal law: 'the criminal law should be used, and only used, to censure persons for substantial wrongdoing'. This claim certainly has bite and substance. For example, it would rule out the penchant of governments for hybrid offences like the ASBO, or the plethora of 'administrative offences' with diluted culpability requirements. However, it clearly raises the issue of whether there is or can be agreement on what constitutes culpable 'substantial wrongdoing', and Ashworth's explicit purpose is 'to re-kindle debate about the functions and characteristics that the criminal law ought to have'[39] if criminal law is to have principled coherence and integrity. As Tadros and Tierney argue, despite recent theoretical advances, 'fully coherent and well defended principles that could be used to identify and distinguish wrongs are yet to emerge, let alone principles that might govern incorporation of those distinctions into the criminal law'.[40]

This implicitly leaves to social scientists, historians, philosophers, and people on Clapham omnibuses, the task of explaining and evaluating its substantive scope. Some critical theorists of criminal law have sought to transcend this divide,[41] analysing the processes of criminalization 'as a set of interlocking practices in which the moments of "defining" and

---

[36] A Ashworth, n 34 above, 277.   [37] Ramsay, n 34 above, 918.
[38] Ashworth, n 27 above, 253.   [39] ibid 256.
[40] V Tadros and S Tierney, 'The Presumption of Innocence and the Human Rights Act' (2004) 67(3) *Modern Law Review* 411.
[41] D Nelken, 'Critical Criminal Law' (1987) 14(1) *Journal of Law and Society* 105; I Dennis (ed), *Criminal Law and Justice* (London: Sweet and Maxwell, 1987); I Loveland (ed), *Frontiers of Criminality* (London: Sweet and Maxwell, 1995); A Norrie, *Crime, Reason and History* (2nd edn) (London: Butterworths, 2001).

Law and Order 137

"responding to" crime can rarely be completely distinguished and in which legal and social extra-legal constructions of crime constantly interact'.[42] This points to the variety of alternative, often conflicting, conceptions of crime apart from, and often in conflict with, the legal.

Normative Constructions

Positivist or formalist legal definitions of crime open themselves to normative critique. Does criminal law proscribe and sanction behaviours that ought not to be punished, because they are acceptable or desirable, or even if regarded as wrong, because criminalization is for a variety of possible reasons not regarded as the appropriate means of control? Conversely, the scope of criminal law can be criticized normatively for failing to include behaviours that should be proscribed and punished.

There are many jurisprudential and criminological debates about the normative limits of criminal law. Perhaps the most familiar argument about alleged over-reach of criminal law is the claim from liberal political philosophy that 'private [im]moral behaviour' should not be subject to criminal law, for both principled and pragmatic reasons, the subject of the famous 'debates' between Mill and Fitzjames Stephen, and Hart and Devlin.[43] On the other hand, critical criminologists have frequently argued that criminal law fails to define as criminal very serious and wilful harm committed by the powerful, states, and corporations.[44] This has developed into the recent claim that criminology should be replaced by 'zemiology', the study of serious culpable harms, rendering as problematic whether or not they are proscribed by criminal law.[45] The definition of 'harms' is, of course, as socially contentious as notions of 'crime', but it explicitly involves normative evaluation, not authoritative declaration.

---

[42] Lacey, n 25 above, 282.

[43] J S Mill, *On Liberty* (Oxford: Oxford University Press, 1998); J F Stephens, *Liberty, Equality, Fraternity* (London: Elder, 1873); H L A Hart, *Law, Liberty and Morality* (Oxford: Oxford University Press, 1963); P Devlin, *The Enforcement of Morals* (Oxford: Oxford University Press; 1965); J Feinberg, *The Moral Limits of the Criminal Law Vols 1–4* (New York: Oxford University Press, 1984–90); S Lee, *Law and Morals* (Oxford: Oxford University Press, 1987).

[44] E Sutherland, *White-Collar Crime* (New York: Holt, Rinehart and Winston, 1949); H Schwendinger and J Schwendinger, 'Defenders of Order or Guardians of Human Rights?' in I Taylor, P Walton and J Young (eds), *Critical Criminology* (London: Routledge, 1975); G Slapper and S Tombs, *Corporate Crime* (London: Longman, 1999); S Tombs and D Whyte (eds), *Unmasking the Crimes of the Powerful* (New York: Lang, 2003); P Green and T Ward, *State Crime* (London: Pluto, 2004). For a discussion of the problems of defining and regulating white-collar or corporate crime, see D Nelken, 'White-Collar Crime' in Maguire *et al*, n 5 above; J Gobert and M Punch, *Rethinking Corporate Crime* (London: Lexis Nexis, 2003).   [45] Hillyard *et al*, n 24 above.

Social/Cultural Constructions

Emile Durkheim's famous attempt to provide a sociological definition of crime suggested that 'Crime shocks sentiments which, for a given social system are found in all healthy consciences . . . an act is criminal when it offends strong and defined states of the collective conscience'.[46] This is as positivist, tautologous, and formal a definition as the standard criminal law textbook's, albeit emphasizing social/cultural rather than legal construction. Moreover, it is even more explicitly based on a consensus model of society. As Durkheim himself recognized, conceptions of the criminal vary considerably between and within societies, and over time. What is typically sanctioned as deviant will vary from the formal definitions of law, and also be hotly contested between different groups. An occupational hazard for a criminologist at parties is to deal with irate demands to explain why the police and courts harass the speeding motorist instead of 'real' criminals. Is drink-driving socially deviant? While it is in most circles nowadays, it was not in England until three decades ago, but it was even then in countries such as, for example, Scandinavia. Will driving under the influence of mobile phones go the same way? Who is 'really' criminal—the 'honest, victimized' householder Tony Martin, or the young burglar he was convicted of murdering?

Criminal Justice Constructions

Who gets formally processed by the criminal justice system as criminal, and for what offences, offers yet another construction of crime and criminality. Recorded crimes and criminals are a very small and almost certainly unrepresentative sample of all law-breaking. The official statistics and research evidence have been well summed up in the title of Jeffrey Reiman's critical classic *The Rich Get Richer and the Poor Get Prison*.[47] They are in prison mainly for a variety of street crimes, not suite crimes— car theft and burglary, not insider trading or pensions mis-selling. The imbalance starts with what is reported and gets more marked as cases go through each stage of the criminal justice process. The overwhelming majority of those in prison (and *a fortiori* those executed in the USA) are male and from economically underprivileged groups, with a huge disproportion of black and other ethnic minority people.[48]

---

[46] Durkheim, n 12 above, 73, 80.

[47] J Reiman, *The Rich Get Richer and the Poor Get Prison* (7th edition) (Boston: Allyn and Bacon, 2004).

[48] R Morgan, 'Imprisonment' in Maguire *et al*, n 5 above, 1132.

The pattern of offences for which people are processed and convicted is almost the obverse of the amount of space they get in typical criminal law books and journals. Most are charged with driving offences, thefts, and only a minority with the serious violent and sexual offences and homicide that occupy the attention of criminal law texts.

Mass Media and Policy Constructions

The constructions of crime offered by the mass media, those that inform most policy debates, are again a very different pattern. Mass media representations follow a 'law of opposites'.[49] They are the obverse of what official statistics on recorded crime and criminals portray—although neither are likely to be a 'true' picture of overall patterns of offending, most of which never comes to light at all.

The mass media—'factual', 'fictional', and hybrid forms—overwhelmingly focus on the most serious violent and sexual offences, above all murder, even though these are thankfully rare.[50] Victims and offenders portrayed in media accounts are disproportionately older and higher in the social scale than their counterparts in official statistics, although they share the common feature of being overwhelmingly male. The criminal justice system is primarily represented by the police, and is mainly presented as successful, law-abiding, and morally virtuous; negative portrayals have certainly increased over the last fifty years but they remain a small minority. In news and fiction stories the police almost invariably get their man, although in reality only a tiny proportion of crimes are cleared up.

It is this mass media picture that informs most contemporary public and policy debate. Politicians generally are highly sensitive to the sensational but rare crimes that are the focus of most media attention, and policy-making is often jolted by them. Increasingly the main attention is on the suffering of massively injured, vulnerable, and ideal-typically innocent victims, as reflected in the new tendency to name laws after them.

An Overlapping Core Construction?

I have distinguished between five different constructions of crime in contemporary discourse, all offering a very different picture: the legal; different moral views; the socially/culturally sanctioned; the criminal justice

---

[49] R Surette, *Media, Crime and Criminal Justice* (2nd edn) (Belmont: Wadsworth, 1998).
[50] For a summary of research on media representation of crime see R Reiner, 'Media Made Criminality' in Maguire, n 5 above. Changes since 1945 are analysed in R Reiner,

process; and the mass media/public policy focus. It is difficult to see any common core. Some ideal-typical cases may in Durkheimian fashion unite all 'healthy consciences', say the Jamie Bulger or Soham murders. These highly unusual crimes are clearly regarded as such on all dimensions. But there will be alternative views on the gravity and even the 'really' criminal nature of most other cases, even if there is no doubt about their legal status. So much policy and popular debate about crime and control involves people talking past each other.

What Happened?—Unravelling Crime Trends

As anyone who has studied even a week of criminology knows, official crime statistics have to be approached with extreme caution.[51] The key official national statistics, going back to the 1850s, are compiled from returns by police forces of crimes they have recorded as known to them. These are both an incomplete and a biased sample of all crimes that occur. There is a substantial 'dark figure' of unrecorded crime, constituting a variable multiple of the recorded rate. Many crimes are not recorded because victims do not report them, the police do not record them even if they are reported, or they have no individual victims and are not discovered by the police. Recorded trends and patterns must be interpreted sceptically because they may reflect changes in recording practices rather than criminals committing crimes. Officially recorded offenders are also a tiny and biased sample of all law-breakers, the lottery losers of the criminal justice process.

Having said this, very substantial steps have been taken in recent decades to alleviate these problems. The most important is the development of alternative ways of measuring crime and offending, above all the regular British Crime Surveys[52] since the early 1980s. There have also been two recent reforms of the police recording process, intended to make it more complete, reliable, and victim-oriented. The first was a revised set of counting rules issued to police forces by the Home Office in 1998, increasing the range of offences that had to be recorded, and specifying more tightly how to calculate the number of offences to record

S Livingstone, and J Allen, 'Casino Culture: Media and Crime in a Winner-Loser Society' in K Stenson and R Sullivan (eds), *Crime, Risk and Justice* (Cullompton: Willan, 2001); R Reiner, S Livingstone, and J Allen, 'From Law and Order to Lynch Mobs: Crime News since the Second World War' in Mason, n 9 above.

[51] For a comprehensive review of the issues see M Maguire, 'Crime Statistics: The "Data Explosion" and its Implications' in Maguire *et al*, n 5 above.   [52] Hereafter 'BCS'.

Law and Order   141

in particular cases. This had the expected and inevitable effect of increasing the recorded crime rate. The second reform, the 2002 National Crime Recording Standard, aimed to achieve greater consistency between different areas in recording practices, above all by requiring that incidents be recorded according to the victim's perception irrespective of the police view of its accuracy. Again this was expected to boost recording, as it restricted officers' discretion not to record offences if they doubted the victim's versions of events. These are desirable reforms but do make comparison over time more problematic, although the Home Office calculated the 1998 statistics using both old and new versions of the counting rules in order to estimate the effect of the changes.

The advent of the BCS twenty-five years ago has shed much light on reporting and recording practices, allowing statistics to be interpreted more confidently. Above all they offer two alternative measures of trends for offences covered by the survey, which gives greater confidence when they point in the same direction, as they did for most of the history of the BCS. However, in recent years the trends indicated by the police statistics and the BCS have begun to diverge, producing a politicization of the debate about their interpretation and the relative merits of different measuring instruments.

Putting together the different sorts of data available, what can be said about the trends in the last half century? The most apparent trend is the spectacular rise in recorded crime since the late 1950s. In the early 1950s the police recorded less than half a million offences per annum. By the mid-1960s this had increased to around one million, and by the mid-1970s to two million. The 1980s showed even more staggering rises, with recorded crime peaking in 1992 at over 5.5 million—a tenfold increase in less than four decades.[53] By 1997 recorded crime had fallen back to 4.5 million. The counting rule changes introduced in 1998 and 2002 make comparison of the subsequent figures especially fraught, but on the new rules, which undoubtedly exaggerate the increase, just under six million offences were recorded by the police for 2003–4—the highest on record—but this had fallen back to just over 5.5 million in 2004–5.[54] Until the 1970s there were no alternatives to the police statistics. Criminologists were wont to give cautionary warnings about whether crime really was increasing as the figures indicated, but it was impossible

[53] G Barclay and C Tavares, *Digest 4—Information about the Criminal Justice System in England and Wales* (London: Home Office, 1999), 2.

[54] S Nicholas, D Povey, A Walker, and C Kershaw, *Crime in England and Wales 2004/05* Statistical Bulletin 11/05 (London: Home Office, 2005), 13.

to know how much of any change was due to new patterns of reporting and/or recording crime rather than offending behaviour.

During the 1970s the General Household Survey[55] asked respondents about their experience of burglary. This allowed an estimate of changes in victimization and reporting patterns for this common offence, which was of crucial importance for public anxieties about crime and the politics of law and order. In the 1970s the increase in recorded burglaries was mainly accounted for by an increase in victims' propensity to report them to the police, not an increase in victimization by burglary. Between 1972 and 1983 recorded burglaries doubled, but victimization increased by only 20 per cent according to the surveys.[56] There was a considerable increase in the proportion of victims reporting burglaries to the police, and the reason is plain from the GHS. In 1972 the property stolen was insured in only 19 per cent of burglary incidents, but by 1980 this had increased to 42 per cent.[57] Thus, the first set of victimization statistics, from the GHS in the 1970s, reinforced criminological scepticism about how much of the huge increase in recorded crime statistics was really due to increased offending.

However, as the BCS came to be repeated in several sweeps during the 1980s and early 1990s the discrepancy in the trends recorded by the surveys and by the police figures began to lessen. Although there was still some increase in reporting and recording, most of the huge rise in recorded crime in the 1980s and early 1990s corresponded to an increase in victimization. Between 1981 and 1993, the number of crimes recorded by the police increased 111 per cent, whilst BCS offences rose by 77 per cent. The proportion of offences reported to the police by victims increased from 31 per cent in 1981 to 41 per cent in 1993 according to the BCS. In the most common types of property crime, such as car thefts and burglary with loss, reporting and recording rates had reached almost 100 per cent.[58] When there is almost complete recording by the police of victimization the trends in the BCS and police figures will of course be almost identical.

From the early 1990s, however, the two sets of statistics begin to diverge once more. Between 1992 and 1995 the police statistics begin to decline

[55] Hereafter 'GHS'.

[56] M Hough and P Mayhew, *Taking Account of Crime: Key Findings from the Second British Crime Survey* (London: Home Office, 1985), 16.

[57] P Mayhew, D Elliott, and L Dowds, *The 1988 British Crime Survey* (London: Home Office, 1989), 19–22; G Barclay, C Tavares, and A Prout, *Digest 3—Information on the Criminal Justice System in England and Wales* (London: Home Office, 1995), 7.

[58] Barclay *et al*, ibid, 6.

Law and Order   143

from their record height of 5.5 million. But the BCS continued to register increasing victimization in these years.[59] The 'missing crimes' in the police statistics are due to a reversal of the trend towards saturation reporting of the most common property offences. Paradoxically, the very high levels of crime set in train processes that led victims to report less, and the police to record fewer of the crimes reported to them.[60] Victims in higher risk categories faced more onerous conditions for insurance, reducing the incentive to report crimes. The police were coming under a tighter performance measurement regime, encouraging under-recording where possible.

After 1997 the divergence between the police and BCS statistics has continued, but in the reverse direction. The police figures increased from 1997 to 2003–4, slightly dropping in 2004–5. This is largely accounted for by the two changes in counting rules over this period. The BCS figures, however, show continuing declines in total victimization from 1995 to 2004–5.

It is hardly surprising that this has made the relative significance of the two sets of statistics highly politicized, with the Conservatives attempting to undermine the validity of the BCS in the 2005 General Election campaign, aided by publications from sympathetic think-tanks.[61] The official crime statistics show crime rising almost continuously from the late 1950s, until they begin to fall sharply during Michael Howard's period as Home Secretary, but then rise again to new record levels under New Labour. The GHS and BCS victimization statistics, by contrast, suggest that until the Thatcher government much of the rise in recorded crime was due to increased reporting.

The spectacular rise in the 1980s and early 1990s was a genuine increase in offending, confirmed by both measures. The apparent decline in recorded crime under Michael Howard, however, was again largely a product of changes in recording—BCS crime continued to rise. But the growth of recorded crime under New Labour is mainly due to recording changes attributable to the revised counting rules. Victimization as measured by the BCS has declined to its lowest level since 1979, when Mrs Thatcher defeated the previous Labour government.

So whether Michael Howard or Tony Blair wins the accolade of the most successful crime-buster since Batman turns on which figures are more reliable. The BCS cannot and does not claim to be a perfect

[59] Nicholas *et al*, n 54 above, 18.

[60] R Reiner, 'The Case of the Missing Crimes' in R Levitas and W Guy (eds), *Interpreting Official Statistics* (London: Routledge, 1996).

[61] N Dennis and G Erdos, *Cultures and Crime* (London: Civitas, 2005).

barometer of crime—this is not possible. Most criminologists would argue, however, that as a measure of trends it is more reliable than the police statistics, which are notoriously subject to the vicissitudes of victims' reporting and police recording behaviour. But then most criminologists are probably not fans of Mrs Thatcher, Michael Howard, or Tony Blair!

A New Leviathan? Crime Control Policies

During the 1970s and 1980s law and order was the exclusive slogan of the political Right.[62] David Downes vividly labelled this as the 'theft of an issue'.[63] As the emerging school of New Left Realism argued, the primary victims of crime were the poorest and most vulnerable groups in society, those that the Left had traditionally seen as its constituency.[64] Crime could also be explained by the social ethos and conditions of unbridled capitalism that the Left had traditionally attacked.[65] The missing link that New Left Realists urged was serious consideration by the Left of short-term crime control policies that might offer some protection whilst waiting for long-term reforms addressing the basic causes.[66]

In the early 1990s Labour tried in earnest to recapture the ground lost on the issue of law and order, especially once Tony Blair became Shadow Home Secretary. They began to attack the Tories not only with the old social democratic arguments about crime being produced by inequality, egoism, and exclusion, but by pointing to failures of Conservative criminal justice policies. Given the record increases in crime in the 1980s, despite burgeoning expenditure on policing and punishment, this was an open goal—as even Tory cabinet ministers privately conceded.[67]

The wrong-footing of the Tories on law and order came to a head in 1993, with Tony Blair's emblematic pledge to be 'tough on crime, tough on the causes of crime'—covering all bases at the same time.[68] Michael

---

[62] R Reiner and M Cross (eds), *Beyond Law and Order* (London: Macmillan, 1991); M Brake and C Hale, *Public Order and Private Lives: The Politics of Law and Order* (London: Routledge, 1992).

[63] D Downes, *Law and Order—Theft of an Issue* (London: Fabian Society, 1983).

[64] J Lea and J Young, *What is to be Done about Law and Order?* (London: Penguin, 1984).

[65] I Taylor, *Law and Order: Arguments for Socialism* (London: Macmillan, 1981).

[66] R Matthews and J Young (eds), *Confronting Crime* (London: Sage, 1986).

[67] K Baker, *The Turbulent Years* (London: Faber, 1993), 450.

[68] This celebrated soundbite was first aired in speeches and articles in early 1993 by Tony Blair as Shadow Home Secretary, outlining the Labour Party's approach to law and

Howard fought back vigorously with his 'prison works' speech to the 1993 Conservative Party Conference, and policies inspired by it. Nonetheless the game had changed dramatically. Having ditched its electoral 'hostages to fortune' such as exclusive association with civil liberties, trade union- ism, and analysis of crime primarily in terms of social justice,[69] Labour was making the political running on what had been one of the Tories' most secure policy areas. As with the whole New Labour project, the ditching of old commitments was seen as a price worth paying for its electoral rewards.

The period 1992–3 was a decisive watershed for the politics of law and order, as for other policy areas. Whilst during the late 1970s and 1980s neo-liberal and neo-conservative political parties, ideas, and policies became dominant in Britain, the US and most of the Western world, they were fiercely if unsuccessfully contested. On a world scale the New Right's ascendancy was marked by the fall of the Soviet Union in 1989. But what really confirmed the global hegemony of neo-liberalism was the accept- ance of the fundamentals of its economic and social policy framework by the erstwhile social democratic or New Deal parties of the West. The Clinton Democrats, New Labour, and their embrace of the 'third way'— neo-liberalism to a cool beat—marked a new, deep consensus, delivering the death-knell of the post-war mixed economy, Keynesian settlement that the conservative parties had accepted when they returned to power in the early 1950s: Blatcherism was Butskellism in reverse.

As argued earlier, in relation to crime the new 'second order' consensus, predicated on an auction of toughness,[70] had five core elements:

(i) Crime, disorder, and now terrorism, are *the* major threats to society and to individual citizens;

(ii) Crime is the fault of offenders, due to their free choice, individual or cultural pathology, or to intrinsic evil. It is *not* caused by social structural factors;

(iii) The victim is the iconic centre of discourse about crime, ideal- typically portrayed as totally innocent. Crime policy is predicated

order, in the wake of the national agonizing stirred by the tragic abduction and murder of the Liverpool toddler James Bulger by two older boys. See Blair, n 21 above. Its significance is discussed usefully in Downes and Morgan, n 5 above, 296–7; T Newburn, *Handbook of Policing* (Cullompton: Willan, 2003), 206–7; C Hale, 'The Politics of Law and Order' in Hale *et al*, n 24 above, 439–41.

[69] Downes and Morgan, n 5 above.

[70] ibid; R Matthews and J Young (eds), *The New Politics of Crime and Punishment* (Cullompton: Willan, 2003).

146   *Robert Reiner*

on a zero-sum game: concern for victims precludes understanding of—let alone any sympathy for—offenders;

(iv) Criminal justice *can* control crime provided it is tough *and* smart. Criminal justice controls crime through effective deterrence, prevention, and incapacitation. 'Prison works', as does 'zero tolerance' policing, and 'responsibilizing' citizens to take self-protective measures against victimization. Civil liberties are at best marginal issues, and deeper social causes of crime are denied; and

(v) Popular culture and the routines of everyday life are increasingly focused on crime risks; politics is dominated by fears about crime, disorder, and the threat of alien evil.

This new hegemonic 'culture of control'[71] has displaced the welfare/rehabilitative consensus that prevailed for most of the twentieth century in the Western world. This is part of a broader shift in politics and culture, the 'death of the social'.[72] The rise of neo-liberalism, individualism, and the 'risk society'[73] has eclipsed the Keynesian, mixed economy, welfare state consensus that prevailed for the first three post-war decades.[74] In the sphere of domestic politics this has been exemplified above all by the ascendancy of New Labour in the 1990s and early twenty-first century, with its promise of a 'third way' 'beyond Left and Right'.[75]

New Labour's crime control policies embodied this triangulation, epitomized by the flagship 1998 Crime and Disorder Act.[76] It was a characteristic 'third way' synthesis of the tough and the smart. It provided 'evidence-led', 'joined up' policy in the duties it placed on police, local authorities, and other relevant agencies to develop a coordinated 'strategy for the reduction of crime and disorder in the area', culminating in the ambitious Crime Reduction Programme launched in 1999. But it also offered tabloid-appeasing toughness: minimum mandatory sentences, ASBOs, and curfews.

The Janus-faced tough/smart policy combination is encapsulated above all in the restructuring of youth justice in the 1998 Act: systematic,

[71] Garland, n 23 above.

[72] N Rose, 'The Death of the Social?' (1996) 25(3) *Economy and Society* 327.

[73] U Beck, *Risk Society* (London: Sage, 1992).

[74] For economic analyses of the sources and implications see: M Blyth, *Great Transformations* (Cambridge: Cambridge University Press, 2002); G Dumenil and D Levy, *Capital Resurgent* (Cambridge, Mass: Harvard University Press, 2004); D Harvey, *A Brief History of Neoliberalism*, (Oxford: Oxford University Press, 2005); A Glyn, *Capitalism Unleashed* (Oxford: Oxford University Press, 2006).

[75] A Giddens, *The Third Way* (Cambridge: Polity, 1998); C Leys, *Market-Driven Politics* (London: Verso, 2003); M Bevir, *New Labour: A Critique* (London: Routledge, 2005).

[76] Hereafter 'the 1998 Act'.

Law and Order　　　　147

evidence-based attempts to address and prevent offending by early pre-diction of risks and appropriate remedies, coordinated by inter-agency teams in the form of the local Youth Offending Teams, and centrally by the Youth Justice Board.[77] Alongside this, however, were a variety of new powers for the police and the courts to control youth crime and disorder, such as ASBOs, child curfew schemes, abolition of *doli incapax*, deten-tion and training orders. The net result was an increase in the use of custodial penalties for young offenders.

Gradually 'tough on crime' has eclipsed 'tough on the causes of crime'. For example, there has been a remorseless growth of police powers. The legislative trend since 1993 has been extensions of police powers without corresponding safeguards, with the Human Rights Act of 1998 con-stituting the only exception. New powers to intercept communications, conduct covert operations, stop and search and arrest, and new public order offences were created in the early years of New Labour by the Police Act 1997, Crime and Disorder Act 1998, Regulation of Investigatory Powers Act 2000, Terrorism Act 2000, and the Criminal Justice and Public Order Act 2001. In 2002 the Home Office conducted a review of PACE, premised on the view that the regime of safeguards it had insti-tuted created a regime of procedures adequately protecting suspects. The concern was to provide a 'useful tool supporting the police and providing them with the powers they need to combat crime'.[78] It was deemed neces-sary to 'simplify police procedures; reduce administrative burdens on the police; save police resources; speed up the process of justice'.[79] Accordingly the Review floated a number of proposals to dilute the safeguards of PACE. The Criminal Justice Act 2003 authorized detention for 36 hours for all, not just 'serious', arrestable offences, and added criminal damage to the possible grounds for stop and search. The Serious Organized Crime and Police Act 2005 created a power of arrest for all offences, ending the category of non-arrestable offences. It enhanced powers of search, and to take fingerprints. It also allowed for the creation of civilian custody officers, overturning the PACE requirement that they should normally be police sergeants. The clear trend is for enhanced police powers and reduced safeguards, reflecting the law and order politics that have prevailed since the early 1990s.

Contrary to the 1984 forebodings of Freeman and others cited at the start of this chapter, the regime of safeguards established since PACE had

[77] J Pitts, *The New Politics of Youth Crime* (London: Palgrave, 2001); T Newburn, 'Young People, Crime and Youth Justice' in Maguire *et al*, n 5 above, 559.
[78] D Blunkett and Lord Macdonald, 'Foreword' in *Report of the Joint Home Office/Cabinet Office: Review of Police and Criminal Evidence Act 1984* (Home Office, November 2002).　　　　[79] ibid, para 8.

a substantial impact on police practice, inhibiting gross violations of suspects' rights. However, the pressures on the police to achieve results have intensified in the new crime control climate, and they are increasingly armed with new powers unfettered by safeguards. This is likely to reduce the legal accountability of the police, despite the welcome enhancement of the complaints process represented by the creation of the Independent Police Complaints Commission.

Prison numbers have risen to record-breaking levels. During the first half of the twentieth century the trend had been for the number of prisoners to fall. From the late 1950s to the early 1980s it doubled from around 20,000 to 40,000, and had grown to around 50,000 by the late 1980s. Following a short period of reduction in the wake of the Criminal Justice Act 1991, there has been a relentless, massive increase of around two-thirds since 1993. In 1993 the rate of imprisonment was 90 per 100,000 population, but it rose to 143 per 100,000 by 2003, and is now over 75,000. This is largely the result of tougher sentencing policy and practice. The proportion of offenders found guilty of an indictable offence that received custodial sentences increased from 15 per cent in 1991 to 25 per cent in 2001. A variety of changes in sentencing powers under New Labour, following in the wake of Michael Howard's 'prison works' approach, from the Crime and Disorder Act 1998 to the Criminal Justice Act of 2003, have resulted in large increases in the proportion and numbers of prisoners serving long sentences.[80]

New Labour has been repeatedly jolted into new 'tough' laws and initiatives by particular media-driven moral panics, and since 2001—and *a fortiori* 2005—the threat of terrorism. This has been epitomized by Tony Blair's 'street crimes summit' at Downing Street in March 2002, and the accompanying initiative pledging to get robbery 'under control' by September.[81] Michael Tonry has documented no less than 33 such get-tough-on-crime initiatives announced between June 2001 and May 2003 alone,[82] with thirteen 'crime summits' between 1999 and 2003.[83] It has been estimated that over 700 new criminal offences have been created by New Labour.[84]

These measures, and the law and order paradigm with its 'can-do' confidence about bringing crime under control by toughness, might get some superficial vindication from the overall fall in crime in the last decade that is indicated by the British Crime Survey, although less clearly

---

[80] A Ashworth, 'Sentencing' in Maguire *et al*, n 5 above; M Tonry, *Punishment and Politics* (Cullompton: Willan, 2004).   [81] For details, see Tonry, ibid 47.
[82] ibid 41–7.   [83] ibid 39–41.
[84] H Kennedy, *Just Law* (London: Vintage, 2005).

by the recorded crime figures. However, the fall has mainly been in the less serious 'volume' crimes, whilst robbery and more serious violent crimes have increased.[85] The role of criminal justice policy in explaining these crime trends is in any case complex and debatable.

Explaining Crime Trends

The predominant account offered by the media and by politicians of the rise in crime since the late 1950s has been the one advanced by the New Right.[86] This blames crime on the personal moral and other defects of offenders, that used to be held in check by effective social controls until post-war liberal social policies culminating in 1960s 'permissiveness' undermined them.

The theme of permissiveness as the basic cause of rising crime has been emphasized recently by Tony Blair, in a speech launching the Home Office's five-year Strategic Plan for law and order. Blair claimed it 'marks the end of the 1960s liberal, social consensus on law and order'.[87] He explicitly blamed the '1960s revolution' for encouraging 'freedom without responsibility', when 'a society of different lifestyles spawned a group of young people who were brought up without parental discipline, without proper role models and without any sense of responsibility to or for others'.[88]

Blair's speech represents the quintessential conservative analysis of rising crime. In this account, the Enlightenment values of personal liberty, autonomy, and self-realization were dangerously democratized by 1960s 'permissiveness'. As this spread to the masses it brought the destruction of family, responsibility, and self- control—the bulwarks of any civilization.[89] This narrative overlooks the ways in which the 'permissive' legislation of the 1960s embodied a restructuring rather than relaxation of control.[90] It cannot explain why tolerant and liberal cultures like those of Holland and the Scandinavian countries were not racked by crime, violence, and law and order politics[91]—though these are emerging

---

[85] D Rose, 'Violent Crime' *The Observer* 28 May 2006, 20–2.

[86] For a crisp demolition see S Hallsworth, *Street Crime* (Cullompton: Willan, 2005), ch 4.

[87] T Blair, 'A New Consensus on Law and Order', Speech launching Home Office Strategic Plan for Criminal Justice, 19 July 2004. Available via <www.labour.org.uk/news/tbcrimespeech>.   [88] ibid.

[89] Dennis and Erdos, n 61 above.

[90] T Newburn, *Permission and Regulation* (London: Routledge, 1991).

[91] D Downes, *Contrasts in Tolerance* (Oxford: Oxford University Press, 1998); H Tham, 'Law and Order as a Leftist Project—The Case of Sweden' (2001) 3 *Punishment*

150   *Robert Reiner*

with the impact of neo-liberalism and the weakening of social democracy since the 1980s.

There have been huge cultural changes since the 1950s in all Western societies—greater individualism, autonomy, concern with self-realization, more scepticism about authority, and less deference.[92] But whilst this 'desubordination'[93] may have reduced internalized controls restraining deviance, it cannot by itself explain rising crime. Other factors need to be examined, including shifts in motivation, opportunity, formal controls, and the labelling of offences.[94]

To understand why crime rates have increased over the last fifty years, in terms of both 'actual' crime and 'recorded' crime, we need to consider all the necessary ingredients both of offending, and of perceptions of crime—controls are only one part of the picture. There are at least four necessary conditions of existence for the occurrence of behaviour that is regarded and recorded as criminal.

Labelling

For behaviour to be treated as 'criminal' it is necessary first for there to be an authoritative construction of the general category of crime it falls under. If it is to be recorded as a crime, the behaviour must then be interpreted as such by victims and/or witnesses, and official criminal justice agents. Shifts in criminal law, and in patterns of reporting and recording incidents, can be major influences on apparent patterns and trends in crime for numerous possible reasons.

Motivation

Social, cultural, and economic changes affect the pressures and attractions of behaviour labelled as criminal, increasing or decreasing the numbers of people motivated to commit them. The most influential and plausible account of how macro-social structures can affect variations in

---

and Society 409; U Bondeson, 'Levels of Punitiveness in Scandinavia: description and explanations' in J Pratt, D Brown, M Brown, S Hallsworth, and W Morrison (eds), *The New Punitiveness* (Cullompton: Willan, 2005).

[92] A Giddens, *Modernity and Self-Identity* (Cambridge: Polity, 1991).

[93] R Miliband, 'A State of Desubordination' (1978) 29(4) *British Journal of Sociology* 399.

[94] R Reiner, 'Crime and Control in Britain' (2000) 34(1) *Sociology* 71; Hallsworth, n 86 above, part 2; R Reiner, 'Political Economy, Crime and Criminal Justice' in M Maguire, R Morgan and R Reiner (eds), *The Oxford Handbook of Criminology* (4th edn) (Oxford: Oxford University Press, forthcoming).

motivations to commit crime between cultures and over time is Merton's theory of anomie.[95] This suggests how cultures that emphasize material success, especially if this is defined primarily in monetary terms, and ones that encourage widespread aspirations in a context of structurally limited legitimate opportunities for achievement, generate strains towards deviance and crime.

Criminal Opportunities

Social and economic changes can increase or reduce the availability of criminal opportunities. These opportunities can be analysed in terms of targets for crime, and the capacity to commit offences. In this sense 'opportunity makes the thief'.[96] Criminal opportunities can be expanded by a proliferation of targets—for example, the spread of ownership of mobile phones—or shifts in 'routine activities'.[97]

Controls

People with motives and opportunities to engage in criminal behaviour may be more or less restrained by controls, both formal and informal. Changes in the efficacy of formal controls through, for example, more or less successful policing strategies, will alter the attractions or possibility of crime. Cultural trends such as liberalization may affect the operations of internalized restraints, 'conscience'—Eysenck's 'inner policeman'[98]—in the way that proponents of the 'permissiveness' thesis argue.

Explaining recent trends in crime requires us to consider how changes in political economy, social structure, and culture have impacted on all these elements of offending. To recap briefly, the pattern we have to explain is: rising recorded crime from the late 1950s to the early 1970s, when there was no alternative to the official police figures; rising recorded crime during the 1970s, but with the GHS burglary victimization statistics suggesting this was largely a product of more reporting by victims; rising recorded crime 1981–92 which was probably mainly due to increased offending, as it was supported by the BCS; falling recorded crime 1992–7, but with the BCS suggesting this was largely a recording phenomenon,

---

[95] R Merton, 'Social Structure and Anomie' (1938) 3 *American Sociological Review* 672.
[96] M Felson and R Clarke, *Opportunity Makes the Thief: Practical Theory for Crime Prevention* (London: Home Office, 1998).
[97] M Felson, *Crime and Everyday Life* (3rd edn) (London: Pine Forge, 2002).
[98] H Eysenck, *Crime and Personality* (2nd edn) (London: Granada, 1970).

and crime was still rising; rising recorded crime since 1997—but with the BCS suggesting this was mainly due to increased recording, largely because of the major changes in counting rules.

This suggests the following broad three sub-periods:

Late 1950s–1970s—Rapid Crime Rise:　The rise in recorded crime was mainly a product of the new mass consumer society. The GHS figures for the 1970s suggest that some at any rate of the recorded increase was due to more reporting and recording of victimization by property crime, a plausible process in a society in which high value consumer goods were proliferating and increasingly insured against theft. However, the culture and social structure of mass consumerism would also plausibly generate higher offending levels. Most obviously this would result from the spread of tempting targets for crime: cars, radios, and other equipment in cars, television sets, videos, computers, mobile phones, and so on. These all increased the opportunities for relatively easy, lucrative thefts.

Although unemployment and inequality were at a historic low point and diminishing, and general living standards rising, Mertonian anomie may well have been increasing motivations to steal. The increasingly materialistic culture of mass affluence emphasized monetary success rather than the means of achieving it. The stimulation of consumption by advertising explicitly undermined norms of deferred gratification—'Live Now, Pay Later', 'Take the Waiting Out of Wanting'. This could have eroded inhibitions about illicit access and not just the legitimate use of credit cards.[99] The pervasive stress on the desirability of must-have consumer products for all would have increased the sense of relative deprivation amongst those sectors lacking in legitimate opportunities. All this was predicted by social democratic criminologists at the dawn of the era of mass affluence,[100] and doubtless continues to fuel crime.[101]

The beginnings of youth culture and broader aspects of de-subordination would have reduced internalized restraints against offending. As recorded crime began to rise, pressures on the police increased, leading to lower clear-up rates and hence a decline in the deterrence and incapacitation

---

[99] Access cards were the first commonly available credit cards in Britain, marketed under the slogan 'Take the waiting out of wanting'.

[100] R Reiner, 'Beyond Risk: A Lament for Social Democratic Criminology' in T Newburn and P Rock (eds), *The Politics of Crime Control* (Oxford: Oxford University Press, 2006).

[101] On consumerism and crime, see J Young, *The Exclusive Society* (London: Sage, 1999); J Lea, *Crime and Modernity* (London: Sage, 2002), 78–81; M Fitzgerald and C Hale, *Young People and Street Crime* (London: Youth Justice Board, 2002); K Hayward, *City Limits* (London: Glasshouse Press, 2004); Hallsworth, n 86 above.

effects of criminal justice. In sum, after the late 1950s a variety of inter-linked consequences of mass consumerism fed rising crime rates. These increased the labelling of crime, opportunities and motivations for offending, and weakened both informal and formal controls.

1980s—Crime Explosion: All these processes continued in the 1980s and early 1990s, during which recorded crime reached historical record heights, and the new BCS confirmed that this was primarily a rise in victimization by crime not a recording change. The key change, however, was the brutal displacement of the consensus, Keynesian, welfare state policies of the post-war decades by neo-liberal monetarist policies. This produced the massive social dislocations of de-industrialization and resurgent mass unemployment—indeed long-term never-employment for increasing numbers of young men, especially amongst ethnic minorities and in inner-city areas. Inequality sharpened into a yawning chasm between the top and bottom of the economic hierarchy, and poverty began to rise after a long historical process of increasing social incorporation and inclusion. Industrial and political conflict was sparked on a scale not experienced for half a century or more, with much more violent disorders.

Informal social controls of all kinds were eroded as whole communities lost the material basis of settled life, with incomparably greater ramifications for stable or any family life and 'morality' than the 'permissiveness' that the Right railed against. Moral *laissez-faire* followed the economic. A culture of egoism, the 'me society', was stimulated under the guise of the ethic of individual responsibility. 'Greed is good' was the infamous watchword of a new Gilded Age. The unbridled turbo-capitalism of the Thatcher years had devastating consequences for order that far outweighed the strong state measures introduced to control it in a Canute-like effort to stem the social tsunami.[102]

---

[102] For evidence about the links between inequality, long-term unemployment, and crime and violence, see, for example, C Hale, 'The Labour Market and Post-War Crime Trends in England and Wales' in P Carlen and R Morgan (eds), *Crime Unlimited* (London: Macmillan, 1999); C Hale, 'Economic Marginalisation, Social Exclusion and Crime' in Hale *et al*, n 24 above; S Hall and S Winlow, 'Rehabilitating Leviathan: Reflections on the State, Economic Management and Violence Reduction' (2003) 7(2) *Theoretical Criminology* 139; S Hall and S Winlow, 'Crime and Violence in the Breakdown of the Pseudo-Pacification Process' in J Ferrell, K Hayward, W Morrison, and M Presdee (eds), *Cultural Criminology Unleashed* (London: Glasshouse Press, 2005); D Dorling, 'Prime Suspect: Murder in Britain' in P Hillyard, C Pantazis, S Tombs, and D Gordon (eds), *Beyond Criminology* (London: Pluto, 2004); R Wilkinson, *The Impact of Inequality* (New York: New Press, 2005), 47–51, ch 5; Reiner, 'Political Economy', n 94 above.

154   *Robert Reiner*

1992—Falling Crime, Rising Fear: The drop in recorded crime during 1993–6 was probably a recording phenomenon rather than a real decline in offending, as argued earlier. Michael Howard may not have succeeded in his aims to be tough on crime, but the 'business-like' police managerialism he sponsored was certainly tough on the recording of crime.

However, after 1997 the BCS points to a sustained and substantial fall in victimization, returning to the levels of the early 1980s. The rising recorded rates of crime overall since 1997 are primarily due to the new counting rules, and in any event have also reduced in the last year. This has not, however, been accompanied by a decline in fear of crime.[103] Falls in recorded crime, and often victimization statistics, are a world-wide phenomenon of the 1990s, not least in the USA and the much trumpeted New York miracle. In the next section we will consider the possible factors that explain the 1990s crime drop.

Tough on Crime? Assessing the New Punitiveness

Explaining 'Law and Order'

As seen earlier, since the late 1970s there has been greater public concern about crime, and increasing support for a tough, 'law and order' approach to it. Crime and criminal justice policy are couched within a 'culture of control'.[104] As David Garland's analysis shows, this had at least three principal sources.

First, is the greater reality of victimization. It is not just that crime has increased, but that it has victimized middle-class and elite groups that were previously relatively immune to risks of crime.[105] As has often been quipped, a conservative is a liberal who has been mugged.

Secondly, the crime drop of the mid-1990s[106] was used by the police, many politicians, and conservative criminologists, to refute the 'nothing works' pessimism of the 1970s and 1980s. They claimed that tough criminal justice policies can contain crime without addressing social root causes—if these existed at all. We shall consider the evidence for such claims below. Thirdly, however, the new public and political support for

---

[103] M Hough, 'Modernisation and Public Opinion: Some Criminal Justice Paradoxes' (2003) 9(1) *Contemporary Politics* 143.   [104] Garland, n 23 above.

[105] ibid 154–6.

[106] Both the recorded drop of the early 1990s, and the later fall in victimization, have been used in this way, albeit with somewhat different party political biases. The Conservatives emphasized the former, New Labour the latter.

tough law and order politics can at best only be explained to a very limited extent by a 'truth will out' narrative about its validity. Public support for 'law and order' in the USA has been shown to be much more closely tied to prior media and political campaigns than by objective changes in crime rates.[107] Media narratives—news and fictional—have increasingly been framed in 'law and order' terms since the 1970s.[108] As inequality and social divisions have been exacerbated in the last quarter of a century, politicians have found crime concerns to be a way of constructing consensus in limited areas through focusing attention on fear of criminal folk-devils.[109]

Assessing 'Law and Order'

To what extent, if any, can the 1990s crime drop, in Britain and the US, be attributed to the politics of law and order—tougher policing and the new punitiveness? The police, particularly in the US, and especially those associated with the crime drop in New York City, have not been slow to claim credit. As William Bratton, the NYPD Commissioner between 1994–6, unabashedly trumpeted, 'Crime is down: blame the police'.[110] Throughout the world this has stimulated a new 'can-do' confidence amongst the police, palpably relieved that after two decades in which 'nothing works' seemed to be the clear conclusion of research on policing and punishment, new policing tactics seemed at last to be vindicating their crime-busting credentials.[111] The broad coincidence of falling crime rates and record imprisonment levels, especially in the USA and Britain, also encouraged those who had claimed that 'prison works'.

Independent research suggests a much more complex and indeed enigmatic picture than the prophets of 'zero-tolerance' and toughness. Most do not question that substantial declines in crime have occurred in the USA and in Britain, but explaining this is far more problematic.[112] It is

---

[107] Beckett, n 10 above; J Roberts and M Hough, *Understanding Public Attitudes to Criminal Justice* (Maidenhead: Open University Press, 2005).

[108] Reiner *et al*, n 9 above.

[109] As anticipated in S Hall, C Critcher, T Jefferson, J Clarke, and B Roberts, *Policing the Crisis* (London: Macmillan, 1978).

[110] W Bratton, 'Crime is Down: Blame the Police' in N Dennis (ed), *Zero Tolerance* (2nd edn) (London: IEA, 1998).

[111] D Dixon and L Maher, 'Policing, Crime and Public Health' (2005) 5(2) *Criminal Justice* 115.

[112] Indeed, so puzzling is the crime fall at a time when the major supposed drivers of crime such as inequality and deprivation have not declined, and in many ways have got worse, that some experts have felt renewed scepticism about the measurement of crime

precisely the widespread character of the crime-drop that calls into question some of the most popular explanations, in particular 'zero-tolerance' policing. As many commentators have argued, crime fell in most parts of the USA despite the considerable variations in policing styles. Whilst the celebrated New York City drop was especially marked, crime declined to a comparable extent even in cities that did not pursue the same, or any, reform strategy.

Close analysis of the New York experience itself suggests problems in attributing most of the falls in homicide and other serious crime to policing changes, because of the timing of these.[113] Certainly some of the huge decline in New York City is plausibly due to policing changes, but there is considerable doubt about how much is attributable to the much-celebrated 'zero-tolerance' aspect of the changes. Even Bratton plays down the label of 'zero-tolerance' for his reforms, and most analysts see the much more rigorous and speedy analysis of crime, and the stricter local managerial accountability for crime trends, summed up as 'COMPSTAT', as the most important element in the NYPD's success.[114]

At the national level, the most rigorous assessment of the 1990s crime drop in America finds that socio-economic and demographic changes—particularly the more buoyant labour market, and the decline in the high-crime age groups in the population—made a more significant impact than criminal justice policies, although these played some part.[115] In Britain too, the success of New Labour in maintaining relatively low levels of unemployment, and reducing poverty to a limited extent, but not inequality, are probably key factors.[116] More intelligence-based assessments of risk underlying patterns of policing, prevention, and punishment have also played a part. Certainly, the marked reductions in the

even by victim surveys, eg R Garside, *Crime, Persistent Offenders and the Justice Gap* (London: Crime and Society Foundation, 2004).

[113] B Bowling, 'The Rise and Fall of New York Murder' (1999) 39(4) *British Journal of Criminology* 531; A Karmen, *New York Murder Mystery* (New York: New York University Press, 2000).

[114] D Weisburd, S Mastrofski, A McNally, R Greenspan, and J Willis, 'Reforming to Preserve: Compstat and Strategic Problem Solving in American Policing' (2003) 2(3) *Criminology and Public Policy* 421; M Moore, 'Sizing Up Compstat' (2003) 2(3) *Criminology and Public Policy* 469.

[115] A Blumstein and J Wallman (eds), *The Crime Drop in America* (Cambridge: Cambridge University Press, 2000).

[116] D Downes, 'New Labour and the Lost Causes of Crime' (2004) 55 *Criminal Justice Matters* 4; R Garside, 'Is it the Economy?' (2004) 55 *Criminal Justice Matters* 32; C Hale, 'Economic Marginalisation, Social Exclusion and Crime' in Hale *et al*, n 24 above.

highest volume property crimes such as car crime and burglary owe much to vastly improved prevention practices.

Whilst emphasizing that crime overall has been declining, New Labour and senior police officers have struggled to benefit from this, above all because of the evidence from surveys and from media discussions that public fears have not declined. This has been labelled the 'reassurance gap' by policy-makers, and stimulated the so-called 'reassurance policing' agenda to try and plug it.[117] A key concept is Martin Innes' and Nigel Fielding's notion of 'signal crimes',[118] that particular offences have special power to symbolize broader crime and disorder and stimulate anxiety, outweighing the general statistical decline in crime—not a million miles away from the old Marxist notion of false consciousness.

There may, however, be a rational kernel to the stubborn refusal of public anxiety to decline with the crime rate, beyond blaming the messengers of the sensationalist and bad news-addicted media, although they are very significant. Within the decline in overall crime, the most worrying serious violent crimes have continued to rise.[119] In so far as the decline in crime overall is due to what Garland has called the 'criminologies of everyday life'[120]—more successful adoption of protective equipment and preventive routines by crime-conscious citizens, rather than any reduction in the root causes of offending—the burden falls on potential victims above all. Whilst prevention tactics, burdensome as they may be, are preferable to victimization, they are a product of insecurity, and indeed may reinforce rather than reduce fear. What is required is not reassurance about crime but about the causes of crime.

Conclusion

The trends I have outlined are dystopian in the extreme: increasing inequality, social polarization, egoism, all fuelling more serious crime. These can be contained—if at all—in fragile ways, by exclusionary and

---

[117] A Millie and V Herrington, 'Bridging the Gap: Understanding Reassurance Policing' (2005) 44(1) *Howard Journal* 41; M Hough, 'Policing, New Public Management and Legitimacy in Britain' in J Fagan and T Tyler (eds), *Legitimacy, Criminal Justice, and the Law* (New York: Russell Sage Foundation Press, 2006).

[118] M Innes and N Fielding, 'From Community to Communicative Policing: "Signal Crimes" and the Problem of Public Reassurance' (2002) 7(2) *Sociological Research Online*, available via <www.socresonline.org.uk>; M Innes, ' "Signal Crimes": Detective Work, Mass Media and Constructing Collective Memory' in Mason, n 9 above.

[119] Hallsworth, n 86 above; Rose, n 85 above.

[120] Garland, n 23 above, 127–31.

preventive routines that reflect and exacerbate fear. Enhanced physical security—locks, fences, window-bars—may protect particular targets, but there is evidence that they divert some offenders to more serious crimes,[121] and may exacerbate fear by offering constant physical reminders of the threats they are intended to control.[122] The use of apparently neutral technological surveillance by CCTV largely reproduces the patterns of discriminatory suspiciousness of traditional policing culture, focusing on the socially disadvantaged.[123] The life of the respectable majority takes place increasingly in 'mass private property',[124] spaces that are legally private but cater to large numbers of people, such as shopping malls or amusement parks. The safety of such 'security bubbles' is largely achieved by the expulsion of people perceived as threatening, whether or not they have acted suspiciously.[125] In the long run such measures exacerbate social divisions and disadvantage, and are likely to increase the pressures driving crime as they accentuate the social exclusion that fuels anomie and resistance.[126]

Rosa Luxemburg's stark choice, socialism or barbarism,[127] remains apposite. But actually, existing socialism as practised in Eastern Europe was barbarism. Its collapse pulled down in its wake the more ethical democratic socialism in the West that had produced more peaceful and just societies, and the promise of further improvement. Whether there is any possibility of its revival, in the face of the globalizing tendencies that have made more difficult if not impossible the agenda of social democracy in one country, and the more individualistic ethos engendered by three decades of neo-liberal hegemony, is a crucial question, not least for crime and criminal justice.[128]

A major difficulty is that neo-liberalism has relinquished the tools available to social democratic states to try and remedy inequality and

---

[121] The growth of street robbery, for example, has been explained as in part a result of the better protection of cars and homes. See Hallsworth, n 86 above.

[122] L Zedner, 'Liquid Security: Managing the Market for Crime Control' (2006) 6(2) *Criminology and Criminal Justice* 267.

[123] M McCahill, *The Surveillance Web* (Cullompton: Willan, 2002); R Coleman, *Reclaiming the Streets* (Cullompton: Willan, 2004).

[124] C Shearing and P Stenning, 'Private Security: Implications for Social Control' (1983) 30(5) *Social Problems* 493.

[125] ibid. See also A Wakefield, *Selling Security* (Cullompton: Willan, 2003). Shearing and Stenning refer to this accentuation of social divisions as a 'new feudalism'.

[126] The classic demonstration of this is M Davis, *City of Quartz* (New York: Vintage, 1992).

[127] R Luxemburg, 'The Junius Pamphlet: The Crisis in German Social Democracy' in P Hindis and K Anderson (eds), *The Rosa Luxemburg Reader* (New York: Monthly Review Press, 2004).   [128] This argument is elaborated in Reiner, n 100 above.

Law and Order 159

exclusion. For example, greater mobility of capital flows, partly because of technological and cultural changes associated with globalization, but crucially because of liberalization of controls over financial movements, has weakened the regulatory and taxation capacity of individual governments in relation to corporations. However, the extent to which this has systematically and irretrievably weakened governments' abilities to tax for redistributive and welfare purposes is debatable, and the position still varies considerably between different countries.[129] There is considerable evidence that variations in the political economy of different states are associated with the character of their penal systems, and with their patterns of serious and violent crime.[130] The more neo-liberal states tend to be the most punitive, whilst more social democratic and welfare-oriented states have less harsh penal regimes.[131] There is also both historical and comparative evidence of links between serious violent crime, inequality, and social exclusion.[132] The combination of general economic prosperity, low unemployment, and some mitigation of the worst levels of poverty,[133] together with more effectively targeted crime prevention and policing, and the huge growth in imprisonment, have bought an overall reduction in crime during the late 1990s. But serious violent crime remains a growing threat, and the containment of volume crime is fragile in the face of the continuing resilience of its basic causes, in particular the anomie of a consumerist society that fuels egoistic aspirations whilst bracketing off issues of the legitimacy of means, and with widening

[129] R Goodin, B Headey, R Muffels, and H-J Dirven, *The Real Worlds of Welfare Capitalism* (Cambridge: Cambridge University Press, 1999); P Hall and D Soskice (eds), *Varieties of Capitalism* (Oxford: Oxford University Press, 2001); A Glyn (ed), *Social Democracy in Neoliberal Times* (Oxford: Oxford University Press, 2001); D Held, *Global Governance* (Cambridge: Polity, 2004); R Taylor, *Sweden's New Social Democratic Model* (London: Compass, 2005). [130] Reiner, 'Political Economy', n 94 above.

[131] K Beckett and B Western, 'Governing Social Marginality: Welfare, Incarceration and the Transformation of State Policy' (2001) 3(1) *Punishment and Society* 43; M Cavadino and P Dignan, *Penal Systems: A Comparative Approach* (London: Sage, 2006); D Downes and K Hansen, 'Welfare and Punishment in Comparative Perspective' in S Armstrong and L McAra (eds), *Perspectives on Punishment* (Oxford: Oxford University Press, 2006).

[132] E Currie, 'Market, Crime and Community: Towards a Mid-Range Theory of Post-Industrial Violence' (1997) 1(2) *Theoretical Criminology* 147; S Hall and S Winlow, 'Barbarians at the Gate: Crime and Violence in the Breakdown of the Pseudo-Pacification Process' in J Ferrell *et al*, n 102 above; Hale, n 68 above; S Hall and C McLean, 'A Tale of Two Capitalisms: A Preliminary Comparison of Violence Rates in European and Anglo-American Market Societies' (University of Northumbria: Division of Sociology and Criminology, 2005); Reiner, 'Political Economy', n 94 above.

[133] J Hills, *Inequality and the State* (Oxford: Oxford University Press, 2004); J Hills and K Stewart (eds), *A More Equal Society?* (Bristol: Policy Press, 2005).

inequality.[134] Economic collapse, an ever present threat in market economies, with a return of mass unemployment and deprivation, would almost certainly trigger a repeat of the 1980s explosion of crime and disorder—or worse—and more authoritarian control efforts.

Certainly the regulative capacity of states to achieve social democratic ends has been undermined by globalization under the neo-liberal auspices of the 'Washington consensus'. But this could be seen as a challenge not a fatal conclusion.[135] The social democratic deficit of states could lead to a search to develop 'collaborative mechanisms of governance at supranational and global levels'.[136] Unless there is some mitigation of neo-liberalism, and the inequality and egoism it carries with it, there is no real hope of reversing the deep pressures that have driven crime up, and assured the ascendancy of law and order politics. Law and order in 2020 would realize the worst visions of 1984.

[134] J Young, *The Exclusive Society* (London: Sage, 1999).
[135] Lea, n 101 above; Hall and Winlow, n 102 above.
[136] Held, n 129 above, 15; Harvey, n 74 above, ch 7.

[16]
Neo-liberalism, Crime and Criminal Justice

What is neo-liberalism?

Neo-liberalism is the most common label for the economic theory and practice that has swept the world since the early 1970s, displacing communism in eastern Europe and China, as well as the Keynesian, mixed economy, welfare state consensus that had prevailed in western liberal democracies since the Second World War (Dumenil and Levy, 2004; Harvey, 2005; Glyn, 2006). As an economic doctrine it postulates that free markets maximise economic efficiency and prosperity, by signalling consumer wants to producers, optimising the allocation of resources, and providing incentives for entrepreneurs and workers (Kay, 2004).

Neo-liberalism as culture and ethic

Advocates of neo-liberalism see it as promoting not only economic efficiency, but also political and personal virtue. (The classic exposition is Hayek, [1944] 2001; for critical assessments see Tomlinson, 1990; Gamble, 1996.) To neo-liberals, free markets are associated with democracy and liberty. They also see markets as encouraging responsibility. On their analysis, welfare states have many moral hazards: they undermine personal responsibility, and meet the sectional interests of public sector workers, not the goals of public service. Neo-liberals advocate market disciplines, workfare and new public management to counteract this (Osborne and Gaebler, 1992); McLaughlin, Muncie and Hughes (2001) analyse the impact of new public management on criminal justice policy; Leys (2001) is a comprehensive critical analysis.

Neo-liberalism has spread from the economic sphere to the social and cultural. The roots of contemporary consumer culture predate neo-liberal dominance, but it has now become hegemonic (Sennett, 2006). Aspirations and conceptions of the good life have become thoroughly permeated by materialist and acquisitive values (Hayward, 2004; Hall and Winlow, 2004, 2006; Lawson, 2006). Business solutions and business models permeate all spheres of activity from sport and entertainment to charities, NGOs and even crime control (Zedner, 2006). The 'Rich List' and its many variations have ousted all other rankings of status.

The dysfunctions of markets

The benefits of neo-liberalism (supposedly economic growth, dynamism, efficiency and responsibility) have been familiarised as common sense by its cheerleaders, and indeed in most public discussion Mrs Thatcher's TINA rules. There are however many negative consequences of unbridled markets and materialism that used to be widely perceived. They were stressed by a variety of traditions, above all the various forms of socialism, and many religions. They were also understood by classical liberal political economy, from Adam Smith to Alfred Marshall and Pigou. As with the trumpeted virtues of markets, their dysfunctions transcend the economic, and include moral, social and political harms. Briefly, in the absence of countervailing interventions markets may produce a variety of negative consequences: economic, ethical, and social and political.

ECONOMIC DISFUNCTIONS

There are five economic disfunctions of markets:

— Left to themselves competitive markets will become increasingly dominated by monopolistic accumulations of power, as the winners use their resources to drive out competitors.
— Inequality of wealth and income will become ever greater as again the winners of early competition multiply their advantages.
— Allocation of resources increasingly reflects the consumer power of the rich, not human need, with the Galbraithian juxtaposition of private affluence and public squalor.
— Market systems are prone to macro-economic cyclical fluctuations (although their sources and the appropriate modes of regulation are of course hotly contested, for example between Keynesians and monetarists).
— Insecurities caused by the vicissitudes and adversities of ill-health, old age and so on are widespread, hard to predict at the level of the individual, and not solely attributable to personal responsibility. They are better protected against by collective rather than individual insurance and other strategies.

ETHICAL DISFUNCTIONS

Materialistic market societies generate cultures of egoism, short-termism and *irresponsibility* to others. They encourage lack of concern about the wider ramifications of action, in the present, but above all for posterity (as the issue of climate change illustrates most obviously). Bakan's analysis of company law shows that it requires corporations to act in ways psychiatrists would diagnose as psychopathic in an individual (Bakan, 2005, pp56–59). The most stirring expression of this claim remains Tawney's quintessential statement of ethical socialism in *The Acquisitive Society*. Competitive market society:

> suspends a golden prize, which not all can attain, but for which each may strive, the enchanting vision of infinite expression. It assures men that there are no ends other than their ends, no law other than their desires, no limit other than that which they think advisable. Thus it makes the individual the centre of his own universe, and dissolves moral principles into a choice of expediencies.
>
> (Tawney, [1921] 1961, p33).

SOCIAL AND POLITICAL DISFUNCTIONS

Inequality and competitiveness produce many adverse social consequences, notably poor health, social conflict and violence. Wilkinson (2005) provides a comprehensive recent review of the voluminous empirical evidence.

12   *Renewal* Vol.14 No.3 2006

'Free' markets have complex institutional, cultural and legal conditions of existence. These include state suppression of the disorder that may be sparked by market-generated social dislocations. As Karl Polanyi forecast in 1944, the same year that Hayek published his *Road to Serfdom* warning of the perils of socialism, markets can *threaten* freedom and democracy (Polanyi, [1944] 2001). In Andrew Gamble's famous formulation, the 'free' market needs the strong state (1994) – and the 'strong' state may well become authoritarian. Democracy is threatened and undermined by wide inequality (Jacobs and Skocpol, 2005). It leads to the 'best democracy money can buy' (Palast, 2004), as the costs of campaigning and media access spiral beyond the reach of all but the wealthy and corporate interests.

Neo-liberalism and crime: theoretical interpretations

The broader economic, social, political, cultural and moral dysfunctions of neo-liberalism produce more crime and more authoritarian criminal justice policy. Both the positive and the negative consequences of neo-liberalism generate processes that criminological theories of various kinds have identified as sources of crime.

Crimes have complex and multiple origins. A crime will not occur unless five necessary conditions are satisfied:

1. *Labelling*: Troublesome, dangerous, harmful acts may occur in profusion, but they are only seen as *crimes* if they are labelled as such. This involves the creation of the necessary legal categories, *and* the reporting of incidents by victims or witnesses, *and* their recording by the police. This means that what appear to be new trends in crime may really be the result of shifting laws, or changing social and official perceptions and practices.

2. *Motive*: A crime cannot occur unless someone has formed a motive to commit what lawyers call the *actus reus*. In the last 150 years criminologists have offered many theories of the sources of these motives. They may be quite normal desires for widely sought property or pleasures, or (by definition much more rarely) deeply deviant pathologies. But the crime will not occur unless somehow biology, psychology or social structure has produced someone with the wish to commit an act that is seen as criminal.

3. *Means*: The motivated potential offender must have the capacity to commit the crime. The means of crime change as technology and social routines alter.

4. *Opportunity*: A motivated, capable potential offender cannot carry out a crime unless there is a suitable victim or physical target.

5. *Absence of controls*: The crime will not occur if the perpetrator is prevented by social controls. These may be *formal*: the presence or threat of codes, courts or constables; or *informal*: the internalised residue of Sunday school sermons perhaps – the inhibitions of conscience that Eysenck called the 'inner policeman'.

Impact of neo-liberalism on the conditions of crime

Neo-liberalism has an impact on all these conditions in ways that make the commission and/or recording of crimes more likely.

LABELLING

A consumerist culture makes the reporting of property crime more likely. The theft of valuable consumer durables is much more likely to be reported to the police and recorded by them, especially if they are insured. This can produce apparent crime waves that are largely recording phenomena. For example the General Household Survey in the 1970s showed that the huge growth of burglaries was primarily due to increased recording, caused by the spread of domestic contents insurance (Hough and Mayhew, 1985, p16). Thus much (although certainly not all) of the increase in recorded crime that fuelled the politics of law and order and helped propel Mrs Thatcher into Downing Street was illusory.

MOTIVE

The most plausible (and venerable) sociological account of crime is Robert Merton's extension of Durkheim's celebrated concept of 'anomie' (for a contemporary reformulation see Messner and Rosenfeld, 2006). In a materialistic culture aspirations are fuelled beyond any possibility of attainment, at all levels of society, and the legitimacy of the means adopted to pursue them are accorded little weight. Monetary success is everything, and crime and anti-social behaviour multiply in the suites as well as the streets. When a meritocratic culture, holding out the dream of affluence to everyone, is combined with a structural reality of rampant inequality of opportunity and attainment, the anomic pressures of unfulfilled aspirations multiply.

It is this perspective that has always been at the heart of social democratic criminology, not a simplistic materialistic determinism linking poverty or unemployment straightforwardly with crime (Reiner, 2006). The link between objective economic conditions and criminality is morality. Materialism and inequality foster a culture of egoistic grasping and cynical pragmatism, and that makes crime and anti-social behaviour more likely. If callous, ends-justifies-the-means practices are celebrated as dynamic entrepreneurialism at the top of society (think *The Apprentice*) it is hardly surprising if this is mirrored by the young and excluded. The Henley Centre's recent findings of increasing self-centredness and selfishness among young people, registered by its regular surveys, illustrate this (Aitkenhead, 2006, pp23–24).

This future was anticipated clearly forty years ago by the Longford Study Group whose report informed the Wilson government's thinking on criminal justice, in the days when Labour was concerned to crack down on the causes of crime. The 'get rich quick ethos' (not a yet unheard of 1960s permissiveness) led, it argued, to a

> weakening of moral fibre ... The values that prevail among those who
> dominate society may be expected to spread to all its levels. If men and
> women are brought up from childhood to regard personal
> advancement and ruthless self interest as the main considerations,
> material success will certainly not train them in social responsibility,
> and worldly failure may lead to social inadequacy and a resentful sense
> of inferiority.
>
> (Longford Study Group, 1966, pp4–5)

14   *Renewal* Vol.14 No.3 2006

Tony Blair and the *Daily Mail* are right to agonise about 'weakening moral fibre'. But they finger the wrong culprits. The ruthless pursuit of profit, not permissiveness, has strained and undermined family life and the other underpinnings of civil society (Currie, 1985, 1998a, 1998b; James, 1995). The deification of the commercial destroys cultural capital.

MEANS

Technological advances and globalisation vastly expand and accelerate illegitimate alongside legitimate communications. They increase capacities to commit old types of crime, and provide spaces for new forms of offending. Internet fraud, grooming by paedophiles, identity theft, drugs, arms and people trafficking, terrorist networks and many other examples are the stuff of contemporary media nightmares. This is recognised by, and reflected in, the proliferation of new international policing bodies and security co-operation (Castells, 2000, chapter 3; Sheptycki and Wardack, 2005).

OPPORTUNITY

The huge proliferation of glittering, mobile, anonymously mass-produced, 'must-have' goodies of popular affluence and consumerism simultaneously constitute tempting targets for crime. From cars and TVs in the 1950s, to mobiles and iPods today, property crime patterns have tracked these conspicuous objects of desire (Lawson, 2006).

ABSENCE OF CONTROLS

— *Formal controls*: Neo-liberalism is not likely to weaken formal controls directly. On the contrary, attempts to stabilise the social tsunami unleashed by neo-liberalism lead to toughening the strong arm of the state. However, as crime rates are likely to rise faster than police numbers, clear-up rates will fall *ceteris paribus*. Even if the severity of punishment increases, *certainty* of punishment, the crucial element of deterrence (Farrington and Jolliffe, 2005, pp70–72), will weaken.

— *Informal and internalised controls*: As argued earlier, the anomic and egoistic culture shaped by neo-liberalism, with its sole emphasis on aspirations rather than on legitimate or ethical means, weakens institutions and inhibitions regulating anti-social or criminal conduct. 'All that is solid melts into air' with the unrestrained sway of market forces, as Marx famously put it (Marx and Engels, [1848] 1998, p38). The dominant theories of conservative criminologists stress the inability to control impulses and defer gratification as the key ingredients of criminality (Wilson and Herrnstein, 1985). In the words of one influential text, criminals 'tend to be impulsive, insensitive ... risk-taking, short-sighted' (Gottfredson and Hirschi, 1990, pp89–91). Remember some iconic catchphrases of the early consumer credit expansion: 'Live now, pay later' or 'Take the waiting out of wanting' (the advertising slogan for Access, the first widely available credit card). Are these not explicit calls to cultivate the characteristics of criminality? Is it any coincidence that the remorseless rise of recorded crime began simultaneously with the 1955 birth of commercial television in the UK?

Much research energy and expenditure has been devoted to assessing the effects of supposed media glorification of deviance and violence (Reiner, 2002). But the culprit is much more likely to be the saturation of the ratings by cupidity-inflaming shows from *Double Your Money* in the 1950s to *Who Wants to be a Millionaire?* and its ilk today.

Crime and neo-liberalism: empirical evidence

There is a plethora of empirical evidence demonstrating that neo-liberalism produces more crime *and* law and order politics, promising and delivering more punitive and authoritarian crime control practices; Reiner (2007a) reviews this in detail. Twenty years ago the late Steven Box wrote an important book assessing the impact of economic recession on crime and punishment (Box, 1987). This included a thorough review of the empirical literature up to that time analysing the relationship between crime and the economy.

Unemployment and crime

Box examined fifty studies on unemployment and crime (eighteen looked at the relationship over time, thirty-two compared different areas cross-sectionally). Thirty-three of these found a positive relationship – that as unemployment increased crime rose. Thus a bare majority pointed in the direction that would be predicted by anomie theory (or indeed the neo-classical rational choice perspective), in which more unemployment would be expected to increase the motives for property crime. However, the majority was slight, and the relationships found were generally weak. The same was true of the American empirical evidence at that time (Chiricos, 1987).

This does not mean that these studies demolish the view that unemployment is linked to crime, as the Thatcher and Reagan governments emphatically claimed. Criminological theories predict that unemployment has contradictory consequences for crime, partly cancelling each other out. It increases motivations for crime, proffers opportunities in the sense of the Devil finding work for idle hands, and reduces the disciplinary effects of work. On the other hand, it is linked to recession and fewer goods available to steal. More people at home also results in better guarded property.

Unemployment can involve a plethora of different social experiences in different contexts, with very different meanings for criminal motivation. Transitional voluntary unemployment in a buoyant economy would not be likely to increase motivations for crime, but long-term, possibly permanent, exclusion from the labour market would. The studies reviewed by Box and Chiricos in 1987 were predominantly examining data from the full-employment post Second World War decades, when unemployment did not involve the long-term social exclusion that affected increasing numbers of poor young men (especially from ethnic minorities) after the advent of neo-liberalism in the late 1970s. Most studies carried out since the mid-1980s show the expected positive relation between unemployment and crime (Farrington et al., 1986; Pyle and Deadman, 1994; Land, Cantor and Russell, 1995; Fielding, Clarke and Witt, 2000; Hale, 1998, 2005; Deadman and Macdonald, 2002; Kleck and Chiricos, 2002; Farrington and Jolliffe, 2005, pp65–69). This is especially so when *voluntary* unemployment is controlled for (Marris, 2000, pp73–74).

16   *Renewal* Vol.14 No.3 2006

Since the 1970s there has been the growth of a casual, poorly paid secondary labour market, increasingly displacing long-term manual work. This lessens the stark contrast between unemployment and employment, attenuating the statistical correlation between the former and relative deprivation and crime. Several studies show a link between the advent of the dual labour market and property crime (Hale, 1999). There are also clear relationships between economic downturns and an increase in property crime (Field, 1990, 1999) – although this finds that unemployment *per se* does not increase crime once its effect on reducing consumption as a proxy for living standards is controlled for; but Hale (1998) questions this conclusion.

Inequality and crime

Box also looked at seventeen studies of the relationship between inequality and crime (all but one were cross-sectional studies). Twelve of these found a positive relationship between inequality and property or non-fatal violent crime (see also Braithwaite, 1979). The five negative results were studies of homicide (Box, 1987, p87).

Studies conducted since 1987 confirm the overall relationship between inequality, market society and crime (Messner and Rosenfeld, 2000, 2006; Hale, 2005, pp334–336). However, there is now also overwhelming evidence that inequality and neo-liberalism are causally linked to homicide (Messner, 1997; Beckett and Sasson, 2000, pp32–35; Dorling, 2004; Wilkinson, 2005). A recent cross-sectional study of US states and Canadian provinces found a clear positive relationship between the degree of income inequality (measured by the Gini coefficient) and homicide rates (Daly, Wilson and Vasdev, 2001). Another recent comparative study of thirty-nine countries found the same relationship (Fajnzylber, Lederman and Loayza, 2002). A recent review of the literature concludes that there 'have now been over fifty studies showing a clear tendency for violence to be more common in societies where income differences are larger' (Wilkinson, 2005, p47).

A definitive study of homicide trends in Britain in the last quarter of a century finds that homicide is increasingly concentrated among poor males who have entered the labour market since the summer of 1981, when the recession induced by Mrs Thatcher's neo-liberal policies first bit (Dorling, 2004). All other groups in the population are now safer from risks of murder than they were. But the risks of serious violence and death facing these cohorts of poor young men, growing out of fights between them, are a testimony to the social and cultural destruction wreaked by neo-liberal policies (see also Davies, 1998):

> [The] woman who only noticed 'those inner cities' some six years after
> the summer of 1981, and the people who voted to keep her in office ...
> Those who perpetrated the social violence that was done to the lives of
> young men starting some 20 years ago are the prime suspects for most of
> the murders in Britain.
>
> (Dorling, 2004, p191).

A more optimistic recent finding is that the introduction of the minimum wage reduced crime in the areas where it had the greatest impact (Hansen and

Machin, 2002). This confirms the link between inequality, relative deprivation and crime, while pointing a tangible way forward.

Political economy, crime, justice: comparative studies
A number of recent studies have demonstrated clear links between neo-liberalism and harsher, more punitive penal policies. Beckett and Western (2001) showed in a comparative analysis of states in the USA between 1975 and 1995 that there was an association between high incarceration and declining in welfare spending, both over time, and cross-sectionally. Downes and Hansen (2006) found the same in a cross-national comparison: welfare spending and punishment were inversely related. A major recent book studied penal policies in twelve countries in depth (Cavadino and Dignan, 2006). It demonstrates that imprisonment and punitive cultural attitudes and policies are highest in the most neo-liberal societies studied (Australia, England and Wales, New Zealand, South Africa and USA), and much lower in social democracies.
　　Although the Scandinavian social democracies remain less characterised by law and order politics and by punitive policies, they are moving in that direction as globalisation exposes them to more pressure to adopt neo-liberalism (Tham, 1998, 2001; Bondeson, 2005). This is only partly related to rising crime. It has already been seen that social democracies are much less prone to serious violent crime, although they do have comparatively high rates of more minor and property crime – possibly because of greater civility actually producing more reporting in surveys and to the police (Young, 2003, p37). Fluctuations in the salience of crime and law and order as public concerns generally have been shown to be a function of media and political campaigning, rather than changes in crime rates (Beckett, 1997, chapter 2; Roberts and Hough, 2005). In sum, contemporary comparisons suggest that neo-liberalism tends to be more punitive than social democracy.

Historical trends
Historical research has demonstrated a long-term association between the growth of social inclusion in the late 19th and early 20th centuries, and a secular trend of falling crime and violence (Gatrell, 1980; Gurr, 1981; Hall and Winlow, 2003, 2004). The advent of mass consumerism in the late 1950s saw a reversal of this process, although some of the increase in recorded crime may have been the result of greater reporting and recording; Reiner (2000 and 2007b) examines the post-war crime trends in detail. In the 1980s and early 1990s, coinciding with the deepest impact of neo-liberalism and the huge growth of inequality, poverty and exclusion it entailed, recorded crime rose to a record level, with the annual British Crime Surveys from 1981 confirming that this was a real increase in victimisation.
　　Since the mid-1990s, however, the police recorded crime figures and the British Crime Survey data have diverged. From 1993 to 1996 the recorded crime statistics fell, but the British Crime Surveys suggested that this was because of increased reporting by victims and recording by the police, rather than less victimisation. Since 1996, however, the British Crime Survey has registered a continuous decline in victimisation, taking it back to 1981 levels. The police recorded data showed several years of rising crime after 1998, primarily because of new counting rules and procedures introduced between

18   *Renewal* Vol.14 No.3 2006

1998 and 2002. The crossing over of the trends indicated by the series coincided with the 1997 election of New Labour. So whether Michael Howard (home secretary from 1993 to 1997) or Tony Blair is the greatest crime-buster since Batman turns on which figures we see as more reliable. Unsurprisingly Tory think-tanks have recently begun questioning the British Crime Survey methodology (Dennis and Erdos, 2005; Green, Grove and Martin, 2005), while New Labour supporters reiterate the well-known problems of the police figures as rehearsed in most criminology texts.

In sum, recent British experience suggests that the social and cultural fallout of neo-liberalism produced massively rising crime in the 1980s and early 1990s. This accentuated already existing tendencies for crime and criminal justice to become increasingly politically polarised issues, with the tough 'law and order' line promulgated by Thatcherism prevailing over the previous cross-party consensus (Taylor, 1999; Young, 1999; Garland, 2001; Downes and Morgan, 2002).

After 1993 the politicisation of law and order was displaced by a new higher level consensus (Downes and Morgan, 2002). New Labour sought to remedy its electorally damaging image as 'soft' on crime, attempting to cover all bases with the legendary formula 'tough on crime, tough on the causes of crime'. As this began to pay dividends in New Labour's gathering popularity, Michael Howard responded with his 'prison works' return to tough Tory fundamentalism on penal matters. Since then there has been fundamental consensus on the importance of crime as an issue, and the need for toughness. At first after the 1997 Labour victory this was balanced a little by a search for 'smart', evidence-led, joined-up, partnership-based policies that could be shown to 'work'. Over time, however, toughness has tended to edge-out smartness in a stream of knee-jerk initiatives responding to red-top rages (Hough, 2004; Tonry, 2004; Roberts, 2005–6). Blatcherite consensus, in which New Labour accepts the fundamentals of Thatcherism with some nuances of difference, is a sad reverse echo of the Butskellism in the 1950s when the Tories were forced to adjust to Labour's mixed economy and welfare state. Nonetheless under Labour enough has changed to help explain the British crime drop of the late 1990s. Unemployment has been consistently low, and there has been some reduction in poverty if not overall inequality (Downes, 2004; Garside, 2004; Hills and Stewart, 2005). The 'smart', 'what works' approach to policing and crime prevention has also contributed to reductions of property crimes, notably burglary and car theft – although possibly producing some displacement to more serious and harder to prevent crimes such as robbery (Fitzgerald, Stockdale and Hale, 2003; Hallsworth, 2005). This indicates the general lesson that technological fixes can never be the silver bullet solution to crime (Marx, 1995).

Soft on the causes of crime?

Political economy – whether a society is organised on neo-liberal or social democratic lines – helps explain much of the British and comparative patterns of serious crime and punishment. But the sharp 1990s crime drop in the USA, most famously in New York City, is something of a mystery. Most American academic analyses give some weight to political economy (Blumstein and Wallman, 2000; Karmen, 2000), but see it as marginal compared with criminal justice and other factors. Popular culture sees 'zero-tolerance' policing as the panacea, though academic research questions the contribution of policing policy to the crime drop (Bowling, 1999). Even those who give policing significant weight in the explanation see the crucial reforms as being intelligence-led management (exemplified by New York's COMPSTAT system) not 'zero tolerance' (Newburn, 2005, chapters 27–31 sum up the debates).

The American analyses of the mystery of the disappearing crime rate resemble Agatha Christie's *Murder on the Orient Express*: everybody dunnit. British analyses are more like *Prime Suspect* (the title of Dorling's study of homicide, in which one offender – in his case Margaret Thatcher – is unmasked at the end).

There is a deeper puzzle: how can 1990s US experience be reconciled with the strong evidence of links between inequality and violence? The 1990s US crime drop has resulted in a resurgence of 'can do' optimism among police and criminal justice policy-makers, inspiring their colleagues around the world. The New York Police Department is credited with finding the Holy Grail of effective but democratic policing. No-one can fail to welcome policies that have saved many lives. But has a new paradigm really been achieved, refuting all previous experience – or is this like the mythical 'new economy' of the 1990s?

Raymond Chandler in *The Long Goodbye* expressed what used to be taken as a traditional criminological truism: 'Crime isn't a disease, it's a symptom. Cops are like a doctor that gives you aspirin for a brain tumour.' In the light of the extensive evidence of the relationship between inequality and violence, it would be hazardous to conclude that the lid can be held down indefinitely on injustice. The comparative evidence clearly suggests that there *are* 'root causes' shaping crime and penal trends, related to variations in political economy.

Social democracy is associated with less homicide, violence and serious crime, and fewer punitive penal policies. This is related to cultural differences in the moral quality of individualism. Social democracies reflect and encourage *reciprocal* individualism, with mutual concern for the welfare of all, as distinct from the *competitive* individualism of neo-liberalism, fostering a Darwinian struggle in which only the strongest flourish.

Suppression neglecting structural causes is what in the context of the 'war on terror' Paul Rogers has called 'liddism' (Rogers, 2002). Are new smarter and tougher policing and penal policies a panacea for holding down the lid on inequality and exclusion? Or do they just offer a temporary breathing space? We cannot afford to be soft on the causes of crime.

Robert Reiner is Professor of Criminology in the Law Department, London School of Economics. He is currently writing a book on trends in law and order.

References and further reading
Aitkenhead, D. (2006), 'It's all about me', *Guardian*, 8 Jul, pp23–24.
Bakan, J. (2005), *The Corporation*, London, Constable.
Beckett, K. (1997), *Making Crime Pay*, New York, Oxford University Press.
Beckett, K. and Sasson, T. (2000), *The Politics of Injustice*, Thousand Oaks, Pine Forge.
Beckett, K. and Western, B. (2001), 'Governing social marginality, welfare, incarceration and the transformation of state policy', *Punishment and Society*, Vol. 3, pp43–59.
Blumstein, A. and Wallman, J. (eds) (2000), *The Crime Drop in America*, Cambridge, Cambridge University Press.

20   *Renewal* Vol.14 No.3 2006

Bondeson, U. (2005), 'Levels of punitiveness in Scandinavia: description and explanations', in J. Pratt, D. Brown, M. Brown, S. Hallsworth and W. Morrison (eds), *The New Punitiveness*, Cullompton, Willan.

Bowling, B. (1999), 'The rise and fall of New York murder', *British Journal of Criminology*, Vol. 39, pp531–554.

Box, S. (1987), *Recession, Crime and Punishment*, London, Macmillan.

Braithwaite, J. (1979), *Inequality, Crime and Public Policy*, London, Routledge.

Castells, M. (2000), *End of Millennium*, Oxford, Blackwell.

Cavadino, M. and Dignan, J. (2006), *Penal Systems: a comparative approach*, London, Sage.

Chiricos, T. G. (1987), 'Rates of crime and unemployment', *Social Problems*, Vol. 34, pp187–211.

Currie, E. (1985), *Confronting Crime*, New York, Pantheon.

Currie, E. (1998a), 'Crime and market society: lessons from the United States', in P. Walton and J. Young (eds), *The New Criminology Revisited*, London, Macmillan.

Currie, E. (1998b), *Crime and Punishment in America*, New York, Holt.

Daly, M., Wilson, M. and Vasdev, S. (2001), 'Income inequality and homicide rates in Canada and the United States', *Canadian Journal of Criminology*, Vol. 43, pp219–236.

Davies, N. (1998), *Dark Heart*, London, Verso.

Deadman, D. and Macdonald, Z. (2002), 'Why has crime fallen? An economic perspective', *Economic Affairs*, Vol. 22, pp5–14.

Dennis, N. and Erdos, G. (2005), *Cultures and Crimes*, London, Civitas.

Dorling, D. (2004), 'Prime suspect: murder in Britain', in P. Hillyard, C. Pantazis, S. Tombs and D. Gordon (eds), *Beyond Criminology*, London, Pluto.

Downes, D. (2004), 'New Labour and the lost causes of crime', *Criminal Justice Matters*, Vol. 55, pp4–5.

Downes, D. and Hansen, K. (2006), 'Welfare and punishment in comparative perspective', in S. Armstrong and L. McAra (eds), *Perspectives on Punishment*, Oxford, Oxford University Press.

Downes, D. and Morgan, R. (2002), 'The skeletons in the cupboard: the politics of law and order at the turn of the millennium', in M. Maguire, R. Morgan and R. Reiner (eds), *The Oxford Handbook of Criminology*, 3rd edn, Oxford, Oxford University Press.

Dumenil, G. and Levy, D. (2004), *Capital Resurgent: roots of the neoliberal revolution*, Cambridge, Harvard University Press.

Fajnzylber, P., Lederman, D. and Loayza, N. (2002), 'Inequality and violent crime', *Journal of Law and Economics*, Vol. 45, No. 1, pp1–40.

Farrington, D. and Jolliffe, D. (2005), 'Crime and punishment in England and Wales 1981–99', in M. Tonry and D. Farrington (eds), *Crime and Punishment in Western Countries 1980–1999*, Chicago, Chicago University Press.

Farrington, D., Galagher, B., Morley, L., St Ledger, R. J. and West, D. J. (1986), 'Unemployment, school leaving and crime', *British Journal of Criminology*, Vol. 26, No. 4, pp335–356.

Field, S. (1990), *Trends in Crime and Their Interpretation: a study of recorded crime in post-war England and Wales*, London, Home Office.

Field, S. (1999), *Trends in Crime Revisited*, London, Home Office.

Fielding, N., Clarke, A. and Witt, R. (eds) (2000), *The Economic Dimensions of Crime*, London, Macmillan.

Fitzgerald, M., Stockdale, J. and Hale, C. (2003), *Young People and Street Crime*, London, Youth Justice Board.

Gamble, A. (1994), *The Free Economy and the Strong State*, London, Macmillan.

Gamble, A. (1996), *Hayek: the iron cage of liberty*, Cambridge, Polity.

Garland, D. (2001), *The Culture of Control*, Oxford, Oxford University Press.

Garside, R. (2004), 'Is it the economy?', *Criminal Justice Matters*, Vol. 55, pp32–33.

Gatrell, V. (1980), 'The decline of theft and violence in Victorian and Edwardian England', in V. Gatrell, B. Lenman and G. Parker (eds), *Crime and the Law*, London, Europa.

Glyn, A. (2006), *Capitalism Unleashed*, Oxford, Oxford University Press.

Gottfredson, M. and Hirschi, T. (1990), *A General Theory of Crime*, Stanford, Stanford University Press.

Green, D., Grove, E. and Martin, N. (2005), *Crime and Civil Society*, London, Civitas.

Gurr, T. R. (1981), 'Historical trends in violent crime', in M. Tonry and N. Morris (eds), *Crime and Justice 3*, Chicago, Chicago University Press.

Hale, C. (1998), 'Crime and the business cycle in post-war Britain revisited', *British Journal of Criminology*, Vol. 38, pp681–698.

Hale, C. (1999), 'The labour market and post-war crime trends in England and Wales', in P. Carlen and R. Morgan (eds), *Crime Unlimited*, London, Macmillan.

Hale, C. (2005), 'Economic marginalization and social exclusion', in C. Hale, K. Hayward, A. Wahidin and E. Wincup (eds), *Criminology*, Oxford, Oxford University Press.

Hall, S. and Winlow, S. (2003), 'Rehabilitating Leviathan: reflections on the state, economic regulation and violence reduction', *Theoretical Criminology*, Vol. 7, pp139–162.

Hall, S. and Winlow, S. (2004), 'Barbarians at the gates: crime and violence in the breakdown of the pseudo-pacification process', in J. Ferrell, K. Hayward, W. Morrison and M. Presdee (eds), *Cultural Criminology Unleashed*, London, Glasshouse.

Hall, S. and Winlow, S. (2006), *Violent Night: urban leisure and contemporary culture*, London, Berg.

Hallsworth, S. (2005), *Street Crime*, Cullompton, Willan.

Hansen, K. and Machin, S. (2002), 'Spatial crime patterns and the introduction of the UK minimum wage', *Oxford Bulletin of Economics and Statistics*, Vol. 64, pp677–697.

Harvey, D. (2005), *A Brief History of Neoliberalism*, Oxford, Oxford University Press.

Hayek, F. ([1944] 2001), *The Road to Serfdom*, London, Routledge.

Hayward, K. (2004), *City Limits: crime, consumer culture and the urban experience*, London, Glasshouse.

Hills, J. and Stewart, K. (eds) (2005), *A More Equal Society?*, Bristol, Policy Press.

Hough, M. (ed.) (2004), 'Evaluating the crime reduction programme in England and Wales', *Criminal Justice*, special issue, Vol. 4, No. 3.

Hough, M. and Mayhew, P. (1985), *Taking Account of Crime: key findings from the second British Crime Survey*, London, Home Office.

Jacobs, L. and Skocpol, T. (2005), *Inequality and American Democracy*, New York, Russell Sage Foundation.

James, O. (1995), *Juvenile Violence in a Winner-Loser Culture: socio-economic and familial origins of the rise in vilence against the person*, London, Free Association Books.

Karmen, A. (2000), *New York Murder Mystery*, New York, New York University Press.

Kay, J. (2004), *The Truth About Markets*, London, Penguin.

Kleck, G. and Chiricos, T. (2002), 'Unemployment and property crime: a target-specific assessment of opportunity and motivation as mediating factors', *Criminology*, Vol. 40, pp649–679.

Land, K., Cantor, D. and Russell, S. (1995), 'Unemployment and crime rate fluctuations in the post-World War II United States', in J. Hagan and R. Peterson (eds), *Crime and Inequality*, Stanford, Stanford University Press.

Lawson, N. (2006), 'Turbo-consumerism is the driving force behind crime', *Guardian*, 29 Jun.

Leys, C. (2001), *Market-Driven Politics*, London, Verso.

Longford Study Group (1966), *Crime: a challenge to us all*, London, Labour Party.

Marris, R. (2000), *Survey of the Research Literature on the Economic and Criminological Factors Influencing Crime Trends*, London, Volterra Consulting.

Marx, G. (1995), 'The engineering of social control: the search for the silver bullet', in J. Hagan and R. Peterson (eds), *Crime and Inequality*, Stanford, Stanford University Press.

Marx, K. and Engels, F. ([1848] 1998), *The Communist Manifesto*, London, Verso.

McLaughlin, E., Muncie, J. and Hughes, G. (2001), 'The permanent revolution: New Labour, new public management and the modernization of criminal justice', *Criminal Justice*, Vol. 1, pp301–318.

Messner, S. (1997), 'Political restraint of the market and levels of criminal homicide: a cross-national application of institutional-anomie theory', *Social Forces*, Vol. 75, pp1393–1416.

Messner, S. and Rosenfeld, R. (2000), 'Market dominance, crime and globalisation', in S. Karstedt and K.-D. Bussmann (eds), *Social Dynamics of Crime and Control*, Oxford, Hart.

Messner, S. and Rosenfeld, R. (2006), *Crime and the American Dream*, 4th edn, Belmont, California.

Newburn, T. (ed.) (2005), *Policing – Key Readings*, Cullompton, Willan.

Newburn, T. and Rock, P. (eds) (2006, in press), *The Politics of Crime Control*, Oxford, Oxford University Press.

Osborne, D. and Gaebler, T. (1992), *Reinventing Government*, New York, Persaeus.

Palast, G. (2004), *The Best Democracy Money Can Buy*, New York, Plume.

Polanyi, K. ([1944] 2001), *The Great Transformation*, Boston, Beacon.

Pyle, D. and Deadman, D. (1994), 'Crime and the business cycle in post-war Britain', *British Journal of Criminology*, Vol. 34, pp339–357.

Reiner, R. (2000), 'Crime and control in Britain', *Sociology*, Vol. 34, pp71–94.

Reiner, R. (2002), 'Media made criminality', in M. Maguire, R. Morgan and R. Reiner (eds), *The Oxford Handbook of Criminology*, 3rd edn, Oxford, Oxford University Press.

Reiner, R. (2006), 'Beyond risk: a lament for social democratic criminology', in T. Newburn and P. Rock (eds), *The Politics of Crime Control*, Oxford, Oxford University Press.

22   *Renewal* Vol.14 No.3 2006

Reiner, R. (2007a), 'Political economy, crime and criminal justice', in M. Maguire, R. Morgan and R. Reiner (eds) *The Oxford Handbook of Criminology*, 4th edn, Oxford, Oxford University Press.

Reiner, R. (2007b), 'Law and order: a 20:20 vision', *Current Legal Problems 2006*, Oxford, Oxford University Press.

Roberts, J. and Hough, M. (2005), *Understanding Public Attitudes to Criminal Justice*, Maidenhead, Open University Press.

Roberts, R. (ed.) (2005–6), 'Uses of research', *Criminal Justice Matters*, special issue, Vol. 62, winter 2005–6.

Rogers, P. (2002), *Losing Control: global security in the twenty-first century*, London, Pluto.

Sennett, R. (2006), *The Culture of the New Capitalism*, New Haven, Yale University Press.

Sheptycki, J. and Wardack, A. (eds) (2005), *Transnational and Comparative Criminology*, London, Glasshouse.

Tawney, R. H. ([1921] 1961), *The Acquisitive Society*, London, Fontana.

Taylor, I. (1999), *Crime in Context*, Cambridge, Polity.

Tham, H. (1998), 'Crime and the welfare state: the case of the United Kingdom and Sweden', in V. Ruggiero, N. South and I. Taylor (eds), *The New European Criminology*, London, Routledge.

Tham, H. (2001), 'Law and order as a leftist project: the case of Sweden', *Punishment and Society*, Vol. 3, pp409–426.

Tomlinson, J. (1990), *Hayek and the Market*, London, Pluto.

Tonry, M. (2004), *Punishment and Politics*, Cullompton, Willan.

Wilkinson, R. (2005), *The Impact of Inequality*, New York, New Press.

Wilson, J. Q. and Herrnstein, R. (1985), *Crime and Human Nature*, New York, Simon and Schuster.

Witt, R., Clarke, A. and Fielding, N. (1999), 'Crime and economic activity: a panel data approach', *British Journal of Criminology*, Vol. 39, pp391–400.

Young, J. (1999), *The Exclusive Society*, London, Sage.

Young, J. (2003), 'Winning the fight against crime? New Labour, populism and lost opportunities', in R. Matthews and J. Young (eds), *The New Politics of Crime and Punishment*, Cullompton, Willan.

Zedner, L. (2006), 'Opportunity makes the thief-taker: the influence of economic analysis on crime control', in T. Newburn and P. Rock (eds), *The Politics of Crime Control*, Oxford, Oxford University Press.

[17]
The Law and Order Trap

Contemporary popular discourses on crime continuously feed an authoritarian law and order agenda

——

L aw and order has been central to the New Labour project from the outset. The template for all the subsequent Clause 4 moments that transformed the electoral frog of Old Labour into the triumphant New Labour prince of 1997 was Tony Blair's successful assault on the Tory stronghold of law and order politics in 1992-3.

The quintessential New Labour slogan 'tough on crime, tough on the causes of crime' was the rallying cry for a concerted campaign to establish in voters' minds that crime was really a Labour issue; even - as Blair was not ashamed to say fifteen years ago - a 'socialist issue'. The slogan managed to hit all bases at once, appeasing the populist desire for punitiveness whilst allaying public fears about victimisation. Its success lay largely in its ambiguities, which allowed everyone to see in it what they wanted. Did 'tough on crime' mean what worked in crime reduction - smart, evidence-led crime prevention? Or did it mean harsh punishment of criminals? Was 'tough on the causes of crime' a nod to the traditional social democratic idea that crime had deep social root causes, or just an underlining of the need to rectify failings of criminal justice? But the ultimate political payoff from the celebrated soundbite lay in its subtext: a double-whammy of toughness locked into one short, sharp sentence, cutting at a stroke the accusation that Labour was soft on crime. It is ironic that this legendary soundbite

Soundings

may have been 'borrowed' from its original author Gordon Brown. But whatever its provenance, for a time it did the business.

Law and order first became a political issue in Britain during the early 1970s, and played a massive part in Margaret Thatcher's 1979 victory. Since then the Tories have almost always dominated as the party of law and order.[1] MORI polls tracking which party was seen as having the best policies on law and order showed the Conservatives in a commanding lead during the Thatcher years (despite massive increases in recorded crime). Blair was able to capture the issue after 1993, but only for an interlude, despite an intensification of tabloid-pleasing toughness as well as remarkable drops in crime levels.[2]

My argument is that law and order is necessarily a liability for Labour, and this cannot be changed without dramatic and undesirable changes in policy and presentation that would undermine any pretension it has to being a party of justice - or indeed one that can successfully improve security for citizens. Yet, ironically, Labour's crime reduction record and potential are far superior to the that of the Tories, and fair and effective protection against crime could be an electoral asset.

The problem is that the crime issue has come to be framed in terms of law and order. It appears in media and political discourse as a series of shocking cases of horrifying harms done to vulnerable victims, with no linking theme apart from the threat from evil individuals. If social roots are recognised at all, reference is made to specific pockets of social deprivation and disorganisation, or to a broader c/Conservative theme of increasing 'permissiveness' due to excessive liberalism (as in David Cameron's 'broken society' talk, which conveniently forgets that it was his predecessor Margaret Thatcher who denied that there was such a thing as society - and made this a self-fulfilling prophecy). Excluded from media and political debate is any connection between the social and economic structure as a whole, or the way of life of the privileged and respectable, and the roots of criminality. The media engage in exquisitely voyeuristic excavation of the details of spectacularly gory incidents and exceptionally frightening types of crime (currently gangs, guns and knives), and canvass limited tactical solutions. Yet neoliberalism - the key source both of the crime explosion of recent decades and the repressive reactions to it - remains outside the discussion (although many of its other deleterious consequences have become prominent in public awareness since credit crunched). Public discourse on crime, framed in law and order terms, cannot see the picture for the pixels.

The law and order trap

Defining crime

In view of the legions of bleeding and anguished victims that are portrayed on the nightly news, it might appear obscurantist to suggest that the concept of crime itself is ambiguous to the point of incoherence. And it is of course vital to recognise the agonies inflicted by what is ordinarily understood by the term crime. But 'crime' carries an ambiguous multiplicity of meanings, and debate frequently confuses these, with baleful consequences: the way crime is understood and publicly discussed has crucial implications for policy and politics. It is therefore helpful to devote some space to analysing the way it is defined.

In contemporary public discourse at least five meanings of 'crime' can be distinguished. The most commonly espoused is the legal: it is defined as 'an offence against an individual or the state which is punishable by law' (in the words of the *Compact Oxford English Dictionary*). The limitation of this definition is its circularity: crime is whatever criminal procedure may process. But what criminal law proscribes is often very different from what is widely held to be seriously wrong or harmful. The culture wars raging in the contemporary world include heated conflicts about what activities ought to be treated as criminal. Normative views about the ambit of crime are also deeply contentious and socially variable. Critical criminologists have long pointed out that the harms perpetrated by corporations and states - which may or may not be proscribed by criminal law in principle but typically go unsanctioned - vastly outweigh in quantity and seriousness the harms treated by criminal justice.[3]

There is also a difference between these legal and normative views about what ought to be criminalised and what is in practice socially proscribed and censured. A hazard of being a criminologist is to be button-holed at parties by red-faced, glass-holding individuals demanding to know why the police waste their time on those driving under the influence of drink or mobile phones - unequivocally illegal and demonstrably dangerous activities - rather than chasing 'real' criminals. 'Criminals' are conceptually other, not 'one of us'. And the criminalised 'others' are not generally those with the power to influence law-making - they are those who are subject to it.

Moving down from the objective heights of law and ethics, a huge volume of research demonstrates that criminal law in action is structured by social divisions and inequalities: class, race, age, gender, sexuality. Those that are suspected and sentenced through criminal justice constructions of crime represent a tiny

Soundings

and highly biased sample of all who participate in crime as it is legally defined; and they are predominantly those without power or property. Offences that are disproportionately committed by the powerful and privileged loom large within the massive body of unrecorded and unprosecuted crime: an incalculable volume of offences are committed in the normal functioning of organisations. These come to light only by chance or through proactive policing tactics that may target a small range of the total. And identified offenders are an even more minute and unrepresentative proportion of those who commit crimes. Only 2 per cent of the minority of crimes that are picked up by the British Crime Survey result in a conviction. Criminal 'justice' at every stage - reporting by victims, police stop and search, arrest, prosecution, sentencing - exhibits huge inequalities along the lines of class, age, race, gender and other social disparities. Three quarters of the prison population were either unemployed or employed in the most marginal sectors prior to arrest. Over 95 per cent are male. Some 16 per cent are from ethnic minorities - more than three times their proportion in the population. Nearly half are under 25 years old. It is the deprived that typically get labelled as depraved. Criminal justice is an apparatus for regulating the offences of the poor, not for enforcing criminal law as such.

Public discourse is focused on a tiny minority of the offences processed by criminal justice. Media and policy constructions of crime concentrate almost exclusively on serious violent and sex crime, in particular murder. This vastly exaggerates the gravity of crime in general. Policy towards mundane offending is driven by emotions and fears generated by the rare frightening cases that dominate media and political attention. A short-circuited picture of crime, portraying no-holds-barred 'law and order' as the source of security in the face of an increasing menace of violent predators, underpins most media and policy debate nowadays.

Though it may be difficult to discern, there is a core concept that is widely invoked in discussion of crime - albeit one that is rarely articulated - and it extends even to relatively minor 'volume' crimes. This is the idea of physical 'trespass': literally 'breaking-in' to the person or property of another. Trespass, physical violation, seems to lurk lingeringly behind popular notions of 'real' crime today. And this is the primary reason for the concentration of criminal justice on the poor and powerless, prior to any issues of discrimination, direct or institutional. The crimes that involve the element of obvious physical trespass upon the property or persons

The law and order trap

of others are rarely resorted to except by the poor. Moreover, the image of crime as trespass also underpins media and political focus on the most dramatic cases of violence and spectacular robbery - paradigm instances of physical 'break-in' to the person or property of others.

The concentration of popular culture and criminal justice practice on the most clear-cut types of trespass, committed disproportionately by the poor and excluded, serves important ideological and control functions for societies characterised by inequalities of power and advantage. The frustrations, pain, anger, insecurity and rage that are engendered by the illegitimate (though largely undiscovered) crimes of the powerful, as well as the many legitimate harms arising from the everyday exercise of economic and political power, are thereby focused onto a scapegoat class of offenders, whose trespasses, evil as they may be, pale into insignificance relative to other sources of misery. The risks of physical or material harm from ordinary crime are dwarfed by those posed by either corporate or state crime, or the routine activities of a turbo-charged neo-capitalist society. A burglary can be a frightening and often traumatic experience, in addition to any material loss and inconvenience suffered. But it rarely has life-trashing effects for whole families or communities, whereas - for example - the downsizing of a business in pursuit of increased profitability can destroy the lives of large numbers of people. Yet the former is a crime, the latter the basis for wealth, celebrity, and a peerage.

The diversion of fear and anger onto ordinary criminals by media and politicians helps secure the structures that generate insecurity. Because of this, many critical voices have argued for the abandonment of criminology, tied as it is to a concept of crime that is embedded more in the discriminatory functioning of criminal justice and media processes than it is in the law itself. Nonetheless the analysis that follows is based on trends and patterns in crime conceived of in this ultimately indefensible way, because it is these that are the focus of officially recorded crime, and the politics of law and order.

The political arithmetic of crime

Criminal statistics are notoriously riddled with pitfalls. Changes in the recorded figures may be due not to changes in offence levels but to fluctuations in reporting or recording, or in the rules for counting. However very substantial steps have

Soundings

been taken in recent decades to alleviate these problems by developing alternative measures. And putting together the different sorts of data available shows - contrary to the popular perception of the Tories as the party of law and order - that crime is very much a product of Conservative policies.

The most apparent trend in crime is the spectacular and remorseless rise in recorded offences since the late 1950s. In the early 1950s the police recorded less than half a million offences per annum. By the mid 1970s this had risen to 2 million. The 1980s showed even more staggering rises, with recorded crime peaking in 1992 at over 5.5 million; but by 1997 recorded crime had fallen back to 4.5 million. Major counting rule changes introduced in 1998 and 2002 make comparison of the subsequent figures especially fraught, but on the new rules (which undoubtedly exaggerate the increase) just under 6 million offences were recorded by the police for 2003-4. This has now fallen back again, to 4.95 million in 2007-8.

Contrasting the police recorded statistics with victim surveys suggests a more complex picture than a remorselessly rising trend. It clearly pinpoints Thatcherite neoliberalism as the accelerant behind a crime explosion in the 1980s and early 1990s, with much more attenuated increases before and after. Three distinct phases can be distinguished since the mid-1950s.

1955-83: recorded crime rise

Until the 1970s there was no other measurement of trends apart from police statistics. But during the 1970s the General Household Survey began to ask about burglary victimisation, and its data showed that most of the increase in recorded burglary was due to greater reporting by victims. In the 1970s recorded burglaries doubled, but victimisation increased by only 20 per cent. Victims reported more burglaries mainly because of the spread of household contents insurance, and it is plausible to infer that this applied to property crimes more generally. So the rise of crime in the heyday of the mixed economy, welfarist consensus was probably substantially less than the recorded statistics suggested - although, no doubt, the first stirrings of consumerism in the 'live now pay later' era would have stimulated acquisitiveness and crime. As the growth of consumer credit urged people to 'take the waiting out of wanting', those without legitimate Access cards were tempted to find illicit routes to the must-have glittering prizes.

The law and order trap

1983-1992: crime explosion

The British Crime Survey, which was first published in 1982, showed huge increases in offending in its first decade, roughly in line with the police statistics. BCS crime rose 77 per cent from 1981 to 1993, whilst police-recorded crime increased by 111 per cent. By both measures crime rose at an explosive rate during the Thatcher and early Major years. The one clearly booming industry during the decade and a half in which neoliberalism destroyed Britain's industrial base was crime.

1993- : ambiguously falling crime

After the early 1990s the trends indicated by the police statistics and the BCS began to diverge. The BCS continued to chart a rise until 1995, but the police data fell from 1992 to 1997. Paradoxically, this was because of the extraordinarily high levels of victimisation. The police recorded fewer crimes as insurance companies made claiming more onerous, thus discouraging reporting by victims; and at the same time more 'businesslike' managerial accountability for policing implicitly introduced incentives against recording. Michael Howard was certainly tough on the causes of *recording* crime.

After New Labour came to power in 1997 the two measures continued to diverge - but in the opposite direction. BCS-recorded crime has fallen rapidly since 1995, and in 2007-8 was below the level of the first BCS, conducted in 1981. The police-recorded statistics, however, began to rise again from 1998 up to 2004, since when they have declined a little.

The rise in the police-recorded rate was due overwhelmingly to two major changes in police procedures for counting crimes, and was a predicted consequence of the changes. New Home Office Counting Rules in 1998 made 'notifiable' a number of offences (such as common assault) that had hitherto not been included in the recorded rate. In 2002, the National Crime Recording Standard required police to record 'any notifiable offence which comes to the attention of the police', even in the absence of evidence supporting the victim's report. These counting-rule reforms indicate concern, in the early optimistic days of New Labour, to develop evidence-based crime policy, even at the price of a politically sensitive rise in recorded crime. A more recent revision, in 2006, restores some discretion to the police not to record

Soundings

offences that are reported without supporting evidence. This would tend to reduce the recorded rate, and may be a factor in the recent decline.

The BCS is free from the particular problems that make the police figures unreliable as a measure of trends. However, it is not (and has never claimed to be) a definitive index. As a survey of individual victims, it necessarily omits many offences: homicide - the supreme example of personal victimisation; crimes with individual victims who are unaware of what happened (such as successful frauds); crimes against organisations or the public at large; consensual offences such as drug-taking. Its sampling frame also excludes certain highly victimised groups, such as children under 16, and the homeless. So the government's tendency to treat the BCS as definitive is as problematic as the earlier exclusive reliance on the police statistics, although it is a more reliable indicator of trends.

The dramatic overall fall in the BCS under New Labour also masks increases in some of the most alarming offences. Murder and other serious crimes of violence have increased in the last thirty years, and are now a higher proportion of all crimes. During the 1960s and early 1970s annual recorded homicides remained between 300 and 400, but this has roughly doubled. The number of homicides has been over 700 in all years since the millennium, and was 784 in 2007-8. In 1976 just 5 per cent of recorded offences were classified as violent, but by 2007-8 it had increased to 19 per cent. Recorded robberies have also risen sharply since the early 1990s, although they have been falling (erratically) in the last few years, from a peak in 2001-2. The current hot topics, gun and knife crime, show similar trajectories. Recorded offences involving firearms have risen sharply in the last thirty years. The latest Home Office statistics show they doubled from 1998-9 to 2005-6 (from just over 5000 to nearly 11,000), but have since fallen back to just under 10,000. Knife crime figures have only recently started to be collected, but murders involving knives or other sharp instruments increased by 28 per cent in the last decade, from 202 in 1997-8 to 258 in 2006-7. So the trends are certainly not as rosy as the BCS total suggests. The next section will analyse the relationship of this to the politics of law and order.

Accounting for law and order

Tony Blair's tough on crime stance represented a decisive watershed for the politics of law and order, and can be seen as part of the onward march of neoliberal ideas.

The law and order trap

One of the things that really confirmed the global hegemony of neoliberalism was the increasing acceptance by western social democratic parties of the fundamentals of its economic and social policy framework. This new political terrain was heralded in Britain in 1992-3 by Labour's seizure of the law and order agenda. A new crime control consensus has subsequently emerged.

There are five core elements in this consensus. Firstly, crime is coming to be seen as public enemy Number 1. It is increasingly seen as *the* major threat to society and to individual citizens. MORI has conducted polls on what people see as 'the three most important issues facing Britain today' for more than thirty years. In the early 1970s, just as law and order was emerging as a political issue, less than 10 per cent rated it amongst the top three. Since 1993 the proportion putting crime in the top three issues has usually been above 30 per cent - despite falling crime. Secondly, there has been a move towards seeing responsibility for crime as being individual rather than social: the crime control consensus views crime as solely the fault of offenders, due to their free choice, individual or cultural pathology, or to intrinsic evil. Social structural factors are denied. Thirdly, there has been a foregrounding of a 'victims v. offenders' approach. The victim has become the iconic centre of discourse about crime, and discourse and policy are predicated on a zero-sum game: concern for victims precludes any understanding of - let alone sympathy for - offenders. This was a particularly pronounced theme of Blair's speeches on criminal justice, such as the one which launched the Home Office's *Five-Year Strategy for Criminal Justice* on 19 July 2004: 'The purpose of the criminal justice reforms is to re-balance the system radically in favour of the victim ... our first duty is to the law-abiding citizen. They are our boss ... That is the new consensus on law and order for our times'.

A fourth element of the new consensus is that policies predicated on crime control are effective. Since the early 1990s can-do optimism has reinvigorated law enforcement agencies around the world: criminal justice *can* control crime, provided it is tough enough. Criminal justice professionals and conservative politicians celebrate this as a triumph of common sense over the 'nothing works' pessimism and over sensitivity to civil liberties that are said to have previously hampered crime control. 'Prison works', as does 'zero tolerance' policing, and the 'responsibilisation' of citizens to take self-protective measures against victimisation.

Finally, a view that we live in a high-crime society has been normalised. Popular culture and routine activities have become increasingly focused on crime risks.

Soundings

Crime concerns have penetrated everyday life, embodied in CCTVs, gated estates, SUVs and other proliferating security kit - all of which, paradoxically, enhance fear at least as much as security. All five elements in the new consensus serve to displace a focus on the social causes of crime and increase feelings of insecurity.

The Thatcher years saw what was largely a phoney war on crime. The Iron Lady talked like Vlad the Impaler, and she certainly oversaw a militarisation of public order policing. But her Home Secretaries, in particular William Whitelaw and Douglas Hurd, tended to adopt more subtle and balanced policies for everyday crime. New Labour's crime policy largely aped the Tory rhetoric of the Thatcher years, but it then delivered on its tough on crime promises. The UK now spends more on law and order as a percentage of GDP than any other OECD country, including the USA.[4] Police numbers are at a record high of over 143,000, and they are armed with ever-expanding powers. Since 1997 the prison population has increased by over one-third, from 60,000 to 83,000, largely because of expansions in the range of criminal offences and the mandating or encouragement of tougher sentences.[5] Well over 40 major Acts of Parliament since 1997 have focused on criminal justice matters, and some 3000 new criminal offences have been created.

It is important to understand whether or not the fall in crime under New Labour shows that toughness works (though it certainly hasn't in relation to public opinion, which stopped seeing Labour as the best party on crime nearly ten years ago). And in fact, though the new crime control consensus is that tough policing and punishment *are* instrumental in bringing crime down, research continues to paint a much more complex picture. Policing and penal policy (including increased imprisonment) have certainly played some part in bringing crime rates down. But the bulk of research suggests that it was the 'smart' rather than the 'tough' elements of policing, prevention and punishment changes that had the most significant impact - measures such as intelligence- and evidence-led targeting of resources on the most vulnerable targets and most serious offenders. Moreover, it remains the case that criminal justice interventions of even the most effective kind play only a limited role in comparison to policies based on 'getting tough on the causes of crime', in political economy and culture. A plethora of evidence indicts the record of neoliberalism: inequality is strongly related to violent crime; unemployment and marginal employment to property crime; and both are strongly accentuated by the egoistic and narcissistic culture of consumerism.[6]

The law and order trap

The cruel irony is that the Labour government knows this. A recent review by
the Prime Minister's Strategy Unit concluded that 80 per cent of the crime reduction
was due to economic factors, although this estimate was somehow omitted from the
version of the report displayed on the Cabinet website, which concentrated almost
entirely on criminal justice solutions.[7] Labour has been moderately successful in
reducing crime, even with its very cautious approach to containing inequality and
exclusion. But it is so locked into the politics of law and order that this is a success
that dare not speak its name.

Law and order: lessons for Labour

New Labour has pursued populist policies on law and order since 1992, embedding
the discourse of toughness ever more deeply. It has largely given the public what
it said it wanted: more policing and punishment. It has even achieved reductions
in overall crime (though not because of those measures). But it has increasingly
lost public confidence in its policies, and there is widespread disbelief about the
generally benign crime trends.

The main reason for this is that discourses and practices of law and order
are based on premises diametrically opposed to social democratic values. They
embody an image of people as necessarily selfishly egoistic and asocial, requiring
tough, exclusionary forms of discipline to maintain order and security. This is quite
different from the social democratic conception of criminals as people who have
acted wrongly, but are capable of rehabilitation and reintegration; and whose actions
have been influenced by socio-economic and cultural pressures that themselves must
be targets of reform. New Labour's espousal of law and order was a Faustian pact to
secure re-election, which now (together with its broader embrace of neoliberalism)
threatens its destruction.

The paradox is that social democratic policies - coupled with smarter crime
prevention, policing, and penal policy, as first-aid responses to crime - *can* deliver
lower crime rates. Periods of Labour government have generally been associated
with lower crime, and social democratic countries more widely enjoy lower
levels of serious violent crime, as well as more humane criminal justice systems.[8]
Neoliberalism has fanned the flames of social breakdown and crime, stimulating
an ever more insatiable popular lust for harsher punishments. The media have

Soundings

of course been important cheerleaders for this. But New Labour has connived in keeping secret that Labour had better policies to provide public protection, and that a social democratic attack on the deep causes of crime is ultimately the only basis for security.

Notes

1. D. Downes and R. Morgan, 'No Turning Back: The Politics of Law and Order into the Millennium', in M. Maguire, R. Morgan and R. Reiner (eds), *The Oxford Handbook of Criminology* (4th ed), Oxford University Press 2007.

2. B. Duffy, R. Wake, T. Burrows and P. Bremner, 'Closing the Gaps - Crime and Public Perceptions', *International Review of Law, Computers and Technology*, 22:1, 2008, p18.

3. In recent years this has provoked an important critique of conventional criminology under the banner of 'zemiology': P. Hillyard, C. Pantazis, S. Tombs and D. Gordon (eds), *Beyond Criminology: Taking Harm Seriously*, Pluto Press 2004.

4. E. Solomon, C. Eades and R. Garside, *Ten Years of Criminal Justice Under Labour: An Independent Audit*, Kings College Centre for Crime and Justice Studies 2007, Figure 3.

5. C. Hedderman, 'Building on Sand: Why Expanding the Prison Estate is Not the Way to "Secure the Future"', Kings College Centre for Crime and Justice Studies 2008.

6. R. Reiner, *Law and Order: An Honest Citizen's Guide to Crime and Control*, Polity, 2007; S. Hall, S. Winlow and C. Ancrum, *Criminal Identities and Consumer Culture*, Willan 2008.

7. *Ten Years of Criminal Justice Under Labour*, n8, p14.

8. D. Downes and J. Young, 'A Criminal Failure: The Tories' Law and Order Record', *New Society*, 13.5.87; *Law and Order: An Honest Citizen's Guide* ..., n4.

[18]
Citizenship, Crime, Criminalization: Marshalling a Social Democratic Perspective

This paper argues that criminalization, in the double sense of more perceived (and probably actual) crime and of the tough crime control policies brought by the politics of law and order, are consequences of the reversal some thirty years ago of the centuries-long progress toward universal incorporation into social, political, and civil citizenship. By contrast, the hundred years before that had witnessed the spread of social rights and greater inclusiveness, and experienced a benign coupling of lower crime and disorder with more consensual and welfare-oriented policing and penality. The necessary condition of restoring that more benign climate of greater security is a reversal of the neoliberalism that undermined social democracy. Since the 2007 credit crash, neoliberalism has been challenged increasingly, as practice and as ideology, yet it remains deeply embedded. The ideas and organization to restore social democracy have not been developed. Nonetheless it remains the precondition for security and humane criminal justice, as envisaged by T.H. Marshall's citizenship lectures fifty years ago.

When the Bush-Cheney administration proposed to replace Social Security with a system of individually accumulated, individually owned, and individually invested accounts, my first thought was that its goal was to take the Social out of Social Security. It took a few minutes longer to realize that it also intended to take the Security out of Social Security.[1]

---

1. R. Solow, Trapped in the New "You're On Your Own" World, New York Review of Books, Nov. 20, 2008, 79–81, reviewing P. Gosselin, High Wire: The Precarious Financial

242 | NEW CRIMINAL LAW REVIEW | VOL. 13 | NO. 2 | SPRING 2010

I. CITIZENSHIP VS. MARKETS: THE MARSHALLIAN PERSPECTIVE

> "Citizenship," like the ideal of "community," is widely attractive just because it disguises hard choices. Everyone would like to be a citizen; nobody wants to be isolated and alienated. But beyond the platitudes, agreement vanishes. . . . [I]f left, right and centre start talking about citizenship, community and allegiance, it will be left, right and centre versions of those good things that they will offer.[2]

During the late 1980s the term "citizenship" became a focal point for political discussion, following on the vogue for the cognate idea of "community." As the philosopher Alan Ryan's somewhat acerbic comments indicate, this was largely because both terms could be called in aid of positions at all points on the spectrum of political debate.[3] The rising stock of citizenship and community can be attributed to the varying needs of conservatives, liberals, and socialists at the turn of the 1990s, as the Soviet empire tumbled and neoliberal hegemony became embedded globally.[4] To the then firmly dominant Thatcher-Reagan neoconservatives and neoliberals, embracing the need for citizenship and community offered a cosy legitimation of the thrust to egoistic individualism unleashed in tandem with the "freeing" of the economy. For all shades of socialism, demoralized by political defeat, it suggested a narrative about what had gone wrong with the predominant earlier approaches: Soviet-style state socialism and Fabian-style top-down dirigiste planning and welfarism. It was widely felt that both statist varieties of socialism had neglected the importance of constitutional and practical respect for individual autonomy, diversity, and democracy. The fracturing of economic security and of communal bonds from the

---

Lives of American Families (2008), http://www.nybooks.com/articles/22080 (last visited Mar. 2, 2010).

2. A. Ryan, Citizens of All Persuasions, London Times, Oct. 25, 1988.

3. In another *London Times* article a couple of years later, Ryan expressed this even more vituperatively: "Goering reached for his revolver when he heard the word culture. Now it is tempting to do the same when people talk about citizenship: the great, but wholly indistinct, good thing that parties and voters agree we should have more of.. . . But is there anything concrete hidden in the clouds of rhetoric, or has the idea of citizenship reached a state of vacuity?" A. Ryan, State and Citizen, London Times, Sept. 12, 1990.

4. G. Andrews ed., Citizenship (1991); B.S. Turner ed., Citizenship and Social Theory (1993).

impact of neoliberalism and globalization accentuated anomie. This stimulated the 1990s search for a "third way," "beyond Left and Right," reconciling the supposed economic success of free-market policies and globalization with social and cultural strategies to promote new forms of citizenship and community that could alleviate the "ontological insecurity" engendered by neoliberalism and egoistic individualism.[5]

For all the ambiguous and diverse meanings that can be coded into the concept of citizenship, it is possible to delineate a core idea, although it is one that opens rather than forecloses argument. David Held has expressed this most succinctly: "From the ancient world to the present day, all forms of citizenship have had certain common attributes. Citizenship has meant a reciprocity of rights against, and duties towards, the community. Citizenship has entailed membership, membership of the community in which one lives one's life. And membership has invariably involved degrees of participation in the community. The question of who should participate and at what level is a question as old as the ancient world itself."[6] If citizenship means community membership, then certain key questions are raised[7]: Who is counted as a member, and how did they get this status? What are the boundaries of community: who is in and who is out? Are there degrees of membership? What rights and duties are entailed?

Different political positions and sociological analyses have answered these questions in fundamentally conflicting ways. A recent overview of debates about citizenship has distinguished seven contemporary perspectives: "revisited," liberal, communitarian, social democratic, nationalist, multiculturalist, feminist, and multiple.[8] Some of these distinctions raise fundamental issues of principle; others are primarily critiques of omissions and emphases in the core perspectives. The most fundamental question of all is membership: who is included in the framework of citizenship? There is an unbridgeable gulf between perspectives that are in principle universalistic, seeking ultimately to include all people in citizenship, "inclusive" theories, and those that would limit it to particular groups, "exclusive"

---

5. A. Giddens, Modernity and Self Identity (1991); A. Giddens, Beyond Left and Right (1995); A. Giddens, The Third Way (1998).

6. D. Held, Between State and Civil Society: Citizenship, in Citizenship 20 (G. Andrews ed., 1991).

7. J.M. Barbalet, Citizenship (1988).

8. G. Shafir ed., The Citizenship Debates (1998).

244 | **NEW CRIMINAL LAW REVIEW** | VOL. 13 | NO. 2 | SPRING 2010

theories. Almost equally vexing is the question of what rights or duties are entailed by citizenship, and how they are prioritized. The last half century has seen something of a reversal in the predominant usage and connotation of the term "citizenship." The social democratic interpretation of citizenship, expressed most influentially by T.H. Marshall and a central reference point for this paper, emphasized a process of inclusion of all people in a common status with civil, political, and social rights (and concomitant responsibilities) by virtue of their humanity. It embodied a universalistic and inclusive ideal. However, the term "citizenship" is now more often used in political discussion in exclusive, nationalistic, and particularistic terms, focusing on barriers to the status of citizen, with the stress on hurdles, testing, pedigree, and desert.[9]

The locus classicus for much debate about citizenship in the last half-century has been Marshall's seminal 1949 lecture "Citizenship and Social Class," delivered in Cambridge in honor of his illustrious (unrelated) namesake Alfred Marshall, the dominant figure in the articulation of the neoclassical synthesis in economics.[10]. These sixty pages of text have generated many volumes of debate that continues to flourish.[11] Marshall's analysis is a quintessential embodiment of an ethical socialist perspective,[12] and its fortunes have ebbed and flowed with the vicissitudes of social democracy, although it has

---

9. New U.K. Citizenship Testing Starts, BBC Website, Nov. 1, 2005, http://bbc.co.uk/1/hi/uk_politics/4391710.stm (last visited Mar. 7, 2010); British Citizenship Tests Planned, BBC Website, 20 February 2008, http://bbc.co.uk/1/hi/uk_politics/7253933.stm (last visited Mar. 7, 2010).

10. T.H. Marshall, Citizenship and Social Class; reprinted in T.H. Marshall, Sociology at the Crossroads (1963 [1950]).

11. For example: M. Bulmer & A.M. Rees eds., Citizenship Today: The Contemporary Relevance of T.H. Marshall (1996); J. Holmwood, Three Pillars of Welfare State Theory: T.H. Marshall, Karl Polanyi, & Alva Myrdal in Defence of the National Welfare State, 3 Eur. J. Soc. Theory 23–50 (Jan.–Mar. 2000); R. White & J. Donoghue, Marshall, Mannheim and Modern Citizenship, Paper presented at the Jubilee Conference of the Australasian Political Studies Association, Canberra, Australian National University (2002); M. Lister, "Marshall-ing" Social and Political Citizenship: Towards a Unified Conception of Citizenship, 40 Gov't & Opposition 471–91 (Oct.–Dec. 2005); P. Breiner, Is Social Citizenship Really Outdated? T.H. Marshall Revisited, Paper presented at the Western Political Science Association Annual Meeting, Albuquerque, New Mexico (2006), www.allacademic.com (last visited Feb. 25, 2010).

12. N. Dennis & A.H. Halsey, English Ethical Socialism (1988); Shafir, supra n. 8; R. Reiner, Beyond Risk: A Lament for Social Democratic Criminology, in The Politics of Crime Control (T. Newburn & P. Rock eds., 2006).

remained a lodestar even for many critics. The most striking aspects of Marshall's work are the threefold categorization of citizenship into civil, political, and social rights, and the evolutionary sequence in which he presents their historical development in the British case: very crudely, that civil rights were the achievement of the eighteenth century, political rights of the nineteenth, and social rights an ongoing process (in 1949).

Marshall's conceptual and historical schema has attracted criticism from a variety of positions. The most common themes among those broadly sympathetic to Marshall's political values have been accusations of Anglocentrism, Whiggism, and a focus on class inequality (implicit in his title) that neglects other dimensions of diversity—primarily gender, ethnicity, and sexual preference. Critics have emphasized the variety of ways in which citizenship rights have developed in the Western industrial world, with many different routes, stages, and forms.[13] They have questioned Marshall's historical account of the British case, especially the implicit Whiggish perspective attributed to Marshall, with its apparent assumptions of steady and smooth progress toward an inevitable goal of the Welfare State, mixed economy consensus that prevailed for a time after the Second World War, when Marshall's lectures were delivered.[14] He has been attacked most strongly for neglect of the complexities of inequality, in particular its gender, ethnic, and sexuality dimensions.[15] Related to this is the charge that he conceives of inequality primarily in economic terms, and is concerned with material redistribution rather than cultural recognition.

The criticisms cited in the previous paragraph are not really fundamental rebuttals of Marshall's position, but extensions and developments of it. "Citizenship and Social Class" is a relatively brief sketch rather than an attempt at a comprehensive analysis. The focus on the British experience is as a case study rather than any suggestion that it offers a universal template, so Marshall would no doubt have welcomed research on the variety of forms of development of citizenship in different places, as elaborated by Mann and others.[16] Although it is true that Marshall suggests a clear long-term

---

13. M. Mann, Ruling Class Strategies and Citizenship, in Citizenship Today (M. Bulmer & A.M. Rees eds., 1996).

14. A. Giddens, T.H. Marshall, the State and Democracy, in Citizenship Today (M. Bulmer & A.M. Rees eds., 1996).

15. Shafir, supra n. 8.

16. Mann, supra n. 13.

246 | **NEW CRIMINAL LAW REVIEW** | **VOL. 13** | **NO. 2** | **SPRING 2010**

trajectory of the extension of citizenship, he does not claim its inevitability and is aware of how its development was uneven and achieved by many conflicts. Whereas he focuses on class inequality and does not discuss issues of ethnicity, gender, or other divisions, the struggles to extend citizenship rights to all people is fully in line with his position.[17] Contrary to the claim that Marshall is primarily concerned with economic redistribution rather than cultural recognition, one of his central arguments is that quantitative economic differences are not problematic if they do not threaten a fundamentally shared status of citizenship as achieved (he believed) by the welfare state. This has plausibly been interpreted as making the crucial problem of class not material difference in itself, but emotional resentment if financial inequalities signify qualitative differences of status.[18]

A more fundamental criticism of Marshall has always come from the political Right, and the increasing purchase of this argument did for a time, in the 1970s and early 1980s, threaten to eclipse the relevance of his work altogether. This is the claim that Marshall's interpretation of citizenship stressed rights at the expense of responsibilities, promulgating a welfare state that has exacerbated the problems it purported to remedy by undermining the compulsion to work and to contribute to society as a core concomitant of citizenship. In fact Marshall anticipated this issue in the conclusion of his essay, citing the arguments of Colquhoun and Mandeville in the eighteenth century that laborers' wages must remain low enough to act as a goad to work, and to prevent poverty from sliding into indigence. He wrote explicitly that it was "no easy matter to revive the sense of the personal obligation to work in a new form in which it is attached to the status of citizenship," and especially to maintain the duty "to put one's heart into one's job and work hard."[19] As he grew older, this problem vexed him more and more. It has been suggested that Marshall ultimately abandoned the more socialist 1949 version of his theory and came to see citizenship rights as primarily civil and political, with economic welfare predicated on performance of responsibilities rather than an absolute right.[20]

---

17. Passing references to Catholic Emancipation and to the struggle for the enfranchisement of women support this, but the overwhelming emphasis is on economic class differences.

18. J.M. Barbalet, Citizenship, Class Inequality and Resentment, in Citizenship and Social Theory (B.S. Turner ed., 1993).

19. Marshall, supra n. 10, at 124.

20. A.M. Rees, The Other T.H. Marshall, 24 J. Soc. Pol'y 341–62 (July–Sept. 1995).

But the most crucial issue in assessing Marshall and the social democratic notion of citizenship he advanced in 1949 is whether it still has any relevance or purchase today, after four decades in which the tide of history has moved very much in the opposite direction (whether or not this won the approbation of Marshall himself in later life). Falling short of seeing the march of citizenship as inevitable, automatic or irreversible, Marshall clearly conveys a sense that the consolidation and further extension of the most controversial social dimension of citizenship was going with the grain of history.

On a recent rereading this came out most forcefully to me in his opening remarks, which at the time probably would have been seen as perfunctory pleasantries. The lectures were part of an annual series in commemoration of Alfred Marshall, and Tom Marshall harked back to a paper Alfred had delivered in 1873 to the Cambridge Reform Club on "The Future of the Working Classes."[21] Alfred Marshall posed the question, "whether there be valid ground for the opinion that the amelioration of the working classes has limits beyond which it cannot pass." And he argued that there were no such limits. "The question is not whether all men will ultimately be equal—that they certainly will not—but whether progress may not go on steadily, if slowly, till, by occupation at least, every man is a gentleman. I hold that it may, and that it will." He supported this conclusion primarily by an analysis of trends in the occupational structure that were reducing the proportion of unskilled laboring jobs in favor of skilled and nonmanual ones, with a concomitant reduction in economic inequality. This would continue, he forecast, but he also advocated some forms of state intervention, in particular compulsory education, to facilitate the trend. He was at pains to distance this from socialism, although he acknowledged that "[t]he picture . . . will resemble in some respects those which have been shown to us by the Socialists, that noble set of untutored enthusiasts who attributed to all men an unlimited capacity for those self-forgetting virtues that they found in their own breasts."[22]

---

21. Marshall, supra n. 10, at 69–73.

22. Tom Marshall notes that the *published* version of Alfred Marshall's lecture tones down the critique of the "socialists" (removing the distancing capital S), and deletes the phrase "untutored enthusiasts." It also changed the tense to the present, eliminating the implication that these views were past history only (Marshall, supra n. 10, at 70 n.3).

248 | **NEW CRIMINAL LAW REVIEW** | VOL. 13 | NO. 2 | SPRING 2010

Tom Marshall builds his 1949 lectures around the same question as Alfred Marshall's 1873 paper: whether "there were limits beyond which the amelioration of the working classes could not pass." And he adopts the same sociological hypothesis: that quantitative economic inequalities were not incompatible with a fundamental equality of status as citizens. But he stresses that the progress toward the realization of social rights of citizenship in the seventy-five years that divided the Cambridge lectures by the two Marshalls had (rightly, in his view) involved a degree of state interference in the market that the leading architect of neoclassical economics would have condemned. "Our modern system is frankly a Socialist system, not one whose authors are, as [Alfred] Marshall was, eager to distinguish it from socialism," although "the market still functions—within limits."[23]

So Tom Marshall's 1949 lectures do convey a strong sense of the further consolidation of citizenship in this social democratic mould through the welfare state and mixed economy, as likely although not inevitable, and certainly desirable. But what is striking some sixty years later and after decades of reversal of this trend, is how deeply embedded it then was. The reference back seventy-five years to Alfred Marshall's lecture shows that the view that growing economic and social equality was progressive, in the double sense that it went with the grain of history *and* represented a desirable advance, was not merely a reflection of the high point of Labourism during the postwar Attlee government. It was a perspective that had long been accepted across a broad sweep of the political spectrum, including even the leading figure in the formulation of neoclassical economics and champion of the virtues of markets.

So does Tom Marshall's analysis still have any relevance? After all, his optimistic view of the advance of citizenship in his sense has been reversed, first by the 1980s neoliberal blitzkrieg and its arch enthusiasts under Margaret Thatcher and Ronald Reagan, and then in the 1990s by the acceptance of neoliberalism's fundamentals by the erstwhile parties of the democratic Left, born again in "New" market-embracing versions. I believe that the core themes of Marshall's work remain valid: above all his basic theoretical and normative position that the two terms in the title of his lectures, "citizenship" and "social class," represent "opposing principles," the former tending toward equality, the latter being "a system of inequality."[24] Indeed, he states

---

23. Marshall, supra n. 10, at 73.
24. Id. at 87.

twice that "in the twentieth century, citizenship and the capitalist class system have been at war."[25] It is this conception of a fundamental war between the principles of class and the market, on the one hand, and citizenship on the other, that is Marshall's primary point, underlying the more obvious evolutionary schema that occupies most of the essay.[26]

Indeed the salience of this "war" between the principles of capitalism and citizenship runs through the historical narrative. In his narrative, the extension of civil and political rights from the eighteenth century onward, desirable as it was, remained largely formal and empty until the development of social rights in the twentieth century. For example, the discussion of the advance of state education and legal aid shows that these are necessary to breathe life and substance into civil and political rights. Much of this is reminiscent of Marx, but the crucial differences are Marshall's unremitting assumption that only peaceful democratic means are acceptable, and that a good enough measure of citizenship is compatible with some room for markets to operate and the degree of economic inequality that entails. Marshall does not develop these theoretical assumptions except by placing them in a historical narrative. But the work of explicating and justifying them has been done by other theorists of social democracy and welfarism whose positions are very similar, notably Karl Polanyi,[27] and indeed by welfarist liberals, above all John Rawls.[28] And the principles of ethical, democratic socialism underpinning Marshall's lectures remain inspirational to many, including myself.[29]

The rest of this paper will seek to defend the continuing relevance of Marshall's social democratic analysis and principles to understanding developments in criminalization, in the double sense of the occurrence of criminalized conduct, and the labelling and punishment of this by criminal law and criminal justice. This is a specific but crucial aspect of Marshall's general depiction of a war between citizenship and capitalist markets. Erosion of the social dimensions of citizenship vitiates the realization of civil and political rights even if these remain formally intact— although it poses a threat to that too.

---

25. Id. at 87, 115.

26. Lister, supra n. 11; Breiner, supra n. 11.

27. K. Polanyi, The Great Transformation (1944 [2001]); Holmwood, supra n. 11; B. Barry, Why Social Justice Matters (2005).

28. J. Rawls, A Theory of Justice (1971).

29. Dennis & Halsey, supra n. 12, ch. 6; Reiner, supra n. 12.

250 | **NEW CRIMINAL LAW REVIEW** | VOL. 13 | NO. 2 | SPRING 2010

II. CITIZENSHIP AND CRIMINALIZATION

"[C]riminalization" constitutes an appropriate conceptual framework within which to gather together the constellation of social practices which form the subject matter of criminal law on the one hand and criminal justice and criminological studies on the other. . . . Escaping the notion of crimes as "given," the idea of criminalization captures the dynamic nature of the field as a set of interlocking practices in which the moments of "defining" and "responding" to crime can rarely be completely distinguished and in which legal and social (extra-legal) constructions of crime constantly interact . . . [I]t allows the instrumental and symbolic aspects of the field to be addressed, as well as encompassing empirical, interpretive, and normative projects. It embraces questions about offenders and victims, individuals and collectivities, state and society.[30]

The rise of Marshallian citizenship over the three centuries between the mid-eighteenth and the mid-twentieth centuries, and its decline over the last forty years (hopefully not irreversible), are closely related to the long-term trends and patterns of criminalization, shaping it in profound and complex ways. The flow and ebb of citizenship is the vital context for understanding the trajectory of criminal behavior (in so far as we can make reasonable guesses about it), criminal law, and criminal justice. This section will concentrate on the experience of the last half-century in Britain, beginning with a very broad overview of earlier patterns.

A. Citizenship and Criminalization in Britain: The Long View

Between the mid-nineteenth and mid-twentieth centuries in Britain, there developed a system of modern criminal justice that broadly sought to emphasize welfare, rehabilitation and reincorporation, consensus, and legitimacy. As any criminal justice system, it was based on the delivery of doses of pain where this was deemed necessary, but compared with what came before and after there was an attempt, however imperfectly realized and often hypocritical, at minimizing this and achieving a measure of consent. Welfarist social policy and amelioration, not exclusion and harsh sanctions, were seen as the basis of order and crime control, with policing and punishment as regrettably necessary stopgaps until root causes could be

---

30. N. Lacey, Legal Constructions of Crime, in The Oxford Handbook of Criminology 197 (M. Maguire, R. Morgan, & R. Reiner eds., 2007).

tackled. This was the heyday of what has been analyzed as policing by consent[31] and penal welfarism.[32]

The backdrop and necessary condition was that crime and disorder seemed to be contained and were indeed reducing problems. National crime statistics only began to be collected and published by the Home Office after the 1856 County and Borough Police Act, which established modern police forces throughout the country. From the 1850s until the 1920s, the crime levels recorded by the police remained on a plateau. Although there are no figures for crimes that were not prosecuted prior to 1856, on the basis of the judicial statistics, historians generally believe that the mid-Victorian levels represent a decline from much higher levels in the early nineteenth century.[33] There is some debate about whether the flat trend from the 1850s to the 1920s is attributable to a low level of offending or to supply-side rationing of the figures driven both by fiscal parsimony and by the wish to present an appearance of success for the new police forces and other nineteenth-century criminal justice reforms.[34] But what is clear is that there was a steady state of criminalization and at least the appearance of success in crime control. Criminologists and policymakers at the turn of the twentieth century (like their U.S. counterparts in the 1990s and early twenty-first century) were perplexed about how to explain the great crime drop.[35] Political and industrial disorder also seemed both less frequent and less violent—a match rather than a battle—compared to the earlier nineteenth century or later twentieth century.[36]

---

31. R. Reiner, The Politics of the Police (2000).

32. D. Garland, Punishment and Welfare (1985).

33. V. Gatrell, The Decline of Theft and Violence in Victorian and Edwardian England, in Crime and the Law (V. Gatrell, B. Lenman, & G. Parker eds., 1980); C. Emsley, The History of Crime and Crime Control Institutions, in The Oxford Handbook of Criminology 204–7 (M. Maguire, R. Morgan, & R. Reiner eds., 2002).

34. H. Taylor, Rising Crime: The Political Economy of Criminal Statistics Since the 1850s, 51 Econ. Hist. Rev. 569–90 (1998); H. Taylor, Forging the Job: A Crisis of "Modernisation" or Redundancy for the Police in England and Wales 1900–39, 39 Brit. J. Criminology 113–15 (1999); R. Morris, "Lies, Damned Lies and Criminal Statistics": Reinterpreting the Criminal Statistics in England and Wales, 5 Crime, Hist. & Societies 111–27 (2001); Emsley, id.

35. L. Radzinowicz & R. Hood, A History of English Criminal Law, Vol. V: The Emergence of Penal Policy in Victorian and Edwardian England (1986).

36. R. Geary, Policing Industrial Disputes (1985).

252 | NEW CRIMINAL LAW REVIEW | VOL. 13 | NO. 2 | SPRING 2010

During the century between the 1850s and 1950s, "policing by consent"[37] became the prevalent system, and "penal welfarism"[38] became the prevailing response to apprehended offenders. Although these had complex conditions of existence, the underlying context was the gradual incorporation of the mass of the population into social as well as civil and political citizenship—what David Garland has called the "solidarity project."[39] The rise of Marshallian citizenship was the bedrock of contained crime and disorder, policing by consent, and penal welfarism.[40] And the reversal of the trend toward greater inclusion with the advent of neoliberalism over the last thirty years is what has generated the explosions in crime and disorder explosions, and the harsher politics of law and order of recent times.[41]

B. The Calculus of Crime: Charting Recent Trends

Criminal statistics are notoriously riddled with pitfalls, as students learn within a few weeks of Criminology 101. The problem is the huge extent of unrecorded crime, resulting from nonreporting by victims, nonrecording by the police, and an incalculable volume of offending that victims and police never even become aware of (although they may encompass severe harms, including poverty or deaths). Changes in the recorded figures may result not only from changes in offense levels but also from fluctuations in reporting or recording them or from the rules for counting them. Very substantial steps have been taken in recent decades to alleviate these problems by developing alternative measures, above all the regular British Crime Surveys (BCSs) since the early 1980s.

The BCSs shed much light on reporting and recording practices, allowing statistics to be interpreted more confidently. Above all, the availability of two alternative measures of trends gives greater confidence when they point in the same direction, as they did for the first decade of the

---

37. Reiner, supra n. 31, ch. 2.

38. Garland, supra n. 32.

39. D. Garland, The Culture of Control 199 (2001).

40. V. Bailey ed., Policing and Punishment in the 19th Century (1981); V. Bailey, Delinquency and Citizenship: Reclaiming the Young Offender, 1914–48 (1987); Reiner, supra n. 31, at 58–59; Garland, supra nn. 32 & 39; Radzinowicz & Hood, supra n. 35.

41. R. Reiner, Law and Order: An Honest Citizen's Guide to Crime and Control (2007).

Survey. However, in the 1990s the trends indicated by the police statistics and the BCSs began to diverge, generating a politicized debate about their relative merits.

Putting together the different sorts of data available, what can be said about the trends in the last half century? The most apparent trend is the spectacular rise in recorded crime since the late 1950s. In the early 1950s, the police recorded less than half a million offenses per annum. By the mid 1970s, this had risen to 2 million. The 1980s showed even more staggering rises, with recorded crime peaking in 1992 at over 5.5 million. By 1997, recorded crime had fallen back to 4.5 million. Major counting rule changes introduced in 1998 and 2002 make comparison of the subsequent figures especially fraught, but according to the new rules (which undoubtedly exaggerate the increase), just under 6 million offenses were recorded by the police for 2003–2004. This has now fallen back again to 4.95 million in 2007–2008.

Contrasting the recorded police statistics with victim surveys suggests a more complex picture, but clearly pinpoints the reversal of Marshallian citizenship by neoliberalism as the accelerant behind a crime explosion. Three distinct phases can be distinguished on the basis of the victim survey evidence, qualifying the relentless rise in the recorded crime rate since the mid-1950s:

1. 1955–1983: Recorded Crime Rise. Until the 1970s, there was no other measurement of trends apart from the police statistics. During the 1970s, the General Household Survey (GHS) began to ask about burglary victimization. Its data showed that most of the increase in recorded burglary resulted from greater reporting by victims. Between 1972 and 1983, recorded burglaries doubled, but victimization increased by only 20 percent. Victims reported more burglaries mainly because of the prevalence of household contents insurance. This cannot be extrapolated necessarily to other crimes, or even to burglary in previous decades, but the GHS indicates that the increased rate for this highly significant crime was mainly a recording phenomenon. It is plausible that this applied to volume property crimes more generally, so the rise of crime was probably substantially less than the recorded statistics suggested.

2. 1983–1992: Crime Explosion. The BCS in the 1980s showed the reverse: although recorded crime still increased more rapidly be-

254 | NEW CRIMINAL LAW REVIEW | VOL. 13 | NO. 2 | SPRING 2010

tween 1981 and 1993 than BCS crime (111 percent compared to 77 percent), the trends were similar. By both measures crime rose at an explosive rate during the 1980s and early 1990s, the Thatcher and early Major years. The decade and a half during which neoliberalism destroyed Britain's industrial base and defined whole areas and generations out of the edifice of citizenship, creating a new excluded underclass,[42] stimulated record growth for one industry: crime.

3. 1993–present: Ambiguously Falling Crime. From the early 1990s, the trends indicated by the police statistics and the BCS began to diverge. The BCS continued to chart a rise until 1995, but the police-recorded data fell from 1992 to 1997. Insurance companies made claiming more onerous, thus discouraging reporting by victims, and more "businesslike" managerial accountability for policing implicitly introduced incentives to keep crime recording down. Michael Howard, the Home Secretary in those years who had announced a harsher approach with his notorious "prison works" speech to the 1993 Conservative Party Conference, certainly succeeded in getting tough on the causes of recording crime, even if not on crime itself.

After New Labour came to power in 1997, the two measures continued to diverge—but in the opposite direction. BCS recorded crime has fallen rapidly since 1995, and by 2007–2008 had dropped below the first BCS data gathered in 1981. The police-recorded statistics, however, began to rise again from 1998 to 2004, since when they have declined a little.

The rise in the recorded rate resulted overwhelmingly from two major changes in police procedures for counting crimes: new Home Office Counting Rules in 1998, and the 2002 National Crime Recording Standard (NCRS). These reforms boosted the recorded rate substantially compared to previous measures. This was a predicted consequence of the changes, because the 1998 rules made "notifiable" a number of offenses (such as common assault) that hitherto had not been included in the recorded rate, and the NCRS mandated the "prima facie" rather than "evidential" principle, requiring police to record "any notifiable offence which comes to the attention of the police" even in the absence of evidence supporting the victim's report.

---

42. R. Dahrendorf, Law and Order (1985); J. Young, The Exclusive Society (1999).

The counting rule reforms indicate concern in the early optimistic days of New Labour to develop evidence-based crime policy, even at the price of a politically sensitive rise in recorded crime.[43] A further revision in the rules in 2006 restored some discretion to the police not to record offenses reported to them in the absence of supporting evidence. This would reduce the recorded rate, other things being equal, and may be a factor in the recent decline.

The BCS is free from the particular problems that make the police figures unreliable as a measure of trends. However, it is not (and has never claimed to be), a definitive index. It necessarily omits many offenses: homicide, the supreme example of personal victimization, crimes with individual victims who are unaware of what happened (such as successful frauds), crimes against organizations or the public at large, consensual offenses such as drug-taking, among other serious examples. Its sampling frame excludes certain highly victimized groups such as children under age sixteen and the homeless. So the government's tendency to treat the BCS as definitive is as problematic as the earlier exclusive reliance on the police statistics.

The dramatic overall fall in BCS data under New Labour also masks increases in some of the most alarming offenses. Murder and other serious crimes of violence have increased in the last thirty years and now comprise a higher proportion of all crimes, even though their overall incidence has fallen recently. During the 1960s and early 1970s, the number of homicides recorded per year remained between 300 and 400, but this has now roughly doubled. The number of homicides has remained well over 700 in all years since the millennium, and was 784 in 2007–2008. In 1976, only 5 percent of recorded offenses were classified as violent, but by 2007–2008, that had increased to 19 percent (partly because the counting rule changes had lowered the threshold for recording violence). Recorded robberies have risen sharply since the early 1990s, although they have been falling (erratically) in the last few years from a peak in 2001–2002. The current hot topics, gun and knife crime, show similar trajectories. Recorded offenses involving firearms have risen sharply in the last thirty years. The latest

---

43. This is also true of the recent revision of the violence figures after it was revealed that the police had not implemented the new rules appropriately, which produced a dramatic leap in the recorded rate. R. Reiner, Why the Violent Crime Figures Are Not as Bad as They Look, Comment Is Free, The Guardian, Oct. 23, 2008. www.guardian.co.uk/commentisfree/2008/oct/23/ukcrime-justice (last visited Mar. 16, 2010).

256 | NEW CRIMINAL LAW REVIEW | VOL. 13 | NO. 2 | SPRING 2010

Home Office statistics show they doubled from 1998–1999 to 2005–2006, from just over 5,000 to nearly 11,000, but have since fallen back to just under 10,000. Knife crime figures have only recently been collected, but murders involving knives or other sharp instruments increased by 28 percent in the last decade, from 202 in 1997–1998 to 258 in 2006–2007. So the trends are certainly not as rosy as the BCS total suggests, and the failure of public anxiety about crime to fall in line with the statistics results not merely from an irrational "reassurance gap." The next section will analyze the relationship of the crime trends to the politics of law and order.

III. ACCOUNTING FOR LAW AND ORDER

When Tony Blair became Shadow Home Secretary in 1992, his tough-on-crime stance represented a decisive watershed for the politics of law and order. Although during the late 1970s and 1980s, neoliberal and neoconservative political parties, ideas, and policies became dominant in Britain, the United States, and most of the Western world, they were fiercely if unsuccessfully contested. On a world scale neoliberalism's ascendancy was crowned by the 1991 fall of the Soviet Union. But what really confirmed the global hegemony of neoliberalism was the acceptance of the fundamentals of its economic and social policy framework by the erstwhile social democratic or New Deal parties of the West. The Clinton Democrats, New Labour, and their embrace of the "third way"—neoliberalism to a cool beat—marked a new, deep consensus and sounded the death knell of the postwar mixed economy, the Keynesian settlement that was the context for Marshall's analysis of citizenship and that the conservative parties had accepted when they returned to power in the early 1950s. "Blatcherism" was Butskellism in reverse.[44]

This new political terrain of neoliberal triumphalism was heralded in Britain in 1992–1993 by Labour's seizure of the law-and-order agenda. A new crime control consensus emerged, with five core elements:

---

44. "Butskellism" refers to the acceptance by the Conservatives of the postwar welfarist Keynesian settlement. R.A.B. Butler was a Conservative Minister of Parliament, Hugh Gaitskell was leader of the Labour Party, so "Butskellism" suggested their positions had converged. With "Blatcherism," I suggest the reverse: the acceptance of Blair's New Labour of the changes of Margaret Thatcher's administration.

1. Crime is Public Enemy No. 1. Crime has increasingly come to be seen as *the* major threat to society and to individual citizens. MORI (now Ipsos MORI), for example, has for more than thirty years conducted polls on what people see as "the three most important issues facing Britain today." In the early 1970s, just as law and order was emerging as a political issue, less than 10 percent rated it among the top three. Since 1993, the proportion putting crime among the top three issues was usually above 30 percent, despite the falling crime rate. Crime is often catapulted to the top by some egregiously shocking incident; for example, the shooting of an eleven-year-old Liverpool boy, Rhys Jones, was associated with a 20-percent jump in August 2007 that saw well over 50 percent of the population rate crime as the number one issue.[45]

2. Individual, not Social, Responsibility for Crime. In the crime control consensus, crime is exclusively the fault of offenders because of their free choice, individual or cultural pathology, or intrinsic evil. Social structural factors and other root cause explanations have been banished from public discourse.

3. Foregrounding Victims vs. Offenders. The victim has become the iconic center of discourse about crime, ideally and typically portrayed as totally innocent. Crime discourse and policy are predicated on a zero-sum game: concern for victims precludes understanding, let alone allowing any sympathy for, offenders. This was a particularly pronounced theme of Blair's speeches on criminal justice, such as the one that launched the Home Office's Five-Year Strategy for Criminal Justice on July 19, 2004: "The purpose of the criminal justice reforms is to re-balance the system radically in favour of the victim, protecting the innocent but ensuring the guilty know the odds have changed. . . . [O]ur first duty is to the law-abiding citizen. They are our boss. It's time to put them at the centre of the criminal justice system. That is the new consensus on law and order for our times."[46]

4. Crime Control Works. Since the early 1990s, can-do optimism has reinvigorated law enforcement agencies around the world: criminal justice *can* control crime provided it is tough (*and* smart).

---

45. B. Duffy, R. Wake, T. Burrows, & P. Bremner, Closing the Gaps—Crime and Public Perceptions, 22 Int'l Rev. Law, Computers & Tech. 17 (Jan. 2008).

46. Tony Blair, "PM's speech on the five-year crime strategy," July 19, 2004, www.number10.gov.uk/page6129 (last visited Mar. 16, 2010).

258 | NEW CRIMINAL LAW REVIEW | VOL. 13 | NO. 2 | SPRING 2010

Criminal justice professionals and conservative politicians cele-brate this as a triumph of common sense over the purported "nothing works" pessimism and over-sensitivity to civil liberties said to have hampered crime control for much of the twentieth century. Policing and punishment, they claim, can control crime through effective deterrence, prevention, and incapacitation, if given sufficient powers and resources. "Prison works," as does "zero tolerance" policing, and the "responsibilization" of citizens to take self-protective measures against victimization. Civil liberties and human rights are at best marginal issues, to be subordinated to crime control exigencies, and deeper social causes of crime are denied or played down.

5. High-Crime Society Normalized. Popular culture and routine ac-tivities have become increasingly focused on crime risks and the perception that we live in a "high-crime society."[47] Crime concerns have penetrated everyday life, embodied in closed-circuit video sur-veillance, gated estates, SUVs, and other proliferating security ap-paratus, paradoxically enhancing fear at least as much as security. "The more provision for security is made, the more people regard as normal or necessary, and the greater their anxiety when it is not available. And for those who cannot afford to buy into these 'bub-bles of security' in the first place, the sense of standing outside pro-tection, of inhabiting dangerous places only increases."[48]

A. Delivering Law and Order

The issue of law and order first became politicized in Britain by the Tory campaign against the Labour government of the late 1970s,[49] but the years of the Thatcher government were largely a phoney war on crime. The Iron Lady talked tough, and certainly she oversaw a militarization of policing in relation to public disorder. But her Home Secretaries, in particular William Whitelaw and Douglas Hurd, adopted much more subtle and balanced policies in relation to everyday crime.

New Labour's crime policy largely aped the Thatcher rhetoric, stitching to-gether something borrowed, something blue. But it has certainly delivered on

47. Garland, supra n. 39, at 161–63.

48. L. Zedner, Too Much Security?, 31 Int'l J. Soc. Law 165 (Jan.–Mar. 2003).

49. D. Downes & R. Morgan, No Turning Back: The Politics of Law and Order into the Millennium, in The Oxford Handbook of Criminology (M. Maguire, R. Morgan, & R. Reiner eds., 2007).

its tough-on-crime promises. The United Kingdom now spends more on law and order as a percentage of gross national product than any other member of the Organization for Economic Cooperation and Development, including the United States.[50] Police numbers are at a record high of over 143,000, and they are armed with ever-expanding powers. Since 1997, the prison population has increased by over one-third, from 60,000 to 83,000, largely because of expansions of the range of criminal offenses and the mandating or encouragement of tougher sentences.[51] Well over forty major Acts of Parliament since 1997 have focused on criminal justice matters, almost all resulting in expanding the powers of the system. Over three thousand new criminal offenses have been created, about one for every day the government has been in power.[52] The potential reach of criminal justice has also been extended by the development of hybrid procedures whereby breach of civil preventative orders, most famously the Anti-Social Behaviour Order (ASBO), can result in criminal penalties. These have been interpreted as embodying the version of a neoliberal conception of citizens as responsibilised individuals, vulnerable to each other's autonomy.[53]

B. Has Law and Order Delivered Security?

It was shown above that overall crime has fallen in the New Labour years, but with worrying increases in some of the most serious and frightening offenses. Does this show that toughness works? It certainly hasn't in relation to public opinion, which has not accepted that crime has fallen, according to the BCS and other surveys.[54]

---

50. E. Solomon, C. Eades, & R. Garside, Ten Years of Criminal Justice Under Labour: An Independent Audit, Fig. 3 (2008), Kings College Centre for Crime and Justice Studies.

51. T. Newburn, "Tough on Crime": Penal Policy in England and Wales, in Crime and Justice 36 (M. Tonry & A. Doob eds., 2007); N. Lacey, The Prisoners' Dilemma: Political Economy and Punishment in Contemporary Democracies (2008); C. Hedderman, Building on Sand: Why Expanding the Prison Estate is Not the Way to "Secure the Future," Kings College Centre for Crime and Justice Studies (2008).

52. N. Morris, Blair's Frenzied Law-Making, The Independent, Aug. 16, 2006.

53. P. Ramsay, The Responsible Subject As Citizen: Criminal Law, Democracy and the Welfare State, 69 Mod. L. Rev. 29–58 (Jan.–Mar. 2006); P. Ramsay, The Theory of Vulnerable Autonomy and the Legitimacy of the Civil Preventative Order, Law, Society and Economy Working Papers (2008).

54. Duffy et al., supra n. 44.

260 | NEW CRIMINAL LAW REVIEW | VOL. 13 | NO. 2 | SPRING 2010

The question of why crime has fallen in the United Kingdom (and even more so, in the United States) is a vexing one and highly debated. As noted above, a central part of the new crime control consensus is that tough policing and punishment *do* work and have been instrumental in bringing crime rates down. However, the bulk of the research continues to paint a much more complex picture. It is certainly widely conceded that policing and penal policy (including increased imprisonment) have played some part in bringing crime rates down, and that the "nothing works" conclusions of the 1970s and early 1980s were not warranted. The bulk of research suggests, however, that it was the smart rather than the tough elements of policing, prevention, and punishment changes that had the most significant impact: intelligence- and evidence-led targeting of resources on the most vulnerable targets and most serious offenders. Moreover, it remains the case that criminal justice interventions of even the most effective kind play only a limited role compared to the importance of "getting tough on the causes of crime"—the root causes in political economy and culture. A plethora of evidence indicts the key aspects of neoliberalism as causes of crime: inequality is strongly related to violent crime, as are unemployment and marginal employment to property crime, and both are strongly accentuated by the egoistic and narcissistic culture of consumerism.[55] In so far as crime has been suppressed by more effective security while the root causes of criminality remain virulent, it is unsurprising that public anxiety remains strong. Only the restoration of progress toward realizing Marshallian citizenship can restore security.

The cruel irony is that the Labour government knows all this, but feels so trapped by the wilderness years of the 1980s, when Labour's espousal of the social democratic argument that the key to crime control was social and economic policy came to be seen as an electoral liability.[56] A recent review by the Prime Minister's Strategy Unit concluded that 80 percent of the crime reduction of the last decade resulted from economic factors—although this estimate is omitted from the version of the report currently on the Cabinet website, which concentrates almost entirely on criminal justice solutions.[57] Thus Labour has been moderately successful in reducing

---

55. Reiner, supra n. 41; S. Hall, S. Winlow, & C. Ancrum, Criminal Identities and Consumer Culture: Crime, Exclusion and the New Culture of Narcissism (2008).

56. Downes & Morgan, supra n. 47.

57. Solomon et al., supra n. 48, 14.

crime, even with its very limited success in containing inequality and exclusion, but it is so locked into the politics of law and order that this is a success that dare not speak its name.

IV. CONCLUSION: REMARSHALLING CITIZENSHIP

This paper has tried to show that criminalization, in the double sense of more perceived (and probably actual) crime and the tough crime control policies brought by the politics of law and order, are consequences of the reversal some thirty years ago of the centuries-long progress toward universal incorporation into social, political, and civil citizenship. The hundred years before that, which had witnessed the spread of social rights and greater inclusiveness, experienced a more benign coupling of lower crime and disorder, and more consensual and welfare-oriented policing and penality. The necessary condition of restoring that more benign climate of greater security is a reversal of the neoliberalism that undermined social democracy.

When I have argued this before,[58] it seemed a quixotic tilting against a solid, deeply embedded edifice, for all the theoretical arguments and empirical evidence of its negative consequences. However, since credit crunched some eighteen months ago, it is evident that neoliberalism is crumbling, as practice and as ideology. But it is not at all evident what will succeed it. Unfortunately the ideas and organization to restore social democracy have not been developed during the wilderness years to a point where there can be any real confidence that this direction will prevail. Nonetheless it remains the precondition for security and humane criminal justice, as envisaged by Marshall's citizenship lectures fifty years ago.

---

58. Reiner, supra n. 31, ch. 7; Reiner, supra n. 12; Reiner, supra n. 41.

List of Publications

Books

The Blue-Coated Worker: A Sociological Study of Police Unionism, Cambridge: Cambridge University Press, 1978. Re-issued 2010.
The Politics of the Police, Brighton and New York: Wheatsheaf/ St Martin's Press, 1985; 2nd.edn Hemel Hempstead and Toronto: Wheatsheaf/University of Toronto Press, 1992; 3rd.edn Oxford: Oxford University Press, 2000; 4th.edn Oxford: Oxford University Press, 2010.
Chief Constables: Bobbies, Bosses or Bureaucrats?, Oxford: Oxford University Press, 1991.
Law and Order: An Honest Citizen's Guide to Crime and Control, Cambridge: Polity Press, 2007.

Edited Books

Beyond Law and Order (ed. with M. Cross), London: Macmillan, 1991.
Criminal Justice: Theory and Practice (ed. with K. Bottomley and T. Fowles), Hull: British Society of Criminology, 1992.
Accountable Policing: Effectiveness, Empowerment and Equity (ed. with S. Spencer), London: Institute for Public Policy Research, 1993.
The Oxford Handbook of Criminology (ed. with M. Maguire and R. Morgan) Oxford: Oxford University Press, 1994; 2nd edn 1997; 3rd edn 2002; 4th edn 2007.
Policing. Vol. I: Cops, Crime and Control: Analysing the Police Function, International Library of Criminology, Criminal Justice and Penology, Aldershot: Dartmouth, 1996.
Policing. Vol. II: Controlling the Controllers: Police Discretion and Accountability, International Library of Criminology, Criminal Justice and Penology, Aldershot: Dartmouth, 1996.

Edited Journals

Editor (with J. Shapland), Special Issue of *British Journal of Criminology* on 'Policing', January 1987.
Review Editor, *British Journal of Criminology*, 1987–1995.
Editor, *Policing and Society: An International Journal*, 1990–1998.
Editorial Board, *Sociology*, 1987–1991.
Academic Advisory Board, *New Society*, 1987–1988.
Editorial Board, *Modern Law Review*, 1991–1997.
Editorial Board, *Policing and Society*, 1998–.
Editorial Board, *Crime, Media and Culture*, 2004–.

Editorial Board, *Journal of Crime, Conflict and Media Culture*, 2004–2007.
Editorial Board, *Policing: A Journal of Policy and Practice*, 2006–.
Editorial Board, *The Police Journal*, 2008–.

Book Chapters

'Police Unionism', in S. Holdaway (ed.), *The British Police*, London: Edward Arnold, 1978, pp. 150–67.

'Keystone to Kojak: The Hollywood Cop', in P. Davies and B. Neve (eds), *Politics, Society and Cinema in America*, Manchester: Manchester University Press, 1981, pp. 195–220.

'The Politics of Police Power', in *Politics and Power 4: Law, Politics and Justice*, London: Routledge and Kegan Paul, 1981, pp. 27–52.

'The Politicisation of the Police in Britain', in M. Punch (ed.), *Control of the Police Organisation*, Cambridge, MA: MIT Press, 1983, pp. 126–48.

'Crime, Law and Deviance: The Durkheim Legacy', in S. Fenton with R. Reiner and I. Hamnett (eds), *Durkheim and Modern Sociology*, Cambridge: Cambridge University Press, 1984, pp. 175–201.

'Police and Race Relations', in J. Baxter and L. Koffmann (eds), *The Police, Constitution and Community*, Abingdon: Professional Books, 1985, pp. 149–87.

'Policing, Order and Legitimacy in Britain', in S. Spitzer and A. Scull (eds), *Research in Law, Deviance and Social Control*, Vol. 8, Greenwich, CT: JAI Press, 1986, pp. 173–94.

'Looking at Policing: A Commentary', in R. Hood (ed.), *Crime and Criminal Policy in Europe*, Oxford: Oxford University Centre for Criminological Research, 1989, pp. 47–49.

'The Politics of Police Research', in M. Weatheritt (ed.), *Police Research: Some Future Prospects*, Aldershot: Gower, 1989, pp. 3–20.

'Where the Buck Stops: Chief Constables' Views on Police Accountability'. in R. Morgan and D. Smith (eds), *Coming To Terms With Policing*, London: Routledge, 1989, pp. 195–216.

'Police and Public Order in 1989', in P. Catterall (ed.), *Contemporary Britain: An Annual Review*, Oxford: Blackwell, 1990, pp. 93–105.

'Policing and Crime', in S. MacGregor and B. Pimlott (eds), *Tackling The Inner Cities*, Oxford: Oxford University Press, 1990, pp. 44–63.

'Beyond Law and Order: Crime and Criminology into the 1990s' (with M. Cross), in R. Reiner and M. Cross (eds), *Beyond Law and Order: Criminal Justice Policy and Politics into the 1990s*, London: Macmillan, 1991, pp. 1–17.

'Chief Constables in England and Wales: A Social Portrait of a Criminal Justice Elite', in R. Reiner and M. Cross (eds), *Beyond Law and Order: Criminal Justice Policy and Politics into the 1990s*, London: Macmillan, 1991, pp. 59–77.

'Multiple Realities, Divided Worlds: Chief Constables' Perspectives on the Police Complaints System', in A. Goldsmith (ed.), *Complaints Against the Police*, Oxford: Oxford University Press, 1991, pp. 211–31.

'Police Research in the United Kingdom: A Critical Review', in N. Morris and M. Tonry (eds), *Modern Policing: A 'Crime and Justice' Thematic Volume*, Chicago, IL: Chicago University Press, 1992, pp. 435–508.

'This Society of Ours is Nose-Diving Rapidly: Chief Constables' Perceptions of Crime, Order and Control', in R. Morgan (ed.), *Policing, Organised Crime and Crime Prevention*, Bristol: Bristol University Centre for Criminal Justice, 1991, pp. 19–36.

'Police and Public Order in 1990', in P. Catterall (ed.), *Contemporary Britain: An Annual Review*, Oxford: Blackwell, 1991, pp. 107–18.

'History, Sociology and Policing', in P. Robert and C. Emsley (eds), *History and Sociology of Crime*, Hamburg: Centaurus, 1991, pp. 121–4.

'Police and Public Order in 1991', in P. Catterall (ed.), *Contemporary Britain: An Annual Review*, Oxford: Blackwell, 1992, pp. 95–104.

'Accountability and Effectiveness', in R. Dingwall and J. Shapland (eds), *Reforming British Police Missions and Structures*, Sheffield: University of Sheffield Faculty of Law, 1993, pp. 33–50.

'Police Accountability: Principles, Patterns and Practices', in R. Reiner and S. Spencer (eds), *Accountable Policing: Effectiveness, Empowerment and Equity*, London: IPPR, 1993, pp. 1–23.

'Conclusions and Recommendations' (with S. Spencer), in R. Reiner and S. Spencer (eds), *Accountable Policing: Effectiveness, Empowerment and Equity*, London: IPPR, 1993, pp. 172–91.

'Race, Crime and Justice: Models of Interpretation', in L. Gelsthorpe (ed.), *Minority Ethnic Groups and the Criminal Justice System*, Cropwood Papers No. 21, Cambridge: Cambridge University Institute of Criminology, 1993, pp. 1–25.

'Crime Control', in C. Martin (ed.), *Changing Policing: Business or Service?*, London: Institute for the Study and Treatment of Delinquency, 1994, pp. 25–28.

'Police Power' (with L. Leigh), in C. McCrudden and G. Chambers (eds), *Individual Rights in the UK Since 1945*, Oxford: Oxford University Press, 1994, pp. 69–108.

'The Dialectics of Dixon: Changing Television Images of the Police', in M. Stephens and S. Becker (eds), *Police Force, Police Service: Care and Control*, London: Macmillan, 1994, pp. 11–32.

'Police and Policing', in M. Maguire, R. Morgan and R. Reiner (eds), *The Oxford Handbook of Criminology*, Oxford: Oxford University Press, 1994, pp. 705–72; 2nd revised edn, 1997, pp. 997–1049.

'Introduction' (with M. Maguire and R. Morgan), in M. Maguire, R. Morgan and R. Reiner (eds), *The Oxford Handbook of Criminology*, Oxford: Oxford University Press, 1994, pp. 1–13.

'The British Police Tradition: Model or Myth?', in J. Vigh and G. Katona (eds), *Social Changes, Crime and Police*, Budapest: Eotvos Lorand University Press, 1993, pp. 31–41. Reprinted in L. Shelley and J. Vigh (eds), *Social Changes, Crime and the Police*, Chur: Harwood Academic Publishers, 1995, pp. 27–36.

'Police and Public Order', in P. Catterall (ed.), *Contemporary Britain 1994*, London: Institute of Contemporary British History, 1994, pp. 96–106.

'Myth vs. Modernity: Reality and Unreality in the English Model of Policing', in J-P. Brodeur (ed.), *Comparisons in Policing: An International Perspective*, Aldershot: Avebury, 1995, pp. 16–48.

'Community Policing in England and Wales', in J-P. Brodeur (ed.), *Comparisons in Policing: An International Perspective*, Aldershot: Avebury, 1995, pp. 161–5.

'The Case for the Prosecution: Police Suspects and the Construction of Criminality', in L. Noaks, M. Levi and M. Maguire (eds), *Contemporary Issues in Criminology*, Cardiff: University of Wales Press, 1995, pp. 231–34.

'Counting the Coppers: Antinomies of Accountability in Policing', in P. Stenning (ed.), *Accountability for Criminal Justice*, Toronto: University of Toronto Press, 1995, pp. 74–92.

'The Case of the Missing Crimes', in R. Levitas and W. Guy (eds), *Interpreting Official Statistics*, London: Routledge, 1996, pp. 185–205.

'Crime and the Media', in H. Sasson and D. Diamond (eds), *LSE on Social Science: A Centenary Anthology*, London: LSE Publishing, 1996, pp. 135–55.

'Have the Police Got a Future?', in C. Critcher and D. Waddington(eds), *Policing Public Order: Theoretical and Practical Issues*, Aldershot: Dartmouth, 1996, pp. 261–27.

'Media Made Criminality', in M. Maguire, R. Morgan and R. Reiner (eds), *The Oxford Handbook of Criminology*, Oxford: Oxford University Press, 1997, pp. 189–231.

'Policing, Protest and Disorder in Britain', in D. Della Porta and H. Reiter (eds), *Policing Protest*, Minneapolis: University of Minnesota Press, 1998, pp. 35–48.

'Paragon, Panacea or Pariah? Changing Images of the British Police', in A. Wright (ed.), *Police and Society*, Portsmouth: Portsmouth University Institute of Police and Criminological Studies, 1998, pp. 41–60.

'Process or Product? Problems of Assessing Individual Police Performance', in J-P. Brodeur (ed.), *Evaluating Police Service Delivery*, Beverly Hills, CA: Sage, 1998, pp. 55–72.

'Copping A Plea', in P. Rock and S. Holdaway (eds), *The Social Theory of Modern Criminology*, London: UCL Press, 1998, pp. 73–98.

'Order and Discipline', in I. Holliday, A. Gamble and G. Parry (eds), *Fundamentals in British Politics*, London: Palgrave Macmillan, 1999, pp. 163–81.

'Policing and the Media', in F. Leishman, B. Loveday and S. Savage (eds), *Core Issues in British Policing*, London: Macmillan, 2000, pp. 52–66.

'Police Research', in R. King and E. Wincup (eds), *Doing Research on Crime and Justice*, Oxford: Oxford University Press, 2000, pp. 205–36.

'Casino Culture: Media and Crime in a Winner-Loser Society' (with S. Livingstone and J. Allen), in K. Stenson and R. Sullivan (eds), *Crime, Risk and Justice: The Politics of Crime Control in Liberal Democracies*, Cullompton: Willan Publishing, 2000, pp. 175–93.

'No More Happy Endings? The Media and Popular Concern about Crime since the Second World War' (with S. Livingstone and J. Allen), in T. Hope and R. Sparks (eds), *Crime, Risk and Insecurity: Law and Order in Everyday Life and Political Discourse*, London: Routledge, 2000, pp. 107–25.

'British Police Organisation 2000', in D. Lawday (ed.), *Policing in France and Britain: Restoring Confidence Locally and Nationally*, London: Franco-British Council, 2001, pp. 17–19.

'The First Cut is the Deepest: Criminological Texts and the Return of the Repressed', in I. McKenzie and R. Bull (eds), *Criminal Justice Research*, Aldershot: Dartmouth, 2002, pp. 3–30.

'Classical Social Theory and Law', in J. Penner, D. Schiff and R. Nobles (eds), *Jurisprudence and Legal Theory*, London: Butterworths, 2002, pp. 230–78.

'Justice', in J. Penner, D. Schiff and R. Nobles (eds), *Jurisprudence and Legal Theory*, London: Butterworths, 2002, pp. 719–78.

'The Organisation and Accountability of the Police', in M. McConville and G. Wilson (eds), *The Handbook of the Criminal Justice Process*, Oxford: Oxford University Press, 2002, pp. 21–42.

'Media Made Criminality', in M. Maguire, R. Morgan and R. Reiner (eds), *The Oxford Handbook of Criminology* (3rd edn), Oxford: Oxford University Press, 2002, pp. 376–416.

'Policing and the Media', in T. Newburn (ed.), *Handbook of Policing*, Collompton: Willan Publishing, 2003, pp. 259–81.

'From Law and Order to Lynch Mobs: Crime News since the Second World War' (with S. Livingstone and J. Allen), in P. Mason (ed.), *Criminal Visions: Media Representations of Crime and Justice*, Collompton: Willan Publishing, 2003, pp. 13–32.

'Political Economy, Crime and Criminal Justice', in M. Maguire, R. Morgan and R. Reiner (eds), *The Oxford Handbook of Criminology* (4th edn), Oxford: Oxford University Press, 2007, pp. 341–80.

'Media Made Criminality', in M. Maguire, R. Morgan and R. Reiner (eds), *The Oxford Handbook of Criminology* (4th edn), Oxford: Oxford University Press, 2007, pp. 302–37.

'Policing and the Police' (with T. Newburn), in M. Maguire, R. Morgan and R. Reiner (eds), *The Oxford Handbook of Criminology* (4th edn), Oxford: Oxford University Press, 2007, pp. 910–52.

'Beyond Risk: A Lament for Social Democratic Criminology', in T. Newburn and P. Rock (eds), *The Politics of Crime Control*, Oxford: Oxford University Press, 2006, pp. 7–49.

'Police Research' (with T. Newburn), in R. King and E. Wincup (eds), *Doing Criminological Research* (2nd edn), Oxford: Oxford University Press, 2007, pp. 343–74.

'Criminology as a Vocation', in D. Downes, P. Rock, C. Chinkin and C. Gearty (eds), *Crime, Social Control and Human Rights*, Cullompton: Willan Publishing, 2007, pp. 395–409.

'Crime and Penal Policy' (with T. Newburn), in A. Seldon (ed.), *Blair's Britain, 1997–2007*, Cambridge: Cambridge University Press, 2007, pp. 318–40.

'Policing and the Media', in T. Newburn (ed.), *Handbook of Policing*, Cullompton: Willan Publishing, 2008, pp. 313–35.

'Preface', in T. Serassis, H. Kania and H. Albrecht (eds), *Images of Crime III*, Freiburg: Max Planck Institute, 2009, pp. v–vi.

'New Theories of Policing: A Social Democratic Critique', in T. Newburn, D. Downes and D. Hobbs (eds), *The Eternal Recurrence of Crime and Control: Essays for Paul Rock*, Oxford: Oxford University Press, 2010, pp. 141–82.

Academic Journal Articles

'The Police in the Class Structure', *British Journal of Law and Society*, **5**(2), Winter 1978, pp. 166–84.

'Fuzzy Thoughts: The Police and "Law and Order" Politics', *Sociological Review*, **28**(2), May 1980, pp. 377–413. Reprinted in R. Reiner (ed.), *Policing*, Aldershot: Gower, 1996.

'Assisting with Enquiries: Problems of Research on the Police', *Quantitative Sociology Newsletter*, No. 22, Summer 1979, pp. 37–67.

'Who are the Police?', *Political Quarterly*, **53**(2), April–June 1982, pp. 165–80.

'A Watershed in Policing', *Political Quarterly*, May 1985, pp. 122–31. Reprinted in *Journal of the Police History Society*, 1986, pp. 10–21.

'Policing Strikes: A Historical U-Turn', *Policing*, **1**(3), Summer 1985, pp. 138–48.

'The Politics of the Act', *Public Law*, Autumn 1985, pp. 394–402.

'Le développement de la police Britannique moderne: une analyse sociologique', *Revue Internationale de Criminologie et de Police Technique*, **4**, 1986, pp. 458–75.

'The Modern Bobby: The Development of the British Police', *Policing*, Winter 1986, pp. 258–75.

'Why Police?', *British Journal of Criminology*, Winter 1986–1987, pp. 1–3.

'Opportunism, Partisanship or Scholarship? Studies of Policing in the UK', *Faculty of Law Occasional Papers*, University College, London, 1987.

'Keeping the Home Office Happy', *Policing*, Spring 1988, pp. 28–36.

'The State and British Criminology', *British Journal of Criminology*, Spring 1988, pp. 138–58.

'In the Office of Chief Constable', *Current Legal Problems*, **41**, 1988, pp. 135–68.

'Dixon's Decline: Why Policing Has Become So Controversial', *Contemporary Record: The Journal of the Institute of Contemporary British History*, **3**(1), Autumn 1989, pp. 2–6.

'Thinking at the Top', *Policing*, **5**(3), Autumn 1989, pp. 181–99.

'Race and Criminal Justice', *New Community*, **16**(1), October 1989, pp. 5–21. Reprinted in B. Hudson (ed.), *Race, Crime and Justice*, Aldershot: Dartmouth, 1996.

'Helping the Police with their Enquiries: The Necessity Principle and Voluntary Attendance at the Police Station' (with I. McKenzie and R. Morgan), *Criminal Law Review*, January 1990, pp. 22–33.

'Top Cop Class', *Howard Journal of Criminal Justice*, August 1990, pp. 215–19.

'Policing and Criminal Justice in Great Britain', *Co-Existence*, Winter 1991, pp. 107–17.

'A Much Lower Pedestal', *Policing*, **7**, Autumn 1991, pp. 225–38.

'Fin de Siècle Blues: The Police Face the Millennium', *Political Quarterly*, **63**(1), January–March 1992, pp. 37–49.

'Codes, Courts and Constables: Police Powers Since 1984', *Public Money and Management*, **11**(1), Spring 1992, pp. 11–15. Reprinted in R. Reiner (ed.), *Policing*, Aldershot: Gower, 1996.

'La tradition policière Britannique: modèle ou mythe?', *Les Cahiers de la Securité Intérieure*, January–March 1992, pp. 29–40.

'Policing a Postmodern Society', *Modern Law Review*, **55**(6), November 1992, pp. 761–81. Reprinted in R. Reiner (ed.), *Policing*, Aldershot: Gower, 1996, and in T. Newburn (ed.), *Policing: Key Readings*, Cullompton: Willan Publishing, 2005.

'Du mythe à la realité: le modèle Britannique', *Les Cahiers de la Securité Intérieure*, May–July 1993, pp. 25–59.

'The Royal Commission on Criminal Justice: Investigative Powers and Safeguards for Suspects', *Criminal Law Review*, November 1993, pp. 808–816.

'From Sacred to Profane: The Thirty Years' War of the British Police', *Policing and Society*, **5**(1), 1995, pp. 121–28.

'Crime and Control: An Honest Citizen's Guide', *Sociology Review*, April 1996, pp. 2–6.

'Policing, Protest, and Disorder in Britain', *EUI Working Papers RSC 97/2*, Florence: European University Institute, January 1997, pp. 1–20.

'The Changing Generic Location of Crime in Film' (with J. Allen and S. Livingstone), *Journal of Communication*, **47**(4), Autumn 1997, pp. 89–101.

'True Lies: Changing Images of Crime in British Postwar Cinema', (with J. Allen and S. Livingstone), *European Journal of Communication*, **13**(1), March 1998, pp. 53–75.

'Crime and Control in Britain', *Sociology*, **34**(1), 2000, pp. 71–94.

'Audiences for Crime Media 1946–91: A Historical Approach to Reception Studies' (with S. Livingstone and J. Allen), *Communication Review*, **4**(2), 2001, pp. 165–92.

'From PC Dixon to Dixon PLC: Policing and Police Powers Since 1954' (with T. Newburn), *Criminal Law Review*, August 2004, pp. 601–18.

'Neophilia or Back to Basics? Policing Research and the Seductions of Crime Control', *Policing and Society*, **17**(1), 2007, pp. 89–101.

'Media, Crime, Law and Order', *Scottish Journal of Criminal Justice Studies*, **12**, July 2006, pp. 5–21.

'Neo-liberalism, Crime and Criminal Justice', *Renewal*, **14**(3), 2006, pp. 10–22.

'Law and Order: A 20:20 Vision', *Current Legal Problems*, **59**, 2006, pp. 129–60.

'The Law and Order Trap', *Soundings: A Journal of Politics and Culture*, **40**, December 2008, pp. 123–34.

'Citizenship, Crime, Criminalisation: Marshalling a Social Democratic Perspective', *New Criminal Law Review*, **13**(2), 2010, pp. 241–61.

'Political Economy, Crime and Criminal Justice: A Plea for a Social Democratic Perspective', *Kriminologisches Journal*, **42**(1), 2010, pp. 41–58.

Shorter Articles

'Reds in Blue', *New Society*, 7 October 1976, pp. 14–16. Reprinted in *Police*, October–November 1976, pp. 22–25, and in *Crime, Deviance and Social Control*, 1979, pp. 26–28.

'Police and Picketing', *New Society*, 7 July 1977, pp. 14–15.

'Police Rules OK', *Contemporary Review*, **231**(1338), July 1977, pp. 17–21.

'Scarborough Conference 1977', *The Police Journal*, January–March 1978, pp. 18–23.

'The New Blue Films', *New Society*, **43**, 30 March 1978, pp. 706–708. Reprinted in *The Media*, 1980, pp. 18–20.

'The Police, Class and Politics', *Marxism Today*, March 1978, pp. 69–80.

'Political Conflict and the British Police Tradition', *Contemporary Review*, April 1980, pp. 191–200.

'Forces of Disorder', *New Society*, 10 April 1980, pp. 51–54. Reprinted in *Hibernia National Review*, May 1980.

'Policing in the United States', *State Research*, **4**(20), October–November 1980, pp. 15–27.

'The Law Enforcers', *The Movie*, No.77, 19 June 1981, pp. 1521–25. Reprinted in A. Lloyd (ed.), *Movies of the Seventies*, London: Orbis, 1984, pp. 167–72.

'Black and Blue: Race and the Police', *New Society*, 17 September 1981, pp. 466–69. Reprinted in *Race and Riots '81*, 1981, pp. 18–20.

'Is Britain Turning into a Police State?', *New Society*, 2 August 1984, pp. 51–56. Reprinted in *Crime and Social Control*, 1985, pp. 8–11.

'Retrospect on the Riots', *New Society*, 25 October 1985, pp. 148–50.

'Response to Review Symposium on *The Politics of the Police*', *British Journal of Criminology*, January 1986, pp. 103–105.

'Talking Tough: The Politics and Practice of Law and Order', *Prison Reform Trust/Christian Action Journal*, Special Issue on 'Crime and Social Justice', Autumn 1986, pp. 5–7.

'Helping with Inquiries' (with I. McKenzie and R. Morgan), *Police Review*, 23 March 1990, pp. 600–601.

'When Necessity is the Mother of Detention' (with I. McKenzie and R. Morgan), *Police Review*, 20 April 1990, pp. 800–801.

'Responsibilities and Reforms', *New Law Journal*, **143**(6611), 30 July 1993, pp. 1096–126. Reprinted in R. Reiner (ed.), *Policing*, Aldershot: Gower, 1996.
'Handcuffing Britain's Police', *Parliamentary Brief*, August–September 1993, pp. 35–36.
'Georgian Britain: Rediscovering the Age of Rape and Violence', *Parliamentary Brief*, November–December 1993, pp. 26–27.
'Crime and Control: An Honest Citizen's Guide to Crime', *LSE Magazine*, **6**(1), Spring 1994, pp. 10–13.
'What Should the Police be Doing?', *Policing*, **10**(3), Autumn 1994, pp. 151–57.
'The Government's Policing Proposals: Some Critical Notes', *Criminal Justice Matters*, Autumn 1994, pp. 24–25.
'A Truce in the War Between Police and Academe', *Policing Today*, October 1994, pp. 30–32.
'The Mystery of the Missing Crimes', *Policing Today*, December 1994, pp. 16–18.
'Policing By Numbers: The Feel Good Fallacy', *Policing Today*, February 1995, pp. 22–24.
'Accentuating the Positive: What Makes a Good Police Officer?', *Policing Today*, April 1995, pp. 26–28.
'Looking Through the Glass (of a Crystal Ball) Darkly', *Policing Today*, June 1995, pp. 17–20. Reprinted in R. Reiner (ed.), *Policing*, Aldershot: Gower, 1996.
'Allowing Moral Panic to Thrive', *Policing Today*, August 1995, pp. 14–16.
'Knights Errant in the Naked City', *Criminal Justice Matters*, **32**, Summer 1998, pp. 27–28.
'The Rise of Virtual Vigilantism: Crime Reporting since World War II', *Criminal Justice Matters*, **43**, Spring 2001, pp. 4–5.
'Success or Statistics? New Labour and Crime Control', *Criminal Justice Matters*, **67**, Spring 2007, pp. 4–5, 37.
'It's the Political Economy, Stupid! A Neo-Clintonian Criminology', *Criminal Justice Matters*, **70**, Winter 2007–2008, pp. 7–8.

Encyclopedia/Dictionary Articles

'Chandler' and 'Hammett', in A. Bullock and R. Woddings (eds), *The Fontana Biographical Comparison to Modern Thought*, London: Fontana, 1983, pp. 139–40 and p. 303.
'Policing', in A. Kuper and J. Kuper (eds), *The Social Science Encyclopedia* (3rd edn), London: Routledge, 2004.
'Crime and the Media', in P. Cane and J. Conaghan (eds), *The New Oxford Companion to Law*, Oxford: Oxford University Press, 2008, pp. 260–61.
'Crime Rates', in P. Cane and J. Conaghan (eds), *The New Oxford Companion to Law*, Oxford: Oxford University Press, 2008, pp. 267–68.
'Dixon of Dock Green', in T. Newburn and P. Neyroud (eds), *Dictionary of Policing*, Cullompton: Willan Publishing, 2008, p. 85.
'Media and Policing', in T. Newburn and P. Neyroud (eds), *Dictionary of Policing*, Cullompton: Willan Publishing, 2008, pp. 161–62.
'Consent', in A. Wakefield and J. Fleming (eds), *The Sage Dictionary of Policing*, London: Sage, 2009, pp. 52–54.
'Police Property', in A. Wakefield and J. Fleming (eds), *The Sage Dictionary of Policing*, London: Sage, 2009, pp. 230–31.

Short Journalistic Articles

'A Consideration of the Political Implications of American Country Music', *New Edinburgh Review*, August 1973, pp. 10–11.

'What Kind of Police?', *New Society*, 25 August 1977, p. 378.

'The Law and Order Campaign', *Tribune*, **42**(38), 22 September 1978, p. 20.

'The Blue-Coated Worker' (serialization), *Police Review*, Nos. 4479–84, 17 November–22 December 1978.

'Marksism Today?', *Marxism Today*, December 1978, pp. 365–56.

'Tops of the Cops', *New Society*, 21 June 1979, p. 716.

'Police United', *New Society*, 2 October 1980, pp. 20–21.

'A Mysterious Affair', *New Society*, 7 May 1981, pp. 234–35.

'McNee Jerks', *New Society*, 25 June 1981, p. 528.

'Shaft', *The Movie*, No. 83, 31 July 1981, pp. 1648–49.

'Riots and the Police', *Marxism Today*, August 1981, p. 6.

'To be Continued … The Rise of the Serial', *The Movie*, No. 110, 5 February 1982, pp. 2181–85.

'Kings of the Wild Frontier', *The Movie*, No. 118, 2 April, 1982, pp. 2356–60.

'Bobbies Take the Lobby Beat', *New Society*, 25 March 1982, pp. 469–71.

'Getting Guns Under Control', *New Society*, 27 October 1983, p. 167.

'The Police Party', *New Society*, 11 October 1984, p. 44.

'Undermining Our Rights?', *New Society*, 13 December 1984, p. 423.

'Closed Prisons, Closed Minds', *New Society*, 14 March 1985, p. 415.

'From "Plods" to "Pigs"', *Police*, March 1985, pp. 26–32.

'Sauce for the Cops', *New Society*, 26 July 1985, p. 126.

'How Safe Will Suspects Be?', *New Society*, 22 November 1985, p. 332.

'Today's Chief Constables Belong to the Nation's Elite', *Police*, August 1988, pp. 28–29.

'Law and Order', *Channel 4 Election Brief*, London: Channel 4 TV, 1987, p. 17.

'Where Does the Met. Go Now?', *Police Review*, 31 July 1987, p. 1526.

'Whatever Happened to Police Accountability?', *Samizdat 4*, Law and Order Special Issue, May–June 1989, pp. 5–6.

'Pulling Rank on the Police File', *Guardian*, 4 July 1990, p. 21.

'Unhappiest Lot of All', *The Times*, 5 September 1991, p. 16.

'Beaten by the Big Stick', *Times Higher Education Supplement*, 20 March 1992, p. 15.

'The Perfidy of the Paramour: How the Police Fell out of Love with the Conservatives', *Times Literary Supplement*, 1 September 1995, pp. 9–10.

'Selling the Family Copper: The British Police Plc', *The Independent*, Section Two, 12 October 1995, pp. 2–3.

'Criminal Investigation', *Guardian* (Society Section), 16 October 1996, p. 8.

'Be Tough on a Crucial Cause of Crime – Neoliberalism', *Guardian*, 24 November 2005, p. 32.

'A Policeman's Lot', *Guardian*, 3 October 2008. Available at: http://www.guardian.co.uk/commentisfree/2008/oct/03/blair.london.

'Not as Bad as it Looks', *Guardian*, 23 October 2008. Available at: http://www.guardian.co.uk/commentisfree/2008/oct/23/ukcrime-justice.

'Law-and-Order Politics', *Guardian*, 22 December 2008. Available at: http://www.guardian.co.uk/commentisfree/2008/dec/22/police-conservatives.

'The Crime Wave is yet to Come', *Guardian*, 23 January 2009. Available at: http://www.guardian.co.uk/commentisfree/2009/jan/23/ukcrime-justice.

'Police v Citizen: The Orwellian Struggle', *Guardian*, 8 April 2009. Available at: http://www.guardian.co.uk/commentisfree/libertycentral/2009/apr/08/ian-tomlinson-police-g20.

'Labour Has Not Broken Britain', *Guardian*, 22 January 2010. Available at: http://www.guardian.co.uk/commentisfree/2010/jan/22/david-cameron-labour-crime.

'Who Put the Politics Into the Police?', *LSE Research*, March 2010, pp. 32–3.

Review Articles

'T. Bunyan: *The History and Practice of the Political Police in Britain*', *British Journal of Law and Society*, Winter 1976, pp. 290–93.

'N. Alex: *New York Cops Talk Back*'; 'D.H. Bayley: *Forces of Order*'; 'W. Ker-Muir Jr: *Police – Street Corner Politicians*'; 'R. Lewis: *A Force for the Future*'; 'R. Mark: *Policing a Perplexed Society*'; 'C. Potholm and R. Morgan: *Focus on Police*'; *Sociology*, January 1978, pp. 165–68.

'T. Bunyan: *The Political Police in Britain* (2nd edn)', *Crime and Social Justice*, Summer 1980, pp. 55–58.

'J. Alderson: *Policing Freedom*', *International Journal of the Sociology of Law*, November 1980, pp. 449–54.

'Books on the Police and Criminal Evidence Act', *British Journal of Criminology*, July 1986, pp. 299–302.

'Lodging Under Her Majesty's Roof', *Times Higher Education Supplement* 16 May 1986, p. 16.

'J. Benyon and C. Bourn (eds): *The Police: Powers, Procedures and Proprieties*', *Policing*, Winter 1986, pp. 329–32.

'Lore and Order', *New Society*, 27 March 1987, pp. 27–29.

'Four Books on Criminology', *Critical Social Policy*, Autumn 1987, pp. 103–106.

'Tackling Crime', *Political Quarterly*, **61**(4), 1990, pp. 477–79.

'Prisoners in the Cage: The Fear of Crime and the End of Social Optimism', *Times Literary Supplement*, 25 January 2002, pp. 3–4.

'How Does It Feel?', *Times Literary Supplement*, 20 June 2008, p. 28.

Book Reviews

In numerous journals, including: *British Journal of Criminology*; *Crime, Media, Culture*; *Sociology*; *British Journal of Sociology*; *Howard Journal of Criminal Justice*; *Public Law*; *Criminal Law Review*; *Criminal Justice History*; *Sociological Review*; *Journal of Law and Society*; *Social Work Today*; *New Law Journal*; *Jewish Journal of Sociology*; *International Journal of the Sociology of Law*; *New Society*; *The Listener*; *The Independent*; *Times Higher Education Supplement*; *Marxism Today*; *Labour Weekly*; *The Tablet*; *Police Review*; *Policing*; *Journal of Social Welfare Law*; *British Book News*; *Critical Social Policy*; *Journal of Social Policy*; *Times Literary Supplement*; *The Independent on Sunday*; *Guardian*.

Name Index